MAR CARIBE

NICARAGUA

COSTA
RICA

PANAMÁ

Barranquilla

Maracaibo

Caracas

Río Orinoco

VENEZUELA

Georgetown

GUYANA

Paramaribo

Cayenne

Medellín

Bogotá

Cali

COLOMBIA

GUAYANA FRANCESA

SURINAME

OCÉANO
ATLÁNTICO

Quito

ECUADOR

Ecuador

Guayaquil

Manaus

Belém

Río Amazonas

PERÚ

BRASIL

Recife

Lima

Machu Picchu
Cuzco

CORDILLERA DE LOS ANDES

Lago Titicaca

BOLIVIA

La Paz

Brasília

OCÉANO
PACÍFICO

Arequipa

Sucre

OCÉANO PACÍFICO

Isla Pinta

Isla Marchena

Isla San Salvador

Isla Santa Cruz

Isla
Isabela

Isla San
Cristóbal

Puerto
Baquerizo
Moreno

LAS ISLAS
GALÁPAGOS
(ECUADOR)

0   100 MILLAS

0   100 KILÓMETROS

Antofagasta

CHILE

Asunción

PARAGUAY

São Paulo

Puerto Iguazú

Rio de Janeiro

Trópico de
Capricornio

Río Paraná

0   8 MILLAS

0   8 KILÓMETROS

Valparaíso

Córdoba

Rosario

URUGUAY

OCÉANO
ATLÁNTICO

Cabo
Cummings

Hanga Roa

Mataveri

Cabo Sur

Cabo

Santiago

ARGENTINA

Buenos
Aires

Montevideo

Río de la Plata

OCÉANO
PACÍFICO

ISLA DE PASCUA
(CHILE)

Concepción

Bahía Blanca

San Carlos de
Bariloche

OCÉANO
PACÍFICO

Islas
Malvinas

Estrecho de
Magallanes

Punta Arenas

Tierra del Fuego

Cabo de Hornos

AMÉRICA DEL SUR

0   250   500   750 MILLAS

0   250   500   750 KILÓMETROS

ELEVACIÓN

METROS	PIES
3050	10000
1525	5000
610	2000
305	1000
152.5	500
0	0

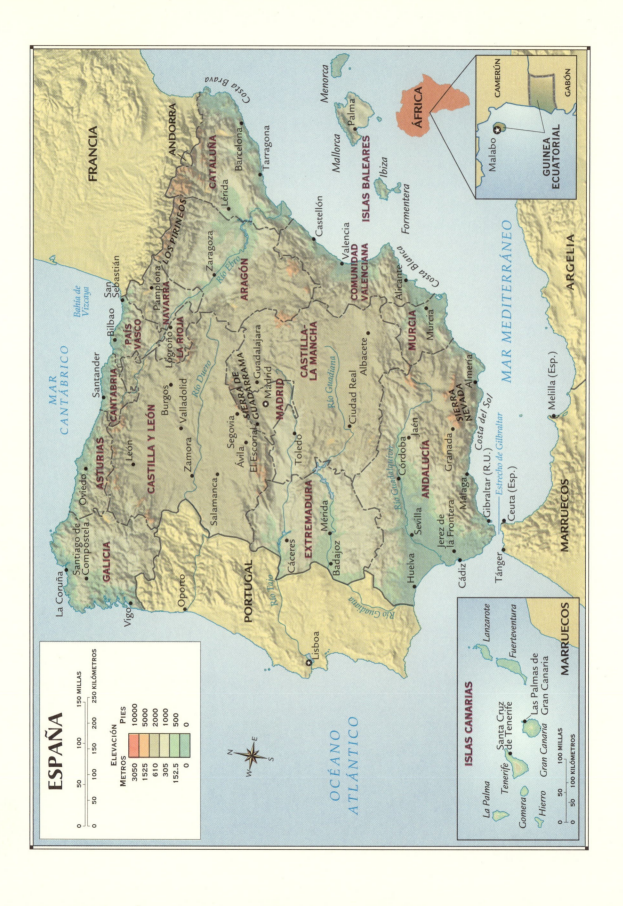

ESPAÑA

ELEVACIÓN

METROS	PIES
3050	10000
1525	5000
610	2000
305	1000
152.5	500
0	0

0   50   100   150 MILLAS
0   50   100   150   200   250 KILÓMETROS

N E S W

OCÉANO ATLÁNTICO

MAR CANTÁBRICO

Bahía de Vizcaya

FRANCIA

ANDORRA

LOS PIRINEOS

Costa Brava

MAR MEDITERRÁNEO

Menorca

Palma

Mallorca

Ibiza

Formentera

ISLAS BALEARES

Costa Blanca

ÁFRICA

CAMERÚN

GABÓN

Malabo

GUINEA ECUATORIAL

ARGELIA

MARRUECOS

Melilla (Esp.)

Ceuta (Esp.)

Estrecho de Gibraltar

Gibraltar (R.U.)

Costa del Sol

Tánger

GALICIA
La Coruña
Santiago de Compostela
Vigo
Oporto

ASTURIAS
Oviedo
Santander
CANTABRIA

PAÍS VASCO
Bilbao
San Sebastián
Pamplona
NAVARRA
LA RIOJA
Logroño

CASTILLA Y LEÓN
León
Zamora
Valladolid
Burgos
Salamanca
Segovia
Ávila

ARAGÓN
Zaragoza
Río Ebro

CATALUÑA
Lérida
Barcelona
Tarragona

Castellón

COMUNIDAD VALENCIANA
Valencia
Alicante

MURCIA
Murcia
Almería

SIERRA DE GUADARRAMA
El Escorial
MADRID
Madrid
Guadalajara
Toledo
Río Tajo

CASTILLA-LA MANCHA
Ciudad Real
Albacete
Río Guadiana

EXTREMADURA
Cáceres
Mérida
Badajoz

ANDALUCÍA
Córdoba
Jaén
Sevilla
Granada
SIERRA NEVADA
Huelva
Málaga
Jerez de la Frontera
Cádiz
Río Guadalquivir

PORTUGAL
Lisboa

Río Duero

MARRUECOS

ISLAS CANARIAS
Lanzarote
Fuerteventura
La Palma
Tenerife
Santa Cruz de Tenerife
Gomera
Hierro
Gran Canaria
Las Palmas de Gran Canaria

0   50   100 MILLAS
0   50   100 KILÓMETROS

¿Sabías que...?

Sicuani (2002) *por Rossmary Valverde*

ABOUT THE COVER ARTIST AND HER ART Rossmary Valverde was born in Lima, Peru in 1969 and currently makes her home in San Francisco, California. A self-taught artist, her paintings consist of bright, bold colors and reflect her childhood memories of Peru. She often mixes sand or small stones into the paint, adding texture and complexity to the apparent simplicity of form in her paintings. Valverde's art has been exported to Australia, Canada, several European countries, Hong Kong, Israel, Japan, Mexico, and to every region of the United States. She can be contacted through Gallery 444 (**www.gallery444.com**) in San Francisco.

¿Sabías que...?

Beginning Spanish

FIFTH EDITION

Bill VanPatten

James F. Lee
University of New South Wales, Sydney, Australia

Terry L. Ballman
California State University, Channel Islands

Andrew P. Farley
Texas Tech University

Boston   Burr Ridge, IL   Dubuque, IA   Madison, WI   New York   San Francisco   St. Louis
Bangkok   Bogotá   Caracas   Kuala Lumpur   Lisbon   London   Madrid   Mexico City
Milan   Montreal   New Delhi   Santiago   Seoul   Singapore   Sydney   Taipei   Toronto

The _McGraw·Hill_ Companies

Higher Education

Published by McGraw-Hill, an imprint of The McGraw-Hill Companies, Inc., 1221 Avenue of the Americas, New York, NY 10020. Copyright © 2008 by The McGraw-Hill Companies, Inc. All rights reserved. No part of this publication may be reproduced or distributed in any form or by any means, or stored in a database or retrieval system, without the prior written consent of The McGraw-Hill Companies, Inc., including, but not limited to, in any network or other electronic storage or transmission, or broadcast for distance learning.

This book is printed on acid-free paper.

1 2 3 4 5 6 7 8 9 0 CCI CCI 0 9 8 7

Student **ISBN:**   978-0-07-351316-4   **Instructor's**   ISBN: 978-0-07-328932-8
Edition MHID: 0-07-351316-4   **Edition (not for resale)** MHID: 0-07-328932-9

Vice president and Editor-in-chief: _Emily G. Barrosse_   Senior production supervisor: _Richard DeVitto_
Publisher: _William R. Glass_   Senior supplement coordinator: _Louis Swaim_
Sponsoring editor: _Katherine K. Crouch_   Design director: _Jeanne M. Schreiber_
Director of development: _Scott Tinetti_   Senior designer: _Violeta Díaz_
Senior development editor: _Allen J. Bernier_   Photo research coordinator: _Natalia Peschiera_
Editorial coordinator: _Amanda Peabody_   Art editors: _Jackie Henry_ and _Robin Mouat_
Senior media producer: _Allison Hawco_   Permissions coordinator: _Veronica Oliva_
Executive marketing manager: _Nick Agnew_   Compositor: _Techbooks_
Project managers: _David M. Staloch_ and _Jackie Henry_   Printer: _Courier_

Because this page cannot legibly accommodate all the copyright notices, credits are listed after the index and constitute an extension of the copyright page.

LIBRARY OF CONGRESS CATALOGING-IN-PUBLICATION DATA

  Sabías que— ?: beginning Spanish / Bill VanPatten … [et al]. —5th ed.
     p. cm.
   Includes index.
   ISBN-13: 978-0-07-351316-4
   ISBN-10: 0-07-351316-4
    1. Spanish language—Textbooks for foreign speakers—English. I. VanPatten, Bill. II.
VanPatten, Bill. Sabías que—?

PC419.E5V36 2008
468.2'421—dc21   2006046964

www.mhhe.com

CONTENTS

Preface   xix

LECCIÓN PRELIMINAR ¿Quién eres?   1

Ideas para explorar ¿Quién eres?   2
Vocabulario
¿Cómo te llamas? ¿De dónde eres? Introducing yourself   2
Gramática
¿Ser o no ser? Forms and uses of **ser**   4

Ideas para explorar Las carreras y las materias   7
Vocabulario
¿Qué estudias? Courses of study and school subjects   7
Gramática
¿Te gusta? Discussing likes and dislikes   10
Vocabulario
¿Qué carrera haces? Talking about your major   13
¿Sabías que... ? Courses of study in Hispanic universities   13

Ideas para explorar Más sobre las clases   14
Gramática
¿Son buenas tus clases? Describing   14
Descriptive Adjectives   14
Possessive Adjectives   15
Vocabulario
¿Cuántos créditos? Numbers 0–30   17
Gramática
¿Hay muchos estudiantes en tu universidad? The verb form **hay**   19
¿Sabías que... ? Grading systems in Hispanic universities   20

Intercambio
 Para mi profesor(a)   21

Vistazos culturales
El español como lengua mundial   22
 Navegando la Red   24

UNIDAD UNO: ENTRE NOSOTROS   28

	Vocabulario	Gramática

LECCIÓN 1

¿Cómo es tu horario?   29

IDEAS PARA EXPLORAR: La vida de todos los días   30

¿Cómo es una rutina?
  Talking about daily routines   30

¿Trabaja o no?
  Talking about what someone else does   33

IDEAS PARA EXPLORAR: Durante la semana   35

¿Con qué frecuencia?
  Talking about how often people do things   35
¿Qué día de la semana?
  Days of the week   38

¿Y yo?
  Talking about your own activities   39

IDEAS PARA EXPLORAR: Más sobre las rutinas   42

¿A qué hora... ?
  Telling when something happens   42

¿Y tú? ¿Y usted?
  Addressing others   45
¿Qué necesitas hacer?
  Talking about what you need or have to do on a regular basis   47

LECCIÓN 2

¿Qué haces los fines de semana?   55

IDEAS PARA EXPLORAR: Actividades para el fin de semana   56

¿Qué hace una persona los sábados?
  Talking about someone's weekend routine   56
¿No haces nada?
  Negation and negative words   58

¿A quien le gusta... ?
  More about likes and dislikes   60

IDEAS PARA EXPLORAR: Las otras personas   61

¿Qué hacen?
  Talking about the activities of two or more people   61
¿Qué hacemos nosotros?
  Talking about activities that you and others do   64

IDEAS PARA EXPLORAR: El tiempo y las estaciones   66

¿Qué tiempo hace?
  Talking about the weather   66
¿Cuándo comienza el verano?
  Talking about seasons of the year   71

¿Qué vas a hacer?
  Introduction to expressing future events   73

LECCIÓN 3

¿Qué hiciste ayer?   80

IDEAS PARA EXPLORAR: Ayer y anoche (I)   81

¿Qué hizo Elena ayer?
  Talking about activities in the past   81

¿Salió o se quedó en casa?
  Talking about what someone else did recently   84
¿Salí o me quedé en casa?
  Talking about what you did recently   89

IDEAS PARA EXPLORAR: Ayer y anoche (II)   96

¿Qué hiciste anoche?
  Talking to a friend about what he or she did recently   96
¿Salieron ellos anoche?
  Talking about what two or more people did recently   97
¿Qué hicimos nosotros?
  Talking about what you and someone else did recently   99

Lecturas culturales y otras actividades

¿Sabías que... ?
Daily schedules 44

 Intercambio

Preguntas para un examen 49
    Forming a series of questions about two schedules

¿Sabías que... ?
Seasons in the northern and southern
    hemispheres 72

 Intercambio

¡Un fin de semana ideal! 75
    Guessing the authorship of various descriptions of
    an ideal weekend

¿Sabías que... ?
Grabbing the reader's attention 91

Vamos a ver 92
Desi Arnaz: La primera superestrella latina 94

 Intercambio

¿Es típico esto? 101
    Writing about what a classmate did

Vistazos culturales

La vida diaria en el mundo hispano 50
Meal schedules
The 24-hour clock
Social schedules
Work schedules
- *España*
- *México*
- *los Estados Unidos y el Canadá*

 Navegando la Red 52

La música y la danza en el mundo hispano 76
Cultural influences

El tango   *El merengue*
El flamenco   *El tamborito*
La salsa y el son   *La cumbia*
El mambo y el chachachá   *El vallenato*
- *la Argentina*   - *la República*
- *España*   *Dominicana*
- *Cuba, Puerto Rico,*   - *Panamá*
   los Estados Unidos   - *Colombia*
   y Venezuela

 Navegando la Red 78

El folclor en el mundo hispano 102
Legends and myths: **La Llorona** *and the* **Popol Vuh**
Religion
Handicrafts
- *la Guinea Ecuatorial*   - *México*
- *Panamá*   - *Nicaragua*
- *Cuba, Puerto Rico y los Estados Unidos*

 Navegando la Red 104

Grammar Summary for **Lección preliminar–Lección 3** 106

UNIDAD DOS: NUESTRAS FAMILIAS   110

	Vocabulario	**Gramática**

LECCIÓN 4

¿Cómo es tu familia?   111

IDEAS PARA EXPLORAR: La familia nuclear   112

¿Cómo es tu familia?
 Talking about your immediate family   112

¿Cuántas hijas… ?
 Question words: A summary   115

IDEAS PARA EXPLORAR: La familia «extendida»   118

¿Y los otros parientes?
 Talking about your extended family   118
¿Tienes sobrinos?
 Additional vocabulary related to family members   121

¿Están casados?
 More on **estar** + adjectives   122

IDEAS PARA EXPLORAR: Mis relaciones con la familia   123

¿Te conocen bien?
 First and second person direct object pronouns   123
¿La quieres?
 Third person direct object pronouns   128
Llamo a mis padres
 The personal **a**   131

LECCIÓN 5

¿A quién te pareces?   138

IDEAS PARA EXPLORAR: Características físicas   139

¿Cómo es? (I)
 Describing people's physical features   139
¿Nos parecemos?
 Talking about family resemblances   142

¿Quién es más alto?
 Making comparisons   141

IDEAS PARA EXPLORAR: Otras características   144

¿Cómo es? (II)
 More on describing people   144

¿Cómo está?
 Describing people's physical or mental state   145
¿La conoces?
 Talking about knowing someone   147

IDEAS PARA EXPLORAR: Más sobre las relaciones familiares   148

¿Te conoces bien?
 True reflexive constructions   148
¿Se abrazan Uds.?
 Reciprocal reflexives   152

LECCIÓN 6

¿Y el tamaño de la familia?   160

IDEAS PARA EXPLORAR: Años y épocas   161

¿Qué edad?
 Numbers 30–199 and talking about people's age   161
¿En qué año… ?
 Numbers 200–2030 and Expressing years   163

¿Está cambiando?
 The present progressive   165

IDEAS PARA EXPLORAR: Épocas anteriores   170

¿Era diferente la vida? (I)
 Introduction to the imperfect tense: Singular forms   170
¿Era diferente la vida? (II)
 More on the imperfect tense: Plural forms   173
¿Tienes tantos hermanos como yo?
 Comparisons of equality   176

Lecturas culturales y otras actividades

¿Sabías que... ?
Hispanic last names   117

 Intercambio
¿Cómo es la familia de... ?   133
Drawing the family tree of a classmate

¿Sabías que... ?
Physical contact in the Spanish-speaking world   153

 Intercambio
¿Cómo son?   155
Describing classmates and their family members

¿Sabías que... ?
Life expectancy in various countries   162

Vamos a ver   166
Está disminuyendo el tamaño de la familia: Datos del
Censo 2000   168

Composición   177

Vistazos culturales

El bilingüismo en el mundo hispano   134
El catalán
El quechua
El gallego
El vasco
El guaraní
El mapuche
- *el Canadá y los Estados Unidos*
- *España*
- *Bolivia, Chile, el Ecuador y el Perú*
- *el Paraguay*
- *la Argentina*

 Navegando la Red   136

El mestizaje en el mundo hispano   156
Spanish and indigenous influences
European influence
Incan influence
Mayan influence
African influence
- *México, Chile, el Paraguay y el Uruguay*
- *Sudamérica*
- *Centroamérica*
- *Cuba, Puerto Rico, la República Dominicana, Colombia, Panamá y Venezuela*

 Navegando la Red   158

La inmigración y emigración en el mundo hispano   180
Hispanic population statistics in the United States
European immigrants in South America
- *el Uruguay y el Paraguay*   - *la Argentina*

 Navegando la Red   182

Grammar Summary for **Lecciones 4–6**   184

UNIDAD TRES: EN LA MESA   186

	Vocabulario	Gramática

LECCIÓN 7

¿Qué sueles comer?   187

IDEAS PARA EXPLORAR: Los hábitos de comer   188

¿Cuáles son algunos alimentos básicos?
  Talking about basic foods in Spanish   188

¿Que si me importan los aditivos?
  Other verbs like **gustar** and the indirect object pronoun **me**   191
¿Te importan los aditivos?
  Te and **nos** as indirect object pronouns   194

IDEAS PARA EXPLORAR: A la hora de comer   196

¿Qué desayunas?
  Talking about what you eat for breakfast   196
¿Qué comes para el almuerzo y para la cena?
  Talking about what you eat for lunch and dinner   199

IDEAS PARA EXPLORAR: Los gustos   201

¿Qué meriendas?
  Talking about snacks and snacking   201

¿Le pones sal a la comida?
  Le and **les** as third person indirect object pronouns   204
¡Está muy salada!
  More about **estar** + adjectives   207

LECCIÓN 8

¿Qué se hace con los brazos?   217

IDEAS PARA EXPLORAR: Los buenos modales   218

¿Qué hay en la mesa?
  Talking about eating at the table   218

¿Se debe… ?
  The impersonal **se**   220

IDEAS PARA EXPLORAR: Las dietas nacionales   222

¿Hay que… ?
  Expressing impersonal obligation   222

¿Se consumen muchas verduras?
  The passive **se**   223

IDEAS PARA EXPLORAR: En un restaurante   227

¿Está todo bien?
  Talking about eating in restaurants   227

¿Para quién es?
  Using **para**   229

LECCIÓN 9

¿Y para beber?   236

IDEAS PARA EXPLORAR: Las bebidas   237

¿Qué bebes?
  Talking about favorite beverages   237

¿Qué bebiste?
  Review of regular preterite tense verb forms and use   238

IDEAS PARA EXPLORAR: Prohibiciones y responsabilidades   245

¿Qué se prohíbe?
  Review of impersonal and passive **se**   245

Lecturas culturales y otras actividades

¿Sabías que... ?
Spanish **tapas**   203

 Intercambio

Preferencias alimenticias   210
   Writing about the preferences and eating habits
   of a classmate

¿Sabías que... ?
The Mediterranean diet   225

 Intercambio

¡Atención, turistas!   231
   Listing good and bad eating habits for Hispanic
   visitors to this country

Vamos a ver   241
Las bebidas nacionales   243

¿Sabías que... ?
A brief history of tequila   248

Composición   249

Vistazos culturales

La cocina en el mundo hispano   212
*Cultural and geographical influences on
      Hispanic cuisine*
Spanish cuisine: **la paella**
Mexican cuisine: Common ingredients and
      los chiles rellenos
Some "less traditional" Hispanic dishes
■ *Puerto Rico*
■ *España*
■ *México*
■ *el Perú*
■ *Colombia*

 Navegando la Red   214

La influencia hispana en el mundo   232
Hispanic influences on the English language
The origin and influence of Don Juan
Literary influences of some Hispanic writers
■ *México*
■ *el Paraguay*
■ *Bolivia, Chile, el Ecuador y el Perú*
■ *Cuba, Puerto Rico y la República Dominicana*
■ *España*
■ *Nicaragua*

 Navegando la Red   234

El arte y la literatura en el mundo hispano   252
Hispanic winners of the Nobel Prize in Literature
Hispanic influences in world art and some noted
      Hispanic painters
■ *España*   ■ *Chile*   ■ *Guatemala*
■ *Colombia* ■ *México*   ■ *los Estados Unidos*

 Navegando la Red   254

Grammar Summary for **Lecciones 7–9**   256

Contents   **xi**

UNIDAD CUATRO: EL BIENESTAR 258

	Vocabulario	Gramática

LECCIÓN 10

¿Cómo te sientes? 259

IDEAS PARA EXPLORAR: Los estados de ánimo 260

¿Cómo se siente?
  Talking about how someone
  feels 260

¿Te sientes bien?
  "Reflexive" verbs 263

IDEAS PARA EXPLORAR: Reacciones 266

¿Cómo se revelan las emociones?
  Talking about how people show
  their feelings 266

¿Te falta energía?
  The verbs **faltar** and **quedar** 270

IDEAS PARA EXPLORAR: Para sentirte bien 274

¿Qué haces para sentirte bien?
  Talking about leisure
  activities 274

¿Qué hacías de niño/a para sentirte bien?
  Using the imperfect for habitual
  events: A review 278

LECCIÓN 11

¿Cómo te relajas? 288

IDEAS PARA EXPLORAR: El tiempo libre 289

¿Qué haces para relajarte?
  More activities for talking about
  relaxation 289
¿Adónde vas para relajarte?
  Talking about places and related
  leisure activities 291

Relajarse es bueno
  When to use an infinitive or an
  -ndo Form 295

IDEAS PARA EXPLORAR: En el pasado 297

¿Qué hicieron el fin de semana
  pasado para relajarse?
  Review of third person
  preterite 297
¿Y qué hiciste tú para relajarte?
  Review of first and second person
  preterite 299

IDEAS PARA EXPLORAR: La última vez... 302

¿Qué hacías que causó tanta risa?
  Narrating in the past: Using both
  preterite and imperfect 302

LECCIÓN 12

¿En qué consiste el abuso? 312

IDEAS PARA EXPLORAR: Hay que tener cuidado 313

¿Qué es una lesión?
  More vocabulary related to
  activities 313

¿Veías la televisión de niño/a?
  Imperfect forms of the
  verb **ver** 316

IDEAS PARA EXPLORAR: Saliendo de la adicción 324

¿Qué debo hacer? —Escucha esto.
  Telling others what to do:
    Affirmative **tú** commands 324
¿Qué no debo hacer? —¡No hagas eso!
  Telling others what *not* to do:
    Negative **tú** commands 326

Lecturas culturales y otras actividades

¿Sabías que... ?
Weather and emotions   272

 Intercambio
Entrevistas   281
   Obtaining information for a composition

¿Sabías que... ?
Baseball in the Caribbean   294

 Intercambio
La tensión y el estrés   307
   Presenting a narration about a classmate to a group

¿Sabías que... ?
Television in the Spanish-speaking world   317

Vamos a ver   319
¿Eres adicto al celular?   321

Composición   328

Vistazos culturales

La globalización en el mundo hispano   284
Various impacts of globalization on Latin America
- *México*
- *Venezuela*
- *Bolivia*

 Navegando la Red   286

Las civilizaciones prehispánicas   308
Various facts about the Aztec, Mayan, and Incan empires
Territorial expanse, art, agriculture, trade, mathematics, and science
- *México*
- *Guatemala*
- *Colombia, el Ecuador, el Perú, Bolivia y Chile*

 Navegando la Red   310

La presencia indígena en el mundo hispano   330
Indigenous influences in Hispanic countries
Artistic and literary works with indigenous themes
Spanish words of indigenous origin
- *México, Guatemala, Bolivia, el Ecuador y el Perú*
- *la Argentina y el Uruguay*
- *Chile*

 Navegando la Red   332

Grammar Summary for **Lecciones 10–12**   334

UNIDAD CINCO: SOMOS LO QUE SOMOS   338

	Vocabulario	Gramática

LECCIÓN 13

¿Cómo te describes? 339

IDEAS PARA EXPLORAR: La personalidad   340

¿Cómo eres tú? (I)
   Describing personalities   340
¿Cómo eres tú? (II)
   More on describing
      personalities   343

IDEAS PARA EXPLORAR: La expresión de la personalidad   345

¿Qué has hecho? (I)
   Introduction to the present
      perfect   345
¿Qué has hecho? (II)
   More on the present perfect   347

IDEAS PARA EXPLORAR: Más sobre tu personalidad   349

¿Te atreves a… ?
   More verbs that require a
      reflexive pronoun   349
¿Es reflexivo?
   Review of the pronoun **se**   351

LECCIÓN 14

¿A quién te gustaría conocer? 362

IDEAS PARA EXPLORAR: La personalidad de los famosos   363

¿Qué cualidades poseían?
   More adjectives to describe
      people   363

IDEAS PARA EXPLORAR: Situaciones hipotéticas   367

¿Qué harías? (I)
   Introduction to the
      conditional tense   367
¿Y si pudieras… ?
   Introduction to the
      past subjunctive   369

IDEAS PARA EXPLORAR: En busca de personas conocidas   373

¿A quién… ?
   Review of the object marker **a**   373
¿Te gustaría… ?
   Review of the verb **gustar**   374

LECCIÓN 15

¿Innato o aprendido? 382

IDEAS PARA EXPLORAR: De aquí para allá   383

¿Dónde está la biblioteca?
   Telling where things are   383
¿Cómo se llega al zoológico?
   Giving and receiving
      directions   384

IDEAS PARA EXPLORAR: Lo interesante   388

¿Por dónde?
   Por and **para** with spatial
      relationships   388
¿Qué es lo curioso de esto?
   Lo + adjective   389

Lecturas culturales y otras actividades

¿Sabías que... ?
The Chinese horoscope   354

 Intercambio
La personalidad de tu compañero/a de clase   356
   Describing the personality of a classmate

¿Sabías que... ?
Don Quijote de la Mancha   366

 Intercambio
¿A quién te gustaría conocer?   377
   Comparing what a classmate says with what
you think

¿Sabías que... ?
Sense of direction in animals   386

Vamos a ver   391
Lo innato frente a lo aprendido: el «dedónde» de
   nuestra personalidad   392

Composición   396

Vistazos culturales

El medio ambiente en el mundo hispano   358
Ecological and economic effects of El Niño
National parks and wildlife reserves
Ecotourism
Endangered species
- ■ *el Perú y el Ecuador*
- ■ *Costa Rica*
- ■ *México*

 Navegando la Red   360

Las ciencias en el mundo hispano   378
Hispanic winners of the Nobel Prize in Science
Paleontology in Patagonia
- ■ *España, la Argentina, los Estados Unidos y Venezuela*

 Navegando la Red   380

La economía en el mundo hispano   398
Import and export products of some Hispanic countries
Comparing gross national products
Economic crises in Latin America
- ■ *Puerto Rico, la República Dominicana y Cuba*
- ■ *Honduras, El Salvador y Nicaragua*
- ■ *Venezuela*   ■ *el Ecuador*
- ■ *Chile*   ■ *la Argentina*

 Navegando la Red   400

Grammar Summary for **Lecciones 13–15**   401

UNIDAD SEIS: HACIA EL FUTURO   404

	Vocabulario	Gramática

LECCIÓN 16

¿Adónde vamos?   405

IDEAS PARA EXPLORAR: La ropa   406

¿Cómo te vistes?
  Talking about clothing   406

¿Qué te pones?
  More on reflexive verbs   409

IDEAS PARA EXPLORAR: De viaje   411

¿En tren o en auto?
  Talking about trips and
    traveling   411
¿Dónde nos quedamos?
  Talking more about trips and
    traveling   414

IDEAS PARA EXPLORAR: En el extranjero   418

Firme aquí.
  Telling others what to do:
    Formal commands   418
¿Qué harías? (II)
  Review of the conditional tense   420

LECCIÓN 17

¿A qué profesión u ocupación quieres dedicarte?   429

IDEAS PARA EXPLORAR: Las profesiones (I)   430

¿Qué profesión?
  Talking about professions   430

¿Qué tipo de trabajo buscas?
  The subjunctive after indefinite
    antecedents   435

IDEAS PARA EXPLORAR: Las profesiones (II)   439

¿Qué características y habilidades
  se necesitan?
  Talking about traits needed for
    particular professions   439

No hay nadie que...
  The subjunctive after negative and
    nonexistent antecedents   441

IDEAS PARA EXPLORAR: Algunas aspiraciones   443

¿Qué piensas hacer cuando... ?
  The subjunctive after expressions
    of future intent   443

LECCIÓN 18

¿Qué nos espera en el futuro?   453

IDEAS PARA EXPLORAR: Las posibilidades y probabilidades del futuro   454

¿Cómo será nuestra vida?
  Introduction to the simple
    future tense   454
¿Es probable? ¿Es posible?
  The subjunctive with expressions
    of uncertainty   457

IDEAS PARA EXPLORAR: Más posibilidades y probabilidades   463

¿Cómo será el futuro?
  Talking about the future   463

Lecturas culturales y otras actividades

¿Sabías que... ?
Lodging in the United States and Spain   417

 Intercambio
Un viaje al extranjero   423
    Determining with whom to travel abroad for
    a month

¿Sabías que... ?
Gender in names of professions   434

 Intercambio
Recomendaciones para elegir una profesión   447
    Recommending to classmates what profession they
    should follow

¿Sabías que... ?
Women in professional fields   457

Vamos a ver   460
«Apocalipsis» por Marco Denevi   461

Composición   466

Vistazos culturales

La moda en el mundo hispano   424
Two internationally known Hispanic designers:
    Cristóbal Balenciaga and Carolina Herrera
Importance of fashion in everyday dress in
    Hispanic culture
La china poblana
El sarape
Importance of vicuña wool
- *España*
- *Venezuela*
- *México*
- *el Perú*

 Navegando la Red   426

La revolución y la guerra civil en el mundo hispano   448
Revolution in Central America
The Mexican Revolution
Zapatista rebels in Chiapas, Mexico
The Spanish Civil War
The Revolution in Cuba
- *Nicaragua*
- *Cuba*
- *México*
- *España*

 Navegando la Red   450

El futuro del español en los Estados Unidos   468
Some related facts from U.S. Census 2000
Bilingual education
Foreign language enrollments in U.S. high schools
- *los Estados Unidos*

 Navegando la Red   470

Grammar Summary for **Lecciones 16–18**   472

Appendix: Verbs   A1

Spanish-English Vocabulary   V1

English-Spanish Vocabulary   V32

Index   I1

PREFACE

We are delighted to publish the Fifth Edition of the innovative and communicatively oriented textbook *¿Sabías que... ?* When we wrote the First Edition, we were responding to what we saw as a real need in the field: a package of materials that was truly oriented toward communication in the classroom and that broke away from traditional presentations and practice of grammar. We wanted to demonstrate that classrooms could be places where the language was used to talk about real things without sacrificing coverage of basic grammatical points that most instructors have come to expect from beginning Spanish textbooks. We also wanted to create a book that incorporated the ideas behind the roles of both input and output in language learning and fashioned them into a coherent approach. Our concern was simply this: Without new materials and with severe constraints on their time, how could instructors move classes toward the kinds of instructional interactions that theory and research were showing to be beneficial to language learning? We believed that without a change in approach, there could be no change in language instruction.

Now, sixteen years later, we find that the description of the First Edition of *¿Sabías que... ?* is still appropriate for this Fifth Edition.

Are you looking for a Spanish textbook that

- encourages students to concentrate on exchanging real-life information about each other and the world around them?
- makes as much use of class time as possible to communicate ideas?
- is at times provocative?
- is filled with engaging activities?

Are you looking for a textbook that is all those things but doesn't sacrifice basic grammar? Then welcome to *¿Sabías que... ?* and the world of information-based instruction! *¿Sabías que... ?* is an innovative package of materials for introductory Spanish courses. It weaves together content language learning and interactive tasks in which information is exchanged—and it gives a complete package to instructors who want to develop students' communicative proficiency in all four skills from the first day of instruction.

Are you also looking for a textbook that can help you focus on the five Cs of the Standards for Foreign Language Learning: *Communication, Cultures, Connections, Comparisons,* and *Communities*? In as much as a beginning university level textbook can reflect the spirit of the Standards, *¿Sabías que... ?* does an excellent job.

- **Communication:** *¿Sabías que... ?* is ideal as a starting point in terms of communication for learners of Spanish because of the meaningful and communicative tasks that form the core of its pedagogy. Communication in *¿Sabías que... ?* occurs in all skills and pushes learners to use what they have learned in a purposeful manner.
- **Cultures:** *¿Sabías que... ?* introduces learners to both *big C* and *little c* cultural information through the **¿Sabías que... ?** boxes, the **Vistazos culturales** sections, and elsewhere.
- **Connections:** Learners frequently make connections with other disciplines through the readings as well as through tasks that ask them to bring in knowledge from other areas.
- **Comparisons:** Learners compare and contrast aspects of grammar, vocabulary, and usage not only between English and Spanish but also between dialects of Spanish.
- **Communities:** Finally, learners are encouraged to use Spanish outside the classroom with assignments that get them to interview people and use the Web. In this way, they are pushed to use Spanish in a non-academic setting and to seek connections with communities beyond classroom walls.

Both instructors and students will find *¿Sabías que... ?* to be a *real* book. It contains universal topics and contemporary themes that are meaningful to students. Many of its readings were culled from magazines that were written for Spanish speakers and not contrived for grammar or vocabulary practice. Spanish is actually used, not just talked about. We hope that you'll share our enthusiasm for these materials, and that you and your class will enjoy many hours of both learning Spanish and learning about each other.

The Information-Based Task Approach

The information-based task approach is a communicative approach. It springs from the idea that languages are best learned when real-world information becomes the focus of student activities. The organization of an information-based approach is simple:

1. Formulate a question or set of questions for the student to answer.
2. Give the student the linguistic tools necessary to get the answer.
3. Provide the student with a source or sources for the information.

For more on this unique and innovative approach, please consult the *Instructor's Manual*.

Organization of the Text

¿Sabías que... ?, Fifth Edition, consists of a preliminary lesson (**Lección preliminar**) and six units of three lessons each. Each unit presents a general theme that is explored in its three lessons.

The organization of the major sections of each lesson allows instructors to organize class meetings better and develop course syllabi (see the *Instructor's Manual* for ideas on lesson and syllabus planning). Each of these major sections is described in the Guided Tour Through *¿Sabías que... ?* on the following pages. The first two lessons of every unit include:

- three **Ideas para explorar** sections
- vocabulary (**Vocabulario**) and grammar (**Gramática**) presentations within each **Ideas para explorar** section
- **Intercambio**
- **Vistazos culturales**

The third lesson of each unit includes:

- two **Ideas para explorar** sections
- **Vocabulario** and **Gramática** presentations
- **Vamos a ver**
- **Composición***
- **Vistazos culturales**

*Lección 3 contains an **Intercambio** activity instead of **Composición.**

A Guided Tour Through

¿Sabías que…?

Lesson-Opening Page Each lesson-opening page contains an advance organizer that informs students about what they will be focusing on in the current lesson. Another feature included on each lesson-opening page is a stop-sign icon that references the **Intercambio** or **Composición** activity at the end of the lesson. This offers students a preview of what they will learn in the lesson and gives them a task to work toward.

Ideas para explorar Each **Ideas para explorar** section introduces a subtopic of the lesson theme through the **Vocabulario** and **Gramática** presentations.

Vocabulario Each **Vocabulario** presents new active vocabulary related to the lesson theme and is followed by activities that encourage students to use the new vocabulary in context.

Some **Vocabulario** sections include **Vocabulario útil** boxes. These boxes highlight additional active vocabulary that students can use in the activities of the lesson.

Gramática A highlighted box accompanying many **Gramática** sections focuses on the presentation material in an easy-to-follow format. Grammar explanations are succinct and the activities that follow allow students to use the grammar in meaning-based exchanges.

¿Sabías que… ? does not offer purely mechanical grammar practice, such as transformation and substitution drills. Grammar is presented bit by bit, with points explained only as necessary for students to perform the various tasks in the lesson.

VAMOS A VER

ANTICIPACIÓN

Paso 1 The reading on page 94 is adapted from a magazine for general readership. Look at the title and the photo without reading anything else. Can you guess the meaning of the word **superestrella?** Select from these two options: (a) *superhit;* (b) *superstar.* Read the first paragraph of the reading to see if you're right.

Paso 2 By now you know the article is about Desi Arnaz. What do you know about him already? Thinking about this will help you better guess words in context as well as comprehend more of what you read. Look at the following statements and select the correct answer for each. Share with the class.

1. Desi Arnaz nació en _____
   a. Puerto Rico   b. Cuba   c. México
2. Se mudó (*He moved*) a los Estados Unidos por razones _____
   a. políticas   b. económicas   c. personales
3. Comenzó su carrera profesional con _____
   a. la música   b. el teatro   c. la televisión

Desi Arnaz

La primera superestrella latina

Desi Arnaz con Lucille Ball

¿En quién piensas cuando oyes la frase «superestrella latina»? ¿Piensas en Jennifer López? ¿en Ricky Martin? ¿en Selma Hayek? ¿en Gloria Estefan? Aunque es cierto que estas personas y muchas otras de ascendencia latina tienen gran fama hoy en día, el primer latino de gran fama en la música, el cine y la televisión de los Estados Unidos fue Desi Arnaz de la serie *I Love Lucy.*

De Cuba a Hollywood

Arnaz nació con el nombre de Desiderio Alberto Arnaz de Acha III, en Santiago, Cuba, en 1917. Debido a la revolución de Batista en 1933, la familia Arnaz huyó de Cuba para instalarse en Miami. Puesto que tuvieron que abandonar sus propiedades y dinero, los Arnaz llegaron a Miami con muy poco. Aceptaron trabajos mínimos y uno de los primeros trabajos de Desi fue limpiar jaulas de canarios. Pero la música siempre fue su pasión y decidió lanzarse a la carrera de músico y cantante, siguiendo las huellas de Xavier Cugat, «el rey de música latina». Formó su propio grupo musical y con éxitos como «Babalú» hizo muy popular la conga entre el público norteamericano. Su carrera lo llevó a Broadway y después a Hollywood.

De las películas a la televisión

En 1940 conoció a Lucille Ball durante la filmación de *Too Many Girls.* Se casó con ella y en diez años los dos fundaron la compañía «Desilu». La serie *I Love Lucy* se estrenó en 1951 y aunque Lucy era la estrella, el genio creativo de esa y muchas otras producciones televisivas era Desi. Gracias al personaje de Ricky Ricardo, la presencia latina en la televisión y la cultura norteamericana en general se estableció. Pero el matrimonio entre Desi y Lucille no duró y se divorciaron en 1960, después de tener dos hijos. En 1976, Arnaz publicó su autobiografía, *A Book,* y diez años más tarde murió de cáncer. Muchos críticos contemporáneos dicen que las superestrellas latinas de hoy le deben mucho a Desi, quien abrió la puerta para los latinos que llegaron después.

INTERCAMBIO

¿Cómo es la familia de...?

 Propósito: dibujar (*to draw*) el árbol genealógico de alguna persona en la clase.

 Papeles: una persona entrevistada; el resto de la clase dividido en cinco grupos.

Paso 1 El profesor (La profesora) le va a asignar a cada grupo una de las siguientes categorías.

Categoría 1: miembros de la familia nuclear
Categoría 2: abuelos
Categoría 3: tíos, incluyendo a los esposos y esposas
Categoría 4: primos
Categoría 5: características particulares de los diferentes parientes (por ejemplo, la persona más loca [*craziest*]; ver **Así se dice**) y sus pasatiempos especiales

Cada grupo debe hacer las preguntas necesarias para obtener toda la información sobre su categoría. Por ejemplo, se puede preguntar sobre los nombres de los parientes, su edad, dónde viven, etcétera.

Paso 2 Los grupos deben entrevistar a la persona seleccionada. Toda la clase debe escuchar sus respuestas y apuntar (*jot down*) toda la información. **¡OJO!** Si no entiendes algo, debes pedir aclaración.

Paso 3 En casa, dibuja el árbol genealógico de la persona entrevistada. Incluye todos los detalles. A continuación hay un ejemplo de cómo se puede poner el nombre de un pariente en el árbol genealógico.
Si hay tiempo, uno o dos voluntarios debe(n) presentar su dibujo a la clase y dar una descripción de dos o tres minutos de varios miembros de la familia.

Así se dice

To say the *biggest, the smallest,* and so forth, Spanish uses the *definite article* + **más** + *adjective.*
To say *the least intelligent, the least shy,* and so forth, Spanish uses the *definite article* + **menos** + *adjective.* Two exceptions are **mayor** and **menor.**

el/la más inteligente
the smartest

el/la menos tímido/a
the least shy

el/la mayor
the oldest

el/la menor
the youngest

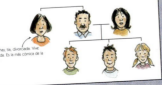

María Shav, tía, divorciada. Vive en Florida. Es la más cómica de la familia.

Vamos a ver The reading selections in **Vamos a ver** are based on authentic materials.

Pre- and postreading activities help students learn such strategies as reading for content, summarizing information, and guessing contextually. Practice in recognizing cognates is often an important part of these activities.

In **Anticipación** students think about the topic they are to read, make predictions about the content of the reading, preview vocabulary, and perform other activities that will help maximize their comprehension.

In **Exploración** students read and gather information—a process accomplished by scanning for specific information, verifying predictions from the **Anticipación** section, skimming for general meaning, and so forth. Students also begin to read for detail, usually by tackling the reading a section at a time.

In **Síntesis** students pull together the information that they have gathered from the reading. Typical activities include completing information grids, creating outlines, creating semantic maps, and writing compositions.

In **Trabajando con el texto** (not included in every **Vamos a ver** section) students go back to the reading to examine features of language or discourse, such as recurring grammatical forms or structures, the organizational structure of the text, or the author's purpose in writing the text.

In **¡Sigamos!,** which concludes **Vamos a ver,** students work further with the themes and topics of the reading.

Intercambio **Intercambio** is the culminating activity found in most lessons. Designed for partner/pair or small group work, **Intercambio** draws upon the vocabulary and grammar structures presented within the lesson to summarize the material in an exciting and engaging lesson-ending task.

Composición The third lesson of most units culminates in **Composición,** a guided writing assignment that integrates vocabulary and grammatical structures of the lesson.

In **Antes de escribir,** students think about the writing topic through brainstorming and organize the information in their composition.

Al escribir helps students draft their compositions. In this section, students not only write, but they also reflect upon what they have written and seek feedback from peers.

In **Después de escribir,** students edit their final draft for vocabulary and grammar, and they create a clean, final version to hand in to their instructor.

Comunicación These activities are done with a partner or in small groups. Although all activities in ¿Sabías que… ? are meaning-based in nature, **Comunicación** activities involve more interaction with classmates. A **Comunicación** icon in the margin signals the beginning of the **Comunicación** activities for each **Vocabulario** and **Gramática** section.

¿Sabías que… ? **¿Sabías que… ?** boxes highlight facts about Hispanic cultures as well as the world around us. All **¿Sabías que… ?** boxes are accompanied by an activity or appear as part of the new **Vistazos culturales** sections.

Así se dice, Consejo práctico, Nota comunicativa **Así se dice** boxes provide additional information about Spanish vocabulary and grammar. **Consejo práctico** boxes point out key difference between Spanish and English and offer helpful advice to students. **Nota comunicativa** boxes present words and phrases to help students complete communicative tasks.

Icons Icons identify Web, listening, video, and online *ActivityPak* activities and features as well as classroom activities that require a separate sheet of paper or group work.

COMPOSICIÓN

En esta lección has examinado cuestiones sobre el futuro. En esta composición vas a escribir sobre «La vida diaria en el año 2050».

Antes de escribir

Paso 1 El propósito de la composición es predecir ciertos aspectos del futuro y describir cómo será la vida diaria en 2050. Vas a dirigirte a la clase. El tono que adoptes puede ser cómico o serio. La composición deberá limitarse a unas 250 palabras.

Paso 2 Como se trata de la vida diaria, ¿qué temas vas a tratar? ¿Qué temas vas a excluir? Haz una lista de los aspectos que se pueden considerar «de la vida diaria». ¿Cuántos vas a incluir?

Paso 3 Debes prestar atención al aspecto lingüístico. ¿Sabes usar los puntos gramaticales que estudiaste en esta lección?

- el futuro
- el subjuntivo con expresiones de duda, posibilidad, etcétera

Al escribir

Paso 1 A continuación hay algunas expresiones que pueden ayudarte a expresar tus ideas. No te olvides de tomar en cuenta el tono de tu composición antes de usarlas.

más que nada	above all
se caracterizará por	will probably be characterized by
por _____ que + *subjunctive*	as _____ as may (be)
(por contentos que estemos)	(as happy as we may be)

Paso 2 Las siguientes expresiones te pueden resultar útiles al escribir la conclusión.

venga lo que venga	come what may . . .
pase lo que pase	come what may . . .
lo que pasará, pasará, pero…	whatever happens will happen, but . . .

Paso 3 Escribe la composición dos días antes de entregársela al profesor (a la profesora).

COMUNICACIÓN

ACTIVIDAD C ¿Qué prefieres?

Paso 1 Entrevista a tres personas para saber qué bebidas prefieren o les gusta tomar en cada ocasión a continuación. Apunta sus respuestas.

	E1	E2	E3
1. para el desayuno (por la mañana)			
2. con una hamburguesa			
3. para la merienda			
4. cuando sale con unos amigos por la noche			
5. mientras estudia (trabaja, lee)			

Paso 2 La clase debe entrevistar al profesor (a la profesora). ¿Son diferentes sus preferencias de las de Uds o son iguales?

¿Sabías que… en España se vive más? Según los nuevos datos, la esperanza de vida¹ en España es de 78,1 años, mientras que en los Estados Unidos es menos: 76,6 años. Sin embargo, los nuevos cálculos de la Organización Mundial de la Salud² ofrecen un nuevo tipo de dato: esperanza de vida saludable.³ Con este cálculo, se establece el número de años que una persona puede esperar vivir en buena salud. En España esta cifra es de 72,8 años, mientras que en los Estados Unidos es de 70 años. En Latinoamérica, el país con mayor esperanza de vida saludable es Cuba: 68,4 años. ¿Y cuál es el país de mayor esperanza de vida saludable en el mundo? El Japón, con unos 74,5 años.

Campol, España

¹esperanza… *life expectancy* ²Organización… *World Health Organization* ³*healthy*

Así se dice

Why are some verbs preceded by *se?* Such verbs are called reflexive verbs, and you will learn about them in **Lección 5.** For now, take note of which verbs are used with *se.* ¡OJO! (*Careful!*) *Se* does not mean *he* or *she.* **Él** and **ella** mean *he* and *she.*

(Ella) Se levanta.
She gets up.

(Él) Se acuesta.
He goes to bed.

Consejo práctico

Although learning how to speak is the goal of many students of Spanish, acquisition of a language is actually dependent on opportunities to hear or read language in context. For this reason, in *¿Sabías que… ?* you always begin learning new vocabulary or grammar by listening to or reading the new items in context.

Nota comunicativa

Here are two expressions you may find useful in the classroom. To ask a question, you can say

Tengo una pregunta, por favor.
I have a question, please.

To ask how to say a particular word in Spanish, you can ask

¿Cómo se dice _____ en español?
How do you say _____ in Spanish?

Vistazos culturales

This informative and colorful two-page cultural section appears near the end of each lesson and addresses a specific theme as it applies to a variety of Spanish-speaking countries. Each **Vistazos culturales** is followed by comprehension questions in **¿Qué recuerdas?** and a **Navegando la Red** activity in which students complete a project and present their findings to the class. This complete **Navegando la Red** activity is available in the Student Edition of the *¿Sabías que… ?* Online Learning Center at **www. mhhe.com/sabiasque5**.

Grammar Summary A grammar summary concluding each unit highlights the major grammar points presented in the preceding lessons and offers students a handy summary guide to help them improve upon their knowledge of grammatical structures in Spanish.

What's New in the Fifth Edition?

We have made the following changes to *¿Sabías que... ?* in response to instructor feedback on the Fourth Edition.

- Some of the **Vamos a ver** reading selections have been updated or replaced. The reading in **Lección 3** continues the theme of Latin superstars in North America, but now discusses the first one ever, Desi Arnaz. The theme of "something good turning into something bad if abused" has been retained in **Lección 12,** but now the reading addresses cell phone addiction instead of addiction to computers.

- Many of the **Vistazos culturales** spreads now contain more visuals and fewer text boxes to make them more intelligible and meaningful to beginning students.

- More production-based activities provide students with additional opportunities to speak and interact from the first lesson. Beginning with **Lección 7,** three new recurring activity types that allow for open-ended discussion and interaction begin to appear.

  1. **En tu opinión:** Students read about a situation and then offer their reactions to it.
  2. **¿Qué haces?:** Students read about a situation and explain how they would react or respond.
  3. **En el escenario:** Students role-play different situations.
  4. **Una historia:** Students examine a series of drawings and create a story based on what they see. They are encouraged to go beyond the drawings and add background information on the characters and settings.

- New on-page annotations in the early lessons serve to explain some of the philosophical and methodological aspects of *¿Sabías que... ?* to first-time instructors. For example, annotations for activities in **Lección 1** are now flagged with "Input Activity" or "Production Activity" to help familiarize first-time instructors with the natural progression from input to production activities within each **Vocabulario** or **Gramática** section that is a key element of the *¿Sabías que... ?* methodology.

- The **Los hispanos hablan** testimonials have been renamed **Videoteca** and moved to the student *Manual.* Audio-only versions of these testimonials are included in the *Audio Program,* and the video segments can still be seen on the *Video, Video on CD,* or *Online Learning Center.*

- The *Interactive CD-ROM* from the Fourth Edition has been updated and redesigned and is now an online product called the *"ActivityPak,"* which is available on the *Online Learning Center.*

- Finally, activities and other proven features have been revised to keep the program fresh and up-to-date for the many loyal users of *¿Sabías que... ?*

Supplements

As a full-service publisher of quality educational products, McGraw-Hill does much more than just sell textbooks to your students. We create and publish an extensive array of print, video, and digital supplements to support instruction on your campus. Orders of new (versus used) textbooks help us to defray the cost of developing such supplements, which is substantial. Please consult your local McGraw-Hill representative to learn about the availability of the supplements that accompany this Fifth Edition of *¿Sabías que... ?*

For Instructors *and* for Students

- The *Manual que acompaña ¿Sabías que... ?,* Volumes 1 and 2, offers additional practice with vocabulary, grammar, and listening comprehension. A distinguishing feature of the *Manual* is the **Vamos a ver** section near the end of every third lesson that provides non-conversational listening practice. Students listen to a short presentation about a topic related to the unit themes, thus practicing the skills needed to comprehend a lecture. The *Manual* also offers a **Videoteca** activity at the end of every lesson. Formerly the **Los hispanos hablan** from the Fourth Edition, these activities offer video interviews with Spanish speakers from around the world as well as pre- and post-viewing activities.

- McGraw-Hill is proud to partner with **Quia™** in the development of the *Online Manual que acompaña ¿Sabías que... ?,* Fifth Edition Volumes 1 and 2. Carefully integrated with the textbook, this robust digital version of the printed *Manual* is easy for students to use and great for instructors who want to manage students' coursework online. Identical in practice material to the print version, the *Online*

Manual contains the full audio program, as well as the **Videoteca** video segments, and provides students with automatic feedback and scoring of their work. The Instructor's Workstation contains an easy-to-use gradebook and class roster system that facilitates course management.

■ The *Audio Program* that accompanies the *Manual* provides additional listening comprehension practice outside of the classroom.

■ The new online *ActivityPak*, available on the *Online Learning Center*, offers students opportunities to review the grammar, vocabulary, and cultural topics presented in the textbook, all in an engaging multimedia environment.

■ Through the new online *ActivityPak* as well as other discrete-point exercises, the *Online Learning Center* provides practice with the grammar and vocabulary presented in the textbook. It also helps students bring the Spanish-speaking world into their language-learning experience through a variety of cultural resources.

■ The *Video Program* contains the **Videoteca** interviews as well as six exciting segments shot on location that examine particular themes within each unit and include interviews with Spanish speakers.

■ Three *cultural and literary readers* are available to supplement first- and second-year Spanish instruction. Written in Spanish, these readers offer the chance for students to broaden their knowledge of the richness of the cultures of the Spanish-speaking world as well as to increase their developing reading skills.

1. *El mundo hispano: An Introductory Cultural and Literary Reader* contains cultural information on the six major regions of the Spanish-speaking world, including the United States, as well as excerpts from Spanish-language literary classics with accompanying comprehension questions.
2. *Mundos de fantasía: Fábulas, cuentos de hadas y leyendas* contains popular Hispanic fables, fairy tales, and legends.
3. *Cocina y comidas hispanas* highlights favorite recipes from around the Hispanic world.

For Instructors *Only*

■ The annotated *Instructor's Edition* contains detailed suggestions for carrying out activities in class. It also offers options for expansion and follow-up.

■ The combined *Instructor's Manual and Testing Program* expands on the methodology of *¿Sabías que... ?* Among other things, it offers suggestions for carrying out the activities in the textbook and suggests ways to provide students with appropriate feedback on their compositions. The *Testing Program* includes sample quizzes for each lesson as well as unit tests.

■ The Instructor's Edition of the *Online Learning Center* contains the following resources to assist instructors in getting the most out of the *¿Sabías que... ?* program.

1. *Instructor's Manual* (Word files of the print version)
2. *Testing Program* (Word files of the print version)
3. *Audioscript* (transcript of the *Audio Program*)
4. *Videoscript* (transcript of the *Video Program*)
5. *Digital Transparencies* (line art from the textbook)

■ *Making Communicative Language Teaching Happen*, Second Edition, by James F. Lee and Bill VanPatten presents and explains current theories and research in the field of Second Language Acquisition. It is a natural companion volume for instructors using *¿Sabías que... ?*

■ *From input to output*, edited by James F. Lee and Bill VanPatten, explains in everyday, non-academic language the progression from input to output that is central to the methodology of *¿Sabías que... ?*

Acknowledgments

We would like to thank the following instructors for completing reviews that were indispensable in the development of *¿Sabías que... ?*, Fifth Edition. The appearance of their names does not necessarily constitute an endorsement of the text or its methodology.

Paloma Borreguero, *University of Washington*
Angela DeLutis-Eichenberger, *University of Maryland—College Park*

Loredana Margaret Di Stravolo, *University of Maryland*
Rafael Durmett, *University of San Francisco*
Elena González Ros, *Brandeis University*
Anthony Houston, *St. Louis University*
Martin Laina, *University of Notre Dame*
Rachel Ann Linville, *University of Maryland*
Kristina McCollam Wiebe, *Kansas State University*
Alice A. Miano, *Stanford University*
Michael Morris, *Northern Illinois University*
Zara Pastos, *Whitworth College*
Kelly Roberton, *Whitworth College*
Regina Roebuck, *University of Louisville*
Cristina Sanz, *Georgetown University*
Jennie Sevedge, *Whitworth College*
Joseph R. Weyers, *College of Charleston*
Julie Wilhelm, *Iowa State University*

Many other individuals deserve our thanks and appreciation for their help and support. First, we thank Gregory Keating for his work on the original manuscript for the **Vistazos culturales** sections. Thanks go to Michael J. Leeser, Mark Overstreet, and Julie Sellers for their work on portions of the original manuscript for the Online *ActivityPak*. For creating the original quizzes found on the *Online Learning Center*, we thank Deborah Gill, Gayle Vierma, and Julie Sellers. We extend special thanks to the people who shared their thoughts and generously gave their time to be interviewed for the **Vamos a ver** and **Los hispanos hablan** video segments. We also thank Laura Chastain, whose careful reading of the manuscript for details of style, clarity, and language added considerably to the quality of the final version.

Thanks are due to the entire production team at McGraw-Hill, especially David Staloch, Jackie Henry (Techbooks), Natalia Peschiera, Robin Mouat, Rich DeVitto, Louis Swaim, and Violeta Díaz.

We are grateful to our publisher William R. Glass, our sponsoring editor Katherine K. Crouch, and to Nick Agnew and the rest of the McGraw-Hill Marketing and Sales team for their unflagging support and promotion of the *¿Sabías que... ?* program. Very special thanks are also due to the editorial team of Scott Tinetti, Allen J. Bernier, Mara Brown, Pennie Nichols, and Amanda Peabody for a wonderful editing job and helping this edition move so smoothly on its path from manuscript to publication.

Last, but not least, we would like to thank our family and friends who have given us a great deal of support over the years. You know who you are and we care a great deal about you all!

LECCIÓN
preliminar

Check out the following media resources to complement this lesson:

 Online *Manual*

 Online Learning Center

 Video on CD

 ActivityPak

¿Quién eres?

In this lesson, as you will get to know your classmates, you will share information about yourself and

◆ ask your classmates their names and where they are from

◆ ask about their majors, what classes they are taking, and which subjects they especially like or dislike

◆ learn the forms and uses of the verb **ser**

◆ learn the subject-pronoun system in Spanish

◆ learn to use the verb **gustar** to talk about yourself and someone you know

◆ learn about gender and number of articles as well as descriptive and possessive adjectives

◆ learn the numbers 0–30

◆ learn the verb form **hay**

ALTO Before beginning this lesson, look over the **Intercambio** activity on page 21. This is the activity you will be working toward throughout the lesson.

Un saludo típico en Bogotá

VOCABULARIO

¿Cómo te llamas? ¿De dónde eres?

Introducing yourself

—**Hola. Me llamo** Luz.
 ¿Cómo te llamas?
—**Soy** Ricardo.
—**¿De dónde eres,** Ricardo?
—**De** Puerto Rico. **¿Y tú?**
—**Soy de** California. **Mucho
 gusto.**
—**Encantado.**

In Spanish, you can use the following expressions to introduce yourself to others.

> Hola. Soy _____.
> *or* Me llamo _____.
> *or* Mi nombre es _____.

To find out another person's name, you can ask

> ¿Cómo te llamas?
> *or* ¿Cómo se llama usted?

¿Cómo te llamas? is used with a person your own age or with a friend or someone with whom you are on familiar speaking terms. **¿Cómo se llama usted?** is generally used with someone older than yourself or when there is a bit of formality or social distance between you and the other person.

To find out where someone is from, you can ask

> ¿De dónde eres?
> *or* ¿De dónde es usted?

¿De dónde eres? is used with the same people as **¿Cómo te llamas? ¿De dónde es usted?** is used with the same people as **¿Cómo se llama usted?** (You will learn more about this in **Lección 1.**)

To respond to these questions, say

> Soy de _____ (*place*).

or simply

> De _____ (*place*).

To report someone else's information, you can say

> Se llama _____ (*name*).
> Es de _____ (*place*).

To respond to an introduction, you can say

> Mucho gusto.
> Encantado. (*if you're a man*)
> *or* Encantada. (*if you're a woman*)

Así se dice

Me llamo literally means *I call myself*. (Don't make the mistake of thinking **me** = *my* and **llamo** = *name!*) **Mi nombre es,** literally translated, means *My name is*. Study the following expressions.

Me llamo…
I call myself . . .

Mi nombre es…
My name is . . .

¿Cómo te llamas?
What do you call yourself?

¿Cuál es tu nombre?
What is your name?

Se llama…
He/She calls himself/herself . . .

Su nombre es…
His/Her name is . . .

ACTIVIDAD A ¡Hola!

Here are the beginnings of several conversations. Choose the expression that would most likely follow each one.

1. **E1:*** ¿Cómo te llamas?
   E2: _____
   ☐ Mi nombre es Carlos.
   ☐ Mucho gusto.
   ☐ Soy de Chicago.

2. **E1:** Hola. Soy Adriana.
   E2: _____
   ☐ Hola. ¿Cómo te llamas?
   ☐ De Minnesota.
   ☐ Mucho gusto. Soy Daniel.

3. **E1:** ¿De dónde eres?
   E2: _____
   ☐ Me llamo Ana.
   ☐ Encantado.
   ☐ Soy de Miami.

4. **E1:** Soy de Cincinnati. ¿Y usted?
   E2: _____
   ☐ De Houston.
   ☐ ¿De dónde es usted?
   ☐ Mucho gusto.

Nota comunicativa

You know how to say *hello* to a friend, but there are a variety of other greetings that you will find useful in Spanish. Here are some very common ones.

Hola. ¿Qué tal?	*Hi. What's up? (How's it going?)*
Buenos días.	*Good morning.*
Buenas tardes.	*Good afternoon.*
Buenas noches.	*Good evening.*

To say *good-bye,* there are a number of leave-taking expressions that you can use, depending on the situation. Here are some frequently used ones.

Adiós. Hasta pronto.	*Good-bye. See you soon.*
Hasta mañana.	*See you tomorrow.*
Chau. Nos vemos.	*Ciao. We'll be seeing each other.*

*****E1** and **E2** will be used throughout *¿Sabías que… ?* as abbreviations for **Estudiante 1** and **Estudiante 2.**

ACTIVIDAD B ¿Qué sigue?°

¿Qué... What follows?

Match each expression from column A with a logical response from column B.

A
1. _____ Hola. ¿Cómo te llamas?
2. _____ ¿De dónde eres?
3. _____ Soy de Tucson.
4. _____ Mi nombre es Teresa.
5. _____ ¿Cómo se llama usted?

B
a. De Nueva York.
b. Mucho gusto.
c. Soy Rodrigo. ¿Y tú?
d. Soy la profesora Gómez.
e. Ah, de Arizona.

 ACTIVIDAD C ¿Qué sigue ahora°?

now

Your instructor will read the first part of several conversations. Choose the letter of the most logical response for each.

1. **a.** De Texas.   **b.** Mucho gusto.   **c.** Se llama Rafael.

2. **a.** ¡Hola!   **b.** Soy del Canadá.   **c.** Mi amigo se llama Jorge.

3. **a.** ¿Cuál es tu nombre?   **b.** Encantado.   **c.** Soy el profesor Ruiz.

COMUNICACIÓN

ACTIVIDAD D ¿Cómo te llamas? ¿De dónde eres?

Paso (*Step*) **1** Introduce yourself to three people you don't know in your class, and find out where each is from. Write down their names and hometowns.

1...   **2**...   **3**...

Paso 2 Now be prepared to introduce one or two of your classmates to everyone else. Follow the model.

MODELO   Clase, les presento a (*I'd like to introduce you to*) un amigo (una amiga). Se llama _____ y es de _____.

GRAMÁTICA

¿Ser o no ser?

Forms and uses of **ser**

—¡Ramón! **¿Eres** tú?
—Sí, **soy** yo.

yo (*I*)	soy	nosotros/nosotras (*we*)	somos
tú (*you*)	eres	vosotros/vosotras (*you* [*pl.*])	sois*
usted (*you*)	es	ustedes (*you* [*pl.*])	son
él (*he*) / ella (*she*)	es	ellos/ellas (*they*)	son

---

*Vosotros** forms are not actively used in *¿Sabías que... ?* They are provided for recognition only. It will be for your instructor to decide whether or not he or she wishes for you to learn these forms.

The verb **ser** generally translates into English as *to be*. (Another verb, **estar,** also translates as *to be*. You will learn the differences between the two in later lessons.) In this lesson you have already seen some forms of **ser.** See the shaded box on the previous page for all of its forms.

Ser is a common verb in Spanish and serves to express a variety of concepts.

1. to tell what someone or something is

   María **es** estudiante.

2. to say where someone or something comes from

   Soy de California. ¿De dónde **eres** tú?

3. to indicate possession

   ¿Las fotografías? **Son** de Carmen.

4. to describe what someone or something is like

   Ana Alicia **es** inteligente.

By now, you have noticed subject pronouns such as **tú** (*you*). The complete list of subject pronouns in Spanish is provided on the previous page. In contrast to English, Spanish allows for the deletion of subject pronouns. In many instances, subject pronouns are used only to emphasize or clarify to whom the speaker is referring. Compare the following.

Soy estudiante.	*I am a student.* (It is obvious from the verb that you are only talking about yourself.)
Yo soy estudiante pero **él** es profesor.	*I am a student but he is a professor.* (Here you are emphasizing the differences.)

ACTIVIDAD E ¿Sí o no?

Do you agree or disagree? Check each statement accordingly. As you do the activity, take note of the forms and uses of **ser**.

	SÍ	NO
1. Soy una persona extrovertida (no introvertida).	☐	☐
2. El presidente (La presidenta) de la universidad es inteligente.	☐	☐
3. Los estudiantes de la universidad son estudiosos.	☐	☐
4. Mis amigos y yo somos conservadores (*conservative*).	☐	☐

ACTIVIDAD F ¿Qué opinas?°

°¿Qué... *What do you think?*

Paso 1 Tell how you feel about each item or person listed. Choose from the list of adjectives provided. Use the correct form of **ser** in your responses.

MODELO el presidente
     a. tonto (*foolish*) **b.** inteligente **c.** sincero →
     El presidente es inteligente.

1. mis clases
   a. interesantes **b.** buenas (*good*) **c.** aburridas (*boring*)

2. Nueva York
   a. atractiva **b.** cosmopolita **c.** espantosa (*scary*)

3. mi familia
   a. aburrida **b.** atractiva **c.** simpática (*nice*)

4. yo
   a. una persona optimista **b.** una persona pesimista **c.** una persona realista

Paso 2 Compare your opinions with those of two classmates. How many opinions do you have in common?

Consejo práctico

Spanish and English share many cognates, words that look or sound alike in various languages. Generally, these words have the same meaning. See whether you can guess the meanings of these Spanish words.

bicicleta	confusión	examinar
cámara	diccionario	malicioso
cancelar	disco	revolución

When spoken, some cognates may not sound like cognates to you because of the differences between Spanish and English pronunciation. Here are some examples.

gen (*gene*)	jirafa (*giraffe*)	rifle

Some cognates are "false" cognates; their meanings are different in the two languages. Here are four common examples.

conferencia	*lecture*	librería	*bookstore*
fábrica	*factory*	pariente	*relative*

Most cognates, however, will share the same meaning and thus will be useful tools in helping you comprehend written and spoken Spanish.

 **ACTIVIDAD G ¡A conocernos!°**   ¡A... *Let's get acquainted!*

Paso 1 Interview someone in the class you do not know. Be sure to greet the person, introduce yourself, find out where he or she is from, and tell where you are from.

Paso 2 With the information you obtained in **Paso 1,** complete the following paragraph.

Mi nombre es _____ y mi compañero/a de clase se llama _____. Él (Ella) es de _____ y yo soy de _____.

 # IDEAS PARA EXPLORAR
Las carreras y las materias

VOCABULARIO

¿Qué estudias?

Courses of study and school subjects

Here is a list of courses of study and subjects in Spanish.

Las ciencias naturales

la astronomía
la biología

la física
la química

Las ciencias sociales

la antropología
las ciencias políticas
la economía
la geografía

la historia
la psicología
la sociología

Las humanidades (Las letras)

el arte
la composición
las comunicaciones
la filosofía
los idiomas, las lenguas extranjeras
  (*foreign languages*)
  el alemán (*German*)
  el español
  el francés
  el inglés
  el italiano
  el japonés
  el portugués

la literatura
la música
la oratoria (*speech*)
la religión
el teatro

Otras materias y especializaciones

la administración de empresas (*business administration*)	**la enfermería** (*nursing*)
	la ingeniería
la agricultura, la agronomía	**la justicia criminal**
el cálculo	**las matemáticas**
la computación, la informática (*computer science*)	**el mercadeo** (*marketing*)
	el periodismo (*journalism*)
la contabilidad (*accounting*)	
la educación física	

Estudiando en EE.UU. ...

Carreras preferidas por los estudiantes extranjeros en EE.UU. Porcentaje de alumnos en cada carrera:

20.1% — Negocios/ management
17.6% — Ingeniería
9.0% — Física/ ciencias
8.4% — Informática

Fuente: Instituto de Educación Internacional

 ACTIVIDAD A ¿Quién?° *Who?*

Listen as your instructor names a subject or field of study. Can you identify who in the following list is most closely associated with each subject named?

1. Albert Einstein
2. Picasso
3. Galileo
4. Margaret Mead
5. Florence Nightingale
6. Marie Curie
7. Sigmund Freud
8. Cervantes
9. Mozart

ACTIVIDAD B ¿Qué materia?

Looking at the following lists, make logical associations by matching the items in column A with the subjects in column B.

A	B
1. _____ Dell o Macintosh	**a.** el periodismo
2. _____ fórmulas y ecuaciones	**b.** la psicología
3. _____ un mapa	**c.** la astronomía
4. _____ un telescopio	**d.** la geografía
5. _____ el psicoanálisis	**e.** la computación
6. _____ el *Washington Post*	**f.** la justicia criminal
7. _____ la publicidad	**g.** las matemáticas
8. _____ la policía	**h.** el mercadeo

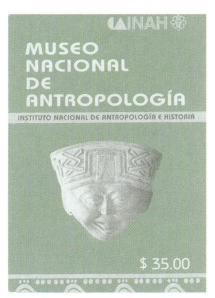

COMUNICACIÓN

✍ ACTIVIDAD C Las clases populares

Paso 1 For each major area of study, write down the name of the subject that you think is the most popular and the one that is the least popular:

	LA MÁS POPULAR	LA MENOS POPULAR
MODELO las lenguas extranjeras	el español	el japonés
1. las ciencias naturales	_____	_____
2. las ciencias sociales	_____	_____
3. las humanidades	_____	_____

Paso 2 Circulate around the room and write down the names of as many people as you can who are taking the most popular classes you listed in **Paso 1.** If someone mentions a subject that you have listed as the least popular, write down that person's name. Do the number of names you collect support your opinion of the most and least popular subjects? Share your results with the class when you have finished.

MODELO ¿Tienes una clase de _____ este semestre?

Así se dice

Have you noticed that in Spanish all nouns have grammatical gender and number? Gender means that all nouns are considered either masculine or feminine, whether they have masculine or feminine qualities or not. Number means they are either singular or plural. Like English, Spanish has articles that are used with nouns. In English, the articles are *the* (definite article) and *a/an* (indefinite articles).

DEFINITE ARTICLE	MASCULINE	FEMININE
SINGULAR	**el** diccionario	**la** computadora
PLURAL	**los** diccionarios	**las** computadoras

INDEFINITE ARTICLE	MASCULINE	FEMININE
SINGULAR	**un** profesor	**una** profesora
PLURAL	**unos** profesores	**unas** profesoras

Note that **unos** and **unas** are the equivalent of *some* in English.

 As a general rule, nouns that end in **-o** are masculine and those that end in **-a** are feminine. When you learn a new noun, be sure to learn the definite article that goes with it!

Nota comunicativa

Here are several expressions you will find useful when you simply don't understand what someone says to you, and you would like clarification.

No entiendo. ⎫
No comprendo. ⎬ *I don't understand.*

If you understand what's been said, but don't know the answer, you can simply say

No sé.   *I don't know.*

Look at the website of a Spanish-language university. Print out a page from its catalog and bring it to class. How many new vocabulary items can you identify and understand?

GRAMÁTICA

¿Te gusta?

Discussing likes and dislikes

me gusta(n)	nos gusta(n)
te gusta(n)	os gusta(n)
le gusta(n)	les gusta(n)
le gusta(n)	les gusta(n)

—¿Qué materias **te gustan**?
—Pues, **me gusta** mucho la educación física y...

—¿Y **te gustan** las ciencias políticas?

—¡Huy, no! **¡No me gustan para nada!**

Spanish has no exact equivalent for the English verb *to like.* Instead, the verb **gustar** (lit. *to please* or *to be pleasing*) is used. For example, to say that you like history, you would say

> **Me gusta** la historia.   *History is pleasing to me.*

If more than one thing pleases you, the verb takes the plural form **gustan.**

> **Me gustan** las ciencias.   *Sciences are pleasing to me.*

To ask another person about his or her likes, you can say

> **¿Te gusta** la clase de español?
> **¿Te gustan** las matemáticas?

To report on what he or she says, you can say

Le gusta la clase de español.   *Spanish class pleases him (her).*
Le gustan las matemáticas.   *Math pleases him (her).*

If you mention the person's name, you must place an **a** before the name.

A Roberto **le gustan** las ciencias.
A Luisa **le gusta** la clase de oratoria.

Me, te, and **le** are called indirect object pronouns. As you can see, they precede the verb forms **gusta** or **gustan.** (You will learn more about indirect object pronouns in later lessons.)

ACTIVIDAD D ¿La misma persona?

For each pair of sentences, indicate what subject best completes each sentence. Then indicate whether each pair of sentences is likely to be said by the same person (**Probablemente es la misma persona**) or by different persons (**Probablemente son dos personas diferentes**).

1. Me gustan _____.

    a. la química   **b.** las matemáticas   **c.** el arte

No me gusta _____.

    a. el cálculo   **b.** las ciencias sociales   **c.** los idiomas

Probablemente _____.

    a. es la misma persona   **b.** son dos personas diferentes

2. Me gusta mucho _____.

    a. los cursos de computación   **b.** la sociología   **c.** las humanidades

En general, me gustan _____.

    a. el francés   **b.** la ingeniería   **c.** las ciencias sociales

Probablemente _____.

    a. es la misma persona   **b.** son dos personas diferentes

3. Me gusta _____ bastante.

    a. la religión   **b.** las letras   **c.** la biología y la física

Por lo general, me gustan _____.

    a. la administración de empresas   **b.** las ciencias naturales   **c.** la filosofía

Probablemente _____.

    a. es la misma persona   **b.** son dos personas diferentes

ACTIVIDAD E Una encuesta°

survey

Here is a rating scale for your likes and dislikes regarding subjects of study. Circle a number to indicate how you feel about each subject. Fill in the blank with any other subject you may be taking.

	5 (CINCO) *Me gusta(n) mucho.*	4 (CUATRO) *Me gusta(n).*	3 (TRES) *Me da igual.* (It's all the same to me.)	2 (DOS) *No me gusta(n).*	1 (UNO) *No me gusta(n) para nada.*
Administración de empresas	5	4	3	2	1
Computación	5	4	3	2	1
Física	5	4	3	2	1
Historia	5	4	3	2	1
Idiomas	5	4	3	2	1
Inglés	5	4	3	2	1
Matemáticas	5	4	3	2	1
Química	5	4	3	2	1
_____	5	4	3	2	1

 ACTIVIDAD F Me gusta(n)...

Paso 1 Based on your responses in **Actividad E,** complete the following sentences. Make sure one of your answers is *not* true!

    a. Me gusta(n) mucho...   **c.** No me gusta(n) para nada...
    b. Me gusta(n)...

Paso 2 Read your statements to a partner. Can he or she guess which statement is false?

    MODELO   E1: Me gusta mucho la física.
            E2: Sí. Eso es cierto. (*That's true.*)
              o ¡Eso es falso! (*That's false!*)

COMUNICACIÓN

ACTIVIDAD G ¿Te gusta(n)... ?

Paso 1 Pair up with a classmate to ask about his or her likes or dislikes with regard to the subjects in the survey in **Actividad E.** Be sure to introduce yourself if you haven't already done so.

    MODELO   E1: ¿Te gusta(n)... ?
            E2: Sí, mucho. (No, para nada. / Sí. Me gusta[n], pero no mucho.)

Paso 2 Based on your classmate's responses in **Paso 1,** report to the class how he or she feels about the following subjects.

    a. los idiomas   **c.** la historia
    b. la física   **d.** las matemáticas

    MODELO   A Tatiana le gusta(n) mucho...

VOCABULARIO

¿Qué carrera haces?

Talking about your major

—Mamá, quiero presentarte a^a
Segismundo, mi **compañero de cuarto.**
—Mucho gusto, Segismundo.
—Igualmente, señora Méndez.
—**¿Qué carrera haces,** Segismundo?
—**Estudio** ingeniería.
—¡Qué bien!

^aquiero… *I want to introduce you to*

To inquire about a classmate's major, you can ask

¿Qué estudias?	*What are you studying?*
¿Qué carrera haces?	*What's your major?* (Lit. *What career are you doing?*)

To tell what your major is, you can use either of the following expressions.

Estudio biología.	*I'm studying biology.*
Soy estudiante de historia.	*I'm a history student.*

If you don't have a major yet, you can say

No lo sé todavía.	*I don't know yet.* (*I still don't know.*)

ACTIVIDAD H ¿Cómo respondes?° ¿Cómo… *How do you answer?*

Give a logical response based on the contexts provided.

1. —¿Qué estudias?
   —_____. (*You're a history major.*)
2. —¿Qué carrera haces?
   —_____. (*You haven't declared a major.*)
3. —¿Estudias psicología?
   —_____. (*No, you're studying journalism.*)

ACTIVIDAD I ¿Sabías que… ?

Read the **¿Sabías que… ?** selection. Then answer these questions.

1. ¿Es administración de empresas la carrera más popular en tu universidad?
2. ¿Es posible tomar (*to take*) «cursos electivos» en tu carrera? Si existe un requisito (*requirement*), ¿es posible seleccionar entre (*among*) varios cursos diferentes?

¿Sabías que... la carrera más popular entre los estudiantes universitarios de Latinoamérica es derecho^a? En los Estados Unidos,^b la carrera más popular es administración de empresas.

En muchos países de habla española,^c un estudiante escoge^d la carrera al comienzo^e de los estudios universitarios. En esta situación, el plan de estudios es predeterminado y el estudiante no tiene muchas oportunidades para explorar «cursos electivos». No existe el concepto de «educación general».

^a*law* ^b*Estados… United States* ^c*países… Spanish-speaking countries* ^d*chooses* ^e*al… at the beginning*

COMUNICACIÓN

ACTIVIDAD J ¡A conocernos mejor!°

¡A... *Let's get better acquainted!*

Using everything you now know how to say in Spanish, introduce yourself to three people in the class whom you haven't met yet. Ask them for the information requested in the chart and fill it in.

NOMBRE	DE...	CARRERA
_____	_____	_____
_____	_____	_____
_____	_____	_____

NAVEGANDO LA RED

Find the website of a Spanish-language university (e.g., **la Universidad Autónoma de Madrid, la Universidad de las Américas en Puebla**). Look up a particular area of specialization. Are the courses offered required or optional? Print out a page and bring it to class.

IDEAS PARA EXPLORAR

Más sobre las clases

GRAMÁTICA

¿Son buenas tus clases?

Descriptive Adjectives

sincer**o**	interesant**e**
sincer**a**	interesant**e**
sincer**os**	interesant**es**
sincer**as**	interesant**es**

As you have probably noticed, Spanish nouns (for example, **la historia, los idiomas**) show gender and number. Similarly, descriptive adjectives, which are words that describe someone or something (for example, **interesante, sincero, optimista**), also show gender and number.

	MASCULINE	FEMININE
Singular	un amigo sincero	una clase aburrida
Plural	unos amigos sinceros	unas clases aburridas

Lección preliminar   ¿Quién eres?

Adjectives that end in **-e** and most that end in consonants only show number.

	MASCULINE	FEMININE
Singular	un amigo inteligente	una clase difícil
Plural	unos amigos inteligentes	unas clases difíciles

Have you noticed that these descriptive adjectives tend to follow the noun rather than precede it?

Possessive Adjectives

SINGULAR	PLURAL
mi	mis
tu	tus
su	sus
nuestro/a	nuestros/as

You may have noticed that certain possessive adjectives, those that indicate ownership, show number (singular or plural) only. One exception is **nuestro** (*our*), which reflects both number and gender agreement: **nuestro profesor, nuestras clases.**

> **Mi clase** es interesante.
> ¿Son aburridas **tus clases**?
> **Nuestra profesora** es inteligente.
> **Nuestros compañeros** son dedicados.

Notice that **su** and **sus** can be used to describe what belongs to him, her, or them. Do not think that **sus** means only *their!* (You will learn more about the possessive adjectives **su** and **sus** in later lessons.)

> **su**   clase   *his (her, their) class*
> **sus**   clases   *his (her, their) classes*

ACTIVIDAD A ¿Cuál° es tu opinión?   *What*

Indicate your opinion by checking each statement as true (**cierto**) or false (**falso**). As you do the activity, notice the form and placement of the adjectives.

	CIERTO	FALSO
1. La cafetería de la universidad es buena.	☐	☐
2. Mis profesores son justos (*fair*).	☐	☐
3. Los estudiantes de mi clase de español son dedicados.	☐	☐
4. Mi clase de español es interesante.	☐	☐

ACTIVIDAD B ¿De qué habla tu profesor(a)?°

¿De... What is your professor talking about?

Listen as your instructor makes a statement. Based on what you know about descriptive adjectives, decide which of the choices given refers to what the statement is talking about.

MODELO **PROFESOR(A):** Son muy serios.
ESTUDIANTE: **a.** la profesora   **c.** el libro
b. las enciclopedias   **(d.)** los profesores

1. a. la historia
b. las comunicaciones
c. el arte
d. los idiomas

2. a. la profesora
b. las profesoras
c. el profesor
d. los profesores

3. a. la estudiante
b. las profesionales
c. el estudiante
d. los actores

4. a. la clase
b. las computadoras
c. el inglés
d. los estudiantes

5. a. la música
b. las ciencias políticas
c. el cálculo
d. los estudios

COMUNICACIÓN

ACTIVIDAD C Entrevista

Interview two classmates to find out how they feel about each item or person listed. The people interviewed can choose an adjective from the list provided. Make sure your classmates use logical adjectives in their correct form. Jot down each person's responses. Remember to greet each person before asking him or her the question below.

MODELO **E1:** ¡Hola! ¿Qué opinas de tus clases (profesores)?
E2: Son...

Adjetivos

| aburrido/a | divertido/a *(fun)* | interesante | regular |
| bueno/a | inteligente | malo/a *(bad)* | tonto/a |

	E1	E2
1. tus clases (profesores) este semestre	____	____
2. la pizza de (nombre de un restaurante)	____	____
3. los políticos *(politicians)* en la capital	____	____
4. la MTV	____	____
5. tu compañero/a de cuarto	____	____

Así se dice

Not all adjectives in Spanish follow a noun. Here are some adjectives that generally precede nouns.

poco/a (*little*)   Juan tiene **poco** tiempo (*time*) para estudiar.
pocos/as (*few*)   Hay **pocas** profesoras de ingeniería.
mucho/a (*much*)   El chico (*boy*) tiene **mucha** paciencia.
muchos/as (*many*)   **Muchos** estudiantes son de California.
algunos/as (*some*)   **Algunos** estudiantes son de Colorado.
este/a (*this*)   **Este** libro es interesante.
ese/a (*that*)   **Esa** materia es fascinante.
estos/as (*these*)   **Estos** estudiantes son de China.
esos/as (*those*)   **Esas** chicas son de Bolivia.

VOCABULARIO

¿Cuántos créditos?

Numbers 0–30

—¿**Cuántas** clases **tienes** este semestre, Vicente?
—**Cuatro. Tengo doce** créditos en total.

—Pues yo **tengo diecinueve.** ¡Mucho trabajo!

—¿**Diecinueve** créditos? ¡Pobrecito!

Knowing the numbers 0 through 30 will enable you to talk about the number of classes and credits you are taking this term.

0 cero	8 ocho	16 dieciséis	24 veinticuatro
1 uno	9 nueve	17 diecisiete	25 veinticinco
2 dos	10 diez	18 dieciocho	26 veintiséis
3 tres	11 once	19 diecinueve	27 veintisiete
4 cuatro	12 doce	20 veinte	28 veintiocho
5 cinco	13 trece	21 veintiuno*	29 veintinueve
6 seis	14 catorce	22 veintidós	30 treinta
7 siete	15 quince	23 veintitrés	

---

*Veintiuno becomes **veintiún** when used with masculine nouns (**veintiún profesores**) and **veintiuna** when used with feminine nouns (**veintiuna profesoras**).

ACTIVIDAD D ¿Cuántos créditos?

Your instructor will read a series of questions. Base your answer on the courses and credit systems at your institution.

MODELO **PROFESOR(A):** Si un estudiante tiene una clase de matemáticas, una de biología y una de alemán, ¿cuántos créditos tiene?

ESTUDIANTE: Tiene doce.

1... 2... 3... 4... 5...

ACTIVIDAD E ¿Qué número?

Divide into pairs. **Estudiante 1** chooses five numbers from the list on the previous page and says them aloud. **Estudiante 2** writes down the numbers he or she hears. Are the numbers correct? Then, switch roles.

1... 2... 3... 4... 5...

COMUNICACIÓN

ACTIVIDAD F ¿Cuántas clases?

¿Cuántas? is used to express *How many?* when the item in question is feminine plural (**las clases, las ciencias**). **¿Cuántos?** is used with masculine plural items (**los estudiantes, los números**). Following the model, interview as many classmates as possible and fill in the chart. Don't forget to introduce yourself if you haven't met the person yet!

MODELO **E1:** | **E2:**

Hola. Me llamo _____.
¿Cómo te llamas? | Me llamo _____.
¿Cuántas clases tienes? | Tengo _____.
¿Y cuántos créditos? | _____ créditos.

NOMBRE DEL ESTUDIANTE (DE LA ESTUDIANTE)	NÚMERO DE CLASES	NÚMERO DE CRÉDITOS
_____	_____	_____
_____	_____	_____
_____	_____	_____
_____	_____	_____
_____	_____	_____

GRAMÁTICA

¿Hay muchos estudiantes en tu universidad?

The verb form **hay**

—¿Cuántos estudiantes **hay** en tu clase de inglés?
—**Hay** veintiocho.

To express the concept *there is* or *there are,* Spanish uses the verb form **hay** (pronounced like English *eye*). **Hay** is used for both singular (*there is*) and plural (*there are*). In Spanish, **h** is silent, so do not pronounce it when you say the word **hay.**

ACTIVIDAD G ¿Cierto o falso?

Is each statement about your Spanish class true (**cierto**) or false (**falso**)?

	CIERTO	FALSO
1. Hay treinta estudiantes en mi clase de español.	☐	☐
2. Hay más hombres (*men*) que mujeres (*women*) en esta clase.	☐	☐
3. Hay en total tres exámenes (*tests*) en esta clase.	☐	☐
4. Hay estudiantes que tienen seis clases este semestre (trimestre).	☐	☐
5. Hay estudiantes que tienen diecinueve créditos este semestre (trimestre).	☐	☐

ACTIVIDAD H ¿Sabías que... ?

Read the **¿Sabías que... ?** selection on page 20 before answering the following questions.

1. Mira (*Look at*) el expediente académico (*transcript*) de un estudiante universitario de México.

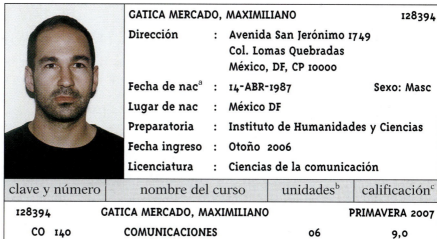

GATICA MERCADO, MAXIMILIANO   128394

Dirección   :   Avenida San Jerónimo 1749
                     Col. Lomas Quebradas
                     México, DF, CP 10000

Fecha de nac[a] :   14-ABR-1987   Sexo: Masc
Lugar de nac   :   México DF
Preparatoria   :   Instituto de Humanidades y Ciencias
Fecha ingreso   :   Otoño 2006
Licenciatura   :   Ciencias de la comunicación

clave y número	nombre del curso	unidades[b]	calificación[c]
128394	GATICA MERCADO, MAXIMILIANO		PRIMAVERA 2007
CO 140	COMUNICACIONES	06	9,0
DL 100	INGLÉS BÁSICO	07	9,4
LI 111	REDACCIÓN[d] I	06	10,0

Universidad del Tepozteco
Avenida Juárez 122
Tepoztlán, Morelos, 62038

[a]nacimiento (*birth*) [b]credits [c]grade [d]Writing

¿Qué tipo de calificaciones saca este estudiante (*does this student get*)?

a. ☐ Las tres calificaciones son sobresalientes.

b. ☐ Dos de las calificaciones son muy buenas y una es sobresaliente.

c. ☐ Las tres calificaciones son malas.

2. ¿En qué clase saca el estudiante la mejor (*best*) calificación?

3. Think about the grading system used at your university and the one described in this **¿Sabías que... ?** activity. In your opinion, which statement best describes the two systems?

a. ☐ Hay muchas diferencias entre (*between*) los dos sistemas.

b. ☐ Hay algunas diferencias entre los dos sistemas.

c. ☐ Hay pocas diferencias entre los dos sistemas.

COMUNICACIÓN

ACTIVIDAD I ¿Dónde hay... ?

Interview a classmate to find out his or her responses to the following questions. Jot down your partner's answers. Then, switch roles. Do you agree?

1. ¿En qué clases hay muchos estudiantes?

2. ¿En qué clases hay pocos estudiantes?

3. ¿Dónde hay mucha actividad en el *campus*?

4. ¿Dónde hay poca actividad en el *campus*?

5. ¿ ?

NAVEGANDO LA RED

Look at the website of at least one university in the Spanish-speaking world. Try to find the answers to at least one of the following questions.

1. How many specializations (majors) does the university offer?

2. What is the average class size?

3. How many total students does the university enroll?

Print out the page(s) and be ready to share your information with the class.

INTERCAMBIO

Para mi profesor(a)

Propósito (*Purpose*): to provide your instructor with some basic information on a classmate

Papeles (*Roles*): two people, the interviewer and one who is interviewed

Paso 1 Look over the following chart. A little later you will fill in a similar chart with information about a classmate (**un compañero [una compañera] de clase**).

Paso 2 Before you begin, think about the questions you will need to ask your classmate. How do you ask in Spanish what a person's major is? How do you find out how many credits someone is taking? Think through all of your questions before you interview your partner.

Paso 3 Pair up with someone. As you conduct the interview, jot down all the information you receive.

> Me llamo _____.
> ### Mi compañero/a de clase
> Mi compañero/a de clase se llama _____.
> Es de _____ (*place*).
> Su especialización: _____
> Clases que tiene este semestre (trimestre): _____
> _____
> _____
> _____
> _____
> _____
> Total de sus créditos este semestre (trimestre): _____
> Su materia favorita: _____

Paso 4 Turn in the chart to your instructor. You have just done your instructor a big favor—you've helped him or her get to know the members of the class!

¿De dónde eres?

Vistazos culturales

El español como lengua mundial

¿Sabías que... después del inglés el español es la lengua de más difusión mundial[a]? Aunque muchos dicen que el chino es la lengua más hablada[b] del mundo, con más de mil millones[c] de hablantes,[d] el español se habla en muchos otros países[e] en cinco continentes. En total, unos 450 millones de personas hablan español en el mundo entero. Con tantos[f] hablantes y con tanta difusión, hay mucha variación dialectal.

[a]*in the world* [b]*spoken* [c]*mil... one billion* [d]*speakers* [e]*countries* [f]*so many*

El español se habla en los continentes de Europa, África, América del Norte, América del Sur y Asia.

El español tiene su origen en una pequeña región en el norte de España.
La región hoy[a] se llama Cantabria.

[a]*today*

Países de habla española y su población en millones de habitantes*

Argentina	37,3	El Salvador	6,2	Panamá	2,8
Bolivia	8,3	España	40,0	Paraguay	5,7
Chile	15,3	Guatemala	12,9	Perú	27,4
Colombia	40,3	Guinea Ecuatorial	0,45	Puerto Rico	3,9
Costa Rica	3,7	Honduras	6,4	República Dominicana	8,5
Cuba	11,1	México	101,8	Uruguay	3,3
Ecuador	13,1	Nicaragua	4,9	Venezuela	23,9
Estados Unidos	28,1				

*Poblaciones estimadas en el año 2001.

En México, Venezuela y muchos otros países: **una naranja**[a]

En Puerto Rico: **una china**

————
[a]*orange*

El vocabulario

En España: **guisantes**[a]

En México: **chícharos**

————
[a]*peas*

En Colombia, Cuba, el Perú y los Estados Unidos: **Uds. son**

En España: **vosotros sois** o **Uds. son**

La gramática

En España, México y muchos otros países: **tú eres**

En la Argentina, el Uruguay y Costa Rica: **vos sos**

En Nicaragua: **un niño**[a]

En España: **un nene**

En Chile: **una guagua**

————
[a]*child (young boy, infant)*

Las diferencias dialectales

La pronunciación

En el Perú, México y muchos otros países: **s** final pronunciado casi siempre[a]

- tú ere**s**
- lo**s** e**s**tudiante**s**
- veintidó**s** libro**s**

En el Caribe y el sur de España: **s** final no pronunciado con mucha frecuencia

- tú ere'
- lo' e'tudiante'
- veintidó' libro'

————
[a]*always*

En el Paraguay, El Salvador y muchos otros países:
- Hasta **lue**go.[a]

En el norte de España:
- Hasta **luo**go.

————
[a]*Hasta… See you later.*

En Los Ángeles (chicanos) y muchos otros lugares:[a] **ll** y **y** pronunciados como la *y* de *yoga* en inglés
- **Y**o me **y**amo [llamo] Juan.

En la Argentina y el Uruguay: **ll** y **y** pronunciados como la *s* de *treasure* o como la *ss* de *mission* en inglés
- **Zh**o me **zh**amo Juan.
- **Sh**o me **sh**amo Juan.

————
[a]*places*

ACTIVIDAD ¿Qué recuerdas?

Indicate whether each statement is true (**cierto**) or false (**falso**).

	CIERTO	FALSO
1. En Puerto Rico una **china** es una naranja.	☐	☐
2. Hay más hispanohablantes (personas que hablan español) en México que en cualquier otro (*any other*) país del mundo.	☐	☐
3. El chino se habla en más países que el español.	☐	☐
4. En el Caribe la tendencia es pronunciar claramente la **-s** final de las palabras.	☐	☐
5. En la Argentina y el Uruguay se dice **vos sos** y en Cuba y España se dice **tú eres.**	☐	☐
6. El español se originó en Sevilla, España.	☐	☐
7. El país de habla española más pequeño (por su población total) es la Guinea Ecuatorial.	☐	☐

NAVEGANDO LA RED

Complete *one* of the following activities. Then present your information to the class.

1. Look for about eight Spanish words spoken by Chicanos in the United States and jot down their equivalents in English.

2. Look for information about the **Real Academia Española.** Then jot down the following details.
 a. cuándo se fundó (*when it was founded*)
 b. en qué ciudad (*city*) está
 c. su misión

3. Choose a country or dialect from the Spanish-speaking world and look for 5–6 Spanish words that are unique to that country or dialect.

¡Hola! — Hello!

¿Cómo te llamas? }
¿Cómo se llama usted? } What's your name?
¿Cuál es tu nombre? }

Me llamo ____. } My name is ____.
Mi nombre es ____. }

Soy ____. — I'm ____.

Se llama ____. } His/Her name is ____.
Su nombre es ____. }

Mucho gusto. } Pleased to meet you.
Encantado/a. }

Igualmente. — Likewise.

¿De dónde eres? } Where are you from?
¿De dónde es usted? }

Soy de ____. — I'm from ____.

¿Y tú? } And you?
¿Y usted? }

Saludos y despedidas — Greetings and Leave-takings

Buenos días. — Good morning.
Buenas tardes. — Good afternoon.
Buenas noches. — Good evening.
¿Qué tal? — What's up? How's it going?

Adiós. — Good-bye.
Chau. — Ciao.
Hasta mañana. — See you tomorrow.
Hasta pronto. — See you soon.
Nos vemos. — We'll be seeing each other.

En (la) clase — In Class

¿Cómo? — Pardon me?
¿Cómo dice? — What did you say?
¿Cómo se dice ____ en español? — How do you say ____ in Spanish?

No comprendo. } I don't understand.
No entiendo. }

No sé. — I don't know.
Otra vez, por favor. — Again, please.
Repita, por favor. — Repeat, please.
Tengo una pregunta, por favor. — I have a question, please.

Verbos — Verbs

hay — there is, there are
ser (irreg.) — to be
tengo — I have
tienes — you have

Carreras y materias — Majors and Subjects

Las ciencias naturales — Natural Sciences

la astronomía — astronomy
la biología — biology
la física — physics
la geografía — geography
la química — chemistry

Las ciencias sociales — Social Sciences

la antropología — anthropology
las ciencias políticas — political science
la economía — economics
la historia — history
la psicología — psychology
la sociología — sociology

Las humanidades (las letras) — Humanities (Letters)

el arte — art
la composición — writing
las comunicaciones — communications
la filosofía — philosophy

los idiomas } foreign languages
las lenguas extranjeras }

  el alemán — German
  el español — Spanish
  el francés — French
  el inglés — English
  el italiano — Italian
  el japonés — Japanese
  el portugués — Portuguese
la literatura — literature
la música — music
la oratoria — speech
la religión — religion
el teatro — theater

Otras materias y especializaciones	Other Subjects and Majors
la administración de empresas	business administration
la agricultura } la agronomía }	agriculture
el cálculo	calculus
la computación	computer science
la contabilidad	accounting
la educación física	physical education
la enfermería	nursing
la informática	computer science
la ingeniería	engineering
la justicia criminal	criminal justice
las matemáticas	mathematics
el mercadeo	marketing
el periodismo	journalism

Más sobre las clases	More About Classes
el/la compañero/a de clase	classmate
el/la estudiante	student
el libro	book
el/la profesor(a)	professor

¿Qué carrera haces?	What is your major?
¿Qué estudias?	What are you studying?
Estudio _____.	I am studying _____.
Soy estudiante de _____.	I am a(n) _____ student.
No lo sé todavía.	I don't know yet.

Preferencias	Preferences
¿Te gusta(n) _____?	Do you like _____?
Sí. Me gusta(n) _____.	Yes, I like _____.
No me gusta(n) _____.	I don't like _____.
No me gusta(n) para nada.	I don't like it (them) at all.

Los números 0 a 30	Numbers 0–30

cero	ocho	dieciséis	veinticuatro
uno	nueve	diecisiete	veinticinco
dos	diez	dieciocho	veintiséis
tres	once	diecinueve	veintisiete
cuatro	doce	veinte	veintiocho
cinco	trece	veintiuno	veintinueve
seis	catorce	veintidós	treinta
siete	quince	veintitrés	

Pronombres de sujeto	Subject Pronouns
yo	I
tú	you (*fam. s.*)
usted, Ud.	you (*form. s.*)
él, ella	he, she
nosotros/as	we
vosotros/as	you (*fam. pl. Sp.*)
ustedes, Uds.	you (*form. pl.*)
ellos, ellas	they

Adjetivos descriptivos	Descriptive Adjectives
aburrido/a	boring
bueno/a	good
espantoso/a	scary
malo/a	bad
tonto/a	foolish

Cognados: atractivo/a, cómico/a, cosmopolita, famoso/a, favorito/a, insincero/a, inteligente, interesante, optimista, pesimista, raro/a, realista, serio/a, sincero/a

Adjetivos de posesión	Possessive Adjectives
mi(s)	my
tu(s)	your (*fam. s.*)
su(s)	your (*form. s., pl.*), his, her, their

Adjetivos de cantidad	Quantifying Adjectives
algunos/as	some
mucho/a	much
muchos/as	many
poco/a	little
pocos/as	few

Adjetivos demostrativos	Demonstrative Adjectives
este/a	this
estos/as	these
ese/a	that
esos/as	those

Artículos indefinidos

Indefinite Articles

un(a)	a, an
unos/as	some

Artículos definidos

Definite Articles

el, la	the
los, las	

Otras palabras y expresiones útiles

Other Useful Words and Expressions

el/la amigo/a	friend
el/la chico/a	boy, girl
el/la compañero/a de cuarto	roommate
el examen	test
el país	country
aquí	here
¿cuántos/as?	how many?
de	of; from
gracias	thank you, thanks
mucho	a lot, very much
muy	very
no	no
o	or
por favor	please
que	that, when
¿qué?	what?
¿quién?	who?, whom?
sí	yes
y	and

Entre nosotros

El camión (*1929*) *por Frida Kahlo*

Perfil[a] *de la artista*

NOMBRE: Frida Kahlo

PAÍS DE ORIGEN: México

FECHA DE NACIMIENTO: 6 de julio, 1907

FECHA DE MUERTE: 13 de julio, 1954

Frida Kahlo, pintora de extraordinarias imágenes, es hoy día la pintora mexicana más conocida[b] del mundo. Su vida fue[c] una aventura fascinante, lo cual se captó en la película *Frida*, con Salma Hayek como protagonista.

———

[a]*Profile*   [b]*la… the most well-known female Mexican painter*   [c]*su… her life was*

LECCIÓN 1

Check out the following media resources to complement this lesson:

  Online *Manual*

 Video on CD

 Online Learning Center

ActivityPak

¿Cómo es tu horario?

In this lesson, you'll focus on daily routines and schedules. You will also

◆ describe, ask, and answer questions and make comparisons related to people's daily routines

◆ talk about time and the days of the week

◆ learn how to form the singular forms of present tense verbs

◆ learn to express when and how often you do something

ALTO Before beginning this lesson, look over the **Intercambio** activity on page 49. This is the activity you will be working toward throughout the lesson.

En una cafetería en México, D.F. (Quecas = Quesadillas)

VOCABULARIO

¿Cómo es una rutina?

Talking about daily routines

El horario de Elena Chávez, estudiante de biología en la Universidad de Miami.

1. Elena **se levanta** temprano.

2. **Hace** ejercicio aeróbico.

3. **Desayuna** café con leche.

4. **Asiste** a clase.

5. **Trabaja** en un laboratorio por la tarde.

6. **Regresa** a casa.

7. **Da** un paseo con su perro Duque.

8. **Juega** con el perro.

9. **Come** pizza en casa.

10. **Lee** su correo electrónico.

11. **Estudia** mucho.

12. **Se acuesta** a las once.

El horario de Tomás Menéndez, diseñador (*designer*) de software y estudiante de noche en la Universidad de Santo Domingo.

1. Tomás **se despierta** tarde.

2. **Lee** el periódico.

3. **Va** en carro a la oficina La Computación.

4. **Habla** por teléfono.

5. **Almuerza** con una amiga.

6. **Sale** de la oficina.

7. **Asiste** a una clase.

8. **Duerme** en clase.

9. **Cena** con dos amigos.

10. **Mira** la televisión en casa.

11. **Escucha** música y **estudia.**

12. **Se acuesta** muy tarde.

Vocabulario útil

¿Cuándo?	When?		
por la mañana	in the morning	**temprano**	early
por la tarde	in the afternoon	**tarde**	late
por la noche	in the evening, at night		

Otros términos	Other Terms		
enviar (envío), **mandar**	to send	**recibir**	to receive
navegar **la Red**	to surf the Net	**los** **mensajes**	(e-mail) messages

Note in the **Vocabulario útil** box above that the word **tarde** as a noun means *afternoon* (**la tarde**), and as an adverb means *late*. **(Tomás se despierta tarde.)**

ACTIVIDAD A El horario de Elena

Look at the drawings of Elena on page 30. As your instructor describes each one, give the number of the drawing.

> MODELO   **PROFESOR(A):** Elena hace ejercicio aeróbico.
> **ESTUDIANTE:** Número dos.

1...   2...   3...   4...   5...   6...   7...   8...   9...   10...   11...   12...

ACTIVIDAD B El horario de Tomás

Look at the drawings of Tomás on page 31. As your instructor describes each one, give the number of the drawing.

1...   2...   3...   4...   5...   6...   7...   8...   9...   10...   11...   12...

COMUNICACIÓN

ACTIVIDAD C El estudioso y el relajado

Paso 1 Alberto is a studious, responsible university student. What might his daily routine look like? Mention at least three activities that you think he does.

> MODELO   Estudia por la noche.

Paso 2 Andrés is a more relaxed, easygoing university student. How might his daily routine be different than Alberto's? Mention at least three activities that Andrés probably does.

> MODELO   Mira la televisión por la noche.

Paso 3 Now compare your ideas with those of a classmate. Did both come up with similar descriptions for Alberto and Andrés? Compile a master list with all of your ideas and be ready to report to the class.

ACTIVIDAD D ¿Y otra persona?

With what you know now, how many things can you say about another person's daily routine? Using the vocabulary for daily routines, present five statements to the class about someone you all know. The class will decide if you are correct or not. Here are some suggestions, but feel free to use other people.

el presidente de los Estados Unidos
la primera dama (*First Lady*)
un actor o una actriz
el profesor (la profesora)

MODELO   El presidente de los Estados Unidos se levanta temprano todos los días.

1...   **2**...   **3**...   **4**...   **5**...

GRAMÁTICA

¿Trabaja o no?

Talking about what someone else does

(yo)	-o	(nosotros/as)	-amos, -emos, -imos
(tú)	-as, -es	(vosotros/as)	-áis, -éis, -ís
(usted)	-a, -e	(ustedes)	-an, -en
(él/ella)	trabaj**a**	(ellos/ellas)	-an, -en
	se acuest**a**		
	com**e**		
	escrib**e**		

As in many languages, Spanish verbs (words that express actions, states, processes, and other events) consist of a stem (the part that indicates the action, state, or event) and an ending. In the verb form **trabaja, trabaj-** is the stem (it means *work*) and **-a** is the ending that tells you several things: present tense, third person singular (some other person is doing the working).

Verbs can be conjugated, that is, they can indicate who or what the subject is (as in **trabaja**) or they can be in the infinitive. Infinitives in English are usually indicated with *to: to run, to get up, to sleep*. Spanish infinitives end in **-r** and belong to one of three classes: **-ar (trabajar), -er (leer),** or **-ir (salir).**

To talk about someone else, a conjugated verb is used. It is called *third person singular*. Take the stem and add **-a** or **-e** as shown in the shaded box. (Note that **-er** and **-ir** verbs share the same ending in this case.)

Consejo práctico

Remember that the best way to learn a new Spanish word is by associating it with its meaning. For example, to learn **se levanta,** you might visualize someone getting out of bed. Try to avoid relating Spanish words to English words.

Consejo práctico

Why are the verb presentations in *¿Sabías que… ?* broken up? Why do you only learn one piece of the verb (e.g., third person singular) at a time? In this part of the lesson, you are focusing on hearing, reading, and talking about someone else's daily routine (e.g., that of Elena or Tomás). Later in this lesson you will talk about your own daily routine and will then learn the first person, or **yo,** verb forms. By focusing your attention on one verb form at a time, your chances of learning the verb forms and the context in which they are used are greatly increased!

Some Spanish verbs have stem vowel changes. You will simply have to memorize these.

o → ue
ac**o**starse → se ac**ue**sta
d**o**rmir → d**ue**rme

e → ie
t**e**ner (*to have*) → t**ie**ne

e → i
p**e**dir (*to ask for, request*) → p**i**de

If you see a third person singular verb form that has a **ue, ie,** or **i** in the stem, chances are that in the stem of the infinitive there is an **o, e,** or **e,** respectively!

Here are other stem changing verbs you will find useful.

o → ue	e → ie
jugar* (*to play*)	pensar (*to think*)
poder (*to be able to, can*)	entender (*to understand*)
volver (*to return*)	querer (*to want*)
	preferir (*to prefer*)
e → i	venir (*to come*)
vestirse (*to get dressed*)	

Notice that the present tense in Spanish is used to talk about (1) habitual actions and (2) things that are happening *right now*.

ACTIVIDAD E   ¿Son típicos o no?

Based on your general assumptions about professors and students, decide if each of the following statements relates more to a typical professor or a typical student. Which statements apply to both? (Note that all verbs in the following statements are stem changers.)

P = El profesor típico (La profesora típica)…
E = El estudiante típico (La estudiante típica)…

1. _____ se acuesta temprano.
2. _____ se viste de manera (*manner*) informal.
3. _____ prefiere la música *rock* a (*to*) la música clásica.
4. _____ almuerza en la cafetería.
5. _____ juega al tenis.
6. _____ pide explicación cuando no entiende la lección.
7. _____ piensa en (*thinks about*) su futuro.
8. _____ no duerme lo suficiente (*enough*).†

***Jugar** follows the pattern of **o** → **ue** verbs although its stem vowel is **u.** It is the only verb in Spanish that does so.

†Negative sentences are formed by placing **no** before the conjugated verb. If there is a reflexive verb like **se levanta** or **se acuesta,** the **no** precedes the **se.** Notice that Spanish does not have a support verb equivalent to *does* or *do.*

Tomás **no se acuesta** temprano. *Tomás doesn't go to bed early.*
Elena **no trabaja** por la mañana. *Elena doesn't work mornings.*

ACTIVIDAD F ¿Y los perros°?

dogs

See whether you can talk about the daily life of a dog by using correct verb forms in logical sentences. Although you may use any of the daily activities and verbs you have learned so far, here are some new verbs and words that may be useful. Afterwards, decide if the same is true for a cat (**un gato**).

Vocabulario útil

beber	to drink	**el agua**	water	**al...**	to the . . . / at the . . .
correr	to run	**el cartero**	mail carrier	**con**	with
ladrar	to bark	**la pelota**	ball		

IDEAS PARA EXPLORAR

Durante la semana

V O C A B U L A R I O

¿Con qué frecuencia?

Talking about how often people do things

Tomás lee el periódico **todas las mañanas.**

You have learned how to say whether an event takes place in the morning, afternoon, or evening. To talk about routine activities that occur every day (night, and so forth) you can use either **todos los** _____ or **todas las** _____.*

Tomás...

se levanta tarde **todas las mañanas.**
almuerza en un café **todas las tardes.**
se acuesta tarde **todas las noches.**
escucha música **todos los días.**

To refer to a frequent activity, you can use the words **frecuentemente, generalmente, regularmente,** and **normalmente.**

Elena come pizza **frecuentemente.**

To talk about how often you do an activity, you may use the following expressions.

siempre	*always*
con frecuencia	*frequently*
a veces	*sometimes*
de vez en cuando	*from time to time*
pocas (raras) veces	*rarely*
nunca	*never*

****Todos los** and **todas las** are equivalent to *every* in English in these contexts.

Así se dice

Do you remember the irregular verb **ser** from **Lección preliminar (soy, eres, es, es, somos, sois, son, son)**? Another highly irregular verb is **ir** (*to go*).

(yo)	voy	(nosotros/as)	vamos
(tú)	vas	(vosotros/as)	vais
(Ud.)	va	(Uds.)	van
(él/ella)	va	(ellos/ellas)	van

ACTIVIDAD A ¿Cierto o falso?

Read the following statements about a typical week in the life of a student at your institution. Are they **cierto** or **falso** in your opinion?

El estudiante norteamericano
(La estudiante norteamericana)…

	C	F
1. se levanta temprano todos los días.	☐	☐
2. no va a clases regularmente y frecuentemente está ausente (*is absent*).	☐	☐
3. siempre duerme ocho horas todas las noches.	☐	☐
4. normalmente escribe sus composiciones a computadora.	☐	☐
5. no mira (*doesn't watch*) nunca la televisión.	☐	☐
6. lee novelas cuando (*when*) no estudia.	☐	☐
7. raras veces almuerza en McDonald's.	☐	☐
8. se acuesta muy tarde con frecuencia.	☐	☐

ACTIVIDAD B ¿Con qué frecuencia?

How often does your best friend do certain activities? Put an X in the appropriate column to indicate what is true for him (her).

	SIEMPRE	CON FRECUENCIA	DE VEZ EN CUANDO	RARAS VECES	NUNCA
1. Lee su correo electrónico.					
2. Se acuesta a las dos de la mañana.					
3. Va a la biblioteca.					
4. Se levanta a las cinco de la mañana.					
5. Hace ejercicio aeróbico.					
6. Duerme en clase.					

Lección 1   ¿Cómo es tu horario?

ACTIVIDAD C Mi profesor(a) de español

Paso 1 Interview a classmate to find out how often he or she thinks your Spanish instructor does the following activities. Use a different expression from the following list in each question and answer.

todos los días
todas las mañanas (tardes, noches)
frecuentemente, regularmente, generalmente
a veces
pocas (raras) veces
nunca

MODELO   mira la televisión →
E1: ¿Mira la televisión frecuentemente el profesor (la profesora)?
E2: Sí, todos los días.
(No, no mira la televisión frecuentemente.)

1. desayuna
2. come chocolates
3. mira la televisión en español
4. habla por teléfono
5. se acuesta temprano
6. navega la Red

Paso 2 Be prepared to read aloud to the class your questions and answers from **Paso 1.** After your classmates share their opinions about the instructor's routine, he or she will say if you were right!

1 de cada 10 españoles ve todos los días TV3

VOCABULARIO

¿Qué día de la semana?

Days of the week

LOS **DÍAS LABORALES** (*WORKDAYS*)

lunes   martes   miércoles   jueves   viernes

LOS DÍAS DEL **FIN DE SEMANA** (*WEEKEND DAYS*)

sábado   domingo

To ask what day it is, you say

¿Qué día es hoy?

To respond, say

Hoy es domingo.
(**Mañana es** lunes.)

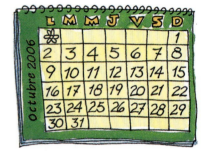

ACTIVIDAD D Las clases de Elena

Your instructor will make a series of statements about Elena's class schedule. Indicate whether they are **cierto** or **falso,** according to the schedule below.

1... **2**... **3**... **4**... **5**... **6**...

LUNES	MARTES	MIÉRCOLES	JUEVES	VIERNES
Biología II	Biología II	Biología II	Biología II	
	Cálculo avanzado		Cálculo avanzado	
Entomología		Entomología		Entomología
Geografía de las Américas		Geografía de las Américas	La destrucción del planeta	Geografía de las Américas

COMUNICACIÓN

ACTIVIDAD E La semana del profesor (de la profesora)

As a class, see whether you can piece together your instructor's weekly schedule by asking only yes/no questions. Several examples are provided for you. As you get information, write it into a calendar like the one on the following page. See how much the class can find out in eight to ten minutes.

MODELOS   ¿Tiene usted una clase los lunes por la mañana?

¿Tiene usted horas de oficina los lunes? ¿los martes?

	LUNES	MARTES	MIÉRCOLES	JUEVES	VIERNES
por la mañana					
por la tarde					
por la noche					

NAVEGANDO LA RED

Look up the office hours of a professor at a university in a Spanish-speaking country and bring this information to class. Are this person's office hours comparable to those of your Spanish professor?

GRAMÁTICA

¿Y yo?

Talking about your own activities

(yo)	trabaj**o** me acuest**o** com**o** escrib**o**	(nosotros/as)	-amos, -emos, -imos
(tú)	-as, -es	(vosotros/as)	-áis, -éis, -ís
(usted)	-a, -e	(ustedes)	-an, -en
(él/ella)	-a, -e	(ellos/ellas)	-an, -en

—**Estudio** por la tarde o por la noche. No **salgo** porque **me levanto** muy temprano todas las mañanas.

—Normalmente no **duermo** mucho porque **trabajo** mucho y **estudio.**

Así se dice

You will encounter another irregularity in Spanish. Most verbs in Spanish that end in **-cer** or **-cir** will end in **-zco** in the **yo** form.

> **conocer** (*to know*):
> No **conozco** al
> presidente.

> **conducir** (*to drive*):
> **Conduzco** rápidamente.

See whether you can give the **yo** form for the following verbs.

> **producir** (*to produce*)
> **traducir** (*to translate*)
> **deducir** (*to deduce*)

Así se dice

An important use of **por** is with expressions of time to mean *during*.

> **por** la mañana (tarde, noche)

Por can also be used to express a period of time during which something happens. In this case, its equivalent expression in English is *for*.

> Estudio **por** dos horas
> cada noche.
> Hago ejercicio **por** una
> hora al día.

Don't be fooled that *for* is always expressed by **por**. As you will learn, Spanish has at least two equivalents for *for*, **por** and **para**. You will learn more about **por** and **para** as you work through ¿*Sabías que… ?*

You have already learned to form verbs ending in **-a** and **-e** to talk about someone else's daily activities. To talk about what *you* do, most verbs will end in **-o**, as illustrated in the shaded box. Note that stem vowel changes also appear in the **yo** form of the verb, also called *first person singular*.

> Normalmente, **estudio** por la noche.
> **Duermo** una hora todas las tardes.
> **Me levanto** temprano los sábados.

Did you catch that a verb that takes **se** in the third person form will take **me** in the first person singular form? Here is another example.

> Normalmente, **me acuesto** a las once y media.

Several of the verbs with which you are familiar have slightly altered stems.

> **Hago** ejercicio con frecuencia.
> No **salgo** mucho con mis amigos.
> **Tengo** mucho trabajo esta semana.

Remember the irregularity of **ir**?

> **Voy** al laboratorio para practicar el español.

Another common verb, **decir** (*to say; to tell*) is also highly irregular. It has more than one kind of change!

> —¿Qué **dices**?
> —¿Yo? Yo no **digo** nada.

ACTIVIDAD F ¿En qué orden?

Paso 1 Number these activities from 1 to 10 in the order in which *you* would do them.

_____ Me acuesto.
_____ Voy en carro a la universidad.
_____ Ceno.
_____ Regreso a casa (al apartamento, a la residencia [*dormitory*]).
_____ Leo el periódico.
_____ Estudio.
_____ Almuerzo.
_____ Desayuno.
_____ Navego la Red.
_____ Hago ejercicio por quince minutos.

Paso 2 Tell the class the order you decided on. Did many of your classmates put the activities in a similar order? Is there a more logical order than the one you came up with?

Paso 3 Given the information you received from your classmates, which statement applies to you?

☐ Mi horario es un horario típico.

☐ Mi horario no es un horario típico.

ACTIVIDAD G Mis actividades

Paso 1 Indicate whether each statement is **cierto** or **falso** for you.

	C	F
1. Voy a clase los lunes, miércoles y viernes.	☐	☐
2. Duermo cinco horas por la noche generalmente.	☐	☐
3. Compro revistas (*I buy magazines*) todas las semanas.	☐	☐
4. Estudio en la biblioteca porque necesito (*I need*) silencio.	☐	☐
5. Me acuesto temprano los días de clase.	☐	☐
6. No hago ejercicio frecuentemente.	☐	☐
7. Almuerzo con mis amigos todos los días.	☐	☐
8. Como pizza para el desayuno frecuentemente.	☐	☐
9. Escucho y tomo apuntes (*I take notes*) en mis clases.	☐	☐

Paso 2 Read the statements to a classmate. Your classmate will guess whether the statement is **cierto** or **falso** for you. Then trade places and you do the guessing.

COMUNICACIÓN

ACTIVIDAD H Restaurantes y cafés

Paso 1 Everyone has favorite places to eat. Think about the spots where you enjoy eating out. When you have time and money to spare, where do you like to eat out for breakfast, lunch, or dinner? Do you go to a special café or store for a particular snack between meals? Use the following verbs to explain where you eat for each occasion.

desayunar   almorzar   cenar   comer

MODELO   Desayuno en McDonald's.

Paso 2 Share your statements with a classmate. Do you have any hot spots in common? Be ready to report some of your favorite places to the class.

Esta mujer lee su correo electrónico mientras toma su primer (first) café del día.

ACTIVIDAD I Tú y yo

Paso 1 Here is a list of typical daily activities. See if you can find someone in the class who matches you on at least three. Follow the model.

caminar (*to walk*) a la universidad
dormir en una clase
llegar (*to arrive*) tarde al trabajo (a una clase)
soñar (ue) despierto (*to daydream*)
tomar (*to drink*) café

MODELOS E1: Siempre tomo café por la mañana. ¿Y tú?
E2: Yo también. / Yo no.

E1: No duermo en la clase de español.
E3: Yo sí. / Yo tampoco. (*Neither do I.*)

Paso 2 When you have found someone with whom you share three activities, report to the class.

MODELO Yo siempre tomo café. Roberto también.

 # IDEAS PARA EXPLORAR
Más sobre las rutinas

VOCABULARIO

¿A qué hora... ?

Telling when something happens

To express what time of day you do something, use the expressions **a la** and **a las.**

—Asisto a mi primera clase **a las ocho.**

—Almuerzo con mi amigo **a la una.**

Use **cuarto** and **media** to express *quarter hour* and *half hour*.

y cuarto
y media
menos cuarto

—Llego a la oficina **a las diez menos cuarto.**

—Estudio **a las once y media.**

To express other times, add the number of minutes to the hour or subtract the number of minutes from the next hour.

—Leo mi correo electrónico **a las seis menos diez.**

—Hablo con una amiga **a las diez y veinte.**

ACTIVIDAD A ¿A qué hora?

Elena mentions at what time she does certain activities. How does she logically complete each statement? Match the time to the appropriate activity. (See the drawings on page 30 for reference.)

1. _____ Hago ejercicio aeróbico…
2. _____ Trabajo en el laboratorio…
3. _____ Prefiero levantarme…
4. _____ Escribo la tarea…
5. _____ Me acuesto…

a. a las once de la noche.
b. a las nueve de la noche.
c. a las seis de la mañana.
d. a las dos de la tarde.
e. a las seis y media de la mañana.

¿A qué hora sale el autobús?

ACTIVIDAD B ¿Sabías que... ?

Paso 1 Read the **¿Sabías que... ?** selection. Then answer the following questions.

1. ¿Quién tiene una vida «más activa» por la noche, el español o el norteamericano?

2. ¿Quién cena (*eats dinner*) temprano y quién cena tarde?

3. ¿Quién pasa (*spends*) todo el día en el trabajo sin salir?

Paso 2 Using the following question, see whether you can find five people in class who prefer the Spanish schedule.

MODELO ¿Cuál de los dos horarios prefieres, el horario español o el norteamericano?

¿Sabías que...
el horario de actividades diarias de un individuo varía de cultura a cultura?

En España y otros países hispanos, por ejemplo, generalmente uno se levanta por la mañana, trabaja hasta[a] la 1.00 o las 2.00 y va a almorzar a casa. Después, descansa[b] hasta las 4.00 y regresa al trabajo. No termina de trabajar hasta las 8.00 ó 9.00 de la noche. Cena tarde, normalmente a las 10.00, y frecuentemente sale después con sus amigos.

En este país, en cambio, una persona generalmente se levanta por la mañana, pasa ocho horas en el trabajo, regresa a casa a las 5.00, cena a las 6.00 ó 6.30, mira la televisión y se acuesta a las 11.00.

¿Cuál de los dos horarios prefieres?

[a]*until* [b]*Después,... Afterward, he or she rests*

 ACTIVIDAD C Tu primera clase

Get into pairs. In two minutes, ask your partner when his or her first class is on each day of the week. Jot down his or her responses. Be prepared to report the results to the class.

MODELO   E1: ¿A qué hora es tu primera clase los lunes?
E2: A las nueve.

NAVEGANDO LA RED

Look up the banking hours of a bank in a Spanish-speaking country. **¿A qué hora abre** (*opens*) **el banco? ¿A qué hora cierra** (*does it close*)**?** Print out the information and bring it to class.

GRAMÁTICA

¿Y tú? ¿Y usted?

Addressing others

—Pepe, **tú sales** de la universidad a las dos, ¿no?
—Sí. ¿Por qué **preguntas**?

(yo)	-o	(nosotros/as)	-amos, -emos, -imos
(tú)	estudi**as** te levant**as** le**es** asist**es**	(vosotros/as)	-áis, -éis, -ís
(Ud.)	estudi**a** se levant**a** le**e** asist**e**	(Uds.)	-an, -en
(él/ella)	-a, -e	(ellos/ellas)	-an, -en

—Profesora, ¿**es Ud.** del Perú?
—No, Eva. Soy de Bolivia. ¿Y **tú**?

You may have noticed that Spanish has several ways of expressing *you*. **Tú** implies less social distance between the speakers. **Usted** (generally abbreviated **Ud.**) indicates a more formal relationship and more social distance. The rules of usage vary from country to country and even within countries, but you can follow this rule of thumb: Use **tú** with your family, friends, anyone close to your own age—and with your pets. Use **Ud.** with everyone else.

For example, to ask a classmate about something, use **tú.** To get the **tú** verb form, add an **-s** to the final vowels **-a** or **-e** of the third person forms.

¿**Miras** la televisión todas las noches?
¿**Cenas** en restaurantes frecuentemente?

Certain verbs are used with **te.**

> ¿A qué hora **te levantas**?
> ¿**Te acuestas** tarde o temprano?

When speaking with someone whom you address as **Ud.,** use the same verb form as with **él** or **ella.**

> ¿**Trabaja** Ud. en la biblioteca?
> Ud. **sale** con los amigos todos los días.

Note the use of **se** with some verbs in the **Ud.** form.

> ¿**Se levanta** Ud. tarde frecuentemente?
> ¿A qué hora **se acuesta** Ud.?

ACTIVIDAD D ¿Y tú? ¿Y usted?

Paso 1 Look at the following questions. Check the box that indicates whether each question is appropriate to ask a friend (**Para un amigo [una amiga]**) or your instructor (**Para mi profesor[a]**).

	PARA UN AMIGO (UNA AMIGA)	PARA MI PROFESOR(A)
1. ¿Te levantas temprano los lunes?	☐	☐
2. ¿Habla varios idiomas?	☐	☐
3. ¿Va frecuentemente al cine (*movies*)?	☐	☐
4. ¿Miras la televisión todos los días?	☐	☐
5. ¿Haces ejercicio regularmente?	☐	☐
6. ¿Empiezas (*Do you begin*) todas las mañanas de buen humor (*in a good mood*)?	☐	☐
7. ¿Lee el periódico todos los días?	☐	☐

Paso 2 Choose two of the questions from **Paso 1** that you checked as being appropriate to ask a friend. Pose these two questions to a classmate.

Paso 3 Now, choose two of the questions from **Paso 1** that you checked as being appropriate to ask your professor. Be ready to ask these questions if called on.

ACTIVIDAD E ¿A qué hora?

Pair up with a classmate you haven't already interviewed to find out at what time (**a qué hora**) he or she does the following things. Write down the information. Then switch roles.

> MODELO E1: ¿A qué hora almuerzas?
> E2: A las doce.

Consejo práctico

Are you speaking Spanish with anyone outside of class? If not, get the phone numbers of three or four of your classmates. Then, call one and do any one of the activities that asks you to interview someone. You might be asked to do this at times in the Workbook. This is a good habit to get into. Ten minutes on the phone once a day and you've added significant practice over the course of your language study!

COMUNICACIÓN

¿A qué hora...

1. te levantas los lunes?
2. vas a tu clase favorita?
3. te acuestas los jueves?
4. vas a la universidad los miércoles?
5. regresas a casa los viernes?
6. miras la televisión, generalmente?
7. ¿ ?

GRAMÁTICA

¿Qué necesitas hacer?

Talking about what you need or have to do on a regular basis

Tomás **tiene que trabajar...**

In order to talk about activities that you have to do, need to do, should (ought) to do, prefer to do, want to do, and can do, use the appropriate verb in its conjugated form followed by an infinitive. Look at the following examples:

Elena **tiene que** (*has*) trabajar todas las tardes.
¿**Necesitas** (*Do you need*) estudiar mucho?
Debo (*I should*) leer el periódico más.
Prefiero (*I prefer*) estudiar en la biblioteca (*library*).

Notice that when a reflexive verb such as **acostarse** or **levantarse** is used, the pronoun can follow and be attached to the infinitive:

Tomás **no puede** (*cannot*) acostarse temprano.
Elena **quiere** (*wants*) levantarse temprano todos los días.

(Reflexive verbs will be discussed in more detail in later chapters.)

...y **estudiar** todos los días.

ACTIVIDAD F ¿Quién?

Read each of the following statements, then indicate whether each more likely refers to a student, a dog, or a professor.

a. una estudiante **b.** un perro **c.** un profesor

1. _____ Debe estudiar todos los días.
2. _____ Necesita corregir (*correct*) tarea con frecuencia.
3. _____ Puede dormir dieciocho horas al día.
4. _____ Quiere sacar buenas notas (*grades*) en sus clases.
5. _____ Tiene que proteger (*protect*) la casa.
6. _____ Prefiere salir con los amigos, pero (*but*) no sale porque tiene que estudiar para un examen.
7. _____ Debe memorizar los nombres de sus estudiantes.
8. _____ No puede hablar por teléfono, ni (*nor*) navegar la Red ni leer el correo electrónico.

ACTIVIDAD G ¿Qué haces regularmente?

Think of activities you do regularly, whether you want to do them or not. Then complete each of the following statements with truthful information about your activities. Try to think of a different activity for each item.

1. Debo ＿＿＿ todos los días, pero generalmente no lo hago (*I don't do it*).
2. Tengo que ＿＿＿ todas las tardes, pero no me gusta.
3. Prefiero ＿＿＿ más, pero no tengo que hacerlo (*to do it*).
4. Quiero ＿＿＿ frecuentemente, pero no debo hacerlo.
5. Necesito ＿＿＿ todos los días.
6. No puedo ＿＿＿ todas las tardes.

Así se dice

You have already learned several useful expressions such as **con frecuencia, frecuentemente, generalmente, normalmente,** and **regularmente** to express habitual or recurring actions. Another way to express actions you perform regularly is to use a form of the verb **soler** plus an infinitive. Note that **soler** has several English equivalents.

Suelo estudiar por la mañana.	*I generally study in the morning.*
¿Cuántas horas **sueles** dormir?	*How many hours do you normally sleep?*
Suelo dormir seis horas.	*I usually sleep six hours.*

COMUNICACIÓN

ACTIVIDAD H Más actividades

Paso 1 Complete each sentence with the correct form of one of the following verbs to form truthful statements about yourself: **(no) deber, necesitar, poder, preferir, querer, soler, tener que.** Follow the model.

MODELO   Necesito dormir ocho horas todas las noches, pero no puedo.

1. ＿＿＿ recibir mensajes de correo electrónico,...
2. ＿＿＿ hacer ejercicio,...
3. ＿＿＿ tocar (*to play*) un instrumento musical,...
4. ＿＿＿ asistir a clase,...
5. ＿＿＿ dormir más,...
6. ＿＿＿ jugar a videojuegos (*video games*),...

Paso 2 Share your responses with a classmate. How much do you have in common with him (her)?

NAVEGANDO LA RED

Look up the website of a university in a Spanish-speaking country. Are classes offered all day long? What's the earliest morning class? What's the latest evening class?

INTERCAMBIO

Preguntas para un examen

Propósito: to form series of questions about two schedules

Papeles: two people, the interviewer and one who is interviewed

Paso 1 Fill in a schedule with at least two things you do in the morning, afternoon, or evening any two days of the week (except weekends). Include such things as when you get up, when you go to bed, when you arrive at school, and when you have lunch.

	LUNES	MARTES	MIÉRCOLES	JUEVES	VIERNES
por la mañana					
por la tarde					
por la noche					

Paso 2 Interview someone with whom you have not worked in this lesson. Find out when he or she does the same or similar things as you on the same two days and jot down the information in the chart. Then make clean copies of your schedule and the schedule of the person you have just interviewed. (Don't forget to use **yo** forms for yourself and **él/ella** forms for your partner.)

	LUNES	MARTES	MIÉRCOLES	JUEVES	VIERNES
por la mañana					
por la tarde					
por la noche					

Paso 3 Using the two schedules, make up the following test items.

three true/false statements of a comparative nature

MODELOS   Yo me levanto muy temprano por la mañana, pero Juan se levanta tarde.

Yo tengo que trabajar todos los días, pero Ana sólo necesita trabajar los jueves y viernes.

two questions that require an answer with a specific activity

MODELO   Yo prefiero hacer esta actividad por la mañana, pero Juan prefiere hacer esto por la tarde. ¿Qué es? (estudiar)

Paso 4 Turn in both the schedules and the test items to your instructor.

Vistazos culturales
La vida diaria en el mundo hispano

¿Sabías que... el horario diario en el mundo hispano es muy diferente que el de este país? En muchos países hispanos la gente[a] come, trabaja, va de compras,[b] y sale con amigos más tarde. Por ejemplo, en España es común cenar entre las 9.00 y 10.00 de la noche, mientras que[c] aquí la costumbre es cenar entre las 5.00 y 7.00 de la tarde. Sin embargo, en el mundo hispano hay diferencias de costumbre de país a país y de individuo a individuo como es el caso en este país.

[a]la... people   [b]va... *going shopping*   [c]mientras... *whereas*

En la mayoría de los países hispanos la comida más fuerte[a] del día es el almuerzo. Por lo general la gente hispana come el almuerzo más tarde que la gente norteamericana. La siguiente tabla resume las diferencias generales entre los horarios de este país, España y México.

[a]comida... *heaviest meal*

Un almuerzo típico en México

En los Estados Unidos y el Canadá el almuerzo típico es una comida rápida que dura entre 30 minutos y una hora. En muchos países hispanos, el almuerzo puede durar un par[a] de horas. La gente no se marcha[b] inmediatamente después de comer. Se queda un rato[c] para conversar con la familia.

[a]un... *a couple*   [b]no... *don't leave*   [c]Se... *They stay awhile*

PAÍS	EL DESAYUNO	EL ALMUERZO	LA CENA
los Estados Unidos y el Canadá	7.00–9.00	11.00–1.00	5.00–7.00
España	9.00–11.00	2.00–4.00	9.00–11.00
México (parte central)	7.00–9.00	2.00–4.00	8.00–10.00

You can investigate these cultural topics in more detail on the *¿Sabías que... ?* Online Learning Center: **www.mhhe.com/sabiasque5**.

El horario oficial en muchos países hispanos se divide[a] en veinticuatro horas y no hay distinción entre A.M. y P.M. Este sistema de tiempo se usa en los horarios del cine, del transporte público, de las tiendas,[b] y de los bancos, etcétera.

---

[a]se... *is divided*   [b]*stores*

¡ Placer al Viajar !

Pullman de Morelos

CUERNAVACA
AEROPUERTO DE LA CD. DE MEXICO

AEROPUERTO - CUERNAVACA		CUERNAVACA - AEROPUERTO	
6:30	15:45	4:00	12:00
7:30	16:30	4:30	12:40
8:15	17:15	5:00	13:20
9:15	18:00	5:30	14:15
10:30	18:45	6:00	15:00
11:15	19:30	7:00	16:00
12:00	20:15	8:00	16:40
12:45	21:00	9:00	17:15
13:30	22:00	10:00	18:15
14:15	23:00	10:40	19:30
15:00		11:20	

MEXICO D.F. **55-49-35-05 AL 08**
CUERNAVACA (73) **18-46-38 Ó 18-91-87**
TIEMPO APROX. DE RECORRIDO: **1 HR. 40 min.**

En este país el día laboral comienza a eso de las 8.00 de la mañana y termina a eso de las 6.00 de la tarde. En España el día laboral comienza a las 8.00 de la mañana pero termina a eso de la 1.30 cuando la gente come y toma una siesta. Después de la siesta, a eso de las 3.00 ó 4.00 de la tarde, la gente vuelve al trabajo donde permanece[a] hasta las 7.00 u[b] 8.00 de la tarde.

---

[a]*(they) stay*   [b]*or*

La **siesta** es un descanso de un par de horas en que los trabajadores suelen regresar a casa para almorzar, convivir[a] con la familia y descansar antes de regresar al trabajo. (Desafortunadamente, esta costumbre está desapareciendo con las demandas y el ritmo acelerado de la sociedad del siglo XXI.)

---

[a]*spend time*

La hora

Los horarios diferentes

El día laboral

En una discoteca de Madrid

La vida nocturna

En España, México y otros países las discotecas suelen abrirse[a] a las 11.30 de la noche y se cierran a eso de[b] las 4.30 ó 5.00 de la mañana. En este país muchos clubes y discotecas se abren y se cierran más temprano.

---

[a]*open*   [b]a... *around*

ACTIVIDAD ¿Qué recuerdas?

Answer the following questions by completing each sentence.

1. ¿A qué hora termina el día laboral en España?

   Termina a eso de las _____ u _____ de la noche.

2. ¿A qué hora suele almorzar la gente de México?

   Suele almorzar a las _____ de la tarde.

3. ¿En qué país se cierran más tarde las discotecas, en España o en los Estados Unidos?

   Se cierran más tarde en _____.

4. ¿A qué hora se suele cenar en España?

   Se suele cenar entre las _____ y las _____ de la noche.

5. Si necesitas tomar un tren en España que sale a las 11.30 de la noche, ¿qué hora se indicará (*will be indicated*) en el horario de trenes?

   Se indicará: _____.

NAVEGANDO LA RED

Complete *one* of the following activities. Then present your information to the class.

1. Look for information about a bank in the Spanish-speaking world. Then compare the schedule of your bank in this country with that of the bank in that country and present your findings to the class. Answer the following questions.
   a. ¿Cuál banco se abre más temprano?
   b. ¿Cuál banco se cierra más tarde?
   c. ¿Cuál banco está abierto los fines de semana? (Da los horarios.)
2. Look for information about academic calendars in two different universities, each in a different Spanish-speaking country. Then compare your university's academic calendar with the calendars of the two universities you find on the Web and present your findings to the class. Answer the following questions.
   a. ¿Cuándo empieza el año académico en cada universidad y cuándo termina?
   b. ¿Cuántos días o semanas libres (*free*) tienen durante el calendario académico?

VOCABULARIO COMPRENSIVO

La vida de todos los días — Everyday Life

abrir	to open
acostarse (ue)	to go to bed
almorzar (ue)	to have lunch
asistir (a)	to attend
cenar	to have dinner
cerrar (ie)	to close
comer	to eat
conducir (conduzco)	to drive
conocer (conozco)	to know (*someone*)
deber + *inf.*	ought to, should, must (*do something*)
desayunar	to have breakfast
descansar	to rest
despertarse (ie)	to wake up
dormir (ue)	to sleep
entender (ie)	to understand
enviar (envío)	to send
escribir	to write
escuchar	to listen to
estudiar (R)*	to study
hablar	to speak
hablar por teléfono	to talk on the phone
hacer (*irreg.*)	to do; to make
hacer ejercicio	to exercise
hacer ejercicio aeróbico	to do aerobics
ir (*irreg.*)	to go
jugar (ue) (a)	to play (*sports*)
leer	to read
levantarse	to get up
mandar	to send
manejar	to drive
mirar (la televisión)	to look at, watch (TV)
navegar la Red	to surf the net
necesitar	to need
pasar	to spend (*time*)
pedir (i)	to ask for, request
pensar (ie) (en)	to think (about)
poder (ue)	to be able, can
preferir (ie)	to prefer
preguntar	to ask (*a question*)
querer (ie)	to want
recibir	to receive
regresar	to return (*to a place*)
salir (*irreg.*)	to go out, leave
soler (ue) + *inf.* (*doing something*)	to be in the habit of

tener (*irreg.*)	to have
tener que + *inf.*	to have to (*do something*)
tocar (la guitarra)	to play (the guitar)
trabajar	to work
venir (*irreg.*)	to come
vestirse (i)	to get dressed
volver (ue)	to return (*to a place*)

¿Cuándo? — When?

durante	during
mañana	tomorrow
(muy) tarde	(very) late
(muy) temprano	(very) early
por la mañana	in the morning
por la tarde	in the afternoon
por la noche	in the evening, at night

¿Con qué frecuencia? — How Often?

a veces	sometimes
con frecuencia	often
de vez en cuando	from time to time
frecuentemente	frequently
generalmente	generally
normalmente	normally
nunca	never
pocas (raras) veces	rarely
regularmente	regularly
siempre	always
todas las mañanas (tardes, noches)	every morning (afternoon, night)
todos los días	every day

¿Qué día es hoy? — What Day Is It Today?

lunes	Monday
martes	Tuesday
miércoles	Wednesday
jueves	Thursday
viernes	Friday
sábado	Saturday
domingo	Sunday
el día laboral	workday
el fin de semana	weekend
Hoy es...	Today is . . .
Mañana es...	Tomorrow is . . .

---

*Words that appear with an (R) in a lesson vocabulary list are review (**Repaso**) words that were active in a previous lesson. They are included in these lists when they thematically fit the lesson.

¿Qué hora es?

Es la una.
Son las (dos, tres).
  menos cuarto
  y cuarto
  y media

What Time Is It?

It's one o'clock.
It's (two, three) o'clock.
  quarter to
  quarter past
  half past

¿A qué hora?

A la una.
A las (dos, tres).

At What Time?

At one o'clock.
At (two, three) o'clock.

Otras palabras y expresiones útiles

la biblioteca	library
el correo electrónico	e-mail

el cuarto	room
el laboratorio	laboratory
el mensaje	(e-mail) message
el periódico	newspaper
la rutina	routine
la tarea	homework
bueno/a (buen) (R)	good
en casa	at home
con	with
en	in; at
más	more
menos	less
para	for
pero	but
por	during; for
porque	because

LECCIÓN 2

Check out the following media resources to complement this lesson:

 Online *Manual*

 Online Learning Center

 Video on CD

 ActivityPak

¿Qué haces los fines de semana?

The focus of this lesson is weekend activities. In exploring this topic, you will

- learn how to talk about weekend activities
- describe your ideal weekend and make comparisons about how people spend their leisure time
- learn words of negation and how to use them
- learn more about the verb **gustar** and how to talk about likes and dislikes
- talk about the weather and discuss how it affects your free time

- learn more present tense verb forms as well as the present progressive
- talk about the seasons and months
- learn to talk about things you are going to do

ALTO Before beginning this lesson, look over the **Intercambio** activity on page 75. This is the activity you will be working toward throughout the lesson.

En un lago de Sevilla, España

IDEAS PARA EXPLORAR

Actividades para el fin de semana

VOCABULARIO

¿Qué hace una persona los sábados?

Talking about someone's weekend routine

El sábado de Elena

1. Por la mañana, Elena **corre** tres millas.

2. Despúes, **chatea** con los amigos.

3. Por la tarde, **toma** café con dos amigos.

4. Por la noche, **baila** en un club de música latina.

El sábado de Tomás

1. Por la mañana, Tomás **limpia** su apartamento.

2. Luego **hace de voluntario.**

3. Por la tarde, **saca** vídeos.

4. Por la noche, **se queda** en casa. (No **sale.**)

El domingo de Elena

1. Por la mañana, Elena **va** a la iglesia.

2. Después, **juega** al voleibol con sus amigas.

3. Luego **nada** en el mar.

4. Más tarde, **charla** con una amiga.

El domingo de Tomás

1. Por la mañana, Tomás **lava** su ropa.

2. Luego **no hace nada** en particular.

3. Por la tarde, **va de compras** al supermercado.

4. Por la noche, **hace** la tarea para mañana.

Así se dice

As you know, the phrase **dar un paseo** means *to take a walk.* The simple verb **dar** is usually translated as *to give,* but in expressions like **dar un paseo,** you will not see the word *give* in the translation. Here are some other expressions that use **dar.**

dar igual
to be all the same, make no difference

dar la mano
to shake hands

darse cuenta de
to realize (make a mental note of)

ACTIVIDAD A ¿Qué día es?

Listen as your instructor reads statements about the typical weekend activities of Elena and Tomás. Then identify which day each statement refers to, according to the information in the drawings.

MODELO   **PROFESOR(A):** Tomás limpia su apartamento.
          ESTUDIANTE: Es sábado.

1…   2…   3…   4…   5…   6…

ACTIVIDAD B ¿Quién es?

Look again at the drawings. Your instructor will read several statements. Give the name of the person doing the activities described in each statement.

1…   2…   3…   4…   5…   6…   7…   8…

✎ ACTIVIDAD C ¿Elena o Tomás?

Look again at the pictures of Elena and Tomás. Indicate two or three activities you have in common with either Elena or Tomás and two or three you don't have in common. Write your activities down, using the following models. Remember to put the verbs in the correct **yo** form. In class, compare your activities to those of your classmates.

MODELOS   Yo también corro los sábados.

Normalmente no lavo mi ropa los domingos.

ACTIVIDAD D Mis fines de semana

This activity is a version of **Veinte preguntas.** Think of something that you normally do on the weekends. (If you do not know the Spanish expression for it, ask your instructor for help.) Your classmates will try to guess what the activity is by asking you yes/no questions.

MODELOS   ¿Haces la actividad con un amigo? ¿con una amiga? ¿solo/a (*alone*)?

¿Haces la actividad en casa? ¿en la universidad? ¿en un café? ¿en la playa (*beach*)?

¿Haces la actividad por la mañana, normalmente? ¿por la tarde? ¿por la noche? ¿a cualquier (*any*) hora?

¿Haces la actividad los sábados? ¿los domingos?

VOCABULARIO

¿No haces nada?

Negation and negative words

—Esto **no me gusta para nada. No quiero hacer nada** esta noche.
—Ay, eres imposible. **No hay nadie** como tú.

You know that the word **nunca** means *never.* A synonym of **nunca** is **jamás.** Note that **nunca** or **jamás** can precede a verb or follow it. If they follow a verb, then a **no** is required before the verb.

> **Nunca** puedo dormir bien. / **No** puedo dormir bien **nunca.**
> **Jamás** me quedo en casa los sábados. / **No** me quedo en casa los sábados **jamás.**

Here are some other negative words that function like **nunca** and **jamás.** Note how in English some of these words have several translations.

nada	*nothing, not anything*
nadie	*no one, not anyone*
ninguno/a	*none, not any*
tampoco	*neither, not either*

Así se dice

You have learned that **por** is used in expressions of time to mean *during* and *for:*

Elena toma café **por** la tarde y después estudia **por** dos horas.
Elena drinks coffee during the afternoon and then studies for two hours.

One of the uses of **para** is in reference to a future deadline:

Tomás hace la tarea **para** mañana.
Tomás is doing the homework for tomorrow.

(You will learn more about **por** and **para** in future lessons of *¿Sabías que... ?*)

No quiero hacer **nada.**	*I don't want to do anything.*
¿Quién se levanta temprano? **¿Nadie?** ¿**Nadie** se levanta temprano? / ¿**No** se levanta **nadie** temprano?	*Who gets up early? No one? Doesn't anyone get up early?*
No voy a **ningún*** lugar este fin de semana.	*I'm not going anywhere this weekend.*
Yo (**no** voy a **ningún** lugar) **tampoco.**	*I'm not (going anywhere) either.*

 ACTIVIDAD E ¿Qué hace los fines de semana?

Listen as your instructor reads statements about several types of students. Circle the letter of the person described.

1. **a.** el estudiante dedicado   **b.** el estudiante no dedicado
2. **a.** el estudiante sociable   **b.** el estudiante solitario
3. **a.** el estudiante activo   **b.** el estudiante sedentario

ACTIVIDAD F Mis fines de semana

Indicate whether each statement is true or false according to your weekend routines.

	C	F
1. Nunca me acuesto antes de (*before*) la 1.00 de la mañana los sábados.	☐	☐
2. No limpio la casa los fines de semana.	☐	☐
3. Nunca me quedo en casa los viernes por la noche.	☐	☐
4. Tampoco me quedo en casa los sábados por la noche.	☐	☐
5. No saco vídeos con mucha frecuencia.	☐	☐
6. Tampoco veo la televisión mucho.	☐	☐
7. No hago ejercicio nunca los domingos.	☐	☐
8. Jamás voy a la biblioteca los sábados.	☐	☐

COMUNICACIÓN

ACTIVIDAD G Los fines de semana del profesor (de la profesora)

Paso 1 What are your instructor's weekends like? With two other people, make up four statements using some negative expressions (**nada, nadie, nunca,** and so forth) to describe your instructor's typical weekend.

Paso 2 Each group should present its statements to the rest of the class, who then decide if each statement is true or not. Your instructor will react. Who knows him or her the best?

***Ninguno** is shortened to **ningún** before singular masculine nouns.

GRAMÁTICA

¿A quién le gusta... ?

More about likes and dislikes

A Elena y a sus amigos **les gusta** bailar.

To talk about another person's likes or dislikes in Spanish is to talk about what pleases him or her. To do this, use **le gusta** or **le gustan.**

> A Elena **le gusta** hacer ejercicio temprano.
> A mi compañero de cuarto **no le gustan** los lunes.

Note that in the first example, **gustar** is in the singular form (**gusta**) because **hacer ejercicio** is singular and is the subject of the sentence. Translated literally, the sentence means *Exercising early is pleasing to Elena.*

To talk about what is pleasing to two or more people, you can use **les gusta** or **les gustan.**

> A mis amigos **no les gusta** levantarse temprano nunca.
> A muchos argentinos **les gustan** las películas norteamericanas.

To express what is pleasing to you and someone else (pleasing to us), you should use **nos gusta** or **nos gustan.**

> **Nos gusta** mucho pasar tiempo con la familia los fines de semana.
> **No nos gustan** los quehaceres domésticos (*household chores*).

Remember that **gustar** does not mean *to like,* although it is often translated that way. Remember that **le, les,** or **nos** is used depending on to whom something is pleasing, and **gusta** or **gustan** is used depending on who or what is pleasing.

ACTIVIDAD H ¿Qué les gusta?

Paso 1 Like people, cats and dogs differ in their likes and dislikes. Decide which of the following statements refer to dogs (**los perros**), which to cats (**los gatos**), and which to both (**los dos**). The last item is for you to make up and see what your classmates think.

> MODELO   PROFESOR(A): Les gusta dormir mucho.
> TÚ: Eso se refiere (se puede referir) a los dos.

1. Les gusta dormir con su dueño (*owner*).
2. Les gusta mucho el pescado (*fish*).
3. No les gusta nadar mucho.
4. Les gusta salir por la noche.
5. Les gusta cazar (*to hunt*).
6. Les gusta hacer trucos (*tricks*).
7. No les gusta ir en coche.
8. No les gusta _____.

Paso 2 If you have a pet, use items from **Paso 1** to talk about its likes and dislikes.

> MODELO   Tengo un perro. Se llama Nikki. A Nikki le gusta nadar. También le gusta mucho andar en carro.

Así se dice

Did you notice the **a** before names or the mention of specific people in the sentences with **gustar?** Since **gustar** actually means *to please* or *be pleasing,* the **a** is used to mark *to* whom or *to* what something is pleasing.

> **A los profesores** les gusta explicar la gramática.

> **¿A quiénes** les gusta no hacer nada por la noche?

> **A nosotros** nos gusta lavar la ropa los sábados.

> **¿A Uds.** les gusta limpiar la casa?

ACTIVIDAD I Estudiantes y profesores

The following are four statements that you might make as students. First decide in groups of three or as a class if they are true. Make any changes necessary. Then complete the second sentence in a logical manner and see how your instructor responds. (**¡OJO!** Be sure to pay attention to how **gustar** is used in each sentence and what the word order looks like!)

1. A nosotros los estudiantes no nos gusta tomar (*to take*) exámenes finales. No sabemos (*We don't know*) si a los profesores les gusta...

2. A nosotros los estudiantes no nos gusta levantarnos temprano para ir a clases. No sabemos si a los profesores les gusta...

3. A nosotros los estudiantes no nos gusta tener clases los viernes por la tarde. No sabemos si a los profesores les gusta...

4. A nosotros los estudiantes no nos gusta estudiar los sábados. Probablemente a los profesores no les gusta...

COMUNICACIÓN

ACTIVIDAD J Una encuesta

Paso 1 Find two people who answer **Sí** to the following questions and report your findings to the class.

1. ¿Te gusta levantarte muy tarde los sábados?
2. ¿Te gusta quedarte en casa los fines de semana?
3. ¿Te gustan los conciertos de música *rock*?

Paso 2 How would you and your friends respond to the questions in **Paso 1?**

MODELOS Sí. Nos gustan los conciertos de música *rock*.

No. Nos gusta quedarnos en casa los fines de semana.

IDEAS PARA EXPLORAR

Las otras personas

GRAMÁTICA

¿Qué hacen?

Talking about the activities of two or more people

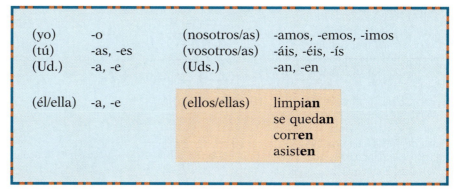

(yo)	-o	(nosotros/as)	-amos, -emos, -imos
(tú)	-as, -es	(vosotros/as)	-áis, -éis, -ís
(Ud.)	-a, -e	(Uds.)	-an, -en
(él/ella)	-a, -e	(ellos/ellas)	limpi**an**
			se qued**an**
			corr**en**
			asist**en**

When your instructor describes the actions of two or more people, you may have noticed that a particular verb form is used. That is, if more than one person is the subject of the sentence, an **-n** is added to the final vowel of the verb. For example, **estudia → estudian; come → comen.** This is known as the *third person plural* or **ellos/ellas** form.

Los domingos por la tarde, Elena y sus amigas siempre **juegan** al voleibol.
Los domingos por la tarde, Tomás y un amigo **van** al supermercado.

Note that **se** is used before the third person plural form of verbs like **acostarse.**

El sábado, Tomás y sus amigos **sacan** vídeos y **se quedan** en casa por la tarde.

ACTIVIDAD A ¿Qué hacen y por qué?

Tomás and his friend from work have a lot of weekend plans. Match their activity in column A with a logical reason in column B.

Tomás y un compañero de trabajo…

A
1. sacan un vídeo porque _____
2. van al cine porque _____
3. van de compras porque _____
4. corren porque _____
5. se levantan tarde porque _____

B
a. necesitan ropa nueva (*new*).
b. quieren ver la última (*latest*) película (*film*) de acción.
c. necesitan hacer ejercicio.
d. quieren ver una película en casa.
e. no tienen que trabajar por la mañana.

ACTIVIDAD B ¿Quiénes?

For each statement, decide whether the weekend activity is typical of students, of people who work full-time, or could easily refer to both groups.

1. Juegan a los videojuegos.
2. Limpian la casa.
3. Se quedan en casa y miran la televisión por la noche.
4. Lavan la ropa.
5. Visitan a parientes.
6. Trabajan en el jardín (*yard*).
7. Duermen más que (*more than*) durante la semana y se levantan más tarde.
8. Van de compras.
9. Dan un paseo con su perro.
10. Salen a bailar.

---

*In Latin America **Uds.** is used for *you all*. In Spain **vosotros/as** is used for two or more people singularly addressed as **tú; Uds.** is used for two or more people singularly addressed as **Ud.**

ACTIVIDAD C Las rutinas en la casa

Paso 1 Write down at least three chores that spouses or partners do as part of their home life.

> MODELO Limpian la casa.

Paso 2 Are celebrities' lives different? Choose one of the following couples and write sentences that indicate whether or not you think they do the things that you listed in **Paso 1.**

> Ozzie y Sharon   Dr. Phil y Robin   Jay y Mavis Leno
>   Osbourne   McGraw
>
> MODELO Ozzie y Sharon no limpian la casa.

Paso 3 Report on the famous couple that you selected and how they may be similar to or different from the average couple.

ACTIVIDAD D ¿Qué actividades tienen en común°?

en... *in common*

Paso 1 Here is a list of activities that some people do on weekends. Read the list and make sure you understand each item before going on to **Paso 2.**

1. Sacan muchos vídeos del videoclub y se quedan enfrente del televisor (*in front of the TV set*) todo el fin de semana.
2. Limpian la casa, lavan la ropa y van al supermercado porque no tienen tiempo durante la semana.
3. Se quedan en casa, escuchan la radio y leen sin parar (*without stopping*).
4. Practican un deporte (*sport*) o hacen ejercicio.
5. No hacen absolutamente nada. Son perezosos (*lazy*).
6. Van al cine.

Paso 2 Make a list of six questions to ask classmates about their weekend activities, based on the preceding statements.

> MODELOS ¿Practicas algún deporte los fines de semana?
>   ¿Haces ejercicio?

Leave space for two people's names after each question.

Paso 3 For each question on your list, find two people who answer **Sí** to that question and write down their names.

Paso 4 The first person who finds two people who answer **Sí** for each of the six questions shouts **"¡Ya lo tengo! ¡Ya lo tengo!"** and presents the findings to the class, following the model.

> MODELO _____ y _____ sacan vídeos del videoclub y se quedan enfrente del televisor todo el fin de semana.

GRAMÁTICA

¿Qué hacemos nosotros?

Talking about activities that you and others do

(yo)	-o	(nosotros/as)	**limpiamos**
			nos qued**amos**
			corr**emos**
			asist**imos**
(tú)	-as, -es	(vosotros/as)	-áis, -éis, -ís
(Ud.)	-a, -e	(Uds.)	-an, -en
(él/ella)	-a, -e	(ellos/ellas)	-an, -en

When talking about the actions of a group of people that includes yourself, use the following verb forms.

> For **-ar** verbs, add **-amos** to the stem.
> For **-er** verbs, add **-emos** to the stem.
> For **-ir** verbs, add **-imos** to the stem.

For example:

> gastar → **gastamos**
> leer → **leemos**
> salir → **salimos**

This is known as the *first person plural* or **nosotros/nosotras** form of the verb.

> Todos los sábados, mi compañera de cuarto y yo **vamos*** de compras y **gastamos** (*we spend*) mucho dinero.
> Luego **almorzamos** en un restaurante.
> Frecuentemente, por la tarde **asistimos** a una conferencia (*lecture*) en el museo de arte.
> Cuando **salimos** del museo, **regresamos** al apartamento.

Verbs with a vowel change in the stem, such as **me acuesto** and **suelo,** don't have a vowel change in the **nosotros/as** form.

> **Nos acostamos** muy tarde todos los sábados porque **solemos** salir con los amigos.

---

*Note the **nosotros/as** forms for two irregular verbs you know: **vamos (ir)** and **somos (ser).**

Lección 2   ¿Qué haces los fines de semana?

ACTIVIDAD E Dos estudiantes argentinos

Paso 1 In a recent interview, two brothers, both Argentine college students, described their typical weekend activities. But the activities they mentioned are not in logical order. Assign the following activities a number from 1 to 6, with 1 being the first and 6 being the last they do.

_____ Dormimos hasta muy tarde el domingo.

_____ Damos un paseo por las calles (*streets*) el viernes por la noche. Siempre hay muchas personas allí.

_____ Leemos y estudiamos el domingo por la noche.

_____ Regresamos a la universidad el domingo por la tarde.

_____ El viernes por la tarde salimos de la universidad y vamos a visitar a la familia.

_____ Salimos a bailar el sábado. Volvemos a casa a las 4.00 ó 5.00 de la mañana.

Paso 2 Now, analyze the activities in **Paso 1** from the perspective of yourself and your friends. Which activities do you and your friends tend to do? Which do you tend not to do? Make two lists.

Nosotros/as también…

Nosotros/as no…

 **ACTIVIDAD F** **¿Qué hacemos los fines de semana?**

Paso 1 Write three statements that describe what you and your friends or family tend to do on weekends.

MODELO Practicamos un deporte los fines de semana.

Paso 2 Now, search for at least one classmate with whom you have in common two activities from **Paso 1.** Ask questions using **Uds.**

MODELO Tus amigos y tú, ¿practican un deporte los fines de semana?

Paso 3 Now share your information with the class. What activities do *most* people have in common?

IDEAS PARA EXPLORAR

El tiempo y las estaciones

VOCABULARIO

¿Qué tiempo hace?

Talking about the weather

To talk about the weather and how it affects what people do, the following expressions are used in Spanish.

Hace sol. Hace buen tiempo. Está despejado.

Llueve. (Está lloviendo.) Hace mal* tiempo. Está nublado.

---

*Malo/a (*Bad*) is shortened to **mal** before a masculine singular noun: **un mal día, una mala semana.**

Hace viento.

Nieva. (Está nevando.)

La temperatura   El tiempo

Hace mucho calor.

Hace calor.

Hace fresco.

Hace frío.

Hace mucho frío.

Grados   Grados
centígrados   Fahrenheit

Note that the verbs **hacer** and **estar** are both translated as *to be* in these expressions. (You will learn more about **estar** later in this lesson.)

Así se dice

The Spanish word **tiempo** has at least two translations in English: *weather* and *time* (not a specific time, but time in general).

¿Qué **tiempo** hace en Buenos Aires ahora?	*What's the weather like in Buenos Aires right now?*
¿Cómo pasas el **tiempo** los fines de semana?	*How do you spend your time on weekends?*

Time in English has at least two translations into Spanish, **hora** and **tiempo**.

What time is it?	¿Qué **hora** es?
I don't have any free time these days.	No tengo **tiempo** libre en estos días.

ACTIVIDAD A El tiempo

Listen as your instructor describes the weather conditions in the drawings on the following page. Match the letter of each description with the corresponding drawing.

1. _____

2. _____

3. _____

4. _____

5. _____

6. _____

7. _____

8. _____

Así se dice

Did you notice that Spanish does not use an equivalent of *it* in phrases like *it's raining* or *it's sunny*? These are both examples of the indefinite *it* used as a subject of a verb in English. While English requires the indefinite subject *it*, Spanish does not. Here are some examples of sentences in which Spanish prohibits the subject *it*.

> Hace calor.
> Está lloviendo.
> Va a nevar.
> Es la una y cuarto.
> Es necesario leer este libro.

ACTIVIDAD B Asociaciones

Certain activities are typically associated with specific weather conditions. Match the activities in column A with an appropriate weather condition in column B. Then compare your associations with those of another person. Are your associations similar?

A	B
1. _____ quedarse en casa (no salir)	**a.** Hace mucho calor.
2. _____ practicar un deporte	**b.** Hace mucho frío.
3. _____ correr	**c.** Está nevando.
4. _____ dar un paseo	**d.** Está lloviendo.
5. _____ nadar o ir a la playa	**e.** Hace fresco.
6. _____ ir al cine	**f.** Está despejado.
7. _____ limpiar la casa (el apartamento)	

ACTIVIDAD C ¿Qué tiempo hace?

Look over the weather information on the following page for Buenos Aires, Argentina, for a Monday. See whether you can guess the meaning of several terms, such as **parcialmente nublado, humedad, visibilidad,** and **soleado.** Then answer the questions.

Ciudad de Buenos Aires

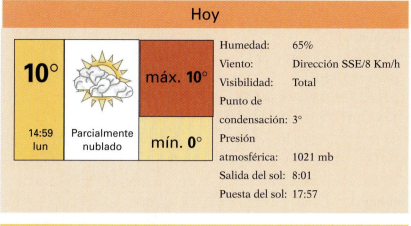

1. ¿Qué tiempo hace hoy en Buenos Aires?
   a. Hace buen tiempo.
   b. Hace mal tiempo.
   c. No hace ni buen tiempo ni mal tiempo.

2. ¿En qué ciudad hace más frío?
   a. Buenos Aires   b. Córdoba   c. Mendoza   d. Río Gallegos

3. ¿Está lloviendo en alguna ciudad?
   ☐ Sí   ☐ No

4. ¿Está nevando en alguna ciudad?
   ☐ Sí   ☐ No

COMUNICACIÓN

ACTIVIDAD D ¿Qué te gusta hacer los fines de semana?

Paso 1 Take the survey on the following page. Then interview someone else and note his or her responses.

MODELO   ¿Te gusta estudiar hasta muy tarde los sábados si hace buen tiempo? ¿y si hace mal tiempo?

	...SI HACE BUEN TIEMPO.		...SI HACE MAL TIEMPO.	
	SÍ	NO	SÍ	NO

Los sábados

1. Me gusta estudiar hasta muy tarde...	☐	☐	☐	☐
2. Me gusta ir al cine...	☐	☐	☐	☐
3. Me gusta hacer ejercicio aeróbico...	☐	☐	☐	☐
4. Me gusta lavar la ropa...	☐	☐	☐	☐
5. Me gusta dormir mucho...	☐	☐	☐	☐
6. Me gusta ir de compras y gastar dinero...	☐	☐	☐	☐
7. Me gusta _____...	☐	☐	☐	☐

Los domingos

1. Me gusta ir a la playa...	☐	☐	☐	☐
2. Me gusta charlar con mis amigos...	☐	☐	☐	☐
3. Me gusta sacar vídeos...	☐	☐	☐	☐
4. Me gusta no hacer nada...	☐	☐	☐	☐
5. Me gusta practicar un deporte...	☐	☐	☐	☐
6. Me gusta escuchar música *rock*...	☐	☐	☐	☐
7. Me gusta _____...	☐	☐	☐	☐

Paso 2 Now decide where you fall on the following scale.

NUESTRA REACCIÓN AL TIEMPO Y LAS ACTIVIDADES QUE HACEMOS SON IGUALES.			NUESTRA REACCIÓN AL TIEMPO Y LAS ACTIVIDADES QUE HACEMOS SON MUY DIFERENTES.	
5	4	3	2	1

NAVEGANDO LA RED

Find a current weather report in Spanish. Present the report (**el pronóstico del tiempo**) to the class, answering the following questions.
1. ¿Qué tiempo hace en dos o tres ciudades principales?
2. ¿Cuál es la temperatura en la capital?
You should also be prepared to present one other fact about the weather in the report.

VOCABULARIO

¿Cuándo comienza el verano?

Talking about seasons of the year

To talk about the months and seasons of the year, you can use these terms.

Los meses y las estaciones del año

el otoño	el invierno	la primavera	el verano

septiembre, octubre, noviembre   **diciembre, enero, febrero**   **marzo, abril, mayo**   **junio, julio, agosto**

Así se dice

You have learned that **está lloviendo** means *it's raining*. The **-ndo** forms of many verbs can be used with **estar** to express something that is occurring *right now*. Some **-ndo** forms have slight irregularities.

¿Qué estás **haciendo**?
What are you doing?

Estoy **leyendo** el
   periódico.

Estoy **viendo** la
   televisión.

ACTIVIDAD E ¿Qué estación es?

Read over the following statements and decide which season is being described.

1. En los meses de junio, julio y agosto, suele hacer mucho calor. En esta estación, muchos estudiantes están de vacaciones.

2. Esta estación se asocia con la lluvia, las flores y el amor. Comprende los meses de marzo, abril y mayo.

3. En esta estación hay viento y las hojas (*leaves*) cambian (*change*) de color. Incluye los meses de septiembre, octubre y noviembre.

4. Los meses de esta estación son diciembre, enero y febrero, y hace frío.

ACTIVIDAD F ¿Sabías que... ?

Read the **¿Sabías que... ?** selection on the following page. Then listen to the statements your instructor reads and say whether each refers to **España** or **la Argentina.**

MODELO   **PROFESOR(A):** Es enero y hace calor.
          ESTUDIANTE: Estamos en la Argentina.

¿Sabías que...

en lugares como la Argentina las estaciones están invertidas en relación con la época en que ocurren en países como España y México? El mundo está dividido en dos hemisferios: el hemisferio norte y el hemisferio sur. Cuando es verano en el hemisferio norte, es invierno en el hemisferio sur. Y cuando es invierno en el hemisferio norte, es verano en el hemisferio sur. Durante las Navidades (25 de diciembre), por ejemplo, en Buenos Aires hace mucho calor y los estudiantes tienen las vacaciones de verano. ¡No hay clases y todos van a la playa!

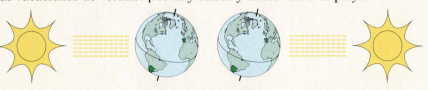

COMUNICACIÓN

ACTIVIDAD G Encuesta

Using the following table as a guide, find out from two people about their favorite and least favorite seasons and weather. Then fill in the same information for yourself. How do the three of you compare? Write a short paragraph with the results. Here are some questions to help you begin your interview.

MODELOS ¿Cuál es tu estación preferida?

¿Qué estación prefieres más?

¿Te gusta el invierno?

¿ ?

	E1	E2	YO
nombre			
estación preferida			
tiempo preferido			
estación menos preferida			
tiempo menos preferido			

Así se dice

You can also use **pasar** with **-ndo** forms to talk about how you or other people spend time. See if you can determine the meaning of the following sentences.

Paso mucho tiempo **estudiando.**
I spend a lot of time studying.

Mi perro **pasa** mucho tiempo **durmiendo.**

Paso todo el día **trabajando.**

GRAMÁTICA

¿Qué vas a hacer?

—El pronóstico es que **va a llover** mucho este fin de semana.

	ir			a	+ *infinitive*
(yo)	voy	(nosotros/as)	vamos		
					estudiar
(tú)	vas	(vosotros/as)	vais	a	leer
(Ud.)	va	(Uds.)	van		
					salir
(él/ella)	va	(ellos/as)	van		

One of the ways to talk about what you are going to do in the future is to use the **ir a** + *infinitive* construction. **Ir** is conjugated to agree with the subject, followed by **a** and an infinitive.

El sábado mis amigos y yo **vamos a nadar.**
Elena **va a tomar** clases de verano.
Tomás y sus colegas de la oficina **van a trabajar** mucho.

ACTIVIDAD H ¿Qué van a hacer?

Elena y sus amigas tienen planes para las próximas vacaciones. ¿En qué orden van a hacer las siguientes actividades (1 = la primera actividad, 6 = la última actividad)?

Elena y sus amigas…

_____ van a ir al cine.
_____ van de compras.
_____ van a despertarse entre las 8.00 y 8.30.
_____ van a desayunar en un café.
_____ van a acostarse tarde.
_____ van a cenar en un restaurante cubano.

ACTIVIDAD I ¿Qué va a hacer?

Elena has specific plans for the weekend. Complete each statement in column A with the most logical activity from column B.

A

1. _____ Elena tiene mucha ropa sucia (*dirty*)…
2. _____ Quiere pasar tiempo con su perro…
3. _____ Si no llueve,…
4. _____ Como quiere hacer algo espiritual,…
5. _____ Tiene que hacer investigaciones (*research*),…

B

a. va a tomar el sol.
b. va a ir a la iglesia.
c. y va a usar mucho detergente.
d. y va a buscar información en la biblioteca o en la Red.
e. y va a dar un paseo con él.

ACTIVIDAD J ¿Qué van a hacer Uds.?

Paso 1 Think of a particular season (**la primavera, el verano, el otoño** or **el invierno**). Make a list of six activities, five that you plan to do during this season, and one that you do *not* plan to do. Do not mention the season in your descriptions.

> MODELO   Voy a _____, pero no voy a _____.

Paso 2 Read your statements to a partner, who will identify the season in which you plan (do not plan) to do your activities. Then, switch roles.

Paso 3 Complete the following paragraph, based on your partner's and your information.

> _____ (*Name of partner*) y yo vamos a _____ y _____, pero no vamos a _____. _____ (Él/Ella) va a _____ y yo voy a _____.

ACTIVIDAD K Después de graduarme

Paso 1 We all need time to relax and wind down after life's major events. Take a moment to think about what you might do during the first few months after you graduate. List at least three things that you plan to do to celebrate, relax, or prepare for your future.

> MODELO   Voy a viajar mucho.

Paso 2 Ask a classmate what he or she plans to do after graduation. Do you have any ideas in common? Be ready to report any similarities in the plans you both have when your instructor surveys the class.

> MODELO   **PROFESOR(A):** ¿Qué vas a hacer después de graduarte?
>
>   **ESTUDIANTE:** Los (Las) dos vamos a viajar.

Paso 3 You have had the opportunity to hear your classmates' ideas. Do the most popular ideas involve traveling, relaxing with family, looking for a job, or something else?

> MODELO   Las ideas populares son...

Paso 4 Now that you have taken note of one or two ideas that seem most popular, indicate whether you are a typical student compared with the rest of the class.

☐ Soy típico/a.   ☐ No soy típico/a.

NAVEGANDO LA RED

Some countries have a lot of temperature and climate variation because they are large or because their geography is so varied. On the Web, locate two Spanish-speaking countries, one that does not seem to have much variation in temperature and climate within its borders and one that does. Present your findings to the class.

INTERCAMBIO

¡Un fin de semana ideal!

Propósito: to guess the authorship of various descriptions of an ideal weekend

Papeles: Everyone writes something and the entire class guesses.

Paso 1 Sit back and visualize yourself spending an ideal weekend. What are you doing? For how long? With whom? What is the weather like? What month is it? Are you imagining a Saturday or Sunday?

Paso 2 Write a paragraph describing a day of your ideal weekend. Include all the information suggested in **Paso 1.** Then place your composition face down on your instructor's desk. Do not write your name on it.

Paso 3 One by one, each person in the class goes up to the instructor's desk and selects a composition other than his or her own. Read the one you have chosen and try to find the person in the class who wrote it.

1. First, think of all the questions you can ask to find the author. The only question you cannot ask is **¿Qué te gusta hacer los fines de semana?** It may help to write out some of the questions. You can begin the process of elimination by asking people whether they prefer Saturday or Sunday.

2. Do not show the composition to anyone.

3. When you think you have found the author, write that person's name at the top of the composition and write your name underneath it. Do not tell the author that you think you have found him or her. Place the composition face down on the instructor's desk.

Paso 4 When all compositions have been returned to the instructor, he or she will call on you to announce the author of the composition and to tell the clues that led you to your decision (for example, **porque le gusta practicar deportes los sábados**). Your instructor will then ask that person if he or she is the author.

Vistazos culturales
La música y la danza en el mundo hispano

¿Sabías que... en el mundo hispano el mestizaje (mezcla[a] de razas y culturas diferentes) se refleja[b] no sólo en las características físicas de la gente sino también[c] en su música y danza? En España, por ejemplo, la música y la danza tienen sus raíces[d] en la cultura árabe, ya que[e] los moros[f] ocuparon ese país desde el año 711 hasta 1492. En el Caribe, las varias corrientes[g] musicales reflejan la influencia africana gracias a los esclavos[h] traídos[i] a la región durante el período colonial.

[a]*blend* [b]*se... is reflected* [c]*sino... but also* [d]*roots* [e]*ya... because* [f]*Moors* [g]*trends* [h]*slaves*
[i]*brought*

La Argentina

El **tango** comenzó como un baile[a] en los arrabales[b] de Buenos Aires a finales del siglo XIX. Al principio, el tango tenía mala fama[c] por asociarse con la clase baja y con los burdeles.[d]

[a]*dance* [b]*slums* [c]*tenía... had a bad reputation* [d]*brothels*

España

El baile flamenco se caracteriza por movimientos y golpes[a] rítmicos de los pies[b] contra el suelo.[c] Esta técnica se llama «el zapateado». La música **flamenca** para guitarra tiene armonías influídas por los árabes y ritmos de tipo africano.

[a]*stomps* [b]*feet* [c]*floor*

Bailando tango en Buenos Aires

You can investigate these cultural topics in more detail on the *¿Sabías que… ?* Online Learning Center: **www.mhhe.com/sabiasque5**.

La **salsa** se ha hecho[a] muy popular en Cuba, Puerto Rico, Nueva York, Venezuela y otros lugares.

[a]se… *has become*

El **merengue** es el baile nacional de la República Dominicana. Su música se conoce por ser muy rápida.

Bailando en la Calle Ocho durante el Carnaval en Miami

Los cubanos y puertorrique-ños también popularizaron el **mambo** y el **chachachá** durante los años 50.[a]

[a]los… *the 50s*

ESTADOS UNIDOS

Golfo de México

La Habana

CUBA

MÉXICO

ISLAS BAHAMAS

Nassau

OCÉANO ATLÁNTICO

Santo Domingo

PUERTO RICO

San Juan

HAITÍ

JAMAICA

Kingston

REPÚBLICA DOMINICANA

Puerto Príncipe

ANTILLAS MENORES

BELICE

Belmopan

GUATEMALA

Guatemala

HONDURAS

Tegucigalpa

MAR CARIBE

EL SALVADOR

San Salvador

NICARAGUA

Managua

Caracas

San José

VENEZUELA

OCÉANO PACÍFICO

COSTA RICA

Panamá

PANAMÁ

COLOMBIA

Bogotá

El **tamborito** es un tipo de música tradicional de Panamá que tiene influencias africanas, españolas, indígenas[a] y norteamericanas.*

[a]*indigenous*

La **cumbia,** un baile y música de origen colombiano, es muy popular en toda Latinoamérica.

El **vallenato** es un tipo de música colombiana que combina música mestiza con ritmos afrocaribeños. El instrumento principal del vallenato es el acordeón.

*Throughout *¿Sabías que… ?*, the term **norteamericano/a** is used to refer to citizens of either Canada and the United States or the United States only. Context will determine the intended meaning.

ACTIVIDAD ¿Qué recuerdas?

Indicate whether each statement is **cierto** o **falso.**

	C	F
1. El instrumento principal del vallenato es la trompeta.	☐	☐
2. El baile nacional de la República Dominicana es la salsa.	☐	☐
3. El tamborito es típico de Panamá.	☐	☐
4. La música y el baile flamencos tienen influencia árabe.	☐	☐
5. Los árabes ocuparon España por aproximadamente 100 años.	☐	☐
6. El tango tiene su origen en las zonas más pobres de Buenos Aires.	☐	☐

NAVEGANDO LA RED

Complete *one* of the following activities. Then present your information to the class.

1. Look for information about the **Ballet Folklórico* de México.** Then jot down the following details.
    a. Explica qué es el Ballet Folklórico.
    b. Describe el vestuario (*apparel*) que usan los bailadores.
    c. Menciona dónde se puede ver el Ballet Folklórico en este país.

2. Look for information about the **corridos mexicanos.** Then jot down the following details.
    a. Define qué es un corrido.
    b. Resume brevemente la historia de los corridos en México y en los Estados Unidos. Es decir, menciona los eventos históricos que influyeron en (*that influenced*) los compositores de los corridos.
    c. Menciona los temas principales de los corridos.
    d. Menciona en qué ciudades mexicanas y norteamericanas se tocan los corridos.

---

*Here **Folklórico** is spelled with a **k** because it is part of the official name of Mexico's Folkloric Ballet. Elsewhere in *¿Sabías que... ?* you will see this word spelled **folclórico.**

Actividades para el fin de semana — Weekend Activities

bailar	to dance
correr (R)	to run
charlar	to chat
chatear	to chat, participate in a chat room
dar (*irreg.*) **un paseo**	to take a walk
gastar (dinero)	to spend (money)
ir (R)	to go
a la iglesia	to church
al cine	to the movies
de compras	shopping
jugar (ue) (R)	to play
al fútbol	soccer
al fútbol americano	football
lavar (la ropa)	to wash (clothes)
limpiar	to clean
(el apartamento)	(the apartment)
nadar	to swim
no hacer nada	to do nothing
practicar un deporte	to practice, play a sport
quedarse (en casa)	to stay (at home)
sacar vídeos	to rent videos
tomar (un café)	to drink (a cup of coffee)
ver (*irreg.*) **la televisión**	to watch television

Palabras de negación — Words of Negation

jamás / **nunca** (R)	never
nada	nothing, not anything
nadie	no one, not anyone
ninguno/a	none, not any
tampoco	neither, not either

¿Qué tiempo hace? — What's the Weather Like?

Hace (mucho) calor.	It's (very) hot.
Hace fresco.	It's cool.
Hace (mucho) frío.	It's (very) cold.
Hace sol.	It's sunny.
Hace viento.	It's windy.
Hace buen tiempo.	The weather's good.
Hace mal tiempo.	The weather's bad.
Está despejado.	It's clear.
Está nublado.	It's cloudy.
Llueve. (Está lloviendo.)	It's raining.
Nieva. (Está nevando.)	It's snowing.
la temperatura	temperature

Los meses y las estaciones del año — Months and Seasons of the Year

enero, febrero, marzo, abril, mayo, junio, julio, agosto, septiembre, octubre, noviembre, diciembre

la primavera	spring
el verano	summer
el otoño	fall, autumn
el invierno	winter

Otras palabras y expresiones útiles

la discoteca	discotheque
la fiesta	party
cada	each
después	after
hasta (muy) tarde	until (very) late
luego	then; therefore
también	also

LECCIÓN  **3**

Check out the following media resources to complement this lesson:

 Online *Manual*

 Video on CD

 Online Learning Center

 ActivityPak

¿Qué hiciste ayer?

En un café de Madrid, España

In this lesson, you will look into what you and your classmates did in the recent past. As part of this lesson, you will

◆ ask and answer questions about last night's activities

◆ ask and answer questions about last weekend's activities

◆ talk about some special events from the past

◆ learn how to use a past tense called the *preterite* to ask questions and to talk about yourself and others

ALTO Before beginning this lesson, look over the **Intercambio** activity on page 101. This is the activity you will be working toward throughout the lesson.

VOCABULARIO

¿Qué hizo Elena ayer?

Talking about activities in the past

Ayer Elena...

1. **...se levantó** temprano.

2. **...hizo** ejercicio aeróbico.

3. **...caminó** a la universidad.

4. **...participó** en clase.

5. **...trabajó** en el laboratorio por la tarde.

6. **...volvió** a casa a las 5.00.

7. **...dio** un paseo con su perro.

8. **...leyó** su correo electrónico.

9. **...pagó** unas cuentas.

10. **...hizo** su tarea.

11. **...cenó** tarde.

12. **...se acostó** temprano.

Ayer Tomás...

1. **...se levantó** tarde.

2. **...leyó** el periódico.

3. **...fue** en carro a la oficina.

4. **...trabajó** mucho en la computadora.

5. **...almorzó** con una clienta en un restaurante.

6. **...salió** de la oficina.

7. **...llegó** tarde a una clase.

8. **...se durmió** en clase.

9. **...llamó** a una amiga.

10. **...vio** la televisión y **comió.**

11. **...escuchó** música y **estudió.**

12. **...se acostó** muy tarde.

Vocabulario útil

el fin de semana pasado	last weekend
la semana pasada	last week
anoche	last night
ayer	yesterday

Lección 3   ¿Qué hiciste ayer?

ACTIVIDAD A ¿Elena o Tomás?

Paso 1 Here is a list of things that either Elena or Tomás did yesterday. According to the drawings at the beginning of this section and what you know from previous lessons, was it Elena or Tomás who did each activity?

	ELENA	TOMÁS
1. Trabajó en el laboratorio.	☐	☐
2. Hizo ejercicio aeróbico.	☐	☐
3. Se durmió en clase.	☐	☐
4. Dio un paseo en el parque.	☐	☐
5. Caminó a la universidad.	☐	☐
6. Se levantó temprano por la mañana.	☐	☐
7. Se acostó tarde por la noche.	☐	☐
8. Almorzó en un restaurante.	☐	☐
9. Trabajó muchas horas en la oficina.	☐	☐

Paso 2 Ahora explica tus respuestas, utilizando el siguiente modelo.

MODELO Creo que (*I think that*) _____ hizo ejercicio porque suele hacer ejercicio todos los días.

Así se dice

As you may have noticed, **fue** is the past tense of **va** (*he or she goes*).

Ayer Elena **fue** a la biblioteca.

Tomás **fue** a la oficina ayer por la mañana.

You have also seen **hizo** in the expression **hizo ejercicio.** Because **hacer** often means *to do,* the form **hizo** can be used to ask what someone *did.*

¿Qué **hizo** Elena ayer?

¿Qué **hizo** la profesora anoche?

ACTIVIDAD B ¿En qué orden?

Read over the following list of activities that Tomás did yesterday. Number them from 1 to 8, with 1 being the first activity Tomás did in the day and 8 being the last.

Tomás...

_____ fue a la oficina.   _____ almorzó con una clienta.
_____ se acostó.   _____ se levantó.
_____ salió de la oficina.   _____ se durmió en clase.
_____ vio la televisión.   _____ estudió.

COMUNICACIÓN

Your instructor will select a student to come to the front of the class. Last night, did he or she do anything similar to Elena or Tomás in the drawings?

MODELO

E1: Creo que Roberto vio la televisión anoche.
PROFESOR(A): Roberto, ¿es verdad?
ROBERTO: No, no es verdad.

GRAMÁTICA

¿Salió o se quedó en casa?

Talking about what someone else did recently

—¿**Salió** Alicia anoche?
—No, pero sí **estudió** hasta muy tarde.

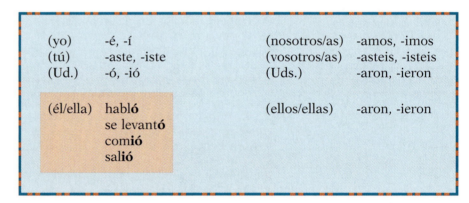

(yo)	-é, -í	(nosotros/as)	-amos, -imos
(tú)	-aste, -iste	(vosotros/as)	-asteis, -isteis
(Ud.)	-ó, -ió	(Uds.)	-aron, -ieron
(él/ella)	habl**ó**	(ellos/ellas)	-aron, -ieron
	se levant**ó**		
	com**ió**		
	sal**ió**		

Spanish has a past tense called the *preterite* (**el pretérito**), which has different forms from those of the present tense.

The preterite has several equivalents in English. For example, **se acostó** can either mean *he went to bed* or *he did go to bed*. Normally the preterite is used to report actions, events, and states that are viewed as having been completed in the past. You will learn other meanings of the preterite in subsequent lessons. For now, you only need to know how to talk about what another person did last night, last weekend, or last week, that is, to express actions completed at some point in the past.

As you have seen, most third person preterite verbs end in a stressed or accented vowel, with **-ar** verbs ending in **-ó,** and **-er** and **-ir** verbs ending in **-ió.** (That's right, **-er** and **-ir** verbs share the same endings, making it easier for you to remember them!)

El estudiante **se levantó** tarde, **comió** en la cafetería y **salió.**

When talking about Tomás' activities, did you happen to notice that the verb **leyó** has a **y** in it? This is a spelling convention used to keep from having three consecutive vowels (**le-** + **-ió** = **leyó**).

Another aspect of the preterite is that no stem vowel changes are carried over from the present tense for **-ar** and **-er** verbs. However, **-ir** verbs with stem changes do have a vowel shift in the third person preterite forms. Two examples are **durmió** (**u** instead of **o** in the stem), and **pidió** (**i** instead of **e** in the stem).

Así se dice

In this **Gramática** section, you learned about third person singular **-ir** preterite verbs that have a stem vowel change. Here are several verbs that experience this change.

durmió (dormir)
pidió (pedir)
sirvió (servir = *to serve*)
corrigió (corregir = *to correct*)
se vistió (vestirse)

You have already learned two irregular preterite forms, **hizo** (**hacer**) and **fue** (**ir**). Note that **ser** has the same forms as **ir** in the preterite; context will help you understand the meaning (**Ana fue al cine** vs. **José fue estudiante**). Although regular third person preterite forms have a stressed vowel at the end, most irregular verbs do not. You will learn other irregular preterite forms later.

Here is a list of verbs you will find useful. They are organized by infinitive endings, **-ar, -er,** and **-ir.**

	-ó (-ar)	-ió (-er)	-ió (-ir)
él/ella	almorzó	comió	asistió
	charló	leyó	salió
	escuchó	vio	
	estudió	volvió	
	manejó		
	sacó		
	se despertó		
	se quedó		

If you're wondering why **vio** doesn't have a written accent, it's because it's a one syllable word and doesn't need one.

ACTIVIDAD D ¿Cómo fue la noche del profesor (de la profesora)?

Paso 1 In groups of three, guess what your instructor did last night. Here are some possibilities. Your instructor may add to the list! (Make sure to pay close attention to the verb forms.)

☐ Corrigió (*He/She corrected*) unas composiciones.

☐ Preparó un examen.

☐ Salió con unos amigos (unas amigas).

☐ Charló con los vecinos.

☐ Preparó la cena.

☐ Leyó un libro interesante.

☐ Leyó un periódico o una revista de noticias internacionales.

☐ Practicó un deporte.

☐ Habló con un(a) colega (*colleague*) por teléfono.

☐ Pagó unas cuentas (*bills*).

Paso 2 A person from one group stands up and presents that group's list of possibilities to the class. Does everyone agree with that list?

Paso 3 Once you have identified the correct activities, put them in the order in which your instructor most likely did them.

ACTIVIDAD E ¡Pobre° Juanito!

Poor

Read about what happened to Juanito last night.

Paso 1 Form groups of three and read **"Una historia verdadera"** quickly. Your instructor will set a time limit for the reading (three minutes maximum).

Una historia verdadera (*true*)

Pobre Juanito. Anoche se quedó en casa sin tener mucho que hacer. Preparó su cena (un sándwich y una ensalada), comió y después estudió unas cuantas[a] horas. A las 10.00 fue al café Casablanca, pero no encontró a ninguno de sus amigos. Después de quince minutos, volvió a casa. Miró las noticias en el canal 4 (cree que los reporteros de ese canal son muy buenos) y luego se acostó.

Pero Juanito no se durmió inmediatamente. Se levantó, buscó entre sus libros una novela de Stephen King y comenzó a leer. Gracias al insomnio y a una novela muy interesante, se pasó toda la noche leyendo. Leyó hasta la última página del libro.

Cuando miró el despertador, exclamó: «¡Ay no! ¡Es hora de ir a la clase de química!». Se tomó tres tazas de café (para no dormirse en clase) y corrió al edificio de Ciencias Naturales. Cuando llegó, notó algo raro: «¿Dónde están los otros estudiantes? ¿Por qué no hay nadie aquí?» Entonces recordó la fecha[b] y pensó: «¡Rayos! Hoy es día de fiesta. ¡No hay clases!»

[a]unas... *a few*   [b]*date*

Paso 2 After reading the story, close your book and list as many actions and details as you can recall. The group with the longest list wins!

Así se dice

Most irregular preterite verbs do not have a stressed vowel ending. Here is a list of some common irregular third person preterite verbs.

anduvo (andar = *to walk*)	estuvo (estar)	supo (saber = *to know*)
condujo (conducir)	fue (ir, ser)	tuvo (tener)
dio (dar = *to give*)	hizo (hacer)	vino (venir)
dijo (decir = *to say, tell*)	pudo (poder)	

¡OJO! The preterite of **saber** means *found out* and not *knew*. The preterite of **poder** means *managed* or *was finally able to.*

Supo eso anoche.   *She found that out last night.*
Por fin **pudo** dormir bien.   *He finally managed to sleep well.*

ACTIVIDAD F De joven...

Paso 1 Imagine what the life of one of your parents was like as a teenager. What about the life of another relative? Read the statements on the following page and indicate whether each individual likely did these things at least once in his or her life.

	PADRE/MADRE		OTRO PARIENTE	
	SÍ	**NO**	**SÍ**	**NO**
1. Condujo sin licencia.	☐	☐	☐	☐
2. Hizo algo ilegal.	☐	☐	☐	☐
3. Anduvo desnudo/a (*nude*) en público.	☐	☐	☐	☐
4. Sacó F en un examen.	☐	☐	☐	☐
5. Protestó contra (*against*) algo en público.	☐	☐	☐	☐
6. Escribió un poema romántico.	☐	☐	☐	☐
7. Dio una fiesta durante la ausencia de sus padres.	☐	☐	☐	☐
8. Le* dijo algo ofensivo a un profesor (una profesora).	☐	☐	☐	☐

Paso 2 Share one or two statements with the class regarding a parent or another relative. Whose parent (relative) did the most audacious thing?

COMUNICACIÓN

ACTIVIDAD G Personas históricas

Paso 1 Match each person in column A with the reason they are remembered today in column B. Then write a sentence for each.

MODELO   Cristóbal Colón hizo viajes por el Atlántico.

A

1. _e_ Cristóbal Colón
2. ____ César Chávez
3. ____ Neil Armstrong
4. ____ George Washington
5. ____ Desi Arnaz
6. ____ Martin Luther King, hijo (*Jr.*)

B

a. andar en la luna
b. decir: «Yo tengo un sueño (*dream*)».
c. defender los derechos (*rights*) de los obreros del campo (*farmworkers*)
d. crear (*to create*) programas de televisión
e. hacer viajes por el Atlántico
f. ser general y presidente

Paso 2 In your opinion, which historical person is the most important? Compare your opinion with that of a classmate and be ready to report to the class.

MODELOS   En mi opinión, Cristóbal Colón es la persona más importante.

En la opinión de Neal, Martin Luther King, hijo es la persona más importante.

---

*Le is an indirect object pronoun meaning roughly *to him* (*her, you* [Ud.], *it*) that you will learn about in **Unidad tres.**

ACTIVIDAD H ¿Qué hizo ayer?

In groups of four, agree on a famous person. (You may choose someone from the following list or think of someone else.) Using the table provided, create a list of at least eight activities that this person probably did yesterday. Do not mention the person's name in your description. Can the class guess who you are describing?

el presidente de los Estados Unidos

el gobernador (la gobernadora) de tu estado

Enrique Iglesias

Penélope Cruz

tu profesor(a) de español

¿otra persona? _____

	AYER
por la mañana	
por la tarde	
por la noche	

NAVEGANDO LA RED

Find information in Spanish on movies, theater, or some other event that you would like to attend. Be prepared to share what you found with the class.

GRAMÁTICA

¿Salí o me quedé en casa?

Talking about what you did recently

(yo)	hablé		(nosotros/as)	-amos, -imos
	me quedé			
	comí			
	salí			
(tú)	-aste, -iste		(vosotros/as)	-asteis, -isteis
(Ud.)	-ó, -ió		(Uds.)	-aron, -ieron
(él/ella)	-ó, -ió		(ellos/ellas)	-aron, -ieron

—Mire Ud., profesor, no **escribí** mi composición por muy buenas razones. Ayer **trabajé** cuatro horas en el Café San Francisco. Y anoche **toqué** la guitarra en un club, pues me gustaría ser músico, ¿sabe? Cuando **llegué** a casa, mi mamá llamó con unas noticias muy importantes y...

To talk about things you did in the past, use the first person singular (**yo**) preterite verb forms. The verb endings are **-é** for **-ar** verbs (**hablar → hablé**), and **-í** for **-er** and **-ir** verbs (**comer → comí** and **salir → salí**).

> Anoche no **hice** nada especial. **Me quedé** en casa sin tener nada que hacer. **Miré** la televisión un rato y **leí** el periódico. **Me acosté** temprano y **dormí** unas siete horas.

As you probably noticed, **hice** is the preterite **yo** form of **hacer.** To talk about where you went, use **fui,** a form of **ir.** Note that **ser** has the same forms as **ir** in the preterite, so **fui** can mean *I went* or *I was.* Context will determine the meaning.

> Anoche **fui** a un concierto de música andina.
> En el pasado (*past*) **fui** estudiante de francés.

Note that irregular verb forms like **hice** and **fui** have no written accent. You will become familiar with other irregular preterite verbs in this lesson.

You will notice that some verb stems undergo spelling changes in the **yo** form. Among these are **saqué, jugué,** and **llegué.** You will soon learn the reasons for these spelling changes.

You will be delighted to know that there are no stem vowel changes of any sort with preterite **yo** forms!

Here is a list of a few useful regular verbs.

	-é (-ar)	-í (-er)	-í (-ir)
yo	hablé	comí	asistí
	llamé	leí	dormí
	trabajé	corrí	salí
	estudié	volví	
	me desperté	vi	
	me quedé		

Vi, because it is a one syllable verb, does not have a written accent.

ACTIVIDAD I ¿Qué hiciste ayer?

Indicate whether you did the following activities yesterday.

		SÍ	NO
1.	Fui a una fiesta.	☐	☐
2.	Me acosté a las 10.00.	☐	☐
3.	Participé en una sala de charla.	☐	☐
4.	Almorcé en una cafetería.	☐	☐
5.	Vi un programa de noticias.	☐	☐
6.	Limpié mi cuarto (apartamento).	☐	☐

Now, compare your responses with those of a classmate. How many of the same activities did you both do?

ACTIVIDAD J Yo también...

Here is a list of things done yesterday by a student who attends the same university as Elena. For each of his statements, write whether or not you did the same thing.

MODELO Asistí a una clase de lenguas extranjeras. →
Yo también asistí a una clase de lenguas extranjeras. Asistí a la clase de español.

1. Estudié un poco en la biblioteca.

2. Durante el día, comí en un restaurante de comida rápida.

3. Asistí a cuatro clases.

4. Fui a una conferencia pública en la universidad.

5. Llamé a un amigo y hablé con él por quince minutos.

6. Jugué a los videojuegos y gasté mucho dinero.

7. Hice ejercicio.

8. Saqué un vídeo y lo vi (*I watched it*).

9. Me acosté a las 12.00.

10. Vi un programa de noticias en la televisión.

Así se dice

Here are the **yo** forms for some common verbs that are irregular in the preterite.

anduve (andar)
conduje (conducir)
di (dar)
dije (decir)
estuve (estar)
fui (ir, ser)
hice (hacer)
pude (poder)
supe (saber)
tuve (tener)
vine (venir)

ACTIVIDAD K ¿Sabías que... ?

Paso 1 Read the **¿Sabías que... ?** selection. Then go back and circle all the preterite **yo** forms that you can find. Do you know what each one means?

¿Sabías que...

muchos escritores usan la primera persona al narrar una historia en vez de usar la tercera[a] persona? El uso de la primera persona ayuda[b] al escritor a «entrar» más en la personalidad de los personajes y a darle otra perspectiva del mundo.[c] En *El túnel*, una novela muy conocida,[d] el escritor argentino Ernesto Sábato usa esta técnica, como se puede ver en el ejemplo a continuación.

> Todos saben que maté[e] a María Iribarne Hunter. Pero nadie sabe cómo la conocí, qué relaciones hubo[f] exactamente entre nosotros y cómo fui haciéndome a[g] la idea de matarla. Trataré[h] de relatar todo imparcialmente porque, aunque sufrí mucho por su culpa,[i] no tengo la necia[j] pretensión de ser perfecto...

¿Te llamó la atención? ¿Crees que te gustaría leer esta novela?

---

[a]*third* [b]*helps* [c]*world* [d]*muy... very well-known* [e]*I killed* [f]*pasado de* **hay**
[g]*fui... I went about formulating* [h]*I'll try* [i]*fault* [j]*foolish*

Paso 2 How would you begin a novel in the first person? Create a sentence based on this excerpt from *El túnel*. Then, as a class, vote on which sentence is most likely to grab a reader's attention.

MODELO Todos saben que...

ACTIVIDAD L Una vez...

With a partner, describe three or four activities from the following list that you have (supposedly) done in the past. Make sure at least one of the activities you describe is *not* true! It will be up to your partner to decide if each activity is true or not. The last one is for you to invent.

MODELO Una vez yo...

1. conocer (*to meet*) a una persona famosa.
2. hacer un viaje (*to take a trip*) a un país de habla española.
3. escribir un poema de amor.
4. recibir un poema de amor.
5. mentirle* (*to lie*) a un profesor (una profesora).
6. ¿ ?

***Le** is an indirect object pronoun that means *to, for,* or *from him* (*her*). In Spanish it is usually obligatory with **entregar** (*to turn in, hand over*), **dar,** and certain other verbs. **Le mentí** = *I lied to him* (*her*).

VAMOS A VER

Paso 1 The reading on page 94 is adapted from a magazine for general readership. Look at the title and the photo without reading anything else. Can you guess the meaning of the word **superestrella?** Select from these two options: (a) *superhit;* (b) *superstar.* Read the first paragraph of the reading to see if you're right.

Paso 2 By now you know the article is about Desi Arnaz. What do you know about him already? Thinking about this will help you better guess words in context as well as comprehend more of what you read. Look at the following statements and select the correct answer for each. Share with the class.

1. Desi Arnaz nació en _____.

    a. Puerto Rico   **b.** Cuba   **c.** México

2. Se mudó (*He moved*) a los Estados Unidos por razones _____.

    a. políticas   **b.** económicas   **c.** personales

3. Comenzó su carrera profesional con _____.

    a. la música   **b.** el teatro   **c.** la televisión

Paso 3 Now read the subheadings contained in the reading. In which of the two sections do you expect to find the answers to the statements in **Paso 2?**

Paso 4 An important strategy to develop while learning to read is to guess words in context and to skip over other words if you can grasp their meaning. Reread the first paragraph and see if you can give a rough English equivalent of the following words and phrases.

1. ascendencia latina

2. gran fama

Paso 1 It is always good to read something in sections and to think about what you have read before continuing. For the article on Desi Arnaz, read the section **De Cuba a Hollywood.** Once you have done so, go back to **Paso 2** of **Anticipación** and verify your answers.

Paso 2 Before continuing, determine whether the following statements are true or false based on what you just read.

	C	F
1. La familia de Desi abandonó todo en Cuba cuando se mudó a los Estados Unidos.	☐	☐
2. El modelo para la carrera de Desi fue Xaviera Cugat.	☐	☐
3. Desi hizo muy popular la música salsa en los Estados Unidos.	☐	☐

Paso 3 Now read the section **De las películas a la televisión.** Then complete the following sentences with a word or phrase based on what you have read.

1. Desi se casó con _____.
2. La compañía que fundaron Desi y su esposa se llamaba _____.
3. Desi era el genio _____ de *I Love Lucy* y varios otros programas.
4. En 1986 Desi _____ de cáncer.
5. Desi _____ la puerta para la presencia latina en la televisión y en la música popular en los Estados Unidos.

SÍNTESIS

Paso 1 One way to remember information from a reading is to select key concepts and then write a short note about each. Here are some key concepts from the reading. Jot down something that will help you remember what you have read about Desi Arnaz.

1. su nacimiento _____
2. su muerte _____
3. el comienzo de su carrera _____
4. eventos importantes en su vida _____

Paso 2 Another excellent way to remember something you have read is to compare it to something else you already know. In this case, you might compare Desi Arnaz to another famous Latino celebrity or to any other famous person, comparing them on the major concepts from **Paso 1.**

TRABAJANDO CON EL TEXTO

Paso 1 Readings are a rich source of both vocabulary and grammar. When you are actively comprehending written text, you are actually picking up new words and phrases. This process will be aided if you think a little more deeply about the new words you encounter. The following words appear in the reading. First, see if you were able to guess their meaning as you read. You will probably need to reread the sentences in which they occur. After doing this, create a multiple-choice test to give to a classmate to see if he or she understood the words. For example, if the word is **propiedad** you might write a test item as shown in the model.

MODELO propiedad: **a.** appropriate **b.** propriety **c.** property

1. canarios   3. genio
2. éxitos   4. duró

Desi Arnaz
La primera superestrella latina

*Desi Arnaz con
Lucille Ball*

¿En quién piensas cuando oyes la frase «superestrella latina»? ¿Piensas en Jennifer López? ¿en Ricky Martin? ¿en Selma Hayek? ¿en Gloria Estefan? Aunque es cierto que estas personas y muchas otras de ascendencia latina tienen gran fama hoy en día, el primer latino de gran fama en la música, el cine y la televisión de los Estados Unidos fue Desi Arnaz de la serie *I Love Lucy.*

De Cuba a Hollywood

Arnaz nació con el nombre de Desiderio Alberto Arnaz de Acha III, en Santiago, Cuba, en 1917. Debido a la revolución de Batista en 1933, la familia Arnaz huyó de Cuba para instalarse en Miami. Puesto que tuvieron que abandonar sus propiedades y dinero, los Arnaz llegaron a Miami con muy poco. Aceptaron trabajos mínimos y uno de los primeros trabajos de Desi fue limpiar jaulas de canarios. Pero la música siempre fue su pasión y decidió lanzarse a la carrera de músico y cantante, siguiendo las huellas de Xavier Cugat, «el rey de música latina». Formó su propio grupo musical y con éxitos como «Babalú» hizo muy popular la conga entre el público norteamericano. Su carrera lo llevó a Broadway y después a Hollywood.

De las películas a la televisión

En 1940 conoció a Lucille Ball durante la filmación de *Too Many Girls.* Se casó con ella y en diez años los dos fundaron la compañía «Desilu». La serie *I Love Lucy* se estrenó en 1951 y aunque Lucy era la estrella, el genio creativo de esa y muchas otras producciones televisivas era Desi. Gracias al personaje de Ricky Ricardo, la presencia latina en la televisión y la cultura norteamericana en general se estableció. Pero el matrimonio entre Desi y Lucille no duró y se divorciaron en 1960, después de tener dos hijos. En 1976, Arnaz publicó su autobiografía, *A Book,* y diez años más tarde murió de cáncer. Muchos críticos contemporáneos dicen que las superestrellas latinas de hoy le deben mucho a Desi, quien abrió la puerta para los latinos que llegaron después.

Paso 2 Now reread the article and underline each verb in the past tense. When you have finished, stop and review just the verbs. Say each aloud to yourself and then say it within the phrase so that it has some context. For example, **tuvieron: tuvieron que abandonar.** Write down the phrase. When you have finished, close your book and with a classmate, see how much of the information from the reading you can recall just by thinking about these phrases. For example, you might recall **tuvieron que abandonar sus propiedades** and your classmate might add **y dinero** if you forgot this detail. In the end, you will have done two things: remembered even more of what you have read, and worked with the past tense in context!

Consejo práctico

You may remember that cognates are words that look or sound similar to words in another language. Some words are close cognates and look or sound almost exactly alike, such as *independence* and **independencia,** for example. Others are more distant from each other, such as *to desire* and **desear.** See whether you can guess the English equivalents of the following cognates.

corrección	lámpara	resolver
cromosoma	ordenar	tomate
dinosaurio	prestigioso	volumen

At first, you may have to work hard to recognize the more distant cognates. But as you progress, you will begin to read cognates in Spanish and know what they mean without even thinking about it!

Vamos a ver

Now that you've completed the **Vamos a ver** section of **Unidad uno,** watch the corresponding **Vamos a ver** segment on the *¿Sabías que... ?* video to further explore the themes presented in this unit. There are related pre- and post-viewing activities on the *¿Sabías que... ?* Online Learning Center at **www.mhhe.com/sabiasque5.**

NAVEGANDO LA RED

Look for a website about any Spanish-language actor or musical artist. Print out a page and take it to class. Be prepared to present the same type of information about this artist that you read about Desi Arnaz in this lesson.

IDEAS PARA EXPLORAR
Ayer y anoche (II)

GRAMÁTICA

¿Qué hiciste anoche?

Talking to a friend about what he or she did recently

—Sí, sí. Y la última vez que no **hiciste** la tarea fue porque **trabajaste** cinco horas la noche anterior...

(yo)	-é, -í	(nosotros/as)	-amos, -imos
(tú)	trabaj**aste** te qued**aste** com**iste** sal**iste**	(vosotros/as)	-asteis, -isteis
(Ud.) (él/ella)	-ó, -ió -ó, -ió	(Uds.) (ellos/ellas)	-aron, -ieron -aron, -ieron

To ask a classmate what he or she did in the past, use the **tú** form of the preterite. **Tú** forms end in **-aste** for **-ar** verbs and **-iste** for **-er** and **-ir** verbs. **Fuiste** and **hiciste** are useful irregular **tú** forms for you to know.

¿Qué **hiciste** anoche? ¿Te **quedaste** en casa o **saliste**? ¿**Fuiste** a alguna fiesta?

ACTIVIDAD A ¿Y qué más?

Imagine that someone makes the following statements to you. What follow-up question would you logically ask after each statement?

1. ____ Fui al cine anoche.
2. ____ Tuve un examen esta mañana.
3. ____ Hice ejercicio esta mañana.
4. ____ Anoche comí en un restaurante elegante.
5. ____ Anoche llamé a mis padres por teléfono.
6. ____ La semana pasada no asistí a clases.
7. ____ Fui a una fiesta anoche.
8. ____ Anoche decidí salir para escapar de la monotonía.

a. ¿Estuvo buena la comida?
b. ¿Hablaste mucho tiempo con ellos?
c. ¿Por qué? ¿Estuviste enfermo/a?
d. ¿Qué viste?
e. ¿Estudiaste mucho anoche?
f. ¿Corriste o nadaste?
g. ¿Te quedaste hasta muy tarde?
h. ¿Adónde fuiste?

> **Así se dice**
>
> Remember that when talking to someone with whom you have some social distance, you use **Ud.** The Ud. form in all tenses is the same as the **él/ella** verb form.
>
> ¿A qué hora **salió Ud.** de casa?
>
> ¿**Fue** en carro o **caminó** al trabajo?

ACTIVIDAD B El verano pasado

Paso 1 Can you guess how your classmates spent last summer? Choose someone in your class and prepare three guesses to present to him or her about what that person did last summer.

> MODELO Trabajaste en un restaurante.

Paso 2 You and your classmate should present each other's guesses. How many did each of you get right?

Paso 3 Did you and your partner have any summer activities in common? If so, write down the activities that you both did and be ready to report your similarities to the class.

> MODELO Jennifer trabajó en un restaurante, y yo también trabajé en un restaurante.

COMUNICACIÓN

ACTIVIDAD C Tú y yo

Paso 1 Write four sentences about things you did yesterday.

1... **2**... **3**... **4**...

Paso 2 Find different people in the class who did the things you listed in **Paso 1**.

ACTIVIDAD	OTRA PERSONA QUE TAMBIÉN HIZO LA ACTIVIDAD
1. _____	_____
2. _____	_____
3. _____	_____
4. _____	_____

GRAMÁTICA

¿Salieron ellos anoche?

Talking about what two or more people did recently

—¿**Salieron** ellos anoche?
—¡Sí! Y no **regresaron** a casa hasta las 3.00 de la mañana.

(yo)	-é, -í	(nosotros/as)	-amos, -imos
(tú)	-aste, -iste	(vosotros/as)	-asteis, -isteis
(Ud.)	-ó, -ió	(Uds.)	-aron, -ieron
(él/ella)	-ó, -ió	(ellos/ellas)	trabaj**aron**
			com**ieron**
			sal**ieron**
			se vist**ieron**

When you describe what two or more people did in the past, you use the *third person plural* or **ellos/ellas** form of the preterite. All regular preterites end in **-aron** for **-ar** verbs, and **-ieron** for **-er** and **-ir** verbs.

—¿**Salieron** Rodrigo y Sonia anoche?
—No, **se quedaron** en casa y **estudiaron.**

The same stem vowel and spelling changes that occur in the third person singular also occur in the third person plural of the preterite.

Anoche los estudiantes **leyeron** mucho y **durmieron** poco.

Most irregular preterites end in **-ieron,** but there are some exceptions. Two of these are **ir** and **decir.**

Ayer mis compañeros hicieron todos los ejercicios y después **fueron** al cine.
¿**Dijeron** la verdad (*truth*) los estudiantes que estuvieron ausentes?

Así se dice

Remember that stem changes in the preterite that occur in third person singular (**él/ella**) forms also occur in third person plural (**ellos/ellas**) forms. This is also true of irregular preterite verbs. Here are third person plural preterite forms of some common stem changing and irregular verbs.

anduvieron	estuvieron	pudieron
dieron	fueron	supieron
dijeron	hicieron	tuvieron
durmieron	pidieron	vinieron

ACTIVIDAD D ¿Qué hicieron ayer?

Read the following statements and indicate which group(s) probably did each activity yesterday.

	ESTUDIANTES	PROFESORES	SECRETARIOS
1. Se acostaron tarde.	☐	☐	☐
2. Miraron una telenovela (*soap opera*).	☐	☐	☐
3. Durmieron mucho.	☐	☐	☐
4. Fueron a la biblioteca.	☐	☐	☐
5. Navegaron la Red.	☐	☐	☐

COMUNICACIÓN

📝 ACTIVIDAD E ¿Qué hicieron anoche?

Paso 1 Get into groups of four. Take out one sheet of paper to be shared in the group. Everyone in the group will take turns writing a sentence describing an activity some friends did last night. Each person will have 30 seconds to write a sentence. After writing a sentence, each person will fold the page so that others cannot read what has been written. After writing a sentence, that person will pass the folded paper to the person on his or her left (in a clockwise direction).

MODELO Anoche mis amigos…

Paso 2 When your instructor indicates, one member of your group should open the sheet of paper and read the sentences. As a group, put the sentences in logical order, and delete or modify sentences that do not make sense. Be ready to read your list to the class.

Paso 3 Listen to the lists written by the other groups. Be prepared to vote for:

la lista más completa
la lista más cómica

GRAMÁTICA

¿Qué hicimos nosotros?

Talking about what you and someone else did recently

(yo)	-é, -í		(nosotros/as)	almorz**amos** volv**imos** asist**imos** nos vest**imos**
(tú)	-aste, -iste		(vosotros/as)	-asteis, -isteis
(Ud.)	-ó, -ió		(Uds.)	-aron, -ieron
(él/ella)	-ó, -ió		(ellos/ellas)	-aron, -ieron

—¿Recuerdas cuando **fuimos** a España? Ay, ¡qué recuerdos (*memories*)! **Comimos** bien, **conocimos** a tantas personas interesantes, ¡y los lugares que **vimos**! ¡Quiero volver!

When you talk about what you and another person did, you use the *first person plural* or **nosotros/as** form of the preterite. All regular **-ar** preterites end in **-amos** (just like the present tense). All regular **-er** and **-ir nosotros/as** forms end in **-imos.** There are no stem vowel or other changes for these verb forms!

Ayer Pepe y yo **almorzamos** en la cafetería.
Mi compañera de cuarto y yo no **salimos** anoche.

Irregular preterite verbs end in **-imos.**

Fuimos al cine el sábado pasado.
Tuvimos un examen en la clase de química la semana pasada.

ACTIVIDAD F Todos nosotros...

Paso 1 Indicate which of the activities on the following page you think every student in the class did yesterday and/or last night.

COMUNICACIÓN

Todos nosotros...

☐ estudiamos.

☐ fuimos a un bar.

☐ miramos una telenovela.

☐ gastamos dinero en ropa.

☐ tuvimos un examen.

☐ comimos en un restaurante de comida rápida.

☐ fuimos a la biblioteca.

☐ hablamos por teléfono.

☐ nos acostamos antes de las 12.00.

☐ hicimos ejercicio.

☐ leímos el periódico.

☐ asistimos a dos clases (por lo menos).

Paso 2 One of you should volunteer to read aloud the list of items you checked. After each statement, those who did the activities should raise their hands. Was the volunteer correct?

Paso 3 Repeat **Pasos 1** and **2,** this time including your instructor as one of the group!

ACTIVIDAD G ¿Qué actividades hicimos?

Paso 1 Interview a classmate and find out what you each did during the week. Here is a list of sample activities. Feel free to come up with others!

asistir a una conferencia pública   ir a un restaurante
bailar en una fiesta   navegar la Red
correr cinco millas   practicar un deporte
hacer de voluntario/a   ver una telenovela

MODELO   La semana pasada, ¿bailaste en una fiesta? ¿corriste cinco millas?

Paso 2 Now with your partner find two other people who did at least two of the same activities that you two did.

MODELO   **E1:** Nosotros estudiamos para un examen, practicamos un deporte, vimos una telenovela y fuimos a un restaurante.

E2: Nosotros también estudiamos para un examen y practicamos un deporte, pero no vimos una telenovela ni fuimos a un restaurante.

ACTIVIDAD H Esta mañana

Paso 1 There are some essential activities that nearly all of us do every morning before we go out in public. See if you can identify four things that everyone in the class probably did this morning in *addition* to those shown in the model.

MODELO   Todos nos despertamos y nos levantamos.

Paso 2 In groups of four, take turns reading your statements aloud to see how many of them everyone in the group did. How many did you get right? Be ready to read your list to the whole class.

INTERCAMBIO

¿Es típico esto?

Propósito: to write a paragraph on what a classmate did and decide whether it's typical

Papeles: two students, interviewer and person interviewed

Paso 1 Look over the following paragraph. Imagine that you are going to fill it in with information about one of your classmates.

Ayer mi compañero/a de clase _____, _____ y _____. También _____, _____ y _____. Pero no _____ ni _____ ayer. Anoche él (ella) _____ y después _____. ¿Es típico esto? ¡Creo que sí (no)!

Paso 2 Now interview a person you do not know well. Before starting the interview, think of questions that will provide the information you will need to fill in and expand on the model paragraph in **Paso 1.** As you formulate your questions, remember to find out when your partner did the activity, whether he or she did it alone, and other similar details.

Paso 3 Use the paragraph in **Paso 1** as a guide to write up the information you have gathered. Make any adjustments to the format of the paragraph that you feel are necessary.

Paso 4 Before turning in your paragraph, let your partner read it. Does he or she agree with your final sentence (that is, **¿Es típico esto? ¡Creo que sí [no]!**)?

Vistazos culturales

El folclor en el mundo hispano

¿Sabías que...

el mundo hispano tiene una tradición folclórica muy rica? El folclor en el mundo hispano se manifiesta en sus mitos y leyendas,[a] en el arte, en las artesanías,[b] en las canciones[c] y en muchas otras expresiones artísticas. En España, se puede notar la influencia árabe, gitana, romana y de otras culturas. En Latinoamérica, el folclor refleja más que nada[d] el mestizaje, pero también se ve la influencia de otras culturas europeas y africanas que llegaron después de los españoles. En la Guinea Ecuatorial, la influencia africana en el folclor es más fuerte[e] que en cualquier otro país del mundo hispano. ¿Por qué? ¡Porque es un país africano!

[a]mitos... *myths and legends* [b]*handicrafts* [c]*songs* [d]más... *more than anything* [e]más... *stronger*

leyendas y mitos del mundo hispano

La Llorona[a]

La Llorona es una leyenda mexicana que cuenta la historia de una mujer bella y vanidosa[b] llamada María. María se casa con un ranchero, tienen varios hijos y todos están contentos. Pero un día el ranchero empieza a prestarles más atención[c] a los hijos que a María. María se enfada[d] y echa[e] a sus hijos en el río.[f] Cuando María se da cuenta de su horrible acto ya es tarde[g] y sus hijos se ahogan.[h] Al día siguiente la gente del pueblo encuentra a María muerta, cerca del río. Desde ese día en adelante[i] la gente dice que el espíritu de María va por el río de noche, llorando[j] en voz alta. Es por eso que la llaman «La Llorona».

La Llorona (*1987*)
por Diana Bryer
(*norteamericana, 1942–*)

[a]La... *The Weeping Woman* [b]*vain* [c]prestarles... *pay more attention* [d]se... *becomes angry* [e]*she throws* [f]*river* [g]ya... *it's already too late* [h]se... *drown* [i]Desde... *From that day on* [j]*crying*

El Popol Vuh

El *Popol Vuh* es el libro sagrado[a] de los mayas quichés. Parte de este libro cuenta la historia de la creación del mundo. Según este mito, los dioses intentaron[b] crear al hombre de varios materiales incluyendo el lodo[c] y la madera[d] pero nunca quedaron satisfechos[e] con su creación. Al final, hicieron al hombre de maíz[f] y quedaron satisfechos.

[a]*sacred* [b]dioses... *gods tried* [c]*mud* [d]*wood* [e]nunca... *they were never satisfied* [f]*corn*

You can investigate these cultural topics in more detail on the *¿Sabías que... ?* Online Learning Center: **www.mhhe.com/sabiasque5**.

La religión

La **santería** es una religión afrocaribeña parecida al vudú y tiene sus raíces en la cultura yoruba del oeste[a] de África. Aunque la santería es una religión principalmente africana, tiene una gran influencia católica. La santería se practica en Brasil, Cuba, Haití, Trinidad, Puerto Rico y en partes de los Estados Unidos donde viven inmigrantes de estos países.

[a]*western part*

Arte huichol

En México el arte folclórico indígena se vale de[a] varios materiales diferentes. Los tepehuanes usan hilaza[b] de varios colores para crear cuadros decorativos. Los temas representados incluyen animales y objetos celestiales. Los artesanos huicholes, también de México, se especializan en un arte que utiliza abalorios[c] de colores brillantes.

[a]*se... makes use of*   [b]*yarn*   [c]*beads*

Alfarería de San Juan de Oriente

El pueblo de San Juan de Oriente en Nicaragua se conoce por su alfarería,[a] un arte que se ha practicado[b] aquí desde la época colonial.[c] Las piezas representan tanto temas precolombinos como temas modernos con diseños geométricos.

La artesanía

[a]*pottery*   [b]*se... has been practiced*   [c]*desde... since colonial times*

ACTIVIDAD ¿Qué recuerdas?

Select the answer that best fits each of the following sentences.

1. Según la leyenda de La Llorona, María mata (*kills*) a sus hijos porque está _____.

   a. nerviosa **b.** triste **c.** celosa (*jealous*)

2. Según la historia maya de la creación, el hombre ideal se creó de _____.

   a. madera **b.** lodo **c.** maíz

3. La religión de origen yoruba que se practica en Cuba y otros países es _____.

   a. la santería **b.** el catolicismo **c.** el vudú

4. Un país hispano que tiene fama internacional por su larga tradición en el arte de la alfarería es _____.

   a. Panamá **b.** Nicaragua **c.** Cuba

5. Los huicholes de México hacen un tipo de artesanía de _____.

   a. hilaza **b.** tela **c.** abalorios

NAVEGANDO LA RED

Complete *one* of the following activities. Then present your information to the class.

1. Look for information about the legends and myths of the Quiché Mayans. Choose one legend or myth and write a brief summary of the story, including its central themes and the moral (**moraleja**) if it has one.

2. Look for information about a folkloric musical genre (**género**) in the Spanish-speaking world. Jot down the following information.

   a. el país o la región donde se toca esta música

   b. las características generales de la música

   c. los temas principales de la letra que acompaña la música y el título de una canción popular de este género

VOCABULARIO COMPRENSIVO

Ayer y anoche — Yesterday and Last Night

andar (*irreg.*)	to walk
buscar	to look for
dar (*irreg.*)	to give
decir (*irreg.*)	to say; to tell
dormirse (**ue, u**)	to fall asleep
empezar (**ie**)	to begin
estar (*irreg.*)	to be
jugar (**ue**) **a los videojuegos**	to play video games
llamar (**por teléfono**)	to call (on the phone)
llegar	to arrive
pagar (**la cuenta**)	to pay (the bill)
practicar un deporte (R)	to practice, play a sport
preparar (**la cena**)	to prepare (dinner)
recibir (R)	to receive
recordar (**ue**)	to remember
saber (*irreg.*)	to know (*facts, information*)
tener un examen	to have (take) a test
ver (*irreg.*) **una telenovela**	to watch a soap opera

¿Cuándo? — When?

anoche	last night
ayer	yesterday
el fin de semana pasado	last weekend
un rato	little while, short time
la semana pasada	last week
la última vez	last time
una vez	once
hace + *time*	_____ ago

The Verb ser

(yo)	soy	(nosotros/as)	somos
(tú)	eres	(vosotros/as)	sois
(Ud.)	es	(Uds.)	son
(él/ella)	es	(ellos/ellas)	son

The verb **ser** is used to:

1. express origin with **de: ¿De dónde eres?**

2. describe a person's qualities: **Tomás es muy inteligente, ¿no?**

3. state who or what a person is: **Es profesor. Soy estudiante.**

4. tell time: **Es la 1.00. / Son las 2.00.**

Remember that subject pronouns are not always required in Spanish. It is fine to say **soy estudiante.** If you say **yo soy estudiante,** you are adding emphasis or making a contrast.

The Verb estar

One of the uses of **estar** is to describe variable conditions.

Tomás **está** muy contento con su trabajo.

Estoy aburrida de mi clase de inglés.

The Verb gustar

me			nos	
te		gusta(n)	os	gusta(n)
le			les	
le			les	

1. **Gustar** does not mean *to like*. It is closest in meaning to the verb *to please*. Thus **me gusta** actually means (*something*) *pleases me.*

2. Since **gustar** means *to please,* the verb must agree in number with the thing doing the pleasing: **Me gusta esta clase. Me gustan todas las clases.**

3. A phrase with **a** can be used with this construction.

   A mí me gustan las matemáticas.

   ¿A ti te gustan también?

   A los profesores no les gusta corregir exámenes.

Present Tense of Regular Verbs

	-ar	-er	-ir
(yo)	me levanto	como	asisto
(tú)	te levantas	comes	asistes
(Ud.)	se levanta	come	asiste
(él/ella)	se levanta	come	asiste
(nosotros/as)	nos levantamos	comemos	asistimos
(vosotros/as)	os levantáis	coméis	asistís
(Uds.)	se levantan	comen	asisten
(ellos/ellas)	se levantan	comen	asisten

Remember that even though **Ud.** and **él/ella** share the same verb forms, **Ud.** means *you* singular (formal, socially distant) and **él/ella** refers to a third person (*he/she*). Likewise, **Uds.** means *you* plural and **ellos/ellas** refers to some other persons (*they*).

Verbs in the present tense can refer to daily or habitual actions

> Todos los días **me levanto** a las 6.00.

but can also be used to refer to an action in progress.

> —¿Qué **haces**?
> —**Preparo** la cena. ¿Por qué **preguntas**?

Verbs with Stem Vowel Changes

Verbs with stem vowel changes are changed in those forms in which the pronounced accent falls on the stem: **yo, tú, Ud., él/ella, Uds., ellos/ellas.** They do not have the change in those forms where the pronounced accent falls on the ending: **nosotros/as, vosotros/as.**

	o → ue
dormir	d**ue**rme
	dormimos
	dormís

	e → ie
tener	t**ie**ne
	tenemos
	tenéis

	e → i
vestirse	se v**i**ste
	nos vestimos
	os vestís

Verbs with Irregularities

Some verbs have irregularities in the **yo** form.

conduzco (conducir)	hago (hacer)
conozco (conocer)	sé (saber)
doy (dar)	tengo (tener)
estoy (estar)	vengo (venir)

Some verbs don't follow predicted patterns.

ir: voy, vas, va, va,
  vamos, vais, van, van

estar: estoy, estás, está, está,
  estamos, estáis, están, están

Descriptive Adjectives

Adjectives tend to follow nouns. Also, adjectives must agree in gender and in number with the nouns they modify.

> un amig**o** dedicad**o**   unos amig**os** dedicad**os**
> una amig**a** dedicad**a**   unas amig**as** dedicad**as**

However, adjectives that end in **-e** and most that end in a consonant only show number agreement.

> un libro interesante   unas clase**s** difícile**s**

Possessive Adjectives

Possessive adjectives precede the noun and agree in number with the noun.

> mi profesor   mi**s** profesor**es**
> tu amiga   tu**s** amiga**s**
> su perro   su**s** perro**s**

Note that the equivalent of **su** or **sus** in English is *his, her, your,* or *their.*

Nuestro is an exception. It reflects both the number and gender of a noun.

> nuestr**o** profesor   nuestr**os** profesor**es**
> nuestr**a** profesor**a**   nuestr**as** profesor**as**

Negation

Certain negative words like **tampoco, nunca,** and **nadie** can be placed before a verb or after. In the latter case, a **no** before the verb is required.

> Yo **no** me levanto temprano.
>   Yo **tampoco** me levanto temprano.
>   Yo **no** me levanto temprano **tampoco.**
> ¿Quién se levanta temprano?
>   **Nadie** se levanta temprano.
>   **No** se levanta **nadie** temprano.
> ¿Cuándo haces ejercicio?
>   **Nunca** hago ejercicio.
>   **No** hago ejercicio **nunca.**

The negative word **nada** normally follows a verb and will be accompanied by **no.**

> **No** hay **nada.**
> **No** tengo **nada.**

Preterite Tense: Regular Forms

	-ar	-er	-ir
(yo)	me levanté	comí	salí
(tú)	te levantaste	comiste	saliste
(Ud.)	se levantó	comió	salió
(él/ella)	se levantó	comió	salió
(nosotros/as)	nos levantamos	comimos	salimos
(vosotros/as)	os levantasteis	comisteis	salisteis
(Uds.)	se levantaron	comieron	salieron
(ellos/ellas)	se levantaron	comieron	salieron

The preterite tense is used to talk about simple actions and events in the past that are viewed as completed. It is useful when talking about events that happened yesterday, last night, and so forth.

Preterite Tense: Irregular Verbs

Some common verbs do not have the characteristic stress on the verb ending in the preterite. These irregular verbs all share the same endings, regardless of whether they are **-ar, -er,** or **-ir** verbs.

andar:	anduv-		-e (yo)
estar:	estuv-		-iste (tú)
hacer:	hic-*		-o (Ud.)
poder:	pud-		-o (él/ella)
saber:	sup-	+	-imos (nosotros/as)
tener:	tuv-		-isteis (vosotros/as)
venir:	vin-		-ieron (Uds.)
			-ieron (ellos/ellas)

Two other irregular verbs share a common ending in the **Uds.** and **ellos/ellas** form.

conducir → condujeron

decir → dijeron

Saber in the preterite means *to find out* (lit. *at a point in time, to begin to know*)

Entonces **supe** la verdad.
Then I found out the truth.

Poder in the preterite means *to manage to, succeed in* (*doing something*)

Por fin **pude** hablar con ella.
I was finally able to speak with her. (*I had tried before, but had always failed.*)

The verbs **ser** and **ir** share the same forms in the preterite: **fui, fuiste, fue, fue, fuimos, fuisteis, fueron, fueron.** Context will determine meaning.

Lincoln **fue** presidente entre 1861 y 1865.

Lincoln **fue** al teatro.

The Verb Form hay

The verb form **hay** can mean *there is* and *there are.*

¿**Hay** café?

No, no **hay** café. Pero sí **hay** refrescos.

Necesitar + *infinitive* and tener que + *infinitive*

In order to talk about what you *need* or *have* to do, you use a conjugated form of **necesitar** + *infinitive* or **tener que** + *infinitive*.

Necesito estudiar mucho esta tarde.
I need to study a lot this afternoon.

Elena **tiene que trabajar** mañana.
Elena has to work tomorrow.

Other helping verbs that are followed by an infinitive include **deber, preferir,** and **querer.**

Debemos hacer ejercicio todos los días.
We should exercise every day.

Tomás y sus amigos **prefieren cenar** tarde.
Tomás and his friends prefer to eat dinner late.

¿**Quieren** Uds. **ir** al cine o **quedarse** en casa?
Do you (plural) want to go to the movies or stay at home?

---

*Hic- becomes **hiz-** when used with **Ud.** and **él/ella: hizo.**

Grammar Summary for Lección preliminar–Lección 3

Ir a + *infinitive*

One way to discuss future activities is to use the conjugated form of **ir a** + *infinitive*.

Voy a levantarme temprano mañana.
I'm going to get up early tomorrow.

Elena y sus amigos **van a bailar** el sábado.
Elena and her friends are going to dance on Saturday.

"Do"

English requires the support verb *do* to make negatives, ask questions, and to emphasize. Spanish has no such verb, and you should not equate the English support verb *do* with **hacer.**

No sabes la respuesta.
*You **do**n't know the answer.*

¿Sueles levantarte tarde?
***Do** you normally get up late?*

¿Dormiste bien?
***Did** you sleep well?*

¡Tú sí saliste anoche!
*You **did** go out last night!*

"It"

Keep in mind that the subject *it* is not expressed in Spanish as it is in English. English is a language that requires sentences to have expressed subjects, but Spanish does not. English requires "dummy" subjects such as *it*, where Spanish needs no expressed subject.

Llueve.
***It**'s raining.*

Hace frío.
***It**'s cold.*

Son las dos y media.
***It**'s two-thirty.*

Es imposible.
***It**'s impossible.*

Nuestras familias

Las hermanas (*1969*) *por Fernando Botero*

Perfil del artista

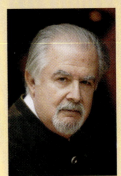

NOMBRE: Fernando Botero

PAÍS DE ORIGEN: Colombia

FECHA DE NACIMIENTO: 1932

Botero, el más conocido de los artistas colombianos y probablemente el más conocido de los artistas latinoamericanos vivientes, nació en Medellín en 1932. Después de terminar sus estudios universitarios en 1950, se fue a España e Italia para estudiar arte. Pero fue en México, durante 1956 y 1957, donde concibió[a] y dio forma a las imágenes rotundas que se identifican con él. En la mayoría de sus obras se encuentran familias, escenas típicas, y también figuras desnudas, a veces con tono satírico. Últimamente,[b] su obra ofrece temas más serios como, por ejemplo, la serie de retratos en que figura el abuso de los presos iraquíes en Abu Ghraib.

_____

[a]*he conceived*   [b]*Recently*

LECCIÓN **4**

Check out the following media resources to complement this lesson:

 Online *Manual*

 Online Learning Center

 Video on CD

 ActivityPak

¿Cómo es tu familia?

In this lesson, you will explore the topic of families. In the process, you will

◆ describe your family (size, members, names)

◆ ask your classmates about their families

◆ learn that speakers of Spanish often use two last names

◆ review interrogatives

◆ learn to use direct object pronouns

◆ learn more about the verb **estar**

ALTO Before beginning this lesson, look over the **Intercambio** activity on page 133. This is the activity you will be working toward throughout the lesson.

Mi familia «extendida» no es muy grande, pero me gusta.

VOCABULARIO

¿Cómo es tu familia?

Talking about your immediate family

La familia de José Luis Gómez

José
45 años

Marta
44 años

José Luis
18 años

Ana
9 años

Rebeca
5 años

Carlos
2 años

Daniel
2 años

Anselmo
3 años

gemelos

José es **el padre** de José Luis.
Marta es **la madre** de José Luis.
José y Marta son **los padres.**
Ana es **una hermana** de José Luis.
Carlos es **un hermano** de José Luis.
Anselmo es **el perro** de José Luis.

José Luis tiene cuatro **hermanos.**
No tiene **hermanastros.**

José Luis, Ana, Rebeca, Carlos y Daniel son **los hijos** de Marta y
José. (Ana es **una hija;** Carlos es **un hijo.**)

Jane	Paul	Laura
42 años	49 años	38 años

Cheryl	Christopher	Brian	Russ
20 años	17 años	6 años	3 años

Paul es **el padre** de Cheryl.
Jane es **la madre** de Cheryl. Es una **madre soltera.**
Paul y Jane son **los padres.**
Cheryl no tiene **hermanas.**
Christopher es **el hermano** de Cheryl.

Cheryl tiene **un hermano** y dos **medio hermanos,** Brian y Russ.
También tiene **una madrastra,** Laura.

Cheryl y Christopher son **los hijos** de Paul y Jane.
Brian y Russ son **los hijos** de Paul y Laura.

Vocabulario útil

la esposa, la mujer	wife	**mayor**	older
el esposo, el marido	husband	**menor**	younger
los esposos	husband and wife	**el/la mayor**	the oldest
los gemelos	twins	**el/la menor**	the youngest
la hermanastra	stepsister		
el hermanastro	stepbrother	**tiene... años**	he/she is . . . years old
el padrastro	stepfather		
el padre soltero	single father		
la pareja	couple; partner		

ACTIVIDAD A ¿Cierto o falso?

Your instructor will make a series of statements about the Gómez family in the previous drawings. According to their family tree, is each statement **cierto** or **falso?**

1... 2... 3... 4... 5... 6... 7...

ACTIVIDAD B ¿Quién es?

Listen as your instructor says a phrase. Relying only on the drawing of Cheryl Fuller's family tree, can you name the person(s) described by your instructor?

1... 2... 3... 4... 5... 6... 7... 8...

ACTIVIDAD C ¿Los Gómez o los Fuller?°

¿Los... The Gómez family or the Fullers?

According to what you know about the Gómez and Fuller families, decide which is being referred to in each statement you hear. See if you can do this activity from memory without looking at the family trees. (Note: **Se refiere a** means *it refers to*.)

MODELO   En esta familia hay cuatro hijos. → Se refiere a los Fuller.

1... 2... 3... 4... 5... 6...

COMUNICACIÓN

ACTIVIDAD D La familia de Alfredo

Alfredo, a friend of José Luis, has written a description of his family. Listen to the description and then draw his family tree, using the Gómez family tree as a guide. Be sure to include everyone's name and age.

ACTIVIDAD E En mi familia...

Prepare a brief oral description of your own family using Alfredo's description in **Actividad D** as a guide. Include all the members of your family and their ages.

Así se dice

By now you may have noticed that there are two ways to express *to know* in Spanish: **conocer** and **saber**. **Conocer** is used to express *to know* (*be acquainted with*) *a person or a place*. **Saber** expresses *to know facts or information*. When followed by an infinitive, **saber** also means *to know how to do something*.

—¿**Conoces** a mi hermano Jaime?
—Sí, **conozco** muy bien a Jaime. **Sabe tocar** la guitarra, ¿verdad?
—Sí. También **sabe jugar** al béisbol, **bailar, hablar** el japonés...

GRAMÁTICA

¿Cuántas hijas... ?

—¿Y **cuántos** hermanos
tienes, José Luis?
—Tengo cuatro: dos herma-
nas y dos hermanitos
gemelos.

> ¿cuántos/as?
> ¿cómo?
> ¿dónde?
> ¿cuál(es)?
> ¿qué?
> ¿quién(es)?
> ¿cuándo?

Interrogatives, or question words, are used to
obtain information from others. You have
already been introduced to the main question
words in Spanish. Here is a summary of them.

¿Cuántos?	¿Cuántos hijos tienes?
¿Cuántas?	¿Cuántas hijas tienes?
¿Cómo?	¿Cómo se llama tu madre?
¿Dónde?	¿Dónde viven tus padres?
¿Cuál?	¿Cuál es tu apellido (*last name*)?
¿Cuáles?	¿Cuáles son los nombres de tus hijos?
¿Qué?	¿Qué familia es más grande, la de los Fuller o la de los Gómez?
¿Quién?	¿Quién es esa chica? ¿Es tu hermana?
¿Quiénes?	¿Quiénes son los padres de José Luis?
¿Cuándo?	¿Cuándo llamas a tu familia?

Note that both **¿qué?** and **¿cuál?** can mean *which?* For now, use **¿qué?**
with a noun and **¿cuál(es)?** with **es (son)** to mean *which.*

> **¿Qué apellido** es más común, García o Gómez?
> **¿Cuál es** el nombre más popular, Juan o José?

ACTIVIDAD F ¿Qué familia?

Silently think of a famous family and write down that family's name
without anyone seeing it. Then team up with a partner who will try to
guess who that family is by asking questions.

MODELOS   ¿Cuántas personas hay en la familia en total?

¿Cuántos hijos (Cuántas hijas) hay?

¿Cuántos años tiene el hijo (la hija) mayor?

Once your partner guesses, switch roles and try to guess the family he
or she has chosen.

Hay once personas en esta familia chilena. ¿Cuántas personas hay en tu familia?

COMUNICACIÓN

ACTIVIDAD G Un breve ensayo°

Un... *A brief essay*

Pair up with someone you do not know well to find out about his or her family.

Paso 1 Read the following paragraphs. Make a note of the type of information that is missing in each blank.

La familia de _____

La familia de mi compañero/a es _____.* En total son _____ personas: _____ padres y _____ hijo(s) (hija[s]). Toda la familia vive en (Los padres viven en)† _____. Su padre tiene _____ años y su madre tiene _____.

Sus hermanos asisten a _____. Se llaman _____ y _____ y tienen _____ y _____ años, respectivamente. _____ es el (la) mayor de la familia y _____ es el (la) menor.

Paso 2 Make up a series of questions to obtain all the missing information needed to construct a composite of your partner's family. It may help to write out the questions first. As you interview, jot down all the information your partner gives.

ACTIVIDAD H ¿Sabías que... ?

Read the **¿Sabías que... ?** selection on the following page. Report to the class what your name would be if you used the system found in Spanish-speaking countries. From now on, use this name on all your assignments in Spanish!

---

*Choose the appropriate word: **pequeña** (*small*), **mediana** (*medium*), **grande.**
†The family may not all live together, so choose accordingly.

¿Sabías que...

muchos hispanos usan dos apellidos? En los países de habla inglesa, las personas generalmente tienen un apellido, por ejemplo, Judd Emerson o Lillian Hoffman.* Pero en los países de habla española, las personas pueden tener dos apellidos, el paterno y el materno: por ejemplo, **Juanita Pérez Trujillo** o **Ramón Sáenz García**. En el primer ejemplo, **Pérez** es el apellido paterno y **Trujillo** es el materno. En el otro ejemplo, **Sáenz** es el apellido paterno y **García** es el materno. En ocasiones formales u oficiales, las personas usan los dos apellidos. Sin embargo,[a] en algunos países, como la Argentina, el doble apellido generalmente no se usa, excepto si el apellido paterno es un nombre muy común (González, Ramírez, Gómez, Pérez, etcétera). En estos casos se incluye el apellido materno para evitar la confusión. Otro punto interesante es que en los países hispanos, las mujeres no cambian sus apellidos cuando se casan. Y en España, si los padres así lo deciden, sus hijos pueden tomar el apellido de la mamá.

Traducciones Dovita
Traducciones español-inglés o inglés-español

Lic. Paloma Novoa García

Avda. Teopanzolco 200
Col. Jacarandas
Cuernavaca, Morelos 62420

Tel. 322-07-90
dovita@infosel.com.mx

BREEN PUBLICIDAD

Félix Hugo Parada Mejía
DIRECTOR GENERAL

FELIX HUGO Y ASOCIADOS, S. A. DE C. V.
Acambay 201, Col. Pirules. C. P. 54040
Edo. de México. Tels: 379 86 01   399 97 07

[a]Sin... *However*

NAVEGANDO LA RED

Look for an online phone book from a Spanish-speaking country. How are women and men listed? Print out a section of the phone book and report your findings to the class.

*También es frecuente en este país ver apellidos «compuestos» (Robert Bley-Vroman, Mary Smith-González). ¿Es este sistema similar o diferente al sistema hispano?

IDEAS PARA EXPLORAR
La familia «extendida»

VOCABULARIO
¿Y los otros parientes?

Talking about your extended family

You have already learned vocabulary related to immediate or nuclear families. Here is a summary of some of the expressions related to extended families.

La familia «extendida» de los Gómez

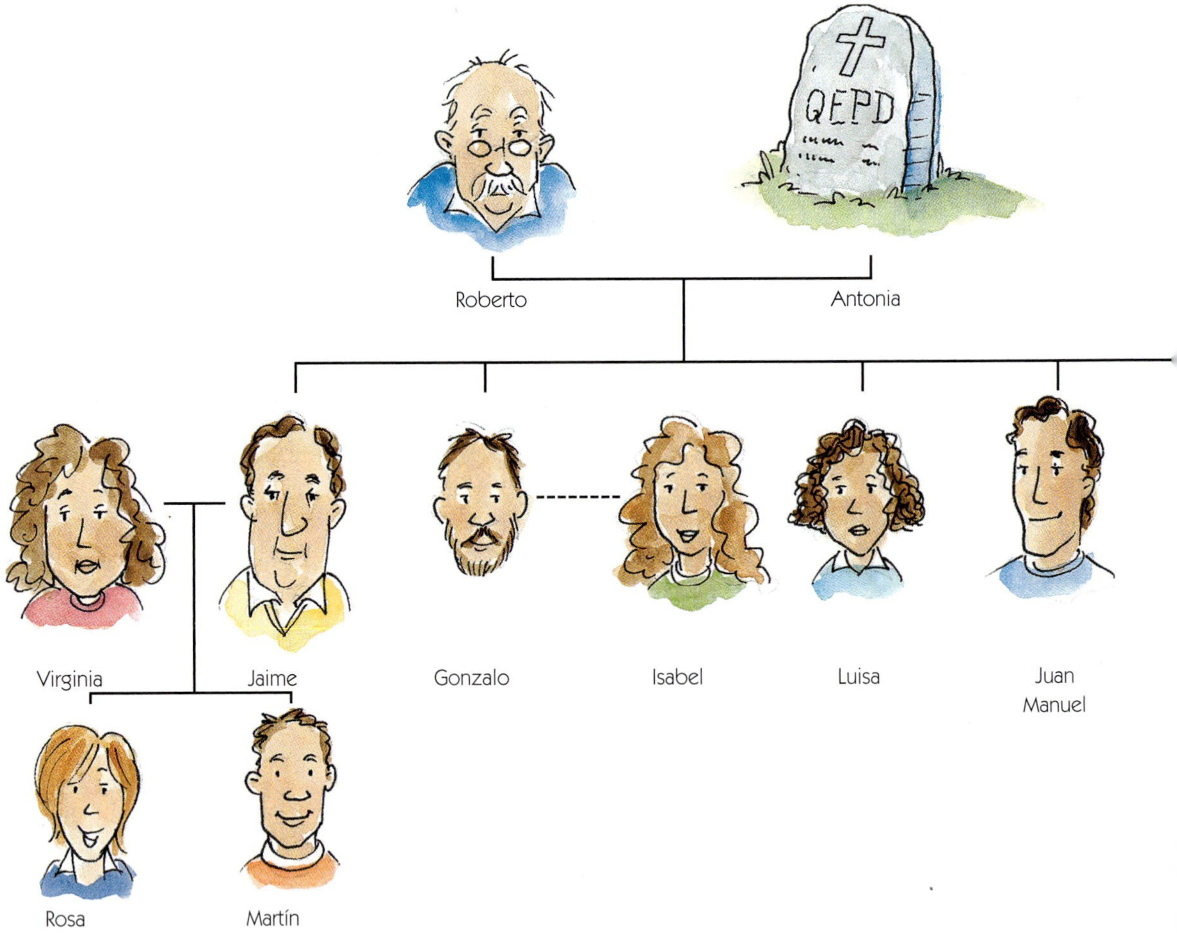

QEPD
Roberto
Antonia
Virginia
Jaime
Gonzalo
Isabel
Luisa
Juan Manuel
Rosa
Martín

Enrique y Teresa y Roberto y Antonia son **los abuelos** de
José Luis.

Roberto y Antonia son sus **abuelos paternos.**

Enrique y Teresa son sus **abuelos maternos.**

Antonia es su **abuela paterna** y Teresa su **abuela materna.**

Antonia, su abuela paterna, **ya murió.**

Enrique, su **abuelo materno, ya murió.**

José Luis tiene varios **tíos:** Gonzalo, Luisa, Jaime, Juan Manuel y
Virginia.

Su **tía** favorita es Luisa. No tiene un **tío** favorito.

Su tío Jaime y su tía Virginia tienen dos hijos, Rosa y Martín.
Ellos son **los primos** de José Luis.

Enrique   Teresa

José   Marta

José Luis   Ana   Rebeca   Carlos   Daniel   Anselmo

ACTIVIDAD A La familia «extendida»

Lee las oraciones de la página 119. Después en el dibujo (*drawing*) de la familia Gómez, busca a las personas mencionadas en las oraciones. ¿Puedes deducir el significado de todas las palabras nuevas?

ACTIVIDAD B Los parientes de José Luis

Estudia el dibujo de la familia Gómez y las palabras nuevas. Luego identifica a los miembros de la familia de la columna A. Contesta con oraciones completas, según (*according to*) el modelo.

MODELO Rosa y Martín son los primos de José Luis.

A		B	
1. _____ Rosa		**a.** una tía	
2. _____ Roberto		**b.** una prima	
3. _____ Enrique		**c.** un tío	
4. _____ Teresa	es (son)	**d.** la abuela materna	de José Luis.
5. _____ Juan Manuel		**e.** el abuelo paterno	
6. _____ Jaime y Gonzalo		**f.** el abuelo materno	
7. _____ Virginia		**g.** dos tíos	
		h. los primos	

COMUNICACIÓN

ACTIVIDAD C El profesor (La profesora)

Usando el nuevo vocabulario y el vocabulario que ya sabes, hazle preguntas (*ask questions*) al profesor (a la profesora). ¿Cuántos datos (*bits of information*) pueden Uds. obtener en sólo cuatro minutos?

MODELOS ¿Tiene Ud. abuelos?
¿Cómo se llaman?

ACTIVIDAD D Familias famosas

Paso 1 Piensa en una familia famosa y escribe una descripción de esa familia. Incluye detalles sobre los miembros de la familia: cuántos son, qué relación hay entre ellos, el nombre de cada uno/a (sin apellido) y el lugar donde viven.

Paso 2 Comparte tu descripción con un compañero (una compañera) de clase para ver si puede adivinar qué familia estás describiendo.

Paso 3 (Optativo) Comparte tu descripción con la clase.

VOCABULARIO

¿Tienes sobrinos?

Additional vocabulary related to family members

Here are some other words related to families. Read each Spanish definition and example. Using the family tree on pages 118–119, can you determine what each new word means?

sobrino/a: hijo o hija de tu hermano/a

José Luis es **el sobrino** de Luisa (la hermana de su padre José).

nieto/a: hijo o hija de tu hijo/a

José Luis es **el nieto** de Enrique y Teresa.

cuñado/a: esposo o esposa de tu hermano/a

Virginia es **la cuñada** de Gonzalo.

suegro/a: padre o madre de tu esposo/a

Roberto es **el suegro** de Marta.

casado/a: cuando una persona tiene esposo/a

Marta está **casada.**

divorciado/a: cuando un esposo y una esposa se separan legalmente

Gonzalo está **divorciado.**

soltero/a: una persona que no tiene esposo/a

Juan Manuel es **soltero.**

ya murió: sin vida, muerto/a

El abuelo materno de José Luis **ya murió.**

viudo/a: cuando el esposo (la esposa) ya murió

Roberto es **viudo.**

vivo/a: que tiene vida

El abuelo paterno de José Luis está **vivo.**

ACTIVIDAD E Más sobre los Gómez

Tu profesor(a) va a leer una serie de preguntas sobre la familia Gómez. Para contestar, puedes consultar el dibujo de las páginas 118–119.

1… 2… 3… 4… 5… 6… 7… 8…

ACTIVIDAD F ¿Cierto o falso?

Estudia otra vez el dibujo de la familia «extendida» de José Luis. Luego escucha las afirmaciones del profesor (de la profesora). ¿Son ciertas o falsas?

1... **2**... **3**... **4**... **5**... **6**... **7**... **8**... **9**... **10**...

COMUNICACIÓN

ACTIVIDAD G Firma aquí, por favor

¿Cómo es tu familia «extendida»? Pregúntaselo a tus compañeros de clase. Cuando alguien contesta afirmativamente, pídele que firme (*ask him* [*her*] *to sign*) tu hoja de papel.

1. ¿Tienes cuñados?
2. ¿Están vivos todos tus abuelos?
3. ¿Tienes un tío soltero o una tía soltera?
4. ¿Tienes sobrinos?
5. ¿Hay más de 30 personas en tu familia «extendida»?
6. ¿Hay una persona divorciada en tu familia?
7. ¿Tienes primos que no conoces?
8. ¿Tienes suegros?

GRAMÁTICA

¿Están casados?

More on **estar** + adjectives

You may remember from the **Lección preliminar** that the verb **estar** can be used with some adjectives when a characteristic or trait is not seen as inherent or defining of a person. However, some adjectives that are almost always used with **estar** include **casado/a, divorciado/a, muerto/a, separado/a,** and **vivo/a.** These adjectives are used with **estar** no matter how long the situation endures. They are not viewed as inherent traits of the person, rather they represent the resultant condition of some process. Interestingly, in Spanish most native speakers use **ser** with the adjective **soltero/a.** Perhaps this is because people are by nature single but then become married.

ACTIVIDAD H ¿Casados o divorciados?

Escucha los nombres de las parejas famosas que menciona tu profesor(a). Indica si **están casados** o **divorciados.**

1... **2**... **3**... **4**... **5**... **6**...

ACTIVIDAD I ¿Vivos o muertos?

Escucha el nombre de cada persona famosa que menciona tu profesor(a). Indica si **está vivo/a** o **muerto/a.**

1... **2**... **3**... **4**... **5**... **6**...

COMUNICACIÓN

 ## ACTIVIDAD J En tu familia...

Piensa en tu familia. ¿Quiénes están casados? ¿Hay personas divorciadas? ¿Están vivos todos tus abuelos? ¿Alguien ya murió? Escribe cinco o seis oraciones para describir el estado de varias personas de tu familia. (Alternativa: Si prefieres, puedes hacer lo mismo [*the same*] con una familia famosa.)

NAVEGANDO LA RED

Find information in Spanish about *one* of the following topics.
1. family makeup (members and size) of Spain's royal family
2. family makeup (members and size) of a current Latin American president or leader
3. family makeup (members and size) of a current Spanish-speaking celebrity

Print out the information and come to class prepared with five or six statements about the family.

IDEAS PARA EXPLORAR

Mis relaciones con la familia

GRAMÁTICA

¿Te conocen bien?

First and second person direct object pronouns

me	nos
te	os
lo/la	los/las
lo/la	los/las

In addition to having a subject, a verb in a sentence will also often have an object. An object is generally defined as a thing or person on which an action or process is performed. Thus, in the sentence *John writes letters, John* is the subject and *letters* is the object (the action of writing is performed on the letters). In the sentence *She has an idea, She* is the subject (pronoun) and *an idea* is the object (the thing on which the process of having is performed). What is the subject and what is the object of the verb **miran** in the following sentence?

Los padres miran a los hijos.

If you said **padres** is the subject (parents are the ones doing the watching) and **hijos** is the object (the people being watched), you were correct. Did you notice that **los hijos** is preceded by **a?** This **a** is called the *personal* **a** and must be used in Spanish before human objects of a verb. (You will learn more about it later.)

What is the subject *pronoun* that corresponds to **padres: ellos, él,** or **nosotros?**

_____ miran a los hijos.

If you said **ellos,** you were correct again. **Los padres** is the subject *noun* and **ellos** is the subject *pronoun.* Subject pronouns are already familiar to you.

yo	nosotros/as
tú	vosotros/as
usted (Ud.)	ustedes (Uds.)
él/ella	ellos/ellas

In Spanish (and English), not only are there subject pronouns, but there are also object pronouns.

Los padres **los** miran (es decir, a los hijos).	*The parents watch **them*** (*that is, the kids*).

Here is the first set of subject and object pronouns in Spanish with which you will become familiar.

PRONOUNS		
	SUBJECT **yo**	OBJECT **me**
1st person singular	**Yo** comprendo (*understand*) a mi hermano.	Mi hermano **me** comprende.
2nd person singular	**tú** **Tú** comprendes a los abuelos.	**te** Los abuelos **te** comprenden.
1st person plural	**nosotros/as** **Nosotros** comprendemos a los parientes.	**nos** Los parientes **nos** comprenden.

Me, te, and **nos** are objects of the verb. Can you figure out who is being understood in the first example in the righthand column? *Me.* In the second, who is being understood? *You.* And in the third, who is being understood? *Us.* Keep in mind the following two facts about object pronouns.

1. They are placed before conjugated verbs.
2. They indicate on whom or what the action or process is performed, not who or what is performing the action or process.

It's also important to keep in mind Spanish word order. In Spanish, subjects can come before or after the verb.

Juan no viene. No viene **Juan.**

Objects marked with **a** generally follow the verb.

María visita **a su hermano.**

Object pronouns must always precede a conjugated verb.

Mis tíos **me fascinan.**

However, they can be attached to the end of an infinitive or a present participle. Note that when a pronoun is attached to a participle, a written accent mark is added to maintain the original pronunciation of the participle.

Mis primos van a **visitarme** en junio.		Mis primos **me** van a visitar en junio.
Mi abuela está **escuchándome.**	*or*	Mi abuela **me** está escuchando.

Spanish also uses the pronouns **me, te,** and **nos** as indirect objects: *to whom, from whom,* and *for whom.*

Mis hermanos **me** escriben cartas muy largas.

To whom are the letters being written? To me.

¿Y **te** dan dinero tus padres?

To whom is money given? To you—or at least that's what is being asked.

You already know how to use indirect objects with the verb **gustar.**

Me gusta recibir cartas de mi familia.	*Receiving letters from my family is pleasing to me.*
¿**Te** gusta escribir cartas?	*Is writing letters pleasing to you?*

What can get tricky in correctly interpreting a sentence is that often you will see or hear a sentence in which the order is object pronoun-verb-subject, just the opposite of English!

Nos invitan a cenar las chicas.	*The girls are inviting us to eat dinner.*
No te comprende el profesor.	*The professor doesn't understand you.*

ACTIVIDAD A Los pronombres

Select the correct interpretation of each sentence. Keep in mind that Spanish has flexible word order and doesn't necessarily follow subject-verb-object order as English does.

1. Mi hermana me llama frecuentemente.

   a. I call my sister frequently.
   b. My sister calls me frequently.

2. ¿Te escriben tus padres?

   a. Do you write to your parents?
   b. Do your parents write to you?

3. No nos escuchan los padres.

   a. Parents don't listen to us.
   b. We don't listen to parents.

4. Me conocen bien mis hermanos.

   a. My siblings know me well.
   b. I know my siblings well.

Nota comunicativa

Here are some ways of saying what you do without using complete sentences. Note: Remember that Spanish does not have a "support verb" equivalent to English *do*.

SOMEONE SAYS	YOU CAN SAY	
No comprendo a mis padres.	Yo sí.	*I do.*
	Yo tampoco.	*Neither do I.*
		(Me neither.)
Veo a mi familia con frecuencia.	Yo también.	*I do, too.*
	Yo no.	*I don't.*

ACTIVIDAD B ¿Objeto o sujeto?

Your instructor will say a series of statements. Match each statement you hear with one of the following sentences. Remember that Spanish does not always follow subject-verb-object word order!

1. a. ☐ A man is calling me.
   b. ☐ I am calling a man.

2. a. ☐ My parents visit me.
   b. ☐ I visit my parents.

3. a. ☐ I follow others.
   b. ☐ Others follow me.

4. a. ☐ We are greeting a friend.
   b. ☐ A friend is greeting us.

5. a. ☐ Our relatives don't understand us.
   b. ☐ We don't understand our relatives.

6. a. ☐ A friend is inviting you to dinner.
   b. ☐ You are inviting a friend to dinner.

7. a. ☐ The professor is watching us.
   b. ☐ We are watching the professor.

8. a. ☐ María is looking for you.
   b. ☐ You are looking for María.

9. a. ☐ Juan believes us.
   b. ☐ We believe Juan.

ACTIVIDAD C Los parientes

What are things that relatives do to us? They can bother us, visit us, criticize us, love us, and so forth.

Paso 1 Read each statement and select the ones that you think are typical.

Los parientes…

a. ☐ nos molestan (*bother*).   **d.** ☐ nos visitan.

b. ☐ nos critican.   **e.** ☐ nos quieren (*love*).

c. ☐ nos ayudan.   **f.** ☐ nos _____.

Paso 2 Now select the alternatives that you think make sense.

Los parientes…

a. ☐ pueden molestarnos, aunque (*although*) no deben hacerlo.

b. ☐ pueden criticarnos, aunque no deben hacerlo.

c. ☐ pueden ayudarnos, aunque no deben hacerlo.

d. ☐ pueden visitarnos, aunque no deben hacerlo.

e. ☐ pueden querernos, aunque no deben hacerlo.

f. ☐ pueden _____nos, aunque no deben hacerlo.

Compare your answers with a classmate's.

ACTIVIDAD D Los perros y los gatos

Para muchas personas, los perros y los gatos son parte de la familia. ¿Qué dices tú en cuanto a (*regarding*) estos animales domésticos? Inventa una o dos oraciones y preséntala(s) a la clase. ¿Están de acuerdo tus compañeros con tus ideas?

MODELOS   Los perros nos quieren. Son nuestros mejores (*best*) amigos.

Los animales no me importan. Son animales nada más.

Vocabulario útil

ayudar	**escuchar**	**molestar**
besar (*to kiss*)	**hablar**	**obedecer** (*to obey*)
comprender	**hacer compañía**	**querer**

GRAMÁTICA

¿La quieres?

Third person direct object pronouns

me	nos
te	os
lo/la	**los/las**
lo/la	**los/las**

The most difficult object pronoun system for students of Spanish is the set of third person object pronouns. The third person direct object pronouns are presented in the second column of the following list of sentences.

SUBJECT	OBJECT*
Ella besa a Juan.	Juan **la** besa.
She kisses Juan.	*Juan kisses her.*
Él besa a María.	María **lo** besa.
He kisses María.	*María kisses him.*
Ellos observan a Marcos.	Marcos **los** observa.
They observe Marcos.	*Marcos observes them.*
Ellas observan a Carlitos.	Carlitos **las** observa.
They observe Carlitos.	*Carlitos observes them.*

Keeping in mind that Spanish has flexible word order, what do you think the following sentence means?

Lo escucha Roberto.

If you said *Roberto listens to him,* you were correct!

Unlike **me, te,** and **nos,** the direct object pronouns **lo, la, los,** and **las** cannot function as indirect object pronouns. This means that they do not normally express *to him, to her, to them, for him, for her, for them,* and so forth, with verbs like **dar, gustar, escribir,** and others. (You will learn about third person indirect object pronouns in a later lesson.)

ACTIVIDAD E La familia de Cheryl

Paso 1 Imagine you overheard the statements on the following page about Cheryl Fuller, whose family tree you studied earlier in this lesson. Indicate to whom each sentence could refer from the choices given.

---

*Third person object pronouns can also refer to animals, things, and ideas.

¿Mi libro? No **lo** tengo.

¿Mis clases? **Las** detesto.

¿Mis dos perros? Ay, **los** quiero muchísimo.

¿Mi personalidad? **La** heredé (*I inherited it*) de mi madre.

Lección 4   ¿Cómo es tu familia?

1. No la quiere para nada.
    a. su madrastra   **b.** su padre
2. Lo ve todos los días.
    a. su hermano Christopher   **b.** su madre
3. Los obedece.
    a. su madre   **b.** sus padres

Paso 2 Now indicate the subject and object of each verb in the sentences in **Paso 1.**

ACTIVIDAD F Mi familia

How do you interact with your parents, children, or siblings? Identify whom you are talking about and indicate whether or not each statement applies to you. Note that **yo** is not used in any of the sentences. This is because the verb form tells who the subject is.

_____ mis padres   _____ mis hijos   _____ mis hermanos

	SÍ. SE ME APLICA.	NO. NO SE ME APLICA.
1. Los llamo con frecuencia por teléfono.	☐	☐
2. Los visito los fines de semana.	☐	☐
3. Los visito una vez al mes.	☐	☐
4. Los abrazo (*hug*) cuando los veo.	☐	☐
5. Los comprendo muy bien.	☐	☐
6. Los aprecio (*appreciate*) mucho.	☐	☐
7. Los admiro.	☐	☐

DEBATE Un drama familiar muy común: Ella se siente[a] dominada, perseguida por su hermano mayor y no sabe qué hacer. El caso de Alicia y Manuel es típico.

ALICIA CUENTA SU PARTE

«Manuel es muy posesivo. No me deja respirar. Cada vez que voy a salir, me pregunta con quién, adónde voy, qué vamos a hacer... A veces me sigue. Cuando un chico viene a visitarme, Manny lo interroga. De veras, mi hermano es peor que mis padres. Por eso peleamos mucho».

MANNY HACE UNA ACLARACIÓN

«Si vigilo a mi hermana, es porque me ha dado[b] motivos para sospechar[c] de ella. En varias ocasiones la sorpendí[d] con un tal Sergio, que es uno de esos rebeldes sin causa con la reputación por el suelo. Ella no conoce a los chicos. Ese tipo sólo busca una cosa».

[a]se... *feels*   [b]ha... *has given*   [c]*to be suspicious*   [d]*I surprised*

ACTIVIDAD G Mis parientes

Select a *female* relative of yours (**madre, hermana, tía, abuela, esposa,** and so forth). Which of the statements describes how you feel about her?

Nombre del pariente: _____ Relación: _____

☐ La admiro.   ☐ La quiero mucho.   ☐ La detesto.
☐ La respeto.   ☐ Trato de imitarla.   ☐ La…

Now select a *male* relative and do the same!

Nombre del pariente: _____ Relación: _____

☐ Lo admiro.   ☐ Lo quiero mucho.   ☐ Lo detesto.
☐ Lo respeto.   ☐ Trato de imitarlo.   ☐ Lo…

Compare your responses with those of two other people. Did you select the same relatives? Did you mark the same feelings?

ACTIVIDAD H Lo respeto porque...

Paso 1 Using a mix of males and females, think of four well-known people that you either admire, detest, hate, or respect. Jot down their names and then write how you feel about that person using the following verbs.

admirar   detestar   odiar (*hate*)   respetar

MODELOS   Barack Obama: Lo admiro porque es inteligente.

Paris Hilton: La detesto porque es tonta y egoísta.

1.   2.   3.   4.

Paso 2 Share your statements with the rest of the class. Are any names repeated? Do you and your classmates have the same opinions?

NAVEGANDO LA RED

In Spanish, find one of the following services: family counseling, reproductive services, child care possibilities, adoption services, or geneological services. Report to the class the following: name, location, type of service, phone number or URL, and anything interesting you learned about the service.

GRAMÁTICA
Llamo a mis padres

Recall that Spanish uses the object marker **a.**

Los padres miran **a** los hijos.
Llamo **a** mis padres.

This object marker has no equivalent in English, but it's important in Spanish because it provides an extra clue about who did what to whom in the sentence. Because Spanish has flexible word order, the **a** reminds you that even if a noun appears before the verb it may not be the subject!

Juan llama **a** María.
A María la llama Juan. } *Juan calls María.*

Note that when an object appears before the verb, the corresponding object pronoun must also be used. If you think that this is redundant, it is! But redundancy is a natural feature of languages. For example, we put past tense endings on verbs even if we also say *yesterday* or *last night*. What does the following sentence mean? Who is doing what to whom?

A la chica la busca el chico.

You were correct if you said *The boy is looking for the girl.*

ACTIVIDAD I ¿Quién?

Select the correct English version of each sentence.

1. A mi mamá la besa mucho mi papá.

   a. My mom kisses my dad a lot.
   b. My dad kisses my mom a lot.

2. A mi papá no lo comprendo yo.

   a. I don't understand my father.
   b. My father doesn't understand me.

3. A la señora la saluda el señor.

   a. The woman greets the man.
   b. The man greets the woman.

4. A los chicos los sorprende la profesora.

   a. The professor surprises the boys.
   b. The boys surprise the professor.

^a*baby*   ^b«quieres» en el dialecto argentino   ^c*I feel*

ACTIVIDAD J ¿A quién?

Paso 1 Contesta las siguientes preguntas. Si no quieres hablar de tu familia, puedes hablar de amigos y otras personas que no son de tu familia.

MODELOS   E1: ¿A quién de tu familia admiras?
E2: A mi madre.

o   Admiro a mi madre.
Admiro a varias personas: a mi padre, a mi madre…

1. ¿A quién de tu familia admiras?
2. ¿A quién de tu familia comprendes mejor?
3. ¿A quién de tu familia no comprendes para nada?

Paso 2 Habla con otra persona en la clase para ver si contesta igual que tú. ¿Hay ciertos sentimientos comunes a la clase, por ejemplo, admiran todos a su abuela? ¿a un tío en particular?

ACTIVIDAD K Variedad de personas

Paso 1 We often find ourselves surrounded by diverse personalities. Some people we understand well and some we don't. Using the verbs provided, write a statement about the following people. If you like, you can write about someone else instead, but you must write about four different people.

admirar   comprender   respetar

MODELOS   Admiro mucho a mi profesora de español.

No admiro mucho a mi compañero de cuarto.

1. tu major amigo/a   3. un(a) profesor(a)
2. tu compañero/a de cuarto   4. un político (una mujer político)

Paso 2 Now share your feelings about each individual with a partner. Be ready to report on your partner's feelings to the class.

MODELO   Kathy admira mucho a su profesora de español.

INTERCAMBIO

¿Cómo es la familia de... ?

Propósito: dibujar (*to draw*) el árbol genealógico de alguna persona en la clase.

Papeles: una persona entrevistada; el resto de la clase dividido en cinco grupos.

Paso 1 El profesor (La profesora) le va a asignar a cada grupo una de las siguientes categorías.

Categoría 1: miembros de la familia nuclear
Categoría 2: abuelos
Categoría 3: tíos, incluyendo a los esposos y esposas
Categoría 4: primos
Categoría 5: características particulares de los diferentes parientes (por ejemplo, la persona más loca [*craziest*]; ver **Así se dice**) y sus pasatiempos especiales

Cada grupo debe hacer las preguntas necesarias para obtener toda la información sobre su categoría. Por ejemplo, se puede preguntar sobre los nombres de los parientes, su edad, dónde viven, etcétera.

Paso 2 Los grupos deben entrevistar a la persona seleccionada. Toda la clase debe escuchar sus respuestas y apuntar (*jot down*) toda la información. **¡OJO!** Si no entiendes algo, debes pedir aclaración.

Paso 3 En casa, dibuja el árbol genealógico de la persona entrevistada. Incluye todos los detalles. A continuación hay un ejemplo de cómo se puede poner el nombre de un pariente en el árbol genealógico.

Si hay tiempo, uno o dos voluntarios debe(n) presentar su dibujo a la clase y dar una descripción de dos o tres minutos de varios miembros de la familia.

Así se dice

To say *the biggest, the smallest,* and so forth, Spanish uses the *definite article* + **más** + *adjective.* To say *the least intelligent, the least shy,* and so forth, Spanish uses the *definite article* + **menos** + *adjective.* Two exceptions are **mayor** and **menor.**

el/la más inteligente
the smartest

el/la menos tímido/a
the least shy

el/la mayor
the oldest

el/la menor
the youngest

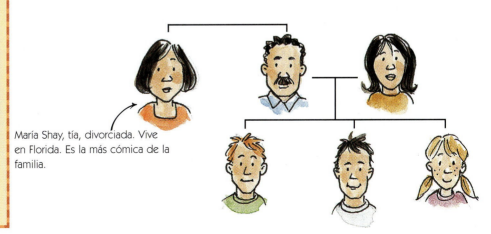

María Shay, tía, divorciada. Vive en Florida. Es la más cómica de la familia.

Vistazos culturales

El bilingüismo en el mundo hispano

¿Sabías que... el bilingüismo es común en la mayoría de los países de habla española? El bilingüismo consiste en el uso habitual de dos lenguas en una misma región. Por ejemplo, Montreal es una ciudad bilingüe porque la vasta mayoría de sus habitantes habla francés e inglés. Es igual en el mundo hispano, sobre todo en España y en algunos países latinoamericanos. ¡Y por supuesto en los Estados Unidos también!

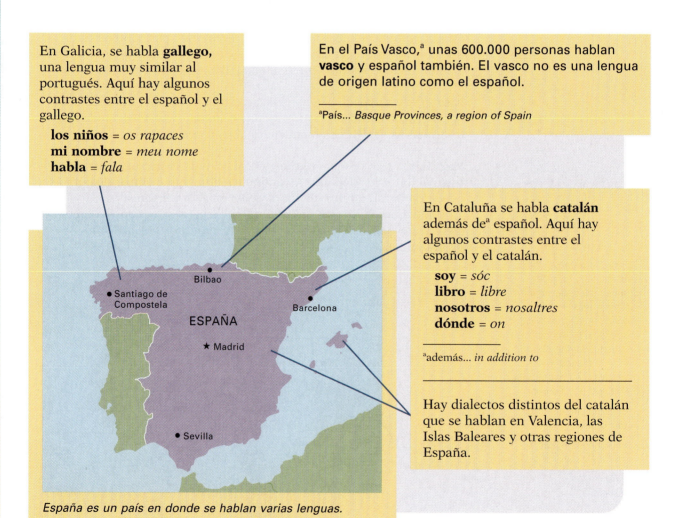

En Galicia, se habla **gallego,** una lengua muy similar al portugués. Aquí hay algunos contrastes entre el español y el gallego.

los niños = *os rapaces*
mi nombre = *meu nome*
habla = *fala*

En el País Vasco,[a] unas 600.000 personas hablan **vasco** y español también. El vasco no es una lengua de origen latino como el español.

[a]País... *Basque Provinces, a region of Spain*

En Cataluña se habla **catalán** además de[a] español. Aquí hay algunos contrastes entre el español y el catalán.

soy = *sóc*
libro = *libre*
nosotros = *nosaltres*
dónde = *on*

[a]además... *in addition to*

Hay dialectos distintos del catalán que se hablan en Valencia, las Islas Baleares y otras regiones de España.

Bilbao
Santiago de Compostela
ESPAÑA
Barcelona
★ Madrid
Sevilla

España es un país en donde se hablan varias lenguas.

WWW

You can investigate these cultural topics in more detail on the *¿Sabías que... ?* Online Learning Center: **www.mhhe.com/sabiasque5**.

COLOMBIA

ECUADOR

PERÚ

BOLIVIA

PARAGUAY

CHILE

ARGENTINA

En la región andina, hay unos 13 millones de hablantes del **quechua,** la lengua de los incas. A diferencia del español, el quechua utiliza muchos sufijos para expresar conceptos como la distancia, la posesión, cuándo, dónde, etcétera.

casa = *wasi*
de la casa = *wasip*
en la casa = *wasipi*
mi casa = *wasii*
casas = *wasikuna*
mis casas = *wasiikuna*

En el sur de Chile y la Argentina vive una tribu indígena llamada los mapuches. Como las demás[a] lenguas indígenas, el **mapuche** es muy diferente de las lenguas europeas.

―――――――
[a]las... *other*

El **guaraní** es una lengua indígena que se habla principalmente en el Paraguay. Es muy diferente de las demás lenguas que se hablan en Sudamérica.

¿Habla español María? = *María piko oñe'ê España ñe'ême?*

ACTIVIDAD ¿Qué recuerdas?

Choose the best answer to the following sentences.

1. El quechua es una lengua indígena que utiliza muchos _____.

   a. adjetivos   b. latinismos   c. sufijos   d. adverbios

2. El guaraní es una lengua hablada en _____.

   a. España   b. Bolivia   c. Colombia   d. el Paraguay

3. En Barcelona, Valencia y las Islas Baleares se hablan dialectos del _____.

   a. gallego   b. catalán   c. vasco   d. portugués

4. El quechua es la lengua de los _____.

   a. mayas   b. incas   c. aztecas   d. mapuches

5. El mapuche se habla en _____.

   a. Chile   b. el Ecuador   c. el Perú   d. España

NAVEGANDO LA RED

Select *one* of the following activities. Then present your findings to the class.

1. Busca la siguiente información sobre una lengua indígena hablada en México o Centroamérica.

   a. el nombre de una tribu indígena y su lengua
   b. el número de hablantes que hay
   c. el nombre de los países o regiones donde se habla esa lengua
   d. Da algunos ejemplos de palabras que son diferentes o similares al español.

2. Busca algunas palabras del español caribeño que son de origen africano y apunta su significado (*meaning*) en inglés.

VOCABULARIO COMPRENSIVO

La familia nuclear — The Immediate Family

la esposa (mujer)	wife
el esposo (marido)	husband
los esposos	married couple
el/la hermanastro/a	stepbrother, stepsister
el/la hermano/a	brother, sister
los hermanos	brothers and sisters, siblings
el/la hijo/a	son, daughter
los hijos	children
la madrastra	stepmother
la madre	mother
la madre soltera	single mother
el/la medio/a hermano/a	half brother, half sister
el padrastro	stepfather
el padre	father
el padre soltero	single father
los padres	parents
la pareja	couple; partner

La familia «extendida» — The Extended Family

el/la abuelo/a	grandfather, grandmother
los abuelos	grandparents
el/la cuñado/a	brother-in-law, sister-in-law
el/la nieto/a	grandson, granddaughter
los nietos	grandchildren
el/la primo/a	cousin
el/la sobrino/a	nephew, niece
el/la suegro/a	father-in-law, mother-in-law
los suegros	in-laws
el/la tío/a	uncle, aunt
los tíos	aunts and uncles

Para describir a los parientes — Describing Relatives

es...	he/she is . . .
soltero/a	single
viudo/a	a widower, widow
está...	he/she is . . .
casado/a	married
divorciado/a	divorced
muerto/a	dead
vivo/a	alive
ya murió	he/she already died
mayor	older
el/la mayor	oldest
menor	younger
el/la menor	youngest

Para hacer preguntas — Asking Questions

¿cómo?	how?
¿cuál?, ¿cuáles?	which?, what?
¿cuándo? (R)	when?
¿cuántos/as? (R)	how many?
¿dónde? (R)	where?
¿qué? (R)	what?, which?
¿quién?, ¿quiénes? (R)	who?

Otras palabras y expresiones útiles

el apellido	last name
el/la gemelo/a	twin
el pariente	relative
el perro	dog
nuevo/a (R)	new
pequeño/a	small
simpático/a (R)	nice, pleasant
tener... años	to be . . . years old

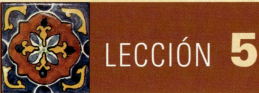

LECCIÓN **5**

Check out the following media resources to complement this lesson:

 Online *Manual*

 Video on CD

 Online Learning Center

 ActivityPak

¿A quién te pareces?

In this lesson, you will explore the topic of family resemblances. As you do so, you will

◆ learn to describe people's physical appearance and to understand descriptions given by others

◆ talk about family resemblances

◆ learn about true reflexives and reciprocal reflexive constructions and use these to talk about relationships among family members and friends

◆ continue to use adjectives

◆ learn the difference between the verbs **saber** and **conocer**

◆ learn more about the verb **estar**

◆ review comparisons with **más** and **menos**

ALTO Before beginning this lesson, look over the **Intercambio** activity on page 155. This is the activity you will be working toward throughout the lesson.

Nos parecemos, ¿no?

Características físicas

VOCABULARIO

¿Cómo es? (I)

Describing people's physical features

el pelo rizado
Es alto.
el pelo lacio
el pelo negro
el pelo rubio
el mentón
los ojos azules

los ojos castaños
Es de estatura mediana.
pelirrojo
las mejillas
los ojos verdes
las orejas
las pecas
el pelo canoso
Es baja.
la nariz grande

Rosario Maira   Heriberto Rodríguez   Evelyn Roman   Bobby Feldman   Marisela González

Vocabulario útil

describir	to describe	**moreno/a**	dark-haired; dark-skinned
la cara	face		
la característica física	physical characteristic, trait	**¿Cómo es?**	What does he (she) look like?
los rasgos	traits (*usually facial features*)	**más alto/a (que)**	taller (than)
		menos grande (que)	smaller (than)
		el/la más alto/a (de)	the tallest
calvo/a	bald	**el/la menos grande (de)**	the smallest

COMUNICACIÓN

ACTIVIDAD A ¿Quién es?

Paso 1 Da el nombre de la persona que ves en los dibujos de la página anterior.

1. ¿Quién tiene los ojos castaños?
2. ¿Quién es pelirrojo?
3. ¿Quién tiene el pelo rubio?
4. ¿Quién es moreno?

5. ¿Quién tiene las orejas grandes?
6. ¿Quién es baja?
7. ¿Quién tiene el pelo rizado?
8. ¿Quién tiene el pelo lacio?

 Paso 2 Tu profesor(a) va a describir a una persona que está en los mismos dibujos. ¿A quién describe?

ACTIVIDAD B Personas famosas

Escucha lo que dice el profesor (la profesora). Para cada característica física, da el nombre de una persona famosa que la tiene o que es así o que la tenía (*had it*) o era (*was*) así si ya murió.

1... **2**... **3**... **4**... **5**... **6**... **7**... **8**...

ACTIVIDAD C Otras personas famosas

Descríbele las características físicas de una persona famosa a un compañero (una compañera) sin decirle el nombre de la persona famosa. Tu compañero/a debe adivinar quién es.

MODELO E1: Es una persona baja. Tiene ojos grandes y pelo azul. Lleva el pelo muy alto. Es madre.
E2: Es Marge Simpson.

ACTIVIDAD D Los compañeros de clase

Paso 1 Mira a las personas de la clase y observa algunas de sus características físicas. Luego cierra los ojos y escucha la descripción que da el profesor (la profesora).

Paso 2 Escribe los nombres de todas las personas en la clase que tienen los rasgos físicos que el profesor (la profesora) describe.

Paso 3 Compara tu lista con la de tus compañeros de clase. La clase debe eliminar los nombres que no deben estar en la lista y preparar una lista de finalistas.

Paso 4 Escucha mientras (*while*) el profesor (la profesora) da más información sobre la persona. De las personas que están en la lista de finalistas, ¿a quién describe?

1. (*La Guajira, Colombia*)

2. (*Madrid, España*)

3. (*Caracas, Venezuela*)

4. (*Mazatlán, México*)

*Las características físicas de los hispanos varían mucho de país a país
y de región a región. ¿Cómo describirías* (would you describe) *a las
personas de las fotos?*

GRAMÁTICA

¿Quién es más alto?

Making comparisons

Remember that **más** and **menos** can be used with adjectives and nouns
to make comparisons. The invariant form of **mucho** can be used to
express that the difference is great when an adjective is used but must
agree when a noun is used.

Mi herman*a* es **más alt*a* que** yo.
Mi pel*o* es **(mucho) más rizad*o* que** el pelo de mis hermanos.
Mi hermano tiene **(much*as*) menos pec*as* que** yo.

Don't forget that adjectives must agree with the person or thing they
describe.

ACTIVIDAD E ¿Cuál es?

Paso 1 Indica qué oraciones se te aplican.

1. **a.** Soy más alto/a que mi padre (hermano, abuelo, tío, etcétera).
   b. Soy menos alto/a que mi padre (hermano, abuelo, tío, etcétera).
   c. Somos de la misma estatura.
2. **a.** Soy más alto/a que mi madre (hermana, abuela, tía, etcétera).
   b. Soy menos alto/a que mi madre (hermana, abuela, tía, etcétera).
   c. Somos de la misma estatura.

Paso 2 ¿Hay diferencias entre los hombres y las mujeres de la clase? ¿Suelen ser todos más altos que su madre o sólo los hombres son más altos? ¿Y en comparación con su padre?

COMUNICACIÓN

ACTIVIDAD F Las parejas

Paso 1 Utilizando los adjetivos a continuación, haz comparaciones entre tu mamá y tu papá, tu abuelo y tu abuela, tu tío y tu tía, etcétera. Puedes sustituir un adjetivo, pero debes usar por lo menos dos de la lista.

cómico/a   delgado/a   extrovertido/a   optimista*

Paso 2 Como clase compartan (*share*) sus comparaciones. Con la información compartida, ¿pueden decir si todos están de acuerdo con lo siguiente?

En un matrimonio, los opuestos se atraen (*attract each other*).

VOCABULARIO

¿Nos parecemos?

Talking about family resemblances

Twins and triplets may be identical, but most of the time brothers and sisters have only some similar physical characteristics. To talk about whether two people resemble each other, the verb **parecerse** is used.

Juan y Roberto **se parecen.**	*Juan and Roberto look like each other.*
Mi hermana y yo **nos parecemos.**	*My sister and I look like each other.*
Me parezco a mi padre.	*I look like my father.*

You can also use the adjective **parecido/a** with the verb **ser** to describe resemblances and similarities.

Mi hermana y mi madre **son** muy **parecidas.**	*My sister and my mother are very similar (much alike).*
Soy muy **parecido** a mi padre.	*I'm very much like my father.*

---

*Adjectives ending in **-ista** do not change according to gender. However, they do for number. Ell**os** son muy optimist**as.**

Julio Iglesias y su hijo Enrique. Los dos son cantantes. ¿En qué más se parecen?

ACTIVIDAD G ¿Es verdad?

¿Cuál de las siguientes oraciones describe tu situación?

SOBRE TUS HERMANOS

1. ☐ Mi(s) hermano(s) y yo nos parecemos.

2. ☐ Me parezco sólo a uno de mis hermanos.

3. ☐ No me parezco a ninguno de mis hermanos.

4. ☐ No tengo hermanos.

SOBRE TUS PADRES

5. ☐ Me parezco a mi padre.

6. ☐ Me parezco a mi madre.

7. ☐ Tengo algunas características de mi padre y otras de mi madre.

8. ☐ No me parezco ni a mi madre ni a mi padre.

SOBRE TUS OTROS PARIENTES (HIJOS, ABUELOS, ETCÉTERA)

9. Mi _____ y yo nos parecemos.

10. Mi _____ se parece más a _____.

Los hijos son la imagen de sus padres

COMUNICACIÓN

ACTIVIDAD H Mi familia y yo

Trae (*Bring*) a la clase una fotografía de un miembro de tu familia.
¿Pueden identificar a la persona de tu fotografía tus compañeros de clase?

MODELO ESTUDIANTE: La persona de la foto es el padre (el hermano, la madre, etcétera) de Jane porque se parecen.

PROFESOR(A): ¿En qué se parecen?

ESTUDIANTE: Los dos tienen los ojos azules y...

ACTIVIDAD I ¿Se parecen?

Paso 1 Selecciona una de las siguientes parejas y haz una lista de las características físicas que tienen en común. Luego haz otra lista de las características que los (las) hace diferentes.

- Danny DeVito y Arnold Schwarzenegger
- Madonna y Marilyn Monroe
- Fred Flintstone y Barney Rubble

- Mary Kate Olson y Ashley Olson
- Kate Hudson y Goldie Hawn
- Ashley Judd y Wynona Judd

Paso 2 Presenta la información del **Paso 1** a la clase. Luego la clase debe decidir si las dos personas se parecen mucho, poco o nada.

NAVEGANDO LA RED

Busca información sobre una persona famosa de habla española que tenga (*has*) hermanos. Imprime (*Print*) algunas fotos de esa persona y sus hermanos y tráelas a clase. Explica en qué se parecen estos hermanos y en qué no se parecen.

IDEAS PARA EXPLORAR

Otras características

VOCABULARIO

¿Cómo es? (II)

More on describing people

En muchos cuentos de hadas (*fairy tales*) el príncipe es **guapo, delgado** y **joven.**

En cambio, el gnomo suele ser **feo, gordo** y **viejo.**

Vocabulario útil

aventurero/a	adventurous	**reservado/a**	
cómico/a		**retraído/a**	reclusive
extrovertido/a		**serio/a**	
feliz	happy	**tímido/a**	shy
gregario/a		**triste**	sad

ACTIVIDAD A ¿De quién hablo?

Escucha el adjetivo que menciona tu profesor(a). ¿A cuál de los siguientes personajes describe? Basa tu respuesta en la película *Blanca Nieves* (*Snow White*) de Disney.

a. Blanca Nieves
b. Doc y Happy (dos enanos [*dwarfs*])
c. la Bruja (*the Witch*)
d. el Príncipe

1... **2**... **3**... **4**... **5**... **6**... **7**... **8**... **9**... **10**...

ACTIVIDAD B Descripciones famosas

Usando el nuevo vocabulario, da unos adjetivos para describir a los siguientes parientes famosos.

1. Martin y Charlie Sheen
2. Bill y Chelsea Clinton
3. Julio y Enrique Iglesias
4. ¿ ?
5. ¿ ?

ACTIVIDAD C Características familiares

Paso 1 Prepara una breve descripción, basándote en los modelos a continuación. La idea es ver si tienes algo en común con los miembros de tu familia en cuanto a la personalidad.

MODELOS   En mi familia nadie es tímido. Todos somos extrovertidos. Hablamos mucho y nos gusta estar con otras personas.

o

En mi familia algunos son reservados y otros no. Por ejemplo, mi papá es un poco reservado pero mi mamá es gregaria y aventurera. Yo no soy muy aventurero pero me parezco más a mi mamá.

Paso 2 Ahora comparte tu descripción con la clase. Después decidan todos si están de acuerdo con la siguiente oración.

De tal palo, tal astilla.   *Like father, like son.*

GRAMÁTICA

¿Cómo está?

Describing people's physical or mental state

You have learned that **ser** is used to describe inherent physical or personality traits—or at least a trait that the speaker views as a definitive characteristic of the person. Many of the same adjectives can be used with **estar** to express some kind of change from what is expected or what is viewed as inherent. Note that English sometimes uses a verb other than *to be* to indicate this change from what is expected.

Paco **es** gregario. Hoy **está** un poco reservado.
Paco is gregarious (by nature). Today he's (he seems) a bit reserved.

Mi tío bajó (*lost*) 30 kilos. ¡Está muy delgado!
My uncle lost 30 kilos. He looks so thin!

—Ángela, ¿qué te pasa? **Estás** muy **seria.**

When someone uses the adjective **guapo/a** with **estar,** the normal meaning is that the person described looks nice or looks better than ever and not that the person is necessarily ugly by nature.

Don't get confused thinking that **ser** implies *permanent* or that **estar** implies *temporary.* A change can be temporary *or* permanent. The matter here is the speaker's expectations and concept of the way the person (or thing) is supposed to be. Twenty years after losing 100 pounds and keeping it off, someone could say to another person:

Todavía (*Still*) estás muy delgado. ¿Cómo lo haces?

(You will learn more about this use of **estar** in later lessons.)

 ## ACTIVIDAD D ¿Esperado o inesperado?°

Expected or unexpected?

Escucha las oraciones que dice tu profesor(a) mientras describe a un amigo. Indica si la descripción representa algo esperado o inesperado.

1... **2**... **3**... **4**... **5**... **6**...

ACTIVIDAD E Correspondencias

En la columna A aparecen algunas oraciones que una persona le dice a otra. Escoge de la columna B la respuesta más lógica para cada oración. Sé cortés. (*Be polite.*)

A	B
1. ____ ¡Estás muy guapo!	**a.** ¡Qué va! Te ves bien. (*No way! You look good.*)
2. ____ Estás un poco retraído.	**b.** ¿Por qué? ¿Qué pasó?
3. ____ Estoy fea.	**c.** Gracias.
4. ____ Estoy muy feliz.	**d.** Tengo un examen mañana y mucha tarea también.

 **COMUNICACIÓN**

 ## ACTIVIDAD F ¿Cuándo cambias de personalidad?

Paso 1 Utilizando el modelo, escribe algunas oraciones sobre cómo eres y cómo cambias de personalidad en ciertas situaciones. Si prefieres, puedes hablar de un hermano (una hermana), tu mamá, tu papá, un tío (una tía), etcétera.

MODELO en una situación formal →
Normalmente soy cómico. Pero en una situación formal, estoy muy serio.

1. entre buenos amigos
2. en público
3. en una fiesta
4. en clase
5. en una entrevista (*interview*)
6. en una primera cita (*date*)

Paso 2 Ahora comparte tus descripciones con la clase. ¿Hay semejanzas (*similarities*) en la clase?

GRAMÁTICA

¿La conoces?

Talking about knowing someone

You have already encountered the verb **saber** to express *to know*. Remember that **saber** is restricted in use to expressing the concept of knowing something such as a fact or knowing that something has happened, will happen, and so forth.

> **Sé** que mi profesor habla español.
> Todos **sabemos** el número de teléfono del profesor, ¿no?
> ¿No **sabes** si viene Tomás?

The verb **conocer** also translates into English as *to know* but means a different kind of knowing. **Conocer** is used when talking about knowing a person (as in having met that person). It can also be used to talk about *being familiar with* a place or thing.

> **Conozco** bien a mis compañeros de clase pero no **conozco** bien al profesor.
> ¿**Conoces** San José? Es muy lindo.
> No **conozco** la música de Shakira. ¿Es buena?

Saber is used to talk about people only when expressing knowledge of information about a person.

> No **sé** si Jaime es inteligente o no. De hecho (*In fact*), no **sé** mucho de Jaime.
> **Sé** muy poco de los Gómez. ¿Dónde viven?

—¿**Conoces** a Elena?
—Sí, pero no muy bien. ¿Por qué?

ACTIVIDAD G ¿Sabemos o conocemos?

Indica si cada oración debe comenzar por **Sabemos** o **Conocemos**. Luego indica si la oración es cierta (C) o falsa (F) para la clase.

	C	F
1. _____ que muchos de esta clase tienen *iPod*.	☐	☐
2. _____ bien el sistema político de este país.	☐	☐
3. _____ al presidente (a la presidenta) de la universidad.	☐	☐
4. No _____ si Jennifer López es puertorriqueña o cubana.	☐	☐
5. No _____ nada de las películas de Steven Spielberg.	☐	☐
6. _____ bastante bien el libro *¿Sabías que... ?*	☐	☐

COMUNICACIÓN

ACTIVIDAD H ¿Conocemos bien al profesor (a la profesora)?

Paso 1 Escribe por lo menos (*at least*) tres cosas que sabes del profesor (de la profesora). Luego escribe tres cosas que *no* sabes de él (ella) con certeza (*certainty*) pero que crees que son ciertas.

> MODELOS   Sé que está casado/a.
>
> Creo que no tiene hijos.

Paso 2 Comparte tus oraciones con la clase mientras tu profesor(a) dice si son ciertas o no.

Paso 3 ¿Cuál de las siguientes ideas expresa mejor los resultados de esta actividad?

☐ Conocemos muy bien al profesor (a la profesora). Es evidente que sabemos mucho de él (ella).

☐ Conocemos al profesor (a la profesora) aunque hay cosas de su vida que no sabemos.

☐ No conocemos al profesor (a la profesora) y parece que no sabemos mucho de él (ella).

ACTIVIDAD I ¿Conoces bien a todos?

Paso 1 ¿Conoces bien a todos tus compañeros de clase? Si no, escoge a una persona que no conoces muy bien y hazle preguntas sobre los siguientes temas.

◆ el tamaño (*size*) de su familia

◆ si prefiere los perros o los gatos

◆ algo de su personalidad

Paso 2 Ahora escribe un breve párrafo sobre la persona, utilizando el modelo a continuación. Uno o dos voluntarios va a leer su párrafo a la clase.

MODELO Yo hablé con ＿＿＿. Ahora lo (la) conozco un poco mejor. Por ejemplo, ahora sé que ＿＿＿. También ＿＿＿.

IDEAS PARA EXPLORAR

Más sobre las relaciones familiares

GRAMÁTICA

¿Te conoces bien?

True reflexive constructions

me	despierto	nos	despertamos
te	despiertas	os	despertáis
se	despierta	se	despiertan
se	despierta	se	despiertan

Cuando un perro **se mira** en el espejo (*mirror*), ¿comprende que no es otro perro?

In **Lección 4,** you learned about objects and object pronouns. These are relatively easy concepts to understand, and objects and object pronouns aren't difficult to distinguish from subjects. But what if subjects and objects refer to the same person or persons? For example, with the verb *to see,* a person can either *see someone else* or can go to a mirror and *see himself or herself* in the reflection. The second type of construction is called a true reflexive.

Any verb that can have an object can be reflexive. To make a verb reflexive, English often uses a pronoun with -*self* or -*selves* (*myself, yourselves,* and so forth). Spanish simply uses the regular object pronouns for first and second person (singular and plural), and the special pronoun **se** for third person.

Comprendo a mi hermanito.	*I understand my little brother.*
Me comprendo.	*I understand myself.*
Juan mira a María.	*Juan looks at María.*
Juan **se** mira.	*Juan looks at himself.*

In **Unidad 1,** you learned some reflexive verbs, including **levantarse** and **despertarse.**

(Yo) **Me levanto** muy temprano.
(Tú) **Te despiertas** a las 6.00 todos los días.
(Ud.) **Se levanta** temprano los fines de semana.
(Él/Ella) **Se acuesta** tarde.
(Nosotros/as) **Nos despertamos** a las 7.30.
(Uds.) **Se acuestan** bastante temprano.
(Ellos/Ellas) **Se levantan** rápidamente.

Levantar literally means *to raise,* so when you say **Me levanto temprano** you are literally saying *I raise me* (i.e., *myself*) *early.* **Acostar** actually means *to put to bed.* When you say **María se acuesta** you are saying *María puts herself to bed.* Knowing that **despertar** means *to awaken* or *to wake up,* how does **Nos despertamos a las 7.30** literally translate in English? You're right if you said *We wake ourselves up at 7:30.*

The reflexive verbs you learned in **Unidad 1** can also be used nonreflexively when the subject and object are not the same. For example, María can wake (herself) up or she can wake up her mother.

María **se despierta.**
María **despierta a su mamá.**

María can also wake (herself) up or someone else can wake her up.

María **se despierta.**
El papá **despierta a María.**

In the following activities, pay attention to how the pronoun **se** indicates a reflexive action or event.

ACTIVIDAD A ¿Acciones reflexivas?

Indica cuál de las opciones capta mejor la idea principal, en cada caso.

1. Marcos tiene muy buena opinión de su primo Roberto. Considera que Roberto es un joven modelo. Marcos...

    a. ☐ admira a otra persona.   **b.** ☐ se admira.

2. Dolores es una persona interesante. Sabe muy bien cuáles son sus puntos fuertes y débiles (*weak*). Sabe lo que quiere de la vida y cómo lograrlo (*to achieve it*). Dolores...

   a. ☐ conoce bien a otra persona.   **b.** ☐ se conoce bien.

3. A Federico no le gusta su compañero de cuarto Rodolfo. Según Federico, Rodolfo no tiene ninguna cualidad buena. Federico...

   a. ☐ detesta a otra persona.   **b.** ☐ se detesta.

4. A Elena le gusta leer los libros de Carl Sagan. Cree que era un hombre muy inteligente y que sus ideas son muy interesantes. Elena...

   a. ☐ respeta a otra persona.   **b.** ☐ se respeta.

5. Mi tío Gregorio siempre habla solo. Y lo más interesante es que contesta sus propias preguntas. Mi tío...

   a. ☐ habla con otra persona.   **b.** ☐ se habla.

6. Marita siempre apunta información en un papel. Dice que si no lo hace ¡nunca recuerda (*remembers*) nada! Marita...

   a. ☐ escribe notas para otras personas.   **b.** ☐ se escribe notas.

7. A las 7.00 de la mañana, Jorge suele entrar en el cuarto de su compañero, Emilio. A Emilio le gusta dormir hasta muy tarde y no tiene energía por la mañana. Pero como tiene que trabajar a las 8.30, Jorge siempre...

   a. ☐ lo despierta.   **b.** ☐ se despierta.

ACTIVIDAD B Correspondencias

Paso 1 Con un compañero (una compañera), haz la correspondencia de cada acción reflexiva de la columna A con una conclusión de la columna B.

Si alguien...

A

1. se habla constantemente _____

2. se mira mucho en el espejo _____

3. se escribe recados (*notes*) todo el tiempo _____

4. se mantiene (*supports financially*) sin la ayuda de otros _____

5. se ofrece como voluntario para todo _____

6. se acuesta siempre a las 3.00 de la madrugada (*early morning*) _____

7. se adapta fácilmente a situaciones nuevas _____

8. se expresa bien _____

9. se impone (*imposes*) límites en lo que gasta cada mes _____

...podemos concluir que...

B

a. está loco.

b. tiene mucho tiempo libre.

c. es flexible.

d. es responsable.

e. es independiente.

f. maneja muy bien el lenguaje.

g. es narcisista.

h. tiene más energía de noche.

i. tiene mala memoria.

Paso 2 Indica si las siguientes oraciones son ciertas (C) o falsas (F) para ti.

	C	F
1. Me miro mucho en el espejo.	☐	☐
2. Me escribo recados para recordar cosas.	☐	☐
3. Me hablo constantemente.	☐	☐
4. Me adapto fácilmente a situaciones nuevas.	☐	☐
5. Me ofrezco como voluntario para todo.	☐	☐
6. Me expreso bien.	☐	☐
7. Me acuesto siempre a las 3.00 de la madrugada.	☐	☐
8. Me impongo límites en lo que gasto cada mes.	☐	☐
9. Me mantengo sin la ayuda de otra persona.	☐	☐

Paso 3 Compara lo que indicaste en el **Paso 2** con las acciones y las conclusiones del **Paso 1.** ¿Crees que tus respuestas reflejan bien algo de tu personalidad?

COMUNICACIÓN

ACTIVIDAD C ¿Se parecen?

Paso 1 Los estudiantes de la clase van a escoger a una persona que quieren entrevistar. Luego van a decidir con cuál de los parientes de esa persona lo (la) quieren comparar. Por ejemplo, pueden compararlo/la con su hermano, su hijo, su madre, etcétera. Utilizando cinco o más de las acciones reflexivas de la **Actividad B,** deben hacerle preguntas y apuntar las respuestas. (Pueden utilizar otras acciones reflexivas.)

MODELOS   ¿A qué hora te acuestas normalmente?
¿Y a qué hora se acuesta _____?

¿Te adaptas fácilmente a... ?
¿Y se adapta _____ fácilmente a... ?

Paso 2 ¿A qué conclusión llegan Uds. sobre su compañero/a y su pariente? ¿Se parecen mucho? ¿poco? ¿Se parecen sólo en ciertas cosas?

NAVEGANDO LA RED

Busca fotos de Frida Kahlo y sus parientes. ¿Tienen todos cejas (*eyebrows*) parecidas?

Mis abuelos, mis padres y yo (árbol genealógico) (*1936*) *por Frida Kahlo (mexicana, 1907–1954)*

GRAMÁTICA

¿Se abrazan Uds.?

(nosotros/as)	**nos comprendemos**
(vosotros/as)	**os comprendéis**
(Uds.)	**se comprenden**
(ellos/ellas)	**se comprenden**

In addition to Spanish reflexive constructions that have English equivalents with *-self* or *-selves,* reflexive constructions in Spanish can express a reciprocal action, that is, when two or more people do something *to each other.*

Los niños **se miran.**	*The children look at each other.*
Los hombres no **se escuchan.**	*The men don't listen to each other.*
¿Nos conocemos?	*Do we know each other?*

What do you think the underlined portion of the following sentence means?

Mi hija y mi esposa <u>no se comprenden</u>. ¿Qué voy a hacer?

The underlined part of the sentence expresses that the speaker's daughter and wife do not understand each other.

Context will usually help you determine whether a third person plural reflexive construction is reciprocal or means *-selves.*

ACTIVIDAD D ¿En qué orden?

Indica el orden (del 1 al 6) en que pasan las acciones en cada situación. Luego compara lo que escribiste con lo que escribió otro compañero (otra compañera).

María y Silvia son dos primas. Hace varias semanas que no tienen contacto la una con la otra. Pero un día...

_____ se abrazan.
_____ se despiden (*they say good-bye*).
_____ se hablan un rato.
_____ se llaman al día siguiente.
_____ se saludan.
_____ se ven.

Así se dice

Although the verb **llevar** usually means *to carry,* the reflexive form of **llevar** is used to express the concept of getting along with someone.

Me llevo bien con toda mi familia.
I get along well with everyone in my family.

Mi padre **no se lleva bien** con su padre, mi abuelo.
My father doesn't get along well with his father, my grandfather.

Llevarse bien/mal can also be used to express a reciprocal action.

Mis padres y yo **nos llevamos** muy bien.
My parents and I get along well (with each other).

ACTIVIDAD E ¿Sabías que... ?

Paso 1 Lee la selección **¿Sabías que... ?** ¿Es típica de este país la costumbre descrita (*described*)? ¿Cómo se saludan los amigos de tu edad en tu grupo?

¿Sabías que...

el contacto corporal entre los hispanos es mayor que entre los de ascendencia anglosajona? En España, por ejemplo, al saludarse y al despedirse dos personas, frecuentemente se besan ligeramente[a] en las mejillas. Esto es típico sobre todo entre dos mujeres y entre una mujer y un hombre pero no es costumbre entre los hombres. El beso es doble; es decir, las dos personas se besan en las dos mejillas. Frecuentemente, cuando se besan, las dos personas también se abrazan. Además, las dos personas no tienen que ser parientes ni amigos íntimos para besarse cuando se saludan.

En otras partes del mundo hispánico, es más común darse un solo beso. Abrazarse o no es cuestión de preferencia individual. Si visitas un país de habla española, deberías[b] observar cómo se saludan y se despiden las personas cuando se encuentran en la calle. Si no comprendes o no tienes oportunidad de observar estas costumbres, ¡pregúntaselo a una persona nativa del lugar que visitas![c]

[a]se... *they kiss lightly*   [b]*you should*   [c]¡pregúntaselo... *ask a native resident about it!*

Dos estudiantes se saludan en Madrid, España.

Paso 2 Lee la selección de nuevo (*again*) y subraya (*underline*) todos los verbos que representan acciones recíprocas. Compara tu trabajo con el de un compañero (una compañera) o con la clase. Luego di cuál sería (*would be*) la frase que le corresponde en inglés a cada frase subrayada. ¿Siempre se dice *each other* en inglés al referirse a una acción recíproca?

Lección 5   ¿A quién te pareces?   ciento cincuenta y tres   **153**

ACTIVIDAD F Una comparación

Paso 1 Indica si las siguientes acciones son típicas o no en tu familia. Puedes añadir (*add*) otra acción si quieres.

En mi familia…

	SÍ	NO
1. nos abrazamos cuando nos vemos.	☐	☐
2. nos besamos cuando nos vemos.	☐	☐
3. nos saludamos por la mañana.	☐	☐
4. nos llamamos mucho por teléfono.	☐	☐
5. nos apoyamos (*support emotionally*).	☐	☐
6. nos comprendemos bien.	☐	☐
7. ¿ ?	☐	☐

Paso 2 Utilizando las ideas del **Paso 1,** formula preguntas para hacerle una entrevista a un compañero (una compañera). Luego entrevista a esa persona.

MODELO   En tu familia, ¿se abrazan Uds. cuando se ven?

Paso 3 Escribe un breve párrafo en el que comparas a tu familia con la de tu compañero/a.

ACTIVIDAD G ¿Se llevan bien?

Paso 1 Lee la explicación **Así se dice** de la página 153. Luego indica si estás de acuerdo o no con cada afirmación a continuación.

	SÍ	NO
1. Las madres y las hijas se llevan mejor que (*better than*) los padres y las hijas.	☐	☐
2. Los padres y los hijos se llevan mejor que las madres y los hijos.	☐	☐
3. Los hermanos se llevan mejor cuando son pocos, por ejemplo, dos o tres.	☐	☐

Paso 2 Toda la clase va a compartir sus experiencias personales. Alguien debe tomar apuntes en la pizarra (*board*).

MODELO   En mi familia, todos se llevan bien. Mi madre y mis hermanos se llevan bien…

Paso 3 Ahora ¿qué cree la clase en cuanto a las afirmaciones del **Paso 1**? ¿Estás tú de acuerdo con tus compañeros/as?

ACTIVIDAD H Las relaciones íntimas

Paso 1 Una relación íntima es un tesoro (*treasure*), pero no es fácil lograr. Prepara una lista de lo que dos personas se hacen para tener una buena relación. Puedes comparar, si quieres, las siguientes relaciones

---

> ### Nota comunicativa
>
> A good way to keep a conversation going (and to hear more Spanish!) is to inquire what the other speaker thinks or how the topic relates to him or her. You can do this in a number of ways.
>
> Y tú, ¿qué crees? *or* Y Ud., ¿qué cree?
>
> ¿Qué crees tú? *or* ¿Qué cree Ud.?
>
> ¿Qué te parece? *or* ¿Qué le parece a Ud.?
>
> ¿Cómo lo ves tú? *or* ¿Cómo lo ve Ud.?

para ver si hay diferencias: dos buenos amigos, dos hermanos, un matrimonio (una pareja).

MODELO En un buen matrimonio, los esposos se comunican bien. Es igual entre dos buenos amigos: se comunican y se comprenden.

Vocabulario útil

abrazar	**besar**	**comunicar**	**hablar**
apoyar	**comprender**	**escuchar**	**respetar**

Paso 2 Basándote en el **Paso 1,** menciona a una pareja que crees que tiene una buena relación íntima.

MODELO Yo creo que ___ y ___ tienen una buena relación porque...

INTERCAMBIO

¿Cómo son?

Propósito: preparar una descripción de un compañero (una compañera) y de un miembro de su familia para contestar dos preguntas.

Papeles: las dos personas hablan y escuchan; una debe apuntar lo que dice la otra.

Paso 1 En esta actividad vas a entrevistar a un compañero (una compañera) para contestar dos preguntas.

1. ¿A quién de su familia se parece más tu compañero/a? ¿En qué sentido?
2. ¿Hay acciones que indican si son muy unidos/as o no? ¿Cuáles son?

Piensa en las preguntas que puedes hacerle para poder contestar estas preguntas. Por ejemplo: «¿Eres tímido/a o extrovertido/a? ¿Quién de tu familia es como tú?» o «¿Se llaman Uds. mucho por teléfono? ¿Se llevan bien?»

Paso 2 Entrevista a tu compañero/a y hazle las preguntas. Apunta toda la información relevante a las preguntas del **Paso 1.**

Paso 3 Con la información obtenida en el **Paso 2,** contesta cada pregunta del **Paso 1** con unas 50 palabras (100 en total). Prepárate bien por si acaso (*just in case*) el profesor (la profesora) te pide que hagas (*asks you to make*) una presentación oral.

MODELOS Juan y su papá se parecen mucho. Los dos son gregarios y nada tímidos. Son aventureros también. Es evidente que son muy unidos. Se abrazan cuando se ven. Se hablan por teléfono cada semana...

o

Juan no se parece mucho a sus hermanos. Sus hermanos son más altos que él. También son más reservados. Pero son bastante unidos...

Vistazos culturales
El mestizaje en el mundo hispano

¿Sabías que... el mestizaje ha influido[a] mucho en la composición racial de muchos países hispanos? El mestizaje se define como la mezcla de razas[b] diferentes. En Latinoamérica el mestizaje se refiere a la mezcla de la herencia[c] española con la herencia indígena, un proceso que se llevó a cabo[d] durante la conquista y el período colonial. Las personas de mezcla española e indígena se llaman **mestizos.** Hay muchos mestizos en México, en muchas partes de Centroamérica y en varios países sudamericanos como Chile y el Paraguay. Sin embargo, en otras regiones, en el Uruguay por ejemplo, el número de mestizos es muy bajo.

[a]*ha... has influenced* [b]*races* [c]*heritage* [d]*se... was carried out*

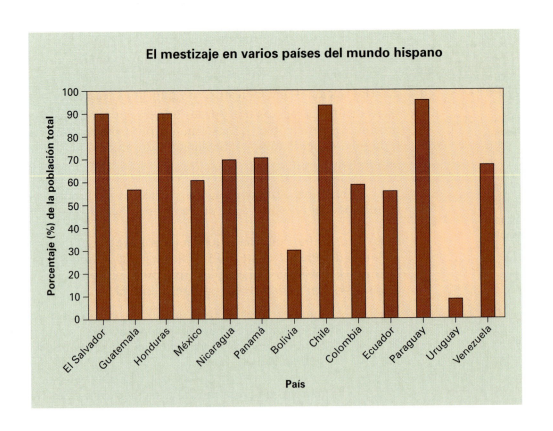

El mestizaje en varios países del mundo hispano

Porcentaje (%) de la población total

País

You can investigate these cultural topics in more detail on the ¿*Sabías que...* ? Online Learning Center: **www.mhhe.com/sabiasque5**.

La influencia europea

En **México** no todas las personas tienen el pelo negro y la piel morena. Muchos mexicanos tienen los ojos y la piel claros,[a] una muestra[b] de la herencia europea en la composición racial del país.

———————
[a]*light-colored*   [b]*indicación*

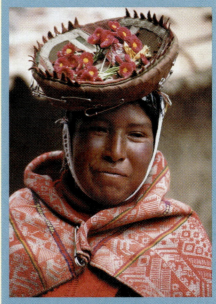

La influencia de los incas

En el **Perú** los mestizos tienen rasgos físicos heredados[a] de los incas y de los españoles.

———————————————
[a]*inherited*

La influencia maya

En **Centroamérica** los indígenas mayas se casaron y tuvieron hijos con los españoles.

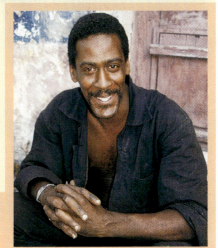

La influencia africana

En el **Caribe** el mestizaje se refiere más que nada a la mezcla de las herencias española y africana. Durante la conquista y el período colonial, muchas poblaciones indígenas del Caribe fueron eliminadas por la viruela.[a] Como consecuencia, se importaron muchos esclavos de África para trabajar en las minas y los cañaverales de azúcar.[b] En Cuba, Puerto Rico, la República Dominicana, así como en partes de Colombia, Panamá y Venezuela, hay muchas personas de herencia española y africana.

———————
[a]*smallpox*   [b]*cañaverales... sugarcane fields*

ACTIVIDAD ¿Qué recuerdas?

Indica si cada oración es cierta (C) o falsa (F).

    C   **F**

1. El porcentaje (%) de la población mestiza es más alto en Chile que en Bolivia. ☐ ☐

2. En el Caribe el mestizaje se refiere más que nada a la mezcla de las herencias indígena y española. ☐ ☐

3. En cuanto a Centroamérica, el porcentaje de la población mestiza es más alto en El Salvador y Honduras. ☐ ☐

4. El mestizaje es un fenómeno que influye mucho en la población del Uruguay. ☐ ☐

5. Las poblaciones indígenas del Caribe fueron eliminadas por la viruela. ☐ ☐

NAVEGANDO LA RED

Escoge *una* de las siguientes actividades. Luego presenta tus resultados a la clase.

1. La composición racial del Uruguay y de la Argentina es influida por la presencia de muchos inmigrantes europeos. Escoge uno de estos países y busca información sobre la inmigración europea en el país para contestar las siguientes preguntas.
   a. ¿Cuándo llegaron de Europa los inmigrantes? ¿En qué año(s)?
   b. ¿Cuántos inmigrantes llegaron y de qué países salieron?
   c. ¿Por qué razones salieron estos grupos de su país natal (*of birth*)?

2. El mestizaje en Cuba está formado por la mezcla de varios grupos étnicos, incluyendo a unas pocas razas indígenas e inmigrantes europeos y africanos. Busca y apunta la siguiente información sobre el mestizaje en Cuba.
   a. Haz una lista de los grupos étnicos que contribuyen a la composición racial de Cuba.
   b. Menciona las fechas de las grandes inmigraciones y el número aproximado de inmigrantes que entraron al país.

VOCABULARIO COMPRENSIVO

Características físicas / Physical Characteristics

la cara	face
las mejillas	cheeks
el mentón	chin
la nariz	nose
las orejas	ears
las pecas	freckles
la estatura	height
alto/a	tall
bajo/a	short
de estatura mediana	of medium height
los ojos	eyes
azules	blue
castaños	brown
verdes	green
el pelo	hair
calvo	bald
canoso	gray
lacio	straight
moreno	dark
negro	black
pelirrojo	red-headed
rizado	curly
rubio	blond
los rasgos	traits (*usually facial features*)
delgado/a	thin
feo/a	ugly
gordo/a	fat
guapo/a	good-looking
joven	young
moreno/a	dark-skinned
viejo/a	old
¿De qué color es (son)... ?	What color is (are) . . . ?
¿De qué estatura es?	What height is he (she)?

Características de la personalidad / Personality Traits

feliz	happy
retraído/a	solitary, reclusive
triste	sad

Cognados: aventurero/a, extrovertido/a, gregario/a, reservado/a, serio/a (R), tímido/a

Para dar opiniones / Giving Opinions

asegurar	to assure
conocer (conozco) (R)	to be acquainted with
creer	to believe
opinar	to think, have the opinion
parecer (parezco)	to seem
pensar (ie) (R)	to think
saber (*irreg.*) (R)	to know (a fact)
es...	it is . . .
cierto	certain
cosa sabida	a known fact
evidente	evident
indudable	without a doubt
obvio	obvious
está claro	it's clear

Otras palabras y expresiones útiles

grande	big
parecido/a	similar
abrazar	to hug
adaptar	to adapt, adjust
afeitar	to shave (*someone*)
apoyar	to support (*emotionally*)
bañar	to bathe (*someone or something*)
besar	to kiss
comprender	to understand
describir	to describe
despedir (i, i)	to say good-bye
imponer (*irreg.*)	to impose
llevar	to carry
llevarse bien (mal)	to get along well (poorly)
mantener (*irreg.*)	to support (*financially*)
parecerse (me parezco)	to resemble, look like
saludar	to greet

¿Cómo es? / What Does He/She Look Like?

más alto/a (que)	taller (than)
menos grande (que)	smaller (than)
el/la más alto/a (de)	the tallest
el/la menos grande (de)	the smallest

LECCIÓN 6

Check out the following media resources to complement this lesson:

 Online *Manual*

 Video on CD

 Online Learning Center

 ActivityPak

¿Y el tamaño de la familia?

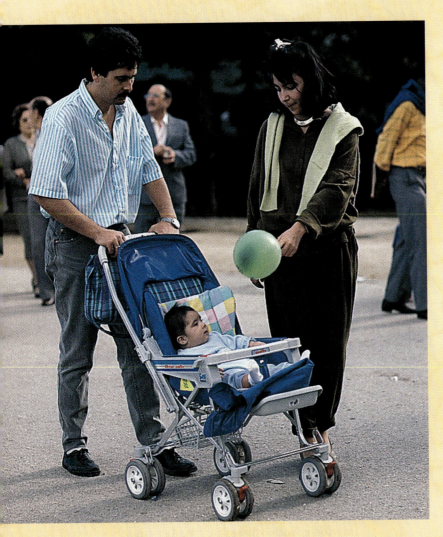

Un matrimonio (married couple) *español de hoy día no tiene una familia tan grande como la que tenían sus abuelos.*

In this lesson, you'll explore how families used to be and how they are now. You will

- read about the changing size of families
- consider how things used to be compared to how they are now
- learn numbers 30–199 in order to talk about ages and decades
- learn numbers 200–2030 in order to talk about dates and centuries
- begin to use the *imperfect* tense
- learn to make comparisons of equality
- learn to use the progressive with **estar**

ALTO Before beginning this lesson, look over the **Composición** activity on pages 177–179. This is the activity you will be working toward throughout the lesson.

VOCABULARIO

¿Qué edad?

Numbers 30–199 and talking about people's age

*¿Quién **tiene** más o menos **cuarenta años** en la fotografía? ¿Quién **tiene sesenta años** o más?*

30	**treinta**	31	**treinta y uno**
40	**cuarenta**	32	**treinta y dos**
50	**cincuenta**	101	**ciento uno**
60	**sesenta**	102	**ciento dos**
70	**setenta**	120	**ciento veinte**
80	**ochenta**		
90	**noventa**		**tener... años**
100	**cien**		to be . . . years old

ACTIVIDAD A ¿Qué número?

Escucha los números que dice el profesor (la profesora). Escribe las cifras (*numbers*) apropiadas.

MODELO   PROFESOR(A): Treinta y cinco
           ESTUDIANTE: 35

1...   **2**...   **3**...   etcétera

ACTIVIDAD B Más números

Sin mirar los números de arriba (*above*), lee cada número a continuación y escribe las cifras correctas. Compáralas con las de otra persona en la clase.

1. _____ cincuenta y cinco
2. _____ noventa y ocho
3. _____ setenta y seis
4. _____ cuarenta y nueve
5. _____ ciento cincuenta y cuatro

ACTIVIDAD C Los números primos

Los números primos son los números que sólo se pueden dividir por ellos mismos o por 1 para obtener un número entero (*whole*). Por ejemplo, 5 es un número primo porque sólo se puede dividir por 5 o por 1 para obtener un número entero: $5 \div 1 = 5$ y $5 \div 5 = 1$, pero $5 \div 2 = 2,5$ y $5 \div 3 = 1,66$. El número 9 no es primo porque se puede dividir por 3 para obtener un numero entero: $9 \div 3 = 3$. ¿Qué números primos existen entre 30 y 199? Con otra persona, haz una lista de por lo menos 5 números primos entre 30 y 199 y compártela con la clase.

COMUNICACIÓN

ACTIVIDAD D Edades

Paso 1 Entrevista a otra persona de la clase para saber la edad de sus padres. Si la persona indicada ya murió, escribe **ya murió.**

Paso 2 Comparen los resultados obtenidos por todos los estudiantes de la clase.

1. ¿Quién de la clase tiene el padre más viejo?
2. ¿Quién tiene la madre más vieja?
3. ¿Quién tiene la madre más joven?
4. ¿Quién tiene el padre más joven?

ACTIVIDAD E ¿Sabías que... ?

Paso 1 Lee la selección **¿Sabías que... ?** Después contesta las siguientes preguntas.

1. ¿En dónde se vive más años de vida saludable, ¿en España, Cuba o los Estados Unidos?
2. ¿Cuántos años de vida saludable pierde (*loses*), más o menos, la persona típica en España?

Paso 2 ¿Llevan una larga vida las personas de tu familia? Habla con tus padres o abuelos y luego reporta su respuesta a la clase.

Así se dice

When 31, 41, 51, and so forth are followed by a noun, the number must end in **un** or **una** to show gender agreement.

treinta y **un** años
treinta y **una** familias
cincuenta y **un**
números
cincuenta y **una** casas

Did you note that the number is not pluralized, that is, no **-s** is added?

¿Sabías que...

en España se vive más? Según los nuevos datos, la esperanza de vida[a] en España es de 78,1 años, mientras que en los Estados Unidos es menos: 76,6 años. Sin embargo, los nuevos cálculos de la Organización Mundial de la Salud[b] ofrecen un nuevo tipo de dato: esperanza de vida saludable.[c] Con este cálculo, se establece el número de años que una persona puede esperar vivir en buena salud. En España esta cifra es de 72,8 años, mientras que en los Estados Unidos es de 70 años. En Latinoamérica, el país con mayor esperanza de vida saludable es Cuba: 68,4 años. ¿Y cuál es el país de mayor esperanza de vida saludable en el mundo? El Japón, con unos 74,5 años.

Campol, España

[a]esperanza... *life expectancy*   [b]Organización... *World Health Organization*   [c]healthy

---

NAVEGANDO LA RED

Busca más información sobre la esperanza de vida saludable en por lo menos otros dos países. ¿Cómo se comparan con lo que se dice de España?

VOCABULARIO

¿En qué año... ?

200	**doscientos**	900	**novecientos**
300	**trescientos**	1000	**mil**
400	**cuatrocientos**	1851	**mil ochocientos cincuenta**
500	**quinientos**		**y uno**
600	**seiscientos**	2000	**dos mil**
700	**setecientos**	2030	**dos mil treinta**
800	**ochocientos**		

Cada vez menos hijos

En sólo dos décadas, el
número de hijos por mujer en España
desciende el 50% del 2,2 al 1,1.

NÚMERO DE HIJOS POR MUJER

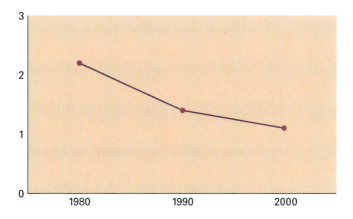

Fuente: Instituto
Nacional de
Estadística de
España

Vocabulario útil

la década   **el siglo** *century*
  la década de los 90   el siglo pasado
la época   el siglo XX
  una época anterior

ACTIVIDAD F ¿Qué siglo?

Escribe el año que oyes. Luego indica a qué siglo corresponde.

1. _____ **a.** el siglo XV   **b.** el siglo XVI
2. _____ **a.** el siglo XVIII   **b.** el siglo XVII
3. _____ **a.** el siglo XIII   **b.** el siglo XIV
4. _____ **a.** el siglo XIX   **b.** el siglo XX
5. _____ **a.** el siglo XVII   **b.** el siglo XVI

Así se dice

A tricky aspect of expressing hundreds in Spanish is that they must agree in gender and number with the noun they modify. Don't be too concerned about this detail. For now, just be aware of it!

doscientos hombres
doscientas mujeres
mil quinient**os** y **un**
perros
mil quinient**as** y **una**
universidades

ACTIVIDAD G Fechas° históricas

Dates

Paso 1 ¿Qué sabes o recuerdas de la historia del mundo hispano? Escribe los años que lee el profesor (la profesora).

1. _____   4. _____
2. _____   5. _____
3. _____   6. _____

Paso 2 Haz la correspondencia entre los años del **Paso 1** y los acontecimientos (*events*) históricos a continuación.

a. Cristóbal Colón llegó a América.
b. Guerra entre México y los Estados Unidos. El territorio desde Texas hasta California pasó a manos (*hands*) norteamericanas.
c. Empezó la Revolución Mexicana.
d. Los moros invadieron España donde permanecieron (*they remained*) hasta el siglo XV.
e. Guerra entre España y los Estados Unidos. Cuba, Puerto Rico, las Islas Filipinas y otros territorios pasaron a manos norteamericanas.
f. Se publicó la primera parte de la novela de Miguel de Cervantes *El ingenioso hidalgo don Quijote de la Mancha.*

Consejo práctico

Numbers are often difficult to learn in another language. For added practice, you might consider the following ideas.

◆ Write out in Spanish telephone numbers you frequently call (**tres, cincuenta y cinco, sesenta y uno, noventa y cuatro** for 355-6194) and keep these by your phone.

◆ Every time you dial a number on the phone, try to say it in Spanish as you dial.

◆ Before doing homework, write out or say aloud in Spanish the number of pages you have to read, what pages you have read, and so forth.

◆ If you are a sports fan, keep track of players' numbers, final scores of a game, and so forth, in Spanish.

Doing this will greatly improve your ability to learn numbers in Spanish!

COMUNICACIÓN

ACTIVIDAD H Datos biográficos

Algunas personas (voluntarias) les dicen a los miembros de la clase cuántos años tienen. La clase debe decir en qué año nació cada persona. ¿Pueden Uds. adivinar en qué año nació el profesor (la profesora)?

GRAMÁTICA

¿Está cambiando?

In Spanish, the verb **estar** can be used with a special verb form to express the present progressive (e.g., *He is working. I am reading. The world is changing.*) In Spanish, this special verb form always ends in **-ando** or **-iendo**.

El mundo está **cambiando.**	*The world is changing.*
Graciela está **comiendo.**	*Graciela is eating.*

With verbs such as **creer, leer,** and **huir** (*to flee*), in which a vowel precedes the **-er** or **-ir** ending, **-yendo** is used to keep from having three vowels together.

El gato está **huyendo.**	*The cat is fleeing.*
Ramón está **leyendo.**	*Ramón is reading.*

The present progressive is used only to express an action or event that is in progress. It can never be used as in English to express future meaning, in which case the simple present tense is used.

Raquel **está saliendo.**	*Raquel is leaving (right now).*
Raquel **sale** mañana.	*Raquel is leaving tomorrow.*

Unlike English, Spanish can also use the simple present tense with a progressive meaning in most circumstances.

¿Qué **haces** en estos días?	*What are you doing these days?*
¿**Sales** ahora?	*Are you leaving now?*
Llueve.	*It's raining.*

ACTIVIDAD I ¿Qué están haciendo?

Indica qué están haciendo las siguientes personas en este momento.

En este momento...

1. mi mamá (abuela, tía, etcétera) está _____.
2. mi papá (abuelo, tío, etcétera) está _____.
3. mi hermano/a (primo/a, hijo/a, etcétera) está _____.
4. mi mejor amigo/a está _____.
5. mi profesor(a) de español está _____.
6. mi vecino/a (*neighbor*) está _____.

a. comiendo algo
b. durmiendo*
c. escribiendo algo
d. leyendo algo
e. preparando algo para comer
f. trabajando
g. viendo la televisión
h. ¿ ?

---

*Verbs that end in **-ir** and have a stem change in the third person preterite tense have the same stem change in the **-ndo** form: **morir** → **m**u**rió** → **m**u**riendo**; **pedir** → **p**i**dió** → **p**i**diendo**.

ACTIVIDAD J ¿Cómo está cambiando la sociedad?

Indica cuál es la respuesta más probable para cada pregunta. Luego compara tus selecciones con un compañero (una compañera) o con la clase.

1. ¿Está cambiando la cantidad de trabajo? Sí, ahora trabajamos _____ que antes.

   a. más   **b.** menos

2. ¿Están cambiando las familias? Sí, son más _____.

   a. grandes   **b.** pequeñas

3. ¿Está cambiando el papel de las mujeres? Sí, ahora son _____ independientes que antes.

   a. más   **b.** menos

4. ¿Está cambiando el papel del hombre? Sí, hay _____ padres solteros.

   a. más   **b.** menos

5. ¿Está cambiando el nivel de educación? Sí, hay más personas que _____.

   a. obtienen (*obtain*)   **b.** no terminan sus
   diplomas universitarios   estudios secundarios

COMUNICACIÓN

ACTIVIDAD K En estos días...

Paso 1 Escribe tres cosas sobre tu vida actual, siguiendo el modelo.

MODELO   En estos días estoy comiendo más de lo normal.

Paso 2 Busca a una persona que tenga* por lo menos *dos* de las mismas acciones. Luego reporta a la clase lo que tienen en común.

VAMOS A VER

ANTICIPACIÓN

Paso 1 The article on page 168 is based on information that appeared in several newspapers. Read the title and the statement below it. You should then have a good idea of the content of the article. (Note: **disminuyendo** = diminishing or decreasing)

Paso 2 Before you read the article for information, you need to know two important words. Can you determine what they mean using the following definitions?

   hogar: domicilio o casa
   vivienda: lugar donde se vive (una casa o un apartamento)

Paso 3 What kind of information would a census reveal about the shrinking size of families in this country? With a partner, list at least three facts from the census that you expect this article to cover.

---

*has; **tenga** is the subjunctive form of **tener.** (You will learn about the subjunctive in a later lesson.)

Paso 1 Scan the text to see whether your three facts are mentioned. How did you do?

Paso 2 Read the first bulleted list. Then answer the following questions.

1. ¿Qué grupo es más grande?
   a. hogares con personas solteras sin hijos
   b. hogares con madres solteras

2. ¿Qué porcentaje de hogares se parece a la imagen tradicional (padres e hijos que viven en una casa)?
   a. casi el 25%   **b.** el 50%   **c.** más del 50%

Paso 3 Read the second bulleted list. Then indicate whether the following statements are **cierto** (C) or **falso** (F).

	C	F
1. Los hombres se casan (*get married*) a una edad menor en comparación con 1900.	☐	☐
2. El «baby-boom» parece afectar el porcentaje de casas donde un matrimonio vive solo, sin hijos.	☐	☐

Paso 4 Now read the article at your own pace. Guess words that you don't know and skip over those you can't guess.

Paso 5 The reading mentions three reasons why household size is down. What are they?

SÍNTESIS

Paso 1 This article can be divided into two sections. With a classmate, decide what these sections are. Share your conclusions with the rest of the class.

Paso 2 The two sections can be the main points in a short outline to summarize the information. Using key words or expressions from the article, write an outline. Make the outline short, but use words that help you recall as much information as possible.

Consejo práctico

Reading comprehension is increased when readers have an idea of what they are going to read. For this reason, you should always: (1) know what the title means and (2) before reading, think about the information the article might contain, based on the title and any visuals.

Consejo práctico

In the various activities in *¿Sabías que... ?,* you will often be asked to recall information from a reading. For this reason, the **Síntesis** section in this lesson asks you to make an outline. To make an outline, search the reading for

◆ key words

◆ key phrases

◆ important names, numbers, and so forth

Then use your outline to see how much of the reading you can recall without looking at the reading itself!

Está disminuyendo el tamaño de la familia
DATOS DEL CENSO 2000

Los hogares estadounidenses han cambiado en los últimos años. Según la información publicada por la Oficina del Censo 2000, la mayoría de las familias en los Estados Unidos no tiene hijos. Algunos datos interesantes del censo se alistan a continuación.

- Sólo el 51,7% de los hogares contiene un matrimonio.
- Sólo el 23,5% de las viviendas pertenece a un matrimonio con hijos menores de dieciocho años. (En 1970, era el 40%.)
- El 12,2% de los hogares contiene una mujer soltera con hijos.
- El 25,8% de las viviendas pertenece a personas solteras sin hijos.
- El tamaño promedio de la familia típica estadounidense por hogar es de 2,59 personas.

En fin, la imagen tradicional de una casa con padre, madre y uno o dos hijos está desapareciendo. Hay varias explicaciones para los datos obtenidos del censo.

- Los matrimonios tienen menos hijos que antes y en muchos casos optan por no tener ningún hijo.
- La edad media en la que los hombres contraen matrimonio es un poco más de los veinticinco años, un récord desde 1900. La situación es igual entre las mujeres.
- La edad media de la población está subiendo y ahora hay más personas mayores que viven solas después de que sus hijos dejan la casa. Estas personas son de la generación llamada el «baby-boom», es decir los que nacieron entre 1950 y 1965.

En 1970 había más casas con padres e hijos. Pero gracias a las tendencias recientes, los hijos viven solos en su propia casa y los padres también viven solos. Así que el mismo número de personas vive ahora en diferentes casas.

Para ver más datos, visite **www.census.gov**.

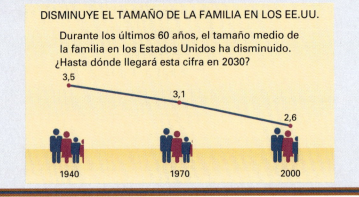

DISMINUYE EL TAMAÑO DE LA FAMILIA EN LOS EE.UU.

Durante los últimos 60 años, el tamaño medio de la familia en los Estados Unidos ha disminuido. ¿Hasta dónde llegará esta cifra en 2030?

3,5

3,1

2,6

1940   1970   2000

ACTIVIDAD El tamaño de nuestra familia

Entrevista a un compañero (una compañera) para averiguar (*find out*) el tamaño de su familia. Tu compañero/a sólo debe incluir padres e hijos. Por ejemplo, si en tu familia son tu mamá, tu papá y tú, son tres. Si en tu familia sólo son tu mamá y tú, son dos. Si en tu familia son tu hijo y tú, son dos, etcétera. No se deben incluir abuelos, tíos ni otros parientes que viven en la misma casa. Después reporta a la clase si tu compañero y tú tienen una familia más o menos grande que el promedio mencionado en la lectura (2,59 personas por familia).

Así se dice

Para hablar del tamaño de tu familia puedes usar **ser** + *número.*

En mi familia **somos** cinco en total.

Somos tres hermanos en mi familia.

¿Cuántos **son** Uds. en su familia?

Vamos a ver

Now that you've completed the **Vamos a ver** section of **Unidad dos,** watch the corresponding **Vamos a ver** segment on the *¿Sabías que... ?* video to further explore the themes presented in this unit. There are related pre- and post-viewing activities on the *¿Sabías que... ?* Online Learning Center at **www.mhhe.com/sabiasque5**.

NAVEGANDO LA RED

Busca información sobre el tamaño de la familia en España, la Argentina y México. ¿Está disminuyendo el tamaño de la familia en estos países también? ¿Qué datos encuentras? Compártelos con la clase.

IDEAS PARA EXPLORAR
Épocas anteriores

GRAMÁTICA

¿Era diferente la vida? (I)

Introduction to the imperfect tense: singular forms

(yo)	me acost**aba** comí**a** escribí**a**	(nosotros/as)	-ábamos -íamos
(tú)	te acost**abas** comí**as** escribí**as**	(vosotros/as)	-abais -íais
(Ud.)	se acost**aba** comí**a** escribí**a**	(Uds.)	-aban -ían
(él/ella)	se acost**aba** comí**a** escribí**a**	(ellos/as)	-aban -ían

When we discuss events, actions, and states of being, we can refer to *when* they occur: This is called *tense*. You already know how to express basic present, past, and future events.

Hablé con mi tío soltero por teléfono. (*past*)
Hablo con mi abuelo materno ahora. (*present*)
Voy a hablar con mi prima favorita pronto. (*future*)

But we can also include information on the status of the event, action, or state. Was it, is it, or will it be *in progress* at the time we refer to it? When we include information about the *progress* of the event, we refer to *aspect*. Can you tell which of these encodes tense and which encodes aspect in an English verb?

will as in "He *will do* it."
-ed as in "He *finished*."
-ing as in "She *was talking*."

If you said the first two encode tense and only the third encodes aspect, you were correct. *Will* encodes future and *-ed* encodes past, but *-ing* encodes that an action was, is, or will be in progress. For example, *He was talking, He is talking,* and *He will be talking.* The tense changes, but the aspect does not: the use of the verb form *talking* encodes the meaning "in progress at the time referred to."

—Sí, cuando yo **tenía** su edad, las cosas **eran** bien diferentes. Yo no **asistía** a la escuela como Uds. **Trabajaba** en el campo con mis padres.

Lección 6   ¿Y el tamaño de la familia?

An important feature of Spanish *past tense* verbs is that they encode aspect. The use of **-aba-** and **-ía-,** for example, indicates *in progress at the time,* while the preterite forms (**-é/-í, -aste/-iste, -ó/-ió,** etc.) do not.

> **Hablaba** con mis abuelos ayer. (*past, but in progress*)
> *I was talking with my grandparents yesterday.*

> **Salía** con mis tíos cuando… (*past, but in progress*)
> *I was leaving with my aunt and uncle when . . .*

This is called the *past imperfect indicative* or simply the *imperfect.*

Spanish also uses the imperfect to refer to actions and events that *occurred repeatedly* in the past, without reference to exactly how often. This corresponds roughly to English *used to* or *would* as in *They used to (would) make fun of me as a child.*

> **Comíamos** en muchos restaurantes diferentes.
> *We used to (We would) eat in many different restaurants.*

> Mis hermanos y yo **nos llevábamos** bien.
> *My siblings and I used to get along well.*

Imperfect verb forms are signaled by **-aba-** (for **-ar** verbs) and **-ía-** (for both **-er** and **-ir** verbs). Examples are given in the shaded box on the previous page.

Ir and **ser** have irregular imperfect stems and unexpected forms but are easy to memorize.

ir	ser
iba	era
ibas	eras
iba	era

In the activities that follow, you will concentrate on using the imperfect when speaking about the way things *used to be* and about actions that *have taken place repeatedly* in the past.

ACTIVIDAD A ¿Sí o no?

Escucha y apunta lo que dice tu profesor(a). Después indica si es cierto o falso para ti. Todas las oraciones tienen que ver con (*deal with*) la vida de tu profesor(a) durante la década anterior.

Yo…

1… **2**… **3**… **4**… **5**… **6**…

ACTIVIDAD B Entrevista

Paso 1 Hazle las siguientes preguntas a un compañero (una compañera) de clase. Apunta sus respuestas. Todas las preguntas tienen que ver con la década anterior.

1. ¿Leías más o menos?
2. ¿Mirabas la televisión más o menos?
3. ¿Te acostabas más temprano que ahora?
4. ¿Te levantabas más temprano que ahora?
5. ¿Salías mucho con tus amigos? ¿más que ahora o menos?

Paso 2 Usando la información del **Paso 1** junto con (*as well as*) la información de la **Actividad A,** haz comparaciones entre el profesor (la profesora) y tu compañero/a.

MODELOS   El profesor (La profesora) leía más y Jorge leía más también.

El profesor (La profesora) comía menos pero Jorge no.

ACTIVIDAD C **Antes y ahora**

Paso 1 ¿Qué cosas hacías tú de niño/a (*as a child*) que no haces de adulto? ¿Qué cosas hacías de niño/a que todavía haces de adulto? ¿Qué cosas no hacías de niño/a que ahora sí haces de adulto? ¿Y qué cosas ni hacías de niño/a ni haces ahora de adulto? Escoge cinco de las situaciones a continuación (puedes añadir cualquier otra si quieres) y escribe unas oraciones para leer en un grupo de otras tres personas.

dormir con la luz prendida (*light turned on*)
tenerles miedo* a los perros grandes
ir al centro comercial (*mall*)
pasar tiempo solo/a
mirar los dibujos animados (*cartoons*) en la televisión
odiar (*to hate*) ciertas verduras (*vegetables*)
montar en bicicleta (*to ride a bike*)
jugar a los videojuegos
hacer la cama (*bed*)
lavar la ropa

Paso 2 Después de leer sus oraciones individuales, los miembros del grupo deben pensar en las siguientes preguntas y luego presentar sus respuestas a la clase.

¿Hay ciertas actividades o cosas que la persona típica...

hacía de niño que no hace de adulto?
no hacía de niño que sí hace de adulto?
hacía de niño y todavía hace de adulto?
ni hacía de niño ni hace ahora de adulto?

***Tener miedo** = *to be afraid of* (lit. *to have fear of*). **Les tengo miedo a los perros grandes.** = *I am afraid of big dogs.*

GRAMÁTICA

¿Era diferente la vida? (II)

More on the imperfect tense: plural forms

—Abuelita, ¿**te llevabas bien** con tus padres?
—¡Claro! **Hacíamos** todo lo que nos **decían** nuestros padres porque si no, ¡qué palizas (*beatings*) **recibíamos**!

(yo)	-aba -ía	(nosotros/as)	nos acost**ábamos** com**íamos** escrib**íamos**
(tú)	-abas -ías	(vosotros/as)	os acost**abais** com**íais** escrib**íais**
(Ud.)	-aba -ía	(Uds.)	se acost**aban** com**ían** escrib**ían**
(él/ella)	-aba -ía	(ellos/ellas)	se acost**aban** com**ían** escrib**ían**

The **-aba-** and **-ía-** markers of the imperfect tense carry over into all forms of the verbs, as you can see in the shaded box above. Remember that with **-ar** verbs, a written accent needs to be placed on the ending for the first person plural (**nosotros**) form (e.g., **-ábamos**) to indicate that the stress falls on the accented vowel and not the one that follows.

The plural forms for **ir** and **ser** follow the same patterns as the singular forms.

ir	**ser**
íbamos	éramos
ibais	erais
iban	eran

Remember that the imperfect, as we are using it here, refers to events, actions, and other "processes" in the past that were habitual and repetitive in nature, things that people would usually do, used to do, generally did, and so forth.

ACTIVIDAD D En las épocas primitivas

Paso 1 Escoge la mejor manera para completar cada oración.

Cuando éramos seres primitivos...

1. No _____ dentistas ni médicos.

    a. teníamos   **b.** practicábamos   **c.** salíamos

2. _____ carne cruda (*raw meat*).

    a. Vivíamos   **b.** Comíamos   **c.** Jugábamos

3. ____ semierectos.

    a. Mirábamos   **b.** Tomábamos   **c.** Caminábamos

4. ____ con gestos y con las manos porque no teníamos idioma oral.

    a. Nos comunicábamos   **b.** Nos acostábamos   **c.** Dormíamos

5. ____ mucho de los animales para comer, vestirnos y para muchas otras cosas importantes.

    a. Comíamos   **b.** Comprábamos   **c.** Dependíamos

6. No ____ con mucha frecuencia.

    a. podíamos   **b.** mirábamos   **c.** nos bañábamos

Paso 2 Ahora escucha al profesor (a la profesora) leer las oraciones completas. ¿Las tienes todas correctas?

ACTIVIDAD E Las mujeres en el siglo XIX

Paso 1 Empareja (*Match*) cada frase de la columna a la izquierda con la más apropiada de la columna a la derecha para formar oraciones completas.

Las mujeres del siglo XIX...

1. enseñaban (*taught*) ____
2. no entraban ____
3. no llevaban* ____
4. no tenían ____

Si estas mujeres...

5. se casaban, tomaban ____
6. trabajaban fuera de (*outside*) casa, ganaban ____
7. trabajaban fuera de casa, no hacían ____

  a. a las fuerzas armadas (*armed services*).

  b. derecho al voto en las elecciones.

  c. el apellido de su esposo.

  d. en las escuelas, pero no en las universidades.

  e. los mismos trabajos que los hombres.

  f. menos que los hombres.

  g. pantalones.

Paso 2 ¿Cuántas situaciones del **Paso 1** ya no son verdaderas? ¿Crees que estos cambios reflejan un cambio grande en cuanto al papel de la mujer en nuestra sociedad? En grupos de tres o cuatro, formen unas oraciones con el imperfecto para describir el papel social de la mujer en el siglo XIX. Luego compartan sus oraciones con la clase y determinen si las mujeres han avanzado (*have advanced*) mucho, poco, nada o sólo en ciertos campos (*fields*).

MODELO   El trabajo principal de la mujer era cuidar a los niños.

ACTIVIDAD F Los años 90

Paso 1 Durante décadas pasadas, eran muchas las cosas y costumbres que estaban de moda (*in style*) en este país que ahora no están de

---

*Llevar** is often used in Spanish to mean *to wear*.

moda. Escribe cuatro oraciones sobre lo que hacíamos en este país en décades anteriores.

MODELOS   Durante los años 40, escuchábamos y bailábamos el *swing*.

Durante los años 60, protestábamos mucho contra la política.

Paso 2 Ahora presenta tus oraciones a la clase sin mencionar la década. ¿Pueden tus compañeros deducir a qué década se refiere cada oración?

COMUNICACIÓN

ACTIVIDAD G Gastos°

Expenses

Paso 1 Estudia el gráfico «Gastos para criar (*raise*) a un hijo… ». Luego contesta las siguientes preguntas por escrito (*in writing*).

1. ¿Las familias gastaban más en la comida para sus hijos en 1960, o menos?

2. ¿Costaba más la vivienda en 1960, o menos?

3. ¿Gastaban más los padres en el cuido (*care*) y en la enseñanza (*education*), o menos?

4. ¿Qué gasto subió más entre 1960 y 2000?

Paso 2 Utilizando las respuestas del **Paso 1** y también mirando el gráfico, prepara un breve informe de 50 palabras, comparando los gastos para criar a un hijo entre 1960 y 2000. Puedes utilizar el modelo si quieres.

MODELO   En 1960 los padres gastaban menos en _____. A la vez, gastaban más en _____. En 2000 el gasto mayor era en _____. Parece que el gasto que subió más entre 1960 y 2000 es en _____.

Paso 3 Alguien debe presentar sus ideas a la clase antes de entregar todos los párrafos al profesor (a la profesora). ¿Tienen todos más o menos la misma información?

Paso 4 Decidan entre todos cuál puede ser la explicación del mayor aumento (*increase*) en los gastos.

Gastos para criar a un hijo hasta los 18 años, clase media, familia con un matrimonio

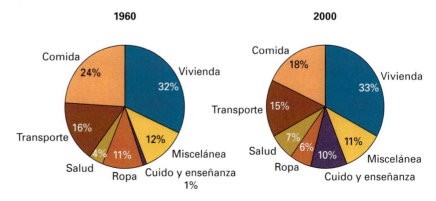

Lección 6   ¿Y el tamaño de la familia?

NAVEGANDO LA RED

Busca información sobre los gastos para criar a los hijos en un país de habla española. ¿Cómo se compara esta información con lo que sabes de esos mismos gastos en tu país?

ACTIVIDAD H Diferencias

Paso 1 Escribe dos oraciones sobre lo que sabes o crees que era típico cuando tus padres eran adolescentes. Una oración debe representar algo que era mejor que ahora y la otra algo que no era mejor. Usa el imperfecto como en el modelo.

> MODELO No tenían computadoras para escribir como nosotros. Esto era más difícil.

Paso 2 En grupos de tres, comparen sus oraciones. Luego escojan tres de las oraciones para presentar a la clase. Alguien del grupo debe escribirlas en la pizarra.

GRAMÁTICA

¿Tienes tantos hermanos como yo?

Comparisons of equality

In readings and in activities you may have noticed the use of **tan... como** and **tanto... como** to express similarities and differences.

> Las familias de hoy no son **tan** grandes **como** las de épocas anteriores.

Use a form of **tanto** when the comparison involves *nouns*. The form of **tanto** must agree in number and gender with the noun.

tanto dinero como   **tantos hijos** como
tanta imaginación como   **tantas familias** como

Use **tan** when the comparison involves *adjectives* (words that modify nouns) or *adverbs* (words that modify verbs).

ADJETIVOS	ADVERBIOS
tan grande como	**tan rápido** como
tan altas como	**tan frecuentemente** como

Tanto como is used when no noun, adjective, or adverb is explicitly mentioned. It means *as much as*.

> Los hombres se ocupan de (*look after*) los niños **tanto como** las mujeres.

ACTIVIDAD I   Familias de ayer, familias de hoy

Paso 1 Completa las siguientes oraciones con **tan** o una forma de **tanto,** según la estructura de la oración. Compara tus respuestas con las de otra persona.

1. La calidad de la vida familiar no es _____ buena hoy día como en los años 50.
2. Las madres modernas no pasan _____ tiempo con sus hijos como las madres de otras épocas.
3. Los hijos de hoy no se adaptan _____ bien como los de épocas anteriores.
4. Las madres que trabajan fuera de casa no son _____ respetadas como las madres «tradicionales».
5. En los años 50, las madres no trabajaban fuera de casa _____ como las madres de hoy.
6. En los años 50, no había _____ divorcios como ahora.
7. En los años 50, los padres no eran _____ permisivos con sus hijos como los padres de hoy.
8. En los años 50, los hijos no tenían _____ problemas sociales y psicológicos como los hijos de hoy.

Paso 2 Ahora la clase va a decidir cuáles de las oraciones son ciertas y cuáles son falsas.

ACTIVIDAD J   Sobre el tamaño de la familia

Repasa rápidamente la lectura de la página 168 y, con un compañero (una compañera), formula tres oraciones con **tanto/tan... como,** a base de la información incluida. ¿Cuántas oraciones diferentes puede inventar la clase?

COMPOSICIÓN

Antes de escribir

In this lesson, you've explored some differences between today's families and those of the past. You have read about the changing family size and completed several activities that focus on changes in women's roles in society, economic pressures, and so forth. In the **pasos** that follow, you will continue to compare previous time periods to the present but in a more personal manner by focusing on the differences (and similarities) between the family of one of your grandparents and that of your own. (If you prefer, you may choose someone other than a grandparent, as long as the person is of a generation older than that of your parents.)

Paso 1 Your purpose in writing is to inform your reader of the many changes that have occurred across the last three generations. As you write and revise, keep in mind who your audience is. For this composition, your audience is someone who is not from this country and does not have firsthand knowledge of the societal changes in this country. Your goal is to make your audience realize that this society's concept of family life has changed in the last 50 years. In order for your audience to come to this realization, you will have to stress the differences between then and now.

Paso 2 What information will support the points you will make?

☐ el tamaño de la familia

☐ la esperanza de vida

☐ el papel de la mujer en la sociedad

☐ las oportunidades económicas

☐ las oportunidades educativas

☐ ¿ ?

Paso 3 In what order will you present the information?

☐ Chronologically: Begin with the past and move to the present, or begin with the present and move to the past.

☐ Point by point: Cover a point about your grandparent's family and then the counterpoint about your own, or cover a point about your own family and then the counterpoint about your grandparent's.

Paso 4 Consider the new grammar presented in this lesson. Can you express yourself by

☐ using the imperfect to express habitual and typical events in the past?

☐ making comparisons?

Al escribir

Paso 1 Draft your composition, keeping its length to about 150 words.

Paso 2 Think about how you will conclude. Here are some words and phrases that may prove useful in emphasizing the final point.

Vocabulario útil

al fin y al cabo	in the end
comoquiera que se examine el hecho	no matter how you look at it
después de todo	after all
en resumen	in summary

Después de escribir

Paso 1 Put your composition aside for a day or two. When you return to it, you will be ready to edit it. Reread what you have written. Focus your editing on specific aspects of the composition. Use the following list as a guide.

1. Information conveyed

   ☐ Number each contrast you make between the two families. Does your wording stress the differences?

2. Language

   ☐ Put a check mark over every verb in the composition. Is the ending on each verb correct?

   ☐ Underline each verb you use to talk about the past. Are the verb tenses correct?

   ☐ Edit your composition for adjective agreement.

Paso 2 Rewrite your composition and make any necessary changes. Before you hand it in, ask someone in class to read it and decide which of the following sums up the central idea.

   a. La familia de tu abuelo/a y tu familia tienen mucho en común.

   b. Hay diferencias y también semejanzas entre la familia de tu abuelo/a y tu familia.

   c. Las diferencias son impresionantes entre la familia de tu abuelo/a y tu familia.

If the third statement is not selected, try to determine where you have not stressed the differences clearly or emphatically enough and modify those places. Once you have done so, hand in your composition.

Vistazos culturales

La inmigración y emigración en el mundo hispano

¿Sabías que...

más de la mitad de los inmigrantes que viven en los Estados Unidos son de Latinoamérica? Actualmenteᵃ hay unos 28,4 millones de inmigrantes en los Estados Unidos. De estos, unos 14,5 millones (el 51%) son de Latinoamérica. La mayoría de los inmigrantes hispanos vive en el Suroeste y el Noreste del país, pero poco a pocoᵇ hay más comunidades de inmigrantes hispanos en lugares distintos como Carolina del Norte, Michigan, Indiana y Tennessee.

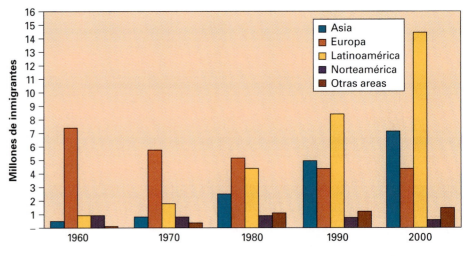

Trabajadores inmigrantes en California

ᵃ*Currently*   ᵇpoco... *little by little*

Origen de inmigrantes en los Estados Unidos

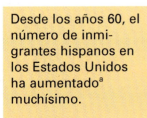

Desde los años 60, el número de inmigrantes hispanos en los Estados Unidos ha aumentadoᵃ muchísimo.

ᵃha... *has increased*

Lección 6   ¿Y el tamaño de la familia?

PARAGUAY

URUGUAY

ARGENTINA

CHILE

Más del 95% de la población del Uruguay viene de inmigrantes europeos, la mayoría de Italia y España. En el Paraguay hay muchos inmigrantes japoneses, portugueses y canadienses.

Entre 1850 y 1940, más de 6,6 milliones de inmigrantes europeos llegaron a la Argentina. Los inmigrantes españoles e italianos predominaron[a] pero también llegaron muchos de Alemania, Francia, Inglaterra, Polonia y Rusia.

[a]*predominated*

La Boca es un barrio de Buenos Aires de mucha influencia italiana.

ACTIVIDAD ¿Qué recuerdas?

Empareja los siguientes datos y las oraciones a continuación.

a. los asiáticos
b. 14,5 millones
c. España e Italia
d. 95%
e. Michigan y Carolina del Norte

1. ____ número de inmigrantes hispanos en los Estados Unidos

2. ____ lugar de origen de muchos de los inmigrantes del Uruguay y del Paraguay

3. ____ otros inmigrantes en los Estados Unidos cuyas (*whose*) poblaciones han aumentando mucho desde los años 60

4. ____ nuevos lugares de asentamiento (*settling places*) para muchos inmigrantes hispanos en los Estados Unidos

5. ____ porcentaje de la población actual del Uruguay y del Paraguay que viene de inmigrantes

NAVEGANDO LA RED

Escoge *una* de las siguientes actividades. Luego presenta tus resultados a la clase.

1. Escoje un estado de los Estados Unidos donde tradicionalmente no se han asentado (*haven't settled*) muchos inmigrantes hispanos (por ejemplo, Michigan, Indiana, Ohio, Carolina del Norte, Carolina del Sur, Tennessee, Wyoming, etcétera) y busca la siguiente información.
   a. número de inmigrantes hispanos en el estado
   b. nombres de las industrias o los trabajos en que trabajan los hispanos

2. Busca la etimología de la palabra **bracero** y haz lo siguiente.
   a. Explica el origen y significado de este término.
   b. Haz una lista de las ventajas (*advantages*) y desventajas (*disadvantages*) del programa de braceros.

3. Busca información en la página Web del *U.S. Census Bureau* (**www.census.gov**) sobre el nivel de educación de los inmigrantes hispanos en los Estados Unidos. Con la información que encuentras, haz una tabla para comparar el nivel de educación de los centroamericanos con el de los caribeños y los sudamericanos.

VOCABULARIO COMPRENSIVO

Las edades / Ages

veinte (R)	twenty
treinta (R)	thirty
cuarenta	forty
cincuenta	fifty
sesenta	sixty
setenta	seventy
ochenta	eighty
noventa	ninety

tener... años (R) — to be . . . years old

Los años y las épocas / Years and Time Periods

cien(to)	one hundred
doscientos	two hundred
trescientos	three hundred
cuatrocientos	four hundred
quinientos	five hundred
seiscientos	six hundred
setecientos	seven hundred
ochocientos	eight hundred
novecientos	nine hundred
mil	one thousand
dos mil	two thousand

los años 20	the twenties
la década	decade
el siglo (pasado)	(last) century

Comparaciones / Comparisons

tan... como	as . . . as
tanto/a... como	as much . . . as
tantos/as... como	as many . . . as

Otras palabras y expresiones útiles

la cifra	number
la gente	people
el promedio	average
el tamaño	size

joven (R)	young
viejo/a (R)	old

GRAMMAR SUMMARY

Question Words

¿cuándo?	¿qué?
¿dónde?	¿quién(es)?
¿cómo?	¿cuánto/a?
¿cuál(es)?	¿cuántos/as?

Remember that prepositions (**a, con, de, en,** and so forth) appear in front of the question word when used. This is unlike English, in which the preposition can "dangle" at the end of a phrase or utterance, far away from the question word.

> ¿**De** dónde es tu amigo?
> *Where is your friend **from**?*

> ¿**Con** quiénes hablas si tienes un problema?
> *Whom do you speak **to** if you have a problem?*

Pronouns

SUBJECT	DIRECT OBJECT	TRUE REFLEXIVE	RECIPROCAL
yo	me	me	
tú	te	te	
Ud.	lo/la	se	
él/ella	lo/la	se	
nosotros/as	nos	nos	nos
vosotros/as	os	os	os
Uds.	los/las	se	se
ellos/ellas	los/las	se	se

1. Remember that object and reflexive pronouns precede conjugated verbs. Don't mistake them for subject pronouns.

   > **Me** llaman los padres.
   > *My parents call me.*

   > **Se** afeita regularmente.
   > *He shaves regularly.*

2. Remember that not all true reflexives in Spanish translate into English with *-self/ -selves*.

   > María **se levanta** temprano.
   > *María gets up early. (We don't say **gets herself up,** even though this would be a literal translation.)*

3. Remember that not all reciprocals in Spanish translate into English as *each other*.

   > **Nos abrazamos** cuando **nos vemos.**
   > *We hug when we see each other. (While both are reciprocal actions, only the second verb in English would normally take **each other**.)*

Object Marker a

Spanish uses **a** to mark objects of a verb when the object could be confused as a subject (i.e., when the object is theoretically capable of performing the action). It helps to indicate who did what to whom in Spanish, especially since Spanish has flexible word order.

> Manuel conoce bien **a** María. (*María is perfectly capable of knowing someone, but she is not the subject in this sentence.*)

> El señor mata **al** león. (*The lion is perfectly capable of killing something else, but he is not the subject in this sentence.*)

Estar

1. Adjectives that reflect a change in status such as **casado** and **divorciado** are normally used with **estar.**

   > Mi hermano **está** divorciado. Su ex mujer vive en Chile.

¿**Estás** casado?

Mis abuelos **están** muertos.

2. Often you can use **estar** with an adjective to show that a trait or characteristic is unexpected.

> Ramona **está** muy seria. (*Ramona seems very serious. Normally she is not.*)
>
> ¿Qué pasó? **Estás** muy delgado.

3. **Estar** can be used with **-ando** or **-iendo** forms to express something in progress.

> **Estoy estudiando.** No puedo hablar.
>
> **Está cambiando** el mundo, ¿no crees?

Saber versus conocer

1. **Saber** is used to express knowledge of a fact or some other kind of information.

> Todos **sabemos** que 2 + 2 = 4.
>
> No **sé** nada de su vida.

2. **Conocer** is used to express familiarity with a person or place and sometimes things.

> **Conozco** muy bien a Elena.
>
> ¿**Conoces** Buenos Aires?

Imperfect Tense

	-ar	-er/-ir	ser	ir
yo	me acostaba	comía/asistía	era	iba
tú	te acostabas	comías/asistías	eras	ibas
Ud.	se acostaba	comía/asistía	era	iba
él/ella	se acostaba	comía/asistía	era	iba
nosotros/as	nos acostábamos	comíamos/asistíamos	éramos	íbamos
vosotros/as	os acostabais	comíais/asistíais	erais	ibais
Uds.	se acostaban	comían/asistían	eran	iban
ellos/ellas	se acostaban	comían/asistían	eran	iban

The imperfect is a past tense that signals that an action, event, or activity occurred habitually in the past. It is frequently, though not always, rendered in English by *used to* and *would*.

> Las familias **eran** más grandes en épocas anteriores.
> *Families used to be / were larger in previous times.*
>
> Las mujeres en otras épocas sólo **trabajaban** en casa.
> *Women in earlier time periods worked (would work) only at home.*

Comparisons of Equality (Similar to English *as . . . as*)

WITH NOUNS	WITH ADJECTIVES AND ADVERBS
tanto dinero **como**	
tantos hijos **como**	**tan** grande **como**
tantas mujeres **como**	**tan** frecuentemente **como**
tanta educación **como**	

Tanto como is used when no noun, adjective, or adverb is explicitly mentioned (similar to English *as much as*).

> Ahora las mujeres trabajan fuera de casa **tanto como** los hombres.

En la mesa

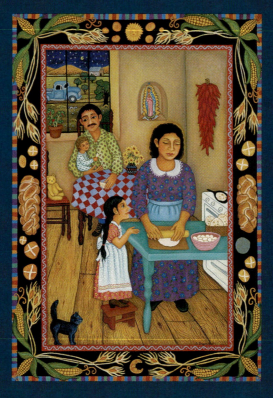

La tortillera *por Diana Bryer*

Perfil de la artista

NOMBRE: Diana Bryer

PAÍS DE ORIGEN: los Estados Unidos

FECHA DE NACIMIENTO: 1942

Bryer nació en Los Ángeles, California pero encontró su inspiración en la belleza e historia de Nuevo México adonde se mudó en 1977. En su obra, en la que abundan los colores vibrantes, ella comunica su pasión por la naturaleza tanto como su fascinación por la historia y las costumbres locales. Un tema que le intriga mucho es la diáspora judía que resultó a causa de la Inquisición Española y la expulsión de los judíos de España a finales del siglo XV. Muchos se establecieron en el Nuevo Mundo y sus descendientes viven en México y Nuevo México. Elementos del judaísmo permanecen[a] en la religión contemporánea de estas zonas. Observa en el cuadro *La tortillera* la pequeña Estrella de David que adorna el nicho en donde está la imagen de la Virgen de Guadalupe.

---

[a]*remain*

LECCIÓN 7

Check out the following media resources to complement this lesson:

 Online *Manual*

 Video on CD

 Online Learning Center

ActivityPak

¿Qué sueles comer?

This lesson focuses on food and eating habits. You will have an opportunity to

- describe some basic foods and snacks
- describe what you generally eat for breakfast, lunch, and dinner
- examine how eating habits in Spanish-speaking countries differ from those in this country
- learn about other verbs like **gustar**
- learn about indirect object pronouns
- learn more about **estar** used with adjectives

 Before beginning this lesson, look over the **Intercambio** activity on pages 210–211. This is the activity you will be working toward throughout the lesson.

El Mercado Libertad en Guadalajara, México

VOCABULARIO

¿Cuáles son algunos alimentos básicos?

Talking about basic foods in Spanish

El calcio

Productos lácteos

el helado

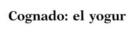

la leche

Cognado: el yogur

el queso

Las proteínas

Carnes

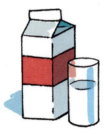

el bistec

Cognado: la hamburguesa

la carne de res

Aves

los huevos

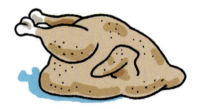

el pollo

la chuleta
de cerdo
(*pork chop*)

el jamón

**Otros
alimentos**

los frijoles

la mantequilla
de cacahuete
(*peanut butter*)

las nueces

Pescados y mariscos

el atún

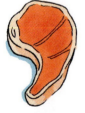

los camarones

Las vitaminas y la fibra

Frutas

Cognados:
la banana
el limón
el tomate

el aguacate
(*avocado*)

las fresas

la manzana

Verduras

la naranja

la toronja
(*grapefruit*)

las uvas

los guisantes

Cognado: las
espinacas

el maíz

**las judías
verdes**

las papas

la lechuga

la zanahoria

Los carbohidratos y la fibra

Cognados: los cereales,
los espaguetis (las pastas
alimenticias)

Las grasas

el arroz
(*rice*)

el pan blanco

el pan integral

**el aceite de
maíz**

**el aceite
de oliva**

la mantequilla
(*butter*)

Vocabulario útil

la comida	meal; food	**agrio/a**	sour	**amarillo/a**	yellow
		amargo/a	bitter	**blanco/a**	white
al horno	baked	**dulce**	sweet	**marrón**	brown
al vapor	steamed	**salado/a**	salty	**negro/a**	black
asado/a	roast(ed)			**rojo/a**	red
cocido/a	cooked			**rosado/a**	pink
crudo/a	raw			**verde**	green

ACTIVIDAD A ¿Cómo es?

El profesor (La profesora) va a mencionar un alimento y luego va a hacer una pregunta sobre el mismo. Contesta la pregunta.

1... **2**... **3**... **4**... **5**... **6**... **7**...

 ACTIVIDAD B Asociaciones

Paso 1 Tu profesor(a) va a nombrar algunos alimentos. ¿Qué color(es) asocias con cada uno?

1... **2**... **3**... **4**... **5**... **6**...

Paso 2 ¿Qué otros alimentos asocias con estos colores?
1. rosado **2.** blanco **3.** amarillo **4.** rojo **5.** marrón

 ACTIVIDAD C Otras asociaciones

El profesor (La profesora) va a nombrar una categoría de alimentos. Di el alimento que se te ocurra (*comes to mind*) primero.

1... **2**... **3**... **4**... **5**... **6**... **7**... **8**...

ACTIVIDAD D ¿Qué alimento es bueno para... ?

Inventa oraciones basándote en el modelo. No olvides (*Don't forget*) usar el artículo definido. (Ver **Así se dice,** a la izquierda.)

MODELO   para el cerebro (*brain*) → El pescado es bueno para el cerebro.

1. para la vista (*vision*)   **4.** para los músculos
2. para los resfriados (*colds*)   **5.** para la tez (*complexion*)
3. para el pelo

COMUNICACIÓN

ACTIVIDAD E Preferencias personales

Paso 1 Describe tus hábitos de comer. Completa cada oración con dos de tus alimentos preferidos, según el caso.

MODELO   Como *yogur* y *pan* a cualquier hora del día.

1. Como _____ y _____ a cualquier hora del día.
2. Nunca o casi nunca como _____ ni _____.
3. Uso _____ y _____ sólo en la preparación de otros platos.
4. Como _____ y _____ solamente acompañados/as de otros alimentos o cuando son parte de una comida más grande.
5. Suelo comer _____ y _____ con pan.
6. Suelo comer _____ y _____ solos/as, sin otra cosa.
7. Me gusta comer _____ y _____ crudos/as.
8. Prefiero comer _____ y _____ cocidos/as.

Paso 2 Ahora, entrevista a un compañero (una compañera) de clase sobre sus hábitos de comer. Hazle preguntas para saber cómo ha completado (*he/she has completed*) las oraciones del **Paso 1.** Apunta sus respuestas. Luego tu compañero/a debe hacerte las mismas preguntas a ti para ver cómo has contestado tú (*you have answered*).

MODELOS ¿Qué alimentos sueles comer con pan?

¿Hay alimentos que te gusta comer crudos?

Paso 3 En conclusión, mi compañero/a y yo…

☐ tenemos hábitos de comer muy parecidos.

☐ tenemos algunos hábitos en común, pero no muchos.

☐ tenemos hábitos de comer muy distintos.

ACTIVIDAD F En su opinión

Paso 1 Trabajando con dos o tres compañeros/as de clase comenta (*discuss*) la siguiente afirmación. Apunten sus ideas.

«El estudiante típico tiene malos hábitos de comer».

Paso 2 Ahora presenten sus ideas al resto de la clase. Según Uds., ¿es verdad que el estudiante típico tiene malos hábitos de comer?

GRAMÁTICA

¿Que si me importan los aditivos?

Other verbs like **gustar** and the indirect object pronoun **me**

me	+	agrada(n) apetece(n) cae(n) bien (mal) encanta(n) importa(n) interesa(n)

—¿Que si **me importan** los aditivos? Todos vamos a morir algún día…
—Pues a mí **me importan** muchísimo.

In Spanish, many verbs require the use of indirect object pronouns to express how a person feels about something or the reaction that something causes in a person. This is true of **gustar,** which you already know means *to please.* (Remember that Spanish does not have a verb that literally means *to like.*)

Here are some others.

agradar *to please*
No **me agrada** la avena.

Oatmeal does not please me.
(I hate oatmeal.)

apetecer *to be appetizing; to appeal (be appealing) (food)*
No **me apetece** el caviar.   *Caviar doesn't appeal to me.*

caer bien *to make a good impression; to agree with (food)*
No **me caen bien** las cebollas.   *Onions don't agree with me.*

encantar *to delight, be extremely pleasing*
¡**Me encantan** las ostras crudas!   *Raw oysters delight me!*
                                                (*I love raw oysters!*)

importar *to be important; to matter*
No **me importan** los aditivos.   *Additives don't matter to me.*

interesar *to be interesting*
Me interesa la cocina española.   *Spanish cuisine interests me.*

Remember that, like **gustar,** these verbs normally appear in the third person singular or plural since someone is affected by something (or things). Do not mistake **me** as a subject pronoun. When used with these verbs, **me** is equivalent to the phrase *to me* and is called an indirect object pronoun. (You will learn about and work with other indirect object pronouns and these verbs later in this lesson.)

ACTIVIDAD G Me importa...

Paso 1 Indica cuánto te importa cada cosa.

	MUCHO	UN POCO	NADA
1. Me importa el color de los alimentos.	☐	☐	☐
2. Me importa el sabor (*flavor*) de los alimentos.	☐	☐	☐
3. Me importa el valor (*value*) nutritivo de los alimentos.	☐	☐	☐
4. Me importa la apariencia de la comida.	☐	☐	☐
5. Me importan las calorías.	☐	☐	☐
6. Me importan los aditivos.	☐	☐	☐
7. Me importan las grasas que contienen los alimentos.	☐	☐	☐
8. Me importan los gustos de otras personas en cuanto a la comida.	☐	☐	☐

Paso 2 Comparte tus respuestas con la clase.

MODELO   Me importan mucho el sabor de los alimentos y las grasas que contienen.

ACTIVIDAD H Mis platos preferidos

Paso 1 En la revista *Noticias* de Buenos Aires, hay una sección en la que personas célebres hablan de las comidas y restaurantes que prefieren. Lee lo que dicen Juan Carlos Harriot y Elsa Serrano en la siguiente página.

Vocabulario útil

alejarse	to go far (away)	**el pulpo**	octopus
		las remolachas	sugar beets
el lenguado	sole		
la parrillada	mixed grill	**relleno/a**	stuffed; filled

Mis platos preferidos

Salgo poco a comer, ya que la mayor parte del tiempo estoy en mi campo de Coronel Suárez. También soy cómodo, así que no me alejo demasiado de mi casa. Frecuento «La Rueda», «Schiaffino», «San Michele». En esas oportunidades pido lo mismo que comería en mi casa: carne asada, preferentemente  un bife de lomo o de «chorizo», y si hay parrillada, bien completa. Algunas veces pescado, como el lenguado frito. Siempre acompaño a la carne con ensaladas, tomates, zanahorias, remolachas. Soy muy simple en mi elección y generalmente como un solo plato.

Juan Carlos Harriott

La Rueda, Av. Quintana 456
Schiaffino, Schiaffino 2183
San Michele, Av. Quintana 257

Soy habitué de «Lola»: una copa de champán primero, luego ensalada Mikada y cerdo con aromas, que son mis preferidos. Postres casi nunca, porque engordan y, además, no soy amante de los dulces. También me encantan las cantinas italianas. Si voy a «Luigi», pido *bocconcino* de pollo con cebollas de verdeo o pulpo al ajo negro. Si como pastas, elijo las simples, fideos, ñoquis, nunca las rellenas. Raras veces tomo vino, pero cuando lo hago prefiero el tinto «Selección López». De «Fechoría», me encanta la pizza de pan alto, pero nunca dejo de comer langostinos, que siempre los tienen fresquísimos.

Elsa Serrano

Fechoría, Córdoba 3921
Luigi, Pringles 1210
Lola, Roberto M. Ortiz 1801

Paso 2 Con un compañero (una compañera) de clase, indica quién diría (*would say*) las siguientes oraciones.

	JUAN CARLOS	ELSA
1. Me encanta la variedad gastronómica.	☐	☐
2. No me agrada salir a comer.	☐	☐
3. Me importa comer bien.	☐	☐
4. Me agrada una copa de vino.	☐	☐

	JUAN CARLOS	ELSA
5. Me encanta salir a comer.	☐	☐
6. Me importan las calorías.	☐	☐
7. Me caen bien las carnes rojas.	☐	☐

Paso 3 ¿Quién tiene gustos más parecidos a los tuyos (*yours*)?

COMUNICACIÓN

ACTIVIDAD I Más sobre los gustos

Paso 1 Completa cada par de oraciones de acuerdo con tus gustos. Esta lección se enfoca (*focuses*) en la comida y los gustos de comer, pero puedes completar las oraciones como quieras (*as you wish*).

1. a. No me cae bien…   **3. a.** No me apetece para nada…

   b. No me caen bien…   **b.** No me apetecen para nada…

2. a. Me encanta…

   b. Me encantan…

Paso 2 Comparte tus oraciones con la clase. ¿Cuántas de las siguientes cosas mencionaron tus compañeros de clase y tú? Si no las mencionaron, di algo sobre algunas de ellas, usando las frases del **Paso 1.**

el ajo (*garlic*)
las ancas de rana (*frog legs*)
los caracoles (los escargots)
la comida casera (*homemade*)

la comida de la residencia
  estudiantil
Mountain Dew
el pescado crudo (el sushi)
la salsa picante

G R A M Á T I C A

¿Te importan los aditivos?

Te and **nos** as indirect object pronouns

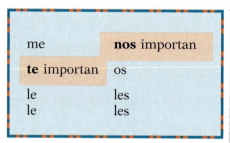

me	**nos** importan
te importan	os
le	les
le	les

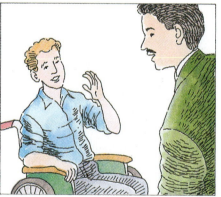

—¿**Te importan** los aditivos?
—Sí.
—A mí, también. **Nos importan** las mismas cosas, ¿no?

Although indirect object pronouns can express a variety of meanings in Spanish, their most frequent English equivalents are *to* or *for* someone. For example, **te** and **nos** are used with many verbs to express *to* or *for you* and *to* or *for us.*

¿**Te** dan dinero tus padres?
La profesora **nos** da mucha tarea.
¿**Te** apetece la comida francesa esta noche?

As you may have noticed with verbs like **gustar,** indirect object pronouns are placed before conjugated verbs. (Remember that Spanish has flexible word order, so do not mistake indirect object pronouns for subjects.) In the following sentence, who is saying something to whom?

Nos dice Manuel que no hay clase mañana.

If you said Manuel was doing the telling and we were the ones being told, you were correct.

Indirect object pronouns can also be attached to the end of an infinitive.

Marta debe **decirnos** a qué hora llegar.
Tienen que **darte** su número de teléfono.

Remember that **le** is used instead of **te** when speaking to someone who you would address as **Ud.**

¿**Le** importa a Ud. si llego tarde?

ACTIVIDAD J Entrevista al profesor (a la profesora)

La clase va a entrevistar al profesor (a la profesora). Primero, lee las preguntas a continuación y agrega (*add*) una más para completar el número 6.

Todas las preguntas tienen que ver con la comida. Quieres averiguar si el profesor (la profesora) es vegetariano/a. Luego la clase debe hacerle las preguntas al profesor (a la profesora) y apuntar sus respuestas. ¿Cuál es la conclusión de la clase?

1. ¿Te (Le) agrada el arroz?
2. ¿Te (Le) caen bien las espinacas?
3. ¿Te (Le) caen bien las frutas?
4. ¿Te (Le) apetece la lechuga?
5. ¿Te (Le) apetecen los frijoles?
6. ¿ ?

COMUNICACIÓN

ACTIVIDAD K Reacciones

Paso 1 Entrevista a un compañero (una compañera) para averiguar sus gustos. Usa los verbos **agradar, apetecer, caer bien, encantar,** etcétera.

MODELO   los mariscos → E1: ¿Te agradan los mariscos?
E2: No. No me agradan para nada. (Ah, sí. Me encantan.)

1. el ajo
2. los refrescos sin azúcar (*sugar*)
3. las espinacas
4. el yogur natural (sin sabor de fruta)
5. el café espresso
6. los meseros (*waiters*) que hablan mucho
7. el hígado (*liver*)
8. el restaurante _____ (nombre)
9. ¿ ?

Paso 2 Prepara un resumen de la entrevista para compartir con la clase los gustos que tienen en común.

MODELO A ninguno/a de los (las) dos nos apetecen las espinacas. Nos caen bien los meseros (las meseras) que hablan mucho porque normalmente son interesantes.

Paso 3 (Optativo) Escucha con atención mientras el profesor (la profesora) describe sus gustos en el **Paso 1.** Luego compara tus gustos con los de él (ella).

MODELO Al profesor (A la profesora) y a mí nos apetece el ajo.

Así se dice

Indirect object pronouns are used with a variety of verbs to express *to* or *for* someone (or something). Be careful, though! English can move the indirect object around with certain common verbs. The result is that the indirect object in English may look like a direct object!

dar	**Me dieron** el premio.	They gave me the prize.
		They gave the prize to me.
decir	**Te dije** la verdad.	I told you the truth.
		I told the truth to you.
servir	**Nos sirvieron** un vino excelente.	They served us a great wine.
		They served a great wine to us.
traer	**¿Te trajeron** algo?	Did they bring you something?
		Did they bring something to you?

NAVEGANDO LA RED

Busca información sobre uno de los siguientes productos alimenticios: el aceite de oliva, el azúcar, la banana, el café, la papa. ¿Puedes encontrar países de habla española que los exportan a este país? Presenta tus resultados a la clase.

 # IDEAS PARA EXPLORAR

A la hora de comer

VOCABULARIO

¿Qué desayunas?

Talking about what you eat for breakfast

Bollería variada (*Assorted rolls*) (1), o **churros** (*type of fried dough*) (2), o **tostada** (3) con mantequilla y **mermelada** (4), **café con leche**

El desayuno español (8.00–10.00 A.M.)

1.   **2.**   **3.**   **4.**

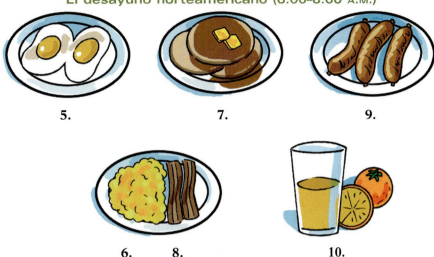

El desayuno norteamericano (6.00–8.00 A.M.)

5.   7.   9.

6.   8.   10.

Dos **huevos fritos** (*fried*) (5) o **revueltos** (*scrambled*) (6), cereal con leche o tres **panqueques** (7), **tocino** (*bacon*) (8) o **salchichas** (9), **jugo de naranja** (10), café, **té** o leche

Vocabulario útil

desayunar	to have breakfast	**el bollo**	roll
		el pan tostado	toast

Así se dice

Confused about the use of **¿qué?** and **¿cuál?** Here's a handy rule that works in most cases: Use **¿qué?** before a noun or to ask for a definition, and use **¿cuál?** everywhere else.

¿Qué alimentos prefieres para el desayuno?
¿Cuál es mejor, el jugo de naranja o el jugo de toronja?

ACTIVIDAD A Dos desayunos muy diferentes

Paso 1 Lee los menús de los dos tipos de desayuno en la sección anterior.

Paso 2 Contesta las siguientes preguntas.

	LOS ESPAÑOLES	LOS NORTEAMERICANOS
1. ¿Quiénes comen más para el desayuno?	☐	☐
2. ¿Quiénes requieren menos tiempo para desayunar?	☐	☐
3. ¿Quiénes no comen huevos por la mañana?	☐	☐
4. ¿Quiénes no comen carne para el desayuno?	☐	☐
5. ¿Quiénes comen alimentos de los cuatro grupos básicos?	☐	☐

ACTIVIDAD B ¿Quién habla?

Escucha las descripciones que va a leer el profesor (la profesora) e indica si se refieren a una persona española o norteamericana.

1... 2... 3... 4...

ACTIVIDAD C Firma aquí, por favor

¿Qué desayunaron los estudiantes de esta clase esta mañana?

1. ¿Comiste sólo un bollo?
2. ¿Comiste pan tostado con café?
3. ¿Comiste huevos?
4. ¿Comiste cereal con leche?
5. ¿Comiste carne?
6. ¿Comiste panqueques?
7. ¿Fuiste a desayunar a McDonald's?
8. ¿Comiste pizza?
9. ¿Tomaste sólo una taza (*cup*) de café o té?
10. ¿No tomaste nada esta mañana?

El delicioso sabor de la fruta con lo mejor de la avena Quaker.

Nota comunicativa

Sometimes you may want to verify what you heard or you may want someone to repeat part of what he or she said. To ask for a verification, you can say **¿Dice(s) que** + *what you want to verify.* To get a partial repetition, use the question words you know to zero in on what you partially heard. Here are some examples.

¿Dices que comiste panqueques?
¿Dice (Ud.) que no tiene azúcar?
¿Comió qué?
¿Fue adónde?

If you need someone to repeat an entire statement, don't say **¿Qué?** In Spanish, **¿Cómo?** is used.

¿Cómo?   *What?*
¿Cómo dice(s)?   *What did you say/are you saying?*

ACTIVIDAD D En su opinión

Paso 1 Trabajando con dos o tres compañeros/as de clase comenta la siguiente afirmación. Apunten sus ideas.

«El desayuno debe ser la comida más importante del día».

Paso 2 Ahora presenten sus ideas al resto de la clase. Según Uds., ¿es verdad que el desayuno debe ser la comida más importante del día?

VOCABULARIO

¿Qué comes para el almuerzo y para la cena?

Talking about what you eat for lunch and dinner

1.
2.
3.
4.
5.
6.
7.
8.
9.

El almuerzo español (2.00–4.00 P.M.)
Menú del día

PRIMER PLATO
lentejas (1) estofadas (*lentil stew*)
tortilla (*omelette*) (2)
ensalada mixta

SEGUNDO PLATO
filete de **ternera** (*veal*) (3) con **patatas** (*potatoes, Sp.*)
emperador (*swordfish*) (4) a la plancha
medio pollo asado

POSTRE
helado
tarta (*pie*) (5)
fruta
flan (6) con nata (*whipped cream*) o café
barrita de pan y **vino** (7)

La cena española (9.00–11.00 P.M.)

huevos fritos, patatas fritas, salchichas, pan y vino

El almuerzo norteamericano (12.00–1.00 P.M.)

sandwich de carne (por ejemplo, jamón, pavo [*turkey*], rosbif) / sandwich de atún, fruta

o hamburguesa con queso, papas fritas

un **refresco** (*soft drink*) / café / leche

La cena norteamericana (5.00–7.00 P.M.)

pollo asado / bistec / langosta (*lobster*) / pescado frito / espaguetis
ensalada mixta
verduras al vapor
arroz / papas al horno / **puré de papas** (*mashed potatoes*) (8)
cerveza (*beer*) (9) / vino y/o **agua**
tarta / helado / gelatina

o pizza

ACTIVIDAD E ¿Español o norteamericano?

Paso 1 Analiza los dos tipos de almuerzos en la sección anterior.

Paso 2 Escucha al profesor (a la profesora). ¿Habla de una persona norteamericana o española?

1...   2...   3...   4...   5...   6...

Paso 3 Mira otra vez los menús para las comidas norteamericanas y españolas en la sección anterior. Luego contesta las preguntas que hace el profesor (la profesora).

1...   2...   3...   4...   5...

ACTIVIDAD F ¿Quién habla?

Escucha al profesor (a la profesora). ¿Expresa las opiniones de una persona española o norteamericana?

1...   2...   3...   4...

ACTIVIDAD G ¿A quién describe?

Paso 1 Revisa los menús típicos para el almuerzo y la cena norteamericanos. ¿Son estos menús típicos del almuerzo y de la cena de un(a) estudiante? Si no, haz los cambios necesarios para mostrar lo que come habitualmente un(a) estudiante de tu universidad. Comparte con la clase tu revisión.

Paso 2 Después de que todos presenten el menú que revisaron, indica tu conclusión.

☐ Hay un almuerzo típico de los estudiantes.

☐ No hay *un* almuerzo típico de los estudiantes.

☐ Hay una cena típica de los estudiantes.

☐ No hay *una* cena típica de los estudiantes.

COMUNICACIÓN

Así se dice

To describe how something tastes, Spanish uses the verb **saber** + **a** or the noun **el sabor.**

Tiene muy buen **sabor.**
No me gusta **el sabor.**
¿A qué **sabe?**
Sabe a pollo.

How would you tell someone from a Spanish-speaking country what Mountain Dew and frozen yogurt taste like?

Nota comunicativa

Earlier you read about using **¿Dice(s) que...?** to verify something you've heard. Another way to verify information is to use a "tag question." A tag question in English can take a variety of forms: You said sardines, *right?* She eats shellfish, *doesn't she?* Spanish has two tag questions: **¿no?** and **¿verdad?** (*right?*). In general, use **¿no?** with affirmative statements and **¿verdad?** with negative ones.

Le gusta la comida rápida, **¿no?**
Prefieres café con leche, **¿no?**
No comió esta mañana, **¿verdad?**
No desea nada más, **¿verdad?**

ACTIVIDAD H Una historia

Paso 1 Trabajando con un compañero (una compañera) de clase, inventa una historia sobre lo que pasa en los siguientes dibujos. A continuación tienen algunas ideas para considerar.

- ◆ ¿Cómo se llama el chico?
- ◆ ¿Qué compra? ¿Por qué va de compras?
- ◆ ¿Cómo se siente mientras prepara la comida?
- ◆ ¿A quiénes invitó a su apartamento?
- ◆ Al final, ¿cómo se siente?

1.   2.   3.   4.

Paso 2 Compartan su historia con el resto de la clase. ¿Quiénes inventaron la mejor historia?

IDEAS PARA EXPLORAR

Los gustos

VOCABULARIO

¿Qué meriendas?

Talking about snacks and snacking

Vocabulario útil

merendar (ie)	to snack (on)	**la máquina vendedora**	vending machine
tener hambre	to be hungry	**la merienda**	snack
		las palomitas	popcorn
los dulces	candies	**las papas (patatas) fritas**	potato chips
las galletas	cookies	**los pasteles**	pastries

ACTIVIDAD A ¿Qué meriendas?

El profesor (La profesora) va a mencionar un alimento. Indica si comes este alimento como merienda o no.

1... **2...** **3...** **4...** **5...** **6...** **7...** **8...** **9...**

¿Con quién meriendas?

COMUNICACIÓN

ACTIVIDAD B Cuando tienes hambre...

Paso 1 Usando los números 1–12, indica con qué frecuencia comes como merienda lo siguiente (**12** = muy frecuentemente, **1** = nunca).

Cuando tengo hambre, meriendo...

_____ una banana.	_____ nueces.
_____ dulces.	_____ palomitas.
_____ galletas.	_____ papas fritas.
_____ una manzana.	_____ un pedazo (*piece*) de pastel.
_____ media toronja.	_____ yogur.
_____ una naranja.	_____ una zanahoria.

Paso 2 Entrevista a otras tres personas en la clase para averiguar qué comen con más frecuencia para merendar y qué comen con menos frecuencia.

MODELOS De los alimentos del **Paso 1,** ¿cuál nunca comes como merienda?

¿Cuál comes con mayor frecuencia para merendar?

Paso 3 Compara tus resultados con los de otra persona (alguien a quien no entrevistaste en el **Paso 2**). Según los resultados, ¿qué suelen merendar las personas y qué no suelen merendar? ¿Pertenecen (*Do* [*they*] *pertain*) las meriendas favoritas a alguna de las categorías de alimentos básicos, como, por ejemplo, a las proteínas?

Así se dice

To say you are hungry or thirsty, Spanish does not use **estar** but rather **tener** with the feminine nouns **hambre** (*hunger*) and **sed** (*thirst*). The literal translations in English are *to have hunger* and *to have thirst*.

Tengo (mucha) hambre.
I'm (*very*) *hungry.*

Tengo (mucha) sed.
I'm (*very*) *thirsty.*

ACTIVIDAD C ¿Sabías que... ?

Paso 1 Lee la selección **¿Sabías que... ?** Luego indica si cada afirmación es cierta (C) o falsa (F).

	C	F
1. Las tapas son un tipo de postre.	☐	☐
2. Las tapas explican cómo es que los españoles pueden cenar muy tarde.	☐	☐
3. En este país no existe ninguna costumbre semejante.	☐	☐

Paso 2 Entrevista a un compañero (una compañera) de clase. ¿Tiene él (ella) la costumbre de merendar cierta comida o a cierta hora?

Paso 3 Ahora piensa en cuando eras niño/a. ¿Qué comidas merendabas? ¿Cuál era la actitud de tu madre hacia merender antes de cenar? Comparte tus respuestas con tu compañero/a.

¿Sabías que...

los españoles tienen la costumbre de merendar a las 5.00 ó 6.00 de la tarde? Dada la hora de la cena española, la merienda consiste en comer tapas, porciones pequeñas de no más de cuatro onzas, perfectas para picar.[a] Entre las tapas más conocidas están las gambas[b] y los champiñones al ajillo,[c] la famosa tortilla española, las croquetas y el jamón serrano. Comiendo unas cuantas tapas, el español se puede sostener hasta la típica hora tarde de comer.

Algunas tapas típicas

Las tapas se originan en la Edad Media.[d] Alfonso X (el Sabio)[e] notó que sus guerreros[f] mostraban poca disposición para la lucha. El Rey descubrió que entre batallas sus soldados aprovechaban[g] el vino que se producía en la región. Entonces, obligó a los taberneros que sirvieran a las tropas a colocarles[h] sobre la copa de vino una rebanada[i] de pan con queso, jamón o chorizo, en porciones que las tropas debían ingerir[j] antes de consumir la bebida alcohólica. Además de empezar la costumbre de las tapas, tal vez Alfonso el Sabio fue el primero en combatir los malos efectos del alcohol.

---

[a]*para... for nibbling* [b]*camarones (Sp.)* [c]*champiñones... mushrooms in garlic* [d]*Edad... Middle Ages* [e]*Alfonso... Alfonso the Tenth (the Wise), an important Spanish king* [f]*warriors, soldiers* [g]*enjoyed* [h]*to place* [i]*slice* [j]*eat*

NAVEGANDO LA RED

Busca información sobre la costumbre española de merendar tapas en la tarde. ¿Puedes encontrar información sobre la historia de las tapas? ¿Se puede conseguir tapas donde tú vives? Presenta tu información a la clase.

GRAMÁTICA

¿Le pones sal a la comida?

Le and **les** as third person indirect object pronouns

me	nos
te	os
le	les

| **le** | pones | **les** | pones |

—¿Te gusta?
—Sí, está riquísima. ¿Qué **le** pusiste?

Así se dice

Remember that Spanish word order is flexible. The subject of a sentence may not always be the first noun before the verb. Don't mistake indirect object pronouns for subjects and don't mistake phrases with **a** for subjects either. In the following sentence, who is not making a good impression on whom?

Al profesor no le cae bien Juanito.

If you said Juanito is not making a good impression on the professor, you were right.

Le and **les** are indirect object pronouns like **me, te,** and **nos.** They frequently mean *to* or *for him* (*her, it*) and *to* or *for them.* (**Les** can also be used to mean *to* or *for you* [*pl.*]).

Tus amigos quieren saber cuáles son los ingredientes especiales.
¿**Les** vas a decir cuáles son? (**les** = a tus amigos)
A Juan no **le** gustan las verduras crudas. (**le** = a Juan)

When **le** and **les** are used with verbs like **poner** (*to put*) and **quitar** (*to remove, take away*), the English equivalent is *to put in* or *on* (*him, her, it,* and so forth) or *to take off of* (*him, her, it,* and so forth).

—¿Qué **le** pones a la comida, mucha sal (*salt*) o poca?
—No **le** pongo nada. (**le** = a la comida)

Cuando preparo el pollo, siempre **le** quito la piel (*skin*). (**le** = al pollo)

Have you noticed that these pronouns are often redundant? That is, **le** and **les** are used even when the person to or for whom something happens is explicitly mentioned in the sentence.

A mi mamá le di algo muy especial para su cumpleaños.
A los perros les encanta comer huesos.

Indirect object pronouns can be used by themselves once the person or thing referred to has been established in context.

—¿Qué **le** vas a decir **a tu compañera de cuarto**?
—No sé. Creo que no **le** voy a decir nada.

In the second part of this exchange, the speaker did not repeat **a mi compañera** because that person had already been referred to in the conversation.

ACTIVIDAD D ¿Qué le pones a la comida?

Paso 1 Marca la(s) respuesta(s) que mejor indica(n) lo que sueles hacer.

1. ¿Qué le pones a la comida?

☐ Le pongo un poco de sal.

☐ Le pongo mucha sal.

☐ No le pongo nada.

☐ Le pongo un poco de pimienta (*pepper*).

☐ Le pongo mucha pimienta.

2. ¿Qué les pones a las hamburguesas?

☐ Les pongo mayonesa.

☐ Les pongo salsa de tomate (*ketchup*).

☐ Les pongo mostaza (*mustard*).

☐ No les pongo nada.

☐ Soy vegetariano/a.

3. ¿Qué les pones a las papas fritas?

☐ Les pongo salsa de tomate.

☐ Les pongo mayonesa.

☐ Les pongo un poco de vinagre.

☐ Les pongo sal.

☐ Les pongo pimienta.

☐ No les pongo nada.

4. ¿Qué les pones a las palomitas?

☐ Les pongo sal.

☐ Les pongo margarina.

☐ Les pongo mantequilla.

☐ Les pongo queso parmesano.

☐ No les pongo nada.

5. Además de leche, ¿qué le pones al cereal preparado?

☐ Le pongo azúcar.

☐ Le pongo miel (*honey*).

☐ Le pongo pasas (*raisins*).

☐ Le pongo fruta fresca (*fresh*).

☐ No le pongo nada.

Paso 2 Usando las respuestas que diste en el **Paso 1,** inventa cinco preguntas para hacerles a tus compañeros de clase de manera que ellos contesten sí o no. (En el **Paso 3,** cada persona va a firmar su nombre al lado de la pregunta.) Por ejemplo, si tú contestaste la pregunta, «No les pongo nada», tu pregunta sería (*would be*) «¿Les pones algo a las palomitas?» Si contestaste «Les pongo mantequilla», tu pregunta sería «¿Les pones mantequilla a las palomitas?»

Paso 3 Ahora hazles las preguntas que escribiste en el **Paso 2** a tus compañeros hasta encontrar a cinco que contesten sí. Cada persona debe firmar su nombre al lado de la pregunta.

ACTIVIDAD E ¿Le pides... ?

El verbo **pedir** (*to request, ask for*) también toma un objeto indirecto aunque el significado no es *to* o *for someone*. Indica lo que haces en las situaciones en la siguiente página.

1. Mañana tienes que entregarle al profesor (a la profesora) un trabajo, pero sabes muy bien que no lo vas a terminar para mañana. ¿Qué haces?

   a. Le pides una prórroga (*extension*) al profesor (a la profesora).
   b. Le pides una prórroga sólo si es un profesor (una profesora) que conoces bien.
   c. No le pides prórroga. Le entregas tarde el trabajo y esperas que lo acepte (*he [she] accepts it*).

2. Es hora de volver a casa. Está lloviendo y no tienes paraguas (*umbrella*). Ves a una persona que conoces subir a (*get in*) su auto. ¿Qué haces?

   a. Le pides que te lleve (*takes you*) a tu casa.
   b. Le pides que te lleve a tu casa sólo si es una persona que conoces muy bien.
   c. No le pides que te lleve a tu casa. Tomas el autobús o un taxi.

3. En un restaurante, se te cae (*you drop*) un tenedor (*fork*). ¿Qué haces?

   a. Le pides otro al mesero.
   b. No le pides otro al mesero. Tomas el tenedor de otra mesa donde no hay clientes.
   c. No le pides otro al mesero. Recoges (*You pick up*) el tenedor del suelo y lo limpias con la servilleta (*napkin*).

COMUNICACIÓN

ACTIVIDAD F Situaciones

Paso 1 En grupos de tres o cuatro, escriban por lo menos tres posibles opciones para cada situación. **¡OJO!** Deben utilizar objetos indirectos.

MODELO	SITUACIÓN:	Estás en un restaurante elegante y el servicio es muy malo.
	POSIBLES OPCIONES:	a. No le doy propina (*tip*) al mesero.
		b. Le digo al gerente (*manager*) que no voy a volver.
		c. Les digo a mis amigos que es un restaurante horrible.

1. Estás en un café con unos amigos. Llega la cuenta y descubres (*you discover*) que no tienes dinero (*money*).
2. Vas al supermercado (*supermarket*) para comprar verduras. Las verduras que tienen no son frescas y, además, son caras.
3. Un amigo te invita a cenar a su casa pero sabes que no cocina (*he doesn't cook*) muy bien.
4. Estás en un café con unos amigos. Llega la cuenta y uno de tus compañeros te dice que no tiene dinero. Es la tercera vez que te pide dinero.
5. Estás en la casa de un amigo (una amiga) y sus padres preparan una cena que no te gusta para nada.

Paso 2 Escojan una situación y escriban las opciones en la pizarra. Presenten las opciones a la clase indicando la opción que prefieren y por qué. ¿Es esta la opción que prefiere la mayoría de la clase?

GRAMÁTICA

¡Está muy salada!

More about **estar** + adjectives

In English, when we use *to be* in talking about foods and other products, we are often referring to how they taste, smell, feel, look, and sometimes sound. In Spanish, **estar** is used in these situations.

La sopa **está** rica.	*The soup is (tastes) really good.*
La sopa **está** salada.	*The soup is (tastes) salty.*
La sopa **está** deliciosa.	*The soup is (tastes) delicious.*
Está muy fuerte el perfume.	*The perfume is (smells) very strong.*
Está fresco el pescado.	*The fish is (looks) fresh.*
Están suaves las toallas.	*The towels are (feel) soft.*

ACTIVIDAD G ¿Fresca o pasada°?

spoiled, old

Completa la información de la columna A con información de la columna B. En algunos casos, hay diferentes combinaciones posibles.

A

1. Si la banana está fresca, _____.
2. Si la banana está pasada, _____.
3. Si la leche está pasada, _____.
4. Si la manzana está fresca, _____.
5. Si la manzana está muy pasada, _____.
6. Si el pollo está pasado, _____.
7. Si el aguacate está listo para comer, _____.

B

a. está marrón
b. está amarilla
c. está olorosa (*odorous*)
d. está blando/a (*soft*)
e. está duro/a (*hard*)
f. está firme pero no duro/a
g. está roja
h. tiene mal olor (*odor*)

ACTIVIDAD H Cuando el pescado está fresco...

Paso 1 Lee la selección «¿Cómo se sabe que un pescado está fresco?» en la siguiente página.

¿Cómo se sabe que un pescado está fresco?

La carne[a]

La firmeza elástica es una garantía de calidad. Presione con el dedo sobre la carne del lomo[b]: si la marca no desaparece o tarda en desaparecer, el pescado no está fresco.

Los ojos

Los ojos nunca deben estar hundidos ni presentar limosidad amarillenta. Rechace los pescados a los que se les han extraído los ojos.[c]

El olor

El pescado fresco huele a mar,[d] un aroma agradable. Si un pescado no está fresco, emite un fuerte olor.

Las agallas

Las agallas deben estar rojas, de una intensidad brillante. Si el pescado está pasado, las agallas presentan un color marrón sucio. En algunos casos los vendedores decapitan los pescados y ya no se puede ver las agallas. Rechace los pescados decapitados.

El vientre

La pared del vientre no debe estar rota.[e] La grasa no debe estar amarilla.

---

[a]*flesh* [b]*back* [c]*a... that have had their eyes extracted* [d]*huele... smells like the sea* [e]*torn*

Vocabulario útil

rechazar	to reject	**la pared**	wall
		el vientre	belly
las agallas	gills		
el dedo	finger	**hundido/a**	sunken
la limosidad	sliminess	**sucio/a**	dirty

Paso 2 Sin volver a mirar la selección, indica a qué parte del pescado se refieren las siguientes oraciones.

1. _____ deben estar rojas y brillantes.   **a.** Las agallas

2. _____ no debe estar roto.   **b.** La carne

3. _____ debe estar firme pero no dura.   **c.** Los ojos

4. _____ no deben estar hundidos.   **d.** El vientre

Paso 3 Con un compañero (una compañera) inventa dos o tres oraciones como las del **Paso 2** sobre otro alimento y cómo debe estar cuando está fresco. Presenten sus oraciones a la clase.

> MODELO   El bistec fresco debe estar rojo y no marrón. Si tiene un olor desagradable no está fresco.

COMUNICACIÓN

ACTIVIDAD I ¡Ay, qué rico!°

My, how delicious!

Paso 1 Piensa en una vez en que comiste un plato muy rico y contesta las siguientes preguntas.

1. ¿Cómo era el plato?

2. ¿Dónde estabas?

3. ¿Con quién estabas?

Paso 2 Ahora, escribe sobre una vez en que dijiste que un plato estaba rico pero no era la verdad. Contesta las mismas preguntas del **Paso 1.**

Paso 3 En grupos de tres, compartan sus experiencias. Al final, una persona del grupo debe presentar dos de las experiencias al resto de la clase.

¡Qué rico está el helado! (La Habana, Cuba)

NAVEGANDO LA RED

Busca una reseña (*review*) en español de un restaurante. Reporta a la clase el nombre del restaurante, dónde se encuentra, quién escribió la reseña y si al final le gustó el restaurante o no.

INTERCAMBIO

Preferencias alimenticias

Propósito: escribir un artículo sobre las preferencias y hábitos de un compañero (una compañera) de clase con relación a la comida.

Papeles: dos estudiantes entrevistan a otro/a; los (las) tres escriben el artículo.

Paso 1 Dos personas deben entrevistar a otra para poder llenar el cuadro (*table*) a continuación. La información tiene que ver con el hecho de salir a comer en vez de (*instead of*) comer en casa.

	EL DESAYUNO	EL ALMUERZO	LA CENA
frecuencia con que sale a comer			
dónde come			
qué suele pedir (orders)			
sus preferencias en cuanto a la comida *qué (no) le encanta* *qué (no) le cae bien* *qué (no) le agrada*			

Paso 2 Ahora los (las) tres tienen que escribir, en forma de un artículo, las preferencias de la persona entrevistada. Pueden utilizar como modelo «Mis platos preferidos» que está en la página 193.

MODELO   Esta persona sale muy poco a comer. Cuando va a un restaurante, suele ir a…

Paso 3 Los grupos deben entregarle al profesor (a la profesora) el artículo **sin indicar el nombre de la persona entrevistada.** El profesor (La profesora) va a leer cada entrevista a la clase para que todos adivinen (*so that everyone can guess*) a quién se refiere.

Vistazos culturales
La cocina en el mundo hispano

¿Sabías que... en el mundo hispano la cocina varía muchísimo de un lugar a otro? La gastronomía de cada país hispano incluye platos tradicionales así como platos especiales que sólo se comen en determinadas regiones. En muchos países la dieta refleja la influencia de varias culturas. En Puerto Rico, por ejemplo, la cocina se llama «criolla» porque tiene influencias caribeñas (frutas tropicales), europeas (el aceite de oliva), indígenas (el chocolate) y africanas (el proceso de freír[a]).

—————————————

[a]*frying*

Plátano frito

Las comidas tradicionales

En **España** la paella es un plato tradicional. Tiene su origen en Valencia pero hay muchas variaciones regionales. La paella es una mezcla de arroz con azafrán[a] y guisantes y puede llevar varios mariscos o carnes.

—————

[a]*saffron*

En **México,** en las comidas más tradicionales se usan ingredientes que se remontan[a] a la época de los imperios azteca y maya. Tal vez el ingrediente más reconocido como «mexicano» es el chile. Hay muchos tipos de chile, algunos muy picantes,[b] otros no tanto. Un plato mexicano tradicional se llama **chile relleno.**[c] Los chiles que se usan en este plato son grandes, verdes y normalmente no pican mucho. El relleno más común es el queso, pero es possible usar otros ingredientes al gusto.

—————————————

[a]*se... date back*   [b]*spicy*   [c]*chiles... stuffed chile*

Chile relleno

Paella

En **México** hay varias especialidades regionales interesantes. En el estado de Oaxaca se comen **chapulines**[a] fritos. En los estados de Chiapas es común comer **armadillo**. En el estado de Guerrero se puede comer **iguana** y en Taxco, una ciudad colonial del estado de Guerrero, una de las delicias locales es una salsa hecha de **jumiles,** un tipo de escarabajo[b] pequeño.

---

[a]*grasshoppers* (Mex.)   [b]*beetle*

Chapulines fritos

Las comidas menos tradicionales

Aunque en este país el **cuy**[a] se considera una mascota,[b] en **el Perú** y otros países andinos el cuy se ha criado[c] como comida por miles de años. El cuy tiene mucho valor nutritivo. Es alto en proteínas y bajo en grasas. Para muchos indígenas pobres que suelen comer papas y arroz, el cuy aporta[d] proteínas a su dieta.

---

[a]*guinea pig*   [b]*pet*   [c]*se... has been raised*   [d]*brings*

Cuy a la parrilla (grilled)

En la provincia de Santander, **Colombia,** se comen **hormigas culonas.**[a] Las hormigas tienen una pulgada de largo[b] y se sirven tostadas. Saben a palomitas de maíz o nueces.

---

[a]*hormigas... fat-bottomed ants*
[b]*tienen... are one inch long*

ACTIVIDAD ¿Qué recuerdas?

Indica si las siguientes oraciones son ciertas (C) o falsas (F).

	C	F
1. La paella española tiene su origen en Sevilla.	☐	☐
2. El cuy es alto en proteínas.	☐	☐
3. Las hormigas culonas son una especialidad de Santander, Colombia.	☐	☐
4. En Oaxaca, México, se come iguana.	☐	☐
5. El maíz es uno de los ingredientes principales de la paella.	☐	☐
6. El aceite de oliva es de origen europeo.	☐	☐

NAVEGANDO LA RED

Escoge *uno* de los siguientes proyectos y presenta tus resultados a la clase.

1. Escoge un país hispano y busca información sobre los platos que se suelen comer allí durante la Navidad. Haz las siguientes cosas.
   a. Menciona el país y haz una breve lista de las comidas y bebidas tradicionales navideñas.
   b. Escribe la receta (*recipe*) de una de las comidas o bebidas de tu lista.
   c. Compara tu lista de comidas con lo que tú sueles comer durante la Navidad, el Janucá (*Hanukkah*) u otra temporada (*season*) especial.

2. Busca información sobre la dieta mediterránea de España y la dieta del Caribe. Haz las siguientes cosas.
   a. Haz dos listas de los ingredientes más comunes, una lista para cada región.
   b. Menciona las semejanzas (*similarities*) y diferencias entre una dieta y la otra.
   c. Menciona las ventajas y desventajas de cada dieta.
   d. Compara la dieta de una de estas dos regiones con la tuya.

3. Busca información sobre los modismos (*idiomatic expressions*) que tienen la comida como tema. Apunta por lo menos tres modismos y da su significado literal y figurado (*figurative*) en inglés. No te olvides de mencionar en qué país o región se usan.
   MODELO **un rábano verde** = *a dirty old man*
   Se usa en México y en otras partes del mundo hispano.

The **Vocabulario comprensivo** list in this lesson is long, since it presents much of the thematic vocabulary that you will have an opportunity to use throughout **Unidad tres.** You will find that the **Vocabulario comprensivo** lists in **Lecciones 8** and **9** are shorter.

Los alimentos básicos
Basic Foods

El calcio — Calcium

los productos lácteos	dairy products
el helado	ice cream
la leche	milk
el queso	cheese
el yogur	yogurt

Las proteínas — Proteins

las carnes	meats
el bistec	steak
la carne de res	beef
la chuleta de cerdo	pork chop
la hamburguesa	hamburger
el jamón	ham
las aves	poultry
el huevo	egg
el pollo	chicken
los pescados y mariscos	fish and shellfish
el atún	tuna
los camarones	shrimp
los frijoles	beans
la mantequilla de cacahuete	peanut butter
las nueces	nuts

Las vitaminas y la fibra — Vitamins and Fiber

las frutas	fruits
el aguacate	avocado
la banana	banana
la fresa	strawberry
el limón	lemon
la manzana	apple
la naranja	orange
el tomate	tomato
la toronja	grapefruit
la uva	grape
las verduras	vegetables
las espinacas	spinach
los guisantes	peas
las judías verdes	green beans
la lechuga	lettuce
el maíz	corn
la papa	potato (*Lat. Am.*)
la patata	potato (*Sp.*)
la zanahoria	carrot

Los carbohidratos y la fibra — Carbohydrates and Fiber

el arroz	rice
los cereales	cereals; grains
los espaguetis	spaghetti
el pan blanco	white bread
el pan integral	whole wheat bread
las pastas alimenticias	pasta

Las grasas — Fats

el aceite de maíz	corn oil
el aceite de oliva	olive oil
la mantequilla	butter

Para describir los alimentos
Describing Foods

agrio/a	sour
amargo/a	bitter
asado/a	roast(ed)
cocinado/a	cooked
crudo/a	raw
dulce	sweet
fresco/a	fresh
pasado/a	spoiled, old
al horno	baked
al vapor	steamed
el gusto	taste (*preference*)
el hábito de comer	eating habit
el sabor	taste (*flavor*)
Sabe a...	It tastes like . . .

¿Qué desayunas?
What Do You Have for Breakfast?

la bollería	assorted breads and rolls
el bollo	roll
el churro	type of fried dough
el huevo frito (revuelto)	fried (scrambled) egg
el jugo (de naranja)	(orange) juice
la mermelada	jam, marmalade

el panqueque	pancake		

el panqueque	pancake
el pan tostado	toast
la salchicha	sausage
el tocino	bacon
la tostada	toast
desayunar (R)	to have breakfast

¿Qué comes para el almuerzo y para la cena?
What Do You Have for Lunch and Dinner?

el emperador	swordfish
la ensalada	salad
el flan	baked custard
las lentejas	lentils
(medio) pollo asado	(half a) roast chicken
el postre	dessert
el puré de papas	mashed potatoes
el sandwich	sandwich
la tarta	pie
la ternera	veal
la tortilla	omelette (Sp.)
almorzar (ue) (R)	to have lunch
cenar (R)	to have dinner
el menú del día	daily menu
el primer (segundo, tercer) plato	first (second, third) course

Las comidas
Meals

el almuerzo	lunch
la cena (R)	dinner
el desayuno	breakfast

¿Qué meriendas?
What Do You Snack On?

los dulces	candy
la galleta	cookie
las palomitas	popcorn
las papas fritas	potato chips; French fries (Lat. Am.)
los pasteles	pastries
las patatas fritas	potato chips; French fries (Sp.)
la máquina vendedora	vending machine
la merienda	snack
merendar (ie)	to snack (on)

Y para tomar...
And To Drink . . .

el agua (f.)	water
el café (R) (con leche)	coffee (with milk)
la cerveza	beer
el refresco	soft drink
el té	tea
el vino	wine

Los condimentos
Condiments

el azúcar	sugar
la mayonesa	mayonnaise
la mostaza	mustard
la pimienta	pepper
la sal	salt
la salsa de tomate	ketchup

Los colores
Colors

amarillo/a	yellow
blanco/a	white
marrón	dark brown
negro/a (R)	black
rojo/a	red
rosado/a	pink
verde (R)	green

Verbos
Verbs

agradar	to please
apetecer	to be appetizing; to appeal, be appealing (food)
caer (irreg.) bien/mal	to make a good/bad impression; to (dis)agree with (food)
encantar	to delight, be extremely pleasing
importar	to be important; to matter
interesar	to be interesting
poner (irreg.)	to put, place
quitar	to remove, take away
tener (mucha) hambre	to be (very) hungry

LECCIÓN **8**

Check out the following media resources to complement this lesson:

 Online *Manual*

 Video on CD

 Online Learning Center

 ActivityPak

¿Qué se hace con los brazos?

In this lesson, you will

- ◆ learn vocabulary related to eating at the table

- ◆ learn some vocabulary related to eating in restaurants

- ◆ note some more differences between eating habits in Spanish-speaking countries and this country

- ◆ learn about the impersonal and passive **se** constructions in Spanish

- ◆ learn more about **por** and **para**

En el mundo hispano es común apoyar **(to support)** *los dos brazos en la mesa.* **(Madrid, España)**

ALTO Before beginning this lesson, look over the **Intercambio** activity on page 231. This is the activity you will be working toward throughout the lesson.

VOCABULARIO

¿Qué hay en la mesa?

Talking about eating at the table

Así se dice

As you know, cognates may not always mean the same thing from one language to another. As you can see in the following **Vocabulario útil** box, *table manners* is rendered in Spanish by the word **modales** and not by the cognate word **maneras** (*ways*). Similarly, you might hear someone described as **muy educado/a,** but this description does not refer to any kind of academic preparation. Note how **educado/a** may be used in Spanish.

Es muy **educada.**
She is very well-mannered.

la jarra
el cuenco
la mesa
la copa
el salero
el vaso
la taza
el pimentero
la cuchara
la servilleta
el platillo
el tenedor
el cuchillo
el plato
el mantel

Vocabulario útil

cortar	to cut	**los brazos**	arms
derramar	to spill	**los buenos modales**	good manners
levantar la mesa	to clear the table	**los codos**	elbows
poner la mesa	to set the table	**los cubiertos**	silverware
		las manos	hands
la boca	mouth		

Lección 8   ¿Qué se hace con los brazos?

ACTIVIDAD A ¿Cómo los utilizamos?

Escucha el nombre del objeto que menciona el profesor (la profesora). Indica para qué lo utilizamos, según el modelo.

MODELO Lo (La) utilizamos para...

1. cubrir (*to cover*) la mesa.
2. tomar café.
3. servir la comida principal.
4. comer la sopa.
5. limpiarnos la boca.
6. comer la comida principal.
7. servir agua o vino.

ACTIVIDAD B Asociaciones

Empareja una palabra o frase de la columna A con otra de la columna B.

A

1. _____ la carne
2. _____ ayudar antes de comer
3. _____ ayudar después de comer
4. _____ ser torpe (*clumsy*)
5. _____ el agua
6. _____ el vino
7. _____ la cuchara

B

a. la copa
b. cortar
c. derramar el vino en la mesa
d. levantar la mesa
e. poner la mesa
f. la sopa
g. el vaso

COMUNICACIÓN

ACTIVIDAD C Con las manos

Paso 1 A continuación hay una lista de comidas típicas. Indica si comes cada una con cubiertos o no. ¿Hay costumbres comunes a la mayoría de la clase?

MODELO las papas fritas → Las como con las manos.

1. las papas fritas
2. los sandwiches de queso
3. las hamburguesas
4. el pollo a la barbacoa
5. las rosquillas (*doughnuts*)
6. la fruta fresca (manzana, naranja)
7. la tarta de manzana

Paso 2 Ahora indica si para tomar alguna de las siguientes bebidas la pones primero en un vaso o no. ¿Hay costumbres comunes a la mayoría de la clase?

MODELO la cerveza → No la pongo en un vaso. La tomo directamente de la botella.

1. la cerveza
2. la leche
3. los jugos
4. el agua mineral
5. los refrescos

---

*La modelo = female fashion model; **el modelo** = any other kind of model.
†La radio = the medium of radio; **el radio** = piece of equipment.

GRAMÁTICA

¿Se debe... ?

—Mira. **Se debe** poner el tenedor al lado izquierdo (*left side*) del plato y el cuchillo al lado derecho (*right*), ¿ves?

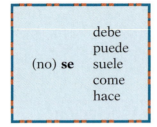

	debe
	puede
(no) **se**	suele
	come
	hace

You have already seen the pronoun **se** used in reflexive sentences. It is also used in Spanish to make impersonal sentences, ones in which the verb is singular and the subject is not specified. In this usage, there is no reflexive meaning similar to *-self* or *-selves*. The rough equivalent in English would be sentences that use the nonspecific subject pronouns *one, you,* or *they.*

No **se debe** comer mucha carne.	*One (You) shouldn't eat a lot of meat.*
Si **se come** bien, **se vive** bien.	*If one eats well, one lives well. (If you eat well, you live well.)*
En Carmon's **se sirve** una pizza magnífica.	*At Carmon's they serve a great pizza.*

What do you think the following sentences mean?

No se debe poner los codos en la mesa.
Se suele almorzar a las 12.00.

If you said *One (You) shouldn't put one's (your) elbows on the table* and *One usually eats lunch at noon (You [They] usually eat lunch at noon),* then you were right.

Los errores que no debes cometer en la mesa

● No comas con los codos apoyados en la mesa. En primer lugar, porque limitas tus movimientos. Y en segundo, porque los alimentos pueden caerse de los cubiertos. Tus brazos tienen que moverse libremente. Sin embargo, cuando no estés comiendo puedes apoyarlos sobre la mesa.
● No dejes las cucharas dentro de la taza del café, del té o de la sopa.
● No pongas alimentos en cantidades exageradas en tu boca. ¡Es de muy mal gusto!
● No mastiques con la boca abierta y no hagas ruido con los labios y la lengua, porque es muy antiestético.
● No hables con la boca llena, porque se saldrá la comida. Si quieres hablar mientras comes, hazlo cuando tengas una mínima cantidad de comida en la boca. De otra manera, habla después de haber tragado los alimentos.

ACTIVIDAD D Los buenos modales

Paso 1 Indica en qué situación se observa cada regla (*rule*).

a. En toda circunstancia.
b. Sólo en ocasiones formales.
c. Sólo con la familia o con amigos muy íntimos.

1. _____ No se debe poner los brazos en la mesa mientras se come.
2. _____ No se debe comer el pollo frito o asado con las manos.
3. _____ Para comer las papas fritas, se debe utilizar tenedor.
4. _____ Al sentarse (*Upon sitting down*) uno a la mesa, se debe colocar la servilleta en el regazo (*lap*) y no dejarla en la mesa.
5. _____ No se debe alcanzar con el brazo (*reach for*) algo en la mesa si está lejos (*far away*).
6. _____ Si alguien quiere sal, se le debe pasar ambos (*both*) el salero y el pimentero.

7. _____ No se debe comenzar a comer si los demás (*the others*) no tienen su comida.

8. _____ Al terminar de comer, uno se debe ofrecer a levantar la mesa para ayudar al anfitrión (a la anfitriona) (*host* [*hostess*]).

Paso 2 Ahora compara tus respuestas con las del resto de la clase. ¿Están todos de acuerdo o no con las afirmaciones?

COMUNICACIÓN

ACTIVIDAD E ¿Cuándo se puede hacer eso?

¿Cuándo se puede hacer las cosas a continuación? Inventa algo para terminar cada oración y compara tus ideas con las de un compañero (una compañera). ¿Qué ideas tienen en común?

1. Se puede interrumpir a otra persona mientras habla cuando (si)…

2. No se tiene que dejar propina cuando (si)…

3. Se le puede pedir a un invitado que traiga (*ask a guest to bring*) algo de comer cuando (si)…

4. Se puede tutear (*address as* **tú**) a un profesor (una profesora) cuando (si)…

ACTIVIDAD F En su opinión

Paso 1 Trabajando con dos o tres compañeros/as de clase, comenta las siguientes afirmaciones. Apunten sus ideas.

«Las madres, no los padres, les enseñan los buenos modales a los niños».
«Las mujeres tienen mejores modales que los hombres».
«Dos hermanos, un niño y una niña, van a tener modales diferentes».

Paso 2 Compartan sus ideas con el resto de la clase. ¿Creen todos que los hombres y las mujeres tienen modales diferentes?

NAVEGANDO LA RED

Busca información sobre una escuela o una página dedicada a enseñar buenos modales y (o) a mejorar el comportamiento social. Reporta a la clase la siguiente información.

◆ el nombre de la escuela o página
◆ tres de los varios tipos de modales que presenta y comenta
◆ lo que dicen de uno de los modales en particular

Así se dice

What if you want to use an impersonal **se** with a reflexive verb? With reflexive verbs and verbs like **quedarse** that always take a **se,** Spanish uses **uno** instead of the impersonal **se.**

Uno se levanta temprano aquí.
Si hay una tormenta (*storm*), **uno** debe **quedarse** en casa.

Uno can also be used instead of the impersonal **se** with all other verbs.

Uno no debe derramar sal. Es mala suerte (*bad luck*).

VOCABULARIO

¿Hay que... ?

Expressing impersonal obligation

—Mira. Aquí dice que **no se puede** visitar Buenos Aires **sin** probar la parrillada.

es imprescindible	it's essential
es (muy) buena idea	it's a (very) good idea
es necesario ⎱	it's necessary
es preciso ⎰	
hay que	one must, it's necessary
no se puede... sin...	you (one) can't . . . without . . .
se debe	you (one) should, must
se tiene que	you have to (one must)

ACTIVIDAD A Nueva York: Lo positivo y lo negativo°

Lo... *The positive and the negative*

Paso 1 Empareja una frase de la columna A con una de la columna B para hablar de lo positivo de Nueva York.

A

1. _____ En Nueva York hay que asistir a...

2. _____ Al visitar Nueva York se tiene que dar un paseo por...

3. _____ Si el dinero no es problema, es preciso quedarse en...

4. _____ Y claro, es necesario probar (*to try*)...

5. _____ No se puede visitar Nueva York sin ver...

B

a. los perritos calientes (*hot dogs*) que se venden (*are sold*) en cada esquina (*corner*).

b. una obra teatral en Broadway.

c. el Hotel Plaza.

d. el Parque Central.

e. la Estatua de la Libertad.

Paso 2 Esta vez, empareja una frase de la columna A con una de la columna B para hablar de lo negativo de Nueva York.

A

1. _____ No se debe caminar...

2. _____ No es buena idea llevar...

3. _____ Hay que evitar (*avoid*)...

B

a. mucho dinero en el bolsillo (*pocket*) o en la bolsa (*purse*).

b. el metro entre las 5.00 y las 6.30 de la tarde.

c. solo/a por la noche.

Así se dice

To enter a room politely, in English we say *Can I come in?* or *May I come in?* In Spanish one simply says **¿Se puede?**, which is short for **¿Se puede pasar?**

—¿**Se puede,** profesora?
—Sí. Pasa.

Paso 3 La clase debe determinar si las cosas negativas del **Paso 2** son exclusivas de Nueva York o si se pueden aplicar a otras ciudades.

COMUNICACIÓN

ACTIVIDAD B Hay que...

Paso 1 Piensa en una ciudad que conoces muy bien. Luego contesta las preguntas a continuación.

Si uno visita _____ (nombre de la ciudad),...

1. ¿hay que comer en algún restaurante en particular? ¿Se debe probar algún plato en particular? ¿Cuáles y por qué?

2. ¿se debe ver algún monumento o edificio (*building*) porque es histórico o interesante? ¿Cuál y por qué?

3. ¿es preciso hacer alguna actividad especial? ¿Cuál y por qué?

Paso 2 Ahora con las respuestas que diste en el **Paso 1,** forma un pequeño párrafo sobre la ciudad en cuestión. Trata de utilizar diferentes expresiones. Añade (*Add*) otros detalles si quieres. Luego si hay tiempo, comparte tu párrafo con la clase.

GRAMÁTICA

¿Se consumen muchas verduras?

The passive **se**

```
          toma(n)
se  +     come(n)
          consume(n)
```

EL VALOR CALÓRICO DE LAS ACTIVIDADES

ACTIVIDAD	CALORÍAS CONSUMIDAS POR HORA	
	MUJER	HOMBRE
Caminar (2–3 km/h.)	200	240
Trabajos caseros[a] (limpiar el piso,[b] barrer,[c] etcétera)	300	360
Correr	800	1.000
Escribir a computadora	200	220
Nadar	600	800
Tenis	440	560
Esquiar	600	700
Leer	40	50
Manejar	120	150
Andar en bicicleta (rápidamente)	460	640
Andar en bicicleta (lentamente)	240	280

¿Cuántas calorías **se consumen** al hacer cada actividad?

[a]Trabajos... *Housework* [b]*floor* [c]*sweeping*

Although you will be working with the passive **se** in a limited context in this lesson, its use in written Spanish is frequent, especially when referring to past events. Here are some typical examples of the passive **se** that you will encounter in readings. The first one's meaning is given to you. Can you figure out the others?

En 1605 **se publicó** la novela *Don Quijote de la Mancha*.
Don Quixote *was published in 1605.*

Se firmó la Declaración de la Independencia de los Estados Unidos en 1776.
Se hicieron varios experimentos.

Earlier you saw **se** used with singular verbs to express impersonal sentences. **Se** can also be used with both singular and plural verbs to form what is called a passive construction. Like an impersonal sentence, a passive sentence with **se** does not contain a stated subject. However, unlike the impersonal **se,** the passive **se** does not translate as *one* or *you* but rather as *is (are)* + *-ed* and sometimes as *they.*

Se queman muchas calorías cuando **se hacen** ejercicios aeróbicos.	*Many calories are burned when doing aerobics.*
Se sirve la cena a las 6.00.	*Dinner is served at 6:00.*
En Gallo's **se sirven** unos mejillones riquísimos.	*At Gallo's they serve some very tasty mussels.*

It is not as important to keep the exact meaning clear as it is to remember that when the object of the verb is plural, verbs in passive **se** constructions are also plural.

En IHOP **se preparan** cantidades enormes de panqueques.	*Enormous quantities of pancakes are prepared at IHOP.*

ACTIVIDAD C ¿En qué país... ?

Paso 1 Por lo general, la geografía y el clima influyen mucho en lo que se come y se toma en un país. Tomando en cuenta lo que sabes de la geografía y el clima en distintas partes del mundo, trata de completar cada oración a continuación.

1. En _____ se comen muchos mariscos.
2. En _____ se toman muchas bebidas calientes.
3. En _____ se preparan muchos platos con carne.
4. En _____ se preparan muchos platos con papas.
5. En _____ se comen muchas frutas tropicales.

Paso 2 Comparte tus oraciones con la clase. ¿Hay compañeros/as que piensan lo mismo que tú? ¿Cuántas veces menciona la clase un país de habla española? ¿Cuántas veces se menciona este país?

ACTIVIDAD D ¿Sabías que... ?

Paso 1 Antes de leer la selección **¿Sabías que... ?** en la siguiente página, piensa un momento en las preguntas a continuación.

1. ¿Qué es un «país mediterráneo»? ¿Puedes nombrar algunos?
2. Basándote en la pregunta anterior, ¿qué tipos de alimentos se consumen en la dieta mediterránea?

Paso 2 Ahora lee la selección. Luego completa lo siguiente.

1. Nombra cuatro alimentos que se consumen en la dieta mediterránea.
2. Según el experimento del Dr. Ancel Keys, ¿qué les pasó a los norteamericanos que siguieron la dieta mediterránea?
   a. Les subió (*Went up*) el nivel de colesterol.
   b. Les bajó (*Went down*) el nivel de colesterol.

¿Sabías que...

hay una dieta conocida como la dieta mediterránea? En esta dieta predominan las legumbres,[a] las pastas alimenticias, el arroz, las verduras, las frutas frescas, el pescado, los mariscos, el aceite de oliva, el pan y condimentos como el ajo, la mejorana[b] y la pimienta. Se llama dieta mediterránea porque es común en los países mediterráneos: España, Italia, Francia y Grecia. Esta dieta también es común en Portugal, aunque no es un país mediterráneo.

La paella española contiene lo típico de la dieta mediterránea: arroz, mariscos, pescado, verduras, aceite de oliva y otros alimentos saludables.

En 1962, el doctor Ancel Keys, conocido nutricionista norteamericano, hizo una investigación sobre la dieta mediterránea. Sus pacientes norteamericanos siguieron[c] esta dieta por varias semanas. Después, fueron sometidos[d] a una serie de exámenes médicos. El doctor Keys pudo comprobar que el nivel[e] de colesterol de sus pacientes había bajado[f] y que la incidencia de enfermedades cardiovasculares también había disminuido.[g] Parece que la dieta mediterránea es bastante saludable, ¿no?

---

[a]*legumes* (La palabra **legumbres** significa también *vegetables*.)   [b]*marjoram*
[c]*followed*   [d]fueron... *they were subjected*   [e]*level*   [f]había... *had dropped*
[g]había... *had diminished*

Paso 3 Mira la foto de la paella que acompaña la selección. ¿Te apetece la paella o no es plato de tu gusto? Entrevista a un compañero (una compañera) de clase para averiguar si le gustaría (*he* [*she*] *would like*) la dieta mediterránea o no. Hazle preguntas sobre los alimentos de esta dieta. Comparte con la clase lo que averiguaste.

MODELO   ¿Te gustan las legumbres? ¿Todas?

COMUNICACIÓN

ACTIVIDAD E La dieta norteamericana

Paso 1 Con otra persona, haz una lista de cinco de los alimentos típicos que se consumen en este país.

MODELO   En este país se consume(n) mucho...

1...   **2**...   **3**...   **4**...   **5**...

Paso 2 Escriban la lista en la pizarra y compárenla con las de otros grupos. ¿Cuáles alimentos se mencionan más? Ahora determinen si la dieta norteamericana es tan saludable como la dieta mediterránea.

ACTIVIDAD F La última vez...

Paso 1 Trabajando con un compañero (una compañera) de clase, habla de la última vez que comiste los cinco alimentos típicos que mencionaron en la **Actividad E.** Utilicen las siguientes preguntas como guía.

- ◆ ¿Qué comieron? ¿Adónde fueron?
- ◆ ¿Lo pasaron bien? (*Did you have a good time?*)
- ◆ ¿Usaron los buenos modales o no? ¿Cometieron algún error?

Paso 2 Compartan las historias con el resto de la clase.

Paso 3 (Optativo) Los estudiantes le preguntan al profesor (a la profesora) sobre la última vez que comió los cinco alimentos típicos.

NAVEGANDO LA RED

Busca la página Web de una Oficina de Turismo de un país de habla española. En particular, busca información sobre la gastronomía del país. ¿Hay recomendaciones para los turistas? ¿Hay una descripción de la dieta típica de los habitantes del país? Imprime la información y compártela con el resto de la clase.

Nota comunicativa

Now that you know the impersonal **se** and the passive **se,** you can expand your repertoire of strategies for communication. When you forget how to say a word or don't know it, you can ask for help by using an impersonal **se.** For example, to ask for help in finding out the Spanish word for *bottle opener,* you can say

¿Cómo se llama esa cosa con que se abre una botella?

Note that the phrase **con que** can be changed to **donde, en que, con quien,** or a number of other phrases depending on what you are saying (e.g., **¿Cómo se llama el lugar donde... ? ¿Cómo se llama la persona a quien... ?**) How would you ask for help during a conversation if you forgot or didn't know the following words? (Note: You can accompany your questions with gestures and anything else that helps!)

cabinet	garage	Post-it notes
dishwasher	knife	Q-tip

IDEAS PARA EXPLORAR

En un restaurante

VOCABULARIO

¿Está todo bien?

Talking about eating in restaurants

*Si el servicio es bueno, **los clientes le dejan una propina al camarero.***

atender (ie)	to wait on (*a customer*)
dejar (una propina)	to leave (a tip)
ordenar	to order
pedir (i, i)	to request, order
traer (*irreg.*)	to bring
el/la camarero/a	waiter, waitress
el/la mesero/a	
el cliente (la clienta)	customer
el/la cocinero/a	chef, cook
la comida para llevar	food to go
la cuenta	bill, check
el primer (segundo, tercer) plato	first (second, third) course
la propina	tip
¿Está todo bien?	Is everything OK?
¿Me podría traer... ?	Could you bring me . . . ?
¿Qué trae... ?	What does . . . come with?

Así se dice

As you already know, learning Spanish is not a simple matter of translating words from English. An example is the verb **invitar.** It can mean *to invite* in the most general sense, such as to invite someone to a party. But in Spanish, it can also mean *to treat* (*pay*).

Pablo: ¿Vamos a tomar un café?
Marisol: Sí. Yo te **invito.**

(*Llega la cuenta.*)
Diego: Bueno, **invito** yo.
Ester: No. **Invito** yo.
Diego: No, no. Tú **invitaste** la última vez.

ACTIVIDAD A Definiciones

Escucha la definición que da el profesor (la profesora). Luego empareja la definición con una palabra o expresión de la sección anterior.

1... **2**... **3**... **4**... **5**... **6**...

ACTIVIDAD B ¿En qué orden?

Paso 1 Pon en orden cronológico las siguientes actividades.

_____ Se pide la cuenta.
_____ El camarero trae el segundo plato.
_____ El cocinero prepara la orden.
_____ Se deja la propina en la mesa.
_____ Se pide la comida.
_____ Se toma un aperitivo.
_____ El camarero trae el primer plato.

Paso 2 Escucha mientras el profesor (la profesora) las lee cronológicamente. ¿Ordenaste bien las actividades?

ACTIVIDAD C ¿Quién lo dice?

Indica quién diría (*would say*) cada oración, un cliente o un camarero.

	CLIENTE	CAMARERO
1. «¿Están listos para pedir?»	☐	☐
2. «¿Qué trae el filete?»	☐	☐
3. «La cuenta, por favor.»	☐	☐
4. «Como primer plato, me gustaría la sopa.»	☐	☐
5. «¿Está todo bien?»	☐	☐
6. «¿Me podría traer otro tenedor, por favor?»	☐	☐

COMUNICACIÓN

ACTIVIDAD D ¿Y la propina?

En los Estados Unidos, es costumbre dejar de propina como mínimo el 15% del total de la cuenta. En esta actividad, vamos a examinar esta costumbre.

Paso 1 Escribe la frase que se te aplica más y entrégasela al profesor (a la profesora). Si no comes mucho en restaurantes, escribe lo que harías (*you would do*) en ese caso.

Con respecto a la propina,…

1. suelo dejar el 15% y nada más.

2. suelo dejar más del 15% si el servicio es excelente.

3. suelo dejar menos del 15%.

4. suelo dejar menos del 15% si el servicio es malo.

5. no suelo dejar nada.

Paso 2 Alguien va a leer las frases en voz alta mientras otra persona lleva la cuenta del (*keeps track of the*) número de ocasiones en que se menciona cada frase. ¿Qué costumbre se menciona más? ¿Cuál se menciona menos?

Paso 3 Ahora entrevista a tres personas sobre lo que hacen en la siguiente situación. **¡OJO!** Hay que responder honestamente.

La cuenta es de $10.00, impuestos (*taxes*) incluidos. Tienes un billete de $10.00 y dos de $1.00. El restaurante no acepta ni cheques personales ni tarjetas de crédito. El servicio fue regular, ni malo ni excelente. ¿Cuánto dejas de propina?

	E1	E2	E3
1. Dejo $1.00 y nada más.	☐	☐	☐
2. Dejo los dos dólares.	☐	☐	☐
3. Pido cambio (*change*) y dejo $1.50.	☐	☐	☐
4. No dejo nada.	☐	☐	☐

Comparte los resultados con el resto de la clase.

ACTIVIDAD E En el escenario

Paso 1 Trabajen en grupos de tres o cuatro. Alguien tiene que hacer el papel de mesero (mesera) y los otros, el de clientes.

SITUACIÓN A

1. El mesero (La mesera) está de mal humor.
2. Los clientes están indecisos (*indecisive*), no saben qué pedir.
3. El mesero (La mesera) les sugiere varias comidas.
4. A los clientes no les gustan las sugerencias del mesero (de la mesera).

SITUACIÓN B

1. El mesero (La mesera) está muy ocupado/a, pero quiere ser cortés (*courteous*).
2. Los clientes le hacen muchas preguntas sobre el menú.

SITUACIÓN C

1. Los clientes entran en un restaurante muy elegante. Están haciendo mucho ruido. No respetan a los otros clientes.
2. El mesero (La mesera) trata de callarlos (*quiet them down*).

Paso 2 Presenten la escena ante (*in front of*) la clase.

GRAMÁTICA

¿Para quién es?

Using **para**

—¿**Para** quién es esa torta?
—Es **para** mi amigo. Es su cumpleaños (*birthday*).

Although you will focus on using **para** in this lesson, it can be helpful to keep in mind that both **por** and **para** can be equivalents of *for* in English.

Para is used to indicate the *destination* or *recipient* of something.

Voy a preparar una sopa **para** Roberto.	*I'm going to make soup for Roberto.* (Roberto will be the recipient of this soup. He is the one who is going to eat it.)
Es una taza **para** café.	*It's a coffee cup (cup for coffee).* (The cup's use is clearly for one beverage over another. Coffee will be served in this cup.)
¿Una mesa? ¿**Para** cuántas personas?	*A table? For how many people?* (The idea here is that someone is going to "receive" a table in the restaurant.)

Por, on the other hand, generally indicates a *source* or a *cause.*

Hago esto **por** mi hermano.	*I do this for my brother.* (The idea here is that my brother is motivating me to do this even though he is not the beneficiary or may never see what I do.)

Perhaps one of the clearest differences between **por** and **para** is when each combines with **que.** Note the different translations in English.

Lo hago **para que** entiendas.*	*I do this so that you will understand.* (Your comprehension is the desired end result: "destination.")
Lo hago **porque** no entiendes.	*I do this because you don't understand.* (Your lack of comprehension is motivating me to do this: "source, cause.")

ACTIVIDAD F ¿Para qué sirve?

Muchas personas creen que hay ciertos alimentos que son buenos para ciertas partes del cuerpo y (o) malos para otras. Indica lo que tú has oído (*you have heard*).

MODELOS El ajo es bueno para la sangre (*blood*).

El ajo es malo para el aliento (*breath*).

1. ____ para el cerebro.

2. ____ para la piel.

3. ____ para los huesos.

4. ____ para los músculos.

5. ____ para los ojos.

ACTIVIDAD G ¿Para qué animal?

¿Conoces el anuncio que dice: «Los Trix son para niños»? ¿Qué alimento es para el conejo (*rabbit*)? Indica para qué animal es cada alimento.

---

*Verbs used after the expression **para que** appear in a form called the subjunctive. (You will learn about the subjunctive in future lessons.)

	A		B
1.	_____ la lechuga	**a.**	para el perro
2.	_____ las zanahorias	**b.**	para el gato
3.	_____ las manzanas	**c.**	para la tortuga (*tortoise*)
4.	_____ la carne	**d.**	para el conejo
5.	_____ el pescado	**e.**	para el caballo (*horse*)
6.	_____ el maíz	**f.**	para la gallina (*chicken*)

COMUNICACIÓN

 ACTIVIDAD H Sugerencias

Paso 1 ¿Qué sabes de los gustos de cada persona en la clase? ¿Qué restaurantes o comidas puedes sugerir para cada una? Utilizando el modelo, inventa tres o cuatro oraciones para diferentes personas. (Optativo: Puedes hacer lo mismo para algunas personas famosas.)

MODELO Para el profesor (la profesora) sugiero Cucina Italiana. Sé que le gusta la comida italiana.

Paso 2 Presenta tus ideas a la clase. ¿Son buenas tus sugerencias? ¿Hay personas que dicen lo mismo?

NAVEGANDO LA RED

Escoge una ciudad como Madrid, España; San José, Costa Rica; Quito, Ecuador; o Santiago, Chile. Busca información sobre el número de restaurantes de origen norteamericano que sirven comida rápida (por ejemplo, McDonald's). Comparte tus resultados con la clase.

INTERCAMBIO

¡Atención, turistas!

Propósito: compilar un folleto (*brochure*) sobre las buenas y malas costumbres de comer para turistas de habla española que visitan este país.

Papeles: tres grupos que hablan entre sí (*among themselves*) para hacer una descripción de lo que se debe y *no* se debe hacer.

Paso 1 La clase debe dividirse en tres grupos. A cada grupo se le va a asignar uno de los siguientes temas.

1. costumbres en la casa

2. costumbres en los restaurantes

3. otras costumbres (saludos, etcétera)

Usando el vocabulario y gramática de esta lección, cada grupo debe escribir dos párrafos (de 100 a 200 palabras) sobre su tema. La idea es dar toda la información posible sobre el tema para incluirla en un folleto para turistas de habla española. Se debe organizar la información según lo que se debe hacer y lo que *no* se debe hacer.

Paso 2 Cada grupo debe presentar su información a los demás. Al terminar, el resto de la clase debe ofrecer comentarios sobre el contenido, sus reacciones, etcétera.

Paso 3 Cada grupo debe escribir de nuevo su información e incorporar las sugerencias e ideas que se presentaron en el **Paso 2.**

Vistazos culturales
La influencia hispana en el mundo

¿Sabías que... los hispanos han tenido[a] un impacto muy grande en las culturas de otros países del mundo? Por ejemplo, en el inglés que se habla en los Estados Unidos hay alrededor de 10.000 palabras prestadas del español. Además, la cultura hispana ha influido en[b] la literatura y el folclor mundiales, sobre todo en Europa.

[a]han... *have had*   [b]ha... *has influenced*

Hay muchas palabras prestadas del español que tienen su origen en la vida ranchera del Oeste de los Estados Unidos. Cuando los pioneros norteamericanos llegaron al Oeste en el siglo XIX, encontraron una cultura ranchera mexicana ya establecida y adoptaron muchos de sus términos.

Del español mexicano:
hoosegow (juzgado)
lasso (lazo)
renegade (renegado)
rodeo
vamoose (vamos)

En un rodeo mexicano

Durante los siglos XVII y XVIII muchos comerciantes[a] de habla inglesa llegaban a los puertos de las Indias Occidentales.[b] Allí aprendieron muchas palabras del español caribeño.

[a]*traders*   [b]Indias... *West Indies*

Muchas palabras del inglés son de origen indígena, pero pasaron al inglés por medio[a] del español.

[a]por... *by way*

Del guaraní:
jaguar (*yaguar*)

Del quechua:
puma
potato

Del náhuatl:
tomate (*tomatl*)
coyote (*coyotl*)
chocolate (*xocolatl*)

Del Caribe:
hurricane (huracán)
tabacco (tabaco)
hammock (hamaca)

Don Juan

Hoy día, si un hombre lleva una vida libertina,[a] se dice que es un «donjuán». El famoso personaje[b] de Don Juan se originó en España en 1630 en el drama *El Burlador de Sevilla,* de Tirso de Molina, y se hizo famoso en la obra de José Zorilla, *Don Juan Tenorio.* Según el relato[c] Don Juan sedujo[d] a la hija del comandante militar de Sevilla. Después de matar al comandante, Don Juan invita a un banquete a la estatua del comandante muerto. Durante la cena, la estatua se anima[e] y se lleva a Don Juan al infierno.[f]

[a]*free of moral and sexual restraint* [b]*character* [c]*story* [d]*seduced* [e]*comes to life* [f]*hell*

Don Juan en otras obras de otros países

FRANCIA: *Le festin de Pierre,* por Molière
INGLATERRA: *The Tragedy of Ovid,* por Sir Aston Cokayne
ITALIA: *Don Giovanni,* una ópera de Mozart
LOS ESTADOS UNIDOS: *Don Juan de Marco,* una película con Johnny Depp

Una presentación de Don Giovanni *en Nueva York*

La literatura modernista de Latinoamérica revolucionó el mundo literario a finales del siglo XIX. Combinó varias corrientes literarias en boga[a] en Francia para crear una literatura única. Los grandes modernistas latinoamericanos incluyen al nicaragüense Rubén Darío y al cubano José Martí.

[a]*vogue*

José Martí:

Cultivo una rosa blanca

Cultivo una rosa blanca
En julio como en enero,
Para el amigo sincero
Que me da su mano franca.

Y para el cruel que me arranca[a]
El corazón con que vivo,
Cardo[b] ni ortiga[c] cultivo,
Cultivo una rosa blanca.

[a]*rips out* [b]*Thistle* [c]*stinging nettle (a plant with thorns)*

ACTIVIDAD ¿Qué recuerdas?

Empareja las frases de la columna A con una de las respuestas de la columna B.

A

1. _____ ópera de Mozart inspirada por el personaje de Don Juan
2. _____ origen de la palabra *coyote* en inglés
3. _____ origen de la palabra *potato* en inglés
4. _____ poeta modernista de Nicaragua
5. _____ el primer drama en el que aparece el personaje de Don Juan

B

a. Rubén Darío
b. el náhuatl
c. *Don Giovanni*
d. el quechua
e. *El Burlador de Sevilla*

NAVEGANDO LA RED

Escoge *uno* de los siguientes proyectos y presenta tus resultados a la clase.

1. Busca información sobre el modernismo literario en Latinoamérica y en España. Después apunta la siguiente información.
   a. una definición del modernismo
   b. algunas características y temas principales de la literatura modernista
   c. los nombres de tres escritores famosos de esta corriente literaria y el título de uno de los libros de cada escritor(a)
2. Busca información sobre el papel de los medios de comunicación (*media*) en difundir (*spreading*) la cultura hispana en este país. Apunta la siguiente información.
   a. el título de por lo menos tres periódicos hispanos que circulan en este país, la ciudad en que circulan y el número aproximado de lectores que tienen
   b. el título y número aproximado de lectores de por lo menos tres revistas norteamericanas que ahora tienen ediciones en español para lectores de habla española en este país
   c. el nombre de dos o tres cadenas (*networks*) de televisión en español en este país y el número aproximado de televidentes (*television viewers*) que tienen

¿Qué hay en la mesa?
What's on the Table?

la copa	(wine) glass
los cubiertos	silverware
la cuchara	spoon
el cuchillo	knife
el cuenco	(*earthenware*) bowl
la jarra	pitcher
el mantel	tablecloth
la mesa	table
el pimentero	pepper shaker
el platillo	saucer
el plato	plate
el salero	salt shaker
la servilleta	napkin
la taza	cup
el tenedor	fork
el vaso	(water) glass

los buenos modales	good manners

cortar	to cut
derramar	to spill
lavar los platos	to wash the dishes
levantar la mesa	to clear the table
poner la mesa	to set the table

En un restaurante
In a Restaurant

el/la camarero/a	waiter, waitress
el cliente (la clienta)	customer
el/la cocinero/a	chef, cook
la comida para llevar	food to go
la cuenta	bill, check
el/la mesero/a	waiter, waitress
el plato del día	daily special
el plato principal	main dish
el primer (segundo, tercer) plato (R)	first (second, third) course
la propina	tip

atender (ie)	to wait on (a customer)
dejar (una propina)	to leave (a tip)
ordenar	to order

pedir (i, i)	to request, order
traer (*irreg.*)	to bring

¿Está todo bien?
Is Everything OK?

¿Me podría traer... ?	Could you bring me . . . ?
¿Qué trae... ?	What does . . . come with?

La obligación impersonal
Impersonal Obligation

es...	it's . . .
imprescindible	essential
(muy) buena idea	a (very) good idea
necesario	
preciso	necessary
hay que	one must, it's necessary
no se puede... sin...	you (one) can't . . . without . . .
se debe	you (one) should, must
se tiene que	you have to (one must)

Otras palabras y expresiones útiles

la boca	mouth
la bolsita para llevar	doggie bag
el brazo	arm
el codo	elbow
la costumbre	custom, habit
la mano	hand
el servicio a domicilio	home delivery

derecho/a	right
educado/a	well-mannered, polite
izquierdo/a	left

invitar	to treat (pay)
probar (ue)	to try, taste
tener buena educación	to be well-mannered

LECCIÓN 9

Check out the following media resources to complement this lesson:

 Online *Manual*

 Video on CD

WWW **Online Learning Center**

WWW **ActivityPak**

¿Y para beber?

Bebiendo con los amigos en la Argentina

In this lesson, you will

◆ learn and review vocabulary related to beverages

◆ examine cultural aspects related to drinking

◆ review regular preterite tense verb forms

◆ learn about the history of some national beverages

◆ discuss responsibilities related to drinking and other matters

◆ review impersonal and passive **se**

ALTO Before beginning this lesson, look over the **Composición** activity on pages 249–251. This is the activity you will be working toward throughout the lesson.

IDEAS PARA EXPLORAR

Las bebidas

VOCABULARIO

¿Qué bebes?

Talking about favorite beverages

Las bebidas alcohólicas

la cerveza
el licor fuerte
el vino (blanco, tinto)

Las bebidas con cafeína

el café
los refrescos
el té (helado)

Las bebidas sin cafeína

algunos refrescos
el café descafeinado
el jugo de manzana
  (naranja, tomate)
la leche
el té de hierbas

Vocabulario útil

tener (mucha) sed	to be (very) thirsty	**(bien) caliente**	(very) hot
		con hielo	with ice
		sin hielo	without ice
(bien) frío/a	(very) cold		

ACTIVIDAD A ¿Qué es?

El profesor (La profesora) va a nombrar una bebida. Di qué tipo de bebida es. **¡OJO!** A veces hay dos posibilidades.

MODELO PROFESOR(A): la leche
ESTUDIANTE: Es una bebida sin cafeína.

1...   2...   3...   4...   5...   6...

ACTIVIDAD B ¿Qué marcas° conoces?   *name brands*

El profesor (La profesora) va a mencionar la marca de una bebida y la clase tiene que decir qué tipo de bebida es.

MODELO PROFESOR(A): Lipton
ESTUDIANTE: té helado

1...   2...   3...   4...   5...   6...   7...   8...

📖 ACTIVIDAD C ¿Qué prefieres?

Paso 1 Entrevista a tres personas para saber qué bebidas prefieren o les gusta tomar en cada ocasión a continuación. Apunta sus respuestas.

	E1	E2	E3
1. para el desayuno (por la mañana)	___	___	___
2. con una hamburguesa	___	___	___
3. para la merienda	___	___	___
4. cuando sale con unos amigos por la noche	___	___	___
5. mientras estudia (trabaja, lee)	___	___	___

Paso 2 La clase debe entrevistar al profesor (a la profesora). ¿Son diferentes sus preferencias de las de Uds. o son iguales?

ACTIVIDAD D Una historia

Paso 1 Trabajando en grupos de tres, cuenten (*tell about*) cómo fue el día de Humberto y Lola. ¿Qué toman y cómo les afecta?

1.　　　　　**2.**　　　　　**3.**　　　　　**4.**

Paso 2 Presenten su historia al resto de la clase. ¿Cuántos grupos interpretaron los dibujos igual que Uds.?

GRAMÁTICA

¿Qué bebiste?

Review of regular preterite tense verb forms and use

—¿Ya **tomaste** la leche que te **preparé**?
—Sí, abuelita.
—Bueno. Anoche no **dormiste** bien y no queremos repetir eso, ¿eh?

	-ar	-er	-ir
(yo)	tom**é**	beb**í**	sal**í**
(tú)	tom**aste**	beb**iste**	sal**iste**
(Ud.)	tom**ó**	beb**ió**	sal**ió**
(él/ella)	tom**ó**	beb**ió**	sal**ió**
(nosotros/as)	tom**amos**	beb**imos**	sal**imos**
(vosotros/as)	tom**asteis**	beb**isteis**	sal**isteis**
(Uds.)	tom**aron**	beb**ieron**	sal**ieron**
(ellos/ellas)	tom**aron**	beb**ieron**	sal**ieron**

As you review the forms of the preterite tense in the shaded box, remember that regular **-er** and **-ir** verbs have the same endings. Also remember that the written accent indicates acoustic stress. In the *present* tense (with the exception of **nosotros** and **vosotros**) all forms carry stress on the stem (TOmo). All forms of the regular *preterite* carry stress somewhere on the ending (toME, tomASte, toMO). This is especially important when distinguishing between present tense (**tomo**) and preterite tense (**tomó**).

The preterite tense is used to talk about single events in the past or a sequence of events, ones that are viewed as having been completed at a particular point in the past.

> **Escribí** la composición.
> **Leí** unos capítulos y luego **miré** la televisión.
> ¿**Lavaste** la ropa ayer? No. La **lavé** esta mañana.
> **Probaron** vinos de todo tipo en su viaje por Chile.

ACTIVIDAD E ¿Qué hiciste?

Mira el dibujo de la abuelita con su nieto de la sección anterior. ¿Qué hiciste tú la última vez que no dormiste bien?

1. ☐ Tomé una pastilla (*pill*).
2. ☐ Leí algo hasta que me dormí.
3. ☐ Miré la televisión.
4. ☐ Conté ovejas (*sheep*).
5. ☐ No hice nada. Me quedé en la cama hasta que me dormí.
6. ☐ Me levanté y empecé a estudiar (leer, trabajar).
7. ☐ ¿ ?

Así se dice

As you know, the irregular verb **hacer** is useful to talk about past events.

—¿Qué **hiciste**?
—No **hice** nada.

To refresh your memory, here are the forms of **hacer** in the preterite tense.

hice	hicimos
hiciste	hicisteis
hizo	hicieron
hizo	hicieron

Así se dice

Remember that **-ir** verbs with **e → i** stem vowel changes in the present tense keep the same stem vowel change in the preterite in the following forms only: **Ud., él/ella, Uds., ellos/ellas.**

The more you see and hear verbs like these, the greater your chances are of internalizing this pattern. For now, you should simply be aware of this detail.

	Ud.	él/ella	Uds.	ellos/ellas
pedir	pidió	pidió	pidieron	pidieron
servir	sirvió	sirvió	sirvieron	sirvieron

The verb **dormir** has an **o → u** stem vowel change in the preterite in these same forms.

	Ud.	él/ella	Uds.	ellos/ellas
dormir	durmió	durmió	durmieron	durmieron

ACTIVIDAD F Firma aquí, por favor

Paso 1 Forma preguntas a base de las oraciones en la página siguiente y házselas a los miembros de la clase. Busca entre tus compañeros a dos que puedan contestar **Sí** a tus preguntas. ¡**OJO**! Haz cada pregunta en la forma de **tú**.

MODELO   ¿Pediste café en un restaurante la semana pasada?

1. Pidió café en un restaurante la semana pasada.
2. Tomó café esta mañana.
3. Tomó más de dos tazas de café esta mañana.
4. Bebió un refresco con cafeína esta mañana.
5. No tomó nada con cafeína esta mañana.
6. Bebió un licor fuerte la semana pasada.
7. Bebió vino con la cena recientemente.

Paso 2 Basándote en los resultados del **Paso 1,** compara las experiencias y preferencias de la clase en cuanto a las bebidas con cafeína y las bebidas alcohólicas.

Así se dice

Do you remember that the verb **conocer** when used in the preterite translates as *met?* With events that theoretically have no real ending (when you know someone, you always know that person), the preterite signals the beginning of the event rather than its completion. What's the beginning of knowing someone? When you meet that person!

Conocí al profesor en agosto.

I met the professor in August.
(I began to know the professor in August.)

Other verbs that work like this are listed below. Using what you know about **conocer,** see if you can restate the translated meaning given for each using the concept of *to begin to.*

VERB	PRESENT TENSE	PRETERITE TENSE
saber	*to know (something)*	*to find out (something)*
poder	*to be able to*	*to manage (to do something)*
comprender	*to understand*	*to grasp (a fact)*

ACTIVIDAD G Experiencias comunes

Paso 1 Completa las siguientes oraciones usando el pretérito. Las oraciones pueden referirse a algo que tomaste, comiste, probaste o hiciste; no importa lo que sea (*it may be*).

MODELO   Una vez bebí mucho licor fuerte y me enfermé (*I got sick*).

1. Una vez ＿＿＿ y me gustó mucho.
2. Una vez ＿＿＿ y no me cayó* bien (no me gustó).
3. Una vez ＿＿＿ y me enfermé.

Paso 2 En grupos de cuatro, compartan las oraciones. Al final deben escribir tres oraciones para describir experiencias verdaderas que han tenido (*have had*) todos los miembros del grupo. Si alguien dice algo que también tú hiciste, debes decirlo. Hay que reescribir cada oración en la forma de **nosotros/as.**

---

*Remember that **-er** verbs whose stems end in a vowel replace the **i** of the **-ió** preterite endings with a **y** to avoid three written vowels (**ca- + -ió → cayó**).

Busca información sobre la exportación de vinos chilenos. Trata de encontrar la siguiente información y preséntala a la clase.

◆ exportación total de vinos (o en dólares o en litros)
◆ marcas de mayor exportación
◆ a qué país(es) exporta Chile más vinos
◆ otra información que te parece interesante

VAMOS A VER

ANTICIPACIÓN

Paso 1 Lee el título de la lectura de esta sección y sólo los primeros dos párrafos. Luego contesta las siguientes preguntas.

1. ¿Cuál es la bebida nacional de los Estados Unidos?
  a. la cerveza
  b. el té helado
  c. no hay solamente una

2. ¿Cuál crees que es el objetivo principal del artículo?
  a. hablar de las bebidas nacionales de varios países de habla española
  b. explicar, región por región, cuáles son las bebidas típicas de los Estados Unidos
  c. hablar de las diferencias entre las bebidas de los Estados Unidos y las de los países de habla española

Si tu respuesta al número **1** es **c**, estás en lo correcto. La respuesta al número **2** es **a**.

Paso 2 Busca los nombres de los países de habla española mencionados en las varias subsecciones de la lectura. Son siete en total. ¿Cuáles son?

Consejo práctico

A good pre-reading strategy is to read and reflect on the first paragraph of an article. Very often the first paragraph can orient your thinking so that you are "on the right track." For this reason, **Paso 1** of **Anticipación** revolves around the first two paragraphs only.

Consejo práctico

Notice that the following **Exploración** section asks you to read the article section by section. Reading bit by bit and then stopping to consolidate the information you have just read is a good habit to get into. The strategy helps you in two ways. First, as you verify and consolidate the information you have read, you are better able to anticipate the upcoming content of the next paragraph or section. Second, by stopping and reviewing as you go, you will remember more when you have finished reading.

EXPLORACIÓN

Paso 1 Lee solamente la primera sección sobre el jerez. Luego completa las siguientes oraciones.

1. El jerez es _____.
  a. un coñac   **b.** un vino   **c.** un té   **d.** un licor fuerte

2. El jerez es de origen _____.
  a. árabe   **b.** español   **c.** inglés   **d.** griego

3. Una manera de pedir un jerez en un restaurante español es decir: «un _____, por favor».

    a. vino   **b.** dulce   **c.** aperitivo   **d.** fino

Paso 2 Ahora lee la sección sobre el ron. Luego indica si las siguientes oraciones son ciertas (C) o falsas (F).

                                                          C   F

1. El ron es un licor fabricado de la caña de azúcar.   ☐ ☐

2. El coco loco es un tipo de ron fuerte.   ☐ ☐

Paso 3 Ahora lee la próxima sección sobre el mate e indica si estas oraciones son ciertas (C) o falsas (F).

                                                          C   F

1. El mate es un tipo de té.   ☐ ☐

2. Se dice que el mate es bueno para la creatividad.   ☐ ☐

Paso 4 Ahora lee la última sección sobre el pisco y luego termina las siguientes oraciones.

1. El pisco es de origen _____.

    a. chileno   **b.** peruano   **c.** ¿ ? (No se sabe.)

2. El nombre **pisco** es de origen _____.

    a. chileno   **b.** peruano   **c.** quechua   **d.** ¿ ? (No se sabe.)

3. Algo que se le añade al pisco sour que no es típico de otros cócteles es _____.

    a. el azúcar   **b.** el brandy   **c.** el agua   **d.** la clara de un huevo

Paso 5 Lee toda la lectura otra vez, desde el comienzo hasta el fin.

SÍNTESIS

Haz las correspondencias correctas entre el país o los países, la bebida y el tipo de bebida. Luego, para cada bebida, añade un dato más como en el modelo.

PAÍS(ES)	BEBIDA	ORIGEN
la Argentina y el Uruguay	el jerez	licor fuerte fabricado de la caña de azúcar
Chile y el Perú	el mate	licor fuerte fabricado de la uva
Cuba y Puerto Rico	el pisco	té herbal
España	el ron	vino

MODELO   En España se toma un vino que se llama «jerez». El jerez es muy conocido en Inglaterra también.

1. la Argentina y el Uruguay

2. Chile y el Perú

3. Cuba y Puerto Rico

Las bebidas nacionales

¿Cuál es la bebida nacional de los Estados Unidos? A muchos norteamericanos les resulta difícil contestar esta pregunta. Quizás sea más fácil dar una respuesta a nivel regional. En el sur, por ejemplo, son típicos el té helado y el famoso *Mint julep*, mientras que en Seattle y sus alrededores el café espresso tiene gran fama. Y claro, California tiene sus excelentes vinos.

A diferencia, en el mundo hispano no es tan difícil contestar tal pregunta. Como su bandera nacional y sus equipos de fútbol, varios países tienen bebidas que les son propias —o por lo menos el nombre de la bebida se asocia de inmediato con su país de origen.

Jerez, reina de las bebidas españolas

El jerez español es un aperitivo excelente.

España tiene la distinción de ser no sólo el país de origen del jerez, sino también su mayor productor. El jerez es un tipo de vino especial que se toma como aperitivo, es decir, antes de comer. También existen tipos de jerez dulce que se toman como digestivo, o sea, después de comer. El jerez se originó en el suroeste de España en una región que se llama Jerez. Hasta los griegos antiguos escribían en su época de los vinos de esta parte del mundo. En la Edad Media, los ingleses empezaron a importar el jerez español, dándole el nombre árabe de la región: *Sherish*. El jerez llegó a ser tan conocido en Inglaterra que en la obra de Shakespeare, *Enrique V*, se encuentra el siguiente fragmento:

> Si yo tuviera mil hijos, el primer principio
> humano que les enseñaría sería
> hacerles abjurar de las bebidas aguadas
> y aficionarlos al jerez.

Hoy en día, se puede entrar en cualquier bar o restaurante español, pedir «un fino», y recibir una copita llena de un espléndido líquido dorado —un buen jerez español.

Ron sobre las rocas

En Puerto Rico, en Cuba y en los países caribeños en general, el ron seguramente ocupa el rango de bebida nacional. La base del ron es la caña de azúcar, una planta que crece en las zonas tropicales. Aunque el ron se conoce en los Estados Unidos por su uso en diferentes cócteles, como los muy conocidos *Daiquirí* y *Piña Colada*, también se toma solo o «sobre las rocas». Hay rones populares y baratos y otros mucho más finos y caros de un sabor y una textura suaves como el Ron de Barrilito Tres Estrellas. Entre los puertorriqueños es muy popular un cóctel que se llama **Coco Loco.** Esta bebida es de sabor muy dulce y se prepara con agua de coco, ron y azúcar. Si no te gustan las bebidas dulces, ¡esta bebida no es para ti!

¿Querés un mate?

No todas las bebidas nacionales son alcohólicas. Si le preguntaras a una persona de la Argentina cuál es la bebida nacional de su país, sin duda te respondería: «¡El mate, claro!» Así también te respondería alguien del Uruguay dado que esta bebida tiene una larga tradición en toda la zona del Río de la Plata. El mate es un tipo de té, hecho de una yerba de sabor distinto y fuerte, que se suele tomar en la tarde, así como el *tea time* de los ingleses. Se dice que el mate es bueno para combatir el estrés y para disminuir el hambre. Es típico tener una taza especial llamada **mate** y una **bombilla** para sorber ligeramente el mate y gozar de esta bebida mientras uno lee o charla con los amigos. Durante sus visitas a los Estados Unidos, el gran escritor argentino, Jorge Luis Borges, tenía fama de insistir en un mate por la tarde durante su reposo diario.

El mate, un té herbal, es típico en la Argentina y el Uruguay.

De los Andes, el pisco

El pisco es un licor fuerte, típico del Perú y Chile.

No se puede visitar ni Chile ni el Perú sin conocer de alguna manera la bebida conocida como el **pisco.** El nombre pisco es de origen quechua, y es un tipo de brandy fabricado de la uva moscatel. En el Perú, esta bebida se produce en la región cerca de Pisco, y en Chile se produce en el Valle del Río Elqui en el centro del país. La producción del pisco data del siglo XVII cuando Chile y el Perú eran parte del Virreinato del Perú, y es probable que esto explique la controversia actual entre el Perú y Chile sobre los derechos al nombre **pisco** —¿Es chileno o peruano? De hecho los dos países producen versiones diferentes de este licor. El del Perú es más seco que su hermano chileno.

El pisco se suele tomar en cócteles, como el típico **Piscola** que es una combinación de este licor con Coca-Cola. Otra bebida popular es el **Pisco sour:** tres medidas de pisco frío, una de jugo de limón, azúcar al gusto y la clara de un huevo. ¡Sabroso!

¡SIGAMOS!

Paso 1 En grupos de tres, indiquen cuál es la bebida nacional de cada país. Luego compartan sus ideas con el resto de la clase. ¿Coinciden sus ideas?

1. Inglaterra
2. Italia
3. Japón
4. México
5. Rusia

Paso 2 La lectura sugiere que no hay una sola bebida nacional en los Estados Unidos sino que hay bebidas regionales. Sigan trabajando (*Keep working*) en grupos de tres para contestar las siguientes preguntas. Luego compartan sus ideas con la clase.

1. ¿Hay una bebida regional que se asocie con el lugar donde viven Uds.?
2. ¿Hay bebidas regionales en otras partes de este país? (No repitan las que se mencionan en la lectura.)

Vamos a ver

Now that you've completed the **Vamos a ver** section of **Unidad tres,** watch the corresponding **Vamos a ver** segment on the *¿Sabías que... ?* video to further explore the themes presented in this unit. There are related pre- and post-viewing activities on the *¿Sabías que... ?* Online Learning Center at **www.mhhe.com/sabiasque5**.

NAVEGANDO LA RED

Busca información sobre el cultivo y la exportación del café en varios países de habla española. Aunque el café se asocia con Colombia, también se produce en otros países. Trae la siguiente información sobre dos o tres países a la clase.

◆ nombre del país
◆ la cantidad que se exporta a los Estados Unidos, el Canadá y Europa
◆ otro dato interesante

IDEAS PARA EXPLORAR

Prohibiciones y responsabilidades

GRAMÁTICA

¿Qué se prohíbe?

Review of impersonal and passive **se**

	permite
(no) **se**	prohíbe
	puede

Nueva York

In **Lección 8** you learned two more uses of **se**—the impersonal and passive. In impersonal sentences, the verb is singular and the subject is not specified. The English counterpart is *you, one,* or *they.*

Se vive más si **se come** bien.	*One lives longer if one eats well. (You live longer if you eat well.)*
No **se puede** entrar.	*One can't enter. (You can't enter.)*

In passive sentences, the verb is either singular or plural, depending on the subject. Singular passives are often indistinguishable from impersonal sentences.

Se comen más verduras ahora que antes.	*More vegetables are eaten now than before.*
Se habla español aquí.	*Spanish is spoken here. (One speaks Spanish here.)*

ACTIVIDAD A ¿Qué se prohíbe?

Paso 1 Indica si las siguientes oraciones son ciertas (C) o falsas (F).

	C	F
1. Se prohíbe el consumo de bebidas alcohólicas en las calles y en los coches.	☐	☐
2. Se prohíbe el consumo de bebidas alcohólicas en las funciones universitarias.	☐	☐
3. No se permite el castigo (*punishment*) físico en las escuelas públicas.	☐	☐
4. No se permite fumar (*to smoke*) en edificios públicos.	☐	☐
5. Se prohíbe fumar en los vuelos (*flights*) nacionales.	☐	☐
6. Se prohíbe declarar que uno es homosexual mientras presta servicio militar.	☐	☐

Paso 2 Ahora indica con qué oraciones está de acuerdo la clase o no. ¿Piensa de la misma manera la mayoría de Uds.?

NÚMERO DE LOS QUE ESTÁN DE ACUERDO	NÚMERO DE LOS QUE NO ESTÁN DE ACUERDO
1. _____	_____
2. _____	_____
3. _____	_____
4. _____	_____
5. _____	_____
6. _____	_____

Paso 3 (Optativo) Inventa una prohibición que te gustaría ver convertida en ley.

ACTIVIDAD B Si se siguen estas recomendaciones...

Paso 1 Escoge las afirmaciones que mejor completen la oración.

Se puede gozar de buena salud si...

☐ se hace ejercicio regularmente.

☐ no se ve mucha televisión.

☐ se comen más carnes rojas y menos carbohidratos complejos.

☐ se toma leche descremada en vez de leche completa.

☐ no se toman bebidas alcohólicas.

☐ se toman refrescos dietéticos en vez de refrescos regulares.

☐ se comen verduras crudas en vez de cocidas.

Paso 2 Inventa otras tres frases lógicas y compártelas con la clase escribiéndolas en la pizarra.

Paso 3 La clase debe agrupar las recomendaciones de los **Pasos 1** y **2** según su grado de importancia: (1) recomendaciones importantes; (2) recomendaciones útiles, pero no muy importantes; (3) recomendaciones poco importantes.

COMUNICACIÓN

ACTIVIDAD C ¿Qué se debe hacer?

Paso 1 Divídanse en grupos de cuatro o cinco. A cada grupo, el profesor (la profesora) le va a asignar una de las siguientes preguntas. El grupo debe contestar la pregunta y preparar una lista de razones que apoyen su opinión.

1. ¿A qué edad se debe legalizar el consumo de bebidas alcohólicas?

   ☐ A los 16 años, la edad de obtener la licencia de manejar.

   ☐ A los 18 años, la edad de ejercer el derecho a votar.

   ☐ A los 21 años, la mayoría de edad.

   ☐ A los 25 años de edad.

   ☐ El alcohol no debe ser legal.

2. ¿Se debe distinguir entre el consumo de cerveza y vino por un lado y de licores fuertes por otro, en cuanto a la legalización del consumo de bebidas alcohólicas?

3. ¿Se debe educar a los alumnos de secundaria (*high school*) en cuanto al consumo de bebidas alcohólicas?

Paso 2 Compartan con la clase sus opiniones y las razones que las apoyan. ¿Cuántos de la clase están de acuerdo con Uds.? ¿Están de acuerdo Uds. con las opiniones de los otros grupos?

ACTIVIDAD D ¿Quién es el responsable?

Paso 1 Contesta lo siguiente:

Si hay un accidente debido a (*due to* [*the fact*]) que un chófer (*driver*) maneja embriagado (*under the influence*), ¿quién es responsable? En otras palabras, ¿a quién se debe castigar (*punish*)?

1. Se debe castigar solamente al chófer embriagado.

2. Se debe castigar al chófer y al cantinero (*bartender*) que le sirvió.

Así se dice

You may notice in **Actividad D** that the personal **a** is used with impersonal and passive **se** to mark objects of the verb.

Se debe castigar **al** chófer.

The personal **a** is used in these sentences because the objects of the verb (the people mentioned) are capable of performing the activity represented by the verb. It is important to mark them clearly as objects and thereby distinguish them from the subject of the verb. Note that if the **a** is mistakenly omitted in some instances, the impersonal or passive **se** would be interpreted as a true reflexive.

Se debe castigar el chófer.
The driver should punish himself.

3. Se debe castigar al chófer y a los otros con quienes tomaba.

4. Se debe castigar al chófer y al anfitrión de la fiesta a que asistía el chófer.

5. ¿ ?

Paso 2 Forma un grupo con otros que comparten la misma opinión. Luego el grupo debe preparar una lista de razones que apoyen su opinión y después escribirlas en la pizarra.

Paso 3 Evalúa las razones que proponen los otros grupos. ¿Te convencen? ¿Quieres cambiar de opinión?

ACTIVIDAD E ¿Sabías que... ?

Paso 1 Lee la selección **¿Sabías que... ?** Luego contesta las siguientes preguntas.

1. ¿Se prohibía o se permitía la fabricación del tequila en el imperio español?

2. ¿Qué quería proteger la Corona española en el Nuevo Mundo?

¿Sabías que...

el tequila, bebida mexicanísima, tiene una larga historia de prohibiciones?

Por mucho tiempo durante el período colonial, la Corona[a] española prohibió la fabricación de licores en México para proteger el mercado de vinos españoles. Esta restricción convirtió el tequila en un licor que sólo se podía comprar en el mercado negro, y como era difícil de obtener, sólo llegó a tener[b] más fama y más demanda.

En 1623, la Corona española, convencida de que se podía aprovechar económicamente si se vendía el tequila abiertamente, inició la producción legal del tequila pero bajo restricciones. Tales restricciones aseguraron que la Corona misma mantendría[c] un estanco[d] total en el mercado tequilero por casi dos siglos.

En 1821, México logró su independencia de España y las restricciones en la producción tequilera desaparecieron. Con el paso del tiempo, y la creciente demanda mundial, el tequila se convirtió en la bebida que más se asocia con México a nivel internacional.

Tequila, la bebida nacional de México

---

[a]*Crown*　[b]*sólo... it only gained (ended up having)*　[c]*would maintain*　[d]*monopoly*

Paso 2 Como sabes, se prohibía la producción y venta del tequila durante el imperio español. ¿Se prohíbe hoy en este país la producción, importación o venta de algo? ¿Qué sabes de los siguientes productos?

1. los puros (*cigars*) cubanos

2. la marihuana para aliviar los síntomas de algunas enfermedades

ACTIVIDAD F ¿Qué haces?

Paso 1 Lee la siguiente situación. Luego coméntala con un compañero (una compañera) de clase.

> Tienes 25 años. Tu hermana menor se gradúa de la escuela secundaria. Ella va a dar una fiesta. Sus padres no van a asistir. Tu hermana te pide que le compres[a] cerveza y licor fuerte para la fiesta. ¿Qué haces?

[a]te... *she asks you to buy her*

Paso 2 Compartan sus reacciones con el resto de la clase. ¿Reaccionaron todos igual?

Paso 3 (Optativo) Aquí tienen otra situación para comentar.

> Tienes 25 años. Vas a entrar en una licorería. Unos chicos de 16 años de edad te piden que les compres[a] cerveza. ¿Qué haces?

[a]te... *they ask you to buy them*

COMPOSICIÓN

Propósito: escribir una composición en la que expreses lo que has aprendido (*you have learned*) sobre las costumbres hispanas; comparar las costumbres hispanas con las de este país.

Título sugerido: ¿Son semejantes o diferentes las costumbres hispanas y norteamericanas?

Antes de escribir

Paso 1 El propósito de la composición es informar al lector (*reader*) sobre las semejanzas y diferencias entre las costumbres hispanas y norteamericanas. Tienes que convencer al lector de que hay más semejanzas que diferencias o viceversa. Primero, decide si vas a hablarle al lector directamente (¿Cree Ud. que... ?), en primera persona (Creo que...) o de forma impersonal (Se cree que...).

Paso 2 A continuación hay una lista de varios temas que exploraste en esta unidad. ¿Qué información vas a incluir?

☐ los desayunos, los almuerzos, las cenas

☐ las meriendas

☐ las comidas en los restaurantes

☐ las dietas nacionales

☐ la dieta mediterránea

☐ los modales

☐ las bebidas nacionales

☐ ¿ ?

Paso 3 Una vez que decidas qué información vas a incluir, tienes que pensar en cómo vas a organizarla. ¿Cuál de las sugerencias te parece buena para esta composición?

☐ presentar las semejanzas y luego las diferencias

☐ presentar las diferencias y luego las semejanzas

☐ presentar las semejanzas y diferencias punto por punto

Paso 4 Basándote en los **Pasos 2** y **3,** haz un breve bosquejo (*outline*) de lo que vas a escribir.

Al escribir

Paso 1 Al escribir el borrador (*draft*), trata de incluir los siguientes puntos gramaticales y expresiones.

1. los pronombres de objeto indirecto

2. **se** impersonal y pasivo

3. expresiones impersonales de obligación

4. **estar**

5. **por** y **para**

Paso 2 Escribe el borrador dos días antes de entregar la composición. A continuación hay una lista de expresiones de transición que te podrán ser (*could be*) útiles en la composición.

a diferencia de	in contrast to
en cambio	on the other hand
en contraste con	in contrast to
igual que	the same as (equal to)
mientras	while
semejante a	similar to

Consejo práctico

Before writing a composition in any language, it is always a good idea to organize your thoughts. Your organization depends primarily on two things. First, what are you writing about? Second, what is your purpose in writing? In this **Composición** your purpose is to express your opinion about Hispanic customs and their similarities to and (or) differences from customs in this country. This significantly narrows the topic you will write about. In general, the more focused your composition, the better it will read to someone else.

Después de escribir

Paso 1 Un día antes de entregar la composición, revisa y corrige el borrador paso por paso. Puedes utilizar el siguiente esquema como guía.

I. Información
 1. Cuenta las semejanzas que aparecen en la composición. Luego cuenta las diferencias. ¿Son suficientes para convencer al lector de tu opinión?
 2. Subraya (*Underline*) las palabras de transición que utilizaste. ¿Ayudan a aclarar la información?

II. Lenguaje
 1. Pon un círculo alrededor de cada pronombre de objeto indirecto.
    a. ¿Es correcta la forma?
    b. ¿Es correcto su uso?

 2. Marca cada **se** que aparece.
    a. ¿Es apropiado el uso de **se**?
    b. ¿Es correcta la forma del verbo?

 3. Revisa los adjetivos que utilizaste. ¿Siempre concuerdan (*agree*) con los sustantivos (*nouns*) que modifican?

 4. Revisa el uso de la **a** personal.
    a. ¿La incluiste?
    b. ¿La usaste correctamente?

Paso 2 Haz los cambios necesarios y entrégale la composición al profesor (a la profesora).

Vistazos culturales
El arte y la literatura en el mundo hispano

¿Sabías que... los hispanos son conocidos mundialmente por su gran talento literario y artístico? Los escritores hispanos han ganado[a] diez Premios Nobel de Literatura en total. De estos diez, cinco fueron ganados por escritores españoles. En el campo del arte, los pintores hispanos han influido[b] mucho en la pintura mundial, sobre todo los cuadros de Picasso. Además, la pintura chicana contemporánea ha producido[c] obras muy conocidas sobre temas relacionados con la vida de los hispanos en el suroeste de los Estados Unidos.

[a]han... *have won*   [b]han... *have influenced*
[c]ha... *has produced*

Gabriel García Márquez

Los Premios Nobel de Literatura

1905: José Echegaray (España), drama

1922: Jacinto Benavente (España), drama

1945: Gabriela Mistral (Chile), poesía

1956: Juan Ramón Jiménez (España), poesía

1967: Miguel Ángel Asturias (Guatemala), prosa

1971: Pablo Neruda (Chile), poesía

1977: Vicente Aleixandre (España): poesía

1982: Gabriel García Márquez (Colombia), prosa

1989: Camilo José Cela (España): prosa

1990: Octavio Paz (México), poesía y ensayo

El pintor colombiano Fernando Botero se conoce por un estilo caracterizado por figuras infladas y rotundas. Las figuras de sus obras son exageradas y reflejan su estilo cómico y voluptuoso.

Las hermanas (*1969*) *por Fernando Botero* (*colombiano, 1932–*)

Coyote Woman (*1985*) *por Diana Bryer* (*norteamericana, 1942–*)

La pintora Diana Bryer de Nuevo México pinta temas sobre la vida diaria y las leyendas del norte de Nuevo México. Un tema común en sus obras es la armonía en que viven los humanos y los animales.

El pintor contemporáneo Ramón Lombarte es un artista realista de Barcelona, España. En sus cuadros figuran[a] personas que parecen ensimismadas,[b] sin darse cuenta de que alguien las está mirando. Las obras de Lombarte tienden a presentar muchas emociones y ansiedades.

[a]*appear*   [b]*lost in thought*

Domingo, medianoche (*1998*) *por Ramón Lombarte* (*español, 1956–*)

ACTIVIDAD ¿Qué recuerdas?

Empareja cada frase de la columna A con una de las respuestas de la columna B.

A

1. _____ poeta chilena que ganó el Premio
Nobel de Literatura en 1945

2. _____ artista español cuyos cuadros se
conocen por presentar muchas
emociones

3. _____ pintor conocido por sus figuras
infladas y rotundas

4. _____ ensayista mexicano que ganó el
Premio Nobel de Literatura en 1990

5. _____ pintora conocida por representar los
mitos y leyendas de los indígenas
de Nuevo México

B

a. Fernando Botero
b. Diana Bryer
c. Ramón Lombarte
d. Gabriela Mistral
e. Octavio Paz

NAVEGANDO LA RED

Escoge *uno* de los siguientes proyectos. Luego presenta tus resultados a la clase.

1. Busca información sobre la corriente literaria latinoamericana
llamada *el realismo mágico* y apunta la siguiente información.
   a. una definición del realismo mágico
   b. algunas características de la literatura mágicorrealista
   c. los nombres de tres escritores famosos de esta corriente y el título
   de uno de los libros de cada escritor(a)
2. Busca información sobre un artista chicano (una artista chicana)
y apunta la siguiente información.
   a. sus datos biográficos (año de nacimiento, lugar de nacimiento,
   etcétera)
   b. el género de arte que hace (escultura, literatura, pintura, etcétera)
   c. los temas principales y los títulos de algunas de sus obras
3. La única mujer hispana que ha ganado (*has won*) un Premio
Nobel de Literatura es Gabriela Mistral. Busca información sobre
su vida y poesía y apunta la siguiente información.
   a. sus datos biográficos
   b. la corriente literaria con que se asocia
   c. los temas centrales y los títulos de algunas de sus obras

VOCABULARIO COMPRENSIVO

Las bebidas / Beverages

la bebida alcohólica	alcoholic beverage
el café (R)	coffee
descafeinado	decaffeinated coffee
la cerveza (R)	beer
el jugo (R)	juice
de manzana	apple juice
de naranja (R)	orange juice
de tomate	tomato juice
la leche (R)	milk
el licor fuerte	hard alcohol
el refresco (R)	soft drink
el té (R)	tea
de hierbas	herbal tea
helado	iced tea
el vino (R)	wine
blanco	white wine
tinto	red wine

Vocabulario relacionado con el tema

la cafeína	caffeine
(bien) frío/a	(very) cold
(bien) caliente	(very) hot
con hielo	with ice
sin hielo	without ice
beber	to drink
tener (mucha) sed	to be (very) thirsty

Otras palabras útiles

castigar	to punish
fumar	to smoke
permitir	to permit, allow
prohibir (prohíbo)	to prohibit

GRAMMAR SUMMARY

Indirect Object Pronouns

SUBJECT PRONOUN	INDIRECT OBJECT PRONOUN
yo	me
tú	te
Ud.	le
él/ella	le
nosotros/as	nos
vosotros/as	os
Uds.	les
ellos/ellas	les

1. Indirect object pronouns have many uses in Spanish that differ from English. In this unit, you have learned to use indirect object pronouns mainly to mean *to* or *for* someone or something.

   No **me** importan los aditivos.
   Additives don't matter to me.

   You have also seen that with **poner,** the meaning in English is *on* and sometimes *in*.

   ¿Qué **les pones** a las papas fritas?
   What do you put on French fries?

   ¿Qué **le pusiste** a la sopa?
   What did you put in the soup?

2. With third person forms as well as with **Ud.** and **Uds., le** and **les** are used even if the person or thing represented by the pronoun is mentioned.

   Al profesor no **le agradan** los vinos franceses.
   French wines aren't pleasing to the instructor.

   Les pongo sal **a las papas fritas.**
   I put salt on French fries.

3. You have also learned a number of verbs that require indirect object pronouns. These verbs are often translated into English with verbs that do not require indirect object pronouns.

   agradar   *to please*
   No **me agrada** eso.
   That doesn't please me. (I don't like that.)

   apetecer   *to appeal, be appealing*
   No **me apetece.**
   It doesn't appeal to me.

   caer (*irreg.*) **bien (mal)**   *to make a good (bad) impression; to (dis)agree with* (food)
   No **me cae** bien el ajo.
   Garlic doesn't agree with me.

   encantar   *to delight, be extremely pleasing*
   Me encantan los vinos chilenos.
   Chilean wines really please me. (I love Chilean wines.)

   importar   *to be important; to matter*
   ¿**Te importa** si le pongo sal?
   Does it matter to you if I put salt on it? (Do you mind if I put salt on it?)

   interesar   *to be interesting*
   ¿**Te interesa** la música clásica?
   Does classical music interest you?

Impersonal and Passive se

1. Impersonal **se** translates into English as *one, they,* and *you,* meaning that there is no particular subject of the verb. The verb is always in the singular form.

   No **se debe** beber tanto café.
   One (You) shouldn't drink so much coffee.

2. Passive **se** translates into English as *is (are) + -ed (-en).* The object of the verb takes on the role of determining whether the verb is singular or plural.

   Se habla español aquí.
   Spanish is spoken here.

   Se hablan varias lenguas aquí.
   Various languages are spoken here.

3. In many instances, the impersonal **se** and a singular passive **se** construction are indistinguishable.

   No **se debe** hacer eso.
   One (You) shouldn't do that. (That shouldn't be done.)

4. With reflexive verbs, impersonal **se** cannot be used. **Uno** is used instead to avoid a "double **se**" construction.

   Uno se levanta tarde por aquí, ¿no?
   Uno no debe **dormirse** en clase.

Uno can also be used with just about any verb as a substitute for the impersonal **se.**

Aquí **uno** toma café con los amigos para ser sociable.
One drinks coffee here with friends to be sociable.

Preterite Review (Regular Forms)

	-ar	-er	-ir
(yo)	tom**é**	beb**í**	sal**í**
(tú)	tom**aste**	beb**iste**	sal**iste**
(Ud.)	tom**ó**	beb**ió**	sal**ió**
(él/ella)	tom**ó**	beb**ió**	sal**ió**
(nosotros/as)	tom**amos**	beb**imos**	sal**imos**
(vosotros/as)	tom**astais**	beb**isteis**	sal**isteis**
(Uds.)	tom**aron**	beb**ieron**	sal**ieron**
(ellos/ellas)	tom**aron**	beb**ieron**	sal**ieron**

1. Remember that in all regular preterite forms, the acoustic stress falls on the verb ending and not on the stem.

2. **-er** and **-ir** verbs share the same endings. Also note that for **-ar** and **-ir** verbs, the regular preterite form for **nosotros** is the same as the present tense form.

3. **-ir** verbs that have an **e → i** stem vowel change in the present tense keep this change in the **Ud., él/ella, Uds.,** and **ellos/ellas** forms in the preterite. **Dormir** also has a stem vowel change (**o → u**) in the **Ud., él/ella, Uds.,** and **ellos/ellas** forms.

pedir

pedí	pedimos
pediste	pedisteis
pidió	**pidieron**
pidió	**pidieron**

servir

serví	servimos
serviste	servisteis
sirvió	**sirvieron**
sirvió	**sirvieron**

dormir

dormí	dormimos
dormiste	dormisteis
durmió	**durmieron**
durmió	**durmieron**

More on estar + Adjectives

With some adjectives, the English equivalent of **estar** can indicate taste, feel, appearance, and smell.

   Esta sopa **está salada.**
   This soup is (tastes) salty.

   Este pescado **está fresco.**
   This fish is (looks) fresh.

Por and para

Para is used to indicate the destination or recipient of something, never the source. Only **por** can indicate source.

   Voy a preparar un cóctel **para** María.
   I'm going to make a drink for María. (She is the recipient of the drink.)

   Trabajo **por** mi familia.
   I'm working for my family. (They are the reason I have to work.)

El bienestar

Domingo, medianoche (1998) por Ramón Lombarte

Perfil del artista

NOMBRE: Ramón Lombarte

PAÍS DE ORIGEN: España

FECHA DE NACIMIENTO: 1956

Ramón Lombarte nació en Barcelona, donde estudió en la Escuela
Massana de Bellas Artes, a la que también asistieron Pablo Picasso
y Joan Miró. El estilo de Lombarte combina el realismo con la sensualidad, como si sus obras
fueran[a] fotografías de escenas privadas donde la luz[b] juega con la sombra[c] para revelar las
emociones de sus sujetos. Por su extraordinario talento, las obras de Lombarte se encuentran
no sólo en galerías y museos sino también en las colecciones privadas del Rey Juan Carlos I de
España, Andrés Segovia y otras personas célebres.

———

[a]*were*　[b]*light*　[c]*shadow*

LECCIÓN 10

Check out the following media resources to complement this lesson:

 Online *Manual*

 Video on CD

 Online Learning Center

 ActivityPak

¿Cómo te sientes?

En esta lección, vas a examinar el tema de los estados de ánimo (*states of mind*). También vas a

◆ describir cómo te sientes

◆ identificar tus estados de ánimo y las circunstancias que los afectan

◆ analizar las maneras en que tú y otros reaccionan frente a varios estados de ánimo

◆ describir nuevos pasatiempos que te hacen sentir mejor

◆ aprender nuevos verbos «reflexivos»

◆ utilizar los verbos **faltar** y **quedar**

◆ repasar el uso del imperfecto para describir los eventos habituales en el pasado

ALTO Before beginning this lesson, look over the **Intercambio** activity on pages 281–283. This is the activity you will be working toward throughout the lesson.

Me siento muy alegre.
(Cerca de Cuzco, Perú)

VOCABULARIO

¿Cómo se siente?

Talking about how someone feels

Las experiencias de Yolanda

1. Son las 10.30 de la mañana. Yolanda se prepara para un examen de física. **Está nerviosa** porque el examen va a ser difícil.

2. Su compañera de cuarto hace mucho ruido. Yolanda no puede concentrarse y **se pone enfadada.**

3. A la 1.00 toma el examen. No tiene idea de cómo va a salir. **Está muy tensa** durante el examen.

4. Después del examen, va al gimnasio a hacer ejercicio. Después, **se siente más relajada.**

5. Por la tarde, va al trabajo. Trabaja hasta muy tarde y, naturalmente, **está cansada.**

6. Al día siguiente, va a la clase de historia. La voz de la profesora es monótona, y Yolanda **está aburrida.**

7. En la clase de física, el profesor le devuelve el examen. Su nota es un 65%. Yolanda **se siente avergonzada** (*ashamed*).

8. Yolanda **se siente deprimida** (*depressed*).

9. Al otro día Yolanda habla de su nota con el profesor. Descubren que el profesor se equivocó (*made a mistake*). La nota debe ser 95%, no 65%. Yolanda **se pone muy contenta.** El profesor le dice, «Perdona, todos nos equivocamos, ¿no?»

10. ¡Ahora Yolanda **se siente muy orgullosa**!

ACTIVIDAD A ¿Cómo se siente Yolanda?

A continuación aparece una lista de los pensamientos (*thoughts*) que tuvo Yolanda durante los tres días que se describen en la sección anterior. Relaciona los estados de ánimo que va a leer tu profesor(a) con los pensamientos de la lista.

MODELO PROFESOR(A): Está nerviosa.
CLASE: Es la letra **a.**

a. Me gustaría dormir diez horas esta noche.
b. ¡Dios mío! ¡Sólo me quedan cuatro horas (*I only have four hours left*) para estudiar!
c. Van a pensar que soy muy tonta.
d. Si esa profesora dice «¡muy bien!» una vez más, me va a dar un ataque cardíaco.
e. ¡Fantástico! ¡Fue un error! Entonces sí saqué (*I got*) una buena nota.
f. No quiero ver a nadie. Quiero estar completamente sola.

Así se dice

When talking about someone else's state of being, you may use **está** or **se siente** with an adjective.

Yolanda **está contenta.**
Yolanda is happy.

Hoy **se siente** un poco **nerviosa.**
Today she feels a bit nervous.

To express the idea of a change in mood, you often can use **se pone** with an adjective.

Su compañera de cuarto hace mucho ruido y Yolanda **se pone enfadada** (*gets mad*).

(You will learn more about these verbs as the lesson progresses.)

Así se dice

Por is often used to mean *because of* or *on account of.*

Me siento mal **por** lo que dijo Rafael.

Yolanda está nerviosa **por** el examen.

In most cases such as these, you can also use **a causa de.**

Yolanda está nerviosa **a causa del** examen.

ACTIVIDAD B ¿Por qué?

El profesor (La profesora) va a leer algunos estados de ánimo comunes a los estudiantes de hoy. Selecciona la situación que puede provocar ese sentimiento en los estudiantes.

1. **a.** Estudia en la biblioteca.
   b. Tiene tres exámenes hoy.
   c. Durmió bien anoche.
2. **a.** Tiene que estudiar, pero su compañero/a de cuarto tiene el radio a todo volumen.
   b. Recibió una carta de una amiga esta mañana.
   c. Va de compras después de clase.
3. **a.** Asiste a clases.
   b. Va a la cafetería a almorzar.
   c. Ganó un millón de dólares en la lotería.
4. **a.** Va a una fiesta con los amigos.
   b. Comió en un buen restaurante anoche.
   c. Sacó F en un examen.

ACTIVIDAD C ¿De buen o mal humor?°

¿De... *In a good or bad mood?*

Paso 1 Cuando sientes las siguientes emociones, ¿generalmente estás de buen o mal humor?

	...ESTOY DE BUEN HUMOR.	...ESTOY DE MAL HUMOR.
1. Si me siento cansado/a	☐	☐
2. Si estoy contento/a	☐	☐
3. Si me siento deprimido/a	☐	☐
4. Si estoy enojado/a (*angry*)	☐	☐
5. Si me siento relajado/a	☐	☐
6. Si me siento orgulloso/a	☐	☐

Paso 2 Ahora compara tus respuestas con las de un compañero (una compañera) de clase.

COMUNICACIÓN

ACTIVIDAD D ¿Cómo estoy? ¡Adivina!

Paso 1 Trabajando con un compañero (una compañera) de clase, escucha bien las instrucciones del profesor (de la profesora) y haz la primera parte de esta actividad.

E1	E2
1.	2.
3.	4.

Paso 2 Ahora dale a tu compañero/a una situación que describa una de las frases que escribiste. Pero antes, lee el modelo. El Estudiante 1 debe comenzar la actividad.

MODELO E1: Mañana tengo dos exámenes difíciles. ¿Cómo estoy?
        E2: Estás nervioso.

GRAMÁTICA

¿Te sientes bien?

"Reflexive" verbs

me	siento aburro	**nos**	sentimos aburrimos
te	sientes aburres	**os**	sentís aburrís
se	siente aburre	**se**	sienten aburren
se	siente aburre	**se**	sienten aburren

—¿Qué te pasa, Jorge? Te ves muy mal. ¿**Te sientes** bien?

—Ay, Lucía... Llegué tarde a mi primera clase y se me olvidó escribir la composición para la clase de inglés. Y al llegar a la clase de matemáticas, supe que íbamos a tener un examen hoy. ¡**Me siento** fatal!

—Ay te comprendo, amigo. Te invito a otro café.

Así se dice

You have seen that there are two ways to express *to get* + condition/state: **ponerse** + *adjective* or a verb that requires a reflexive pronoun. One way of expressing the idea of getting very angry, very upset, very tired, and so forth, is with **ponerse** + **muy** + *adjective.*

> **Me pongo muy enojado.**
> **Se pone muy cansada.**

Another way is to use **mucho** with the verbs that require a reflexive pronoun.

> **Me enojo mucho** cuando…
> **Se cansa mucho si…**

You learned in **Lección 5** that verbs like **sentirse** are not "true reflexives" because no one is doing anything to himself or herself. Nonetheless, these verbs require a reflexive pronoun. Here are some other common verbs that are useful for expressing how a person feels and that require reflexive pronouns.

aburrirse	*to get bored*
alegrarse	*to get happy*
cansarse	*to get tired*
enojarse	*to get angry*
irritarse	*to be (get) irritated*
ofenderse	*to be (get) offended*
preocuparse (por)	*to worry, get worried (about)*

ACTIVIDAD E ¿Cómo te sientes en estas circunstancias?

Indica cada frase que describe tu propia experiencia. Luego inventa una frase de acuerdo con tu personalidad.

1. Me siento bastante tenso/a…

☐ cuando tengo mucho trabajo.

☐ cuando tengo varios exámenes el mismo día.

☐ cuando necesito dinero y no lo tengo.

☐ al final del semestre/trimestre.

☐ ¿ ?

2. Me pongo enojado/a cuando…

☐ saco una mala nota.

☐ alguien habla mal de un amigo mío (una amiga mía).

☐ alguien me promete (*promises*) hacer algo pero no lo hace.

☐ alguien me llama por teléfono mientras duermo.

☐ ¿ ?

3. Me siento muy contento/a cuando…

☐ compro algo nuevo.

☐ me miro en el espejo.

☐ hago ejercicio.

☐ veo a mi familia.

☐ ¿ ?

Así se dice

Remember that most adjectives reflect both gender and number of what or whom they modify.

> **Ana y Raquel** están aburri**das** en la clase de álgebra.
> **Los padres** se ponen enfada**dos** cuando sus hijos no escuchan bien.
> **Jorge** siempre se siente nervios**o** antes de tomar un examen.

ACTIVIDAD F ¿Te aburres fácilmente?

Paso 1 Indica si cada reacción es típica de tu persona o no.

	ES TÍPICA	ES RARA
1. Me aburro fácilmente.	☐	☐
2. Me enojo por cosas pequeñas.	☐	☐
3. Me irrito cuando no duermo lo suficiente.	☐	☐
4. Me preocupo por mi situación económica.	☐	☐
5. Me alegro cuando mis amigos me invitan a una fiesta.	☐	☐
6. Me ofendo cuando la gente fuma.	☐	☐
7. Me canso fácilmente.	☐	☐

Paso 2 Ahora compara tus respuestas con las de un compañero (una compañera). Escribe dos oraciones en las que mencionas una cosa que Uds. tienen en común y otra que no tienen en común.

MODELO Los (Las) dos nos irritamos cuando no dormimos lo suficiente. En cambio, Rick se ofende cuando la gente fuma, y yo no.

COMUNICACIÓN

ACTIVIDAD G Asociaciones

¿Qué emociones asocias con lo que te rodea (*surrounds you*)? Tu compañero/a de clase va a escoger cuatro elementos (uno de cada categoría) y te va a preguntar sobre la emoción o sentimiento que asocias con cada uno. Luego tú le vas a hacer preguntas a tu compañero/a.

MODELO E1: ¿Qué emoción asocias con el color rojo?
E2: Asocio el color rojo con el enojo (*anger*). (Me siento tensa cuando pienso en el color rojo.)

Así se dice

Remember that **tener** + *noun* may be used to express conditions and states of being. Here are two more examples.

tener celos
to be jealous

tener envidia
to be envious

COLORES

amarillo	**café**	**negro**
azul	**gris** (*gray*)	**rojo**
blanco	**morado** (*purple*)	**verde**

COSAS

el chocolate	**la lluvia**	**un objeto de arte**
las computadoras	**las novelas**	**los regalos** (*gifts*)
el dinero		

OCASIONES

una cita con un amigo (una amiga)	**los exámenes**	**los sábados**
mi cumpleaños	**un funeral**	**las vacaciones**
	los lunes	

PERSONAS

mi madre	**mi pareja**	**mi compañero/a de cuarto**
mi padre	**mi hijo/a**	**el profesor (la profesora) de** _____

NAVEGANDO LA RED

Busca la página Web de un hispano famoso (una hispana famosa). ¿Menciona esta persona un color, una comida o un objeto favorito y cómo le hace sentir? ¿Habla de sus emociones? Presenta tus resultados a la clase.

IDEAS PARA EXPLORAR

Reacciones

VOCABULARIO

¿Cómo se revelan las emociones?

Talking about how people show their feelings

Jorge mira una película en la televisión. La película tiene escenas muy variadas.

Un día en la vida de Jorge

Durante las escenas cómicas	**Durante las escenas románticas**	**Durante una escena de suspenso**	**Luego al llegar el final trágico**

1. Jorge **se ríe.**

2. Jorge se siente avergonzado y **se sonroja (se pone rojo).**

3. Jorge **se come las uñas** porque **está asustado.**

4. Jorge **llora** porque **está triste.**

Mientras Yolanda está en su apartamento, ocurre una escena dramática entre su compañera de cuarto y el novio.

Un día en la vida de Yolanda

1. Yolanda está limpiando el apartamento. Se siente muy contenta y por eso **está silbando.**

2. Llega su compañera de cuarto con el novio. **Están muy enojados.**

3. Su compañera **grita,** va directamente al cuarto y **se encierra.**

4. «Silvia, háblame». Silvia **permanece callada** (es decir, no habla, no contesta).

5. Finalmente cuando se va su novio, Silvia sale de su dormitorio y comienza a **quejarse de** él. «No lo puedo creer. Sólo quiere hacer lo que él quiere. ¡Es tan egoísta!»

6. Yolanda piensa: «¡Qué cómicos! No cambian. Siempre la misma historia».

Vocabulario útil

asustar	to frighten	**tener dolor de cabeza**	to have a headache
contar (ue) un chiste	to tell a joke	**tener miedo**	to be afraid (*lit.* to have fear)
gritar	to shout, yell		
pasarlo (muy) mal	to have a (very) bad time	**tener vergüenza**	to be ashamed, embarrassed (*lit.* to have shame)

ACTIVIDAD A ¿Por qué?

Tu profesor(a) va a leer las reacciones de algunos estudiantes. Escoge la letra de la actividad que mejor explica por qué esta persona reaccionó de esta manera.

1. **a.** Tiene dolor de cabeza.

   b. Ve a un buen amigo.

   c. Recibió malas noticias.

2. **a.** Recibió un cheque de sus padres.

   b. Descubre que se ganó la lotería.

   c. El dependiente del supermercado no la trató (*treated*) con respeto.

3. **a.** Se preparó un desayuno saludable.

   b. Ofendió a alguien sin querer hacerlo.

   c. Sabe jugar bien al tenis.

4. **a.** Alguien le contó un chiste.

   b. Ve una escena de horror en la televisión.

   c. Se acostó temprano.

Así se dice

In this section you are working with three more verbs that require a reflexive pronoun. Remember that the use of this pronoun does not mean that these verbs are true reflexives! Here is a quick comparison of reflexive **se** (*himself* [*herself*]) and nonreflexive **se**. The latter has no exact English equivalent.

REFLEXIVE **SE**

Juan **se admira.**
Juan admires himself.

Luis **se baña.**
Luis takes a bath (bathes himself).

María **se ve** en el espejo.
María sees herself in the mirror.

NONREFLEXIVE **SE**

Juan **se queja** mucho.
Juan complains a lot.

Luis **se sonroja** fácilmente.
Luis blushes easily.

María **se ríe** sin motivo.
María laughs for no reason.

ACTIVIDAD B Definiciones

Fíjate otra vez en (*Note once again*) el nuevo vocabulario que aparece con los dibujos de Jorge y Yolanda en las páginas 266–267. Da la palabra que corresponde a cada definición.

MODELO llenarse los ojos de lágrimas (*tears*) → llorar

1. manifestar disgusto o inconformidad con algo o con alguien
2. no decir nada, guardar silencio, no contestar a los demás
3. cambiar de color la cara involuntariamente
4. levantar la voz cuando se está furioso/a
5. entrar en un cuarto y cerrar la puerta para estar solo/a

ACTIVIDAD C ¿Con qué frecuencia?

Entrevista a dos compañeros/as de clase para averiguar con qué
frecuencia reaccionan a las siguientes situaciones.

1 = a menudo (*often*)　　　　**2** = raras veces　　　　**3** = nunca

	E1			E2		
	1	2	3	1	2	3
1. Cuando estás enojado/a, ¿con qué frecuencia gritas?	☐	☐	☐	☐	☐	☐
2. Cuando te sientes triste, ¿con qué frecuencia lloras?	☐	☐	☐	☐	☐	☐
3. Cuando tienes miedo, ¿con qué frecuencia te comes las uñas?	☐	☐	☐	☐	☐	☐
4. Cuando te sientes avergonzado/a, ¿con qué frecuencia te pones rojo/a?	☐	☐	☐	☐	☐	☐
5. Cuando no estás contento/a, ¿con qué frecuencia te quejas?	☐	☐	☐	☐	☐	☐
6. Cuando te sientes muy enfadado/a, ¿con qué frecuencia te encierras en tu cuarto?	☐	☐	☐	☐	☐	☐

COMUNICACIÓN

ACTIVIDAD D ¿Estás de acuerdo?

Paso 1 Indica si estás de acuerdo o no con las siguientes opiniones.

	ESTOY DE ACUERDO.	NO ESTOY DE ACUERDO.	DEPENDE.
1. Es bueno gritar cuando uno está muy enojado.	☐	☐	☐
2. Cuando uno se siente deprimido, es importante llorar.	☐	☐	☐
3. Ponerse rojo es vergonzoso (*embarrassing*).	☐	☐	☐
4. No es malo reírse cuando otra persona se cae (*falls down*).	☐	☐	☐
5. Cuando alguien lo insulta a uno, es mejor permanecer callado en vez de gritar.	☐	☐	☐
6. Es aceptable silbar en un lugar público, como en un supermercado.	☐	☐	☐

Paso 2 Entrevista a otra persona de la clase para ver si está de acuerdo
con tus opiniones. Puedes usar los siguientes modelos.

MODELOS　En tu opinión, ¿es bueno gritar... ?

¿Crees que es bueno gritar... ?

GRAMÁTICA

¿Te falta energía?

The verbs **faltar** and **quedar**

*A esta chica chilena **le falta energía.** No tiene ganas de hacer nada.*

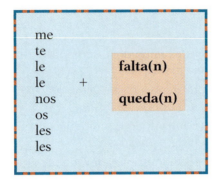

me		
te		
le	+	**falta(n)**
le		
nos		**queda(n)**
os		
les		
les		

The verbs **faltar** and **quedar** are similar to **gustar** in that they require indirect object pronouns. Remember that **gustar** actually means *to please* or *to be pleasing.*

> **Me gusta** ayudar a otras personas.

> Lit. *Helping other people pleases me.*

Faltar actually means *to be absent* or *not to be present.* Like **gustar,** it can be literally rendered in English, but other preferred ways express the same concept.

> Me **faltan** cinco dólares.

> *I'm missing five dollars.*
> (Lit. *Five dollars are absent to me.*)

> Me **falta** energía.

> *I lack energy.*
> (Lit. *Energy is absent to me.*)

Note how you can say that someone is absent from class using **faltar** and that the English equivalent is very close in structure.

> Ángela **falta** hoy.

> *Ángela is absent today.*

The verb **quedar** means *to be remaining.* Like **gustar** and **faltar,** it has literal and preferred English equivalents. Compare the following.

> Me **quedan** diez centavos.

> *I have ten cents left.*
> (Lit. *Ten cents are remaining to me.*)

> ¿Te **quedan** muchas clases para terminar tu carrera?

> *Do you have a lot of classes left to finish your degree?*
> (Lit. *Are there many classes remaining to you to finish your degree?*)

From the previous examples, you may have noticed that **faltar** and **quedar** often appear in third person forms.

ACTIVIDAD E Al llegar a la universidad

Paso 1 Piensa en las cosas que les faltan a muchos cuando llegan a la universidad por primera vez. (Si quieres, puedes hablar de las cosas que les faltan a muchos cuando trabajan por primera vez después de graduarse.) Indica lo que piensas.

A muchos estudiantes cuando llegan por primera vez a la universidad…

☐ les falta confianza (*confidence*).

☐ les falta una buena educación secundaria.

☐ les falta la habilidad de organizar el tiempo.

☐ les falta independencia económica.

☐ les falta(n) _____.

Paso 2 Ahora piensa en las primeras semanas de tus estudios universitarios (o en las primeras semanas en tu trabajo). ¿Cuál(es) de las siguientes oraciones refleja(n) tu situación?

Cuando llegué por primera vez a la universidad…

☐ me faltaba confianza.

☐ me faltaba una buena educación secundaria.

☐ me faltaba la habilidad de organizar el tiempo.

☐ me faltaba independencia económica.

☐ me faltaba(n) _____.

ACTIVIDAD F ¿Te queda algo?

Paso 1 Indica lo que es verdad para ti.

1. Generalmente, al final del mes…
   ☐ me queda dinero.
   ☐ no me queda dinero.

2. Después de estudiar por cuatro horas…
   ☐ me queda energía.
   ☐ no me queda energía.

3. Para terminar la carrera universitaria…
   ☐ me quedan más de 30 créditos.
   ☐ me quedan menos de 30 créditos.

Paso 2 Ahora busca a una persona en la clase que tenga tres de las mismas respuestas que tienes tú. ¿Puedes encontrar a alguien en menos de cuatro minutos hablando sólo en español? **¡OJO!** No te olvides de hacer las preguntas correctamente.

MODELO Generalmente, ¿te queda dinero al final del mes?

ACTIVIDAD G ¿Sabías que... ?

Paso 1 Lee la selección **¿Sabías que... ?** Luego contesta las preguntas a continuación.

1. ¿Por qué se llama el malestar «el síndrome *invernal*»?

2. ¿Cuáles son los tres síntomas mayores de este síndrome?
   a. A muchos les falta…
   b. También les falta…
   c. Se consumen más…

3. ¿Cuál parece ser la causa del síndrome?

4. Según la selección, ¿en cuál de los siguientes países esperas encontrar más casos de este síndrome? Explica tu respuesta.
   a. México
   b. Chile
   c. Costa Rica

Paso 2 Busca los usos de **faltar** en el artículo. ¿Puedes indicar cuál es el sujeto del verbo en cada caso? ¿Puedes dar una equivalencia literal en inglés y también una equivalencia más estándar?

Paso 3 Indica si sufres del síndrome invernal o no. Completa la siguiente frase con dos o tres oraciones. Luego compara lo que escribiste con lo que escribieron otros miembros de la clase.

«Durante el invierno me siento… »

¿Sabías que...

existe algo llamado «el síndrome invernal»? El síndrome invernal se refiere al estado general de depresión en que se encuentran muchas personas durante el invierno. Según estudios psicológicos, los síntomas comienzan a aparecer a finales de otoño. ¿Cuáles son los síntomas? Primero, a muchos les falta energía. Les entra cierto letargo difícil de quitar. Segundo, les falta la habilidad de concentrarse en el trabajo y en los estudios. También se reporta que durante esta época, se consumen más drogas y bebidas alcohólicas que durante los demás meses del año. En fin, el síndrome produce cierto tipo de depresión en sus víctimas. Este síndrome es bastante conocido en Europa, y los países nórdicos son especialmente afectados. También se reporta su existencia en España, aunque no en grado tan alto como en los otros países mencionados.

¿Cuál es la causa del síndrome? Según los científicos, es la falta de luz. Como todos sabemos, el invierno no es solamente una época más fría sino también más oscura.[a] Hay menos luz solar y parece que es esta falta de luz lo que estimula la ocurrencia del síndrome en muchas personas.

_____

[a]más… *darker*

ACTIVIDAD H La falta de ánimo

La palabra **ánimo** es similar a la palabra **energía.** Así que si uno dice: «Me falta ánimo», quiere decir que a esa persona le falta energía. En esta actividad, vas a trabajar con un compañero (una compañera) para formular un cuestionario que luego vas a darles a otras personas en la clase.

Paso 1 En parejas, escriban cinco oraciones a las cuales una persona pueda responder **siempre** (5), **con frecuencia** (4), **a veces** (3), **casi nunca** (2), **nunca** (1). La idea es hacer oraciones que parecen reflejar situaciones típicas para muchas personas. También deben tratar de variar las situaciones.

		5	4	3	2	1
MODELO	Me falta ánimo después de tomar un examen.	☐	☐	☐	☐	☐
1. _____		☐	☐	☐	☐	☐
2. _____		☐	☐	☐	☐	☐
3. _____		☐	☐	☐	☐	☐
4. _____		☐	☐	☐	☐	☐
5. _____		☐	☐	☐	☐	☐

Paso 2 Ahora dale el cuestionario a otra persona. ¿Resultó bien el cuestionario? ¿Necesitas hacer alguna modificación?

ACTIVIDAD I En tu opinión

Paso 1 Trabajando con dos o tres compañeros/as de clase comenta la siguiente afirmación. Apunten sus ideas.

«La depresión es un problema químico».

Paso 2 Presenten sus ideas al resto de la clase. ¿Qué saben Uds. sobre la depresión y sus causas?

NAVEGANDO LA RED

Se dice que el país de habla española con más psiquiatras y psicólogos es la Argentina. Busca una página Web argentina para una clínica de psiquiatría o psicología. ¿Qué servicios se ofrecen? ¿Qué dicen que pueden hacer por ti?

VOCABULARIO

¿Qué haces para sentirte bien?

Talking about leisure activities

Para sentirse bien Yolanda participa en actividades físicas.

Hace ejercicios aeróbicos.

Levanta pesas.

Nada.

Juega al basquetbol.

Camina.

Juega al tenis.

También le gusta hacer otras cosas que la relajan.

Sale con los amigos.

Va al cine.

Va de compras.

Cuando se siente tenso, Jorge, al igual que Yolanda, hace actividades físicas como practicar deportes.

Corre.

Juega al fútbol.

Juega al béisbol.

Juega al boliche.

A veces se dedica a actividades artísticas en su casa.

Pinta.

Toca la guitarra.

Canta.

ACTIVIDAD A Categorías

Paso 1 Tu profesor(a) va a leer una lista de actividades. Escribe cada actividad en la categoría apropiada.

SE PUEDE PRACTICAR A SOLAS (*ALONE*).	SE REQUIEREN DOS O MÁS PERSONAS.

Paso 2 Haz lo que hiciste en el **Paso 1,** pero con otras categorías.

SE REQUIERE UNA HABILIDAD ESPECIAL.	NO SE REQUIERE NINGUNA HABILIDAD.

Paso 3 Compara las respuestas que diste en los **Pasos 1** y **2** con las de un compañero (una compañera) de clase. ¿Están totalmente de acuerdo? ¿En qué actividades no están de acuerdo?

 ACTIVIDAD B Asociaciones

Tu profesor(a) va a leer varias actividades. Empareja los elementos de la siguiente lista con cada actividad.

1. _____ las raquetas
2. _____ los músculos
3. _____ las tarjetas de crédito
4. _____ el agua

5. _____ Pablo Picasso
6. _____ la Serie Mundial
7. _____ la Copa Mundial
8. _____ el violín

COMUNICACIÓN

ACTIVIDAD C ¿Qué les recomiendas?

Paso 1 Las siguientes personas quieren hacer algo, pero no saben exactamente qué. Según lo que dicen, sugiéreles por lo menos una actividad.

> MODELO Me siento triste hoy. Quiero hacer algo para animarme (*cheer me up*). No quiero estar solo. →
> Puedes jugar al boliche o al basquetbol con alguien.

1. Estoy muy tenso. Mañana es sábado y necesito hacer ejercicio, pero nada que requiera mucho esfuerzo (*effort*) físico.
2. No soy una persona activa. Prefiero hacer cosas intelectuales o artísticas.
3. Estoy bastante cansada. No quiero salir de casa, pero necesito hacer algo para relajarme.
4. Quiero hacer alguna actividad física, pero hoy hace mal tiempo. Quiero hacer algo sin tener que salir de la casa.
5. Cuando me siento muy tenso, me encanta participar en cualquier deporte que requiera mucha energía y que sea competitivo.

Paso 2 Ahora inventa dos situaciones como las que aparecen en el **Paso 1.** Luego preséntaselas a otras dos personas. ¿Qué recomendaciones te dan? ¿Cuál es tu reacción personal? ¿Te gusta cada sugerencia?

ACTIVIDAD D ¿Qué actividades te gustan?

Paso 1 Piensa en las siguientes actividades y escribe una reacción.

Vocabulario útil
(no) me gusta
(no) me interesa
(no) tengo la destreza (*skill*) / **el talento**

1. caminar
2. hacer ejercicio
3. ir de compras
4. jugar al boliche

5. levantar pesas
6. nadar
7. pintar
8. tocar la guitarra (el piano)

Paso 2 Entrevista a un compañero (una compañera) para ver su reacción ante las actividades alistadas en el **Paso 1.** ¿Tienen Uds. las mismas reacciones?

MODELO   E1: ¿Qué piensas de levantar pesas?
         E2: No me gusta.
         E1: ¿No? A mí me gusta mucho.
         E2: Yo creo que es aburrido.

Paso 3 (Optativo) Presenta a la clase una breve comparación entre lo que tú piensas de las actividades del **Paso 1** y lo que piensa tu compañero/a.

ACTIVIDAD E Una historia

Paso 1 Trabajando con un compañero (una compañera) de clase, inventa una historia sobre lo que pasa en los siguientes dibujos. A continuación tienen algunas ideas para considerar.

◆ ¿Quiénes son las dos personas? ¿Cómo se llaman?
◆ ¿Cuál es la relación entre ellas?
◆ ¿Cómo se sienten las dos mujeres?
◆ ¿Qué ideas tiene la señora?

1.   2.   3.

4.   5.

Paso 2 Compartan su historia con el resto de la clase. ¿Quiénes inventaron la historia más interesante?

GRAMÁTICA

¿Qué hacías de niño/a para sentirte bien?

Using the imperfect for habitual events: a review

Para sentirse bien, Yolanda **jugaba** con muñecos. Ahora le encanta jugar al tenis.

(yo)	pintaba corría salía	(nosotros/as)	pintábamos corríamos salíamos
(tú)	pintabas corrías salías	(vosotros/as)	pintabais corríais salíais
(Ud.)	pintaba corría salía	(Uds.)	pintaban corrían salían
(él/ella)	pintaba corría salía	(ellos/ellas)	pintaban corrían salían

In **Lección 6** you learned that the imperfect can be used to talk about events that occurred repeatedly in the past. Such habitual events in the past, often translated into English as *used to + verb* or *would + verb*, are rendered in Spanish with a single verb.

Jorge **se aburría** en la escuela secundaria.

¿Qué **hacías** de niño para sentirte bien?

Jorge would get bored (*used to get bored*) in high school.

What did you do (*used to do*) as a child to feel well?

Remember that imperfect verb forms do not have stem vowel changes or repeat any irregularities from either the present or the preterite tense. However, the following verbs are irregular in the imperfect.

ir   iba, ibas, iba, iba, íbamos, ibais, iban, iban

ser   era, eras, era, era, éramos, erais, eran, eran

ACTIVIDAD E Jorge: Antes y ahora

Paso 1 Empareja las frases de la columna A con las de la columna B para expresar lo que Jorge hacía antes y lo que hace ahora.

A

1. _____ Cuando se ponía triste...
2. _____ Cuando quiere relajarse...
3. _____ Cuando estaba con sus amigos y hacía buen tiempo...
4. _____ Cuando le falta energía...
5. _____ Cuando se ponía nervioso...

B

a. nadaba.
b. hablaba con su mamá.
c. pinta o hace otra actividad artística.
d. se comía las uñas (¡todavía lo hace!).
e. hace algo físico para animarse.

Paso 2 Entre las actividades que Jorge hacía antes en el **Paso 1,** escoge una que tú no hacías; y entre las actividades que él hace ahora, escoge una que tú tampoco (también) haces. Ahora escribe un párrafo según el modelo.

MODELO   Antes, cuando Jorge se ponía triste, hablaba con su mamá. A diferencia de Jorge, yo hablaba con mi papá. Ahora, cuando Jorge quiere relajarse, pinta; yo también.

ACTIVIDAD F ¿Qué hacías y qué haces para sentirte mejor?

Paso 1 Completa las siguientes oraciones con detalles de tu vida.

DE ADOLESCENTE	AHORA
1. Cuando me enojaba con mis amigos…	Cuando me enojo con mis amigos…
2. Cuando me faltaba dinero…	Cuando me falta dinero…
3. Cuando me sentía tenso/a…	Cuando me siento tenso/a…
4. Cuando estaba muy alegre (*happy*)…	Cuando estoy muy alegre…
	Cuando lo paso muy mal…
5. Cuando lo pasaba muy mal…	

Paso 2 Trabaja con un compañero (una compañera) de clase. Sin leerle la primera parte de la oración, léele una de las frases que tú escribiste. Él (Ella) tiene que determinar a qué pregunta te refieres.

MODELO   E1: …escuchaba música sentimental en mi cuarto.
         E2: ¿Escuchabas música sentimental cuando lo pasabas mal?
         E1: ¡Exacto!

COMUNICACIÓN

ACTIVIDAD G ¿Cómo se sentían?

Se sabe que hoy día muchas personas viven bajo muchas tensiones. Pero, ¿tenía la gente de otras épocas más tensiones que la gente de hoy?

Paso 1 Con un compañero (una compañera), piensa en la vida de los seres prehistóricos o primitivos. Escojan una de las siguientes oraciones.

Los seres primitivos…

1. ☐ llevaban (*led*) una vida tranquila. No vivían tan tensos como la gente de hoy.

2. ☐ tenían muchas preocupaciones. Sentían las presiones propias de (*belonging to*) su época.

Paso 2 La clase debe dividirse en grupos de cuatro. A cada grupo se le va a asignar uno de los siguientes grupos.

1. los seres prehistóricos
2. los griegos de la época clásica
3. los aztecas antes de la llegada de los españoles
4. las familias de la época medieval
5. los pioneros norteamericanos del siglo XIX
6. los adolescentes norteamericanos típicos de los años 60
7. los adolescentes norteamericanos típicos de los años 20

Paso 3 ¿Qué hacían para sentirse bien? Cada grupo debe escribir por lo menos cinco oraciones sobre los hábitos de las personas de la época que se le ha asignado (*has been assigned to it*).

Vocabulario útil

bailar	**leer**
beber bebidas alcohólicas	**nadar**
cantar	**pintar**
contar chistes (historias)	**tocar algún instrumento musical**
jugar	

Paso 4 Cada grupo debe presentar sus oraciones a la clase. Los otros compañeros deben escuchar cada presentación y, después, indicar sus opiniones sobre la siguiente pregunta.

«¿Era más fácil sentirse bien en el pasado o es más fácil sentirse bien ahora?»

ACTIVIDAD H Cambios en la vida

Paso 1 Piensa en los pasatiempos, juegos y deportes que te gustaban cuando tenías 10 años. Menciona por lo menos cuatro actividades que hacías.

MODELO   A los 10 años, leía mucho.

Paso 2 Indica si hacías las actividades que mencionaste en el **Paso 1** cuando tenías 15 años.

MODELO   A los 15 años, todavía leía mucho.

Paso 3 Indica si todavía haces alguna de esas actividades hoy día.

MODELO   Ahora no leo mucho.

Paso 4 Basándote en los **Pasos 1–3,** explica cómo ha cambiado tu vida o no.

MODELO   Ahora no hago las mismas actividades que hacía de niño/a. Por ejemplo, de niño/a... Durante mi adolescencia,... Ahora...

ACTIVIDAD I En el escenario

Paso 1 Trabajen en grupos de dos o tres. Una persona de cada grupo tiene que ser el psicólogo (la psicóloga) y los otros, los pacientes.

SITUACIÓN A
Dos personas visitan al psicólogo (a la psicóloga) para consultar sobre algunos problemas matrimoniales que tienen. Los dos hablan de su situación y de las emociones que sienten. El psicólogo (la psicóloga) les hace preguntas y les da consejos.

SITUACIÓN B
Una persona visita al psicólogo (a la psicóloga) porque no puede estar entre el público. No se siente cómoda cuando está entre muchas personas. Esta persona habla de incidentes en su vida pasada (posibles causas) y de las emociones que siente hoy. El psicólogo (La psicóloga) le hace preguntas y le da consejos.

SITUACIÓN C
Un padre (Una madre) y su hijo/a visitan al psicólogo (a la psicóloga) porque hay problemas en la casa. El (La) joven no respeta a su padre (madre) y no quiere obedecer «las reglas de la casa». El padre (La madre) se siente frustrado porque no sabe qué hacer con su hijo/a. Ambas personas hablan desde su propia perspectiva y el psicólogo (la psicóloga) les hace preguntas y les da consejos.

Paso 2 Algunos grupos presentan su escena al resto de la clase.

NAVEGANDO LA RED

Busca la página Web de una persona hispana famosa. Luego busca información sobre las actividades que hacía él (ella) de niño/a. Comparte tus resultados con la clase.

INTERCAMBIO

Entrevistas

Propósito: obtener información para luego escribir una composición.

Papeles: una persona que entrevista y una persona entrevistada.

Paso 1 Mira el esquema a continuación. Vas a entrevistar a un compañero (una compañera) de clase y llenar el esquema con los datos obtenidos de la entrevista. Pero antes, escoge un estado de ánimo de la categoría A y después uno de la categoría B y piensa en las preguntas que vas a hacerle a tu compañero/a.

CATEGORÍA A
contento/a
relajado/a

CATEGORÍA B
enojado/a
tenso/a
triste o deprimido/a

MODELO   De adolescente, ¿te sentías tenso/a a menudo? Y ahora, ¿también te sientes tenso/a a menudo? ¿Cuándo te sientes así? ¿En qué circunstancias?

Nombre _____

Especialización _____

CATEGORÍA A

1. De adolescente se sentía _____

    ☐ a menudo   ☐ de vez en cuando   ☐ nunca

2. Ahora se siente _____

    ☐ a menudo   ☐ de vez en cuando   ☐ nunca

Circunstancias:

Indicaciones:

CATEGORÍA B

1. De adolescente se sentía _____

    ☐ a menudo   ☐ de vez en cuando   ☐ nunca

2. Ahora se siente _____

    ☐ a menudo   ☐ de vez en cuando   ☐ nunca

Circunstancias:

Indicaciones:

Lo que debe hacer para cambiar de ánimo:

Paso 2 Entrevista a tu compañero/a y apunta sus respuestas en el esquema.

Paso 3 Con los datos obtenidos en los **Pasos 1** y **2,** escribe una pequeña composición en la que te comparas a ti mismo/a (*yourself*) con tu compañero/a. Utiliza el siguiente modelo para organizar tu composición.

INTRODUCCIÓN
«Acabo de entrevistar a José sobre algunos de sus estados de ánimo. Ahora voy a hacer una comparación entre él y yo».

PÁRRAFO 1
«José… »

PÁRRAFO 2
«Yo… »

CONCLUSIÓN
«Se puede ver que José y yo _____».

Vistazos culturales
La globalización en el mundo hispano

¿Sabías que... la globalización ha tenido[a] un impacto muy grande en el mundo hispano? En términos generales la globalización es un fenómeno económico que se refiere al proceso de desnacionalizar los mercados domésticos para permitir inversiones[b] en mercados extranjeros. Muchas compañías norteamericanas y europeas han invertido[c] en países hispanos. La globalización ha causado[d] muchos cambios en la vida diaria de los hispanos, sobre todo en cuanto a la lengua, la ropa y la dieta.

[a]ha... *has had*   [b]*investments*   [c]han... *have invested*   [d]ha... *has caused*

Desde hace un par de décadas[a] el interés en aprender y hablar inglés ha crecido[b] mucho en Latinoamérica. En varios países hispanos el inglés se oye en los anuncios y en las conversaciones diarios.

[a]Desde... *Over the past two decades*   [b]ha... *has grown*

En el español coloquial de Venezuela es común oír palabras del inglés con sufijos verbales del español como **faxear** o **clickear.** Ademas, algunos restaurantes, gimnasios y clubes nocturnos tienen nombres en inglés como *Crystal Ranch, Sport Center* y *Studio Fifty Four.*

En México algunos productos lácteos sin crema se anuncian con la palabra inglesa *light* en lugar de la palabra española **descremada.** También se oyen muchas expresiones con palabras inglesas. Por ejemplo: «Dame *chance*». o «Me gusta tu *look*».

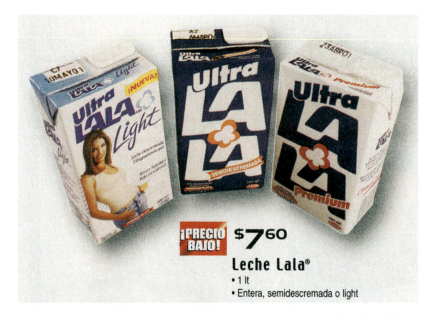

¡PRECIO BAJO! $7⁶⁰

Leche Lala®
• 1 lt
• Entera, semidescremada o light

En muchos lugares, las tiendas pequeñas van desapareciendo mientras se abren más almacenes y supermercados cada año.

Las compras

En muchos países hispanos, la gente va a varios lugares para hacer sus compras semanales.[a] Va a la carnicería para comprar carne, a un mercado abierto para comprar frutas y verduras, a una farmacia para comprar medicina, etcétera. En este país esta costumbre casi no existe. En cambio tenemos, y hemos tenido[b] por muchos años, supermercados y grandes tiendas tipo almacén[c] como Wal-Mart y Target que venden de todo en un solo lugar. Pero por el proceso de la globalización la tienda tipo almacén es cada vez más común en el mundo hispano. Debido a este proceso, la manera en que muchos hispanos hacen sus compras ha cambiado,[d] especialmente en las ciudades grandes.

---

[a]*weekly* [b]*hemos... we've had* [c]*warehouse* [d]*ha... has changed*

La dieta

Además de cambiar la manera en que los hispanos hacen sus compras, la globalización ha cambiado también lo que muchos hispanos comen. La tradición de la comida rápida en los Estados Unidos ha influido en[a] la dieta de muchos hispanos. La franquicia McDonald's, por ejemplo, tiene ocho restaurantes en Bolivia y más de 175 en México. Otras cadenas,[b] ahora comunes en el mundo hispano, son Burger King, Kentucky Fried Chicken, Pizza Hut, Taco Bell y otras.

---

[a]*ha... has influenced* [b]*chains*

Un McDonald's en La Paz, Bolivia

ACTIVIDAD ¿Qué recuerdas?

Termina las siguientes oraciones.

1. En México, se usa la palabra inglesa ＿＿ para nombrar productos bajos en grasa.

2. En ＿＿ es común oír palabras en inglés con sufijos verbales del español como **faxear.**

3. La expresión mexicana «Dame *chance*». quiere decir: «＿＿» en inglés.

4. El sufijo que se les agrega (*is added*) a palabras inglesas para formar nuevos verbos en español es ＿＿.

5. Tres compañías norteamericanas que han influido en la vida hispana son ＿＿, ＿＿ y ＿＿.

NAVEGANDO LA RED

Selecciona *uno* de los siguientes proyectos. Luego presenta tus resultados a la clase.

1. Busca información sobre la historia de la compañía alemana Volkswagen en Latinoamérica. Haz lo siguiente.
   a. Prepara una lista de los países y ciudades hispanos donde hay fábricas de automóviles Volkswagen.
   b. Averigua el número de empleados (*employees*) que trabajan en estas fábricas.
   c. Escoge *uno* de los países de la parte **a** y describe brevemente cómo la presencia de la fábrica Volkswagen ha influido en la vida diaria de los habitantes del país.

2. Busca información sobre el fenómeno de *code switching* en las comunidades hispanas de los Estados Unidos. Haz lo siguiente.
   a. Define el fenómeno de *code switching*.
   b. Menciona en qué partes de los Estados Unidos es común oír *code switching* entre español e inglés.
   c. Da unos ejemplos de *code switching* entre español e inglés.

VOCABULARIO COMPRENSIVO

Los estados de ánimo*
States of Mind

aburrirse	to get bored
alegrarse	to get happy
cansarse	to get tired
enojarse	to get angry
estar	to be
aburrido/a (R)	bored
asustado/a	afraid
cansado/a	tired
enojado/a	angry
nervioso/a	nervous
tenso/a	tense
irritarse	to be (get) irritated
ofenderse	to be (get) offended
ponerse (*irreg.*)	to get
contento/a	happy
enfadado/a	angry
triste	sad
relajarse	to relax
sentirse (ie, i)	to feel
alegre	happy
avergonzado/a	ashamed, embarrassed
deprimido/a	depressed
orgulloso/a	proud
relajado/a	relaxed
¿Cómo te sientes?	How do you feel?
¿Qué te pasa?	What's the matter?

Reacciones
Reactions

asustar	to frighten
comerse las uñas	to bite one's nails
encerrarse (ie) (en su cuarto)	to shut oneself up (in one's room)
gritar	to shout, yell
llorar	to cry
pasarlo (muy) mal	to have a (very) bad time

permanecer callado/a	to keep quiet
ponerse rojo/a	to blush
preocuparse	to worry, get worried
quejarse	to complain
reír(se) (i, i)	to laugh
silbar	to whistle
sonreír (i, i)	to smile
sonrojarse	to blush
tener dolor de cabeza	to have a headache
tener miedo	to be afraid
tener vergüenza	to be ashamed, embarrassed

Para sentirse bien
To Feel Well

caminar	to walk
cantar	to sing
jugar (ue) (R) al	to play
basquetbol	basketball
béisbol	baseball
tenis	tennis
jugar al boliche	to bowl
levantar pesas	to lift weights
pintar	to paint

Repaso: correr, hacer ejercicio, ir al cine, ir de compras, jugar al fútbol, nadar, practicar un deporte, salir con los amigos, tocar la guitarra

Palabras y expresiones útiles

contar (ue) un chiste	to tell a joke
encantar (R)	to be very pleasing
estar de buen (mal) humor	to be in a good (bad) mood
faltar	to be missing, lacking
hacer ruido	to make noise
quedar	to be remaining
sacar una buena (mala) nota	to get a good (bad) grade

---

*Many of the adjectives referring to states of mind can be used with more than one verb. For example, **estar nervioso/a** and **sentirse nervioso/a** are both possible.

Check out the following media resources to complement this lesson:

 Online *Manual*   **Online Learning Center**

 Video on CD   **ActivityPak**

¿Cómo te relajas?

¿Qué actividades te hacen sentir bien? En esta lección vas a examinar un poco más este tema y también vas a

◆ hablar de actividades y lugares que se asocian con relajarse

◆ aprender sobre los usos del infinitivo y la forma **-ndo**

◆ repasar el *pretérito* y aprender nuevas formas

◆ aprender a narrar una historia en el pasado, usando el *pretérito* y el *imperfecto*

◆ examinar algunas diferencias culturales entre los Estados Unidos y el mundo hispano con respecto al humor

 Before beginning this lesson, look over the **Intercambio** activity on page 307. This is the activity you will be working toward throughout the lesson.

Me relajo esquiando con los amigos.

IDEAS PARA EXPLORAR

El tiempo libre

VOCABULARIO

¿Qué haces para relajarte?

More activities for talking about relaxation

Las siguientes personas practican deportes para relajarse.

Juegan al golf,

al voleibol y...

también **saltan a la cuerda.**

Para relajarse, las siguientes personas...

esquían en las montañas o...

esquían en el agua.

A esta persona le gusta...

andar en bicicleta,

patinar y...

andar en patineta.

A esta persona le gusta...

dibujar y también...

trabajar en el jardín.

A este chico le gusta...

meditar o...

bañarse en un jacuzzi.

Vocabulario útil

la aromaterapia		**los patines**	(inline)
el monopatín*	scooter;	**(en línea)**	skates
	skateboard	**la patineta***	skateboard
el patinaje	skating	**el yoga**	

ACTIVIDAD A ¿Qué actividad es?

Escoge la actividad que describe tu profesor(a).

1. **a.** esquiar en el agua **b.** esquiar en las montañas **c.** jugar al golf

2. **a.** jugar al tenis **b.** dibujar **c.** jugar al voleibol

3. **a.** trabajar en el jardín **b.** jugar al tenis **c.** saltar a la cuerda

4. **a.** esquiar en el agua **b.** dibujar **c.** patinar

5. **a.** saltar a la cuerda **b.** trabajar en el jardín **c.** jugar al golf

6. **a.** meditar **b.** bañarse en un jacuzzi **c.** andar en bicicleta

ACTIVIDAD B Actividades inapropiadas

Usando la lista de actividades que se da en la sección anterior, ¿qué actividad *no* le recomiendas a las siguientes personas?

1. a alguien que sufre (*suffers*) de artritis
2. a alguien que tiene problemas cardíacos
3. a alguien a quien le gusta vivir una vida solitaria
4. a alguien que no sabe nadar
5. a alguien que pierde el equilibrio fácilmente
6. a alguien a quien no le gusta sudar (*sweat*)

---

*For many Spanish speakers, **monopatín** means *skateboard*. However, since **monopatín** now also means *scooter*, the word **patineta** with the meaning *skateboard* is gaining popularity to avoid confusion.

Lección 11 ¿Cómo te relajas?

ACTIVIDAD C Firma aquí, por favor

Paso 1 Busca a personas que den (*give*) respuestas afirmativas a tus preguntas.

1. ¿Sabes patinar en línea?
2. ¿Andas mucho en bicicleta?
3. ¿Te gusta trabajar en el jardín?
4. ¿Dibujas bien?
5. ¿Juega al golf tu madre (padre, abuelo)?
6. ¿Medita alguien en tu familia?
7. ¿Haces yoga (Utilizas la aromaterapia)?
8. ¿Te gusta andar en patineta (monopatín)?

Paso 2 Comparte los resultados con el resto de la clase.

VOCABULARIO

¿Adónde vas para relajarte?

Talking about places and related leisure activities

A estas personas les gusta hacer algo en el agua para relajarse. Por ejemplo...

pescan en el **río**,

navegan en un barco en el **lago** y...

bucean en el **mar (océano)**.

Estas personas prefieren...

escalar montañas o...

hacer cámping (acampar) en el **bosque**.

Estas personas se relajan cuando...

dan un paseo por el **desierto** o...

tienen un picnic en el **parque.**

Y estas personas se sienten más relajadas si hacen algo en la ciudad, por ejemplo, cuando...

ven una exposición en el **museo** o...

conversan con los amigos en un café.

ACTIVIDAD D ¿Dónde se hace?

Escoge el lugar que se asocia con la actividad que describe tu profesor(a).

1. **a.** el lago   **b.** el café   **c.** las montañas
2. **a.** el bosque   **b.** el río   **c.** el museo
3. **a.** el museo   **b.** el mar   **c.** el parque
4. **a.** el desierto   **b.** el bosque   **c.** el café
5. **a.** el museo   **b.** el lago   **c.** el gimnasio

ACTIVIDAD E ¿Cierto o falso?

Paso 1 En grupos de dos, una persona va a leerle las siguientes oraciones a un compañero (una compañera). La persona que escucha debe cerrar su libro mientras determina si cada oración es cierta o falsa.

1. Bucear es una actividad con que se asocia el desierto.
2. El acto de visitar un museo se considera como una actividad cultural.
3. Es importante saber nadar si vas a navegar en un barco.
4. Escalar montañas es una actividad apropiada para la persona aventurera.

Paso 2 Ahora inviertan los papeles (*switch roles*) y continúen este **Paso** con las mismas instrucciones del **Paso 1.**

1. Conversar en un café se considera como una actividad física.
2. A muchas personas que tienen un picnic les molestan los insectos.
3. Pescar es una actividad apropiada para el individuo obsesionado con hacer ejercicio.
4. Esquiar en las montañas es una actividad que se asocia con el invierno.

Paso 3 Ahora los (las) dos pueden leer todas las oraciones. ¿Las contestaron bien todas?

ACTIVIDAD F ¿Qué otras actividades?

Paso 1 Usando las varias actividades ya mencionadas en esta lección y otras lecciones anteriores, escribe cinco actividades para cada categoría.

1. actividades acuáticas
2. actividades artísticas o culturales
3. actividades sociales
4. actividades al aire libre
5. otras actividades

Paso 2 Compara lo que escribiste con lo que escribió un compañero (una compañera) de clase. ¿Qué otras actividades escribieron Uds.?

Paso 3 Ahora toda la clase va a pensar en las actividades que ayudan a aliviar la tensión y a relajarse y que se pueden incluir en la categoría de **otras actividades.** No deben ser actividades físicas. ¿Cuántas más pueden añadir?

COMUNICACIÓN

ACTIVIDAD G Para relajarme...

Paso 1 En tres minutos, haz una lista de por lo menos cuatro de las actividades que escribiste en la **Actividad F** que más te gustan. Puede ser algo que haces con frecuencia o sólo de vez en cuando.

MODELO   Para relajarme me gusta nadar en el mar (pescar, navegar en un barco, etcétera).

Paso 2 Compara tus respuestas con las de un compañero (una compañera). Indica las preferencias que los (las) dos tienen en común.

Paso 3 Mira la lista que escribiste en el **Paso 1.** Escoge tres de esas actividades y explica cómo cada una de ellas te ayuda a relajarte. Menciona el lugar donde te gusta hacer la actividad y cuáles son sus beneficios. ¿Son físicos? ¿emocionales? ¿sociales? ¿económicos? (¿Cuesta mucho dinero? ¿poco dinero? ¿Es gratis [*free*]?)

1. ¿Dónde haces la actividad?

2. ¿Cuáles son sus beneficios? Son…

    a. físicos.   **c.** sociales.

    b. emocionales.   **d.** económicos.

> MODELO   Me gusta nadar en el mar. Nadar es una buena actividad porque produce beneficios físicos. También es económico porque es gratis.

Paso 4 Divídanse en grupos de tres o cuatro personas. Una persona va a contestar las preguntas que le hacen los demás del grupo.

ACTIVIDAD H ¿Sabías que… ?

Paso 1 Lee la selección **¿Sabías que… ?** Luego contesta las siguientes preguntas.

1. En general, ¿cuál es el deporte más popular en el mundo hispano?

2. ¿En qué región suele ser el béisbol el deporte más popular?

3. ¿De qué país viene un gran número de beisbolistas que juegan profesionalmente en los Estados Unidos y el Canadá?

¿Sabías que…

el béisbol se considera el deporte nacional en las naciones del Caribe? Mientras que el fútbol es el deporte más popular en el mundo, inclusive en la mayoría de los países hispanos, el béisbol es el más popular en los países caribeños. En lugares como la República Dominicana, Cuba y Puerto Rico el béisbol goza de una tremenda popularidad. Muchos de los beisbolistas de las Grandes Ligas de los Estados Unidos y el Canadá vienen del Caribe, y de la República Dominicana en particular. Algunos de los beisbolistas dominicanos más famosos son Sammy Sosa, Rafael Furcal, Julio Lugo y Manny Ramírez.

El béisbol es el deporte nacional de varios países del Caribe.

Paso 2 Entrevista a dos o tres compañeros/as de clase.

1. Para relajarte, ¿te gusta jugar al béisbol?

2. Para relajarte, ¿te gusta mirar un partido de béisbol?

3. En tu opinión, ¿cuál es el deporte nacional de este país?

GRAMÁTICA

Relajarse es bueno

When to use an infinitive or an **-ndo** form

Ramón se relaja **leyendo** un buen libro, pero Silvia se relaja **haciendo** mucho ejercicio.

Sometimes if you are thinking in English, you may use a wrong verb or verb form. For example, *-ing* in English can either be part of a noun or a verb. In Spanish, **-ndo** can never be a noun. Spanish uses the infinitive with an optional definite article **el** or an actual noun if one exists.

El patinar (Patinar, El patinaje) es divertido.	*Skating is fun.*
El meditar (Meditar, La meditación) alivia el estrés.	*Meditating gets rid of stress.*

Sometimes a word in English ending in *-ing* is an adjective. Spanish can never use an **-ndo** form as an adjective.

El hacer cámping puede ser **relajante.**	*Camping can be relaxing.*
El jugar al tenis es **agobiante.**	*Playing tennis is exhausting.*

The use of a verb ending in **-ndo** is limited to two contexts: (1) to mean something is in progress, as in **Yolanda está haciendo yoga;** and (2) to mean *by doing something,* as in **Luis se relaja meditando** (*Luis relaxes by meditating*).

ACTIVIDAD I Preferencias

Indica cuáles de las siguientes acciones se te aplican.

Prefiero relajarme _____.

- ☐ bañándome con agua caliente
- ☐ haciendo ejercicio físico
- ☐ meditando
- ☐ practicando algún deporte
- ☐ tomando una cerveza
- ☐ viendo la televisión
- ☐ ¿ ?

ACTIVIDAD J ¿Qué crees?

Termina cada oración usando las siguientes frases para indicar lo que piensas. Puedes repetir las frases si quieres.

…es (muy) divertido
…es (muy) aburrido
…es para personas mayores
…es para personas jóvenes

…(no) me entusiasma
…me parece tonto
…me parece bien para relajarse
…(no) me interesa mucho

1. Jugar al golf _____.
2. Andar en monopatín _____.
3. Trabajar en el jardín _____.
4. Pescar _____.
5. Ir a un museo de arte _____.
6. ¿ ? _____.

El festival anual de bicicleta en Madrid, España

ACTIVIDAD K Prefiere relajarse...

Paso 1 Lee el siguiente párrafo.

Juan prefiere relajarse leyendo un buen libro. El hacer ejercicio no le interesa porque no le gusta sudar. María prefiere relajarse haciendo ejercicio aeróbico. Para ella, leer es aburrido.

Piensa en las preguntas que podrías (*you could*) hacerles a tus compañeros para escribir un párrafo similar sobre ellos. Por ejemplo: ¿Cómo prefieres relajarte? ¿Crees que el meditar es bueno?

Paso 2 Entrevista a cuatro personas. Luego escoge dos como sujetos de tu párrafo. ¿Son diferentes?

ACTIVIDAD L ¿Qué haces?

Paso 1 Lee la siguiente situación. Luego coméntala con un compañero (una compañera) de clase.

Tu pareja empieza a trabajar más de lo normal y deja poco tiempo para relajarse. Parece que pasa más tiempo en su trabajo que contigo y te sientes marginado/a. ¿Qué haces?

Paso 2 Compartan sus reacciones con el resto de la clase. ¿Reaccionaron todos igual?

Paso 3 (Optativo) Aquí tienen otra situación para comentar.

Tu pareja sugiere que tomen vacaciones para que los dos se relajen y tú crees que es buena idea. Pero las vacaciones que propone tu pareja no te interesan para nada y prefieres hacer algo diferente. Luego tu pareja propone vacaciones separadas. ¿Qué haces?

NAVEGANDO LA RED

Busca información sobre un equipo (*team*) de béisbol o fútbol de algún país hispano. Presenta la siguiente información a la clase.

◆ el nombre del equipo y la ciudad, región o país que representa

◆ el nombre de tres jugadores del equipo y su edad y lugar de nacimiento

◆ otro detalle interesante

GRAMÁTICA

¿Qué hicieron el fin de semana pasado para relajarse?

Review of the third person preterite

Los chicos **dieron una fiesta** el sábado pasado.

(yo)	-é, -í	(nosotros/as)	-amos, -imos
(tú)	-aste, -iste	(vosotros/as)	-asteis, -isteis
(Ud).	-ó, -ió	(Uds.)	-aron, -ieron

(él/ella)	**jugó** al golf	(ellos/ellas)	**jugaron** al golf
	se bañó en el jacuzzi		**se bañaron** en el jacuzzi
	corrió en el parque		**corrieron** en el parque
	dio un paseo		**dieron** un paseo

Remember that the preterit is used to talk about activities that people completed in the past or events that occurred in the past.

Margarita **meditó** por unas horas ayer.	*Margarita meditated for several hours yesterday.*
Mis amigos **asistieron** a un concierto.	*My friends attended a concert.*

Some verbs have irregular stems and endings. For this lesson, the most important are:

andar (anduvo, anduvieron) **hacer (hizo, hicieron)**
estar (estuvo, estuvieron) **ir (fue, fueron)**

Vocabulario útil

el fin de semana pasado	last weekend	**ayer por la mañana (tarde, noche)**	yesterday morning (afternoon, evening)
el sábado (domingo) pasado	last Saturday (Sunday)	**hace** + (*time*)	(*time*) ago
		hace unos años	a few years ago
anoche	last night	**hace varios meses**	several months ago
ayer	yesterday		

 ## ACTIVIDAD A Un fin de semana activo

Paso 1 Margarita tuvo un fin de semana bastante activo. Tu profesor(a) va a decir la primera parte de algunas oraciones sobre Margarita. Escoge la terminación más lógica de la columna B para cada oración que dice tu profesor(a).

A	B
1. _____	**a.** a la cuerda
2. _____	**b.** en bicicleta
3. _____	**c.** en el agua
4. _____	**d.** en el jacuzzi
5. _____	**e.** en el jardín
6. _____	**f.** voleibol

Paso 2 Con un compañero (una compañera), escribe lo que hizo Margarita tal como lo oíste. ¿Pueden recordar exactamente lo que dijo su profesor(a)?

ACTIVIDAD B ¿Qué hicieron los chicos?

Paso 1 Mira el dibujo sobre los chicos que dieron una fiesta el sábado pasado (página 297). A continuación hay una lista de todas las actividades que hicieron los chicos el sábado pasado. ¿En qué orden las hicieron probablemente? (**1** = la primera cosa que hicieron y **8** = la última cosa que hicieron)

_____ Se acostaron a las 2.00 de la mañana.
_____ Compraron mucha comida.
_____ Sirvieron cosas de beber y comer.
_____ Limpiaron el apartamento antes de acostarse.
_____ Se levantaron relativamente temprano.
_____ Corrieron en el parque por la mañana.
_____ Prepararon varias meriendas para los invitados.
_____ Fueron al supermercado.

Paso 2 Compara tu lista con la de un compañero (una compañera). ¿Están Uds. de acuerdo?

COMUNICACIÓN

 ## ACTIVIDAD C ¿Quiénes hicieron estas actividades?

Paso 1 Piensa en dos personas famosas (o en una pareja o un matrimonio de algún programa de televisión) y en lo que estas personas probablemente hicieron el fin de semana pasado.

Vocabulario útil

bebieron...

cenaron...

durmieron (bien, mal)

fueron a...

hablaron con (una persona)

leyeron...

recibieron una llamada de...

se acostaron...

se relajaron...

tuvieron una visita de...

vieron a (una persona)

volvieron...

Paso 2 Usando las frases del **Paso 1** u otras, si prefieres, describe por lo menos cuatro cosas que estas personas posiblemente hicieron el fin de semana pasado. ¡Pero no menciones los nombres de las personas en tu descripción!

Paso 3 Ahora divídanse en grupos de tres o cuatro. Una persona va a leer lo que escribió en el **Paso 2,** y el resto del grupo tiene que adivinar quiénes son las personas famosas.

GRAMÁTICA

¿Y qué hiciste tú para relajarte?

Review of first and second person preterite

Así se dice

Do you remember that first person singular (**yo**) forms in the preterite experience spelling changes with verbs like **sacar, llegar,** and **empezar?** Verbs whose infinitives end in **-car, -gar,** or **-zar** have the following changes.

-car → -qué
sacar → sa**qué**
buscar → bus**qué**

-gar → -gué
llegar → lle**gué**
jugar → ju**gué**

-zar → -cé
empezar → empe**cé**
almorzar → almor**cé**

(yo)	me relajé comí dormí fui hice	(nosotros/as)	-amos, -imos (*reg.*)
(tú)	te relajaste comiste dormiste fuiste hiciste	(vosotros/as)	-asteis, -isteis (*reg.*)
(Ud.) (él/ella)	-ó, -ió (*reg.*) -ó, -ió (*reg.*)	(Uds.) (ellos/ellas)	-aron, -ieron (*reg.*) -aron, -ieron (*reg.*)

—¿Qué **hiciste** para relajarte el fin de semana pasado?

—Pues, **pasé** casi todo el fin de semana en casa. **Lavé** la ropa, **leí** mucho y **dormí** como un bebé.

In the next set of activities, you will use mostly **yo** and **tú** forms. Your goal should be to be able to talk about what you did in the past as well as to ask someone else about his or her past activities.

Remember that regular preterite **yo** forms have an accented **-é** or **-í** in the ending and that **tú** forms end in **-aste** or **-iste**. Verbs that have one syllable in the **yo** form do not take written accents.

me acosté tarde	**te acostaste** tarde
me quedé en casa	**te quedaste** en casa
dormí mucho	**dormiste** mucho
escribí la tarea	**escribiste** la tarea
vi la televisión	**viste** la televisión

A number of common verbs have irregular stems in the preterite and do not have a stressed ending.

andar	**Anduve** en bici. ¿**Anduviste** en bici?
estar	**Estuve** todo el día en casa. ¿Dónde **estuviste** tú?
hacer	**No hice** nada. ¿Qué **hiciste** tú?
ir	**Fui** al cine. ¿Adónde **fuiste** tú?
poder	**No pude** relajarme. ¿**Pudiste** relajarte?
tener	**Tuve** un sueño. ¿**Tuviste** un sueño?
venir	**Vine** temprano. ¿A qué hora **viniste**?

ACTIVIDAD D ¿Qué hice yo?

Lee cada descripción e indica cuál es la respuesta más lógica.

1. El viernes por la tarde fui al gimnasio y allí...

    a. vi la televisión.
    b. levanté pesas.
    c. fui al museo.

2. El sábado por la tarde compré algo nuevo cuando...

    a. fui de compras.
    b. hice ejercicio aeróbico.
    c. acampé en las montañas.

3. El sábado por la noche salí con mis amigos y me sorprendí cuando...

    a. vi a mi ex novio.
    b. volví tarde a mi casa.
    c. saqué una buena nota en el examen de física.

4. Como soy fanática de las actividades acuáticas, fui al mar donde...

    a. escalé una montaña.
    b. corrí dos millas.
    c. nadé.

5. Me puse triste cuando supe que...

    a. una amiga había sufrido (*had suffered*) un accidente automovilístico.
    b. mis amigos se rieron mucho en el cine.
    c. un niño gritó en el supermercado.

 ACTIVIDAD E El fin de semana pasado

Indica si hiciste las siguientes actividades o no. Si no hiciste alguna de ellas, sustitúyela por (*replace it with*) otra actividad.

MODELO   El fin de semana pasado...

		SÍ	NO
a. fui al cine. _____		☑	☐
b. corrí. *No corrí. Levanté pesas.* _____		☐	☑

El fin de semana pasado...

	SÍ	NO
a. hice ejercicio aeróbico. _____	☐	☐
b. di una fiesta. _____	☐	☐
c. me quedé en casa. _____	☐	☐
d. jugué a los naipes. _____	☐	☐
e. dibujé. _____	☐	☐
f. anduve en bicicleta. _____	☐	☐

COMUNICACIÓN

ACTIVIDAD F ¿Dices la verdad o mientes?

Paso 1 Haz dos descripciones de tus actividades, reales o inventadas, del fin de semana pasado. Puedes usar las expresiones de la siguiente lista en tu narración.

primero
luego (después, entonces)
más tarde

por fin
finalmente

MODELO   El sábado pasado me levanté temprano, fui al gimnasio y allí corrí y nadé. Después fui de compras con un amigo. Finalmente fui al cine y vi una película fabulosa.

Paso 2 Divídanse en grupos de tres o cuatro. Una persona del grupo va a leer su descripción, y los demás tienen que determinar si las actividades descritas (*described*) son reales o inventadas. La persona que más les toma el pelo (*pulls their leg*) a sus compañeros, ¡gana!

NAVEGANDO LA RED

Busca la página Web de un atleta conocido (una atleta conocida) por uno de los siguientes deportes: el tenis, el fútbol, el golf, la natación o el boxeo. Presenta la siguiente información sobre él (ella) a la clase.

- su fecha de nacimiento
- cuándo comenzó a practicar ese deporte
- el nombre de algunos de los premios (*awards*), torneos (*tournaments*), copas (*cups*), títulos, etcétera que ha ganado (*he* [*she*] *has won*)
- otro detalle interesante

La última vez...

GRAMÁTICA

¿Qué hacías que causó tanta risa?

Narrating in the past: using both preterite and imperfect

—Una vez un hombre **entró** en un bar. No **conocía** a nadie y **no tenía** dinero para...
—Ya lo **oí**, Jorge. Ese chiste es película vista...

PRETÉRITO	IMPERFECTO
Cuando mi mamá **llamó,**...	...yo **meditaba.** No **hacía** buen tiempo. **Llovía** y no **quería** salir de mi casa.
Ayer **fui** al gimnasio. **Levanté** pesas y luego **corrí** dos millas.	Mientras yo **hacía** ejercicio, mi compañera de cuarto **trabajaba** en el jardín.

As you know, there are two past tenses in Spanish: the *preterite* and the *imperfect*. Both tenses are needed and are used in combination when narrating events in the past because Spanish encodes what is called *aspect*. Aspect refers not to when an event happened, but to whether or not the event was in progress at the time referred to. As such, the use of the preterite and imperfect depends on how a narration unfolds and what relationship each event has to a time reference in the past.

Of the two, the imperfect signals that an event is being reported in progress at a specific point in time in the past. The point in time can be given as clock time (At 2:00 . . .) or it can be another event (When Daniel arrived . . .).

TIME REFERENCE	EVENT IN PROGRESS
A las 2.00 de la tarde... *At 2:00 in the afternooon . . .*	todavía **dormía.** *I was still sleeping.*
Cuando Daniel **llegó,**... *When Daniel arrived, . . .*	yo **estudiaba.** *I was studying.*

Because the imperfect means "in progress" it can be used to contrast two events occurring simultaneously. Typically, the word **mientras** (*while*) is used to connect these events.

IN PROGRESS	IN PROGRESS
Mientras yo **dormía,...**	mi compañero de cuarto **leía.**
While I was sleeping, . . .	*my roommate was reading.*
Mientras mi mamá **hablaba,...**	yo la **escuchaba** con atención.
While my mom was speaking, . . .	*I was listening to her carefully.*
¿Qué **hacías...**	mientras él **trabajaba?**
What were you doing . . .	*while he was working?*

The preterite does not signal events in progress but is used instead to refer to isolated events in the past, sequences of events, or to pinpoint a time in the past to which other events relate.

ISOLATED EVENT IN THE PAST
Anoche **me quedé** en casa.   *Last night I stayed home.*

SEQUENCE OF EVENTS
Ayer **jugué** al tenis y luego **me**   *Yesterday I played tennis and*
bañé en el jacuzzi.   *then I sat in the jacuzzi.*

PINPOINTING A TIME REFERENCE IN THE PAST
Cuando **salí** del cine...   *When I left the movie theater . . .*

Notice how in the following short narrative, the preterite and imperfect work together to show how the events relate to one another and to the time references included in the narrative. First, underline the preterite forms and circle the imperfect forms you see. Then, for each use of the imperfect, see if you can tell at what point in time the event was in progress. The answers follow, but cover them up before you read.

Ayer hacía mal tiempo, llovía y no tenía ganas de hacer nada. Decidí quedarme en casa. Miraba la televisión cuando sonó el teléfono. No quería hablar con nadie pero lo contesté. Oí la voz de un amigo que parecía estar muy triste...

EVENT IN PROGRESS	POINT IN TIME
hacía mal tiempo	
llovía	decidí quedarme en casa
no tenía ganas	
miraba la televisión	sonó el teléfono
no quería hablar	lo contesté
parecía estar triste	oí la voz

ACTIVIDAD A ¿Qué hizo Yolanda ayer para relajarse?

Empareja cada frase de la columna A con una frase lógica de la columna B.

A

1. _____ Eran las 7.00 de la mañana cuando Yolanda…

2. _____ Se bañó, se vistió y…

3. _____ Hacía sol cuando…

4. _____ Manejó por una hora y después…

5. _____ Yolanda pescaba cuando de repente (*suddenly*) vio una serpiente de cascabel (*rattlesnake*) y…

6. _____ Cuando se repuso (*she recovered*)…

7. _____ Eran las 6.00 de la tarde cuando por fin volvió a casa. Estaba contenta y…

B

a. llegó a las montañas y encontró un lugar ideal para pescar.

b. se asustó y gritó.

c. se despertó.

d. salió de su casa a las 8.00.

e. se sentía relajada después del bonito día en las montañas.

f. desayunó rápidamente.

g. pescó un rato más y después decidió regresar a casa.

ACTIVIDAD B Creando una narrativa

Paso 1 Las siguientes oraciones forman una breve narrativa. La clase debe dividirse en cuatro grupos. Cada grupo debe completar como quiera (*as it wishes*) las oraciones que le corresponden.

GRUPO 1:
   El otro día me sentía muy _____. Tenía ganas de _____.

GRUPO 2:
   Así que decidí _____. Primero _____ y luego _____.

GRUPO 3:
   Eran la(s) _____ de la _____ cuando por fin _____. No sabía si debía _____.

GRUPO 4:
   Entonces empezó a hacer buen tiempo / llover (*escojan uno*). Decidí _____ y estaba muy _____.

Paso 2 Comenzando con el Grupo 1, cada grupo debe leer sus oraciones en voz alta. ¿Forman las oraciones una narrativa coherente y lógica?

Paso 3 Repitan el **Paso 1** pero esta vez la clase debe enfocarse en una de las siguientes situaciones. ¿Cómo resulta la narrativa esta vez?

1. Una estudiante salía de su clase de biología. En la mano tenía el examen del día anterior. La nota era una B+.

2. Un señor estaba en su oficina. Acababa de tener (*He had just had*) una discusión (*argument*) muy fuerte con su jefe.

3. Al final del día, una maestra de secundaria sólo pensaba en olvidarse del día tan difícil que tuvo.

ACTIVIDAD C La última vez que alguien me llamó...

Paso 1 Piensa en la última vez que alguien te llamó por teléfono y contesta las siguientes preguntas.

1. La última vez que alguien me habló por teléfono fue...

    ☐ ayer.   ☐ anoche.   ☐ esta mañana.   ☐ ¿ ?

2. a. Cuando sonó el teléfono, yo...

    ☐ estudiaba.   ☐ dormía.

    ☐ leía.   ☐ miraba la televisión.

    ☐ comía.   ☐ escuchaba música.

    ☐ trabajaba.   ☐ ¿ ?

    b. ...y estaba...

       ☐ solo/a.   ☐ con un amigo (una amiga).

                            ☐ ¿ ?

3. Esa persona y yo hablamos...

    ☐ por unos   ☐ por varios   ☐ por ¿ ?
        segundos.   minutos.

4. Cuando colgué (*I hung up*) el teléfono,...

    ☐ (no) me sentía bien.   ☐ estaba tenso/a.

    ☐ estaba preocupado/a.   ☐ estaba aburrido/a.

    ☐ estaba enfadado/a.   ☐ ¿ ?
       (irritado/a).

Paso 2 Ahora trabaja con un compañero (una compañera). Usando la información del **Paso 1,** cuéntale qué pasó la última vez que alguien te llamó.

COMUNICACIÓN

ACTIVIDAD D La última vez...

Paso 1 Piensa en la última vez que te reíste a carcajadas (*laughed loudly*). ¿Qué hacías? ¿Dónde estabas?

La última vez que me reí a carcajadas...

1. ☐ estaba en mi casa.   ☐ no estaba en mi casa.

2. ☐ estaba solo/a.   ☐ estaba con otra(s) persona(s).

3. ☐ leía algo.   ☐ escuchaba algo.

4. ☐ veía* algo.   ☐ recordaba algo.

---

*Aside from **ir** and **ser, ver** is the only other irregular verb in the imperfect: **veía, veías, veía, veía, veíamos, veíais, veían, veían.** You will learn more about the imperfect of **ver** in **Lección 12.**

Al oír algo gracioso, ¿te ríes como este joven?

Después de reírme tanto...

1. ☐ me sentí muy bien.
2. ☐ me sentí avergonzado/a.
3. ☐ tenía dolor de estómago (*stomachache*).

Paso 2 Usando tus respuestas del **Paso 1,** escribe un breve párrafo.

MODELO   La última vez que me reí a carcajadas estaba solo. Veía...

Paso 3 Presenta una versión oral de tu narración a la clase. ¿Cuántos estaban en una situación similar cuando se rieron a carcajadas? ¿Cuántos se sintieron igual después?

ACTIVIDAD E Un incidente real o ficticio

Paso 1 Describe algo cómico que te pasó recientemente. Escribe por lo menos cuatro oraciones, dando detalles sobre lo que ocurrió. Tienes la opción de inventar algo, es decir, un incidente ficticio.

Paso 2 Presenta tu incidente a un compañero (una compañera). Tu compañero/a tiene que decidir si fue un incidente real o ficticio. Después de que cada uno revele la verdad sobre su incidente, los (las) dos deben seleccionar un incidente para compartir con la clase.

Paso 3 La clase debe votar para escoger el incidente más cómico. ¿Saben si es algo real o ficticio?

ACTIVIDAD F Una historia

Paso 1 Trabaja con un compañero (una compañera). Inventen una historia sobre lo que pasó en los siguientes dibujos. A continuación tienen algunas ideas para considerar.

◆ ¿Quiénes son las personas? ¿Qué relación hay (o había) entre ellos?
◆ ¿Adónde fueron? ¿Cómo fueron a ese lugar? ¿Por qué fueron?
◆ ¿Qué actividades hicieron?
◆ ¿Cómo se sentían al hacer cada actividad?
◆ ¿Qué pasó al final? ¿Por qué?

1.

2.

3.

Lunes, a.m.

Domingo, p.m.

4.   5.

Paso 2 Compartan su historia con el resto de la clase. ¿Quiénes inventaron la historia más interesante?

NAVEGANDO LA RED

Busca una narración cómica o algunos chistes en español. Imprime lo que encuentres y entrégaselo a tu profesor(a).

INTERCAMBIO

La tensión y el estrés

Propósito: presentar una narración sobre un compañero (una compañera) a un grupo de estudiantes.

Papeles: una persona que entrevista, una persona entrevistada y un grupo de estudiantes que escucha la narración.

Paso 1 Entrevista a un compañero (una compañera) de clase sobre la última vez que se sentía tenso/a. Obviamente necesitas hacerle preguntas, pero antes, piensa en qué es lo que quieres averiguar.

◆ cuándo se sentía tenso/a tu compañero/a
◆ dónde estaba
◆ con quién estaba
◆ qué fue lo que le causó la tensión y el estrés
◆ cómo se sentía física y emocionalmente
◆ qué hizo para aliviar la tensión y el estrés

Paso 2 Escribe las preguntas que le vas a hacer a tu compañero/a en la segunda persona singular (tú). ¿Puedes usar correctamente el pretérito y el imperfecto en tus preguntas?

Paso 3 Ahora entrevista a tu compañero/a. Apunta sus respuestas.

Paso 4 Piensa en cómo vas a contar lo que te dijo tu compañero/a a un grupo de tres estudiantes. Después de que todos presenten la narración sobre su compañero/a, determinen quién presentó la narración más interesante del grupo.

¿Qué haces cuando te sientes muy tenso/a?

Vistazos culturales
Las civilizaciones prehispánicas

¿Sabías que... las civilizaciones prehispánicas tenían culturas muy estructuradas y elaboradas? Las tres civilizaciones prehispánicas más grandes eran la azteca de México, la maya de México y Centroamérica y la inca de Sudamérica. Estas civilizaciones contaban con[a] sistemas económicos y sociales muy avanzados. Además, las tres civilizaciones demostraron un alto nivel de creación artística y aportaron[b] grandes avances al conocimiento científico.

[a]contaban... *had*   [b]*contributed*

Durante su período de mayor extensión, el Imperio inca abarcaba[a] lo que hoy es parte de Colombia, el Ecuador, el Perú, Bolivia y Chile. Cuando llegaron los conquistadores españoles, el Imperio inca contaba con más de 9 millones de habitantes.

[a]*encompassed*

Las ciudades principales de los mayas eran Chichén Itzá (México), Tikal (Guatemala) y Palenque (México).

Cuando el conquistador español Hernán Cortés llegó a México en 1519, el Imperio azteca gobernaba más de 25 millones de habitantes. La capital azteca, Tenochtitlán, tenía unos 200.000 habitantes.

You can investigate these cultural topics in more detail on the *¿Sabías que… ?* Online Learning Center: **www.mhhe.com/sabiasque5**.

Los mayas y los incas tenían sociedades agrícolas. Los incas cultivaban papas y quinoa[a] en terrazas en los Andes.

———
[a]*type of grain*

Reproducción del mercado de Tlatelolco (*Museo de Antropología, México, D.F.*)

En Tlatelolco, cuidad vecina de Tenochtitlán, los aztecas dirigían[a] un mercado muy elaborado donde se podía obtener productos de todas partes del imperio.

———
[a]*managed*

La economía

Las culturas prehispánicas

Los mayas usaban un sistema numérico basado en unidades de 1, 5 y 20 con un signo[a] para el 0. Gracias a este sistema y otros conocimientos,[b] pudieron hacer cálculos astronómicos más precisos que los que hicieron los europeos de la misma época.

———
[a]*sign*   [b]*knowledge*

Machu Picchu, ciudad perdida de los incas

La arquitectura

Tanto los incas como los mayas y los aztecas construyeron templos de una belleza[a] impresionante.

———
[a]*beauty*

Las ciencias

Los sacerdotes[a] mayas se interesaban mucho por el tiempo. Tenían dos calendarios: un calendario lunar de 260 días para marcar las ceremonias religiosas y un calendario solar de 365.2422 días para marcar el año.

———
[a]*priests*

El Caracol (Observatorio), Chichén Itzá, México, donde se supone que los mayas hicieron observaciones astronómicas

ACTIVIDAD ¿Qué recuerdas?

Indica si las siguientes frases son ciertas (C) o falsas (F).

		C	F
1.	Los mayas cultivaban papas y quinoa en terrazas.	☐	☐
2.	Los incas construyeron templos impresionantes.	☐	☐
3.	En 1519, el Imperio azteca contaba con unos 200.000 habitantes.	☐	☐
4.	Tikal y Palenque eran ciudades importantes del Imperio maya.	☐	☐
5.	Los mayas tenían un sistema de numeración que incluía el concepto del cero.	☐	☐

NAVEGANDO LA RED

Escoge *uno* de los siguientes proyectos. Luego presenta la información a la clase.

1. Las civilizaciones azteca, inca y maya tenían sociedades muy estructuradas. Busca información sobre la jerarquía (*hierarchy*) social de *dos* de estas civilizaciones. Haz lo siguiente.
   a. Haz dos listas, una para cada civilización, de las diferentes clases sociales que había.
   b. Menciona los privilegios y (o) las desventajas asociadas con cada rango (*rank*) social.
2. Busca información sobre los papeles de los hombres y las mujeres en las civilizaciones azteca, inca y maya. Apunta la siguiente información.
   a. el papel que tenía el hombre comparado con el que tenía la mujer en cada sociedad
   b. las responsabilidades que tenía el hombre comparadas con las que tenía la mujer en cada sociedad
3. Busca más información sobre el calendario lunar (el de 260 días) de los mayas que se usó para ceremonias religiosas. Contesta las siguientes preguntas.
   a. ¿Cómo está organizado el calendario? (días, semanas, meses, etcétera)
   b. ¿Cuál es el uso principal del calendario y cuál es el significado de los *katuns*?
   c. ¿Cuáles son dos de las profecías (*prophecies*) que se encuentran en el calendario?
   d. Según las profecías que encontraste, ¿crees que los mayas eran pesimistas u optimistas?

¿Cómo te relajas?

How Do You Relax?

acampar	to go camping
andar en	to ride a
bicicleta	bicycle
monopatín	scooter; skateboard
patineta	skateboard
bañarse (en un jacuzzi)	to bathe (in a jacuzzi)
bucear	to (scuba) dive
dar una fiesta	to throw (have) a party
dibujar	to draw
escalar montañas	to mountain climb
esquiar	to ski
en el agua	to water ski
en las montañas	to snow ski
hacer cámping	to go camping
hacer yoga	to do yoga
ir al teatro	to go to the theater
jugar (ue) (R)	to play
a los naipes	cards
al golf	golf
al voleibol	volleyball
meditar	to meditate
navegar en un barco	to sail
patinar (en línea)	to (inline) skate
pescar	to fish
saltar a la cuerda	to jump rope
tener un picnic	to have a picnic
trabajar en el jardín	to garden
utilizar la aromaterapia	to use aromatherapy

Repaso: dar un paseo, ir a la iglesia, leer, levantar pesas

Lugares

Places

el bosque	forest
el desierto	desert
el lago	lake
el mar	sea
las montañas	mountains
el museo	museum
el océano	ocean
el parque	park
el río	river

Otras palabras y expresiones útiles

chistoso/a	funny
cómico/a (R)	comic(al), funny
gracioso/a	funny, amusing
el chiste (R)	joke
la risa	laugh; laughter
causar risa	to cause laughter, make laugh
hacer reír	to make laugh
hacerle gracia a uno	to strike someone as funny
reír(se) (i, i) a carcajadas	to laugh loudly
tener gracia	to be funny, charming

LECCIÓN 12

Check out the following media resources to complement this lesson:

 Online *Manual*

 Video on CD

 Online Learning Center

 ActivityPak

¿En qué consiste el abuso?

¿Has pensado (*Have you thought*) en lo que pasa cuando una persona no aprende a hacer las cosas con moderación? ¿Cuáles son las consecuencias de hacer algo en exceso? En esta lección, vas a explorar esta cuestión y vas a

◆ continuar usando el *imperfecto* y el *pretérito* para hablar del pasado

◆ leer algo sobre la adicción a los teléfonos celulares

◆ comenzar a comprender los mandatos (*commands*) orales y escritos

ALTO Before beginning this lesson, look over the **Composición** activity on pages 328–329. This is the activity you will be working toward throughout the lesson.

¿Puede convertirse en abuso una diversión como jugar a los videojuegos?

IDEAS PARA EXPLORAR

Hay que tener cuidado

VOCABULARIO

¿Qué es una lesión?

More vocabulary related to activities

DAÑINO *adj.* Se aplica a lo que causa un daño: *Algunos mariscos son dañinos si se comen crudos.*

DAÑO *m.* Efecto negativo. Detrimento: *Este problema puede causar mucho daño.* Dolor: *Estos zapatos me hacen mucho daño.*

HERIDA *f.* El resultado físico de la acción de herir: *Muchos atletas sufren heridas mientras practican su deporte.*

HERIR *v. tr.* Causar en un organismo un daño en que hay destrucción de los tejidos, como un golpe con un arma, etcétera: *El soldado hirió al enemigo con un disparo de pistola.*

LESIÓN *f.* Sinónimo de herida: *El corredor sufrió una lesión en el tobillo.*[a]

[a] *ankle*

Vocabulario útil

el peligro	danger
peligroso/a	dangerous

ACTIVIDAD A Consecuencias

Paso 1 ¿Cuáles pueden ser las consecuencias de practicar estas actividades si uno no tiene cuidado? Indica tus respuestas y luego compáralas con las de un compañero (una compañera).

	ADICCIÓN FÍSICA	DAÑOS FÍSICOS	ADICCIÓN PSICOLÓGICA	OTROS PELIGROS PSICOLÓGICOS
1. hacer ejercicios aeróbicos	☐	☐	☐	☐
2. ir de compras	☐	☐	☐	☐
3. esquiar	☐	☐	☐	☐
4. comer	☐	☐	☐	☐
5. jugar a los videojuegos	☐	☐	☐	☐
6. ingerir bebidas alcohólicas	☐	☐	☐	☐
7. chatear (participar en un chat [*chat room*])	☐	☐	☐	☐

Paso 2 Ahora compara tus respuestas con las de todos tus compañeros. Un(a) estudiante debe escribir en la pizarra las actividades que indicaron los demás en las cuatro columnas.

 ACTIVIDAD B ¿Peligroso o dañino?

Muchos opinan que las palabras **dañino** y **peligroso** no significan lo mismo. Según ellos, no son sinónimos. En esta actividad vas a ver si para ti significan lo mismo o no.

Paso 1 Indica si las actividades a continuación pueden ser o dañinas o peligrosas.

MODELOS   Ver la televisión puede ser dañino (peligroso).
Escalar montañas puede ser peligroso (dañino).

1. practicar el paracaidismo (*skydiving*)
2. escuchar música a todo volumen con frecuencia
3. salir solo/a de noche en una ciudad grande
4. montar en motocicleta sin casco (*helmet*)
5. tomar el sol (*sunbathing*)
6. tomar más de tres tazas de café diariamente

Paso 2 Piensa en las clasificaciones que hiciste en el **Paso 1.** ¿Qué tendencias notas? ¿Cuál es la diferencia entre una actividad dañina y una peligrosa?

Paso 3 Indica cuál de las siguientes opiniones es la más apropiada.

☐ Para mí, una actividad dañina puede tener consecuencias mucho más graves que una actividad peligrosa. Por ejemplo, una actividad dañina puede conducir a (*lead to*) la muerte.

☐ Para mí, una actividad peligrosa puede tener consecuencias mucho más graves que una actividad dañina. Por ejemplo, una actividad peligrosa puede conducir a la muerte.

COMUNICACIÓN

 ACTIVIDAD C ¡Cuidado!

¡Ciertas actividades, si se hacen en exceso, son más peligrosas que otras!

Paso 1 Haz una clasificación de las actividades en la siguiente página usando la escala a continuación. Escribe el número de cada categoría en el espacio indicado.

1 = No ofrece mucho peligro.
2 = Puede ser peligrosa.
3 = Es muy peligrosa.

a. _____ reírse
b. _____ ir de compras
c. _____ jugar al tenis
d. _____ jugar al fútbol americano
e. _____ trabajar en una oficina
f. _____ trabajar en una fábrica
g. _____ tomar café
h. _____ ingerir bebidas alcohólicas
i. _____ hacer yoga
j. _____ ver la televisión
k. _____ jugar a los videojuegos

Paso 2 Con dos compañeros/as de clase, piensa en otras actividades que podrían agregarse (*could be added*) a las categorías del **Paso 1** y escríbelas.

	NO OFRECE MUCHO PELIGRO.	PUEDE SER PELIGROSA.	ES MUY PELIGROSA.
l. _____	☐	☐	☐
m. _____	☐	☐	☐
n. _____	☐	☐	☐

Paso 3 Con tus compañeros/as del **Paso 2**, sigue el modelo y explica cuál es la más peligrosa de las actividades indicadas en el **Paso 1** y cuál es la que ofrece menos o ningún peligro.

MODELO   Jugar al fútbol americano es la actividad más peligrosa porque puede causar daños físicos graves.

¿Están listos/as tus compañeros/as y tú para defender sus respuestas?

ACTIVIDAD D Una vez...

Paso 1 Escoge uno de los siguientes temas y prepara una breve descripción de 50–75 palabras.

◆ Cuenta alguna actividad peligrosa que hiciste en el pasado. ¿Qué pasó? ¿Te hiciste daño?

◆ Describe un accidente en el que sufriste una herida o una lesión. ¿En qué circunstancias ocurrió? ¿Tuviste que ir al médico/a?

◆ Describe una ocasión en la que una persona que conoces sufrió una herida o lesión.

Paso 2 Entrégale tu descripción a tu profesor(a) y escucha sus comentarios.

GRAMÁTICA

¿Veías la televisión de niño/a?

Imperfect forms of the verb **ver**

veía	veíamos
veías	veíais
veía	veían
veía	veían

Like **ir** and **ser, ver** is a verb that has an irregular stem in the imperfect. For regular **-er** verbs the **-er** ending is dropped and the appropriate **-ía-** ending is added. For **ver,** however, the **e** is retained and **ve-** becomes the stem.

—De niño, yo siempre **veía** mucho la televisión. ¿Y tú?
—En mi familia, no la **veíamos** tanto.

These three verbs are the only irregular Spanish verbs you will encounter in the imperfect. Here is a review of the imperfect forms of **ir** and **ser.**

ir	iba, ibas, iba, iba,	**ser**	era, eras, era, era,
	íbamos, ibais, iban, iban		éramos, erais, eran, eran

ACTIVIDAD E ¿Sabías que... ?

Paso 1 Lee la selección **¿Sabías que... ?** en la siguiente página. Luego contesta las preguntas a continuación.

1. En cuanto a los españoles y su tiempo libre, ¿cuáles son las dos actividades más populares?
2. ¿Cómo crees que se comparan España y este país con respecto al acto de ver la televisión?

Paso 2 Escoge la oración que mejor capte la idea principal de la selección.

☐ La televisión es muy importante en este país, pero no tanto como lo es en otros países del mundo.

☐ La actividad de ver la televisión es popular en este país y lo es también en países del mundo hispano, como España.

¿Sabías que...

al igual que en este país, en el mundo hispano la televisión también tiene un papel muy importante? Todos saben que la televisión es un elemento bien integrado en la cultura norteamericana, pero no muchos saben que también es así en gran parte del mundo hispano. En una encuesta realizada en España en los años 90, por ejemplo, el 85% de los solicitantes dijo que veía la televisión todos o casi todos los días. A este mismo grupo se le hizo la siguiente pregunta: «¿En qué suele emplear, en general, su tiempo libre?» Los participantes respondieron así:

estar con la familia: 76%

ver la televisión: 69%

estar con amigos: 54%

leer libros o revistas: 45%

Además de los que declararon ver la televisión todos o casi todos los días, el 26% admite verla entre dos o tres horas al día.

A los miembros de esta familia española les gusta ver la televisión juntos.

Source: Boletín del Centro de Investigaciones Sociológicas

ACTIVIDAD F Una preocupación materna

Si cuando eras niño/a veías la televisión demasiado, es lógico que tus padres se preocuparan (*worried*). Pero en el **Paso 1,** vas a ver una situación bastante diferente.

Paso 1 Mira la tira cómica en la siguiente página. **¡OJO!** Faltan los últimos dos cuadros (*frames*). La tira no está completa.

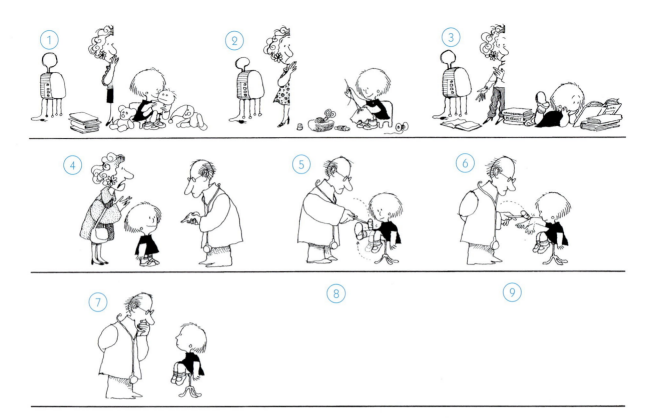

Paso 2 Busca la descripción que corresponde a cada cuadro de la tira cómica y escribe el número del cuadro (de los cuadros) en los espacios apropiados. Hay descripciones que pueden aplicarse a más de un cuadro. (Presta atención al uso de los verbos en el pasado.)

1. _____ Le gustaba coser (*to sew*) porque frecuentemente veía coser a su abuela.

2. _____ El médico escuchaba atentamente mientras Josefina le explicaba todo lo que observaba en María Luisa.

3. _____ Pero el médico no le encontró nada malo y estaba perplejo.

4. _____ Entonces el médico comenzó a examinar a María Luisa.

5. _____ Le examinó el brazo.

6. _____ Le examinó la pierna (*leg*).

7. _____ María Luisa jugaba a solas con sus muñecas (*dolls*).

8. _____ Por fin Josefina no resistió más y llevó a María Luisa al médico.

9. _____ También leía mucho y veía muy poco la televisión.

10. _____ Una vez, Josefina estaba muy preocupada por su hija María Luisa.

Paso 3 Completa la tira cómica. Escribe algunas oraciones para describir lo que pasó al final. Recuerda usar el pretérito para expresar acciones aisladas (*isolated*) y (o) en secuencia y el imperfecto para expresar acciones o eventos en proceso o que eran habituales. ¡Vas a leer tus oraciones en clase!

ACTIVIDAD G Entrevistas

Muchos creen que los niños y los estudiantes universitarios pasan mucho tiempo mirando la televisión. ¿Es verdad?

Paso 1 Entrevista a un compañero (una compañera) de clase. Hazle las siguientes preguntas.

1. ¿Cuál de estas descripciones se te puede aplicar a ti?
   □ De niño/a veía más televisión que ahora.
   □ De niño/a veía menos televisión que ahora.
2. ¿Cuántas horas diarias de televisión veías cuando eras niño/a?
3. ¿Cuántas horas diarias de televisión ves ahora? ¿Crees que en este sentido eres una persona como las demás?

Paso 2 Comparte los resultados obtenidos en el **Paso 1** con los de tus compañeros de clase. ¿Es verdad que los estudiantes ven muchas horas de televisión? ¿Y los niños?

Paso 3 (Optativo) ¿Hay adictos a la televisión en tu clase? ¿Cómo llegaste a esta conclusión?

NAVEGANDO LA RED

Busca la página Web de un hispano famoso (una hispana famosa) y busca información sobre su niñez. ¿Se menciona por lo menos una actividad que hacía de niño/a? Imprime la información y preséntala a la clase.

VAMOS A VER

ANTICIPACIÓN

Paso 1 ¿Sabes lo que es un mapa conceptual? Un mapa conceptual es una representación visual de asociaciones. Por ejemplo, ¿qué asocias con los teléfonos celulares? ¿Usos? ¿Equipo (*equipment*)? ¿Servicios? En un mapa conceptual, comienzas con el concepto central (**los teléfonos celulares**) y le vas agregando (*you proceed to add*) los conceptos relacionados a medida que se te ocurren (*as they come to mind*). La clase entera debe participar en la elaboración de un mapa conceptual de los teléfonos celulares en la pizarra. Deben incluir todo lo que saben acerca de estos aparatos.

1.

llamar a amigos
estar en contacto con la familia
casos urgentes
usos
LOS TELÉFONOS CELULARES

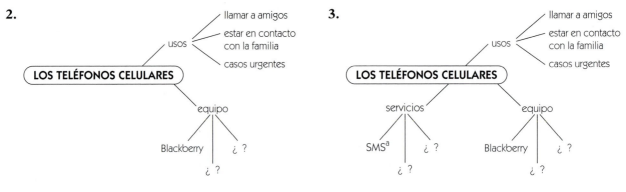

2.

llamar a amigos
estar en contacto con la familia
casos urgentes
usos
LOS TELÉFONOS CELULARES
equipo
Blackberry   ¿ ?
¿ ?

3.

llamar a amigos
estar en contacto con la familia
casos urgentes
usos
LOS TELÉFONOS CELULARES
servicios   equipo
SMS[a]   ¿ ?   Blackberry   ¿ ?
¿ ?   ¿ ?

[a]*Short Message Service (text messaging)*

Paso 2 Ahora deben organizar las ideas para elaborar un mapa en limpio (*clean*). Copien y guarden el mapa.

Consejo práctico

Semantic maps **(mapas conceptuales)** are very useful ways of organizing what you know about a topic or concept. They are an excellent way to free-associate about a topic before reading and even before writing. Most people simply brainstorm the ideas, letting them fall where they will onto the map and organizing them after the period of free-association is over. Each node in the

branch represents a connection between two concepts. When organizing your semantic map, you may wind up with different kinds of branches, as in the following example.

Incidentally, semantic maps are also a good way to organize and study new vocabulary and phrases when learning Spanish.

equipo —— pelota
raqueta
EL TENIS
tenistas   torneos —— «Grand Slam» —— Wimbledon
                                              Abierto de Francia
individuales dobles   Abierto de   Abierto de
                         Australia   los Estados Unidos

EXPLORACIÓN

Paso 1 Fíjate en el título de la lectura que se encuentra en la siguiente página. Mira también la foto y el párrafo introductorio en letra grande. ¿Tienes alguna idea de qué se trata la lectura?

Paso 2 Ahora vuelve al mapa conceptual de **Anticipación.** ¿Incluyeron tus compañeros y tú un efecto emocional negativo de los celulares?

Paso 3 Lee la lectura e indica si las siguientes oraciones se refieren a Alicia, a Roberto o a los dos.

	ALICIA	ROBERTO	LOS DOS
1. Tuvo un accidente.	☐	☐	☐
2. Terminó su amistad con otra persona.	☐	☐	☐
3. Tuvo un conflicto con otra persona.	☐	☐	☐
4. Se puso inconsolablemente triste.	☐	☐	☐

¿Eres adicto al celular?

La adicción al celular es una adicción nueva. Como las víctimas de otras adicciones, el adicto al celular parece no poder controlar su conducta. Aunque esta adicción parece ser benigna, puede causar problemas personales y en algunos casos representar un riesgo serio.

Alicia era una joven de 25 años, enérgica y trabajadora. No era raro verla paseando en la calle con la bolsa en una mano y el teléfono celular en la otra, pegado a su oreja. Aun cuando entraba a una tienda o cualquier lugar de negocios como un banco, seguía con su conversación telefónica cuando un empleado la atendía. Un día, mientras caminaba y hablaba por teléfono, un chico chocó con ella y se le cayó el celular a Alicia. ¡Puaf! El aparato quedó en mil pedazos. Aunque el chico le pidió disculpas, Alicia empezó a gritarle diciéndole cosas que normalmente no se dicen en público. Se agachó para recoger lo que quedaba de su celular y empezó a llorar. No había manera de calmarla. El pobre chico se quedó estupefacto ante la reacción de Alicia.

El celular puede convertirse en una adicción si uno no limita su uso.

Roberto, otro joven de 21 años, salió recientemente con una amiga a comer pizza. Mientras esperaban su comida, sonó el celular de la amiga. Aunque la amiga le dijo a su interlocutor que estaba con Roberto y que iban a comer, la conversación siguió. Llegó la pizza y Roberto empezó a comer. Su amiga continuó hablando por teléfono entre bocados de pizza. Después de media hora terminó la conversación y la amiga puso su celular en la bolsa. Roberto no estaba nada a gusto, creyendo que su amiga había demostrado una tremenda falta de cortesía, no tomándolo en cuenta mientras él comía sin hablar y escuchaba una conversación en la cual no podía participar. Después de esa noche, Roberto no volvió a ver a su amiga.

Estos dos episodios son ejemplos de un nuevo fenómeno que combina la psicología con la comunicación: la adicción al teléfono celular. Mejor dicho, no es una adicción al celular por sí mismo sino más bien una adicción al «estar conectado» con el resto del mundo acompañada de un miedo de «perder algo» si uno no está constantemente conectado. En esta adicción, el celular juega un papel importante. La gente que sufre de esta aflicción pasa horas hablando por el celular y muchos, cuando no están hablando, pasan tiempo leyendo y contestando e-mail. A ellos, no les entra en la cabeza la idea de que el celular se usa en casos de urgencia o en casos especiales. Aunque parece ser una adicción benigna, considera el siguiente caso: Un policía está en la calle dirigiendo el tráfico. Una señora que siempre maneja su auto mientras habla por el celular no lo ve porque está tan metida en su conversación. Choca con el policía y, desafortunadamente, lo mata. A la señora la acusan de haber cometido homicidio involuntario y unas semanas después se aprueba una ley que prohíbe el uso de los celulares mientras uno maneja. Así que hasta un aparato inocuo como un celular puede representar un riesgo serio para el público.

Según los expertos, cualquier persona que usa el celular con regularidad puede convertirse en adicta, como en los casos de Alicia y de la amiga de Roberto. ¿Cuáles son los síntomas de esta adicción?

- Te sientes irritado y ansioso si no tienes el celular disponible, por ejemplo, cuando lo dejas en casa.
- Hablas por el celular aunque estés con otras personas o tengas otras cosas urgentes que hacer, causando problemas entre otra persona y tú.
- Pasas tiempo pensando qué estará haciendo un amigo y sientes la necesidad de llamarlo para ver qué pasa.
- No puedes manejar ni hacer ninguna otra actividad sin hablar por el celular al mismo tiempo.
- Te sientas a una mesa para comer y sacas el celular para ponerlo en la mesa.
- Tu necesidad de estar conectado parece ser incontrolable.
- El celular te controla más a ti de lo que tú lo controlas a él.

Si padeces de uno o más de estos síntomas, es muy probable que seas adicto al celular y a la necesidad de estar conectado. La curación se encuentra en la terapia tradicional para cualquier adicción: consultar con un experto y seguir a la letra sus consejos.

Paso 4 Ahora lee de nuevo el párrafo sobre el caso de Alicia. Luego pon las siguientes oraciones en orden cronológico.

_____ Gritó al chico.

_____ Recogió los pedazos de su teléfono.

_____ Paseaba por la calle.

_____ Se le cayó su objeto favorito.

_____ Un chico chocó con ella.

Paso 5 Según el párrafo que incluye la lista de síntomas, indica si los siguientes individuos sufren de adicción al celular o no.

	SÍ	NO
1. Ramón nunca puede salir de la casa sin su celular. Si se le olvida, regresa a casa inmediatamente.	☐	☐
2. Carlota tiene cuatro muy buenas amigas y habla por el celular con cada una por lo menos tres veces al día.	☐	☐
3. Sonia vive en Arizona, donde muchas carreteras están en el desierto, y prefiere llevar el celular en el coche para sentirse segura.	☐	☐
4. A Marcos se le descompuso (*broke*) el celular esta mañana y los técnicos dicen que van a tardar diez días en arreglarlo. Como Marcos no quiere esperar tanto, compra otro en eBay por $89.	☐	☐
5. Anita era una estudiante excelente. Pero desde que comenzó a pasar mucho tiempo hablando por el celular, sus notas han bajado (*have gone down*) considerablemente.	☐	☐

Paso 6 Ahora lee el último párrafo. Si una persona se considera adicta, ¿qué debe hacer?

Debe...

☐ buscar la ayuda de los amigos y seguir sus recomendaciones

☐ no hacer nada; la vida siempre presenta dificultades

☐ recurrir a un(a) especialista y seguir sus recomendaciones

SÍNTESIS

Paso 1 Colabora con todos tus compañeros de clase para hacer un nuevo mapa conceptual sobre los teléfonos celulares. Contribuye con la información que has aprendido (*you have learned*) al leer la lectura.

LOS TELÉFONOS CELULARES

Paso 2 Compara este nuevo mapa conceptual con el que hicieron todos en la sección **Anticipación.** ¿Es este nuevo mapa más completo?

Paso 3 Haz una copia del nuevo mapa y guárdala. ¡Es posible que necesites esta información más tarde para un examen!

Paso 1 Lee de nuevo lo que le pasó a Alicia. Subraya los verbos que aparecen en el pasado. ¿Qué verbos están en el pretérito y qué verbos están en el imperfecto?

Paso 2 Recuerda que el imperfecto tiene dos funciones importantes: (1) expresar una acción habitual en el pasado y (2) expresar una acción en proceso de realizarse (*happening*). Busca en el párrafo sobre Alicia un ejemplo de cada función.

¿Es posible ser adicto al Internet? ¿Cuánto tiempo pasas tú leyendo el correo electrónico, chateando o haciendo compras en el Internet?

Vamos a ver

Now that you've completed the **Vamos a ver** section of **Unidad cuatro,** watch the corresponding **Vamos a ver** segment on the *¿Sabías que... ?* video to further explore the themes presented in this unit. There are related pre- and post-viewing activities on the *¿Sabías que... ?* Online Learning Center at **www.mhhe.com/sabiasque5**.

NAVEGANDO LA RED

Busca la página Web de un grupo u organización que ayuda a los que sufren de alguna adicción. Puede ser a la Red, al tabaco, al alcohol, a la cocaína, al trabajo, al chocolate, etcétera. Contesta las siguientes preguntas y comparte tu información y tus respuestas con la clase.

◆ ¿Qué tipo de organización es? ¿A qué tipo(s) de adictos ayuda?

◆ ¿Cómo los ayuda? ¿Qué hace la organización y (o) qué tienen que hacer los adictos para ayudarse a sí mismos?

◆ ¿Hay evidencia de que esta organización realmente los ayuda?

IDEAS PARA EXPLORAR

Saliendo de la adicción

GRAMÁTICA

¿Qué debo hacer? —Escucha esto.

> toma
> acuéstate
> come
> escribe
> haz
> di

—Laura, si de veras quieres dejar el vicio del chocolate, primero **admite** que tienes un problema.

Command forms (*Eat! Drink this! Do that!*) come in several forms: **tú, Ud., vosotros/as** (*Sp.*), and **Uds.** The affirmative **tú** forms are relatively easy to learn, since they are in most cases identical to third person singular verb forms. You are already familiar with some of these commands because they have been used in the instructions of many activities in this book.

Come más ensalada si quieres ser más delgado.
Mira más televisión si quieres comprender la cultura de este país.

Many commonly used verbs have irregular affirmative **tú** command forms.

decir	**Di** la verdad.	*Tell the truth.*
hacer	**Haz** dos más.	*Make two more.*
ir	**Ve*** a la tienda.	*Go to the store.*
poner	**Pon** tus libros aquí.	*Put your books here.*
salir	**Sal** si puedes.	*Get out if you can.*
tener	¡**Ten** cuidado!	*Be careful!*
venir	**Ven** conmigo.	*Come with me.*

Both direct and indirect object pronouns, as well as reflexive pronouns, are attached to the end of affirmative **tú** commands. Indirect objects always precede direct objects.

Cómelo, si quieres.	*Eat it if you want.* (*it* = **el sandwich**)
Dámelas, por favor.	*Give them to me, please.* (*them* = **las páginas**)
Cálmate.	*Calm down.*

---

*The regular **tú** command form of the verb **ver** is also **ve.** Context will determine meaning.

Ve a la casa de tus abuelos.   *Go to your grandparents' house.*
¡**Ve** esto!   *Look at this!*

ACTIVIDAD A Minilectura

Paso 1 Lee el artículo «Cómo salir de la adicción». ¿Puedes deducir a qué tipo de adicción se aplican los consejos?

CÓMO SALIR DE LA ADICCIÓN

1. **Admite que eres una adicta.** Según los médicos, nadie puede salir de una adicción si no admite que realmente la tiene. Hazte la siguiente pregunta: ¿El tiempo que empleas para hacer ejercicios, NO está balanceado con el resto de tus actividades? Si la respuesta es sí, eres una adicta.

2. **Empieza a «cortar» tu entrenamiento gradualmente.** Si te sientes dependiente de tu rutina, empieza a eliminar actividades lentamente. Quita primero la que disfrutes menos. Corta un poco el tiempo. Si practicas una hora y media diaria, empieza a cortar 30 minutos. Si te entrenas 5 días a la semana, corta un día. Comienza a tener sentido de la moderación.

3. **Cambia tus actividades.** Sustituye la parte que más te extenúa en tu entrenamiento. Digamos que es el pedaleo o el levantamiento de pesas... deja de hacerlo por un período de tiempo y, en cambio, ve integrando los ejercicios de relajación, toma clases de yoga o ensaya con un ejercicio que te permita socializar, como el tenis, el raquetbol o el baile.

Paso 2 Repasa el artículo y apunta todos los mandatos que encuentras. **¡OJO!** Escribe sólo los verbos; no tienes que escribir toda la frase u oración.

Paso 3 ¿Cuáles de las siguientes recomendaciones parecen lógicas según el artículo? Marca sólo las que te parezcan apropiadas.

☐ *Mírate* en un espejo y *di:* «Tengo un problema».

☐ *Habla* con un amigo y *pídele* el nombre de un doctor (una doctora).

☐ *Limita* tu contacto con otros adictos y *busca* la amistad de personas que tengan otros intereses.

☐ *Busca* otro tipo de ejercicio. Si corres, *toma* una clase de ejercicios aeróbicos. Si pedaleas, *empieza* a correr.

☐ *Come* más y *bebe* menos.

☐ *Elimina* los ejercicios que más te gustan. No vas a triunfar si no te sacrificas.

Nota comunicativa

A command is a very direct way of asking someone to do something. In English, commands are often accompanied by *please* or some other phrase to soften the directness of the command. Sometimes questions are used with *will* or *would: Will you come here, please? Would you let us talk alone for a minute?* Spanish uses the simple present tense in the form of questions to form "soft" commands.

¿Me **pasas** el salero?
¿Me **das** tu número de teléfono?

COMUNICACIÓN

📑 **ACTIVIDAD B Más consejos**

Paso 1 Escoge *una* de las adicciones de la lista a continuación. Escribe por lo menos tres consejos en forma de mandatos afirmativos para dárselos a un amigo (una amiga) que sufre de esa adicción.

adicción al alcohol   adicción a la televisión
adicción al chocolate   adicción a los tranquilizantes
adicción al tabaco (fumar)   adicción a los videojuegos

Paso 2 Reúnete con otras dos personas para presentar tus consejos. Al final, el grupo debe hacer una sola lista de los consejos de los tres y compartirlos con la clase. ¿Son diferentes los consejos para cada adicción, o se repiten los mismos consejos para algunas de ellas?

GRAMÁTICA

¿Qué no debo hacer? —¡No hagas eso!

Telling others what *not* to do: Negative **tú** commands

Así se dice

Negative **Uds.** commands are the same as affirmative **Uds.** commands, with the addition of **no**.

No hablen durante el examen. **No salgan** sin terminarlo todo.

Negative **vosotros** commands are formed using the same stems as all other commands (**mir-, dig-, salg-,** and so forth) and adding **-éis** if the verb is **-ar** and **-áis** if the verb is **-er/-ir:**

No habléis durante el examen. **No salgáis** sin terminarlo todo.

Which does your instructor use when speaking to your classmates and you as a group: **Uds.** or **vosotros** commands?

	tomes
	te acuestes
	comas
no	escribas
	hagas
	digas

—**No pienses** más en el chocolate, Laura, y **no te dejes caer** en la tentación.

Negative **tú** commands are formed by taking the **yo** form of the present tense indicative, dropping the **-o** or **-oy,** and adding what is called *the opposite vowel* + **s.** The opposite vowel is **e** if the verb is an **-ar** verb. The opposite vowel is **a** if the verb is an **-er** or **-ir** verb. Any stem changes or irregularities of the **yo** form in the present tense indicative are retained. And, of course, reflexive verbs have the pronoun **te.**

vengo → veng- + -as → **no vengas**
me acuesto → acuest- + -es → **no te acuestes**
doy → d- + -es → **no des**

Among the handful of verbs whose negative **tú** commands are not formed in this way are **ir** and **ser.**

ir   **no vayas**
ser   **no seas**

Unlike affirmative **tú** commands, negative **tú** commands require all pronouns to precede the verb.

No me digas eso.   *Don't tell me that.*
No te levantes tarde.   *Don't get up late.*
No me lo pidas.   *Don't request it of me.*

ACTIVIDAD C Lo que no debes hacer

Según el artículo «Cómo salir de la adicción» de la página 325, ¿cuáles de las siguientes recomendaciones no te parecen apropiadas?

☐ No pases mucho tiempo con los amigos si quieres salir de la adicción, pues ellos pueden distraerte (*distract you*) de tu propósito.

☐ No elimines por completo los ejercicios de tu rutina.

☐ No hables de tu problema con nadie. Es un asunto personal que a nadie le interesa.

☐ No hagas nada radical. Salir de la adicción requiere tiempo y cambios graduales.

☐ No leas información sobre tu problema, ni tampoco pienses demasiado en él. Es mejor no «intelectualizar» mucho respecto a una adicción.

ACTIVIDAD D Consejos

A continuación hay varios consejos que se le podrían dar (*that could be given*) a un amigo (una amiga) que tiene problemas con el alcohol. Si pudieras (*If you could*) darle un solo consejo, ¿cuál de los cuatro sería (*would it be*)? ¿Puedes explicar por qué?

Ten esperanza.
Llámame cuando sientes la tentación de beber.
No salgas con amigos a quienes les gusta beber mucho.
Busca tratamiento en un centro de rehabilitación.

ACTIVIDAD E La adicción al trabajo

Paso 1 Lee rápidamente el artículo que aparece en el margen.

Paso 2 Ahora completa las siguientes oraciones de una manera lógica.

1. No te mientas;…
2. No seas esclavo de tu trabajo;…
3. No te olvides de los amigos;…
4. No te preocupes por las horas extras;…

Paso 3 Inventa tres o cuatro consejos más para dar a un adicto (una adicta) al trabajo.

MODELO No almuerces en tu oficina.

Paso 4 Con un compañero (una compañera) reúne las ideas de los **Pasos 2** y **3** y formula una serie de cinco a seis consejos más apropiados al adicto (a la adicta) al trabajo.

ACTIVIDAD F En tu opinión

Paso 1 Trabajando con dos o tres compañeros/as de clase comenta la siguiente afirmación. Apunten sus ideas.

«La adicción al trabajo _____ es tan peligrosa como la adicción al alcohol».

a. siempre   **b.** muchas veces   **c.** pocas veces

COMUNICACIÓN

El trabajo como adicción

El adicto al trabajo se miente a sí mismo y les miente, portanto, a los demás. En realidad, hace todo lo posible por no tener un instante libre, por ser un esclavo del trabajo. «No puede» tomar un café con el amigo porque hace horas extras; «no puede» escuchar a sus hijos porque no dispone de tiempo; «no puede» hacer el amor de manera relajada y libre porque está cansado. Mientras él huye de su insatisfacción se convierte, a su vez, en fuente de insatisfacción para los otros.

Christina Peri Rossi

Paso 2 Ahora presenten sus ideas al resto de la clase. ¿Qué opinan Uds. sobre la adicción al trabajo comparada con la adicción al alcohol o la adicción al celular?

ACTIVIDAD G Adicto a...

Paso 1 De hecho, uno podría (*could*) ser adicto a casi cualquier cosa. Con otra persona, inventa una adicción cómica o ridícula y descríbela. Luego inventa cuatro o cinco consejos en forma de mandato para darle al adicto.

MODELO Una adicción nueva es la adicción a las zanahorias. Hay personas que no pueden pasar ni cinco minutos sin abrir el refrigerador y buscar este vegetal. Hasta las esconden (*hide*) en sus bolsillos... Para salir de esta adicción, hay varios consejos: 1. No compres zanahorias cuando vas al supermercado. 2. ...

Paso 2 Presenten sus descripciones a la clase. ¿Hay una en particular que a todos les parece la más graciosa (*funny*)?

NAVEGANDO LA RED

Busca un artículo en un periódico o una revista en español que hable de alguna adicción. Apunta lo siguiente y compártelo con la clase.

◆ el número de personas adictas
◆ las causas
◆ la tasa (*rate*) de curación
◆ otro detalle interesante

COMPOSICIÓN

En esta lección examinaste cómo algunas actividades diarias practicadas en exceso podrían ser dañinas. Leíste un artículo sobre la adicción a los teléfonos celulares y también examinaste los hábitos en cuanto a ver la televisión. Finalmente, te informaste de cómo se puede salir de una adicción y del trabajo como adicción.

Ahora vas a escribir una composición basada en las ideas que se presentaron en esta lección. Utiliza el siguiente título:

La televisión: ¿diversión o adicción?

Antes de escribir

Paso 1 Vas a escribir tu composición tomando en cuenta a las personas que ven la televisión en exceso. Tu propósito es convencer al lector de que existe la adicción a la televisión, describir las consecuencias negativas de esta adicción y después ofrecer algunas sugerencias sobre cómo salir de ella.

Piensa en los artículos que leíste en esta lección. ¿Cómo presentan el tema? ¿Con una pregunta? ¿con una breve historia o narración del caso de una persona adicta (por ejemplo, Alicia, la adicta al celular)? ¿Cómo vas a comenzar tu composición?

También piensa en el propósito de la composición y en el tipo de persona que la va a leer. ¿Quién es el lector típico, adicto a la televisión? ¿En qué forma vas a dirigirte (*address*) a esa persona?

Paso 2 Antes de escribir, haz un bosquejo de tus ideas. Puedes colaborar con un compañero (una compañera) si quieres.

1. Síntomas de adicción a la tele
2. Consecuencias negativas
3. Cómo salir de esta adicción

Paso 3 ¿En qué orden piensas presentar tus ideas? ¿Quieres presentar primero las consecuencias y luego seguir con los síntomas y las sugerencias? ¿O piensas que es mejor presentar primero los síntomas seguidos por las consecuencias y por último las sugerencias?

Al escribir

Paso 1 Hay que prestar atención al aspecto lingüístico de la composición. ¿Puedes utilizar los siguientes aspectos gramaticales?

1. el imperfecto del verbo **ver** (por ejemplo, **veía**)
2. los mandatos afirmativos
3. los mandatos negativos

Paso 2 Escribe la composición con dos días de anticipación. Un día antes de entregársela al profesor (a la profesora), lee la composición de nuevo. ¿Quieres cambiar o modificar...

1. las consecuencias de la adicción que presentaste?
2. la descripción de la adicción?
3. los consejos sobre cómo salir de la adicción?
4. el orden de tus ideas?
5. algún otro aspecto?

Después de escribir

Paso 1 Lee la composición de nuevo para repasar...

1. la concordancia entre formas verbales y sujetos y entre sustantivos y adjetivos.
2. el uso del imperfecto del verbo **ver** y el uso del pasado en general.
3. el uso de los mandatos afirmativos.
4. el uso de los mandatos negativos.

Paso 2 Haz los cambios necesarios y entrégale la composición al profesor (a la profesora).

Vistazos culturales
La presencia indígena en el mundo hispano

¿Sabías que...

en muchos países latinoamericanos las culturas indígenas son una parte importante de la identidad nacional? En México, Guatemala, Bolivia, el Ecuador y el Perú hay poblaciones indígenas muy grandes. En estos países la presencia indígena se refleja en varios aspectos de la cultura nacional como el arte, la literatura, la lengua, la política, etcétera. En otros países latinoamericanos como la Argentina y el Uruguay, la presencia indígena no tiene un papel tan importante.

Poblaciones indígenas

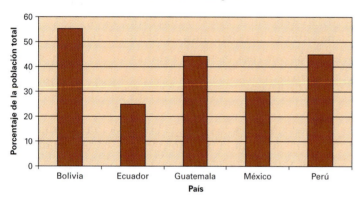

Eje Y: Porcentaje de la población total
Eje X: País
Bolivia, Ecuador, Guatemala, México, Perú

En Bolivia, el Ecuador y el Perú, se habla tanto el español como el quechua, la lengua de los incas. De hecho, en Bolivia, hay tantos hablantes de esta lengua indígena que es uno de los idiomas oficiales del país.

Más de un millón de mexicanos habla náhuatl, la lengua de los aztecas. En México hay más de 100 culturas indígenas.

En una clase de náhuatl cerca de México, D.F.

Una familia quechua en un mercado de Andahuaylillas, Perú

El subcomandante Marcos, líder de los indígenas en Chiapas, México

La política

A veces durante la historia de algunos países latinoamericanos como México, Guatemala, Chile y otros, los indígenas se han sublevado[a] para defender sus derechos. En México, por ejemplo, los indígenas del estado de Chiapas se rebelaron contra el gobierno en 1994 porque vivían en una pobreza[b] inmensa. Querían más tierra[c] para cultivar y más acceso al sistema político.

———————————
[a]se... *have revolted* [b]*poverty* [c]*land*

Las tradiciones

Los descendientes de las tribus indígenas de varios países siguen celebrando las fiestas y tradiciones de sus antepasados.

Lo indígena en la cultura nacional

Los voladores de Papantla, una tradición totonaca, Estado de Veracruz, México

La literatura

Muchos escritores del siglo XX escribieron novelas de temas indígenas para captar la realidad de la población indígena de su país.

- Jorge Icaza (el Ecuador): *Huasipungo* (1934)
- Miguel Ángel Asturias (Guatemala): *Hombres de maíz* (1949)
- José María Arguedas (el Perú): *Los ríos profundos* (1958)

La lengua

Palabras españolas de origen náhuatl:		Palabras españolas de origen quechua:	
aguacate	papalote[b]	cóndor	pampa[b]
chicle[a]	tomate	gaucho[a]	puma
chocolate		llama	

———————————
[a]*chewing gum* [b]*kite (Mex.)*

———————————
[a]*rancher* [b]*grassy plain*

ACTIVIDAD ¿Qué recuerdas?

Completa las siguientes oraciones.

1. Aproximadamente _____ personas habla(n) náhuatl en México.

2. Según la gráfica, el porcentaje de la población indígena es más alto en este país: _____.

3. Además del español, el _____ es uno de los idiomas oficiales de Bolivia.

4. El autor de la novela guatemalteca *Hombres de maíz* se llama _____.

5. En el año _____ hubo una sublevación muy grande de indígenas en contra del gobierno mexicano.

6. La palabra **cóndor** tiene su origen en la lengua de los _____.

NAVEGANDO LA RED

Escoge *uno* de los siguientes proyectos. Luego presenta la información a la clase.

1. Busca información sobre «La Malinche» en la historia del indigenismo mexicano para poder contestar las siguientes preguntas.
   a. ¿Quién era La Malinche y qué papel tuvo en la conquista española de México?
   b. ¿Por qué crees que La Malinche es un símbolo del indigenismo y mestizaje mexicanos para algunos?
   c. Hoy día, **el malinchismo** es un término común en México. ¿Qué crees que significa este término o en qué circunstancias se usa?

2. Busca información sobre los mapuches de Sudamérica. Después haz lo siguiente.
   a. Explica qué quiere decir la palabra **mapuche** en español.
   b. Alista los nombres y la población mapuche aproximada de cada país en el que viven los mapuches.
   c. Explica brevemente cómo es la economía de los mapuches y por qué los mapuches chilenos están inmigrando a Santiago (la capital de Chile).

VOCABULARIO COMPRENSIVO

Los daños físicos — Physical Injuries

la herida	wound, injury
la lesión	
el peligro	danger
dañino/a	harmful
grave	serious
peligroso/a	dangerous
consistir en	to consist of
herir (ie, i)	to wound
tener cuidado	to be careful

¿Eres adicto/a? — Are You Addicted?

el abuso	abuse
la adicción	addiction
el alcoholismo	alcoholism
la consecuencia	consequence
la autoestima	self-esteem
abusar de	to abuse
convertirse (ie, i) en adicto/a	to become addicted
salir de una adicción	to overcome an addiction
ser adicto/a	to be addicted
sufrir	to suffer; to experience

GRAMMAR SUMMARY

Verbs That Require a Reflexive Pronoun

1. Remember that with true reflexive verbs, the subject and the object refer to the same person or thing (**me miro** = *I look at myself,* **se mira** = *she looks at herself*). But you have learned a number of verbs in this unit that require a reflexive pronoun (**me, te, se,** and so forth) even though they are not reflexive in meaning. Review the list of such verbs below.

2. **Ponerse** can be used with a number of adjectives to talk about changes in emotional state.

> **Me puse irritado** con ella.
> *I got irritated with her.*

> **¿Te pusiste contento?**
> *Did you become happy?*

3. Although the verbs in (1) and the use of **ponerse** in (2) are not true reflexives, most of them can be used without a reflexive pronoun to talk about how something affects someone else. Compare the following sentences.

> **Me ofendí.**
> *I got offended.*

> Ese comentario **me ofendió.**
> *That comment offended me.*

> **¿Te aburriste** en la clase?
> *Did you get bored in class?*

> **¿Te aburrió** la clase?
> *Did the class bore you?*

aburrirse	to get bored	**¿Te aburres** fácilmente?	*Do you get bored easily?*
alegrarse	to get happy	**Me alegro** de oír eso.	*I'm happy to hear that.*
cansarse	to get tired	Jaime **se cansa** si hace calor.	*Jaime gets tired if it's hot.*
enojarse	to get angry	No quiero **enojarme.**	*I don't want to get angry.*
irritarse	to be (get) irritated	¡No **te irrites**!	*Don't get irritated!*
ofenderse	to be (get) offended	**¿Se ofendió** Ud.?	*Did you get offended?*
preocuparse	to worry, get worried	**Me preocupo** por eso.	*I worry about that.*
sentirse (ie, i)	to feel	**Me siento** bien.	*I feel good.*

The Verbs faltar and quedar

The verbs **faltar** (*to be missing, lacking*) and **quedar** (*to be remaining*) are generally used with indirect object pronouns to express concepts equivalent to the English *to have something missing* or *to have something remaining.* Note both the literal and the more standard translations in English, which will help you remember how these verbs work in Spanish.

> **Me faltan** $10.
> *I'm short $10.* (Lit. *$10 is lacking to me.*)

> **¿Le falta** algo a Ud.?
> *Are you missing something?* (Lit. *Is something missing to you?*)

> No **nos queda** nada.
> *We have nothing left.* (Lit. *Nothing is remaining to us.*)

> ¿Cuánto dinero **te queda**?
> *How much money do you have left?* (Lit. *How much money is remaining to you?*)

Both **faltar** and **quedar** can be used without indirect object pronouns. Compare the following sentences to those above and at left.

> **¿Queda** pan?
> *Is there any bread left?*

> Algo **falta...**
> *Something is missing . . .*

> ¿Quién **falta**?
> *Who is absent?* (*Who is missing?*)

Estar + Adjective

Remember that to express a condition or state of being, whether emotional or physical, Spanish uses the verb **estar** and not **ser**.

Estoy muy **cansado.**
I am very tired.

Siempre **estoy contento.**
I am always happy.

¿Nunca **estás aburrida**?
Are you ever bored?

-ndo and *-ing*

The verb endings **-ndo** in Spanish and *-ing* in English are not exactly equivalent. Unlike *-ing*, **-ndo** can never be used with a verb to express a subject. The infinitive or a noun is used.

Salir de la adicción no es fácil.
Getting out of addiction is not easy.

El patinaje es buen ejercicio.
Skating is good exercise.

The **-ndo** form can be used to express *by doing something*, but in this case there is no equivalent of the English word *by* in Spanish.

Me preparo para un examen **revisando** mis apuntes.
I prepare for an exam by reviewing my notes.

Tener + Nouns

In this, as well as other units, you have seen **tener** used with nouns to express concepts that would require the verb *to be* in English. Don't make the mistake of using **estar** in these situations.

tener cuidado	*to be careful* (lit. *to have care*)
tener gracia	*to be funny, charming* (lit. *to have charm, wit*)
tener miedo	*to be afraid* (lit. *to have fear*)
tener vergüenza	*to be ashamed, embarrassed* (lit. *to have shame*)

Since these expressions use nouns, **mucho/a** and **poco/a** are used as modifiers, as well as the phrases **un poco de** and **nada de.** Don't make the mistake of using **muy.**

Ten **mucho** cuidado.
Be very careful.

Tengo **un poco de** miedo.
I'm a little bit afraid.

No tiene **nada de** gracia.
He's not at all funny.

The Imperfect and the Preterite

Most students of Spanish have more difficulty with the functions of the imperfect than those of the preterite. However, they also tend to have more problems with the forms of the preterite. For this reason, the functions of the imperfect and the forms of the preterite are emphasized in this summary.

1. The imperfect has two main functions in Spanish. The first is to talk about events that happened habitually in the past.

   De niño **jugaba** mucho.
   As a child I played a lot.

   ¿**Dormías** con la luz prendida?
   Did you used to sleep with the light on?

   Antes Juan **se ofendía** fácilmente.
   Juan used to (would) get offended easily.

   Although *used to* and *would* are often English translations of the Spanish imperfect, note in the first example that this is not always the case.

2. The second basic function of the imperfect is to convey that a past event was in progress at a particular point in time. That point in time can be clock time (at 2:00) or at the time that the event occurred. (When the door opened . . .).

   ¿Qué **hacías** anoche a las 9.00?
   What were you doing last night at 9:00?

   ¿A las 9.00? **Estudiaba.**
   At 9:00? I was studying.

   ¿Y qué **hacías** cuando llamé?
   And what were you doing when I called?

   Veía la televisión.
   I was watching TV.

3. The preterite is used in most other cases, such as when a habitual event is limited by a time frame or by a specific number of times, when an event is not recalled as in progress at a particular point in time, and so forth.

   Jugué todo el verano.
   I played all summer long.

A las 9.00 **empecé** a estudiar.
I started studying at 9:00.

Cuando **volví** a casa, **encontré** una carta en la puerta.
When I got home, I found a letter on the door.

4. A handful of verbs undergo a slight change of meaning depending on whether the preterite or imperfect is used. However, remember that since Spanish can inflect the verb to show whether an event was in progress or not, these "meaning changes" are actually due to the fact that English does not inflect verbs this way and thus uses different words to express the same concepts.

No **sabía** eso.
I didn't know that.
(*My knowing something was in progress at the time inferred.*)

Lo **supe** anoche.
I found out last night.
(*My knowing was not in progress last night. I literally began to know last night.*)

Ya la **conocía.**
I knew her already.
(*My knowing her was in progress at the time inferred.*)

Conocí a Roberto anoche.
I met Roberto last night.
(*My knowing Roberto was not in progress last night. I literally began to know him last night.*)

5. Clock time is always expressed in the imperfect in the past. This is because the hour "was in progress" when something else happened.

Eran las 10.00 cuando oí un sonido raro.
It was 10:00 when I heard a strange sound.

Regular Preterite Stems and Endings

cansarse	beber	salir
me cansé	bebí	salí
te cansaste	bebiste	saliste
se cansó	bebió	salió
se cansó	bebió	salió
nos cansamos	bebimos	salimos
os cansasteis	bebisteis	salisteis
se cansaron	bebieron	salieron
se cansaron	bebieron	salieron

Regular Preterite Verbs with Spelling Changes in the yo Form

buscar →	bus**qué**
criticar →	criti**qué**
pagar →	pa**gué**
jugar →	ju**gué**
almorzar →	almor**cé**

Certain Preterite Stem Vowel Changes with Regular Endings

dormir (**o → ue** in present)
  d**u**rmió
  d**u**rmieron

sentirse (**e → ie** in present)
  se s**i**ntió
  se s**i**ntieron

pedir (**e → i** in present)
  p**i**dió
  p**i**dieron

Irregular Preterite Stems and Irregular Endings

andar:	**anduv-**	**-e**
estar:	**estuv-**	**-iste**
hacer:	**hiz-***	**-o**
poder:	**pud-**	**-o**
poner:	**pus-**	**-imos**
querer:	**quis-**	**-isteis**
saber:	**sup-**	**-ieron**
tener:	**tuv-**	**-ieron**
venir:	**vin-**	

Irregular preterite verbs whose stems end in **j** drop the **i** of **-ieron.**

INFINITIVE	PRETERITE STEM	PRETERITE FORM
conducir	conduj-	condu**jeron**
decir	dij-	di**jeron**
traer	traj-	tra**jeron**

Dar is completely irregular in the preterite and doesn't follow any of the above patterns.

di	dimos
diste	disteis
dio	dieron
dio	dieron

---

*Remember that Spanish does not allow the combination of **ze** or **zi**. The **yo** form of **hacer** in the preterite therefore becomes **hice** (hiz- + -e → hice).

Commands

1. Affirmative **tú** command forms are the same as the present tense **él/ella** forms.

> **Toma.**
> *Here.* (*Take this.*)
>
> **Bebe.**
> *Drink up.*
>
> **Escribe** tu nombre aquí.
> *Write your name here.*

Some common verbs have irregular affirmative **tú** command forms.

decir:	**Di** algo.
hacer:	**Haz** algo.
ir:	**Ve** a clase.
poner:	**Pon** esto allí.
salir:	**Sal** si puedes.
tener:	**¡Ten** cuidado!
venir:	**Ven** conmigo.

2. With few exceptions, all negative **tú** commands are regular. They are formed by taking the **yo** form of the present tense and adding **-es** if the verb is **-ar, -as** if the verb is **-er** or **-ir.**

INFINITIVE	*YO* FORM	NEGATIVE COMMAND STEM	NEGATIVE COMMAND FORM
tomar	tomo	tom-	no **tomes**
venir	vengo	veng-	no **vengas**
hacer	hago	hag-	no **hagas**

Note that the **c → qu, g → gu,** and **z → c** spelling changes apply here as in the case of the preterite **yo** forms.

INFINITIVE	*YO* FORM	NEGATIVE COMMAND STEM	NEGATIVE COMMAND FORM
almorzar	almuerzo	almuerc-	no **almuerces**
pagar	pago	pagu-	no **pagues**
criticar	critico	critiqu-	no **critiques**

Two verbs that have irregular negative command forms are **ir** and **ser.**

> ir → **no vayas**
> ser → **no seas**

3. If an object pronoun or a reflexive pronoun is used with the verb, then

   a. it is attached to the end if the command is affirmative.

   b. it goes in front of the verb if the command is negative.

> **Dime** algo.
> *Tell me something.*
>
> **Levántate** temprano.
> *Get up early.*
>
> **Cálmate.**
> *Calm down.*
>
> **Prúebalo.**
> *Try it.*

> **No me digas** eso.
> *Don't tell me that.*
>
> **No te levantes** tarde.
> *Don't get up late.*
>
> **No te ofendas.**
> *Don't get offended.*
>
> **No lo pruebes.**
> *Don't try it.*

Note that when adding pronouns to affirmative commands, accent marks are required to preserve the stress where it normally falls on the command form.

Somos lo que somos

Las cuatas Diego (*1980*) *por Cecilia Concepción Álvarez.*

Perfil de la artista

NOMBRE: Cecilia Concepción Álvarez

PAÍS DE ORIGEN: los Estados Unidos

FECHA DE NACIMIENTO: 1950

Cecilia Concepción Álvarez se crió en la frontera entre California y México, hija de padre cubano y madre mexicana. Autodidacta en el arte, se graduó de la Universidad Estatal de San Diego en sociología. La mezcla de lo político con lo cultural ha inspirado su obra artística. Además de retratos, también se dedica a la creación de grandes obras de arte público. Trabajando con la juventud de la comunidad ha creado murales, lo cual conlleva una conciencia de la identidad chicanolatina.

LECCIÓN 13

Check out the following media resources to complement this lesson:

 Online *Manual*

 Video on CD

 Online Learning Center

ActivityPak

¿Cómo te describes?

En esta lección, vas a tratar el tema de las cualidades de una persona. Vas a aprender

◆ adjetivos y expresiones para describir la personalidad de una persona

◆ un tiempo verbal nuevo: el *pretérito perfecto* (*present perfect*)

◆ nuevos verbos que requieren el uso de **se,** y luego repasar las verdaderas construcciones reflexivas

ALTO Before beginning this lesson, look over the **Intercambio** activity on pages 356–357. This is the activity you will be working toward throughout the lesson.

¿Te ves a ti mismo/a como te ven las otras personas?

IDEAS PARA EXPLORAR

La personalidad

VOCABULARIO

¿Cómo eres tú? (I)

Describing personalities

¿Cómo ves el mundo y la vida?
idealista ↔ realista
optimista ↔ pesimista

¿Cómo actúas con otras personas?
adaptable, flexible ↔ testarudo/a[a]
callado/a ↔ hablador(a)   impaciente ↔ paciente
calmado/a ↔ explosivo/a   insensible[c] ↔ sensible
chismoso/a[b] ↔ discreto/a   insincero/a ↔ sincero/a

¿Cómo eres tú?

¿Cómo trabajas?
caótico/a ↔ metódico/a
decidido/a[d] ↔ indeciso/a[e]
perezoso/a ↔ trabajador(a)

¿Cómo eres en cuanto a la política y la sociedad?
conformista ↔ rebelde
conservador(a) ↔ liberal

¿Qué otras características tienes?
aburrido/a ↔ divertido/a[f]   ingenuo/a[g] ↔ sabio/a[h]
arrogante ↔ humilde   inseguro/a ↔ seguro/a
gregario/a ↔ tímido/a

[a]*stubborn*   [b]*gossipy*   [c]*insensitive*   [d]*decisive*   [e]*indecisive*   [f]*fun-loving*   [g]*naive*   [h]*wise*

Vocabulario útil

poseer	to possess	**equilibrado/a**	balanced
celoso/a	jealous	**leal**	loyal
creativo/a		**posesivo/a**	

Lección 13   ¿Cómo te describes?

ACTIVIDAD A Correspondencias

Escucha la cualidad que menciona tu profesor(a). Luego escoge la frase que mejor corresponda a la cualidad.

1. **a.** tomas decisiones rápidamente
   b. no tomas decisiones rápidamente

2. **a.** las personas te pueden decir secretos
   b. las personas no deben decirte nada en secreto

3. **a.** aceptas las ideas de otros fácilmente
   b. no aceptas las ideas de otros fácilmente

4. **a.** tienes ideas progresistas
   b. tienes ideas tradicionales

5. **a.** siempre hablas de lo que haces
   b. no hablas mucho de lo que haces

6. **a.** puedes ser actor cómico
   b. no puedes ser actor cómico

7. **a.** eres confidente
   b. no eres confidente

8. **a.** eres buen amigo
   b. no eres buen amigo

ACTIVIDAD B Más correspondencias

Haz la correspondencia entre la columna A y la columna B.

A

Si eres...

1. pesimista, _____
2. flexible, _____
3. rebelde, _____
4. perezoso/a, _____
5. sabio/a, _____
6. insensible, _____
7. celoso/a, _____
8. creativo/a, _____

B

a. dañas los sentimientos de otras personas.
b. ves negro el futuro.
c. evitas (*you avoid*) el trabajo.
d. no te gusta seguir las reglas de otros.
e. probablemente eres posesivo/a también.
f. probablemente tienes mucha experiencia en la vida.
g. inventas cosas sin dificultad.
h. te adaptas fácilmente.

ACTIVIDAD C Personas famosas

Entre todos, nombren personajes de la literatura, del cine o de la televisión que poseen las siguientes cualidades.

1. idealista
2. explosivo/a
3. seguro/a
4. ingenuo/a

COMUNICACIÓN

ACTIVIDAD D ¿Te consideras... ?

Busca a personas que contesten tus preguntas con «sí» como en el modelo.

MODELO E1: ¿Te consideras liberal?
E2: Sí.
E1: Firma aquí, por favor.

1. discreto/a
2. testarudo/a
3. divertido/a
4. decidido/a
5. paciente
6. optimista
7. explosivo/a
8. caótico/a

ACTIVIDAD E ¿Cabezón, metódico u optimista?

Paso 1 Imagina que vas a hacerle algunas preguntas a otra persona para averiguar si es testaruda (flexible), metódica (caótica) u optimista (pesimista). Con un compañero (una compañera), agrupa las preguntas según la cualidad a la que aluden. **¡OJO!** Hay cuatro preguntas para cada cualidad. (Por ejemplo, hay cuatro preguntas para **testarudo [flexible]**.)

1. ¿Crees que la vida es como una gran aventura?
2. ¿Crees que tu manera de hacer las cosas es la mejor?
3. ¿Dicen los demás que sueles estar de buen humor?
4. ¿Discutes (*Do you argue*) hasta que los demás se resignan a tus ideas?
5. ¿Te adaptas fácilmente a nuevas situaciones?
6. ¿Eres muy organizado/a?
7. ¿Mantienes muy limpio el lugar donde vives?
8. ¿Siempre ves lo bueno en una situación?
9. ¿Tienes ideas muy fijas?
10. ¿Escribes de nuevo tus apuntes al final del día?
11. ¿Crees que los problemas más graves del mundo se resolverán (*will be resolved*)?
12. ¿Te gusta hacer listas de las cosas que necesitas hacer?

Paso 2 Ahora entrevista a otra persona usando las preguntas del **Paso 1.** Al final, decide si la persona es muy testaruda, un poco testaruda, flexible, o muy flexible, etcétera, según sus respuestas. Por ejemplo, si contesta afirmativamente las cuatro preguntas sobre **testarudo (flexible)** es muy testaruda. Si contesta afirmativamente sólo una vez, es un poco testaruda, etcétera. Presenta tus resultados a la clase.

"T" ANALIZAMOS

Con la tilde hacia la derecha	$\mathcal{L}^{-}$	Enérgica y productiva
Con la tilde hacia la izquierda	$\mathcal{L}$	Perezosa, poco productiva
Con la tilde inclinada hacia abajo	$\mathcal{t}$	Agresiva y arriesgada
Con la tilde por encima	$\mathcal{T}$	Imaginativa y espiritual
Con la tilde cruzando la letra	$\mathcal{t}$	Disciplinada y responsable
Con forma de estrella y tilde larga	$\mathcal{V}$	Rápida y persistente
Con forma de estrella y tilde corta	$\mathcal{V}$	Insegura

Muchas veces la letra (*handwriting*) de una persona revela su personalidad. Analiza tu letra según «"T" analizamos». ¿Estás de acuerdo con el análisis?

VOCABULARIO

¿Cómo eres tú? (II)

More on describing personalities

Cualidades

el afán de realización	eagerness to get things done
el don de mando	talent for leadership
la tendencia a evitar riesgos	tendency to avoid risks

Adjetivos

arriesgado/a	bold, daring
capaz de dirigir (a otros)	able to direct (others)
retraído/a	solitary, reclusive

Cognados: agresivo/a, aventurero/a, extrovertido/a, gregario/a, imaginativo/a, impulsivo/a, introvertido/a, reservado/a, tímido/a, vulnerable al estrés (a la tensión)

Todos saben que Carlitos es muy **imaginativo.**

Griselda, una mujer **aventurera,** hace una de sus actividades favoritas.

¿Te gusta quedarte en casa en vez de salir? ¿Prefieres estar solo/a más que con otras personas? Entonces eres **retraído/a** como Wanda.

ACTIVIDAD F ¿Semejante u opuesto?

Escucha mientras tu profesor(a) dice una de las palabras o expresiones nuevas. Di si las palabras o expresiones a continuación representan un concepto semejante u opuesto.

1. retraído
2. la tendencia a evitar riesgos
3. el don de mando
4. el afán de realización
5. introvertido
6. gregario

ACTIVIDAD G ¡Bingo!

Escucha las instrucciones de tu profesor(a) para jugar al Bingo.

ACTIVIDAD H ¿Lógica o no?

Indica si cada oración es lógica o no, en tu opinión. Si dices que no, ¿puedes explicar por qué?

	ES LÓGICA.	NO ES LÓGICA.
1. Una persona gregaria no habla mucho.	☐	☐
2. Para ser presidente/a, es bueno tener el don de mando.	☐	☐
3. Las personas retraídas tienden a evitar riesgos.	☐	☐
4. Una persona agresiva no es tímida.	☐	☐
5. Si alguien es vulnerable al estrés, es muy capaz de dirigir a otros.	☐	☐
6. Una persona imaginativa tiene mucha creatividad.	☐	☐
7. Las personas perezosas y las que tienen el afán de realización pueden llevarse muy bien en el trabajo.	☐	☐

COMUNICACIÓN

ACTIVIDAD I ¿Qué es?

El profesor (La profesora) va a darle a una persona de la clase uno de los atributos presentados en esta sección. Todos deben hacerle preguntas a esa persona para averiguar el nombre de ese atributo.

MODELO E1: ¿Te gusta estar solo?
E2: No. Me gusta estar con otras personas.
E3: Si tienes un conflicto con alguien, ¿hablas con esa persona?
E2: Sí.
E4: ¿Eres capaz de dirigir a otros?
E2: ¡Sí!

NAVEGANDO LA RED

¿Tiene cada cultura su propia personalidad? ¿Existe alguna personalidad colectiva que se pueda atribuir a un grupo de personas? Busca información sobre la gente de Costa Rica, Puerto Rico, la Argentina y México. (Sobre todo mira las páginas de las oficinas de turismo de cada país.) ¿Hay descripciones de la gente del país? Presenta tus resultados a la clase.

La expresión de la personalidad

GRAMÁTICA

¿Qué has hecho? (I)

Introduction to the present perfect

—**He tomado** una decisión.
—¿Sí? ¿Cuál es?
—**He decidido** buscar otro trabajo.
—¿Lo **has pensado** bien?

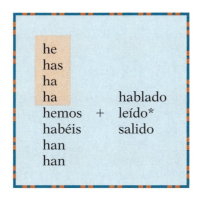

he		
has		
ha		
ha		hablado
hemos	+	leído*
habéis		salido
han		
han		

You may recall encountering in *¿Sabías que… ?* the *present perfect* (**el pretérito perfecto**) tense. Forms such as **ha investigado** and **han investigado,** roughly equivalent to English *has investigated* and *have investigated,* consist of the verb **haber** and a *past participle*.

In most past participles the **-ar, -er,** and **-ir** endings of the infinitive are replaced with **-ado, -ido,** and **-ido,** respectively. There are no stem changes.

probar	**He probado** comidas muy exóticas.
poder	No **he podido** estudiar para el examen.
dormir	No **he dormido** bien esta semana.

A few common verbs have irregular past participles:

hacer:	hecho	¿**Has hecho** la tarea?
escribir:	escrito	No **hemos escrito** la composición.
poner:	puesto	Mi papá ya **ha puesto** la mesa.
decir:	dicho	¿**He dicho** algo incorrecto?
ver:	visto	¿**Has visto** a la profesora recientemente?
morir:	muerto	Su perro **ha muerto.**

Although the verb **ir** is irregular in many tenses, it has a regular past participle. What do you think is the past participle of **ir?** You were right if you guessed **ido.**

As you continue to describe your personality in this lesson, you will find the present perfect useful when talking about things you have and haven't done.

---

*When **-er** and **-ir** verb stems end in **-a, -e,** or **-o,** the **i** in the past participle ending **-ido** carries an accent.

ACTIVIDAD A ¿Quién ha hecho qué?

1. ¿Quién ha recibido el Premio Nobel dos veces?
   - **a.** Marie Curie
   - **b.** Óscar Arias Sánchez
   - **c.** Nelson Mandela
2. ¿Quién *no* ha ganado el Abierto de Francia?
   - **a.** Pete Sampras
   - **b.** Andre Agassi
   - **c.** Sergi Bruguera
3. ¿Quién *no* ha hecho un vídeo musical?
   - **a.** Bette Midler
   - **b.** Madonna
   - **c.** Judy Garland
4. ¿Quién *no* ha sido vicepresidente de los Estados Unidos?
   - **a.** Lyndon Johnson
   - **b.** George W. Bush
   - **c.** Richard Nixon
5. ¿Quién ha escrito obras teatrales?
   - **a.** Neil Simon
   - **b.** Dan Brown
   - **c.** Danielle Steele

ACTIVIDAD B ¿Sí o no?

Empareja una frase de la columna A con una de la columna B para formar oraciones lógicas y gramaticalmente correctas. Luego indica si se te aplican o no.

A

1. He estudiado _____
2. He hablado _____
3. He visto _____
4. He salido _____
5. He conocido _____
6. Me he despertado _____

B

- **a.** a una persona famosa.
- **b.** con algunos amigos esta semana.
- **c.** con algunos familiares por teléfono esta semana.
- **d.** para varios exámenes este semestre.
- **e.** una película recientemente.
- **f.** tarde varias veces esta semana.

ACTIVIDAD C ¿Lo has hecho tú?

Paso 1 Completa las siguientes frases con información que se te aplica.

Esta semana...

1. he escrito _____.
2. he mirado _____.
3. he ido al (a la) _____.
4. he visitado (a) _____.
5. he leído _____.

Paso 2 La clase entera debe convertir las oraciones del **Paso 1** en preguntas y hacérselas al profesor (a la profesora) para averiguar si ha hecho cosas semejantes. ¿Quién tiene más en común con el profesor (la profesora)?

MODELO   ¿Ha escrito Ud. una carta esta semana?

Así se dice

The present perfect in English and Spanish share many meanings and functions; however, they are not exactly equivalent. For example, English *I have lived in Chicago for ten years* would be rendered in Spanish as **Hace diez años que vivo en Chicago.** See whether you can give an English equivalent for each sentence.

Hace un mes que no llueve.
Hace mucho tiempo que no veo a mi familia.
Hace un año que fumo.

ACTIVIDAD D Un perfil

Paso 1 Hazle las siguientes preguntas a un compañero (una compañera) de clase. Luego determina cómo lo (la) clasificarías (*you would classify him* [*her*]) en las siguientes escalas.

seguro/a ⟵⟶ inseguro/a, tímido/a
decidido/a ⟵⟶ indeciso/a

1. ¿Has perdido alguna buena oportunidad porque no pudiste tomar una decisión?
2. ¿Has dicho: «sí» cuando realmente querías decir: «no»?
3. ¿Has pedido la opinión de otras personas antes de comprar algo caro (*expensive*)?
4. ¿Has conocido a alguna persona atractiva pero tuviste miedo de hablarle?
5. ¿Le has escrito una carta a alguien para decirle lo que piensas de algo que esa persona ha hecho?

Paso 2 Ahora contesta las mismas preguntas de tu compañero/a. Después él (ella) va a analizar tus respuestas. ¿Eres tan seguro/a y decidido/a como tu compañero/a o son diferentes?

GRAMÁTICA

¿Qué has hecho? (II)

More on the present perfect

—**Hemos hecho** muchas compras.
—Sí, ¡y ahora tenemos que pagar las cuentas!

he		
has		
ha		
ha		hablado
hemos	+	leído
habéis		salido
han		
han		

In the previous section, you worked with the present perfect to talk about yourself, to ask questions of someone, and to report on someone else. Note the forms of **haber** used in the present perfect to talk about groups of people.

Hemos terminado la tarea.	*We've finished the homework.*
¿**Han (Habéis)** decidido algo?	*Have you all decided something?*
Marta y Paco no **han** escrito nada.	*Marta and Paco have not written anything.*

ACTIVIDAD E ¿Qué hemos hecho?

Entre todos, decidan si cada oración a continuación es cierta o falsa, según lo que han hecho este semestre (trimestre).

		C	F
1.	Hemos escrito una composición.	☐	☐
2.	Hemos hecho reportes orales.	☐	☐
3.	Hemos hablado de las relaciones familiares.	☐	☐
4.	Hemos hablado de nuestra personalidad.	☐	☐
5.	Hemos visto un vídeo o un segmento de un vídeo.	☐	☐
6.	Hemos entrevistado al profesor (a la profesora).	☐	☐

ACTIVIDAD F ¿A quiénes?

Indica a quiénes les harías (*you would ask*) cada pregunta.

1. ¿Qué películas han visto Uds. recientemente?
   a. Ebert y Roeper
   b. Siegfried y Roy
   c. Penn y Teller

2. ¿Qué deportes han practicado Uds. esta semana?
   a. niños de edad preescolar
   b. adolescentes
   c. personas jubiladas

3. ¿A cuántos pacientes han examinado Uds. esta semana?
   a. estudiantes
   b. secretarias
   c. doctores

4. ¿Han estudiado Uds. el nuevo vocabulario para hoy?
   a. estudiantes de química
   b. estudiantes de retórica
   c. estudiantes de español

COMUNICACIÓN

ACTIVIDAD G Le toca al profesor (a la profesora)°

Le... *It's the professor's turn.*

Paso 1 En grupos de cuatro, escriban cinco oraciones sobre lo que creen que su profesor(a) ha hecho junto con su familia o sus amigos en los últimos tres días.

Paso 2 Ahora entrevisten a su profesor(a). ¿Qué grupo tiene todas las oraciones correctas?

MODELO ¿Han cenado su familia y Ud. en algún restaurante?

Busca lo siguiente sobre personas famosas de habla española y presenta tus resultados a la clase.

◆ ¿Quién se ha casado recientemente?

◆ ¿Quién ha tomado unas vacaciones?

◆ Menciona dos o tres detalles sobre el evento.

IDEAS PARA EXPLORAR

Más sobre tu personalidad

GRAMÁTICA

¿Te atreves a... ?

More verbs that require a reflexive pronoun

—...y lo peor es que nunca **se da cuenta de** sus errores.

> atreverse a + *inf.*
> burlarse de
> comportarse
> darse cuenta de
> jactarse de
> portarse

You learned in **Lección 10** that a number of verbs in Spanish that are not reflexive in meaning require a reflexive pronoun. Remember **quejarse (de)** (*to complain* [*about*])? These verbs do not translate into English with -*self* or -*selves,* nor do they denote that someone is doing something to himself or herself. You will always see the following verbs used in Spanish with a reflexive pronoun.

atreverse a + *inf.* to dare to (*do something*)

¿**Te atreves a** decir eso?

burlarse (de) to laugh (*at*), make fun (*of someone*)

Ella siempre **se burla de** mí.

comportarse to behave

Los niños no **se comportan** bien cuando van a la iglesia.

darse cuenta (de) to realize (*something*)

Nunca **se da cuenta de** sus errores.

jactarse (de) to boast (*about something*)

Se jactan de ser los mejores jugadores de fútbol.

portarse to behave

Siempre **me porto** bien en público.

ACTIVIDAD A ¿Quién... ?

Indica la personalidad de la persona que hace cada acción a continuación. ¿Están todos de acuerdo?

¿Quién...

1. se queja de tener que hacer cola (*stand in line*)?

   a. una persona optimista   **b.** una persona impaciente   **c.** una persona sabia

2. se atreve a vestir (*dress*) de una manera extravagante?

   a. una persona conservadora   **b.** una persona humilde   **c.** una persona rebelde

3. se comporta bien en cualquier situación?

   a. una persona adaptable   **b.** una persona ingenua   **c.** una persona insincera

4. se jacta siempre de sí misma o de lo que tiene?

   a. una persona decidida   **b.** una persona arrogante   **c.** una persona realista

5. siempre se da cuenta de cuándo una discusión es inútil?

   a. una persona cabezona   **b.** una persona caótica   **c.** una persona sabia

6. siempre se burla de los demás?

   a. una persona insensible   **b.** una persona metódica   **c.** una persona divertida

ACTIVIDAD B ¿Cómo es?

Completa cada oración de manera lógica, utilizando adjetivos que describan a la persona.

1. Si una persona (no) se queja mucho es porque es _____.

2. Si una persona (no) se jacta mucho es porque es _____.

3. Si una persona (no) se da cuenta de que los demás le mienten es porque es _____.

ACTIVIDAD C ¿Cuándo?

Indica cuándo se podría (*one could*) hacer las siguientes acciones. Si crees que nunca es apropiado hacer una acción en particular, puedes decir: «Nunca es apropiado _____».

1. Es justo quejarse cuando uno _____.

2. Es aceptable jactarse cuando uno _____.

3. Es justo portarse mal cuando uno _____.

4. Es perdonable burlarse de otra persona cuando uno _____.

ACTIVIDAD D En mi vida...

Paso 1 Completa las siguientes oraciones. Puedes escribir frases ciertas o falsas.

1. Me he comportado mal _____.

2. Me he atrevido a _____.

3. Me he quejado de _____.

4. Me he burlado de _____.

5. Me he jactado de _____.

Paso 2 Algunos voluntarios deben leer algunas de sus oraciones a la clase. La clase tiene que determinar si la información es cierta o falsa.

Paso 3 (Optativo) En grupos, escriban oraciones que se le apliquen al profesor (a la profesora). ¿Conocen Uds. bien a su profesor(a)?

ACTIVIDAD E En tu opinión

Paso 1 Trabajando con dos o tres compañeros/as de clase indica si, según tu experiencia, las siguientes afirmaciones son ciertas o falsas. Den ejemplos para apoyar sus decisiones. Apunten sus ideas.

	C	F
1. Las apariencias engañan. El exterior no indica la personalidad que tiene la persona.	☐	☐
2. Los ojos revelan la personalidad de una persona.	☐	☐
3. La ropa indica algo sobre la personalidad de alguien.	☐	☐
4. Los opuestos se atraen.	☐	☐

Paso 2 Presenten sus ideas al resto de la clase. ¿Han tenido todos las mismas experiencias?

GRAMÁTICA

¿Es reflexivo?

Review of the pronoun **se**

ACCIONES REFLEXIVAS	VERBOS QUE REQUIEREN *SE*
Are the subject and the object the same?	Is this one of a handful of verbs that must include **se**?
NO: Juan conoce bien a María. YES: Juan **se conoce** bien.	YES: Enrique **se jacta** demasiado. NO: Enrique habla mucho.
NO: ¿Cómo describes a Marta? YES: ¿Cómo **te describes** a ti mismo?	YES: No **me quejo** mucho de la vida. NO: No comprendo la vida.

You have learned a number of uses of the pronoun **se** and its variants (**me, te, nos, os**), and you may be confused as to what a reflexive is and what a verb that requires **se** is. The preceding chart summarizes the difference. Verbs that are reflexive also appear in nonreflexive forms. Remember that the term *reflexive* means that the subject of the action is also the object of the action. Usually, a version of *-self* is used in an English equivalent.

¿Le hablas a Roberto con frecuencia?	*Do you talk to Roberto frequently?*
¿**Se habla** Roberto con frecuencia?	*Does Roberto talk to himself frequently?*
¿**Te hablas** con frecuencia?	*Do you talk to yourself frequently?*

In the first example, *you* (**tú**) is the subject of the verb and *Roberto* is the object (the person to whom the subject frequently talks). This is a nonreflexive use of the verb. In the second example, *Roberto* is both the subject (He talks.) and the object (*He* is the one to whom he talks!). This is a reflexive use of the verb. Can you tell who the subject and object are in the third example? If you answered that they are the same person, you are right! In this example, *you* (**tú**) talk to *yourself* (**te**)!

With verbs that require **se,** there is no reflexive action. The verbs simply use this pronoun, they cannot appear without it, and it is not possible to use a version of *-self* in an English equivalent.

No **me quejo** mucho.	*I don't complain much.*
¡Qué va! **Te quejas** de todo.	*What do you mean?! You complain about everything.*

ACTIVIDAD F ¿Una acción reflexiva?

Paso 1 Indica si cada oración describe una acción reflexiva o si el verbo simplemente requiere el uso del pronombre reflexivo.

	ACCIÓN REFLEXIVA	REQUIERE SE
1. Me burlo de mis amigos.	☐	☐
2. Me escribo recados para recordar cosas importantes.	☐	☐
3. El profesor (La profesora) se habla en clase.	☐	☐
4. El profesor (La profesora) se jacta de nosotros porque somos muy buenos.	☐	☐
5. Me considero bastante leal.	☐	☐
6. No me atrevo a hablarle al profesor (a la profesora) cuando lo (la) veo en el gimnasio.	☐	☐
7. Siempre me porto bien en público.	☐	☐
8. El profesor (La profesora) no se da cuenta de la hora muchas veces.	☐	☐
9. El profesor (La profesora) se define como muy liberal.	☐	☐

¿De qué te ríes tanto?

Paso 2 Ahora indica si las oraciones del **Paso 1** son ciertas o falsas para ti.

	C	F		C	F
1.	☐	☐	**6.**	☐	☐
2.	☐	☐	**7.**	☐	☐
3.	☐	☐	**8.**	☐	☐
4.	☐	☐	**9.**	☐	☐
5.	☐	☐			

COMUNICACIÓN

ACTIVIDAD G Las acciones y la personalidad

Paso 1 En parejas contesten las siguientes preguntas, usando o verbos reflexivos o verbos que requieren **se.** También pueden agregar una acción no reflexiva para dar una respuesta más completa.

1. Si una persona se define como sabia, ¿qué acciones hace o no hace?

2. Si una persona se define como humilde, ¿qué acciones hace o no hace?

3. Si una persona se define como impaciente, ¿qué acciones hace o no hace?

4. Si una persona se define como arrogante, ¿qué acciones hace o no hace?

Paso 2 Ahora presenten sus ideas a la clase. Después, entre todos, contesten la siguiente pregunta.

¿Revelan las acciones de una persona su personalidad?

ACTIVIDAD H ¿Sabías que... ?

Paso 1 Lee la selección **¿Sabías que... ?** Luego contesta las siguientes preguntas.

1. ¿En qué se basa el horóscopo chino, en el mes o en el año en que uno nace?

2. Según la descripción del buey y del perro, ¿crees que los dos podrían (*could*) ser amigos?

3. La selección menciona los siguientes animales: el delfín, el oso y el león. ¿Qué cualidades asocias con cada uno?

¿Sabías que...

en muchas culturas se han utilizado los animales para representar la personalidad humana? En el horóscopo chino, por ejemplo, se utiliza un sistema a base del año en que uno nace. El año corresponde a un animal. Así que las personas nacidas en 1937, 1949, 1961, 1973, 1985, 1997 y los que nacerán[a] en 2009 se definen como **buey.**[b]

El buey es paciente, metódico, equilibrado, introvertido, sencillo[c] pero inteligente y desconfiado.[d] El perro (1934, 1946, 1958, 1970, 1982, 1994, 2006), en cambio, es alerta,* observador, leal, justo, discreto, honesto y el mayor pesimista del mundo.

En las culturas azteca y maya, el jaguar era un animal muy estimado por sus cualidades. Es feroz y astuto,[e] cualidades importantes para ser un buen guerrero. Los guerreros se ponían trajes y adornos que imitaban al jaguar. En los tiempos modernos la costumbre continúa aunque con variaciones. Por ejemplo, los equipos de fútbol americano y también de béisbol y basquetbol muchas veces llevan nombres de animales: los Delfines de Miami, los Osos de Chicago y los Leones de Detroit son algunos ejemplos.

Las grandes civilizaciones prehispánicas usaban los animales como símbolos, incorporando su imagen en el arte, la arquitectura y en sus trajes ceremoniales.

[a]*will be born* [b]*ox* [c]*simple* [d]*distrustful* [e]*clever*

*****Alerta,** like **optimista** and similar adjectives, does not change its final vowel to an **-o** when used to modify masculine nouns.

Paso 2 A continuación hay una lista de los animales del horóscopo chino y una lista de cualidades. Usando las cualidades que has aprendido en esta lección y las otras que aparecen en la lista, ¿qué cualidades dirías tú (*would you say*) que tiene cada animal?

ANIMALES DEL HORÓSCOPO CHINO

el buey	el conejo	el perro
el caballo	el dragón	la rata (*rat*)
la cabra	el gallo (*rooster*)	la serpiente
el cerdo (*pig*)	el mono (*monkey*)	el tigre

CUALIDADES

ambicioso/a	excéntrico/a	peligroso/a
apasionado/a	filosófico/a	perfeccionista
autoritario/a	impetuoso/a	popular
bello/a (*beautiful*)	independiente	refinado/a
cerebral	inocente	respetuoso/a
criticón, criticona	inquieto/a (*restless*)	simpático/a
egoísta (*self-centered*)	intelectual	sociable
encantador(a) (*charming*)	justo/a	tacaño/a (*stingy*)
escrupuloso/a	malicioso/a	violento/a

Paso 3 (Optativo) Busca información en la Red sobre el horóscopo chino. ¿Son correctas tus ideas del **Paso 2**?

ACTIVIDAD I ¿Cómo te ves?

Paso 1 Trabajando con un compañero (una compañera) de la clase, inventa una historia sobre lo que pasa en los siguientes dibujos. Comenten la personalidad de la chica que se mira en el espejo.

1.

2.   **3.**

4.

Paso 2 Compartan su historia con el resto de la clase. Después, entre todos, contesten la siguiente pregunta.

¿Te ves a ti mismo/a así como te ven los demás?

INTERCAMBIO

La personalidad de tu compañero/a de clase

Propósito: escribir un breve párrafo, describiendo a un compañero (una compañera) de clase.

Papeles: una persona que entrevista y una persona entrevistada.

Paso 1 A continuación hay una encuesta. Vas a entrevistar a un compañero (una compañera) de clase para descubrir su personalidad. Lee la encuesta para tener una idea de su contenido.

UN PERFIL

1. A esta persona le gusta leer...

☐ libros cómicos.   ☐ literatura clásica.

☐ ensayos filosóficos.   ☐ novelas populares (corrientes).

☐ novelas de ciencia ficción.   ☐ _____.

☐ libros de misterio.

2. A esta persona le gustan las películas...

☐ de misterio.   ☐ *western.*

☐ cómicas.   ☐ extranjeras.

☐ documentales.   ☐ _____.

☐ románticas.

3. En cuanto a la música, es probable que esta persona escuche...

☐ *rock.*   ☐ *country.*

☐ música popular.   ☐ *rap.*

☐ *jazz.*   ☐ _____.

☐ música clásica.

4. Esta persona prefiere estar...

☐ solo/a.   ☐ con un grupo pequeño de
                                        amigos íntimos.
☐ con una sola persona.
                                     ☐ con muchas personas.

5. Esta persona busca _____ en una pareja.

☐ una buena apariencia física   ☐ inteligencia

☐ dinero   ☐ una personalidad atractiva

6. Si se enfrenta con un problema, esta persona...

☐ actúa agresivamente.   ☐ actúa con cuidado.

☐ no hace nada.

7. Por lo general, esta persona es...

☐ enérgica.   ☐ ni muy enérgica ni muy
                                        perezosa.
☐ perezosa.

8. Esta persona _____ en el futuro.

☐ piensa mucho   ☐ no piensa para nada

☐ piensa poco

9. Para describir a esta persona con una palabra, yo diría (*I would say*) que es...

☐ razonable.   ☐ excéntrica.

☐ conservadora.   ☐ arriesgada.

10. Los sábados por la noche es probable que esta persona se encuentre...

☐ en casa frente al televisor.   ☐ en una fiesta.

☐ en casa leyendo un libro.   ☐ en casa de unos amigos.

☐ en el cine.   ☐ _____.

☐ en un concierto.

Paso 2 Piensa un momento en las preguntas que le vas a hacer a la persona que entrevistas. **¡OJO!** No debes hacerle preguntas directas, como «¿Lees novelas clásicas?» Hazle preguntas indirectas con la intención de deducir de sus respuestas la información que quieres. Por ejemplo: «¿Cuál es tu novela favorita? ¿Quién es tu escritor preferido (escritora preferida)?»

Paso 3 Entrevista a tu compañero/a. Apunta sus respuestas y luego llena el formulario de la encuesta con los datos obtenidos.

Paso 4 Examina los datos que tienes. ¿Tienes lo suficiente para categorizar a tu compañero/a? Si no, piensa en otras preguntas que le puedes hacer.

Paso 5 Con los datos que has obtenido, escribe un párrafo sobre la persona que has entrevistado. Puedes usar el siguiente modelo si quieres, modificándolo según tus datos.

He entrevistado a ____. Según los datos que me ha dado, ____. Un ejemplo de esto es que (cuando) ____. También he descubierto (*discovered*) que ____. A la pregunta «____» su respuesta fue «____». Finalmente, ____ me ha dicho que ____. Por estas razones, yo diría que ____ es ____.

1 = el nombre de la persona
2 = una descripción de la persona
3 = una oración en la que se mencione algo que la persona hace que revele su personalidad
4 = una oración que lleve por lo menos un adjetivo
5 = una pregunta que le has hecho
6 = su respuesta a la pregunta anterior
7 = algo que revele otro detalle de su personalidad
8 = adjetivos que crees que describen a esa persona

NAVEGANDO LA RED

Busca información sobre la relación entre los colores y la personalidad. Por ejemplo, si el rojo es tu color favorito, ¿qué indica esto de tu personalidad? Como mínimo, busca información sobre la relación entre la personalidad y los siguientes colores: el rojo, el azul y el verde.

Vistazos culturales
El medio ambiente en el mundo hispano

¿Sabías que... el medio ambiente es un tema de mucha importancia en la mayoría de los países hispanos? En cuanto al medio ambiente hay dos cosas que principalmente conciernen a los hispanos: los efectos de El Niño y el ecoturismo. El Niño es un fenómeno climático que afecta el clima de Sudamérica y otras partes del mundo. El ecoturismo es una industria turística lucrativa que tiene la doble meta de estimular la economía y proteger el medio ambiente, sobre todo a las especies en peligro de extinción.

El Niño es un fenómeno climático que ocurre cuando las aguas del Océano Pacífico cerca de las costas del Perú y del Ecuador se calientan.[a] El calentamiento provoca cambios climáticos drásticos por todo el mundo. En Sudamérica hay lluvias torrenciales mientras que en la India, Asia y Sudáfrica, lugares que normalmente reciben mucha lluvia, se sufren sequías[b] fuertes.

[a]se... *warm up* [b]*droughts*

Barco de pesca peruano

La economía de las costas del Perú y del Ecuador depende mucho de la industria pesquera.[a] Durante El Niño las aguas calientes en el Océano Pacífico matan los peces, causando problemas ecológicos y económicos. Además, los pájaros que se alimentan de[b] los peces también se mueren o se van a otros lugares. Esto perjudica[c] muchísimo la industria de fertilizantes que depende del guano de los pájaros.

[a]*fishing* [b]se... *feed on* [c]*jeopardizes*

En las Islas Galápagos cerca del Ecuador existen aves de varios tipos, incluyendo los piqueros de patas rojas o patas azules.

Dos piqueros de patas azules

La Reserva Biológica Limoncocha es un territorio protegido en la Amazonia ecuatoriana. Su atractivo principal son las 350 especies de aves. La reserva es también el hábitat principal de una especie de caimán[a] negro.

[a]*alligator*

El ecoturismo

En la costa de Oaxaca, México, más de 700.000 tortugas llegan a poner huevos[a] entre los meses de mayo y enero. Pero como el huevo de tortuga se considera una delicia[b] todavía, guardias armados patrullan por[c] la costa cuando las tortugas ponen huevos para evitar que la gente los coma[d] y para proteger la especie.

[a]*poner... lay eggs*   [b]*delicacy*   [c]*patrullan... patrol*
[d]*para... to keep people from eating them*

El ecoturismo nació en Costa Rica, país que tiene aproximadamente 30 parques nacionales donde uno puede ver la flora y fauna nativas. Hay muchas especies que amenazan con extinguirse,[a] como es el caso de la rana flecha azul venenosa[b] en el Parque Braulio Carrillo.

[a]*amenazan... are threatened with extinction*
[b]*rana... poison blue dart frog*

Una rana flecha azul venenosa de Costa Rica

ACTIVIDAD ¿Qué recuerdas?

Empareja cada frase de la columna A con la frase correspondiente de la columna B.

A

1. _____ los pájaros se mueren

2. _____ el hábitat principal del piquero de patas azules

3. _____ se trata del calentamiento de las aguas del Océano Pacífico

4. _____ lugar donde más de 700.000 tortugas ponen huevos cada año

5. _____ un plan de desarrollo económico sustentable que utiliza el medio ambiente

B

a. El Niño

b. Oaxaca, México

c. sufre la producción de fertilizantes

d. el ecoturismo

e. las Islas Galápagos

NAVEGANDO LA RED

Selecciona *uno* de los siguientes proyectos y presenta tus resultados a la clase.

1. Busca información sobre las especies en peligro de extinción en el mundo hispano. Haz lo siguiente.
   a. Escoge un país hispano y menciona los nombres de tres especies de animales de este país que amenazan con extinguirse.
   b. Menciona las leyes (*laws*) que hay o los esfuerzos que se hacen para proteger estas especies.

2. Busca información sobre las **maquiladoras** en la frontera entre los Estados Unidos y México. Haz lo siguiente.
   a. Define lo que es una maquiladora e indica cuántas hay en la frontera.
   b. Menciona los problemas ambientales que las maquiladoras han causado.

VOCABULARIO COMPRENSIVO

¿Cómo eres tú?
What Are You Like?

arriesgado/a	bold, daring
calmado/a	calm
caótico/a	messy, chaotic
celoso/a	jealous
chismoso/a	gossipy
confidente	trustworthy
conservador(a)	conservative
creativo/a	creative
decidido/a	decisive; decided
discreto/a	discreet
divertido/a	fun-loving
egoísta	egotistical, self-centered
encantador(a)	charming
equilibrado/a	balanced
hablador(a)	talkative
humilde	humble
indeciso/a	indecisive
ingenuo/a	naive
inquieto/a	restless
inseguro/a	insecure
insensible	insensitive
leal	loyal
metódico/a	methodical
rebelde	rebellious
retraído/a (R)	solitary, reclusive
sabio/a	wise
seguro/a	secure
sensible	sensitive
tacaño/a	stingy
testarudo/a	stubborn
tímido/a	shy, timid
trabajador(a)	hardworking

Verbos para hablar de ciertos comportamientos
Verbs for Talking About Certain Kinds of Behavior

atreverse (a)	to dare (to)
burlarse (de)	to make fun (of), laugh (at)
comportarse	to behave
darse cuenta (de)	to realize (*something*)
jactarse (de)	to boast, brag (about)
portarse	to behave

Otras palabras y expresiones útiles

poseer	to possess
el afán de realización	eagerness to get things done
el don de mando	talent for leadership
la tendencia a evitar riesgos	tendency to avoid risks
capaz de dirigir (a otros)	able to direct (others)
vulnerable al estrés (a la tensión)	vulnerable to stress

LECCIÓN 14

Check out the following media resources to complement this lesson:

 Online *Manual*

 Video on CD

 Online Learning Center

 ActivityPak

¿A quién te gustaría conocer?

¿Has pensado alguna vez en las cualidades de ciertas personas famosas? ¿Qué persona famosa te interesa conocer? Este es el tema de la presente lección y vas a

- aprender más vocabulario relacionado con la personalidad
- aprender un nuevo tiempo verbal: el *condicional*
- aprender un modo verbal: el *pasado de subjuntivo*
- hablar de situaciones hipotéticas
- repasar el verbo **gustar** y la **a** personal

ALTO Before beginning this lesson, look over the **Intercambio** activity on page 377. This is the activity you will be working toward throughout the lesson.

Salvador Dalí, pintor español (1904–1989)

IDEAS PARA EXPLORAR

La personalidad de los famosos

VOCABULARIO

¿Qué cualidades poseían?

More adjectives to describe people

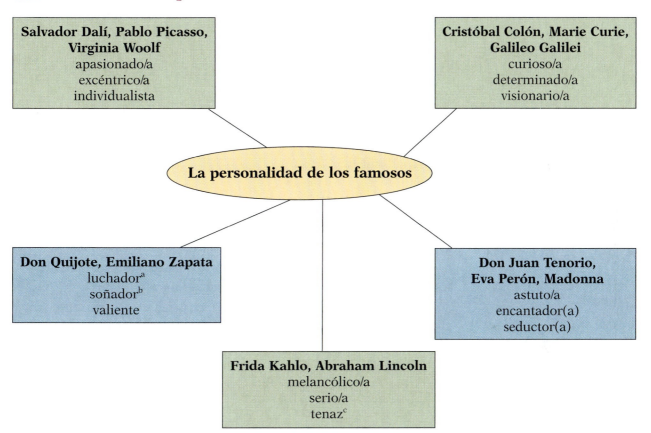

Salvador Dalí, Pablo Picasso, Virginia Woolf
apasionado/a
excéntrico/a
individualista

Cristóbal Colón, Marie Curie, Galileo Galilei
curioso/a
determinado/a
visionario/a

La personalidad de los famosos

Don Quijote, Emiliano Zapata
luchador[a]
soñador[b]
valiente

Don Juan Tenorio, Eva Perón, Madonna
astuto/a
encantador(a)
seductor(a)

Frida Kahlo, Abraham Lincoln
melancólico/a
serio/a
tenaz[c]

[a]*fighter* [b]*dreamer* [c]*tenacious*

Vocabulario útil

ceder	to yield	frívolo/a	
aburrido/a		incierto/a	
ambicioso/a		indiferente	
apático/a		justo/a	
cobarde	coward, cowardly	malévolo/a	evil
conformista		práctico/a	
de poco interés		superficial	
dócil		tonto/a	

ACTIVIDAD A Antónimos

Escucha lo que dice tu profesor(a). Luego indica la palabra opuesta.

1. **a.** visionario
   b. indiferente
   c. de poco interés
2. **a.** incierto
   b. apático
   c. apasionado
3. **a.** indiferente
   b. determinado
   c. superficial
4. **a.** cobarde
   b. luchador
   c. tenaz
5. **a.** seductor
   b. justo
   c. conformista

ACTIVIDAD B Si uno es...

Escoge la cualidad que mejor complete cada oración.

1. Si uno es curioso y (e) _____ puede hacer muchas cosas buenas.
   a. perezoso   **b.** cobarde   **c.** inteligente   **d.** tonto
2. Si uno es soñador y (e) _____ puede tener una vida feliz.
   a. aburrido   **b.** optimista   **c.** indeciso   **d.** retraído
3. Si uno es astuto y (e) _____ puede tener una buena carrera en mercadeo (*marketing*).
   a. imaginativo   **b.** apático   **c.** ingenuo   **d.** tímido
4. Si uno es dócil y _____ siempre hace lo que quieren los demás.
   a. valiente   **b.** justo   **c.** práctico   **d.** conformista
5. Si uno es encantador y (e) _____ puede manipular a los demás para conseguir lo que quiere.
   a. seductor   **b.** individualista   **c.** luchador   **d.** de poco interés

ACTIVIDAD C Personajes de la televisión

Escucha lo que dice tu profesor(a) sobre un personaje de la televisión. Si no estás de acuerdo con lo que dice, da otras cualidades para describir al personaje.

1...   2...   3...   4...   5...

ACTIVIDAD D ¡Entrevisten al profesor (a la profesora)!

La clase se debe dividir en grupos de tres personas. A cada grupo se le debe asignar una de las siguientes cualidades. Cada grupo debe escribir una oración sobre el profesor (la profesora), utilizando el modelo. Al final, el profesor (la profesora) dirá (*will say*) si todos tienen razón o no.

apasionado/a   individualista   soñador(a)
determinado/a   serio/a

MODELO   Nosotros creemos que la profesora es muy determinada.

ACTIVIDAD E Una persona famosa

Escoge una persona famosa de la siguiente lista. Luego escribe algunas oraciones como las del modelo sobre esta persona. Por fin, entrégale tu papel a tu profesor(a).

Vicente Van Gogh   Leonardo da Vinci   Isabel I de Inglaterra
Hillary Clinton   Bill Gates   ¿ ?

MODELO   Creo que _____ es (era) una persona interesante. Es (Era) _____ y (e) _____. Esas cualidades me interesan más que otras…

ACTIVIDAD F ¿Sabías que... ?

Paso 1 Lee la selección **¿Sabías que... ?** en la siguiente página. Luego contesta las preguntas a continuación.

1. Al escribir *Don Quijote,* Cervantes quiso escribir una novela seria sobre el espíritu humano. ¿Sí o no?

2. Don Quijote decidió hacerse caballero después de leer muchas novelas. ¿Sí o no?

3. En realidad, Don Quijote no era soñador ni idealista sino una persona que no sabía la diferencia entre la realidad y la ficción. ¿Sí o no?

4. ¿Has oído las expresiones *tilting at windmills* y *quixotic nature*? ¿Cuál de las siguientes ideas capta mejor el sentido de estas expresiones?

   a. Se dice de alguien determinado, tenaz, valiente, individualista y con afán de realización.

   b. Se dice de alguien quizás un poco ingenuo, que no ve el lado práctico de las cosas y que lucha por causas imposibles.

Paso 2 *Don Quijote* fue una reacción a las novelas populares de los tiempos de Cervantes. ¿Conoces tú obras literarias o películas que son sátiras de algo popular? ¿Qué sabes de estas obras: (1) *Naked Gun;* (2) *Rocky Horror Picture Show;* (3) *Shrek?* ¿Puedes describir a los personajes principales?

¿Sabías que...

el famoso personaje, Don Quijote de la Mancha, se creó como un tipo de antihéroe? Aunque todos conocemos al Quijote como el soñador idealista, en realidad esa no fue la intención de Miguel de Cervantes al crear a este personaje. La idea de Cervantes era escribir una sátira de las novelas corrientes de su época, las novelas de caballería.[a] En estas novelas siempre había un caballero que realizaba[b] hazañas[c] nobles y extraordinarias, salvando a damas y pueblos enteros. Era valiente, luchador, justo y determinado —cualidades ideales pero no muy reales. En cambio, lo que escribió Cervantes es el relato de un hombre enloquecido[d] que en busca de aventuras hace disparates[e] verdaderos.

Al principio de la novela, Don Quijote (que no es su nombre verdadero) es un simple señor con una obsesión por las novelas de caballería. Pasa tanto tiempo leyendo dichas novelas que pierde el juicio[f] y decide hacerse caballero como los que aparecen en las novelas. A causa de su locura,[g] ve lo que quiere ver: molinos[h] que le parecen «gigantes malévolos», sirvientas que ve como «damas nobles y bellas» y un rocín[i] que para él es un «noble caballo». En fin, crea su propio mundo. Muchas de las escenas son bastante cómicas y algunas de ellas son las más conocidas de la historia de la literatura. Al final de la obra Don Quijote regresa a casa, se enferma, recobra el juicio y luego muere. Desde su publicación en 1605, *Don Quijote* se ha traducido a 60 idiomas, ha sido objeto de muchos estudios filosóficos y ha inspirado obras de teatro, películas y canciones. Lo que empezó como una burla, llegó a ser una de las obras más leídas y comentadas del mundo, con un personaje que se ha convertido en el típico soñador optimista.

Don Quijote *se ha traducido a más de 60 idiomas como se ve en este ejemplo de Francia.*

[a]*knighthood* [b]*performed* [c]*deeds* [d]*crazed* [e]*absurdities* [f]*pierde... he loses his mind* [g]*craziness* [h]*windmills* [i]*nag, old workhorse*

NAVEGANDO LA RED

Busca información sobre uno de los siguientes personajes reales o ficticios: Don Quijote, Don Juan Tenorio, Eva Perón, Frida Kahlo, Diego Rivera, Pablo Picasso. ¿Cómo es el personaje? Busca también algunos datos biográficos básicos (por ejemplo, lugar de origen, fechas en que nació y murió, etcétera). Luego presenta tus resultados a la clase.

IDEAS PARA EXPLORAR

Situaciones hipotéticas

GRAMÁTICA

¿Qué harías? (I)

Introduction to the conditional tense

tomar ser vivir	+	-ía -ías -ía -ía -íamos -íais -ían -ían

—¿Qué **harías** tú para conocer a una
  persona famosa?
—No sé. Pero me **gustaría** conocer a
  Brad Pitt.

The *conditional* is used to express hypothetical situations and is roughly equivalent to English *would* + verb. You are probably already familiar with the conditional in the expression **Me gustaría.** Here are other examples.

¿Cómo **sería** el mundo sin
  los idealistas?

*What would the world be like
  without idealists?*

¿Cómo **tratarías** a alguien
  como Don Quijote?

*How would you treat
  someone like Don Quijote?*

The conditional is formed by adding **-ía** and person and number endings to the infinitive.

ser   sería, serías, sería, sería,
        seríamos, seríais, serían, serían

Note that the forms for **yo, él/ella,** and **Ud.** are the same. Context will often help determine the subject. Here are a few common verbs that are irregular in the conditional.

decir → **dir-**   diría, dirías, diría, diría,
                  diríamos, diríais, dirían, dirían

hacer → **har-**   haría, harías, haría, haría,
                  haríamos, haríais, harían, harían

poder → **podr-**   podría, podrías, podría, podría,
                  podríamos, podríais, podrían, podrían

salir → **saldr-** saldría, saldrías, saldría, saldría
saldríamos, saldríais, saldrían, saldrían

tener → **tendr-** tendría, tendrías, tendría, tendría,
tendríamos, tendríais, tendrían, tendrían

haber → **habría** (*there would be*)

You will often see the conditional used with what is called the *past
subjunctive* to make *if . . . then* statements of a hypothetical nature.

Si conocieras a alguien como *If you met someone like Don Quijote,*
Don Quijote, ¿qué le **dirías**? *what would you say to him* (*her*)?

For now, we will concentrate on the conditional. (You will learn more
about the past subjunctive later in this lesson.)

ACTIVIDAD A Nuestros límites

Paso 1 Escoge el verbo que mejor complete cada oración.

Yo...

1. nunca _____ más de $150 por un par de zapatos.
   a. haría **b.** bebería **c.** pagaría

2. nunca _____ con una persona sólo porque es rica.
   a. me casaría **b.** vería **c.** me quejaría

3. nunca _____ la tarea de otra persona para luego entregársela al
   profesor (a la profesora).
   a. copiaría **b.** estudiaría **c.** asistiría

4. nunca _____ a vivir a otro país sin hablar la lengua de ese lugar.
   a. visitaría **b.** iría **c.** sería

5. nunca _____ sólo para proteger a un amigo.
   a. saldría **b.** tendría nada **c.** mentiría

Paso 2 Vuelve a las oraciones del **Paso 1** y escoge la que te parezca
más interesante. Luego indica si para ti es cierta, falsa o si depende de
las circunstancias.

Paso 3 Utilizando la oración que escogiste en el **Paso 2,** entrevista a
cinco compañeros/as. ¿Cómo contestan ellos? ¿Igual que tú?

MODELO ¿Pagarías más de $150 por un par de zapatos?

ACTIVIDAD B ¿Que harías por $10.000?

Indica lo que harías por $10.000. ¿Harían tus compañeros las mismas
acciones?

Por $10.000 yo...

☐ **1.** dormiría solo/a en un cementerio por una semana entera.

☐ **2.** saltaría del edificio más alto del mundo en paracaídas.

☐ **3.** asistiría a mis clases vestido/a de (*dressed like*) gorila por un día
entero.

☐ **4.** nadaría en aguas donde suelen aparecer tiburones (*sharks*).

☐ **5.** comería un plato entero de gusanos (*worms*) vivos.

☐ **6.** viviría en la selva (*jungle*) con una tribu de gorilas por una semana.

☐ **7.** suspendería (*I would fail*) una de mis clases a propósito.

☐ **8.** cantaría solo/a el himno nacional (*national anthem*) en público durante el campeonato (*championship*) de algún deporte.

ACTIVIDAD C ¿Quién lo haría?

Paso 1 Escoge cinco de las acciones de la **Actividad B.** Luego, utilizando el nuevo vocabulario de esta lección y de la lección anterior, indica quién o qué tipo de persona haría esas acciones.

MODELO   Sólo una persona muy valiente nadaría en aguas con tiburones.

Paso 2 Ahora compartan todos sus ideas. ¿Son parecidas?

COMUNICACIÓN

 ACTIVIDAD D ¿Cuánto pagarías por conocerlo/la?

Paso 1 Apunta el nombre de una persona famosa que quieres conocer. Luego escribe dos o tres cosas que harías para conocer a esa persona, utilizando el modelo a continuación. Debes pensar en estas preguntas y otras que se te ocurran (*that come to mind*): ¿Pagarías una cantidad de dinero extraordinaria? ¿Harías algo peligroso? ¿vergonzoso? ¿asqueroso (*disgusting*)? ¿prohibido?

MODELO   Para conocer a _____ yo _____.

Paso 2 Busca a otras personas en la clase que quieran conocer a la misma persona o a otra persona de la misma categoría u ocupación (por ejemplo, actor, político, artista, etcétera). ¿Harían lo mismo para conocer a la persona? ¿Quién es el más atrevido (la más atrevida) de la clase?

GRAMÁTICA

¿Y si pudieras... ?

Introduction to the past subjunctive

(yo)	me acostara comiera viviera	(nosotros/as)	-áramos -iéramos
(tú)	te acostaras comieras vivieras	(vosotros/as)	-arais -ierais
(Ud.)	se acostara comiera viviera	(Uds.)	-aran -ieran
(él/ella)	se acostara comiera viviera	(ellos/ellas)	-aran -ieran

—Ah, **si** sólo **pudiera** conocer a George Clooney.

Very often we need to express concepts that are *contrary to fact* or *hypothetical*. In English, we use the conditional and a form of the past.

I would go to Europe tomorrow if I had the money.
If Juan were here now, I'd tell him what I'm thinking.

These are called hypothetical situations because they express situations in which something does not exist. In the first example, the speaker doesn't have the money and, in the second Juan is not present. The speaker *hypothesizes* what would happen if the conditions were true.

In Spanish, the same constructions exist. You would use the conditional in Spanish where you would use the conditional in English, but in the *if clause* you would use a different verb form called the *past subjunctive*.

Iría a Europa mañana si **tuviera** dinero.
Si Juan **estuviera** presente le diría lo que pienso.

The stem or root of the past subjunctive is the same as that used in the **ellos** form of the preterite, for example: **trabajaron → trabaj-, estuvieron → estuv-, pidieron → pid-,** and so forth. Note that all regularities or irregularities are carried over if they appear in the **ellos** form of the preterite. The endings for the past subjunctive are based on **-ara-** for **-ar** verbs and **-iera-** for **-er** and **-ir** verbs. For example, for the **yo** form, the past subjunctive of **trabajar** would be **trabaj- + -ara → trabajara.** The **tú** form would have the characteristic **-s** on the end, that is, **trabajaras.** For **comer,** the **yo** and **tú** forms would be **comiera** and **comieras.** The **yo, Ud.,** and **él/ella** forms are identical.

As a reminder, here are the common irregular preterite forms with the derivation of the past subjunctive stem. All of these common irregular verbs, whether **-ar, -er,** or **-ir,** take the **-iera-** endings.

estar: estuvieron → estuv- → estuviera, estuvieras, estuviera,…
tener: tuvieron → tuv- → tuviera, tuvieras, tuviera,…
hacer: hicieron → hic- → hiciera, hicieras, hiciera,…
saber: supieron → sup- → supiera, supieras, supiera,…
poder: pudieron → pud- → pudiera, pudieras, pudiera,…
decir: dijeron → dij- → dijera,* dijeras, dijera,…

In this lesson, you will mostly work with singular forms of the past subjunctive as in the following examples.

¿Qué harías **si no tuvieras** que estudiar?
Si pudiera, iría contigo esta noche.
No sé lo que Juan diría **si supiera** la verdad.

What would you do if you didn't have to study?
If I could, I'd go with you tonight.
I don't know what Juan would say if he knew the truth.

---

*With irregular stems that end in **j,** the **i** in the verb ending **-iera** is dropped.

Lección 14   ¿A quién te gustaría conocer?

ACTIVIDAD E Situaciones hipotéticas

Paso 1 Indica lo que harías en cada situación.

1. Si encontrara veinte dólares en el piso...
   - ☐ **a.** los guardaría y no diría nada.
   - ☐ **b.** se los daría a una persona desamparada (*homeless*).
   - ☐ **c.** se los daría a la policía.

2. Si viera un accidente entre dos carros...
   - ☐ **a.** me pararía (*I would stop*) y ofrecería ayuda.
   - ☐ **b.** seguiría mi ruta pensando que la policía se ocuparía del asunto (*would handle the situation*).

3. Si un amigo me confesara que robó una casa...
   - ☐ **a.** lo reportaría a la policía.
   - ☐ **b.** me quedaría callado sin decirle nada a nadie.
   - ☐ **c.** dejaría de ser amigo de esa persona.

4. Si un amigo copiara el examen de otro...
   - ☐ **a.** se lo diría al profesor (a la profesora).
   - ☐ **b.** le diría a mi amigo que debe confesar lo que ha hecho.
   - ☐ **c.** dejaría de ser amigo de esa persona.

5. Si alguien me contara un buen chisme...
   - ☐ **a.** se lo contaría a mis amigos.
   - ☐ **b.** se lo contaría sólo a mi mejor amigo.
   - ☐ **c.** no se lo contaría a nadie.

Paso 2 Ahora comparte tus respuestas del **Paso 1** con otra persona. ¿Son iguales? ¿Qué adjetivos pueden utilizar para describir su personalidad a base de sus respuestas?

ACTIVIDAD F ¿Y tu profesor(a)?

¿Conoces bien a tu profesor(a)? Con otra persona, determina cuál parece ser la opción más lógica. Luego escucha las instrucciones del profesor (de la profesora).

1. Si tu profesor(a) tuviera otra profesión, ¿cuál de las siguientes sería?

a. doctor(a)	**c.** veterinario/a	**e.** artista
b. actor (actriz)	**d.** persona de negocios	

2. Si tu profesor(a) no hablara español, ¿qué otro idioma hablaría?

a. francés	**c.** árabe	**e.** chino
b. japonés	**d.** navajo	

3. Si tu profesor(a) fuera un animal, ¿cuál sería?

a. un perro	**c.** un gato	**e.** un chimpancé
b. un águila (*eagle*)	**d.** un búho (*owl*)	

4. Si tu profesor(a) pudiera hacer un viaje, ¿adónde iría?

    a. a Europa   **c.** a África   **e.** a Australia

    b. al Oriente   **d.** a otro planeta

5. Si tu profesor(a) tuviera la oportunidad de conocer a cualquier persona, ¿a quién conocería?

 ACTIVIDAD G Si yo fuera...

Paso 1 Escribe el nombre de una persona famosa (viva o ya muerta) que te gustaría ser por un día.

Paso 2 Ahora explica en qué sería diferente tu vida si fueras esa persona. Menciona por lo menos dos ideas sin mostrárselas a otra persona.

    MODELO   Me gustaría ser presidente de los Estados Unidos por un día. Si fuera él, no dormiría mucho pero tendría mucho poder.

Paso 3 Entrégale tu papel al profesor (a la profesora). Si él (ella) lee tus ideas a la clase, ¿pueden los demás adivinar que son tuyas (*yours*)?

Paso 4 Para cada persona cuyas ideas lee el profesor (la profesora), los demás deben mencionar por lo menos una idea en que esa persona no ha pensado.

    MODELO   Si fueras presidente, también tendrías que viajar mucho. ¿Te gustaría pasar tanto tiempo en avión?

ACTIVIDAD H ¿Qué cambiarías?

Paso 1 Trabajando con un compañero (una compañera) de clase, explica qué aspectos de personalidad de las siguientes personas les cambiarías y por qué los cambiarías.

    MODELO   A mi madre le combiaría su carácter paranoico. A veces ella... Sería mejor si ella fuera más (menos)...

1. amigo/a   **3.** padre (madre)

2. compañero/a de casa   **4.** profesor(a)

Paso 2 Compartan sus ideas con el resto de la clase. ¿Hay ciertas cualidades que se mencionan mucho?

NAVEGANDO LA RED

Busca información sobre la vida diaria de un político (una mujer político) o un actor (una actriz). Comparte tu información con la clase y luego indica si te gustaría tener una vida semejante.

En busca de personas conocidas

GRAMÁTICA

¿A quién... ?

You may recall from **Lección 4** that the preposition **a** is used to mark objects of a verb when both the subject and object of the verb are equally capable of performing the action. There is no English equivalent.

Jaime ve **a** Ricardo	*Jaime sees Ricardo. (Both Jaime and Ricardo are capable of the act of seeing. **A** is required.)*
Jaime ve el edificio.	*Jaime sees the building. (Only Jaime is capable of the act of seeing. No **a** is required.)*
El perro muerde **al** gato.	*The dog bites the cat. (Both the dog and the cat are capable of the act of biting. **A** is required.)*
El perro muerde la pelota.	*The dog bites the ball. (Only the dog is capable of the act of biting. No **a** is necessary.)*

Having an object marker like **a** gives Spanish more flexible word order than English, so be sure not to mistake an object for a subject just because it precedes the verb. Do you know who is the subject and who is the object in the following sentences?

Al perro lo muerde el gato.*
A María no la entiende bien Juan.
¿A quién busca Reinaldo?

ACTIVIDAD A ¿A quién... ?

Paso 1 Contesta las siguientes preguntas como en el modelo.

MODELO ¿A quién adora Lucy (de *Peanuts*)? A Schroeder (el pianista).

1. ¿A quién amaba secretamente Superman?
2. ¿A quién molestaba siempre Bugs Bunny?
3. ¿A quién engañaba siempre Lucy Ricardo?
4. ¿A quién buscaba el Capitán Hook?
5. ¿A qué detective ayudaba el señor Watson?
6. ¿A quién mató Mark David Chapman en 1980?

---

*When object nouns appear before the verb, a corresponding pronoun is usually inserted. **Al profesor lo** conocemos bien.

Paso 2 Ahora con otra persona, inventa dos preguntas, una fácil y otra más difícil, utilizando las preguntas del **Paso 1** como modelos. Luego preséntenlas a la clase.

COMUNICACIÓN

ACTIVIDAD B La admiración...

Paso 1 Contesta las siguientes preguntas con una oración completa.

1. ¿A qué persona famosa admiras más?

2. ¿A qué persona famosa detestas?

Paso 2 Todos deben contestar las preguntas mientras que el profesor (la profesora) apunta los nombres en la pizarra. ¿Qué tendencias hay en las respuestas?

GRAMÁTICA

¿Te gustaría... ?

Review of the verb **gustar**

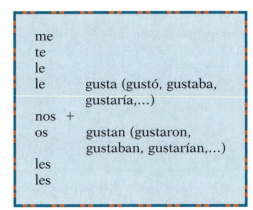

me
te
le
le   gusta (gustó, gustaba, gustaría,...)
nos +
os   gustan (gustaron, gustaban, gustarían,...)
les
les

—Dime, ¿a quién más **te gustaría** conocer?

Remember that there is no Spanish equivalent of the verb *to like*. To express something similar, Spanish uses **gustar,** which means something like *to please*. The person or thing that is pleased almost always precedes the verb. The subject follows. Remember that the thing or person pleased must be marked with an **a** to distinguish it from the subject.

    A mi papá no **le gustan** los políticos.

        los políticos = subject (they are the ones not pleasing)
        mi papá = indirect object (he is the one that is not pleased)
        gustan = plural (because **los políticos** is a plural subject)

When referring to yourself, to a friend, to yourself and other people, or to a group of friends in Spain, you do not need a phrase with **a.** The object pronoun is sufficient.

No **me** gustan las matemáticas.	**Nos** gusta esta película.
¿**Te** gustan tus clases?	¿**Os** gusta la paella?

You may, however, use **a mí, a ti, a nosotros/as,** or **a vosotros/as** for emphasis, similar to, "Well, as for me (you, us, you [all]), . . ."

A mí no me gustan para nada.　　**A nosotras,** sí, nos gustan.
¿**A ti** te gustan?　　　　　　　　¿**A vosotras,** os gusta?

No matter what, you will always need to use **me, te, le, nos, os,** or **les** in your sentence.

Así se dice

You've probably noticed that **gustar** tends to appear in one of two forms: **gusta** or **gustan.** That's because we are usually talking about inanimate things being pleasing to someone. It is possible, however, to use **gustar** in other forms when talking about people, but the connotation may be romantic! Imagine the following exchange between two people on a date.

　—**Me gustas mucho.**
　—**Tú también me gustas.**

To avoid giving someone the wrong impression, if you want to say you are fond of that person in a nonromantic way, you should use **querer** or **caer bien.** (Although **querer** can be used romantically as well.) **Te quiero mucho** could easily be said between family members or friends. **Me caes bien** would be said among friends only. Note that if you are talking about famous people, you aren't usually expressing something romantic.

　Me gusta mucho Shakira. ¿Y a ti?

ACTIVIDAD C Gustos

Escucha lo que dice tu profesor(a). Luego indica cuál de las opciones podría terminar cada oración. Después contesta la pregunta.

1. a. lo típico.　　　　　　**b.** las cosas extrañas (*weird*).

¿Lo diría una persona individualista o conformista?

2. a. luchar.　　　　　　　**b.** los problemas difíciles.

¿Lo diría una persona valiente o pacifista?

3. a. el amor.　　　　　　　**b.** las mujeres.

¿Lo diría una persona seductora o visionaria?

4. a. el trabajo regular.　　**b.** los trabajos intensivos.

¿Lo diría una persona apática o trabajadora?

ACTIVIDAD D Firma aquí

Paso 1 Busca a personas en la clase que contesten afirmativamente las siguientes preguntas. En las preguntas 5 y 6, piensa tú en alguien.

1. ¿Te gusta Shakira? ____

2. ¿Te gusta Enrique Iglesias? ____

3. ¿Te gustan los Black Eyed Peas? ____

4. ¿Te gusta... ? ____

5. ¿Te gustan... ? ____

Paso 2 Reporta lo que aprendiste, utilizando el modelo.

MODELO A Mark le gusta mucho Shakira.

Paso 3 Indica si te gustaría conocer a una de las personas mencionadas.

MODELO A mí me gustaría conocer a los Black Eyed Peas.

ACTIVIDAD E ¿Cómo soy?

Paso 1 Utilizando las cualidades que has aprendido en esta lección y en la anterior, apunta las cualidades que tú crees que posees.

Soy...

Paso 2 En dos o tres oraciones, explica si te gustaría tener otras cualidades.

MODELO Soy conformista pero me gustaría ser un poco más individualista. Me gustaría ser siempre como quiero ser sin pensar en lo que opinan de mí los demás.

Paso 3 Comparte lo que escribiste con otras dos personas. ¿Están todos contentos con ser como son o les gustaría cambiar alguna de sus cualidades?

ACTIVIDAD F En tu opinión

Paso 1 En grupos de tres, comenten la idea de que las personas cambian. A continuación hay una lista de ideas para considerar. Den ejemplos de sus experiencias personales cuando sea posible.

◆ los cambios que ocurren entre la niñez y la adolescencia
◆ los cambios que ocurren debido a nuevas experiencias (viajar al extranjero; asistir a la universidad)
◆ los efectos de una relación amorosa
◆ los efectos de una muerte (un divorcio)

Paso 2 Compartan sus ideas con el resto de la clase. ¿Cuántos dicen que las personas cambian? ¿Cuántos dicen que las personas no cambian?

NAVEGANDO LA RED

Busca información sobre una persona famosa de habla española, por ejemplo, Enrique Iglesias, Shakira, Jennifer López, Luis Miguel. ¿Qué tipo de vida lleva esa persona? Presenta tus resultados a la clase e indica si llevarías una vida igual o diferente si fueras esa persona.

INTERCAMBIO

¿A quién te gustaría conocer?

Propósito: comparar lo que dice un compañero (una compañera) con lo que tú piensas

Papeles: tres personas entrevistadas; el resto de la clase hace preguntas

Paso 1 Tres voluntarios deben pensar en la siguiente pregunta porque la clase los va a entrevistar en unos minutos: ¿A qué persona (viva o muerta) te gustaría conocer y por qué? Los demás deben pensar en otras preguntas para obtener información basada en las siguientes categorías.

1. cualidades de la persona famosa

2. cosas que la persona famosa ha hecho

3. lo que haría la persona entrevistada si conociera a la persona famosa (Por ejemplo, ¿qué podrían hacer juntas las dos?)

4. lo que haría la persona entrevistada si fuera la persona famosa por un día

Paso 2 Escucha las instrucciones de tu profesor(a).

Paso 3 Después escoge *una* de las entrevistas para escribir una breve reacción (de 70 palabras como máximo), utilizando el siguiente modelo.

MODELOS A mí también me gustaría conocer a _____. (Explica por qué y si tú harías las mismas cosas.)
o
A mí no me gustaría conocer a _____. (Explica por qué no y luego a quién te gustaría conocer y por qué.)

Vistazos culturales
Las ciencias en el mundo hispano

¿Sabías que... los hispanos han ganado un total de veintitrés Premios Nobel? Desde principios del siglo XX los hispanos han hecho muchos trabajos pioneros en las ciencias naturales, sobre todo en los campos de la fisiología, la física y la química. Además, en los años 90 y los primeros años del siglo actual, la Argentina se ha hecho mundialmente famosa por sus estudios en la paleontología debido a unos descubrimientos importantes sobre los dinosaurios.

Premios Nobel ganados por hispanos en el mundo

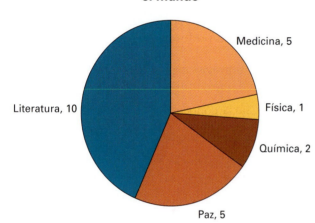

- Medicina, 5
- Física, 1
- Química, 2
- Paz, 5
- Literatura, 10

Octavio Paz (1914–1998) fue el último hispanohablante en recibir el Premio Nobel de Literatura en 1990.

Premios Nobel en las ciencias

- ◆ **1906, Santiago Ramón y Cajal (español):** por su trabajo sobre la estructura del sistema nervioso
- ◆ **1947, Bernardo Houssay (argentino):** por el descubrimiento del papel que hace una hormona en el metabolismo del azúcar
- ◆ **1959, Severo Ochoa (español):** por sus descubrimientos en la síntesis biológica de los ácidos nucleicos
- ◆ **1968, Luis W. Álvarez (norteamericano):** por sus contribuciones a la física de las partículas subatómicas
- ◆ **1970, Luis Leloir (argentino):** por su trabajo en la biosíntesis de los carbohidratos
- ◆ **1980, Baruj Benacerraf (venezolano):** por su trabajo en inmunología
- ◆ **1984, César Milstein (argentino):** por su trabajo y sus descubrimientos en inmunología
- ◆ **1995, Mario Molino (norteamericano):** por su trabajo sobre cómo la producción y el uso de varios productos dañan la capa de ozono

En la Patagonia argentina, unos descubrimientos importantes han cambiado drásticamente nuestros conocimientos[a] sobre los dinosaurios. En la provincia de Neuquén, se ha descubierto una región de miles de huevos fósiles que se extiende por más de 20 kilómetros. Además, se han encontrado huesos fósiles de un tamaño nunca visto antes en la historia de la paleontología.

[a]*knowledge*

En 1987 se descubrió el dinosaurio más grande del mundo, ahora llamado el Argentinosaurio. Medía[a] 30 metros de largo y pesaba más de 100 toneladas. Andaba en cuatro patas[b] y tenía un cuello largo que usaba para comer árboles.

[a]*It measured*   [b]*feet*

NEUQUÉN

Durante el Período Cretáceo, la Patagonia era una zona húmeda. Ahora es un lugar árido.

En 1993 se descubrió el dinosaurio carnívoro más grande del mundo, ahora llamado el Giganotosaurio. Medía 15 metros de largo, 2 metros de alto y pesaba más de 8 toneladas. Andaba en dos patas y comía dinosaurios diez veces más grandes que él, incluyendo el enorme Argentinosaurio.

Reproducción del esqueleto de un Argentinosauro en el Fernbank Museum en Atlanta, Georgia.

ACTIVIDAD ¿Qué recuerdas?

Completa las siguientes oraciones.

1. La _____ es una región árida de Sudamérica donde se han hecho investigaciones sobre los dinosaurios.

2. Los hispanos han ganado _____ Premios Nobel en las ciencias.

3. El dinosaurio carnívoro más grande del mundo era el _____.

4. En la provincia de _____ de la Argentina se han encontrado miles de huevos fósiles de dinosaurios.

5. El dinosaurio más grande del mundo era el _____.

6. _____ ganó el Premio Nobel por su trabajo sobre la capa de ozono.

NAVEGANDO LA RED

Escoge *uno* de los siguientes proyectos. Luego presenta tus resultados a la clase.

1. Busca información sobre el número de casos del Síndrome de Inmunodeficiencia Adquirida (SIDA*) en los países hispanos. Luego haz lo siguiente.
   a. Prepara una lista de todos los países hispanos y el número de personas contagiadas por el Virus de Inmunodeficiencia Humana (VIH[†]).
   b. Indica en qué país o región del mundo hispano es más alto el número de personas con VIH y en qué país o región es más bajo.

2. Busca información sobre el uso de la tecnología en el mundo hispano. Luego haz lo siguiente.
   a. Crea una tabla que muestre los nombres de los países hispanos y el número de usuarios (*users*) de la Red en cada país. Reporta también el porcentaje de la población total que representan estos usuarios.
   b. Agrega otra columna a la tabla que muestre el número de usuarios de teléfono celular en los países hispanos. Reporta también el porcentaje de la población total que representan estos usuarios.
   c. Compara el uso de estas tecnologías en el mundo hispano con su uso en este país.

---

*AIDS
[†]HIV

Lección 14 ¿A quién te gustaría conocer?

VOCABULARIO COMPRENSIVO

Las cualidades personales

	Personal Qualities
aburrido/a (R)	boring
ambicioso/a	ambitious
apasionado/a	passionate
apático/a	apathetic
astuto/a	astute
cobarde	coward, cowardly
conformista	conformist
curioso/a	curious
determinado/a	determined
dócil	docile
encantador(a) (R)	charming
excéntrico/a	eccentric
frívolo/a	frivolous
incierto/a	uncertain

indiferente	indifferent
individualista	individualistic
justo/a	fair, just
luchador(a)	fighter
malévolo/a	evil
melancólico/a	melancholy, sad
práctico/a	practical
seductor(a)	seductive
serio/a	serious
soñador(a)	dreamer
superficial	superficial
tenaz	tenacious
tonto/a	foolish, dumb
valiente	courageous
visionario/a	visionary

 LECCIÓN **15**

 Check out the following media resources to complement this lesson:

Online *Manual* **Online Learning Center**

Video on CD **ActivityPak**

¿Innato o aprendido?

Muchos se han preguntado si el carácter de una persona es algo innato o si es producto del ambiente. ¿Qué crees tú? En esta lección, vas a explorar este tema y vas a

◆ aprender a expresar relaciones espaciales usando preposiciones

◆ aprender a dar y a seguir instrucciones para ir a un lugar

◆ aprender algo más sobre la preposición **por**

◆ usar **lo** + *adjetivo* para expresar tu opinión de algo

◆ leer algo sobre lo que es innato o aprendido en los animales

◆ leer información sobre la personalidad y la genética

ALTO Before beginning this lesson, look over the **Composición** activity on pages 396–397. This is the activity you will be working toward throughout the lesson.

¿Qué rasgos de personalidad crees que comparten estas gemelas de México D.F.?

IDEAS PARA EXPLORAR

De aquí para allá

VOCABULARIO

¿Dónde está la biblioteca?

Telling where things are

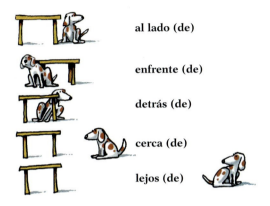

al lado (de)

enfrente (de)

detrás (de)

cerca (de)

lejos (de)

Así se dice

Have you seen the word **quedar** used instead of **estar** to refer to location? Although both **estar** and **quedar** can be used to talk about the location of things (buildings, cities, places), only **estar** can be used to talk about animate beings.

estar (quedar)
¿Dónde **está (queda)** la oficina principal?
Colombia **está (queda)** al norte del Perú.

estar
¿Dónde **está** el secretario?
Manuel **está** en Colombia ahora.

When talking about location, **estar** is normally used.

El perro **está** al lado de la mesa.
—¿Dónde **estás**?
—**Estoy** cerca de la plaza.

Note that the preposition **de** is used with **al lado** (*next to, alongside*), **enfrente** (*in front*), **detrás** (*behind*), **cerca** (*near, close*), and **lejos** (*far*) when a point of reference is mentioned.

La biblioteca está **enfrente de** la cafetería.

You can omit **de** if a point of reference is not explicitly mentioned.

—¿Sabes dónde está la cafetería?
—Sí…
—Pues, la biblioteca está **al lado.**

ACTIVIDAD A ¿Sí o no?

Escucha lo que dice tu profesor(a). ¿Es cierto o falso?

1… **2**… **3**… **4**… **5**… **etcétera**

ACTIVIDAD B ¿Qué edificio es?

Escucha lo que dice tu profesor(a) y da la información que pide.

1... 2... 3... 4... 5... etcétera

ACTIVIDAD C Una prueba

Con un compañero (una compañera), crea una prueba para darle a la clase.

Paso 1 Escojan un punto de referencia en el *campus* o en la ciudad. **¡OJO!** Recuerden que no todos los estudiantes conocen bien la ciudad.

Paso 2 Decidan dónde van a poner a la persona que contesta la pregunta —es decir, si va a estar enfrente, detrás, a la derecha, al norte, etcétera, de este punto de referencia.

Paso 3 Escriban cinco preguntas.

> MODELOS Estás enfrente de las residencias estudiantiles. ¿Qué edificio está detrás?
>
> Estás a la derecha del gimnasio. ¿Qué edificio queda más cerca de allí?

Paso 4 Denle la prueba a la clase.

VOCABULARIO

¿Cómo se llega al zoológico?

Giving and receiving directions

—Por favor, ¿**dónde queda** el parque zoológico?

—A ver... **Siga Ud. por esta calle** hasta que llegue a una **bocacalle** con **semáforo.** Luego **doble a la izquierda** y **siga derecho** por siete **cuadras.** Allí en la **esquina** verá la entrada al parque zoológico. Pero está cerrado hoy...

Here are some useful expressions for requesting, giving, and following directions in Spanish.

¿Me podría decir... ?	Could you tell me . . . ?
Perdón, ¿cómo se llega a... ?	Excuse me, how do you get to . . . ?
¿Dónde está (queda)... ?	Where is . . . ?
Siga (Ud.) por...	Continue . . . , Follow . . .
Siga derecho (recto*)...	Continue (Go) straight . . .
Doble a la derecha (izquierda).	Turn right (left).
Cruce la calle...	Cross . . . Street
una cuadra (manzana*)	block
la bocacalle	intersection
la esquina	corner
el semáforo	traffic light

*****Recto** and **manzana** are dialectal variants used in some places, including Spain and Central America.

If you were giving directions to a friend or if a friend were giving directions to you, the familiar form of the commands would be used (**sigue, dobla,** and so forth).

 ## ACTIVIDAD D ¿Adónde llegas?

Escucha las direcciones* que da tu profesor(a). ¿Adónde llegas?

1… **2**… **3**… **4**… **etcétera**

 ## ACTIVIDAD E ¿Y tú?

Paso 1 Escucha lo que dice tu profesor(a). Indica si cada oración se te aplica siempre, a veces o nunca.

1… **2**… **3**… **4**… **5**… **6**… **7**…

Paso 2 ¿Cuáles son tus reacciones hacia el **Paso 1,** y cómo te comparas con los demás miembros de la clase? ¿Es cierto que a los hombres no les gusta pedir direcciones mientras que a las mujeres no les importa?

COMUNICACIÓN

ACTIVIDAD F ¿Lo pueden hacer?

Una persona voluntaria debe salir de la clase y esperar en el pasillo. Mientras tanto, la clase debe arreglar las sillas y mesas para formar una ruta que esa persona tendrá que (*will have to*) seguir según las direcciones que la clase le dará. Después de arreglar la ruta, alguien debe salir al pasillo y vendarle los ojos (*blindfold*) a la persona voluntaria. Cuando vuelva a la clase, los demás deben darle direcciones para guiarlo/la por la ruta. ¿Lo pueden hacer sin que él (ella) se tropiece con (*bumps into*) una silla?

Vocabulario útil
el paso   step   **¡Cuidado!**   Watch out! Careful!

ACTIVIDAD G ¿Sabías que… ?

Paso 1 ¿Sabes lo que es el sentido de orientación? El sentido de orientación se refiere a la habilidad de saber dónde está uno y no perderse. Indica si tienes tú buen sentido de orientación según la siguiente escala.

MI SENTIDO DE ORIENTACIÓN

excelente									**horrible**
10	9	8	7	6	5	4	3	2	1

Paso 2 Ahora lee la selección **¿Sabías que… ?** en la siguiente página. Luego contesta las preguntas.

---

*Other dialectal variants used to express *directions* include **indicaciones** and **instrucciones.**

¿Sabías que...

muchos animales tienen excelente sentido de orientación? A nosotros los seres humanos nos parece que nunca se pierden, siempre saben dónde están y algunos hacen viajes de miles de millas sin tener problemas en llegar al destino deseado. ¿Cómo lo hacen? Varios animales poseen un «tercer ojo» situado en alguna parte de la cabeza. Es un órgano de origen antiquísimo, que existió en varios animales hace 400 millones de años, según indican los fósiles. Los científicos han descubierto este tercer ojo en diversos animales que existen ahora como la salamandra, varios tipos de peces (como la trucha[a]), las serpientes y otros reptiles. Este tercer ojo es muy sensible a la luz y parece que los animales que lo poseen se orientan por el sol.

Mientras que los seres humanos consultamos una brújula para orientarnos, la abeja se orienta por la posición del sol.

En cambio, las abejas,[b] otra especie que parece tener un excelente sentido de orientación, poseen una «brújula[c] interna». Como en el caso del tercer ojo de los animales, esta brújula les permite a las abejas guiarse por el sol. A diferencia del tercer ojo, la brújula no funciona durante la noche. Como el tercer ojo es muy sensible a la luz, el animal que lo posee puede seguir orientándose por las estrellas.[d] La brújula interna de la abeja no le da esta habilidad.

Muchos creen que el sentido de orientación de los animales y su habilidad para viajar largas distancias son innatos, es decir, instintivos. Sin embargo, experimentos hechos con las abejas demuestran que no lo es. Cada abeja tiene que aprender a usar su brújula interna. Se ha comprobado que aun después de 60 vuelos, la abeja se pierde si no puede ver la colmena.[e] Sólo después de 500 vuelos aprende el funcionamiento de su brújula interna.

---

[a]*trout*   [b]*bees*   [c]*compass*   [d]*stars*   [e]*hive*

1. Explica con tus propias palabras lo que es «el tercer ojo», qué animales lo tienen y qué habilidad le da al animal.

2. Indica cuál(es) de las siguientes afirmaciones sobre la abeja es (son) cierta(s).

   ☐ La abeja nace con la habilidad de guiarse por el sol.

   ☐ La abeja también puede usar las estrellas para guiarse durante la noche.

   ☐ La abeja usa la colmena como punto de referencia.

Paso 3 Describe el sentido de orientación de los miembros de tu familia, usando las palabras y frases a continuación.

PARIENTE	ANIMAL	CATEGORÍA
madre	ave	cuando le dan direcciones
padre	reptil	cuando visita una ciudad
hermano/a	langosta (*locust*)	por primera vez
hijo/a	mariposa	para ir a la casa de un
abuelo/a	abeja	amigo por primera vez
	tortuga	sabe dónde queda el Norte

Mi padre tiene el sentido de orientación de una tortuga. Nunca necesita plano (*city map*). Es un misterio cómo él siempre sabe por dónde ir y cómo llegar a cualquier lugar cuando visitamos por primera vez una ciudad.

¿Cómo se orientan estas aves migratorias?

ACTIVIDAD H Una historia

Paso 1 Trabajando con un compañero (una compañera) de clase, inventa una historia para describir lo que pasa en los siguientes dibujos. A continuación tienen algunas ideas para considerar.

◆ ¿En qué ciudad están las mujeres?

◆ ¿Cómo se llaman las dos mujeres?

◆ ¿Qué cualidades poseen?

◆ ¿Por qué no encuentran el museo de arte?

1.

2.   **3.**

4.   **5.**

Paso 2 Compartan su historia con el resto de la clase. ¿Qué grupo inventó la historia más chistosa?

 NAVEGANDO LA RED

Busca el plano de la capital de un país hispano. Lleva el plano a clase y explica dónde queda el Palacio de Gobierno, el Palacio de Justicia, el Ayuntamiento (*City Hall*), etcétera, y si hay un parque central. ¿Crees que podrías visitar la ciudad sin perderte?

 # IDEAS PARA EXPLORAR
Lo interesante

GRAMÁTICA

¿Por dónde?

Por and **para** with spatial relationships

—Tiene que pasar **por** enfrente del Palacio de la Ópera...

Another distinction between **por** and **para** involves direction and space. In general, **para** is used to indicate a destination or goal. **Por** is used to indicate the space through which one travels or moves (the route). Compare the following sentences.

Salgo **para** Tikal mañana.
I'm leaving for Tikal tomorrow. (Tikal is my destination.)

Para llegar a Tikal, tienes que pasar **por** la selva.
To get to Tikal, you have to go through the jungle.

Para ir a la biblioteca, tienes que pasar **por** enfrente de la cafetería.
To get to the library, you have to go past the front of the cafeteria.

Although the English equivalent of **para** in these cases is generally *to,* the equivalent of **por** can be different expressions: *around, by way of, through,* and others.

ACTIVIDAD A ¿Destino o ruta?

Paso 1 Indica si el lugar mencionado en cada oración es el destino o la ruta de la persona que habla.

	DESTINO	RUTA
1. «Vamos para Oz».	☐	☐
2. «Tendríamos que ir por los Alpes».	☐	☐
3. «Viajo por todos los océanos en mi submarino».	☐	☐
4. «Salí para las Indias pero llegué a un territorio nuevo».	☐	☐
5. «Siempre bajo por la chimenea».	☐	☐

Paso 2 Ahora indica qué persona o personaje famoso podría decir cada oración.

COMUNICACIÓN

ACTIVIDAD B ¿Qué lugar es?

Paso 1 Escribe una oración sobre la universidad, la ciudad o algún lugar muy conocido, utilizando el siguiente modelo.

MODELO   Para ir a _____, tienes que pasar por _____.

Paso 2 Ahora cada persona debe leer su oración en voz alta (*aloud*). ¿Pueden los demás adivinar el destino que describes?

ACTIVIDAD C Para ir al museo...

En grupos de tres, escriban un diálogo para acompañar las situaciones que se ven en los dibujos de la **Actividad H** en las páginas 387–388. Utilicen **por** y **para** en su diálogo. Luego comparten su diálogo con la clase.

GRAMÁTICA

¿Qué es lo curioso de esto?

Lo + adjective

—Y **lo bueno** de esto es que cuesta muy poco.

Although in Spanish you can say **la cosa interesante es que...** there is another way to express "the . . . thing." Normally you can simply use **lo** (called the neuter article) with the adjective. Here are some examples.

Lo impresionante de Juan es su gran honestidad.
Lo interesante de María es que nunca se pierde en lugares desconocidos.
Lo curioso del inglés es que no tiene muchas inflexiones.

Just about any adjective can be used in this manner as long as it makes sense to do so.

Lo bueno de aprender español es que se habla en muchos lugares.
Lo difícil de viajar a Europa es el cambio de hora.

You may also use such phrases as superlatives to express "the most . . . thing" or "the . . . -est thing."

Lo más impresionante de todo es el sistema eficiente del Metro.
Lo más sorprendente del caso es que Roberto nunca se enteró (*found out*).

Notice that the adjective is always in the singular masculine form.

ACTIVIDAD D Lo interesante

Indica la frase que mejor complete la oración de una manera lógica.

1. (Sobre Arizona): Claro, _____ del estado es el Gran Cañón.

   a. lo más ridículo   **b.** lo más eficiente   **c.** lo más espectacular

2. (Sobre Stephen King): _____ de su carrera es el número de sus obras que ha sido base de películas.

   a. Lo ideal   **b.** Lo aburrido   **c.** Lo impresionante

3. (Para ir a Machu Picchu): _____ es subir las montañas donde se sitúa.

   a. Lo bueno   **b.** Lo difícil   **c.** Lo curioso

4. (Sobre las estatuas de la Isla de Pascua [*Easter Island*]): _____ es que su origen es desconocido.

   a. Lo curioso   **b.** Lo cómico   **c.** Lo fácil

5. (Sobre los secretos): _____, claro, es nunca decir lo que no quieres que se repita (*that you don't want repeated*).

   a. Lo prudente   **b.** Lo triste   **c.** Lo interesante

ACTIVIDAD E ¿Qué dices tú?

Paso 1 Indica cuál de las ideas te parece mejor y luego comparte tus respuestas con otras dos personas. ¿Están de acuerdo contigo?

1. Si un amigo (una amiga) te dice una mentira, lo más prudente es...

   ☐ **a.** no decirle nada.

   ☐ **b.** confrontarlo/la con la verdad.

   ☐ **c.** no hablarle más y dejar de ser su amigo/a.

   ☐ **d.** ¿ ?

2. Para impresionar a una persona en la primera cita, lo ideal sería...

   ☐ **a.** ser sincero/a y actuar con naturalidad.

   ☐ **b.** llevarle un regalito.

   ☐ **c.** darle muchos cumplidos (*compliments*).

   ☐ **d.** ¿ ?

3. Si tienes alguna cualidad que no te gusta, lo mejor sería...

   ☐ **a.** observar en otros alguna buena cualidad y tratar de imitarla.

   ☐ **b.** buscar terapia psicológica.

   ☐ **c.** aceptarla porque uno no puede dejar de ser lo que es.

   ☐ **d.** ¿ ?

Lección 15   ¿Innato o aprendido?

Paso 2 En grupos de tres, inventen una situación dejando la conclusión en blanco. Luego preséntenla a los demás para que decidan (*so that they decide*) cuál es la mejor solución.

> MODELO   Si alguien te dice algo negativo sobre tu mejor amigo/a, lo prudente sería...

ACTIVIDAD F ¡Aprender español!

Imagina que vas a contribuir con unas oraciones para un folleto sobre el aprendizaje del español. Utilizando una o dos de las siguientes frases, crea oraciones sobre el español. (Alternativa: Puedes hablar de la universidad.) Después, comparte tus oraciones con la clase.

lo bueno (mejor)	lo interesante	lo importante
lo (más) difícil	lo impresionante	lo ¿ ?

NAVEGANDO LA RED

Busca información sobre la enseñanza del español para extranjeros en países de habla española. ¿Qué institutos hay? ¿Cómo es el curso y cuánto cuesta? Luego completa lo siguiente y presenta tu información a la clase.

◆ Lo bueno de este curso (esta escuela) es...
◆ Lo malo es...

VAMOS A VER

ANTICIPACIÓN

Paso 1 Lee el título del artículo que aparece en las páginas 392–393. ¿Entiendes lo que significa? (la crianza = *upbringing*).

Paso 2 Ahora mira la foto que acompaña el artículo. ¿Recuerdas lo que son los gemelos? ¿En qué se parecen los gemelos idénticos? ¿Se parecen sólo físicamente o también en cuanto a la personalidad?

Paso 3 Ahora lee el párrafo que acompaña el título. ¿Entiendes todo lo que dice? (ambiente = *environment,* proviene = *originates*)

Paso 4 Ya debes tener una buena idea del tema general del artículo. La clase entera debe completar la siguiente oración.

> En este artículo se habla de si nuestra personalidad es producto de _____. Se va a ofrecer evidencia de estudios sobre _____.

Paso 5 Para confirmar lo que han escrito en el **Paso 4,** lee rápidamente la primera parte del artículo hasta llegar a la parte que verifica (o refuta) lo que Uds. han escrito.

Lo innato frente a lo aprendido:
El «dedónde» de nuestra personalidad

¿De dónde proviene nuestra personalidad? ¿Somos producto del ambiente en que nos criamos? ¿O es que la genética determina el carácter de uno tanto como determina sus rasgos físicos? Los estudios sobre los gemelos idénticos quizás ofrezcan una respuesta.

✷ ✷

El curioso caso de los «gemelos Jim»

Jim Lewis y Jim Springer nacieron gemelos idénticos pero fueron adoptados por diferentes familias pocos días después. Al conocerse por primera vez en 1979, ya eran adultos y claro que estaban nerviosos. Pero más tarde dirían que ese día fue el más importante de su vida. Durante las primeras etapas de establecer una relación perdida, se asombraron por las semejanzas entre los dos. A cada uno le pusieron el nombre de «James». Cada uno se casó dos veces. La primera esposa de cada uno se llamaba «Linda» y la segunda se llamaba «Betty». Los dos tenían un hijo llamado «James Allan» y ambos habían tenido un perro con el nombre de «Toy».

Los gemelos idénticos pueden ser la clave en el debate sobre lo innato frente a lo aprendido.

¿Coincidencias? ¿O es posible que exista algún fundamento científico que explique esto? Esta era la pregunta que empujaba al doctor Thomas Bouchard de la Universidad de Minnesota a llevar a cabo un estudio sobre el fenómeno de los gemelos separados después del nacimiento. Bouchard se puso en contacto con los «gemelos Jim» poco después de que estos se habían reunido. Estudió con detalle la personalidad y actitud de cada uno y los resultados fueron asombrosos. En un examen que medía ciertos aspectos de la personalidad, notablemente la tolerancia, la conformidad y la flexibilidad, los resultados eran tan semejantes que parecía que la misma persona había tomado el examen dos veces. Los exámenes sobre su inteligencia, destrezas cognitivas, gustos y otros aspectos de su carácter revelaron otras semejanzas sorprendentes.

Otros estudios

El estudio sobre los «gemelos Jim» inició otros estudios para comparar a gemelos separados después de nacer. En otro estudio, el doctor Bouchard analizó a dos gemelos originarios de Trinidad. Uno se había criado en esa isla caribeña y el otro en Checoslovaquia durante la ocupación nazi. Aunque había claras diferencias a base de las dos culturas en que se habían criado,

Bouchard observó semejanzas de temperamento y la manera en que hacían acciones típicas. Por ejemplo, los dos leían revistas empezando por la última página y ambos tenían la curiosa costumbre de estornudar en público para atraer la atención.

A través de estos estudios, Bouchard y otros han concluido que ciertas cualidades y tendencias son heredadas, incluyendo el don de mando, la imaginación, la vulnerabilidad al estrés, el retraimiento y la tendencia a evitar riesgos. En cambio, ciertos rasgos como la agresividad, la organización, el afán de realización y la impulsividad son adquiridos durante la niñez.

Más recientemente, se ha demostrado que la claustrofobia es común entre los gemelos en general y parece que muchas fobias podrían ser hereditarias. En un libro sobre los gemelos escrito por Lawrence Wright, se ofrece evidencia de que hasta la orientación política y la dedicación a la religión son reguladas por los genes.

Críticas

Por supuesto, las conclusiones de estos y otros estudios no les agradan nada a los que creen que los puntos de vista político, social y moral son la responsabilidad del individuo. Tales personas han denunciado estos estudios, diciendo que disminuyen el impacto y valor de la familia en la crianza de los niños. Pero estos estudios no eliminan por completo la evidencia de la importante influencia del ambiente en cómo somos. De hecho, demuestran que son las experiencias fuera del hogar las que tienen más impacto en las actitudes, los valores y ciertos rasgos de la personalidad no heredados. Así que en algunos aspectos, la crianza dentro del hogar no es tan importante como lo que experimentamos en la sociedad en general.

Otra crítica de los estudios sobre los gemelos es que las conclusiones son más tentativas de lo que indican los investigadores. La verdad es que no se han estudiado bien los hogares ni las comunidades en que se han criado los gemelos separados. En el caso de los «gemelos Jim», por ejemplo, los dos se criaron en Ohio en familias de la misma clase social que vivían a sólo 45 millas la una de la otra. Dicen los críticos que estos ambientes son muy parecidos y pueden provocar muchas de las semejanzas observadas. Sin embargo, existen casos como el de los gemelos de Trinidad que debilitan este argumento. En tales casos la evidencia del efecto de los diferentes ambientes está bien clara.

En fin, es evidente que la genética sí juega un papel importante en el «dedónde» de la personalidad, o en otras palabras, que la personalidad es más que un simple producto del ambiente en que nos criamos.

EXPLORACIÓN

Paso 1 Cada persona debe tomar un número de 1 a 3. A los 1 se les va a asignar la sección «El curioso caso... ». A los 2 se les va a asignar la sección «Otros estudios». A los 3 se les va a asignar la sección «Críticas».

Paso 2 Cada persona debe leer la sección asignada y tomar apuntes. Luego los 1 deben reunirse con otros dos o tres 1. Los 2 deben reunirse con otros dos o tres 2, etcétera. En cada grupo, se debe resumir la sección leída incluyendo por lo menos:

1. la idea principal de la sección

2. dos o tres puntos importantes que explican la idea principal o que la apoyan.

Paso 3 Cada grupo debe presentar su resumen a la clase. Para la presentación, pueden utilizar la pizarra si quieren. Traten de limitarse a cinco minutos por presentación. Como algunos grupos han leído la misma sección, pueden agregar información y (o) ponerla énfasis en algo dicho anteriormente. **¡OJO!** Mientras que los demás grupos presentan su resumen, debes tomar apuntes y pedir una explicación si no entiendes algo.

Consejo práctico

By now you should be familiar with two strategies for handling new words in a reading.

1. deducing the meaning of words relying on
   a. context
   b. cognate status
   c. and relationship to other words (e.g., **alejarse** ↔ **lejos**)
2. skipping words that aren't deducible while seeing if you can get the general idea(s) of the sentence or paragraph

Remember to let the information asked of you guide you in your reading. What am I going to be asked about this reading? Which words are most important for me to understand right now? If necessary, you can look up some words during a second reading.

SÍNTESIS

Ahora lee toda la lectura y revisa tus apuntes del **Paso 3** de **Exploración**. Debes añadir cualquier detalle importante que falte (*that's missing*). Vas a utilizar tus apuntes y las ideas de **Exploración** en la **Composición** al final de esta lección.

¡SIGAMOS!

ACTIVIDAD A ¿En qué se parecen?

Paso 1 Haz una lista de las cualidades que compartes con tus padres (y abuelos) y otra de las que no compartes con ellos. Luego indica si tus hermanos también poseen las mismas cualidades.

Paso 2 En grupos de cuatro, compartan sus listas. ¿En qué se parecen? ¿Hay muchas cualidades comunes en las familias? Reporten al resto de la clase lo que piensan.

Consejo práctico

As you know, jotting down key words and concepts while you read is an important tool for better recall of information. However, don't forget to review your notes as you go! That is, when you finish a section, review your notes and think about what you have just read. Are your notes clear? Do you wish to add something? Will the words and phrases you jotted down help you recall all the main points and a few supporting ideas?

Consejo práctico

By now you may have noticed the relationship between reading and writing as well as listening and writing established in *¿Sabías que... ?* A good academic skill (in any language!) is to be able to use your own words to summarize information that you have received from another source. Can you take others' ideas and express them in your own words? Can you organize information into main ideas, supporting ideas, and details? In *¿Sabías que... ?* you are working on skills that will help you not only in Spanish but in other courses as well!

ACTIVIDAD B Situación

Paso 1 Trabajando en grupos de tres o cuatro, lean la siguiente situación.

Un amigo (una amiga) no quiere hacer nada. Prefiere quedarse en casa todo el tiempo. Tú crees que eso está mal, que él (ella) necesita salir más, hacer más amigos y gozar de la vida. Cuando se lo dices, te contesta: «Lo siento pero así nací».

¿Aceptan Uds. esta respuesta? ¿Qué hacen si la situación tiene que ver con otro factor que puede tener malas consecuencias?

Paso 2 Compartan sus ideas con el resto de la clase. ¿Están todos de acuerdo?

Vamos a ver

Now that you've completed the **Vamos a ver** section of **Unidad cinco,** watch the corresponding **Vamos a ver** segment on the *¿Sabías que... ?* video to further explore the themes presented in this unit. There are related pre- and post-viewing activities on the *¿Sabías que... ?* Online Learning Center at **www.mhhe.com/sabiasque5**.

NAVEGANDO LA RED

Busca información sobre un estudio de gemelos de algún país hispano. Reporta a la clase dónde y cuándo se hizo el estudio, quién lo hizo y cuáles fueron algunos de los resultados o las conclusiones.

COMPOSICIÓN

En esta lección has examinado la idea de que ciertas cualidades son aprendidas, mientras que otras son innatas. Por ejemplo, has visto que entre los animales el sentido de orientación no es necesariamente innato, y que los estudios sobre los gemelos separados han revelado la importancia de la genética en el carácter de uno. Con la información que has aprendido, escribe una composición titulada «Somos lo que somos».

Antes de escribir

Paso 1 El propósito de la composición es presentar ideas de que somos lo que somos por dos factores: lo genético y lo que aprendimos del ambiente en que nos criamos y vivimos. Toma en cuenta que hay personas que no creen en la influencia genética en la personalidad y en el comportamiento de los seres humanos y que también creen que todo lo que hacen los animales es por instinto. ¿Qué ejemplos te pueden servir para demostrar que los dos factores determinan nuestro carácter? Escoge el tono que vas a adoptar. ¿Es apropiado usar la primera persona y dar ejemplos personales? ¿Vas a dirigirte directamente al lector (a la lectora)?

Paso 2 Escribe algunas ideas relacionadas con cada punto a continuación que puedes incluir en la composición. Repasa la lección si no recuerdas todos los datos.

1. El sentido de orientación
   a. las abejas
   b. el «tercer ojo»
2. Los gemelos separados después de nacer
   a. los «gemelos Jim»
   b. los rasgos heredados
   c. los rasgos adquiridos

Paso 3 Escribe el orden en que vas a presentar tus ideas y ejemplos. ¿Es lógica esta organización?

Al escribir

Paso 1 Aquí tienes unas frases que pueden ayudarte a expresar las ideas.

en su mayor parte	*for the most part*
es evidente que	*it is evident that*
es lógico pensar que	*it is logical to think that*
está claro que	*it is clear that*

Paso 2 Al escribir la conclusión, debes tomar en cuenta el propósito de la composición y también el punto de vista de los lectores. Si quieres, puedes usar en la conclusión una de las siguientes frases.

después de todo	*after all*
en definitiva	*definitely*
por lo tanto	*therefore*

Paso 3 Escribe la composición dos días antes de entregársela al profesor (a la profesora).

Después de escribir

Paso 1 Antes de entregar la composición, léela de nuevo. ¿Quieres cambiar o modificar...

◆ las ideas que presentaste?

◆ el orden en que presentaste las ideas?

◆ la conclusión?

◆ el tono?

Paso 2 Lee la composición una vez más para verificar...

◆ la concordancia entre formas verbales y sujetos.

◆ la concordancia entre adjetivos y sustantivos.

◆ el uso de **lo** + *adjetivo*.

Paso 3 Haz todos los cambios necesarios y entrégale la composición al profesor (a la profesora).

Vistazos culturales

La economía en el mundo hispano

¿Sabías que... hay mucha variedad en la economía de los países hispanos? En el Caribe, por ejemplo, la economía de cada país depende de industrias distintas. En Puerto Rico la economía depende de la fabricación de productos electrónicos y farmacéuticos. En cambio, la economía de la República Dominicana se basa en la minería, sobre todo en la extracción de hierro,[a] níquel, oro y plata.[b] La economía de Cuba depende de la exportación de azúcar, petróleo y tabaco.

[a]*iron* [b]*silver*

Cultivando tabaco en Cuba

**Producto Nacional Bruto[a]
por persona de los países latinoamericanos (2000)**

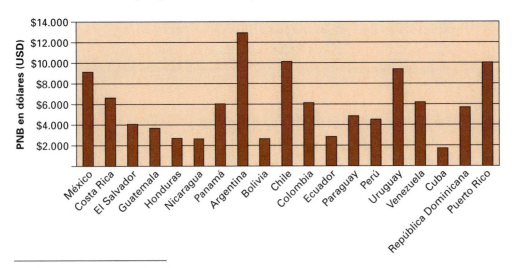

[a]Producto... *Gross National Product*

You can investigate these cultural topics in more detail on the *¿Sabías que... ?* Online Learning Center: **www.mhhe.com/sabiasque5**.

En un pueblo salvadoreño después del terremoto de 2001

Las crisis económicas

- **Honduras, El Salvador y Nicaragua (1998):** La economía ya vulnerable de muchos países centroamericanos sufre pérdidas muy grandes a causa de la destrucción causada por el huracán Mitch.

- **El Salvador (2001):** La economía salvadoreña, todavía recuperándose del huracán Mitch, sufre un golpe[a] más, debido a un fuerte terremoto[b] de magnitud 7,9 en la escala Richter.

[a]*hit* [b]*earthquake*

Durante los años 90 **Venezuela** empieza a sufrir varias crisis a causa de una demanda reducida del petróleo (su exportación principal), la inestabilidad política y una crisis financiera en el sector bancario.

En **el Ecuador (1999)** la moneda nacional se deprecia más del 70% debido a un colapso financiero y a la destrucción causada por El Niño entre 1997 y 1998.

En **Chile (1999)** una fuerte sequía[a] exacerba una recesión ya en progreso. Chile experimenta un crecimiento económico negativo por primera vez en quince años.

[a]*drought*

En **la Argentina (2002)** la economía sufre un colapso fuerte cuando el peso argentino pierde la mayor parte de su valor por deudas[a] de unos 140 mil millones de dólares.

[a]*debts*

ACTIVIDAD ¿Qué recuerdas?

Completa las siguientes oraciones.

1. En Chile, la crisis económica en 1999 fue exacerbada por _____.

   a. inundaciones **b.** un huracán **c.** un terremoto **d.** una sequía

2. _____ sufrió un fuerte terremoto en 2001.

   a. El Salvador **b.** Nicaragua **c.** El Ecuador **d.** La Argentina

3. La crisis en Venezuela durante los años 90 se debió a menos demanda del _____.

   a. café **b.** petróleo **c.** azúcar **d.** oro

4. De los siguientes países, _____ tenía el PNB más alto en el año 2000.

   a. México **b.** Costa Rica **c.** la Argentina **d.** Chile

5. La economía de Puerto Rico depende más de la industria _____.

   a. farmacéutica **b.** petrolera **c.** minera **d.** bancaria

NAVEGANDO LA RED

Escoge *uno* de los proyectos y presenta tus resultados a la clase.

1. Busca información sobre la tasa de desempleo (*unemployment rate*) de los países hispanos. Haz lo siguiente.
   a. Haz una gráfica con el nombre y la tasa de desempleo de cada país hispano.
   b. Menciona qué países tienen la tasa más alta y la más baja.
2. Busca información sobre la moneda de cada país hispano. Después haz una gráfica que muestre la siguiente información.
   a. el nombre de cada país
   b. el nombre de la moneda que se usa en cada país
   c. el tipo de cambio (*exchange rate*) actual con el dólar

VOCABULARIO COMPRENSIVO

¿Dónde está... ?	**Where Is . . . ?**
el este, el oeste,	east, west,
el norte, el sur	north, south
al lado (de)	next to, alongside
cerca (de)	near, close
detrás (de)	behind
enfrente (de)	in front (of)
lejos (de)	far (from)
quedar	to be located
De aquí para allá	**From Here to There**
la bocacalle	intersection
la cuadra	block

la esquina	corner
la manzana	block
el semáforo	traffic light
¿Dónde queda... ?	Where is . . . ?
¿Me podría decir... ?	Could you tell me . . . ?
Perdón, ¿cómo se	Excuse me, how do you
llega a... ?	get to . . . ?
Cruce la calle.	Cross the street.
Doble a la derecha/	Turn right/left.
izquierda.	
Siga derecho (recto).	Continue (Go) straight.
Siga (Ud.) por...	Continue . . . , Follow . . .

The Present Perfect

he
has
ha
ha   almorzado
hemos   +   leído
habéis   salido
han
han

1. The present perfect corresponds roughly to English *have + past participle.*

    Ya **he comido.**
    I have eaten already.

    ¿Te **has mirado**?
    Have you looked at yourself?

2. There are no stem vowel changes with past participles: **almorzar → almorzado, venir → venido,** and so forth.

3. A number of common verbs have irregular past participles that do not end in **-ado** or **-ido.**

    decir →   dicho
    escribir → escrito
    hacer →   hecho
    morir →   muerto
    poner →   puesto
    ver →   visto

4. There are two instances in which the present perfect is used in English where it is not used in Spanish.

    a. to have . . . for + *amount of time*

    Hace varios minutos **que estoy** aquí.
    I have been here for a few minutes.

    Hace dos años **que vivo** en Chicago.
    I have lived in Chicago for two years.

    b. to have just (*done something*)

    Acabo de limpiar eso. No lo toques.
    I have just cleaned that. Don't touch it.

    ¿Acabas de llegar?
    Have you just arrived? / Did you just arrive?

Verbs That Require a Reflexive Pronoun

Some verbs in Spanish require a reflexive pronoun. Because these verbs are not true reflexives or reciprocal reflexives, their English equivalents do not use *-self, -selves,* or *each other.*

atreverse a + *inf.*	*to dare to (do something)*
burlarse (de)	*to make fun (of)*
comportarse	*to behave*
darse cuenta (de)	*to realize*
jactarse (de)	*to boast (about)*
portarse	*to behave*

Note that some of these verbs use prepositions when followed by nouns or verbs.

No me atreví.
No me atreví **a decirlo.**

No me di cuenta.
No me di cuenta **de eso.**

Reflexives

Remember that with some verbs **se** is required. With other verbs, **se** is used only when the meaning is reflexive, that is, when the subject and object of the verb are the same person or thing.

El perro **se** mira en el espejo.
El perro mira al gato.

Me hablo mucho porque vivo solo.
No le hablo a Jorge mucho.

The Conditional Tense

tomaría	me atrevería	viviría
tomarías	te atreverías	vivirías
tomaría	se atrevería	viviría
tomaría	se atrevería	viviría
tomaríamos	nos atreveríamos	viviríamos
tomaríais	os atreveríais	viviríais
tomarían	se atreverían	vivirían
tomarían	se atreverían	vivirían

1. The conditional in Spanish is roughly equivalent to English *would + verb* when the latter expresses a hypothetical event.

> No **viviría** allí nunca.
> *I would never live there.*

> ¿**Te burlarías** de mí?
> *Would you make fun of me?*

2. Remember that *would + verb* in English can also refer to a repeated action in the past. In this situation, you would use the imperfect in Spanish and not the conditional.

> **Iba** y **venía** mucho.
> *He would come and go a lot* (in those days).

> **Nos comportábamos** bien.
> *We would behave* (when we were children).

3. A few common verbs have irregular stems in the conditional tense.

decir →	dir-
hacer →	har-
poder →	podr-
salir →	saldr-
tener →	tendr-
haber →	habría (*there would be*)

Estar + location

Estar, and not **ser,** is normally used to talk about location.

> Buenos Aires **está** en la Argentina.
> Ahora mi mamá **está** en México.
> ¿Dónde **está** la oficina del profesor?

Quedar can be used to talk about the location of immovable inanimate things like buildings and places.

> ¿Dónde **queda la oficina** del profesor?
> **México queda** al sur de los Estados Unidos.

Past Subjunctive

The past subjunctive is used to express hypothetical situations in conjunction with the conditional tense. It is formed using the **ellos** form of the preterite, and all the irregularities found in the **ellos** preterite form are carried over to the past subjunctive forms. For example, with the verb **tener: tener → ellos tuvieron → tuv- → si yo tuviera, si tú tuvieras, si Ud. tuviera,** etc.

tomar	tener	dormirse
ellos tomaron	ellos tuvieron	ellos se durmieron
tomara	tuviera	me durmiera
tomaras	tuvieras	te durmieras
tomara	tuviera	se durmiera
tomara	tuviera	se durmiera
tomáramos	tuviéramos	nos durmiéramos
tomarais	tuvierais	os durmierais
tomaran	tuvieran	se durmieran
tomaran	tuvieran	se durmieran

Lo + Adjective

You can use **lo** + adjective to express the concept of *the curious thing, the interesting thing,* and so forth. The adjective always appears in the masculine singular form.

> **Lo curioso** de este caso...
> **Lo interesante** del estudio...

More on por and para

One use of **por** is to express direction through, around, and so forth. **Para** expresses direction toward a goal or destination.

> Voy **para** los Andes.
> *I'm heading toward the Andes.*

> Voy **por** los Andes.
> *I'm going through the Andes (to get somewhere else).*

Review of the Object Marker a

When two nouns in a sentence are both capable of being a subject, the object of the verb is marked with **a.**

Juan conoció **a** María.
El perro quiere mucho **al** gato.

Review of gustar

Remember that in **gustar** constructions the subject (the action, person, or thing that is pleasing) is generally placed after the verb, whereas the object (the person to whom the subject is pleasing) usually precedes the verb.

A Juanita le gustaría **ser actriz.**

For emphasis or contrast you can add **a mí, a ti, a nosotros/as,** or **a vosotros/as,** as appropriate.

A mí me gustaría conocer a Jennifer López.

Hacia el futuro

Ganas, That Is All You Need (1989) por Wayne Healy y David Botello

Perfil de los artistas

NOMBRES: Wayne Alaniz Healy
David Rivas Botello

PAÍS DE ORIGEN: los Estados Unidos

FECHA DE NACIMIENTO: 1946

Wayne Alaniz Healy y David Rivas Botello se criaron en East Los Ángeles (también llamado «East Los» por los que viven allí). En 1975, fundaron un equipo de muralistas con el nombre East Los Streetscapers. La gran influencia en su arte ha sido el movimiento muralista mexicano, que se ve en las obras de Diego Rivera, David Alfaro Siqueiros y José Clemente Orozco, por ejemplo. Este movimiento combina temas y elementos del socialismo, modernismo e indigenismo. Además de los murales que han pintado en Los Ángeles, Healy y Botello también han realizado trabajos artísticos en Houston, St. Louis, San José (California) y otros lugares en el oeste y suroeste del país. En 1992, Healy y Botello recibieron una beca del Comité para la Cooperación Educativa y Cultural de los Estados Unidos y España para pintar murales en Barcelona.

LECCIÓN **16**

Check out the following media resources to complement this lesson:

 Online *Manual*

 Video on CD

 Online Learning Center

ActivityPak

¿Adónde vamos?

En esta lección, vas a

◆ aprender vocabulario relacionado con la ropa y con los viajes

◆ repasar el *condicional*

◆ hablar de tus preferencias en cuanto a viajar

◆ examinar lo que harías y lo que no harías en varias situaciones hipotéticas

◆ determinar con quién podrías hacer un viaje largo

◆ aprender unos nuevos verbos reflexivos

◆ aprender a formar los mandatos formales.

ALTO Before beginning this lesson, look over the **Intercambio** activity on page 423. This is the activity you will be working toward throughout the lesson.

En la Estación de Santa Justa **(Sevilla, España)**

IDEAS PARA EXPLORAR
La ropa

VOCABULARIO

¿Cómo te vistes?

Talking about clothing

Las prendas de vestir

la chaqueta

1.

el sombrero

las medias

2.   los zapatos

3.   el vestido

El bufón llamado «Don Juan de Austria» (*1632–1633*) *y* La infanta
Margarita de Austria (*1653*) *por Diego Velázquez* (*español, 1599–1660*)

4.   la blusa de rayón

la camisa de algodón

la corbata de seda

el traje de lana

los pantalones

la falda

los calcetines

5.

6.

Vocabulario útil

llevar	to wear
vestirse (i, i)	to dress, get dressed
el abrigo	overcoat
los *bluejeans*	jeans
la camiseta	T-shirt
el cuero	leather
el diseño	design
el jersey	pullover
los pantalones cortos	shorts
la sudadera	sweats, sweatpants
el suéter	sweater
el tacón (alto)	(high) heel
el traje de baño	bathing suit
barato/a	inexpensive
caro/a	expensive

Las telas de fibras naturales	Natural Fabrics
el algodón	cotton
la lana	wool
la seda	silk

Las telas de fibras sintéticas	Synthetic Fabrics
el poliéster	polyester
el rayón	rayon

ACTIVIDAD A ¿Con qué sexo asocias esta ropa?

Paso 1 El profesor (La profesora) va a mencionar algunas prendas de vestir. ¿Con quién asocias cada prenda, con los hombres, con las mujeres o con ambos?

MODELO una sudadera →
La asocio con ambos sexos.

1... **2**... **3**... **4**... **5**... **6**... **7**... **8**... **9**... **10**...

Paso 2 Ahora ¿qué opinas? ¿Quiénes tienen más opciones en cuanto a la ropa, los hombres o las mujeres?

ACTIVIDAD B Cambios

Paso 1 Mira las fotos de la sección anterior y escucha las descripciones del profesor (de la profesora). ¿A cuál de las personas o fotos describe?

1... **2**... **3**... **4**... **5**... **etcétera**

Así se dice

The verb **vestirse** is a true reflexive. When you say **Me visto** you are literally saying *I dress myself*. To talk about what you put on, you may use **vestirse,** or simply **ponerse,** which means literally *to put on one's self.*

¿Qué **te pones** para ir a clase?
Suelo **ponerme** pantalones cortos y camiseta.

	C	F
1. Antiguamente, los hombres llevaban medias. Ahora no.	☐	☐
2. Antes tanto las mujeres como los hombres vestían pantalones así como hoy.	☐	☐
3. Como hoy, los hombres de épocas anteriores llevaban pantalones largos, no cortos.	☐	☐
4. Las telas que se usaban en épocas anteriores eran la seda, la lana y el algodón. No existían las telas sintéticas.	☐	☐
5. Los sombreros no han cambiado mucho a través de la historia.	☐	☐
6. Antiguamente, las mujeres llevaban falda corta.	☐	☐

Paso 3 ¿A qué conclusión llegas?

☐ La ropa ha cambiado mucho para el hombre y la mujer.

☐ La ropa no ha cambiado tanto.

ACTIVIDAD C ¿Quiénes son? ¿Adónde van?

Indica quiénes podrían ser las personas que se describen a continuación y adónde van. En algunos casos hay varias posibilidades.

1. un hombre de 25 años que lleva traje de lana gris, camisa blanca, corbata de seda conservadora y zapatos negros

2. una mujer de 62 años que lleva sombrero negro, vestido negro y largo y zapatos negros

3. una joven de 20 años que lleva blusa de seda, falda de cuero y zapatos de tacón alto

4. un joven de 18 años que lleva sudadera, camiseta y zapatos de tenis

5. una mujer de 35 años que lleva chaqueta de seda color melón, blusa de seda blanca, falda de color crema, zapatos de tacón bajo y medias

 **COMUNICACIÓN**

ACTIVIDAD D Hoy en clase...

Paso 1 Observa la ropa de tus compañeros. Escribe en el cuadro el número de prendas que ves hoy en clase.

LA ROPA QUE LLEVAMOS HOY EN CLASE			
bluejeans	otros tipos de pantalones	faldas	vestidos
jerseys	sudaderas	camisas	camisetas	blusas
zapatos de cuero	zapatos de tenis	zapatos para correr	zapatos de otros tipos

Paso 2 Apunta aquí las tres prendas de vestir más populares entre los estudiantes.

_____   _____   _____

En esta lista se dan algunas razones por las cuales es posible que muchos estudiantes lleven una prenda de ropa en particular.

☐ Es cómodo/a.
☐ Es barato/a.
☐ Es fácil de lavar (cuidar).
☐ Dura (_It lasts_) mucho.

☐ Va bien con cualquier otro tipo de ropa.
☐ Está de moda (_in style_).
☐ ¿ ?

¿Por qué crees que los estudiantes llevan la ropa que apuntaste al principio de este paso? ¿Qué opinan los demás?

ACTIVIDAD E De viaje°

De... _On a trip_

Paso 1 Imagina que este verano vas de viaje por un mes y piensas visitar España, Francia e Italia. ¿Qué prendas de ropa piensas llevar? ¿Cuántas maletas (_suitcases_) llevas? Haz una lista de todo lo que llevas en las maletas y explica por qué. No te olvides de incluir el número de pares de zapatos y de calcetines y otras prendas necesarias.

Paso 2 Intercambia tu lista con otras personas. ¿Se puede agrupar a las personas de la clase por lo que llevan para el viaje?

GRAMÁTICA

¿Qué te pones?

More on reflexive verbs

—Amor, ¿cómo **me veo**?

A number of verbs used to talk about clothing and appearance are used in the reflexive form.

ponerse	to put on	**verse (bien)**	to look (good)
quitarse	to take off	**vestirse (i, i)**	to dress, get dressed

Si quiero **verme** más delgado, **me pongo** ropa de color negro.
If I want to look slimmer, I put on black clothes.

Al llegar a casa, **me quito** los zapatos.
As soon as I get home, I take off my shoes.

¿Cómo **te vistes** cuando sales a bailar?
How do you dress when you go out dancing?

Note that **vestirse** takes the preposition **a, con,** or **de** when the meaning is _to dress in._

Siempre **se viste a** la moda.   _She always dresses in style._
Hoy **se viste de** rojo.   _Today she's dressed in red._
Prefiero **vestirme con** bluejeans.   _I prefer to dress in jeans._

ACTIVIDAD F ¿Quién?

Haz la correspondencia entre las columnas A y B para indicar quién diría qué.

A

1. _____ Tengo que verme bien. Es mi trabajo.
2. _____ Intento verme bien para causar buena impresión en mis clientes.
3. _____ Nos quitamos los zapatos al entrar en la casa. Es nuestra costumbre.
4. _____ Me visto con pantalones negros y camisa blanca porque es el uniforme de mi escuela.

B

a. un niño de 10 años
b. una modelo
c. una mujer de negocios
d. una abuela japonesa

ACTIVIDAD G ¿Cómo lo haces?

Paso 1 Indica lo que haces en cada situación.

1. Zapatos y calcetines
   - ☐ Primero me pongo los dos calcetines. Luego me pongo los dos zapatos.
   - ☐ Me pongo un calcetín y un zapato. Luego me pongo el otro calcetín y el otro zapato.

2. Pantalones y camisa (falda y blusa)
   - ☐ Me pongo primero la camisa (blusa) y luego me pongo los pantalones (la falda).
   - ☐ Me pongo primero los pantalones (la falda) y luego la camisa (blusa).

3. Reloj (*wristwatch*)
   - ☐ Primero me pongo la ropa y luego me pongo el reloj.
   - ☐ Primero me pongo el reloj y luego me pongo la ropa.

Paso 2 Todos deben compartir sus respuestas. ¿Hay muchas respuestas diferentes?

COMUNICACIÓN

ACTIVIDAD H ¿Tratas de verte bien?

Paso 1 Escoge *una* de las siguientes situaciones y contesta la pregunta.

1. Tienes una primera cita con alguien. ¿Tratas de verte bien? ¿Cómo te vistes?
2. Hay una cena familiar y es una ocasión especial. ¿Tratas de verte bien? ¿Cómo te vistes?
3. Te van a sacar una foto especial, por ejemplo, una foto de la familia. ¿Tratas de verte bien? ¿Cómo te vistes?

Paso 2 Busca dos personas del mismo sexo que hayan escogido la misma situación que tú. ¿Repondieron todos de la misma manera?

Paso 3 Los hombres y las mujeres de la clase deben comparar sus respuestas. ¿Hay alguna diferencia entre los sexos en cuanto a lo que significa «verse bien»?

ACTIVIDAD I En tu opinión

Paso 1 Trabajando con dos o tres compañeros/as de clase, comenta las siguientes afirmaciones. ¿Están de acuerdo o no? Apunten sus ideas.

> «El (La) líder de este país debe vestirse de una manera más informal para identificarse más con el pueblo».
> «La ropa y la forma de vestirse son mucho más importantes para las mujeres que para los hombres»

Paso 2 Presenten sus ideas al resto de la clase.

NAVEGANDO LA RED

Busca información sobre un almacén en España, la Argentina u otro país de habla española. Imagina que te compras dos prendas de ropa. ¿Qué prendas son? ¿Cuánto pagas por todo? ¿Sabes a cuánto está (*what the exchange rate is for*) el dólar en ese país?

IDEAS PARA EXPLORAR

De viaje

VOCABULARIO

¿En tren o en auto?

Talking about trips and traveling

¿En qué vamos?	By what means are we traveling?	***¿Quiénes?***	
el autobús	bus	**el/la agente (de viajes)**	(travel) agent
el avión	airplane	**el/la aeromozo/a**	
el barco	boat	**el/la auxiliar de vuelo**	flight attendant
el crucero	cruise ship	**el/la camarero/a**	
el tren	train	**el/la maletero/a**	porter, skycap
		el/la pasajero/a	passenger
¿Dónde?			
el aeropuerto	airport	***¿Qué hacemos?***	
la cabina	cabin	**alquilar**	to rent
la estación	station	**bajar de**	to get off (*a bus, car, plane, etc.*)
el extranjero	abroad		
la sala de espera	waiting room	**facturar el equipaje**	to check luggage
la sección de (no) fumar	(no) smoking section	**hacer autostop**	to hitchhike

hacer cola	to stand in line		
hacer escala	to make a stop (*flight*)		
hacer la maleta	to pack one's suitcase		
hacer un viaje	to take a trip		
marearse	to get sick, become nauseated		
sacar fotos	to take pictures		
subir a	to get on/in (*a bus, car, plane, etc.*)		
viajar	to travel		

¿Qué más?	What else?
el asiento	seat
el boleto (billete*)	ticket
de ida	one-way
de ida y vuelta	round-trip
la clase turística	economy class
la demora	delay
el equipaje	luggage
la llegada	arrival
el pasaje	ticket, passage
la primera clase	first class
la salida	departure
el vuelo	flight

¿Sabes cuál de estos pasajes es para viajar en autobús y cuál es para viajar en avión? ¿Puedes encontrar la hora de salida de cada viaje? ¿y el número del vuelo del viaje en avión?

ACTIVIDAD A Definiciones y descripciones

Escucha la definición o descripción que da el profesor (la profesora) y luego indica a cuál de las opciones se refiere.

1. **a.** el tren **b.** el barco **c.** el avión
2. **a.** la sala de espera **b.** la cabina **c.** la estación
3. **a.** el maletero **b.** el agente de viajes **c.** el pasajero
4. **a.** el asiento **b.** la demora **c.** el billete
5. **a.** el barco **b.** la cabina **c.** el vuelo
6. **a.** hacer cola **b.** hacer escala **c.** hacer la maleta
7. **a.** alquilar **b.** marearse **c.** facturar
8. **a.** el pasaje **b.** la sala de espera **c.** la demora
9. **a.** el billete **b.** de ida y vuelta **c.** la clase turística
10. **a.** la pasajera **b.** la agente de viajes **c.** la auxiliar de vuelo

---

***Boleto** is mostly used in Latin America; **billete** is used in Spain.

ACTIVIDAD B ¿En qué orden?

Cuando viajas en avión, ¿en qué orden haces las siguientes actividades?
Compara tus resultados con los del resto de la clase.

_____ Compro el boleto.   _____ Hago la maleta.
_____ Facturo el equipaje.   _____ Llego al aeropuerto.
_____ Hago cola.   _____ Subo al avión.
_____ Le pido una almohada   _____ Tomo el asiento.
      (*pillow*) al asistente de _____ Voy a la sala de espera.
      vuelo.

 ACTIVIDAD C Firma aquí, por favor

Busca a personas de la clase que contesten afirmativamente las
siguientes preguntas.

1. ¿Has viajado alguna vez en primera clase?

2. ¿Has hecho algún viaje al extranjero?

3. ¿Te has mareado alguna vez durante un vuelo?

4. ¿Has perdido el boleto?

5. ¿Has tenido que esperar más de una hora a causa de una demora?

6. ¿Has hecho un viaje en crucero?

7. ¿Has hecho autostop?

ACTIVIDAD D ¿Molestia o no?

Paso 1 Indica si las siguientes cosas te molestan o te molestarían en un
viaje por avión.

5 = Me molesta mucho y de hecho me enfado.
3 = Me molesta.
0 = No me molesta. Así es la vida.

1. _____ Hay una demora de una hora.

2. _____ Hay una demora de dos horas o más.

3. _____ Tienes que hacer cola por más de 30 minutos para facturar el
equipaje.

4. _____ La persona en el asiento a tu lado se marea y vomita.

5. _____ Según el itinerario, es necesario hacer tres escalas y cambiar
de avión dos veces.

6. _____ Al llegar a tu destino, tus maletas no aparecen. Te dicen que no
van a llegar hasta el día siguiente.

Paso 2 Ahora entrevista a un compañero (una compañera) de clase.
Léele cada oración y pregúntale si le molesta o no (tu compañero/a no
debe mirar su libro). Apunta sus respuestas, pero no le digas lo que has
contestado tú en el **Paso 1.**

Paso 3 Al final, revela tus respuestas y compáralas con las de tu
compañero/a. ¿A quién le molestan más esas situaciones? Entre todos,
¿han pensado en otras situaciones molestas?

COMUNICACIÓN

Así se dice

Para can be used instead
of **a** to indicate *to, toward,
for,* or *in the direction of,*
especially when travel or
distance is involved.

Mañana salgo **para**
París.
¿Cuándo vienes **para**
México?

For now you can use **a,**
but look for uses of **para**
with destination as you
continue to learn Spanish.

ACTIVIDAD E Una historia

Paso 1 Trabajando con un compañero (una compañera) de clase, inventa una historia sobre lo que pasa en los siguientes dibujos. A continuación tienen algunas ideas para considerar.

◆ ¿Quiénes son las dos mujeres? ¿Qué relación hay entre ellas?

◆ ¿Adónde y por cuánto tiempo van?

◆ ¿Cómo lo pasan durante el vuelo?

◆ Al llegar a su destino, ¿qué pasa? ¿Cómo se sienten?

◆ ¿Qué creen Uds. que deben hacer ellas?

1.   2.   3.

4.   5.

Paso 2 Compartan su historia con el resto de la clase. ¿Quiénes inventaron la mejor historia?

VOCABULARIO

¿Dónde nos quedamos?

Talking more about trips and traveling

El alojamiento	Lodging	**el hotel de lujo**	luxury hotel
el armario	closet	**el hotel de cuatro estrellas**	four-star hotel
el botones	bellhop		
la cama matrimonial	double bed	**el/la huésped(a)**	guest
la cama sencilla	twin bed	**el mozo**	bellhop
las comodidades	conveniences, amenities	**la pensión completa**	full room and board
		la pensión	boardinghouse, bed and breakfast
la habitación	room		
con baño (privado)	with a (private) bath	**la media pensión**	room and breakfast (*often with one other meal*)
con ducha	with a shower		

la recepción	front desk	
el servicio de cuarto	room service	
alojarse	to stay, lodge	
confirmar	to confirm	
reservar	to reserve	
con (un mes de)	(one month) in	
anticipación	advance	

tener vista	to have a view
completo/a	full, no vacancy
desocupado/a	vacant, unoccupied

1.

2.

Hay hoteles de todo tipo en el mundo hispano. ¿Qué tipo de hotel te gusta a ti, los hoteles de lujo modernos como este resort *(1) cerca de San José del Cabo, México o prefieres los hoteles más tradicionales como este (2) de Andalucía, España?*

ACTIVIDAD F El alojamiento en un hotel

Paso 1 Indica si las siguientes cosas son necesarias para ti o si sólo son preferibles cuando te alojas en un hotel. Si no te importa algo, indica eso.

	NECESARIO	PREFERIBLE	NO ME IMPORTA(N)
1. una cama matrimonial en vez de una sencilla	☐	☐	☐
2. la ayuda de un botones	☐	☐	☐
3. un baño privado	☐	☐	☐
4. un baño con ducha	☐	☐	☐
5. servicio de cuarto	☐	☐	☐
6. si el precio incluye el desayuno	☐	☐	☐
7. si tiene vista	☐	☐	☐
8. extras como champú gratis y televisión por cable	☐	☐	☐
9. armario grande	☐	☐	☐

Paso 2 ¿Cómo contestarían las siguientes personas a cada número del **Paso 1**?

1. una persona de negocios que viaja frecuentemente y que normalmente se queda tres días en un hotel

2. dos jóvenes ricos y famosos que van a Colorado para esquiar

3. una persona que viaja en carro y que solamente pasa una noche en el hotel antes de continuar su viaje

4. dos personas jubiladas (*retired*) que pasan una semana en Florida

Paso 3 ¿Hay diferencias entre lo que tú consideras necesario y en lo que consideran necesario las personas del **Paso 2**? ¿Hay ciertas cosas que siempre son necesarias si uno se aloja en un hotel? Explica por qué.

ACTIVIDAD G ¿Sabías que... ?

Paso 1 Entre todos, hagan una lista de todas las comodidades que esperan encontrar en un hotel norteamericano. Digan también cuáles son las diferencias entre un hotel y un motel.

Vocabulario útil

el champú y el jabón	shampoo and soap
la televisión por cable	cable television
las toallas	towels
los pisos	floors

Paso 2 Lee la selección **¿Sabías que... ?** en la siguiente página. Luego contesta las preguntas a continuación.

1. El concepto de hotel en el mundo hispano es igual al de este país. ¿Sí o no?

2. ¿Cuál de los siguientes tipos de alojamiento no existen en los países hispanos?

   a. hoteles de lujo
   b. moteles
   c. pensiones

3. ¿Cuáles son las características que distinguen una pensión de un hotel?

Paso 3 Piensa si te gustaría alojarte en una pensión por una semana. En tu opinión, ¿cuáles son las ventajas y desventajas de alojarse en una pensión?

¿Sabías que...

los tipos de alojamiento en el mundo hispano varían mucho de país a país y también son diferentes de los que se encuentran en este país? En todos los países del mundo hispano hay grandes hoteles de lujo y también hoteles de diferentes categorías, pero en ninguna parte hay nada semejante al motel norteamericano. Muchos hoteles norteamericanos tienen piscina,[a] gimnasio y otras comodidades para sus huéspedes. Esto normalmente no se encuentra en los hoteles hispanos, a menos que sean de tipo *resort* como los que hay en Acapulco, Cancún, San Juan y otras ciudades.

Hay un tipo de alojamiento que se encuentra sobre todo en España pero no en este país: la pensión. Las pensiones españolas suelen ser pequeñas y más baratas que un hotel. A veces consisten en nada más que el piso de un alto edificio urbano. Los dueños son una familia y muchas veces las habitaciones no tienen baño privado. Tampoco tienen televisor, radio, reloj despertador ni teléfono. Pero para el turista que quiere un alojamiento barato, una buena pensión cómoda ofrece una alternativa al hotel.

---

[a]*swimming pool*

Una pensión típica en San Pedro de Alcántara. Las pensiones ofrecen alojamiento más económico del que ofrecen los hoteles.

COMUNICACIÓN

ACTIVIDAD H ¿Te alojas allí o no?

Paso 1 Imagina que te encuentras en la siguiente situación.

Estás de viaje y es de noche. Es verano y hace un poco de calor. No has comido y estás muy cansado/a. No has hecho ninguna reservación y encuentras un hotel que tiene un cuarto por $45 la noche. Tu plan es pasar la noche y continuar tu viaje por la mañana.

Indica cuál(es) de los siguientes factores afectaría(n) tu decisión de alojarte en ese hotel. ¿Hay un problema en particular que te haría ir a buscar otro alojamiento?

1. Al entrar en la habitación ves dos cucarachas, una sobre la cama y otra en el lavabo (*sink*).
2. Al inspeccionar la habitación ves que la bañera (*bathtub*) está muy sucia y enmohecida (*mildewed*).
3. Al entrar en la habitación te das cuenta de que se puede oír todo el tráfico incesante de la carretera.
4. Al poner el televisor ves que no funciona.
5. Al probar los grifos (*faucets*) te das cuenta de que no hay agua caliente.
6. Al mirar por la ventana ves a algunos individuos que te hace sospechar que el hotel es un lugar de narcotraficantes (*drug dealers*).
7. Al probar el aire acondicionado, encuentras que no funciona.

Paso 2 En grupos de tres, compartan sus reacciones del **Paso 1.** ¿Están de acuerdo en sus reacciones? ¡No se olviden de la situación! Completen uno de los siguientes párrafos y preséntenselo a los demás miembros de la clase. (Pueden modificar los párrafos según la discusión entre Uds.)

1. Nosotros estamos de acuerdo en que si _____ es suficiente razón para buscar otro alojamiento. Pero si _____ creemos que no es suficiente razón.

2. No nos ponemos de acuerdo en nuestro grupo. Algunos creen (Una persona cree) que si _____ es suficiente razón para buscar otro alojamiento. Otra(s) persona(s) cree(n) que si _____ es suficiente razón para buscar otro alojamiento. Todos estamos de acuerdo en que si _____ no habría problema en quedarnos allí.

ACTIVIDAD I En el escenario

Paso 1 Trabajando en grupos de tres, escojan una de las situaciones del **Paso 1** de la **Actividad H** e inventen un minidrama. Alguien tiene que ser el (la) recepcionista, otra persona el (la) botones y otra persona el cliente (la clienta).

Paso 2 Presentan su minidrama al resto de la clase.

NAVEGANDO LA RED

Busca la siguiente información sobre un hotel en México y compártela con la clase.

◆ el nombre del hotel
◆ la ciudad donde se encuentra
◆ el precio de una habitación para una persona (dos personas) por noche
◆ algunas comodidades que se ofrecen

IDEAS PARA EXPLORAR

En el extranjero

GRAMÁTICA

Firme aquí.

Telling others what to do: Formal commands

In an earlier lesson, you learned about direct commands when you are talking to someone with whom you would use **tú.** Direct commands to persons with whom you would use **Ud.** or **Uds.** take a different form. The stem of both affirmative and negative formal commands is formed by dropping the final **-o** from the first person singular (**yo**) present tense form (e.g., **dormir** → **duermo** → **duerm-; poner** → **pongo** → **pong-**) and adding *the opposite vowel* (**-e/-en** for **-ar** verbs, **-a/-an** for **-er** and **-ir** verbs).

Firme aquí, por favor.	*Sign here, please.*
Salgan por aquí.	*Leave (you [all]) this way.*

Verb stems that end in **-g** will add a **u** to keep the pronunciation of the hard **g** if followed by an **e.** The same is true for verb stems that end in **-c;** they will be spelled **qu** to maintain the hard **k** sound.

Saque su pasaporte, por favor.	*Take out your passport, please.*
¡No **lleguen** tarde!	*Don't arrive late!*

Reflexive and object pronouns are attached to the end of an affirmative command. With negative commands, the pronouns are placed in front.

Vístan**se** bien.	*Dress well.*
No **se** acueste muy tarde.	*Don't go to bed too late.*

Some common irregular commands are those in which the **yo** form ends in **-oy** in the present tense: **ir, ser, dar.**

No **vaya** muy lejos.	*Don't go far away.*
No **sea** ingrato.	*Don't be ungrateful.*
Déme dos boletos.	*Give me two tickets.*

ACTIVIDAD A ¿Quién lo diría?

¿Quién diría cada oración? ¿El recepcionista de un hotel o un huésped?

	RECEPCIONISTA	HUÉSPED
1. Firme aquí, por favor.	☐	☐
2. Para hacer una llamada fuera del hotel, marque el «9» primero.	☐	☐
3. Déme dos llaves, por favor.	☐	☐
4. Por favor, no me despierten antes de las 8.00 de la mañana.	☐	☐

ACTIVIDAD B En la habitación

¿Cuál de las siguientes oraciones esperarías encontrar en la habitación de un hotel?

☐ **1.** Ayúdenos a conservar el agua.

☐ **2.** Por favor, deje abierta la puerta para la mujer de la limpieza.

☐ **3.** En caso de incendio (*fire*), *no* use el ascensor.

☐ **4.** Si no encuentra todo a su satisfacción, escríbanos al volver a su casa.

✎ ACTIVIDAD C Agencia de turismo

En grupos de tres, escojan un lugar en este país que puede ser un lugar de vacaciones o un lugar visitado por turistas. No les digan cuál es ese lugar a los demás miembros de la clase. Luego formulen cinco oraciones basándose en el modelo sin indicar el lugar.

MODELOS   Visite nuestras playas blancas.

Tome una bebida mirando la puesta del sol (*sunset*).

Después cada grupo va a leer sus oraciones. ¿Puede el resto de la clase adivinar a qué lugar se refiere cada grupo?

ACTIVIDAD D ¿Cuándo?

En parejas, indiquen dos circunstancias en las que se diría cada oración. Luego compárenlas con las de sus compañeros. Recibirán (*You will receive*) un punto cada vez que otra pareja tenga (*has*) la misma circunstancia. Si ninguna de las parejas tiene circunstancias iguales, recibirán diez puntos. ¿Quién gana al final?

1. No se preocupe, señor. Yo me ocuparé de (*I'll take care of*) todo.
2. Pase por esas puertas y tome el ascensor a la derecha.
3. Gracias y vuelva pronto.

GRAMÁTICA

¿Qué harías? (II)

Review of the conditional tense

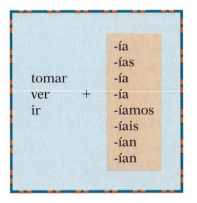

		-ía
		-ías
tomar		-ía
ver	+	-ía
ir		-íamos
		-íais
		-ían
		-ían

In a previous lesson you learned that the conditional is roughly equivalent to English *would* and that one of its functions is talking about hypothetical events.

En ese caso, **me quejaría.**   *In that case, I would complain.*
En un viaje por México,   *On a trip around Mexico, I*
   probaría la comida local.   *would sample the local food.*

The conditional of regular verbs is easily formed. As the shaded box suggests, the conditional consists of the infinitive plus an **-ía-** ending. Here are some examples of regular verbs in the conditional tense.

tomar   tomar**ía,** tomar**ías,** tomar**ía,** tomar**ía,**
        tomar**íamos,** tomar**íais,** tomar**ían,** tomar**ían**

ver	vería, verías, vería, vería,
	veríamos, veríais, verían, verían
ir	iría, irías, iría, iría,
	iríamos, iríais, irían, irían

Remember that a number of verbs have irregular stems in the conditional tense. Here are some useful ones for this lesson.

decir →	dir-	Nunca **diría** eso.
hacer →	har-	No **haría** eso.
poder →	podr-	No **podría** comer eso.
salir →	sald-	No **saldría** con él.
tener →	tend-	No **tendría** que ser caro.
haber →	**habría** (*there would be*)	

You will find the conditional useful in this lesson for talking about hypothetical situations while traveling.

ACTIVIDAD E Con 500 dólares...

Paso 1 Escoge *una* de las opciones a continuación.

Con 500 dólares...

1. me compraría _____.

4. iría a _____.

2. pagaría mi cuenta de _____.

5. me gustaría _____.

3. le compraría un regalo a _____.

Paso 2 Ahora busca a por lo menos dos personas que contestaran más o menos igual que tú. No te olvides de hacerles la pregunta correctamente.

MODELOS   Con 500 dólares, ¿te comprarías un DVD (*DVD player*)?

Con 500 dólares, ¿le comprarías un regalo a tu mamá? ¿Qué le comprarías?

Paso 3 Presenta los resultados del **Paso 2** a la clase.

MODELO   Con 500 dólares, Juan, Silvia y yo nos compraríamos un aparato electrónico. Yo me compraría un DVD, Juan un televisor y Silvia un iPod.

ACTIVIDAD F ¿Y con 5.000 dólares?

Repite la **Actividad E** pero esta vez con otra cantidad de dinero. Específicamente, ¿qué harías con 5.000 dólares? Comprueba si las mismas personas que dieron una respuesta como la tuya en la **Actividad E** también dan una respuesta similar ahora.

ACTIVIDAD G ¿Podrías... ?

Paso 1 Contesta las preguntas en la siguiente página.

3 = ¡Claro que sí! Podría hacerlo sin dificultad.
2 = Sí, creo que podría hacerlo.
1 = No, no podría hacerlo.

1. _____ ¿Podrías vivir sin teléfono por más de tres días?
2. _____ ¿Podrías pasar más de cuatro días sin ver la televisión?
3. _____ ¿Podrías pasar una semana o más sin tener ningún contacto con otra persona?

Ahora escucha y contesta las preguntas que hace tu profesor(a).

4. _____
5. _____
6. _____

Paso 2 Usando tus respuestas del **Paso 1,** indica cuál de las siguientes oraciones te describe mejor.

15–18 puntos:	Podría hacer cámping a solas. De hecho, me gustaría.
10–14 puntos:	No sé si podría hacer cámping a solas. Tendría que pensarlo.
6–9 puntos:	Definitivamente no podría hacer cámping, ¡ni a solas ni con otras personas!

ACTIVIDAD H Lo que (no) harías

Paso 1 Indica lo que harías y lo que *no* harías si alguien te lo pidiera (*asked you to do it*).

	SÍ	NO
1. Comería un plato de gusanos.	☐	☐
2. Me pondría ropa del sexo opuesto y saldría a caminar por la calle.	☐	☐
3. No me bañaría ni me ducharía por un mes.	☐	☐
4. Dejaría que otra persona copiara mi examen.	☐	☐
5. Iría a clase o al trabajo vestido/a de gorila.	☐	☐
6. Suspendería un examen a propósito.	☐	☐

Paso 2 Ahora indica cuál(es) de las cosas del **Paso 1** harías…

_____ por 500 dólares.   _____ por 50.000 dólares.
_____ por 5.000 dólares.   _____ por 500.000 dólares.

¿Cambia tu opinión sobre lo que (no) harías según la cantidad de dinero?

Paso 3 (Optativo) En grupos de tres, inventen tres o cuatro oraciones como las del **Paso 1** para presentar a su profesor(a) y repitan el **Paso 2.** ¿Cuáles son sus respuestas?

COMUNICACIÓN

ACTIVIDAD I En un país hispano

Escribe una breve descripción de lo que harías y de lo que *no* harías durante un viaje a un país hispano. Luego compártela con otras dos personas. ¿Cuál es su reacción? ¿Harían ellos/as las mismas cosas o no? A continuación hay algunas posibilidades.

alojarme en un hotel para turistas norteamericanos
alquilar un carro

beber el agua local sin precaución
comprar muchos recuerdos (*souvenirs*)
hacer autostop
hacer cámping
hablar con personas desconocidas
hablar sólo español
probar toda la comida que se me presente
salir con un chico hispano (una chica hispana)
sacar muchas fotos
visitar las ciudades grandes
visitar los pueblos pequeños

NAVEGANDO LA RED

Busca información sobre una agencia de turismo en un país hispano. ¿Cómo se llama? ¿Se alistan los nombres de los agentes? ¿Cuál es su dirección y su número de teléfono?

INTERCAMBIO

Un viaje al extranjero

Propósito: determinar con quién podrías viajar al extranjero por un mes entero

Papeles: una persona que entrevista y otra persona entrevistada

Paso 1 Piensa en las cosas que serían importantes para ti al viajar al extranjero. Haz una lista de por lo menos cinco cosas.

Paso 2 Basándote en lo que escribiste en el **Paso 1,** escribe varias preguntas para hacerle a otra persona sobre sus preferencias al viajar, para ver si los (las) dos serían compatibles durante un viaje largo. Por ejemplo, si para ti el precio del alojamiento sería un factor importante, puedes hacer preguntas como las siguientes:

¿Cuánto pagarías por noche en un hotel?
¿Harías cámping para ahorrar dinero?
¿Podrías dormir en el tren durante la noche?

Hazle las preguntas a un compañero (una compañera) de clase y apunta sus respuestas. Trata de conseguir todos los detalles posibles.

Paso 3 Escribe un resumen de lo que averiguaste en el **Paso 2.** Puedes seguir el modelo a continuación, haciendo los cambios necesarios.

_____ y yo (no) seríamos buenos compañeros (buenas compañeras) de viaje. En primer lugar, él (ella) (no) _____ y _____. Yo también (tampoco) _____. En segundo lugar,...

Paso 4 Antes de entregar tu resumen, deja que la otra persona lo lea. ¿Está de acuerdo con lo que has escrito?

Vistazos culturales
La moda en el mundo hispano

¿Sabías que... en el mundo hispano hay diseñadores de moda internacionalmente conocidos? Cristóbal Balenciaga y Carolina Herrera son dos diseñadores hispanos que han influido mucho en el desarrollo[a] de la indumentaria[b] moderna. Sus diseños son reconocidos y elogiados[c] en París, Nueva York y otros círculos importantes de la moda internacional.

---

[a]*development* [b]*apparel* [c]*praised*

Un vestido de Cristóbal Balenciaga

Cristóbal Balenciaga (1895–1972) nació en Getaria, provincia de Guipúzcoa, en el País Vasco. Se hizo[a] famoso por sus abrigos y trajes voluminosos con muchas líneas rectas. A lo largo de[b] su carrera, Balenciaga diseñó trajes para una clientela famosa, incluyendo a la reina de Bélgica.

---

[a]*Se... He became* [b]*A... Throughout*

Carolina Herrera con algunas modelos

Carolina Herrera (1936–) nació en Venezuela de ascendencia española. Viene de una familia de hacendados[a] y hombres de estado.[b] Diseña ropa encantadora y sencilla, sin olvidarse de los detalles[c] importantes. El estilo de Herrera es marcado por la elegancia y el lujo, características inspiradas por Balenciaga.

---

[a]*landowners* [b]*hombres... statesmen* [c]*details*

Aunque la moda internacional influye mucho en la indumentaria cotidiana[a] de muchos hispanos, también hay muchas influencias tradicionales que tienen un papel importante en el estilo de las prendas. En muchos lugares de Latinoamérica, por ejemplo, la ropa refleja la mezcla de culturas distintas, sobre todo culturas europeas e indígenas.

_____
[a]*daily*

El **traje de china poblana**[a] es una de las prendas más expresivas del mestizaje colonial en México. Es un traje de camisa blanca con mangas cortas[b] y una falda colorida bordada[c] de lentejuelas.[d]

_____
[a]*del pueblo*   [b]*mangas… short sleeves*   [c]*embroidered*
[d]*sequins*

Un traje de china poblana

Un sarape

El **sarape** es una prenda rectangular que tiene una apertura[a] en el centro que sirve para pasar la cabeza. Por su tamaño grande, el sarape también se considera una cobija.[b] El sarape era una prenda básica para el hombre del campo en México durante el período colonial y se sigue usando mucho hoy día.

_____
[a]*opening*   [b]*blanket*

En el Perú, la nobleza del Imperio inca usaba prendas hechas de lana de vicuña. La vicuña es un animal delgado de pelo rojo anaranjado. Su lana tiene fama de ser muy suave y muy fina. Hoy día todavía se usa mucho la lana de vicuña en la producción de ropa moderna y textiles finos peruanos.

Vicuñas, fuente (source) *de telas para los incas*

ACTIVIDAD ¿Qué recuerdas?

Completa las siguientes oraciones.

1. El diseñador español Cristóbal Balenciaga nació en _____.

   a. Barcelona   **b.** Sevilla   **c.** Madrid   **d.** el País Vasco

2. _____ es un animal de los Andes que se estima por su lana suave.

   a. La llama   **b.** La oveja   **c.** El cuy   **d.** La vicuña

3. La diseñadora Carolina Herrera es de origen _____.

   a. mexicano   **b.** venezolano   **c.** argentino   **d.** colombiano

4. El traje de china poblana consiste en _____.

   a. un vestido   **b.** camisa y falda   **c.** tela   **d.** prendas

5. Una prenda mexicana parecida a una cobija es _____.

   a. el abrigo   **b.** el sarape   **c.** la falda   **d.** la china poblana

NAVEGANDO LA RED

Escoge *uno* de los siguientes proyectos. Luego presenta tus resultados a la clase.

1. Selecciona *uno* de los grupos indígenas ya estudiados en lecciones anteriores: los aztecas, los incas o los mayas. Busca información sobre la ropa que se usaba en esa sociedad indígena y haz un comentario de unas 75 palabras sobre cómo la ropa distinguía las clases sociales. No te olvides de mencionar las diferentes clases sociales y las prendas que se asociaban con cada una.

2. Busca información sobre la influencia de la moda norteamericana en la ropa que usan los jóvenes en los países hispanos. Haz lo siguiente.

   a. Menciona cinco marcas de ropa norteamericana que se venden en las tiendas y almacenes del mundo hispano.

   b. Selecciona tres prendas específicas y menciona cómo son los precios en el mundo hispano. (Tendrás que calcular el tipo de cambio con el dólar.) ¿Cuestan más estas prendas en este país o en el mundo hispano?

VOCABULARIO COMPRENSIVO

Las prendas de vestir — Articles of Clothing

el abrigo	overcoat
los *bluejeans*	jeans
la blusa	blouse
los calcetines	socks
la camisa	shirt
la camiseta	T-shirt
la chaqueta	jacket
la corbata	tie
la falda	skirt
el jersey	pullover
las medias	stockings
los pantalones	pants
los pantalones cortos	shorts
el sombrero	hat
la sudadera	sweats, sweatpants
el suéter	sweater
el traje	suit
el traje de baño	bathing suit
el vestido	dress
los zapatos	shoes
los zapatos de tacón alto	high-heel shoes

llevar	to wear
ponerse (*irreg.*)	to put on (*clothing*)
quitarse	to take off (*clothing*)
verse (bien)	to look (good)
vestir (i, i)	to wear
vestirse (i, i) (R)	to dress, get dressed

Las telas y materiales — Fabrics and Materials

el algodón	cotton
el cuero	leather
la lana	wool
el poliéster	polyester
el rayón	rayon
la seda	silk

Palabras útiles

barato/a	inexpensive
caro/a	expensive
el diseño	design

De viaje — On a Trip

el/la aeromozo/a	flight attendant
el aeropuerto	airport
el/la agente de viajes	travel agent
el autobús	bus
el/la auxiliar de vuelo	flight attendant
el avión	airplane
el barco	boat
la cabina	cabin
el/la camarero/a	flight attendant
el crucero	cruise ship
la estación	station
el extranjero	abroad
el/la maletero/a	porter, skycap
el/la pasajero/a	passenger
la sala de espera	waiting room
la sección de (no) fumar	(no) smoking section
el tren	train

alquilar	to rent
bajar de	to get off (*a bus, car, plane, etc.*)
facturar el equipaje	to check luggage
hacer autostop	to hitchhike
hacer cola	to stand in line
hacer escala	to make a stop (*flight*)
hacer la maleta	to pack one's suitcase
hacer un viaje	to take a trip
marearse	to get sick (nauseated)
sacar fotos	to take pictures
subir a	to get on/in (*a bus, car, plane, etc.*)
viajar	to travel

Palabras útiles para los viajes — Useful Words for Trips

el asiento	seat
el boleto (el billete)	ticket
de ida	one-way ticket
de ida y vuelta	round-trip ticket
la clase turística	economy class
la demora	delay
el equipaje	luggage
el pasaje	ticket; passage
la llegada	arrival
la primera clase	first class
la salida	departure
el vuelo	flight

El alojamiento — Lodging

el armario	closet
el botones	bellhop
la cama	bed
matrimonial	double bed
sencilla	twin bed

las comodidades	conveniences, amenities	**la recepción**	front desk
la habitación	room	**el servicio de cuarto**	room service
con baño (privado)	with a (private) bath		
con ducha	with a shower	**alojarse**	to stay, lodge
el hotel	hotel	**confirmar**	to confirm
de cuatro estrellas	four-star hotel	**reservar**	to reserve
de lujo	luxury hotel	con (*time* + **de**)	(*time*) in advance
el/la huésped(a)	guest	anticipación	
el mozo	bellhop	**tener vista**	to have a view
la media pensión	room and breakfast (*often with one other meal*)		
		completo/a	full, no vacancy
la pensión	boardinghouse, bed and breakfast	**desocupado/a**	vacant, unoccupied
la pensión completa	full room and board		

LECCIÓN 17

Check out the following media resources to complement this lesson:

 Online *Manual*

 Video on CD

WWW **Online Learning Center**

WWW **ActivityPak**

¿A qué profesión u ocupación quieres dedicarte?

En esta lección vas a

◆ aprender el vocabulario relacionado con muchas profesiones y el trabajo

◆ hablar de las cualidades necesarias para practicar ciertas profesiones u ocupaciones

◆ explicar por qué quieres dedicarte a cierta profesión u ocupación

◆ ver una nueva forma verbal: el *subjuntivo*

ALTO Before beginning this lesson, look over the **Intercambio** activity on page 447. This is the activity you will be working toward throughout the lesson.

En tu opinión, ¿cuáles son las profesiones más importantes para el siglo XXI?

IDEAS PARA EXPLORAR

Las profesiones (I)

VOCABULARIO

¿Qué profesión?

Talking about professions

¡VOSª ESTÁS LOCA, MAFALDA! ¿YO ESTUDIAR UNA CARRERA?

¿YO SER INGENIERA, O ARQUITECTA, O ABOGADA, O MÉDICA? ¿YO? ¡JHA'!

¡YO VOY A SER AMA DE CASA Y VOY A APECHUGAR CONᵇ LAS TAREAS DOMÉSTICAS! ¡VOY A SER **MUJER**!

¡Y NO UNA DE ESAS AFEMINADAS QUE TRABAJAN EN COSAS DE HOMBRES!

ᵃvos = you (fam., sing.), used in Argentina and other Latin American countries   ᵇapechugar... put up with

Campos	*Profesiones*	*Campos*	*Profesiones*
la agricultura	el granjero (la granjera)	la computación	el programador (la programadora)
la arquitectura	el arquitecto (la arquitecta)		el/la técnico
el arte	el pintor (la pintora)	la contabilidadª	el contador (la contadora)
	el escultor (la escultora)	los deportes	el/la atleta
la asistencia social	el trabajador (la trabajadora) social		el jugador (la jugadora) de...
la ciencia	el científico (la científica)	el derechoᵇ	el abogado (la abogada)
	el biólogo (la bióloga)	la enseñanza	el profesor (la profesora)
	el físico (la física)		el maestro (la maestra)
	el químico (la química)	la farmacia	el farmacéutico (la farmacéutica)
	el astrónomo (la astrónoma)	el gobierno la política	el político (la política)
el cine el teatro la televisión	el director (la directora)		el senador (la senadora)
	el fotógrafo (la fotógrafa)		el/la representante
	el productor (la productora)		el presidente (la presidenta)
	el actor (la actriz)		

ªaccounting ᵇlaw

Lección 17 ¿A qué profesión u ocupación quieres dedicarte?

Campos	Profesiones		Campos	Profesiones
la ingeniería	el ingeniero (la ingeniera)		la música	el/la músico
	el médico (la médica)		los negocios	el hombre (la mujer) de negocios
la medicina	el enfermero (la enfermera)		el periodismo	el/la periodista
	el veterinario (la veterinaria)		la psicología	el psicólogo (la psicóloga)
la moda^c	el diseñador (la diseñadora)		la terapia física	el/la terapeuta físico/a

^cfashion

Vocabulario útil

consultar	to consult
el/la asesor(a)	consultant
el/la ayudante	assistant
el/la especialista (en algo)	specialist (in something)
el/la gerente	manager
el/la jefe/a	boss

ACTIVIDAD A Asociaciones

Paso 1 El profesor (La profesora) va a mencionar una profesión. Indica el nombre que se asocia con cada profesión.

1. **a.** Lois Lane   **b.** Amelia Earhart   **c.** Bette Midler
2. **a.** Bono   **b.** Perry Mason   **c.** Barbara Walters
3. **a.** Oprah Winfrey   **b.** Donald Trump   **c.** Michael Douglas
4. **a.** Sammy Sosa   **b.** Julio Iglesias   **c.** Juan Valdés
5. **a.** Dr. Phil   **b.** Anderson Cooper   **c.** Donna Karan
6. **a.** Fidel Castro   **b.** Lee Treviño   **c.** Isabel Allende
7. **a.** Johnson y Johnson   **b.** Sara Lee   **c.** Federico García Lorca
8. **a.** Bill Clinton   **b.** Jaime Escalante   **c.** Jane Fonda

Paso 2 Indica lo que asocias con cada profesión que se menciona.

1. **a.** la máquina de escribir   **b.** la ropa especial   **c.** los animales
2. **a.** los pacientes   **b.** el transporte   **c.** la clase
3. **a.** los contratos   **b.** el béisbol   **c.** las revistas
4. **a.** el laboratorio   **b.** el piano   **c.** el dinero
5. **a.** la aspirina   **b.** el Congreso   **c.** los dibujos

Así se dice

Don't be fooled by professions that end in -ista: these can be either masculine or feminine.

Mi **padre** es **dentista.**
Mi **madre** es **dentista.**
Mi **hermano** es **periodista.**
Mi **hermana** es **periodista.**

1. a. la corte   **b.** la clase   **c.** la universidad

2. a. la playa   **b.** la escuela   **c.** el restaurante

3. a. el campo   **b.** la ciudad   **c.** el espacio

4. a. la clínica   **b.** la casa   **c.** el parque

5. a. el hospital   **b.** el océano   **c.** el estudio

ACTIVIDAD B ¿Cuál es?

El profesor (La profesora) va a leer la descripción de una profesión. Indica de qué profesión se habla en cada caso. **¡OJO!** Es posible que exista más de una respuesta.

1...   **2...**   **3...**   **4...**

 ACTIVIDAD C Firma aquí, por favor

Busca entre los estudiantes de la clase a los que tienen familiares que trabajan en campos específicos.

1. ¿Hay algún médico en tu familia?

2. ¿Hay alguna abogada en tu familia?

3. En tu familia, ¿hay alguna profesora?

4. ¿Es contador algún pariente tuyo?

5. ¿Hay alguna enfermera en tu familia?

6. ¿Hay algún ingeniero en tu familia?

7. ¿Es farmacéutica alguna mujer de tu familia?

COMUNICACIÓN

ACTIVIDAD D De niño/a

Muchas personas tienen aspiraciones profesionales cuando son muy jóvenes. ¿Qué pensabas ser tú?

Paso 1 Completa la siguiente oración.

Recuerdo que de niño/a quería ser _____.

Paso 2 ¿Han cambiado tus deseos? ¿Qué quieres ser ahora?

Ahora quiero ser _____.

Paso 3 ¿Cuántas personas en la clase han cambiado de idea también? Comparte tus oraciones con la clase. Apunta lo que dicen tus compañeros. Determina...

1. si algunos de los estudiantes respondieron de una manera semejante.

2. si la mayoría ha cambiado de idea o no.

Así se dice

Spanish does not use the indefinite articles **un** or **una** with the verb **ser** when talking about professions.

Quiero **ser abogado.**
Ella **es arquitecta.**

Un and **una** *are* used, however, when professions are modified in some way.

Quiero ser **un** abogado **famoso.**
Ella es **una** arquitecta bastante **conocida.**

ACTIVIDAD E ¿Cuánto prestigio?

Algunas profesiones tienen más prestigio que otras. ¿Cómo calificas tú las siguientes profesiones?

Paso 1 Pon al lado de cada profesión el número que indique el prestigio que tú crees que tiene en la sociedad.

1 = poco prestigio
2 = algún prestigio
3 = mucho prestigio

_____ trabajador(a) social
_____ abogado/a
_____ maestro/a de secundaria
_____ enfermero/a
_____ piloto
_____ director(a) de cine
_____ policía

_____ veterinario/a
_____ hombre (mujer) de negocios
_____ contador(a)
_____ aeromozo
_____ granjero/a
_____ taxista

Paso 2 Compara lo que escribiste con lo que escribieron otros dos compañeros de clase. ¿Tienen opiniones diferentes? ¿En qué basaron sus respuestas?

NAVEGANDO LA RED

Busca anuncios clasificados en uno o dos periódicos electrónicos publicados en español. ¿Cuáles son los trabajos o profesiones que más se anuncian? Presenta uno de los anuncios a la clase.

ACTIVIDAD F ¿Sabías que... ?

Paso 1 ¿Hay nombres de profesiones u oficios en inglés que indican el sexo de una persona? Por ejemplo, ¿a qué sexo se refiere la palabra *hostess*? Piensa en otros dos ejemplos.

Paso 2 Lee la selección **¿Sabías que… ?** Luego contesta las siguientes preguntas.

1. ¿Es posible *no* indicar el sexo de una persona al referirse a su profesión u oficio en español?

2. La selección se refiere a «la doctrina académica de que deben decirse en femenino los nombres de profesión aplicados a una mujer». ¿Cómo se dirían **médico** o **piloto** si se les aplica la doctrina a estos nombres?

Paso 3 Presenta la siguiente situación a varios amigos que no estén en tu clase de español y pídeles que completen la oración con la primera palabra que se les ocurra. Luego reporta tus resultados a la clase.

Vas con tus amigos a un restaurante y resulta que una mujer los atiende. Tú vas al baño para lavarte las manos y les dices a tus amigos: —*If the _____ comes and takes our order while I'm gone, tell her I want my burger well done.*

¿Cuántos responden con una palabra que indica el sexo de la persona como, por ejemplo, *waitress*? ¿Hay mucho uso de *waitperson* o *server*?

¿Sabías que...

en español resulta problemática la formación del femenino en los nombres de algunas profesiones? Esto se debe a que ahora gran número de mujeres tienen profesiones que por tradición han sido casi exclusivas del sexo masculino. En el idioma inglés, el género[a] de un nombre no tiene la importancia que tiene en español. Por ejemplo, la palabra *doctor* no lleva en sí nada que indique si se refiere a un hombre o a una mujer. Para hacer esta distinción es necesario decir *male doctor* o *female doctor*. En otros casos, para evitar relacionar el sexo con la profesión, se han creado nuevos nombres para ciertas ocupaciones y profesiones, como por ejemplo *flight attendant* en vez de *stewardess*.

En cambio, en español es indispensable distinguir el género, masculino o femenino, del nombre. ¿Y qué pasa cuando los nombres de algunas profesiones, que ahora practican las mujeres, tienen por lo general la forma masculina, como ocurre con **médico** y **piloto**? El resultado es que hay mucha discrepancia en su uso. A pesar de que existe la doctrina académica de que deben decirse en femenino los nombres de profesión aplicados a una mujer, algunos hispanohablantes dicen **una médico** o **la médico, una piloto** o **la piloto,** al referirse a las que tienen título oficial para curar o conducir un avión, respectivamente.

[a]*gender*

Una médica española

GRAMÁTICA

¿Qué tipo de trabajo buscas?

The subjunctive after indefinite antecedents

Busco un trabajo | que me **pague** bien.
Necesito una jefa | que me **comprenda.**
Quiero un trabajo | que **esté** cerca de mi casa.
Prefiero una oficina | que **tenga** más luz.
¿Hay algún puesto | que me **ofrezca** todo esto?

—Necesitamos una persona que **sepa** comunicarse bien, que **escriba** claramente...
—Y que **tenga** don de gentes (*a way with people*)...

We can describe someone or something by using adjectives (**Tengo una secretaria bilingüe**) or using clauses also called subordinate sentences (**Tengo una secretaria que habla varios idiomas**). In each case, **bilingüe** and **habla varios idiomas** both describe the secretary and tell us something about her.

Clauses can describe two kinds of entities: a definite or known entity and an indefinite or unknown entity. A definite entity is someone or something you know personally, have contact with, can name, point to, and so forth. An indefinite entity is someone or something you hope exists, are searching for (but aren't sure exists), would like, and so forth. A verb form called the *subjunctive* is used in clauses that describe such indefinite entities. Compare the following examples.

DEFINITE ENTITIES
Tengo un profesor que me **entiende.**
Hay varios trabajos que **pagan** bien.
Vivo con una persona que **hace** mucho ruido.

INDEFINITE ENTITIES
Quiero un profesor que me **entienda.**
Buscamos trabajos que **paguen** bien.
Prefiero vivir con alguien que no **haga** mucho ruido.

Así se dice

Spelling changes in the subjunctive serve to maintain the pronunciation of certain consonants. Remember that to maintain the hard "**g**" of **pagar, llegar, entregar,** and other verbs, a **u** is added to the stem before the vowel **e**. To maintain the hard "**c**" of **buscar, indicar,** and other verbs, **qu** is added to the stem before the vowel **e**.

Indicative	Subjunctive
entrego	entregue
pago	pague
busco	busque
indico	indique

The forms of the present subjunctive are based on the **yo** form of the present indicative (the present tense verb forms with which you have been working).

tomar → **tomo** → **tom-**
conocer → **conozco** → **conozc-**
salir → **salgo** → **salg-**

What makes the subjunctive different from the indicative is that verbs in the subjunctive use the "opposite vowel" in their endings: **-ar** verbs use an **-e-** and **-er/-ir** verbs use an **-a-.** Here are some examples in the third person singular and plural.

-ar (→ -e-)	**-er (→ -a-)**	**-ir (→ -a-)**
tom**e**, tom**en**	com**a**, com**an**	viv**a**, viv**an**
llegu**e**, llegu**en**	teng**a**, teng**an**	salg**a**, salg**an**
pagu**e**, pagu**en**	entiend**a**, entiend**an**	sirv**a**, sirv**an**

Note that **-ar** verbs whose stem ends in g (pagar → **pag-**, llegar → **lleg-**) will add a **u** to maintain the hard **g** sound.

A few verbs in the present subjunctive have irregular forms. Here are the third person singular and plural forms of some of these verbs.

dar	**dé, den**	saber	**sepa, sepan**
estar	**esté, estén**	ser	**sea, sean**
haber	**haya, hayan**		
ir	**vaya, vayan**		

In this section, you will work with third person forms, both singular and plural.

ACTIVIDAD G ¡Te toca a ti!

Forma todas las oraciones que puedas, tomando palabras o frases de los siguientes grupos como en los modelos. Luego compártelas con la clase. ¿Hay otras personas que formaron oraciones iguales a las tuyas?

GRUPO A	GRUPO B	GRUPO C
Tengo	parientes	que me comprenden.
Prefiero tener	amigos	que me comprendan.
	profesores	
	¿ ?	que no saben nada de nada.
		que no sepan nada de nada.
		que me quieren.
		que me quieran.
		que no tienen problemas en ayudarme.
		que no tengan problemas en ayudarme.
		¿ ?

MODELOS   Tengo parientes que me comprenden.

Prefiero tener profesores que me respeten.

ACTIVIDAD H ¿Qué esperas?

Paso 1 ¿Sabes lo que quieres de tu educación universitaria? Indica las cosas que se te apliquen.

Durante mi educación universitaria, espero encontrar…

1. ☐ clases que me gusten.
2. ☐ profesores interesantes que no sean aburridos.
3. ☐ cursos que me preparen bien para el futuro.
4. ☐ personas que vayan a ser mis amigos para toda la vida.
5. ☐ profesores que me den buenos consejos.
6. ☐ un programa que me permita estudiar en el extranjero.
7. ☐ ¿ ?

Paso 2 Todos deben compartir sus respuestas y luego indicar cuáles de las situaciones del **Paso 1** son más (menos) probables.

Consejo práctico

Are you confused about when to use the indicative and when to use the subjunctive? Don't despair! For many learners of Spanish, it takes a long time to internalize the subjunctive. For now, just familiarize yourself with its forms and uses. Once again, mistakes while speaking are a natural part of learning another language; more than likely, such mistakes won't interfere with communication.

COMUNICACIÓN

ACTIVIDAD I ¿Piensas así?

Paso 1 Indica si las siguientes oraciones expresan tus deseos o no.

1. Quiero un trabajo que…
   ☐ esté cerca de donde vive mi familia.
   ☐ esté lejos de donde vive mi familia.

2. Prefiero un puesto en el que yo…
   ☐ tenga grandes responsabilidades.
   ☐ tenga pocas responsabilidades.

3. Espero entrar en una profesión que…
   ☐ ofrezca la oportunidad de viajar mucho.
   ☐ no requiera viajes frecuentes.

4. Necesito un trabajo en el que…
   ☐ yo tenga que relacionarme con muchas personas todos los días.
   ☐ yo tenga que relacionarme muy poco con otras personas.
   ☐ casi no tenga que relacionarme con nadie.

5. Para mí es importante encontrar un trabajo que…
   ☐ pague bien.
   ☐ contribuya algo a la sociedad.
   ☐ requiera mi inteligencia.

6. Si es posible, quiero un trabajo que _____.

Paso 2 Comparte tus respuestas con el resto de la clase. Alguien debe apuntar las respuestas en la pizarra.

Paso 3 ¿Qué buscan los estudiantes de la clase en un trabajo? ¿Qué aspectos les parece que son de mayor importancia? ¿Se puede generalizar a base de las respuestas dadas en los **Pasos 1** y **2**?

Paso 4 (Optativo) Usa las preguntas del **Paso 1** para hacer una encuesta entre personas que no estén en tu clase. Entrevista a personas de diferentes edades, por ejemplo, adolescentes y recién graduados. Presenta las respuestas a la clase. ¿Cómo se comparan con la información del **Paso 3**?

Así se dice

Remember that most subjunctive forms are based on the present tense **yo** form of verbs. The present tense **yo** stem is the same as the subjunctive stem.

hago	**hag-**
salgo	**salg-**
entiendo	**entiend-**
duermo	**duerm-**
pido	**pid-**
conozco	**conozc-**

What is the subjunctive stem of **repetir? venir?**

ACTIVIDAD J Una historia

Paso 1 Trabajando con un compañero (una compañera) de clase, inventa una historia sobre lo que pasa en los siguientes dibujos. A continuación tienen algunas ideas para considerar.

◆ ¿Cómo se llaman las personas?

◆ ¿Quiénes son y cuántos años tienen?

◆ ¿Dónde está la oficina y por qué está allí el joven?

◆ Al final, ¿cómo se siente el joven? ¿Qué va a pasar?

1.

2.

3.

4.

Lección 17 ¿A qué profesión u ocupación quieres dedicarte?

5.   6.   7.

Paso 2 Compartan su historia con el resto de la clase. ¿Quiénes inventaron la historia más interesante?

NAVEGANDO LA RED

Busca información sobre la distribución de profesiones en un país de habla española. Busca el porcentaje relativo de personas que: (1) son profesionales (médicos, abogados, profesores), (2) trabajan en servicios, (3) son obreros y (4) trabajan en la agricultura. Luego busca la misma información sobre este país. ¿Qué diferencias y semejanzas hay? Presenta tus resultados a la clase.

IDEAS PARA EXPLORAR
Las profesiones (II)

VOCABULARIO

¿Qué características y habilidades se necesitan?

Talking about traits needed for particular professions

—Bueno, quieren saber qué **habilidades** especiales tengo. Voy a poner que **hablo varios idiomas...** y que **sé usar una computadora...**

Here is a list of qualities and skills (or abilities) that are useful for talking about particular professions. Some of these expressions you already know.

Cualidades

pensar de una manera directa	**ser honesto/a**
ser carismático/a	**ser íntegro/a** (*honorable*)
ser compasivo/a (*compassionate*)	**ser listo/a** (*clever, smart*)
ser compulsivo/a	**ser mayor**
ser emprendedor(a) (*aggressive, enterprising*)	**ser organizado/a**
ser físicamente fuerte	**ser paciente**
ser hábil para las matemáticas	**tener don de gentes**

Habilidades

hablar otro idioma	**saber mandar** (*to know how to direct others*)
saber dibujar	
saber escribir bien	**saber usar una computadora**
saber escuchar	
saber expresarse claramente	**tener habilidad manual** (para trabajar con las manos)

Note that **saber** + *infinitive* means *to know how to do something* or *to be able to do something*. Spanish does not normally use **poder** + *infinitive* to talk about being able to do something that is related to talent or knowledge.

Sé escribir bien.	*I know how to write well.*
María **sabe escuchar.**	*María knows how to listen.*

but

María **puede levantar** cien libras fácilmente.	*María can lift a hundred pounds easily.*

ACTIVIDAD A ¿Qué profesional?

La clase entera debe determinar qué profesionales deben tener las siguientes cualidades.

1. Deben pensar de una manera directa.
2. Deben ser emprendedores.
3. Necesitan ser pacientes.
4. Deben ser físicamente fuertes.
5. Necesitan ser hábiles para las matemáticas.
6. Deben ser carismáticos.
7. Deben tener don de gentes.

ACTIVIDAD B Definiciones

El profesor (La profesora) va a dar unas definiciones. ¿De qué cualidad se habla en cada caso?

1...   2...   3...   4...   5...

ACTIVIDAD C ¿Qué cualidades?

Paso 1 La clase debe dividirse en grupos de tres. A cada grupo se le va a asignar una profesión.

Paso 2 Cada grupo debe pensar en por lo menos tres de las cualidades que se requieren para practicar esa profesión. Luego debe llenar el siguiente párrafo.

La profesión de que hablamos es _____. En primer lugar, para practicar esta profesión, una persona tiene que _____. También debe _____. Y es muy bueno _____.

Paso 3 Cada grupo va a leer su párrafo a la clase. ¿Están los otros grupos de acuerdo con sus opiniones?

GRAMÁTICA

No hay nadie que...

The subjunctive after negative and nonexistent antecedents

You learned previously that the subjunctive is used after indefinite antecedents. The subjunctive is also used after negative and nonexistent antecedents. These antecedents are people or things said not to exist. Here are some examples.

No hay familia que no **tenga** problemas.
There is no family that does not have problems.

No existen políticos que realmente **se preocupen** por el pueblo.
There are no politicians that really care about the public.

No tenemos empleados que **hablen** español.
We don't have any employees that speak Spanish.

ACTIVIDAD D En esta oficina

Escucha la frase que dice tu profesor(a). Escoge la frase que mejor precede lo que oyes.

1. **a.** Aquí hay una sola persona...
   b. No hay nadie aquí...

2. **a.** No tenemos nadie...
   b. Tenemos un señor...

3. **a.** En mi oficina hay una mujer...
   b. No hay nadie en mi oficina...

4. **a.** No tenemos líder...
   b. Tenemos un buen líder...

5. **a.** Hay sólo un jefe...
   b. No hay ningún jefe por aquí...

6. **a.** Hemos encontrado a una persona...
   b. No hemos encontrado a nadie...

ACTIVIDAD E No hay nadie que...

Piensa en los demás miembros de la clase. Indica si las siguientes oraciones son ciertas o falsas. Si alguna es falsa, explica por qué.

En la clase, no hay nadie que...　　C　　F

1. sea organizado. ☐ ☐
2. sea físicamente fuerte. ☐ ☐
3. sepa dibujar. ☐ ☐
4. haga yoga. ☐ ☐
5. sepa usar una computadora. ☐ ☐
6. llegue tarde a clase. ☐ ☐
7. viva en una residencia estudiantil. ☐ ☐

 **COMUNICACIÓN**

ACTIVIDAD F En nuestra universidad

Paso 1 ¿Qué tipos de profesores hay en tu universidad? ¿Qué tipos de clases? Completa cada oración con algo verdadero, según tu propia experiencia.

PROFESORES
Hay profesores que...
Hay varios profesores que...
Hay algunos profesores que...
No hay ningún profesor que...

CLASES
Hay clases (en las) que...
Hay varias clases (en las) que...
Hay algunas clases (en las) que...
No hay ninguna clase (en la) que...

Paso 2 Todos deben compartir sus respuestas. ¿Qué tendencias hay? ¿Hay tendencias según la especialización de los miembros de la clase?

ACTIVIDAD G En tu opinión

Paso 1 Trabajando con un compañero (una compañera) de clase, comenta la siguiente afirmación. ¿Cuál ha sido su experiencia? Apunten sus ideas.

«No hay nadie que esté totalmente satisfecho con lo que hace en la vida».

Paso 2 Presenten sus ideas al resto de la clase. ¿Hay personas que no se quejen de lo que hacen en la vida?

 NAVEGANDO LA RED

Busca información sobre un puesto (*position, job*) que te parezca interesante. Presenta la siguiente información a la clase.

◆ el lugar y el nombre del puesto
◆ el tipo de trabajo
◆ las cualidades que buscan
◆ el sueldo y los beneficios que ofrecen

IDEAS PARA EXPLORAR

Algunas aspiraciones

GRAMÁTICA

¿Qué piensas hacer cuando... ?

The subjunctive after expressions of future intent

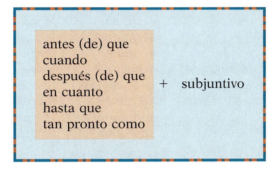

> antes (de) que
> cuando
> después (de) que
> en cuanto + subjuntivo
> hasta que
> tan pronto como

ᵃpara... *why the heck*

You already know a variety of ways to express future intent in Spanish.

> **Quiero ser** arquitecto.
> **Pienso ser** veterinaria.
> **Me gustaría** ser actor.
> **Voy a ser** asesora agrícola.

Whenever you express a future intent with a conjunction that refers to time, the subjunctive mood must follow the conjunction. Conjunctions of time, such as those in the shaded box, are essentially any temporal expressions that relate one event to another.

> No voy a estar contento **hasta que** (*until*) **sea** rico y famoso.
> **Tan pronto como** (*As soon as*) **termine** mis estudios, voy a hacer un viaje a Europa.
> ¿Qué piensas hacer **después de que** (*after*) **recibas** el diploma?

Nota comunicativa

There are a number of formulaic expressions involving the subjunctive that are excellent transition and stalling devices when speaking. Here is one you can use to help string together ideas or to give yourself a slight pause while thinking of how to say something.

o sea... *that is to say* . . .

The following expressions express a noncommittal attitude.

sea lo que sea... *be that as it may* . . .

que yo sepa... *as far as I know* . . .

Compare these projected future events with the following sentences in which either habitual events or something that occurred in the past are mentioned.

Siempre hago la tarea hasta que llega mi novia.
Cuando terminó el año escolar, fui a México para visitar a mis parientes.

Now that you are familiar with the subjunctive, you are ready to see and use other forms. Simply take the **él/ella** form and add the appropriate endings to refer to person and number. Note that the **yo, él/ella,** and **Ud.** forms are the same.

	-ar	**-er**	**-ir**
(yo)	termin**e**	teng**a**	recib**a**
(tú)	termin**es**	teng**as**	recib**as**
(Ud.)	termin**e**	teng**a**	recib**a**
(él/ella)	termin**e**	teng**a**	recib**a**
(nosotros/as)	termin**emos**	teng**amos**	recib**amos**
(vosotros/as)	termin**éis**	teng**áis**	recib**áis**
(Uds.)	termin**en**	teng**an**	recib**an**
(ellos/ellas)	termin**en**	teng**an**	recib**an**

You should now be able to fill in the missing forms for these irregular verbs.

ir: vaya, _____ (tú), _____ (Ud.), vaya, _____ (nosotros/as), vayáis, vayan

ser: sea, _____ (tú), _____ (Ud.), sea, _____ (nosotros/as), seáis, sean

ACTIVIDAD A ¿Quién lo diría?

Indica «quién» diría cada oración si pudiera (¡algunos no pueden hablar!). En algunos casos, es posible que haya más de una respuesta.

a. un bebé de 1 año   **c.** un perro
b. una maestra de primaria   **d.** un chico de 10 años

1. _____ «Me van a dar de comer tan pronto como vuelvan a casa».

2. _____ «No me van a dar dinero hasta que ayude con las tareas domésticas».

3. _____ «Pienso ser abogado como mi mamá cuando sea grande».

4. _____ «No puedo salir hasta que me abran la puerta».

5. _____ «Antes de que se vayan, quiero darles la tarea para mañana».

6. _____ «Después de que comamos, quiero salir a jugar».

7. _____ «Voy a llorar hasta que me den de comer».

8. _____ «Cuando lleguen los invitados, voy a hacer mucho ruido».

9. _____ «Tan pronto como Uds. terminen el ejercicio, vayan a la pizarra a escribir las respuestas».

ACTIVIDAD B Para completar

Completa lógicamente cada oración a continuación. ¿Cuántos de tus compañeros de clase dicen algo similar?

1. _____ tan pronto como (yo) reciba el diploma.
2. _____ después de que terminemos este curso.
3. _____ hasta que digan que es seguro.
4. _____ en cuanto (yo) tenga un poco de dinero.

COMUNICACIÓN

⬚ ACTIVIDAD C Planes profesionales

Paso 1 ¿Qué vas a hacer en las siguientes circunstancias? Indica las respuestas que reflejen mejor tus propias opiniones.

1. Cuando termine los estudios,...
   - ☐ voy a buscar empleo inmediatamente.
   - ☐ voy a seguir estudiando para sacar un diploma avanzado.
   - ☐ pienso volver a casa a vivir con mi familia.
   - ☐ ¿ ?

2. Después de que obtenga cierta experiencia en un puesto,...
   - ☐ me gustaría ser jefe/a.
   - ☐ voy a buscar otro puesto en otro lugar.
   - ☐ creo que me gustaría cambiar de carrera para no aburrirme.
   - ☐ ¿ ?

3. Antes de que me decida a aceptar un puesto,...
   - ☐ pienso consultar con mi familia.
   - ☐ pienso consultar con mis amigos.
   - ☐ pienso consultar con mis profesores.
   - ☐ ¿ ?

---

*Verbs such as **dormir** and **morir (o → ue)** *do* have different stems in these forms (**o → u**): **durmamos** and **muramos.**

4. Cuando por fin alcance todas mis metas (*goals*), yo...

    ☐ voy a estar bastante joven.

    ☐ voy a estar muy viejo/a.

    ☐ voy a tener _____ años.

5. Me gustaría jubilarme (*retire*) cuando tenga...

    ☐ 50 años.   ☐ 60 años.

    ☐ 55 años.   ☐ ¿ ?

Paso 2 Entrevista a un compañero (una compañera) de clase. Formula preguntas basadas en las respuestas que diste en el **Paso 1.** Por ejemplo, si en el número **5** respondiste 55 años, tu pregunta sería «¿Te gustaría jubilarte cuando tengas 55 años?» Escribe tus preguntas antes de la entrevista.

Paso 3 A base de la información obtenida en el **Paso 2,** ¿son semejantes o diferentes tu compañero/a y tú? ¿Qué aspectos de la personalidad de Uds. se revelan a través de las respuestas?

ACTIVIDAD D Otros planes

Paso 1 Todos en la clase deben escoger a una persona famosa. Luego, en grupos de dos, deben terminar las siguientes oraciones desde la perspectiva de esa persona.

1. No voy a _____ hasta que _____.

2. Tan pronto como _____, pienso _____.

3. Antes de que _____, yo debería _____.

Paso 2 Cada pareja debe compartir sus oraciones con el resto de la clase. ¿Son todas iguales? ¿Quiénes captan mejor la personalidad de esa persona?

ACTIVIDAD E ¿Para qué... ?

Paso 1 Revisa el dibujo de Mafalda en la página 443. ¿Entiendes la queja del niño?

Paso 2 Inventa tu propia queja, utilizando el siguiente modelo, y preséntala a la clase. No te olvides de utilizar el infinitivo y el subjuntivo correctamente.

    «¿Para qué cuernos quiero _____ cuando _____ ? ¡Yo quiero _____ ahora!»

¿Cuántas quejas diferentes se expresan? ¿Hay un tema común?

NAVEGANDO LA RED

Busca la página Web de una persona que tenga un puesto profesional. Imprime la página y presenta a la clase la siguiente información.

◆ su nombre

◆ el puesto que tiene

- ◆ dónde estudió
- ◆ qué diplomas tiene
- ◆ otros detalles que te parezcan interesantes

INTERCAMBIO

Recomendaciones para elegir una profesión

Propósito: hacer una recomendación de trabajo o profesión basada en una entrevista

Papeles: una persona que entrevista y otra persona entrevistada

Paso 1 Vas a escribirle unas recomendaciones a un compañero (una compañera) de clase con referencia a la profesión que debe seguir. Primero, lee el siguiente párrafo y piensa en los datos que necesitas obtener para hacer las recomendaciones.

> Según nuestra conversación, veo que tú _____. También he observado que _____. Dices que tus metas personales son _____. Entonces, creo que puedes trabajar en los siguientes campos: _____. Una profesión ideal para ti sería _____.

Paso 2 Vas a entrevistar a una persona en la clase sobre la siguiente lista de temas. Lee la lista y escribe preguntas para cada tema que te ayuden (*will help*) a obtener los datos que deseas sobre esa persona. Tus preguntas deben ayudarte a saber algo sobre la persona sin hacerle preguntas directas sobre su vida privada.

- ☐ la personalidad de la persona
- ☐ las metas de la persona
- ☐ cómo la persona se relaciona con los demás
- ☐ sus intereses
- ☐ sus aptitudes o habilidades especiales
- ☐ ¿ ?

Paso 3 Ahora entrevista a esa persona y apunta sus respuestas mientras habla. Pídele aclaraciones cuando sea necesario.

Paso 4 Completa el párrafo del **Paso 1** con los datos que obtuviste. Agrega otras ideas según tus apuntes de la entrevista. Antes de entregarle tu párrafo al profesor (a la profesora), muéstraselo a la persona que entrevistaste. ¿Qué piensa de lo que escribiste? ¿Dice que le interesa el campo o profesión que le sugeriste?

Vistazos culturales
La revolución y la guerra civil en el mundo hispano

¿Sabías que... en el siglo XX hubo muchas revoluciones y guerras civiles en el mundo hispano? La mayoría de las revoluciones ocurrió durante un período en el que las naciones hispanas querían modernizarse y establecer una economía estable e igualitaria. En algunos casos, la revolución fue el resultado de distintas ideologías políticas.

En Centroamérica, muchas tierras que pertenecían[a] a las comunidades indígenas fueron expropiadas por el gobierno y vendidas a hacendados ricos[b] y compañías extranjeras. Esto provocó grandes rebeliones entre los campesinos[c] y el gobierno.

[a]*belonged*   [b]hacendados... *wealthy landowners*   [c]*peasant farmers*

1979: En **Nicaragua,** los guerrilleros sandinistas derrocaron[a] al dictador Anastasio Somoza y su gobierno militar. El triunfo puso fin a más de 45 años de opresión por las fuerzas paramilitares de la familia Somoza.

[a]*overthrew*

El general Francisco Franco (Madrid, España)

1936–1939: En **España,** durante la Guerra Civil Española, los nacionalistas se enfrentaron a los republicanos por el control del país. En 1939 los nacionalistas, bajo el mando del General Francisco Franco, ganaron la guerra, y Franco se hizo dictador hasta 1975, año de muerte.

You can investigate these cultural topics in more detail on the *¿Sabías que... ?* Online Learning Center: **www.mhhe.com/sabiasque5**.

Revolucionarias mexicanas en 1911

1910–1920: En **México,** durante la Revolución Mexicana, las fuerzas de Pancho Villa y Emiliano Zapata lucharon contra el gobierno del dictador Porfirio Díaz y los hacendados ricos que se habían adueñado de[a] las tierras de los indígenas.

---

[a]se... *had seized*

1959: En **Cuba,** Fidel Castro dirigió un movimiento revolucionario para derrocar el régimen corrupto de Fulgencio Batista. Como presidente, Castro transformó Cuba en una nación socialista.

Fidel Castro, dictador socialista de Cuba

El subcomandante Marcos en Chiapas

1994: En **México,** el Ejército Zapatista de Liberación Nacional (EZLN), guiado por el subcomandante Marcos, se sublevó en contra del gobierno mexicano por las injusticias y la opresión que sufrían los indígenas del estado de Chiapas.

ACTIVIDAD ¿Qué recuerdas?

Indica si las siguientes oraciones son ciertas o falsas.

	C	F
1. Muchos problemas políticos en Centroamérica se deben a la expropiación de la tierra.	☐	☐
2. El EZLN fue un grupo que se sublevó contra el gobierno mexicano.	☐	☐
3. Anastasio Somoza fue dictador de Guatemala.	☐	☐
4. Francisco Franco fue dictador de España por más de 35 años.	☐	☐
5. Entre 1910 y 1920, los campesinos mexicanos se sublevaron en contra del dictador Fulgencio Batista.	☐	☐

NAVEGANDO LA RED

Escoge *uno* de los siguientes proyectos. Luego presenta tus resultados a la clase.
1. Busca información sobre la ocupación francesa de México durante el siglo XIX. Apunta la siguiente información.
   a. las fechas de la ocupación francesa
   b. el nombre y origen del emperador que gobernó México durante la invasión francesa
   c. el significado y la importancia del Cinco de Mayo en México y en este país
2. Busca información sobre la guerra entre España y los Estados Unidos que ocurrió a finales del siglo XIX. Haz lo siguiente.
   a. Apunta cuándo comenzó y cuándo terminó.
   b. Explica algunas de las razones por las que ocurrió.
   c. Resume brevemente el resultado de la guerra y la importancia del mismo para el mundo de hoy.

VOCABULARIO COMPRENSIVO

Campos / Fields

la arquitectura	architecture
la asistencia social	social work
la contabilidad	accounting
el derecho	law
la enseñanza	teaching
la farmacia	pharmacy
el gobierno	government
la medicina	medicine
la moda	fashion
los negocios	business
la política	politics
la terapia física	physical therapy

Repaso: la agricultura, el arte, la ciencia, el cine, la computación, los deportes, la ingeniería, la música, el periodismo, la psicología, el teatro, la televisión

Profesiones / Professions

el/la abogado/a	lawyer
el actor (la actriz)	actor (actress)
el/la arquitecto/a	architect
el/la asesor(a)	consultant
el/la astrónomo/a	astronomer
el/la atleta	athlete
el/la ayudante	assistant
el/la biólogo/a	biologist
el/la científico/a	scientist
el/la contador(a)	accountant
el/la director(a)	director
el/la diseñador(a)	designer
el/la enfermero/a	nurse
el/la escultor(a)	sculptor
el/la especialista	specialist
el/la farmacéutico/a	pharmacist
el/la físico/a	physicist
el/la fotógrafo/a	photographer
el/la gerente	manager
el/la granjero/a	farmer
el hombre (la mujer) de negocios	businessman (business-woman)
el/la ingeniero/a	engineer
el/la jefe/a	boss
el/la jugador(a) de...	. . . player (*sports*)
el/la maestro/a	teacher (*elementary school*)
el/la médico/a	doctor
el/la músico	musician
el/la periodista	journalist
el/la pintor(a)	painter
el/la político/a	politician
el/la presidente/a	president
el/la productor(a)	producer
el/la profesional	professional
el/la profesor(a) (R)	professor; teacher
el/la programador(a)	programmer
el/la psicólogo/a	psychologist
el/la químico/a	chemist
el/la representante	representative
el/la senador(a)	senator
el/la técnico	technician
el/la terapeuta físico/a	physical therapist
el/la trabajador(a) social	social worker
el/la veterinario/a	veterinarian

Cualidades y habilidades / Qualities and Abilities

hablar otro idioma	to speak another language
pensar de una manera directa	to think in a direct (*linear*) manner
saber	to know how
dibujar	to draw
escribir (R) bien	to write well
escuchar (R)	to listen
expresarse claramente	to express oneself clearly
mandar	to direct others
usar una computadora	to use a computer
ser	to be
carismático/a	charismatic
compasivo/a	compassionate
compulsivo/a	compulsive
emprendedor(a)	enterprising, aggressive
físicamente fuerte	physically strong
hábil para las matemáticas	good at math
honesto/a (R)	honest
íntegro/a	honorable
listo/a	clever, smart
mayor (R)	older
organizado/a	organized
paciente (R)	patient
tener	to have
don de gentes	a way with people
habilidad manual	the ability to work with one's hands

Otros verbos

consultar (con)	to consult
dedicarse a	to dedicate oneself to
jubilarse	to retire

Other Verbs

Para expresar la intención futura

antes (de) que	before
cuando (R)	when
después (de) que	after
en cuanto	as soon as

Expressing Future Intent

hasta que	until
tan pronto como	as soon as

Otras palabras y expresiones útiles

la meta	goal
puesto	position, job
o sea	that is to say
que yo sepa	as far as I know
sea lo que sea	be that as it may

LECCIÓN 18

Check out the following media resources to complement this lesson:

 Online *Manual*

 Vídeo on CD

 Online Learning Center

 ActivityPak

¿Qué nos espera en el futuro?

¿Cómo será el futuro? ¿Qué cambios ocurrirán que afectarán al individuo y a la sociedad en general? Mientras examinas estos temas, vas a

◆ aprender algo sobre los posibles avances científicos y tecnológicos

◆ ver cómo se forma el *futuro simple*

◆ ver otros usos del *subjuntivo*

◆ leer un cuento sobre el futuro

ALTO Before beginning this lesson, look over the **Composición** activity on pages 466–467. This is the activity you will be working toward throughout the lesson.

Con la ayuda de las máquinas, este empleado de una fábrica en Quito, Ecuador, puede hacer el trabajo de muchos. ¿Habrá empleo para él en el futuro?

IDEAS PARA EXPLORAR

Las posibilidades y probabilidades del futuro

GRAMÁTICA

¿Cómo será nuestra vida?

Introduction to the simple future tense

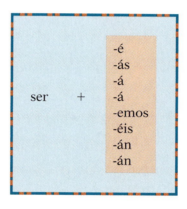

ser + -é
-ás
-á
-á
-emos
-éis
-án
-án

—Creo que en el siglo XXI **habrá** avances médicos muy importantes. **Tendremos** nuevos métodos científicos y una tecnología capaz de curar enfermedades muy graves.

You already know several ways to express future intent in Spanish.

> Muchos estudiantes **piensan especializarse** en las ciencias computacionales.
> La mayoría de la gente **espera llevar** una vida mejor dentro de unos años.
> El mundo **va a ser** muy diferente en el próximo siglo.

Spanish also has a simple future tense, equivalent to English *will + verb*.

> —¿Qué lenguas **serán** importantes en los negocios del siglo XXI?
> —Bueno, el japonés **será** importante.

The *future* tense is formed by adding the endings **-é, -ás, -á, -á, -emos, -éis, -án, -án** to the infinitive of a verb.

> cambiar + é = cambiaré (*I will change*)
> ver + ás = verás (*you* [tú] *will see*)
> vivir + á = vivirá (*he/she/you* [Ud.] *will live*)
> ser + emos = seremos (*we will be*)
> estudiar + éis = estudiaréis (*you* [vosotros/as] *will study*)
> trabajar + án = trabajarán (*they/you* [Uds.] *will work*)

The endings are the same regardless of whether the infinitive ends in **-ar, -er,** or **-ir.** A small number of frequently used verbs have irregular future stems.

decir → **dir-**	diré, dirás, dirá, dirá, diremos, diréis, dirán, dirán
hacer → **har-**	haré, harás, hará, hará, haremos, haréis, harán, harán
poder → **podr-**	podré, podrás, podrá, podrá, podremos, podréis, podrán, podrán
salir → **saldr-**	saldré, saldrás, saldrá, saldrá, saldremos, saldréis, saldrán, saldrán
tener → **tendr-**	tendré, tendrás, tendrá, tendrá, tendremos, tendréis, tendrán, tendrán
haber → **habr-**	habrá (*there will be*)

ACTIVIDAD A ¿Qué predices?°   *What do you predict?*

Paso 1 A continuación hay una lista de predicciones sobre lo que ocurrirá en los próximos diez años. Indica si estás de acuerdo o no.

	ESTOY DE ACUERDO.	NO ESTOY DE ACUERDO.
1. Habrá la posibilidad de seleccionar un «hijo perfecto» por medio de los avances en la genética.	☐	☐
2. No se podrá encontrar comidas con conservantes artificiales, pues estos serán prohibidos definitivamente.	☐	☐
3. Una mujer será presidenta de los Estados Unidos.	☐	☐
4. Desarrollarán una vacuna contra el SIDA.	☐	☐
5. Encontrarán el remedio para el cáncer.	☐	☐
6. Se resolverá el problema del efecto invernadero (*greenhouse effect*).	☐	☐
7. El español llegará a ser* la lengua mundial, reemplazando al inglés como la lengua de los negocios y la tecnología.	☐	☐
8. La ropa será cada vez más unisexual. Por eso, empezarán a desaparecer las secciones separadas para hombres y mujeres en los almacenes (*department stores*).	☐	☐

Paso 2 Usando las ideas del **Paso 1,** averigua las opiniones de tus compañeros de clase.

MODELO   E1: ¿Crees que una mujer será presidenta de los Estados Unidos?
              E2: Creo que sí. (No. No lo creo.)
              E1: Bien. ¿Y crees que... ?

****Llegar a ser** means *to become*, in the sense of a process of evolution, promotion, or change over time.

Mercedes **llegó a ser** jefa después de mucho trabajo.
Buenos Aires **llegó a ser** la ciudad más importante de la Argentina.

Paso 3 Usa las preguntas del **Paso 2** para entrevistar a tres compañeros/as de clase. Apunta sus respuestas.

Paso 4 Llena la tabla a continuación con tus datos del **Paso 3.**

			A	B	C
E1: _____			☐	☐	☐
E2: _____			☐	☐	☐
E3: _____			☐	☐	☐

A = Está de acuerdo con la mayoría de las predicciones.
B = Está de acuerdo con algunas predicciones pero no con otras.
C = No está de acuerdo con ninguna de las predicciones.

 ACTIVIDAD B ¿Y la ropa?

Se dice que si esperas suficiente tiempo la moda de ayer volverá. ¿Qué opinas tú? ¿Qué ropa estará de moda en cinco años? ¿Bajarán o subirán las faldas? ¿Serán anchas (*wide*) o delgadas las corbatas?

Paso 1 Escribe seis oraciones sobre cómo será la moda en veinte años. Comenta por lo menos lo siguiente: los colores, las telas, los tipos de zapatos, dónde y cómo se comprará la ropa.

Paso 2 Compara tus oraciones con las de otras dos personas. ¿Qué semejanzas y diferencias hay entre lo que escribieron Uds.?

ACTIVIDAD C ¿Sabías que... ?

Paso 1 Lee la selección **¿Sabías que... ?** en la siguiente página. Luego contesta las preguntas a continuación.

1. ¿Cuál es el estereotipo de la mujer hispana según la selección?

2. Describe con tus propias palabras lo que está pasando en los países hispanos según lo que has leído y escuchado.

Paso 2 ¿Es la situación en este país igual o diferente de la que se describe en la selección? Los hombres de la clase deben entrevistar a las mujeres, usando las siguientes ideas para formular sus preguntas.

1. la carrera que estudia

2. sus aspiraciones y planes con relación al trabajo y a la vida personal y familiar

Paso 3 Ahora las mujeres deben entrevistar a los hombres, usando las mismas ideas del **Paso 2.** ¿Hay muchas diferencias entre las respuestas de las personas de cada sexo? Después la clase debe comentar lo siguiente y escribir la información en la pizarra.

1. las futuras carreras de los dos sexos

2. planes para el matrimonio u otro tipo de relaciones permanentes con otra persona

3. planes para tener hijos

¿Sabías que...

en muchos países de habla española el futuro está en manos de las mujeres? La imagen estereotípica que se tiene de los países hispanohablantes es que son sociedades «machistas», donde el hombre ocupa todas las posiciones importantes y la mujer queda relegada a hacer los trabajos domésticos y a criar a los hijos. Sin embargo, si analizamos las estadísticas de empleo, todo parece indicar que este estereotipo está muy lejos de la realidad. Según algunos, las mujeres en el mundo hispano están consiguiendo nuevos puestos a un ritmo tres veces mayor que los hombres. Además, cada día más mujeres ocupan puestos administrativos y técnicos en los campos que antes eran territorio exclusivo de los hombres.

Una foto de un folleto distribuido por el Ministerio de Asuntos Sociales de España. ¿Por qué carga tantos sombreros esta mujer? ¿Qué representan?

Parece que esta es una tendencia que continuará en las próximas décadas en todo el mundo hispano. En España, México, Costa Rica, Panamá, el Perú, la Argentina y otros países, las mujeres hispanas están entrando en grandes números en los campos de administración de empresas, derecho, medicina, ingeniería y ciencias. Los investigadores predicen que dentro de pocos años el número de mujeres profesionales empleadas será mayor que el número de hombres.

GRAMÁTICA

¿Es probable? ¿Es posible?

The subjunctive with expressions of uncertainty

(No) Es probable que	
(No) Es posible que	
No es cierto que	+ subjuntivo
Es dudoso que	
Dudo que	
No creo que	

—...y **es poco probable que encontremos** una vacuna contra esta enfermedad en los próximos cinco años, pero hay esperanzas para el futuro lejano.

In previous lessons you learned about the use of the subjunctive with indefinite antecedents and with conjunctions of time. Another important use of the subjunctive is with expressions that indicate uncertainty, doubt, probability, and possibility.

(No) Es probable que una mujer **sea** presidenta de los Estados Unidos en diez años.

(No) Es posible que lleguemos al planeta Marte para el año 2020.

Es dudoso que para el año 2015 **haya** colonias en la luna.

Although negation does not affect the use of the subjunctive with expressions of possibility and probability, it does affect the use of the subjunctive with expressions of doubt, disbelief, and uncertainty.

SUBJUNCTIVE REQUIRED	INDICATIVE REQUIRED
Es dudoso que...	No es dudoso que...
No es cierto que...	Es cierto que...
No creo que...	Creo que...
Dudo que...	No dudo que...

ACTIVIDAD D ¿Estás de acuerdo?

Algunas personas dudan de muchas cosas, no sólo de lo que puede (o no puede) ocurrir en el futuro, sino también del estado de ciertas cosas en el presente. Indica si estás de acuerdo con lo siguiente o no. ¿Y qué piensan tus compañeros?

	ESTOY DE ACUERDO.	NO ESTOY DE ACUERDO.
1. Es dudoso que para el año 2015 les encontremos solución a los problemas del medio ambiente.	☐	☐
2. No es muy cierto que en diez años se pueda seleccionar el sexo de los hijos.	☐	☐
3. Es dudoso que en diez años Quebec sea independiente del resto del Canadá.	☐	☐
4. No es cierto que todas las escuelas públicas sean tan malas como lo dicen las noticias.	☐	☐
5. Es muy dudoso que en este momento el gobierno comprenda los problemas de los que no tienen vivienda.	☐	☐

ACTIVIDAD E ¿Qué es probable que ocurra para el año 2020?

Usando la siguiente «escala de probabilidades» y el subjuntivo, escribe una nueva oración para indicar lo que opinas sobre cada idea.

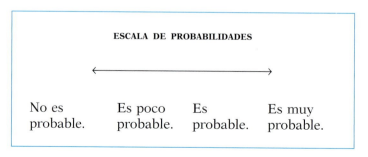

ESCALA DE PROBABILIDADES

No es probable. Es poco probable. Es probable. Es muy probable.

MODELO Los carros dejarán de contaminar el medio ambiente para el año 2020. →
Es poco probable que los carros dejen de contaminar el medio ambiente para el año 2020.

1. Cada estudiante universitario de este país tendrá una computadora personal.
2. Con la eficiencia de la tecnología, el ser humano será más perezoso.
3. Todos usaremos teléfonos celulares.
4. La mayoría de nosotros vivirá en una casa «inteligente».
5. No existirá la institución de la Seguridad Social en los Estados Unidos.
6. México mostrará evidencia de transformarse en el poder económico más importante de Latinoamérica.
7. Todos haremos las compras por la Red.

COMUNICACIÓN

ACTIVIDAD F ¿Dudas?

En la actividad anterior, indicaste la probabilidad de ciertos acontecimientos del futuro. En esta actividad, vas a expresar tus dudas aun más.

Paso 1 Con un compañero (una compañera), indica si las expresiones a continuación implican que se tiene una gran duda, una ligera duda o ninguna duda.

1. Dudo…
2. No creo…
3. Creo…
4. Estoy seguro/a…
5. No estoy seguro/a de…
6. No me parece…

Paso 2 Refiriéndote al año 2020, combina las siguientes oraciones con una de las expresiones del **Paso 1.**

MODELO Creo… / No se venderán libros, sólo vídeos. →
Creo que no se venderán libros, sólo vídeos.

1. La energía solar será más común que la energía nuclear.
2. Los carros funcionarán con electricidad y no con gasolina.
3. La temperatura global subirá de forma permanente debido al efecto invernadero.
4. Habrá una guerra en el espacio.
5. Los hispanos llegarán a ser el grupo mayor de este país.
6. El español será considerado idioma oficial en California, Florida y otros estados de los Estados Unidos.
7. (Inventa una oración relacionada con la condición política o social de este país o con la vida de todos los días.)

Paso 3 Usando la expresión **¿Crees que… ?,** pregúntales a dos compañeros de clase lo que opinan de las afirmaciones del **Paso 2.** Apunta sus respuestas.

Nota comunicativa

Here are some ways you can express your doubt about or rejection of an idea expressed by someone else.

No lo creo.
I don't think so.

¿Hablas en serio?
Are you serious?

¡No puede ser!
That can't be!

A otro perro con ese hueso.
Peddle that story somewhere else.

Sí. Y yo soy el Papa.
Sure. And I'm the Pope.

Paso 4 Escriban siete oraciones en las que describan lo que las otras dos personas y tú creen y lo que no creen.

MODELOS   Todos (no) creemos que (dudamos que...)

Yo (no) creo que..., pero mis compañeros lo creen (dudan).

Marta y yo (no) creemos que..., pero Roberto lo cree (duda).

ACTIVIDAD G En el escenario

Paso 1 Trabajen en grupos de dos. Una persona hará el papel del optimista («Creo que... ») y otra persona será el pesimista («No. Dudo que... »). Inventen un diálogo entre estas dos personas.

Paso 2 Presenten su diálogo al resto de la clase.

NAVEGANDO LA RED

Busca información sobre algún plan para construir un edificio, un parque u otro lugar en un país de habla española. Presenta la información a la clase para describir el plan.

VAMOS A VER

ANTICIPACIÓN

Paso 1 Pronto leerás un cuento titulado «Apocalipsis», del escritor argentino Marco Denevi. Piensa en la palabra **apocalipsis.** En grupos de tres, escriban las ideas que se les ocurren cuando oyen esta palabra. Por ejemplo: fin, final, etcétera.

Paso 2 Comparte tus ideas del **Paso 1** con el resto de la clase. ¿Qué ideas son las más comunes?

Paso 3 Revisa las siguientes palabras y expresiones.

las máquinas	machines	**apretar (ie) un**	to push a
la raza humana	human race	**botón**	button
		bastar (con)	to be enough
alcanzar	to reach; to	**dar un paso**	to take a step
	achieve		

Ahora indica si estás de acuerdo o no con las ideas en la siguiente página. Luego comparte tus respuestas con la clase.

	ESTOY DE ACUERDO.	NO ESTOY DE ACUERDO.
1. Las máquinas ocupan un lugar muy importante en la vida contemporánea.	☐	☐
2. La raza humana se extinguirá algún día.	☐	☐
3. Los seres humanos alcanzaremos la perfección mental y física en el futuro.	☐	☐
4. En un día típico, aprieto por lo menos diez botones.	☐	☐
5. Cada vez que los seres humanos inventan algo nuevo, dan un paso más hacia una vida mejor.	☐	☐

Paso 4 Lee solamente las primeras dos oraciones del cuento a continuación. ¿Qué ideas de los **Pasos 1** y **3** ya aparecen en el cuento?

Paso 5 Contesta las siguientes preguntas.

1. Utilizando la información de la primera oración, ¿en qué año ocurre el cuento?

2. ¿Qué pasa cuando las máquinas «alcanzan tal perfección»?

Apocalipsis

por Marco Denevi

La extinción de la raza de los hombres se sitúa aproximadamente a fines del siglo XXXII. La cosa ocurrió así: las máquinas habían alcanzado tal perfección que los hombres ya no necesitaban comer, ni dormir, ni hablar, ni leer, ni escribir, ni pensar ni hacer nada. Les bastaba apretar un botón y las máquinas lo hacían todo por ellos. Gradualmente fueron desapareciendo las mesas, las sillas, las rosas, los discos con las nueve sinfonías de Beethoven, las tiendas de antigüedades, los vinos de Burdeos, las golondrinas, los tapices flamencos, todo Verdi, el ajedrez, los telescopios, las catedrales góticas, los estadios de fútbol, la Piedad de Miguel Ángel, los mapas, las ruinas del Foro Trajano, los automóviles, el arroz, las sequoias gigantes, el Panteón. Sólo había máquinas. Después los hombres empezaron a notar que ellos mismos iban desapareciendo paulatinamente y que en cambio las máquinas se multiplicaban. Bastó poco tiempo para que el número de los hombres quedase reducido a la mitad y el de las máquinas se duplicase. Las máquinas terminaron por ocupar todos los sitios disponibles. No se podía dar un paso ni hacer un ademán sin tropezarse con una de ellas. Finalmente los hombres fueron eliminados. Como el último se olvidó de desconectar las máquinas, desde entonces seguimos funcionando.

Paso 1 Ahora lee hasta la oración: «Sólo había máquinas».

Paso 2 Como clase, revisen las cosas que fueron desapareciendo y organícenlas según categorías generales, por ejemplo: objetos de uso diario = mesas, sillas. Al final, expliquen qué representan estas cosas y las categorías a las que pertenecen.

Paso 3 Antes de seguir leyendo, expliquen cuáles son algunos de los posibles finales de este cuento. ¿Qué será de los seres humanos?

Paso 4 Lee el resto del cuento y expliquen quién es el narrador (la narradora).

SÍNTESIS

Paso 1 Uds. han leído un cuento sobre el futuro del ser humano. ¿Con cuál de las siguientes películas populares se puede comparar mejor el cuento?

1. *War of the Worlds*
2. *The Terminator, Terminator 2* o *Terminator 3*
3. *Independence Day*
4. *The Time Machine*

Paso 2 En grupos de tres o cuatro personas, traten de explicar por qué desaparecieron los seres humanos. Aquí hay unas ideas para comenzar.

◆ Fueron eliminados por las máquinas.
◆ Se debilitaron (*They got weak*) físicamente hasta que ya no pudieron hacer nada.

 Paso 3 En casa, escribe un breve ensayo de 50 a 75 palabras sobre el tema del cuento.

Paso 4 Revisa tu ensayo y asegúrate del uso correcto de los siguientes puntos gramaticales.

◆ el pretérito
◆ la concordancia entre verbos y sujetos

También, evita el uso excesivo de los pronombres de sujeto (**yo, tú, Ud., él/ella,...**).

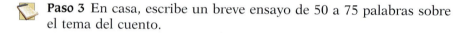

NAVEGANDO LA RED

Busca información sobre el escritor Marco Denevi. Presenta la siguiente información a la clase.

◆ cuándo y dónde nació
◆ qué estudió
◆ los puestos que desempeñó (*had*) además de ser escritor
◆ si ganó algún premio
◆ los nombres de otras obras conocidas que escribió
◆ otros detalles interesantes de su vida

IDEAS PARA EXPLORAR
Más posibilidades y probabilidades

VOCABULARIO

¿Cómo será el futuro?

Talking about the future

Sustantivos	
el beneficio	benefit
la desventaja	disadvantage
el ocio	leisure time
el ordenador	computer (*Sp.*)
el peligro	danger
la ventaja	advantage

Adjetivos	
beneficioso/a	beneficial
peligroso/a	dangerous

*¿Serán **beneficiosos** para el ser humano todos los avances tecnológicos
y científicos? ¿Hay **desventajas** o **peligros** que los acompañen?*

ACTIVIDAD A ¿Cuál es?

Empareja cada palabra con su definición.

1. _____ la desventaja
2. _____ el beneficio
3. _____ el ocio
4. _____ el peligro
5. _____ la ventaja

a. algo que implica consecuencias negativas
b. algo grave, que puede resultar en la muerte
c. algo parecido a un beneficio
d. el tiempo libre
e. una consecuencia positiva

COMUNICACIÓN

ACTIVIDAD B La selección del sexo

Paso 1 Lee la selección titulada «Selección del sexo» en la siguiente página.

Paso 2 Haz una encuesta entre tus compañeros de clase. ¿Qué opinan
de las siguientes afirmaciones? Después la clase debe llegar a una
conclusión sobre el tema.

La selección del sexo de un hijo...

1. será muy beneficiosa para la sociedad en general.

2. será peligrosa para la sociedad en general.

3. tendrá beneficios, pero también consecuencias negativas.

Selección del sexo

Dentro de un par de años será posible elegir el sexo del hijo. Dos días después de la fecundación se podrá conocer la identidad del embrión. Así la pareja o la mamá podrá elegir con toda seguridad el sexo de su hijo. Estos métodos diagnósticos ya son habituales en el Hammersmith Hospital de Londres pero se reservan para esos casos en que una enfermedad se transmite genéticamente por el sexo como, por ejemplo, la hemofilia.

ACTIVIDAD C El ocio

Paso 1 En parejas, hagan una lista de los beneficios de dedicar suficiente tiempo al ocio. También indiquen cuánto tiempo de ocio por semana es suficiente para un adulto.

 Paso 2 Ahora lee la selección «El ocio» y explica con tus propias palabras (25 o menos) lo que pasará con el ocio.

Paso 3 ¿Crees que la disminución del tiempo para el ocio se podrá evitar? ¿Cómo? Todos deben comentar las siguientes posibilidades. Si pueden pensar en otras, coméntenlas también.

◆ reducir las horas laborales de la semana, por ejemplo, de 40 a 30

◆ declarar obligatoria una semana de vacaciones cada tres meses

◆ enseñar en las escuelas secundarias maneras para controlar el ritmo de la vida, incluyendo como enfoque principal el tiempo libre

◆ introducir en el trabajo horas libres con clases gratis de yoga, meditación, ejercicio u otra forma de relajación

El ocio

Aunque parece ilógico, el ocio, o sea el tiempo libre, se convertirá en uno de los bienes más escasos y, por lo tanto, más preciados. Al principio de los años 80 los prospectivistas declararon que la sociedad de los ordenadores, de la robótica y de los satélites nos liberaría del trabajo, dejándonos cada vez más tiempo libre. Hasta el momento ha ocurrido exactamente lo opuesto y lo más probable es que se mantenga la presente aceleración de la vida moderna. La tranquilidad no dependerá de los avances científicos sino de las actitudes personales y sociales.

ACTIVIDAD D ¿Qué haces?

Paso 1 Trabajando con un compañero (una compañera) de clase, comenta la siguiente situación.

Eres miembro del Congreso de esta nación. Un colega presenta una propuesta que obliga a todas las escuelas primarias (públicas) a que ofrezcan cursos de español. La meta es crear una «nación bilingüe» en el futuro. Como miembro del Congreso, ¿qué haces?

Paso 2 Presenten sus reacciones al resto de la clase. ¿Reaccionaron todos igual?

Paso 3 (Optativo) Repitan los pasos anteriores con la siguiente situación.

Eres miembro del Consejo Estatal (Provincial) de Educación. Alguien propone la eliminación de los cursos de idiomas extranjeros a nivel secundario. Parece que el 50% del público está a favor porque quiere más inglés, ciencias y matemáticas, mientras que el 50% está en contra. ¿Qué haces?

Vamos a ver

Now that you've completed the **Vamos a ver** section of **Unidad seis,** watch the corresponding **Vamos a ver** segment on the *¿Sabías que.. ?* video to further explore the themes presented in this unit. There are related pre- and post-viewing activities on the *¿Sabías que... ?* Online Learning Center at **www.mhhe.com/sabiasque5**.

NAVEGANDO LA RED

Busca cualquier información sobre el futuro que a ti te interese. Presenta algunas ideas a la clase y comenta si estás de acuerdo o no con la información.

COMPOSICIÓN

En esta lección has examinado cuestiones sobre el futuro. En esta composición vas a escribir sobre «La vida diaria en el año 2050».

Antes de escribir

Paso 1 El propósito de la composición es predecir ciertos aspectos del futuro y describir cómo será la vida diaria en 2050. Vas a dirigirte a la clase. El tono que adoptes puede ser cómico o serio. La composición deberá limitarse a unas 250 palabras.

Paso 2 Como se trata de la vida diaria, ¿qué temas vas a tratar? ¿Qué temas vas a excluir? Haz una lista de los aspectos que se pueden considerar «de la vida diaria». ¿Cuántos vas a incluir?

Paso 3 Debes prestar atención al aspecto lingüístico. ¿Sabes usar los puntos gramaticales que estudiaste en esta lección?

◆ el futuro

◆ el subjuntivo con expresiones de duda, posibilidad, etcétera

Al escribir

Paso 1 A continuación hay algunas expresiones que pueden ayudarte a expresar tus ideas. No te olvides de tomar en cuenta el tono de tu composición antes de usarlas.

más que nada	*above all*
se caracterizará por	*will probably be characterized by*
por ____ que + *subjunctive*	*as ____ as may ____*
(por contentos que estemos)	(*as happy as we may be*)

Paso 2 Las siguientes expresiones te pueden resultar útiles al escribir la conclusión.

venga lo que venga	*come what may . . .*
pase lo que pase	*come what may . . .*
lo que pasará, pasará, pero…	*whatever happens will happen, but . . .*

Paso 3 Escribe la composición dos días antes de entregársela al profesor (a la profesora).

Después de escribir

Paso 1 Un día antes de entregar la composición, léela de nuevo. ¿Quieres cambiar...

- ☐ los temas?
- ☐ la introducción?
- ☐ la organización?
- ☐ la conclusión?
- ☐ el tono?

Paso 2 Lee la composición una vez más para verificar...

- ◆ la concordancia entre verbos y sujetos.
- ◆ el uso del futuro.
- ◆ el uso del subjuntivo.

Paso 3 Haz todos los cambios necesarios y entrégale la composición al profesor (a la profesora).

Vistazos culturales
El futuro del español en los Estados Unidos

¿Sabías que... el español es uno de los idiomas más hablados en los Estados Unidos? Los datos del Censo 2000 revelan que actualmente hay más de 28,1 millones de norteamericanos que hablan español en casa. Esta cifra representa el 10% de la población total del país. El español también ha sido el idioma elegido por estudiantes que quieren aprender otra lengua. Por lo general, hay más inscripciones[a] en los cursos de español que en los de cualquier otro idioma.

———————————

[a]*enrollments*

EL CENSO 2000					
NÚMERO DE HISPANOHABLANTES EN CASA Y SU PROFICIENCIA (AUTOREPORTADA) EN INGLÉS RESIDENTES DE 5 AÑOS DE EDAD EN ADELANTE					
	1980	**%**	**1990**	**%**	**2000**	**%**
Hispanohablantes en casa	11.116.194	100	17.339.172	100	28.101.052	100
Hablan inglés muy bien	5.534.875	49,8	9.033.407	52,1	14.349.796	51,1
Hablan inglés con dificultad	5.581.319	50,2	8.305.765	47,9	13.751.256	48,9

Una manifestación en el National Mall en Washington, D.C. (abril de 2006)

Hoy día hay un gran debate sobre la necesidad de ofrecer educación bilingüe en los Estados Unidos. Varias propuestas se han formulado en el suroeste del país que fomentan el uso exclusivo del inglés en las escuelas públicas.

Otra cuestión relacionada con el futuro del español en los Estados Unidos es la de la inmigración.

Lección 18   ¿Qué nos espera en el futuro?

You can investigate these cultural topics in more detail on the *¿Sabías que... ?* Online Learning Center: **www.mhhe.com/sabiasque5**.

A pesar de las propuestas para terminar con la educación bilingüe, el número de estudiantes en los Estados Unidos interesados en aprender el español como segunda lengua ha aumentado muchísimo en las últimas décadas. En el año 2000 el *American Council on the Teaching of Foreign Languages* (ACTFL) publicó los resultados de una encuesta sobre las inscripciones en lenguas extranjeras en las escuelas secundarias públicas del país. Como se ve en el cuadro, los estudiantes de las escuelas secundarias se inscriben más en los cursos de español que en los de cualquier otro idioma.

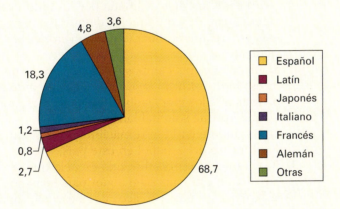

Inscripciones en segundas lenguas como porcentaje de todas las segundas lenguas (adaptado de ACTFL, 2000)

- Español
- Latín
- Japonés
- Italiano
- Francés
- Alemán
- Otras

4,8 3,6 18,3 1,2 0,8 2,7 68,7

Una clase de inmersión total en California

Una celebración mexicana en los Estados Unidos: el Cinco de Mayo, Austin, Texas

ACTIVIDAD ¿Qué recuerdas?

Empareja cada descripción de la columna A con una de las respuestas de la columna B.

A

1. ____: número de personas en el país que hablan español en casa

2. ____: idioma que más se estudia como segunda lengua en las escuelas secundarias del país

3. ____: número de norteamericanos que son bilingües (español/inglés)

B

a. 14,3 millones

b. 28,1 millones

c. el español

NAVEGANDO LA RED

Escoge *uno* de los siguientes proyectos. Luego presenta tus resultados a la clase.

1. La habilidad de hablar y escribir bien el español es una destreza (*skill*) cada día más estimada por las empresas (*businesses*) norteamericanas. Busca anuncios de puestos para profesionales en este país que requieren buen dominio (*proficiency*) del español. Haz lo siguiente.

   a. Menciona tres campos o puestos en los que es necesario saber español y el nivel de dominio que se pide para cada uno.

   b. Indica si los empleados bilingües en español e inglés ganan más que los que sólo hablan inglés.

   c. Basándote en la información que encuentres, da tu opinión sobre el futuro del español en este país.

2. Busca información sobre una escuela que se dedique a enseñar español en este país o en algún país hispano. Haz lo siguiente.

   a. Apunta los datos básicos de la escuela (nombre, dirección, teléfono, etcétera).

   b. Indica los tipos de cursos que se ofrecen (cultura, lengua, español para negocios, etcétera), los horarios de clases y los costos (por curso, de inscripción, etcétera).

   c. Menciona otros detalles que te parezcan interesantes.

VOCABULARIO COMPRENSIVO

Las posibilidades y probabilidades del futuro

Future Possibilities and Probabilities

la duda — doubt

dudar — to doubt
(no) creo que... — I (don't) think that . . .
(no) es cierto que... — it's (not) certain that . . .

es dudoso que... — it's doubtful that . . .
(no) es posible que... — it's (not) possible that . . .

(no) es probable que... — it's (not) probable that . . .

Hablando del futuro

Talking About the Future

el beneficio — benefit
la desventaja — disadvantage
el ocio — leisure time
el ordenador — computer (*Sp.*)
el peligro (R) — danger
la ventaja — advantage

beneficioso/a — beneficial
peligroso/a (R) — dangerous

GRAMMAR SUMMARY

Review of the Conditional Tense

1. The use of the conditional tense in Spanish and English is roughly similar. Both languages use the conditional to refer to hypothetical events, that is, what you *would* do in a given circumstance.

> Con $50.000 me **compraría** una casa.
> *With $50,000 I would buy a house.*

> ¿Qué **harías** tú con $50.000?
> *What would you do with $50,000?*

> **Me encantaría** visitar la Argentina.
> *I would love to visit Argentina. (Lit. Visiting Argentina would really please me.)*

2. Forms of the conditional are highly regular. With the exception of a few verbs, the conditional is formed using the infinitive as the stem plus the endings listed below.

		-ía
		-ías
		-ía
comprar		-ía
comer	+	-íamos
vivir		-íais
		-ían
		-ían

3. The following verbs have irregular stems.

decir	→	**dir-**
hacer	→	**har-**
poder	→	**podr-**
salir	→	**saldr-**
tener	→	**tendr-**
haber	→	**habría** (*there would be*)

Reflexive Verbs and Clothing

The following verbs tend to be used reflexively and are used to talk about clothing: **ponerse, quitarse, verse,** and **vestirse (i, i).**

> —¿**Me pongo** la chaqueta?
> *Should I put on my jacket?*

> —Sí, **pónte**la y no **te quites** el suéter. Va a hacer frío.
> *Yes, put it on and don't take off your sweater. It's going to be cold.*

> Cuando salgo a bailar, me gusta **verme** bien.
> *When I go out dancing, I like to look good.*

Formal Commands

1. Singular and plural formal commands use the **Ud.** and **Uds.** forms of the present subjunctive, respectively. See the FORMS subsection in the section entitled "The Subjunctive" in this grammar summary on pp. 473–474.

2. Remember that direct and indirect object pronouns and reflexive pronouns are attached to the end of affirmative commands and precede negative commands.

> —Profesora, ¿le entregamos la tarea ahora?
> *Professor, should we turn in the homework now?*

> —No. **No me la entreguen** ahora. **Entréguenmela** al final de la hora.
> *No, don't turn it in now. Turn it in at the end of the hour.*

The Subjunctive

USES

The subjunctive has a variety of uses in Spanish; in *¿Sabías que... ?* you have focused on the following uses.

1. The subjunctive with indefinite antecedents: The subjunctive is used in subordinate clauses that modify indefinite antecedents. *Indefinite* means that the person or thing mentioned in the main clause is not known to exist.

> Busco un trabajo **que me permita viajar mucho.**
> *I'm looking for a job that allows me to travel a lot.*

In this example, the speaker is looking for a specific type of job, but he or she does not know if one exists or is hoping that one exists.

Here are some other examples. In each sentence, the indefinite antecedent is italicized and the clause (**que...**) describes the antecedent.

> Necesito *un amigo* **que me comprenda.**
>
> Quiero *un perro* **que no necesite mucho cuido.**
>
> Prefiero ver *una película* **que tenga mucha acción.**

Compare these sentences with the following ones in which the antecedent is not indefinite but rather is known by the speaker.

> Tengo un buen amigo que me comprende.
>
> Existen varias razas de perro que no necesitan mucho cuido.
>
> *Titanic* es una película que tiene mucha acción.

2. The subjunctive is also used in expressions in which the antecedent is claimed not to exist, for example, **No hay nadie, No tengo, No hay trabajo,** and so forth.

> **No hay nadie** que **comprenda** esto.
>
> **No hay trabajo** que **pague** lo que quieres.
>
> **No tenemos** un jefe que **sepa** dirigir a otros.

3. The subjunctive with conjunctions of time: Another use of the subjunctive is with conjunctions of time that express future intent. Here are some of these conjunctions.

antes (de) que	en cuanto
cuando	hasta que
después (de) que	tan pronto como

> **Tan pronto como tenga** dinero, voy a hacer un viaje a Puerto Rico.

In this example, the entire sequence of events is projected into the future. The speaker does not have the money now but thinks he or she will have some in the future. Here are some other examples.

> **Cuando terminen** mis clases, pienso tomar unas vacaciones.
>
> No quiero trabajar **hasta que tenga** que trabajar.

Compare these projected future events with the following sentences in which either habitual events or something that occurred in the past is mentioned.

> Siempre estudio hasta que mi amigo viene a visitarme.
>
> Cuando terminaron las clases, decidí tomar unas vacaciones.

¡OJO! With **antes (de) que** the subjunctive is always used.

4. The subjunctive with expressions of uncertainty: The subjunctive is used with clauses preceded by expressions of doubt, disbelief, uncertainty, probability, possibility, and so on. Here are some expressions that elicit the subjunctive.

dudar que	(no) es probable que
es dudoso que	no creer que
(no) es posible que	no es cierto que

> **No creo que tengas** más días de vacaciones que yo.
>
> **Dudamos que** ella **salga** esta noche.
>
> **Es probable que** ellos **sepan** llegar a este lugar.

Note that if **dudar** and **es dudoso** are negated, then these become expressions of certainty and the subjunctive is not used.

> **No dudo que** tu hermana **es** la mejor cantante de todas.

FORMS

Like **Ud.** commands, the subjunctive stem is the same as that of the **yo** form of the present indicative. The **nosotros/as** and **vosotros/as** forms of most stem changing verbs do not have a stem vowel change.

1. Subjunctive endings take on the "opposite vowel": **-ar** verbs have an **-e-** in the endings and **-er/-ir** verbs have an **-a-**. Spelling changes also appear in the subjunctive in order to maintain pronunciation of certain consonants in the stem (**g → gu, c → qu, z → c**).

	-ar	-er	-ir
(yo)	almuerce	tenga	viva
(tú)	almuerces	tengas	vivas
(Ud.)	almuerce	tenga	viva
(él/ella)	almuerce	tenga	viva
(nosotros/as)	almorcemos	tengamos	vivamos
(vosotros/as)	almorcéis	tengáis	viváis
(Uds.)	almuercen	tengan	vivan
(ellos/ellas)	almuercen	tengan	vivan

2. Verbs with **-ir** endings that have a stem vowel change in the third person preterite have that same stem vowel change in the **nosotros/as** and **vosotros/as** forms of the present subjunctive.

(yo)	me sienta	duerma
(tú)	te sientas	duermas
(Ud.)	se sienta	duerma
(él/ella)	se sienta	duerma
(nosotros/as)	nos sintamos	durmamos
(vosotros/as)	os sintáis	durmáis
(Uds.)	se sientan	duerman
(ellos/ellas)	se sientan	duerman

3. The following verbs have irregular subjunctive stems.

dar	**dé** (but: **des, den,** and so forth)
estar	**esté**
haber	**haya**
ir	**vaya**
saber	**sepa**
ser	**sea**

The Future Tense

1. The Spanish and English future tenses have essentially the same function—to express events that will occur sometime in the future.

> Creo que **estaré** contento.
> *I think I will be happy.*

> Algún día una mujer **será** presidenta de los Estados Unidos.

> *Someday a woman will be president of the United States.*

> ¿**Habrá** clase mañana?
> *Will there be classes tomorrow?*

2. The future is formed like the conditional. The infinitive is used as the stem and the endings shown at the right are added.

		-é
		-ás
estar		-á
ser	+	-á
vivir		**-emos**
		-éis
		-án
		-án

3. Irregular conditional verb stems are irregular in the future tense as well.

decir	→	**dir-**
hacer	→	**har-**
poder	→	**podr-**
salir	→	**saldr-**
tener	→	**tendr-**
haber	→	**habrá** (*there will be*)

APPENDIX

Verbs

A. Regular Verbs: Simple Tenses

INFINITIVE PRESENT PARTICIPLE PAST PARTICIPLE	INDICATIVE					SUBJUNCTIVE		IMPERATIVE
	PRESENT	IMPERFECT	PRETERITE	FUTURE	CONDITIONAL	PRESENT	IMPERFECT	
hablar hablando hablado	hablo hablas habla hablamos habláis hablan	hablaba hablabas hablaba hablábamos hablabais hablaban	hablé hablaste habló hablamos hablasteis hablaron	hablaré hablarás hablará hablaremos hablaréis hablarán	hablaría hablarías hablaría hablaríamos hablaríais hablarían	hable hables hable hablemos habléis hablen	hablara hablaras hablara habláramos hablarais hablaran	habla / no hables hable hablemos hablad / no habléis hablen
comer comiendo comido	como comes come comemos coméis comen	comía comías comía comíamos comíais comían	comí comiste comió comimos comisteis comieron	comeré comerás comerá comeremos comeréis comerán	comería comerías comería comeríamos comeríais comerían	coma comas coma comamos comáis coman	comiera comieras comiera comiéramos comierais comieran	come / no comas coma comamos comed / no comáis coman
vivir viviendo vivido	vivo vives vive vivimos vivís viven	vivía vivías vivía vivíamos vivíais vivían	viví viviste vivió vivimos vivisteis vivieron	viviré vivirás vivirá viviremos viviréis vivirán	viviría vivirías viviría viviríamos viviríais vivirían	viva vivas viva vivamos viváis vivan	viviera vivieras viviera viviéramos vivierais vivieran	vive / no vivas viva vivamos vivid / no viváis vivan

B. Regular Verbs: Perfect Tenses

INDICATIVE										SUBJUNCTIVE			
PRESENT PERFECT		PAST PERFECT		PRETERITE PERFECT		FUTURE PERFECT		CONDITIONAL PERFECT		PRESENT PERFECT		PAST PERFECT	
he has ha hemos habéis han	hablado comido vivido	había habías había habíamos habíais habían	hablado comido vivido	hube hubiste hubo hubimos hubisteis hubieron	hablado comido vivido	habré habrás habrá habremos habréis habrán	hablado comido vivido	habría habrías habría habríamos habríais habrían	hablado comido vivido	haya hayas haya hayamos hayáis hayan	hablado comido vivido	hubiera hubieras hubiera hubiéramos hubierais hubieran	hablado comido vivido

Appendix: Verbs   **A1**

C. Irregular Verbs

INFINITIVE PRESENT PARTICIPLE PAST PARTICIPLE	INDICATIVE					SUBJUNCTIVE		IMPERATIVE
	PRESENT	IMPERFECT	PRETERITE	FUTURE	CONDITIONAL	PRESENT	IMPERFECT	
andar andando andado	ando andas anda andamos andáis andan	andaba andabas andaba andábamos andabais andaban	anduve anduviste anduvo anduvimos anduvisteis anduvieron	andaré andarás andará andaremos andaréis andarán	andaría andarías andaría andaríamos andaríais andarían	ande andes ande andemos andéis anden	anduviera anduvieras anduviera anduviéramos anduvierais anduvieran	anda / no andes ande andemos andad / no andéis anden
caer cayendo caído	caigo caes cae caemos caéis caen	caía caías caía caíamos caíais caían	caí caíste cayó caímos caísteis cayeron	caeré caerás caerá caeremos caeréis caerán	caería caerías caería caeríamos caeríais caerían	caiga caigas caiga caigamos caigáis caigan	cayera cayeras cayera cayéramos cayerais cayeran	cae / no caigas caiga caigamos caed / no caigáis caigan
dar dando dado	doy das da damos dais dan	daba dabas daba dábamos dabais daban	di diste dio dimos disteis dieron	daré darás dará daremos daréis darán	daría darías daría daríamos daríais darían	dé des dé demos deis den	diera dieras diera diéramos dierais dieran	da / no des dé demos dad / no deis den
decir diciendo dicho	digo dices dice decimos decís dicen	decía decías decía decíamos decíais decían	dije dijiste dijo dijimos dijisteis dijeron	diré dirás dirá diremos diréis dirán	diría dirías diría diríamos diríais dirían	diga digas diga digamos digáis digan	dijera dijeras dijera dijéramos dijerais dijeran	di / no digas diga digamos decid / no digáis digan
estar estando estado	estoy estás está estamos estáis están	estaba estabas estaba estábamos estabais estaban	estuve estuviste estuvo estuvimos estuvisteis estuvieron	estaré estarás estará estaremos estaréis estarán	estaría estarías estaría estaríamos estaríais estarían	esté estés esté estemos estéis estén	estuviera estuvieras estuviera estuviéramos estuvierais estuvieran	está / no estés esté estemos estad / no estéis estén
haber habiendo habido	he has ha hemos habéis han	había habías había habíamos habíais habían	hube hubiste hubo hubimos hubisteis hubieron	habré habrás habrá habremos habréis habrán	habría habrías habría habríamos habríais habrían	haya hayas haya hayamos hayáis hayan	hubiera hubieras hubiera hubiéramos hubierais hubieran	
hacer haciendo hecho	hago haces hace hacemos hacéis hacen	hacía hacías hacía hacíamos hacíais hacían	hice hiciste hizo hicimos hicisteis hicieron	haré harás hará haremos haréis harán	haría harías haría haríamos haríais harían	haga hagas haga hagamos hagáis hagan	hiciera hicieras hiciera hiciéramos hicierais hicieran	haz / no hagas haga hagamos haced / no hagáis hagan

C. Irregular Verbs (*continued*)

INFINITIVE / PRESENT PARTICIPLE / PAST PARTICIPLE	INDICATIVE PRESENT	IMPERFECT	PRETERITE	FUTURE	CONDITIONAL	SUBJUNCTIVE PRESENT	IMPERFECT	IMPERATIVE
ir / yendo / ido	voy / vas / va / vamos / vais / van	iba / ibas / iba / íbamos / ibais / iban	fui / fuiste / fue / fuimos / fuisteis / fueron	iré / irás / irá / iremos / iréis / irán	iría / irías / iría / iríamos / iríais / irían	vaya / vayas / vaya / vayamos / vayáis / vayan	fuera / fueras / fuera / fuéramos / fuerais / fueran	ve / no vayas / vaya / vamos / no vayamos / id / no vayáis / vayan
oír / oyendo / oído	oigo / oyes / oye / oímos / oís / oyen	oía / oías / oía / oíamos / oíais / oían	oí / oíste / oyó / oímos / oísteis / oyeron	oiré / oirás / oirá / oiremos / oiréis / oirán	oiría / oirías / oiría / oiríamos / oiríais / oirían	oiga / oigas / oiga / oigamos / oigáis / oigan	oyera / oyeras / oyera / oyéramos / oyerais / oyeran	oye / no oigas / oiga / oigamos / oíd / no oigáis / oigan
poder / pudiendo / podido	puedo / puedes / puede / podemos / podéis / pueden	podía / podías / podía / podíamos / podíais / podían	pude / pudiste / pudo / pudimos / pudisteis / pudieron	podré / podrás / podrá / podremos / podréis / podrán	podría / podrías / podría / podríamos / podríais / podrían	pueda / puedas / pueda / podamos / podáis / puedan	pudiera / pudieras / pudiera / pudiéramos / pudierais / pudieran	
poner / poniendo / puesto	pongo / pones / pone / ponemos / ponéis / ponen	ponía / ponías / ponía / poníamos / poníais / ponían	puse / pusiste / puso / pusimos / pusisteis / pusieron	pondré / pondrás / pondrá / pondremos / pondréis / pondrán	pondría / pondrías / pondría / pondríamos / pondríais / pondrían	ponga / pongas / ponga / pongamos / pongáis / pongan	pusiera / pusieras / pusiera / pusiéramos / pusierais / pusieran	pon / no pongas / ponga / pongamos / poned / no pongáis / pongan
querer / queriendo / querido	quiero / quieres / quiere / queremos / queréis / quieren	quería / querías / quería / queríamos / queríais / querían	quise / quisiste / quiso / quisimos / quisisteis / quisieron	querré / querrás / querrá / querremos / querréis / querrán	querría / querrías / querría / querríamos / querríais / querrían	quiera / quieras / quiera / queramos / queráis / quieran	quisiera / quisieras / quisiera / quisiéramos / quisierais / quisieran	quiere / no quieras / quiera / queramos / quered / no queráis / quieran
saber / sabiendo / sabido	sé / sabes / sabe / sabemos / sabéis / saben	sabía / sabías / sabía / sabíamos / sabíais / sabían	supe / supiste / supo / supimos / supisteis / supieron	sabré / sabrás / sabrá / sabremos / sabréis / sabrán	sabría / sabrías / sabría / sabríamos / sabríais / sabrían	sepa / sepas / sepa / sepamos / sepáis / sepan	supiera / supieras / supiera / supiéramos / supierais / supieran	sabe / no sepas / sepa / sepamos / sabed / no sepáis / sepan
salir / saliendo / salido	salgo / sales / sale / salimos / salís / salen	salía / salías / salía / salíamos / salíais / salían	salí / saliste / salió / salimos / salisteis / salieron	saldré / saldrás / saldrá / saldremos / saldréis / saldrán	saldría / saldrías / saldría / saldríamos / saldríais / saldrían	salga / salgas / salga / salgamos / salgáis / salgan	saliera / salieras / saliera / saliéramos / salierais / salieran	sal / no salgas / salga / salgamos / salid / no salgáis / salgan

C. Irregular Verbs (*continued*)

INFINITIVE PRESENT PARTICIPLE PAST PARTICIPLE	INDICATIVE					SUBJUNCTIVE		IMPERATIVE
	PRESENT	IMPERFECT	PRETERITE	FUTURE	CONDITIONAL	PRESENT	IMPERFECT	
ser siendo sido	soy eres es somos sois son	era eras era éramos erais eran	fui fuiste fue fuimos fuisteis fueron	seré serás será seremos seréis serán	sería serías sería seríamos seríais serían	sea seas sea seamos seáis sean	fuera fueras fuera fuéramos fuerais fueran	sé / no seas sea seamos sed / no seáis sean
tener teniendo tenido	tengo tienes tiene tenemos tenéis tienen	tenía tenías tenía teníamos teníais tenían	tuve tuviste tuvo tuvimos tuvisteis tuvieron	tendré tendrás tendrá tendremos tendréis tendrán	tendría tendrías tendría tendríamos tendríais tendrían	tenga tengas tenga tengamos tengáis tengan	tuviera tuvieras tuviera tuviéramos tuvierais tuvieran	ten / no tengas tenga tengamos tened / no tengáis tengan
traer trayendo traído	traigo traes trae traemos traéis traen	traía traías traía traíamos traíais traían	traje trajiste trajo trajimos trajisteis trajeron	traeré traerás traerá traeremos traeréis traerán	traería traerías traería traeríamos traeríais traerían	traiga traigas traiga traigamos traigáis traigan	trajera trajeras trajera trajéramos trajerais trajeran	trae / no traigas traiga traigamos traed / no traigáis traigan
venir viniendo venido	vengo vienes viene venimos venís vienen	venía venías venía veníamos veníais venían	vine veniste vino vinimos vinisteis vinieron	vendré vendrás vendrá vendremos vendréis vendrán	vendría vendrías vendría vendríamos vendríais vendrían	venga vengas venga vengamos vengáis vengan	viniera vinieras viniera viniéramos vinierais vinieran	ven / no vengas venga vengamos venid / no vengáis vengan
ver viendo visto	veo ves ve vemos veis ven	veía veías veía veíamos veíais veían	vi viste vio vimos visteis vieron	veré verás verá veremos veréis verán	vería verías vería veríamos veríais verían	vea veas vea veamos veáis vean	viera vieras viera viéramos vierais vieran	ve / no veas vea veamos ved / no veáis vean

D. Stem-Changing and Spelling Change Verbs

INFINITIVE PRESENT PARTICIPLE PAST PARTICIPLE	INDICATIVE					SUBJUNCTIVE		IMPERATIVE
	PRESENT	IMPERFECT	PRETERITE	FUTURE	CONDITIONAL	PRESENT	IMPERFECT	
construir (y) construyendo construido	construyo construyes construye construimos construís construyen	construía construías construía construíamos construíais construían	construí construiste construyó construimos construisteis construyeron	construiré construirás construirá construiremos construiréis construirán	construiría construirías construiría construiríamos construiríais construirían	construya construyas construya construyamos construyáis construyan	construyera construyeras construyera construyéramos construyerais construyeran	construye / no construyas construya construyamos construid / no construyáis construyan
dormir (ue, u) durmiendo dormido	duermo duermes duerme dormimos dormís duermen	dormía dormías dormía dormíamos dormíais dormían	dormí dormiste durmió dormimos dormisteis durmieron	dormiré dormirás dormirá dormiremos dormiréis dormirán	dormiría dormirías dormiría dormiríamos dormiríais dormirían	duerma duermas duerma durmamos durmáis duerman	durmiera durmieras durmiera durmiéramos durmierais durmieran	duerme / no duermas duerma durmamos dormid / no durmáis duerman

D. Stem-Changing and Spelling Change Verbs (*continued*)

INFINITIVE / PRESENT PARTICIPLE / PAST PARTICIPLE	INDICATIVE					SUBJUNCTIVE		IMPERATIVE
	PRESENT	IMPERFECT	PRETERITE	FUTURE	CONDITIONAL	PRESENT	IMPERFECT	
pedir (i, i) pidiendo pedido	pido pides pide pedimos pedís piden	pedía pedías pedía pedíamos pedíais pedían	pedí pediste pidió pedimos pedisteis pidieron	pediré pedirás pedirá pediremos pediréis pedirán	pediría pedirías pediría pediríamos pediríais pedirían	pida pidas pida pidamos pidáis pidan	pidiera pidieras pidiera pidiéramos pidierais pidieran	pide / no pidas pida pidamos pedid / no pidáis pidan
pensar (ie) pensando pensado	pienso piensas piensa pensamos pensáis piensan	pensaba pensabas pensaba pensábamos pensabais pensaban	pensé pensaste pensó pensamos pensasteis pensaron	pensaré pensarás pensará pensaremos pensaréis pensarán	pensaría pensarías pensaría pensaríamos pensaríais pensarían	piense pienses piense pensemos penséis piensen	pensara pensaras pensara pensáramos pensarais pensaran	piensa / no pienses piense pensemos pensad / no penséis piensen
producir (zc) produciendo producido	produzco produces produce producimos producís producen	producía producías producía producíamos producíais producían	produje produjiste produjo produjimos produjisteis produjeron	produciré producirás producirá produciremos produciréis producirán	produciría producirías produciría produciríamos produciríais producirían	produzca produzcas produzca produzcamos produzcáis produzcan	produjera produjeras produjera produjéramos produjerais produjeran	produce / no produzcas produzca produzcamos producid / no produzcáis produzcan
reír (i, i) riendo reído	río ríes ríe reímos reís ríen	reía reías reía reíamos reíais reían	reí reíste rió reímos reísteis rieron	reiré reirás reirá reiremos reiréis reirán	reiría reirías reiría reiríamos reiríais reirían	ría rías ría riamos riáis rían	riera rieras riera riéramos rierais rieran	ríe / no rías ría riamos reíd / no riáis rían
seguir (i, i) (g) siguiendo seguido	sigo sigues sigue seguimos seguís siguen	seguía seguías seguía seguíamos seguíais seguían	seguí seguiste siguió seguimos seguisteis siguieron	seguiré seguirás seguirá seguiremos seguiréis seguirán	seguiría seguirías seguiría seguiríamos seguiríais seguirían	siga sigas siga sigamos sigáis sigan	siguiera siguieras siguiera siguiéramos siguierais siguieran	sigue / no sigas siga sigamos seguid / no sigáis sigan
sentir (ie, i) sintiendo sentido	siento sientes siente sentimos sentís sienten	sentía sentías sentía sentíamos sentíais sentían	sentí sentiste sintió sentimos sentisteis sintieron	sentiré sentirás sentirá sentiremos sentiréis sentirán	sentiría sentirías sentiría sentiríamos sentiríais sentirían	sienta sientas sienta sintamos sintáis sientan	sintiera sintieras sintiera sintiéramos sintierais sintieran	siente / no sientas sienta sintamos sentid / no sintáis sientan
volver (ue) volviendo vuelto	vuelvo vuelves vuelve volvemos volvéis vuelven	volvía volvías volvía volvíamos volvíais volvían	volví volviste volvió volvimos volvisteis volvieron	volveré volverás volverá volveremos volveréis volverán	volvería volverías volvería volveríamos volveríais volverían	vuelva vuelvas vuelva volvamos volváis vuelvan	volviera volvieras volviera volviéramos volvierais volvieran	vuelve / no vuelvas vuelva volvamos volved / no volváis vuelvan

VOCABULARIES

The Spanish-English Vocabulary contains all the words that appear in the text, with the following exceptions: (1) most identical cognates that do not appear in the chapter vocabulary lists; (2) verb forms; (3) diminutives ending in **-ito/a;** (4) absolute superlatives ending in **-ísimo/a;** and (5) most adverbs ending in **-mente.** Active vocabulary is indicated by the number of the chapter in which a word or given meaning is first listed (P = **Lección preliminar**). Vocabulary that is glossed in the text is not considered to be active vocabulary, and no chapter number is indicated for it. Only meanings that are used in this text are given. The English-Spanish Vocabulary includes all words and expressions in the end-of-lesson vocabulary lists.

Gender is indicated except for masculine nouns ending in **-o,** feminine nouns ending in **-a,** and invariable adjectives. Stem changes and spelling changes are indicated for verbs: **dormir (ue, u); llegar (gu).**

Because **ch** and **ll** are no longer considered separate letters, words with **ch** and **ll** are alphabetized as they would be in English. The letter **ñ** follows the letter **n: añadir** follows **anuncio,** for example.

The following abbreviations are used:

adj.	adjective	*m.*	masculine
adv.	adverb	*Mex.*	Mexico
Arg.	Argentina	*n.*	noun
aux.	auxiliary	*obj.*	object
conj.	conjunction	*p.p.*	past participle
d.o.	direct object	*pl.*	plural
f.	feminine	*poss.*	possessive
fam.	familiar or colloquial	*prep.*	preposition
form.	formal	*pron.*	pronoun
gram.	grammatical term	*refl.*	reflexive
inf.	infinitive	*rel. pron.*	relative pronoun
inv.	invariable	*s.*	singular
i.o.	indirect object	*Sp.*	Spain
irreg.	irregular	*sub. pron.*	subject pronoun
Lat. Am.	Latin America	*v.*	verb

Spanish-English Vocabulary

A

a to; at (*with time*) (1)
abajo *adv.* below, underneath
abalorio bead
abarcar (qu) to encompass
abeja bee
abierto/a *p.p.* open
abjurar de to renounce
abogado/a lawyer (17)
abrazar (c) to hug (5)
abrigo overcoat (16)
abril *m.* April (2)
abrir (*p.p.* **abierto/a**) to open
absolutamente absolutely

abuelo/a grandfather/grandmother (4)
aburrido/a boring (P); **estar** *irreg.* **aburrido/a** to be bored (10)
aburrirse *refl.* to get bored (10)
abusar de to abuse (12)
abuso abuse (12)
acabar to complete, finish, end; **acabar de** + *inf.* to have just (*done something*)
academia academy
académico/a academic
acampar to go camping (11)
acaso: por si acaso just in case
acceso access

accidente *m.* accident
acción *f.* action
acecho *m.* watching, observation
aceite *m.* oil; **aceite de maíz** corn oil (7); **aceite de oliva** olive oil (7)
aceleración *f.* acceleration
aceptable acceptable
aceptar to accept
acerca de *prep.* about, on, concerning
ácido *n.* acid; **ácido nucléico** nucleic acid
aclaración *f.* clarification

aclarar to clarify

acompañar to accompany

acondicionado/a conditioned; **aire** *m.* **acondicionado** air conditioning

acontecimiento event

acordeón *m.* accordion

acortar to shorten

acostar (ue) to put to bed; **acostarse** *refl.* to go to bed (1)

acostumbrado/a accustomed to

acostumbrar to be accustomed (used) to; **acostumbrarse** *refl.* **a** to get accustomed to; to be (get) used to

actitud *f.* attitude

actividad *f.* activity

activo/a active

acto *m.* act

actor *m.* actor (17)

actriz *f.* actress (17)

actual current

actuar (actúo) to act; to behave; **actuar con naturalidad** to act naturally

acuático/a aquatic

acuerdo agreement; **de acuerdo** in agreement, agreed; **estar** *irreg.* **de acuerdo** to agree; **ponerse** *irreg.* **de acuerdo** to come to an agreement

acusar to accuse

adaptable adaptable

adaptar to adapt, adjust (5)

adecuado/a adequate; appropriate

adelante *adv.* ahead

ademán *m.* gesture

además *adv.* besides, also; **además de** *prep.* besides, in addition to

adicción *f.* addiction (12); **salir** *irreg.* **de una adicción** to overcome an addiction (12)

adicional additional

adicto/a *n.* addict; **convertirse (ie, i) en adicto/a** to become addicted (12); *adj.* addicted; **ser** *irreg.* **adicto/a** to be addicted (12)

adiós good-bye (P)

aditivo additive

adivinar to guess; to predict

adjetivo adjective; **adjetivo de posesión** possessive adjective

administración *f.* **de empresas** business administration (P)

administrativo/a administrative

admiración *f.* admiration

admirar to admire

admitir to admit

adolescente adolescent

adonde *adv., conj.* where

¿adónde? (to) where?

adoptado/a adopted

adoptar to adopt

adoptivo/a: hijo/a adoptivo/a adopted child

adorar to adore, love

adquirir (ie) to acquire

adquisición *f.* acquisition

aduana *s.* customs

adueñarse de to seize, take possession of

adulto adult

adverbio adverb

aeróbico/a aerobic; **hacer** *irreg.* **ejercicio aeróbico** to do aerobics (1)

aeromozo/a flight attendant (16)

aeropuerto airport (16)

afán *m.* preoccupation; urge; enthusiasm; **afán de realización** eagerness to get things done (13)

afectar to affect

afeitar(se) to shave (5)

afeminado/a effeminate

aficionado/a fan

afirmación *f.* affirmation, statement

afirmativo/a affirmative

África Africa

africano/a African

afrocaribeño/a Afro-Caribbean

agacharse to crouch, squat

agalla gill

agave *m.* agave, century plant

agencia agency; **agencia de turismo** travel agency

agente *m., f.* agent; **agente de viajes** travel agent (16)

agobiante *adj.* exhausting

agosto *m.* August (2)

agradar to please

agradecido/a thankful

agrario/a agrarian

agregar (gu) to add (7)

agresividad *f.* aggressivity

agresivo/a aggressive

agrícola *adj. m., f.* agricultural

agricultura agriculture (P)

agrio/a sour (7)

agronomía agriculture (P)

agrupar to group, assemble

agua *f.* (*but* **el agua**) water (7); **agua mineral** mineral water; **esquiar (esquío) en el agua** to water ski (11)

aguacate *m.* avocado (7)

aguantar to bear, put up with, stand

águila *f.* (*but* **el águila**) eagle

ahí *adv.* there

ahogar(se) (gu) to drown

ahora *adv.* now

ahorrar to save

aire *m.* air; **aire acondicionado** air conditioning; **al aire libre** outdoors

aislado/a isolated

ajedrez *m.* chess

ajeno/a of another, belonging to someone else (13)

ajillo: al ajillo cooked in garlic sauce

ajo garlic

al (*contraction of* **a** + **el**) to the; **al** + *inf.* upon, while, when + *verb form*; **al (mes, año)** per (month, year)

alcanzar (c) to reach; to get, obtain; to be sufficient

alcohol *m.* alcohol

alcohólico/a *n., adj.* alcoholic; **bebida alcohólica** alcoholic beverage (9)

alcoholismo alcoholism (12)

alegrar to make happy; **alegrarse** *refl.* to get happy

alegre happy; **sentirse (ie, i) alegre** to feel happy (10)

alegría happiness

alejarse *refl.* to move away; to go far (away)

alemán *m.* German (*language*) (P)

alemán, alemana *n., adj.* German

Alemania Germany

alerta *inv.* alert

alfarería pottery

álgebra *m.* algebra

algo something

algodón *m.* cotton (16)

alguien someone

algún, alguno/a some, any (P); **algunas veces** sometimes

aliento breath

alimentar to feed

alimenticio/a nutritional; **pasta alimenticia** pasta (7)

alimento food; **alimento básico** basic food (7)

alistar to enlist

aliviar to relieve; to lessen

allá *adv.* there; **de aquí para allá** from here to there (15)

allí *adv.* there

almacén *n.* department store; warehouse

almohada pillow
almorzar (ue) (c) to have lunch (1)
almuerzo lunch (7)
alojamiento lodging (16)
alojarse *refl.* to stay, lodge (16)
Alpes *m. pl.* Alps
alpino/a alpine
alquilar to rent
alrededor de *prep.* around
alrededores *n. m. pl.* surroundings
alto/a tall; high; **el/la más alto/a (de)** the tallest (5); **en voz alta** aloud; **más alto/a (que)** taller (than) (5); **zapato de tacón alto** high-heeled shoe (16)
aludir to allude
alumno/a student
amante *m., f.* lover
amar to love (13)
amargo/a bitter (7)
amarillo/a yellow (7)
Amazonia *f.* Amazon region
ambicioso/a ambitious (14)
ambiental environmental
ambiente *m.* surroundings, environment; **medio ambiente** environment, surroundings
ambos/as *adj.* both
amenazar (c) to threaten
América del Norte North America
América del Sur South America
americano/a American; **fútbol** *m.* **americano** football; **jugar (ue) (gu) al fútbol americano** to play football (2)
amigo/a friend (P)
amistad *f.* friendship
amor *m.* love
análisis *m.* analysis
analizar (c) to analyze
anaranjado/a *adj.* orange
ancas *f. pl.* **de rana** frog's legs
ancho/a wide
andaluz(a) *n., adj.* Andalusian
andar *irreg.* to walk (3); to go; **andar en bicicleta** to ride a bicycle (11); **andar en monopatín** to ride a scooter, skateboard (11); **andar en patineta** to skateboard (11)
andino/a *n., adj.* Andean
ángel *m.* angel
anglosajón, anglosajona Anglo-Saxon
animado/a: dibujo animado cartoon
animal *m.* animal; **animal doméstico** domestic animal, pet

animar to vitalize; **animarse** *refl.* to come to life
ánimo spirit; **estado de ánimo** state of mind (10)
anoche *adv.* last night (3)
ansiedad *f.* anxiety
ansioso/a anxious
antepasado ancestor
anterior previous
ante before; in the face of; in front of
antes *adv.* before; **antes (de) que** *prep.* before (17)
anticipación *f.*: **con anticipación** in advance; **reservar con (un mes de) anticipación** to reserve (a month) in advance (16)
antiestético/a unaesthetic
antiguamente long ago; formerly
antigüedad *f.* antique
antiguo/a old; ancient
antihéroe *m.* antihero
antónimo *m.* antonym
antropología anthropology (P)
anual *adj.* annual
anular to overturn
anunciar to announce
anuncio advertisement; **anuncio comercial** commercial (ad)
añadir to add
año year; **hace unos años** a few years ago; **los años 20** the twenties (6); **tener** *irreg.* _____ **años** to be _____ years old (4)
aparato apparatus, device, appliance
aparecer (zc) to appear
apariencia appearance
apartamento apartment; **limpiar el apartamento** to clean the apartment (2)
apasionado/a passionate (14)
apático/a apathetic (14)
apechugar (gu) con to put up with
apellido last name (4)
aperitivo appetizer; aperitif
apertura opening
apetecer (zc) to be appetizing (7), to appeal, to be appealing (*food*) (7); **no me apetece** it doesn't appeal to me
aplicado/a *adj.* devoted; *p.p.* applied
aplicar (qu) to apply
apocalipsis *m.* Apocalypse
aportar to bring
apoyar to rest, lean; to support (*emotionally*) (5)

apoyo support
apreciar to esteem; to appreciate
aprender to learn
aprendizaje *m.* learning period
apretar (ie) to tighten; **apretar un botón** to push a button
aprobar (ue) to pass; to approve
aprobatorio/a passing; **calificación** *f.* **mínima aprobatoria** minimum passing grade
apropiado/a appropriate
aprovechar to take advantage of
aproximado/a approximate
aptitud *f.* aptitude, ability
apuntar to jot down
apuntes *m. pl.* notes; **tomar apuntes** to take notes
aquel, aquella *adj.* that; *pron.* that one
aquí *adv.* here (P); **de aquí para allá** from here to there (15)
árabe *adj.* Arab
árbol *m.* tree; **árbol genealógico** family tree
área *f.* (*but* **el área**) area
argentino/a Argentine
argumento argument; plot
árido/a arid
arma *f.* (*but* **el arma**) weapon
armado/a armed; **fuerzas armadas** armed forces
armario closet (16)
aroma *m.* aroma
aromaterapia *f.* aromatherapy; **utilizar (c) la aromaterapia** to use aromatherapy (11)
arquitecto/a architect (17)
arquitectura architecture (17)
arrabales *m. pl.* slums
arrancar (qu) to rip out
arreglar to arrange; to fix
arrepentir (ie, i): más vale prevenir que arrepentir an ounce of prevention is worth a pound of cure
arriba *adv.* up above
arriesgado/a daring (13)
arrogante arrogant
arroz *m.* rice (7)
arte *m.* art; **objeto de arte** work of art (P)
artesanía *s.* crafts
artesano/a *n.* artisan
artículo article
artificial artificial
artista *m., f.* artist
artístico/a artistic
artritis *f.* arthritis

asado/a roast(ed) (7); **(medio) pollo asado** (half a) roasted chicken (7)

ascendencia ancestry

ascensor *m.* elevator

asco: dar *irreg.* **asco** to disgust

asegurar to assure (5)

asentamiento: lugares *m.* **de asentamiento** settling places

asesinar to assassinate

asesor(a) consultant (17)

así *adv.* thus, so

Asia Asia

asiático/a Asiatic

asiento seat (16); **tomar asiento** to take a seat

asignar to assign

asignatura subject

asistencia social social work (17)

asistente *m., f.* assistent; **asistente social** social worker

asistir (a) to attend (1); to assist

asociación *f.* association

asociar(se) to associate

asombrar to surprise; to astonish

aspecto aspect; appearance

aspiración *f.* aspiration

aspirina aspirin

asqueroso/a disgusting

astilla chip, splinter; **de tal palo, tal astilla** a chip off the old block

astronomía astronomy (P)

astronómico/a astronomical

astrónomo/a astronomer (17)

astuto/a astute (14)

asunto topic, matter

asustado/a afraid (10); **estar** *irreg.* **asustado/a** to be afraid (10)

asustar to frighten (10)

ataque *m.* attack; **ataque cardíaco** heart attack

atención *f.* attention; **llamar la atención** to attract attention; **prestar atención** to pay attention

atender (ie) to wait on (*a customer*) (8)

atentamente attentively

atleta *m., f.* athlete (17)

atmosférico/a: presión atmosférica atmospheric pressure

atractivo/a attractive (P)

atraer (*like* **traer**) to attract

atreverse (a) to dare (to) (13)

atribuir (y) to attribute

atributo attribute

atrocidad *f.* atrocity

atún *m.* tuna (7)

aumentar to increase

aumento *m.* increase

aun *adv.* even

aún *adv.* still, yet

aunque even though

ausente absent

auténtico/a authentic

auto car

autobús *m.* bus (16)

autoestima self-esteem (12)

automático/a automatic; **vendedora automática** vending machine

automóvil *m.* automobile

automovilístico/a *adj.* automobile

autor(a) author

autoreportado/a self-reported

autoritario/a authoritarian

autostop *m.*: **hacer** *irreg.* **autostop** to hitchhike (16)

auxiliar *m., f.* **de vuelo** flight attendant (16)

avance *m.* advance

avanzado/a advanced

avanzar (c) to advance

ave *f.* (*but* **el ave**) bird; *pl.* poultry (7)

avena *s.* oats

avenida avenue

aventura adventure

aventurero/a adventurous (5)

avergonzado/a ashamed, embarrassed (10); **sentirse (ie, i) avergonzado/a** to feel ashamed, embarrassed (10)

averiguar (güe) to find out

avión *m.* airplane (16)

ayer *adv.* yesterday (3); **ayer por la mañana/tarde/noche** yesterday morning/afternoon; last night

ayuda help; *pl.* aids

ayudante assistant (17)

ayudar to help

ayuntamiento city hall

azafrán *m.* saffron

azteca *n., adj. m., f.* Aztec

azúcar *m.* sugar (7)

azul blue; **ojos azules** blue eyes (5)

B

bailador(a) dancer

bailar to dance (2)

baile *m.* dance

bajar to lower; to go down; **bajar de** to get off (*a bus, car, plane*) (16)

bajo *prep.* under

bajo/a short (*height*) (5)

balanceado/a balanced

baleares: Islas Baleares Balearic Islands

banana banana (7)

bancario/a banker

banco bank

bandera flag

banquete *m.* banquet

bañar to bathe (*someone or something*) (5); **bañarse** *refl.* to bathe oneself; **bañarse en un jacuzzi** to bathe in a jacuzzi (11)

bañera bathtub

baño bathroom; **habitación** *f.* **con baño privado** room with a private bath (16); **traje** *m.* **de baño** bathing suit (16)

bar *m.* bar

barato/a inexpensive (6)

barbacoa barbecue

barbilla chin

barco boat (16); **navegar (gu) en un barco** to sail (11)

barra bar

barrer to sweep

barrio neighborhood

barrita small loaf (*bread*)

basar to base; **basarse en** to base one's opinions on

base *f.* base; **a base de** on the basis of

básico/a basic; **alimento básico** basic food

basquetbol *m.* basketball; **jugar (ue) (gu) al basquetbol** to play basketball (10)

bastante *adj., adv.* enough

bastar to be enough

batalla battle

bebé *m., f.* baby

beber to drink (9)

bebida drink, beverage (9); **bebida alcohólica** alcoholic beverage (9)

béisbol *m.* baseball; **jugar (ue) (gu) al béisbol** to play baseball (10)

beisbolista *m., f.* baseball player

Bélgica Belgium

bello/a beautiful

beneficio benefit (18)

beneficioso/a beneficial (18)

benigno/a harmless

benjamín *m.* youngest son/child

besar to kiss (5)

beso kiss

biblioteca library (1)

bicicleta bicycle; **andar** *irreg.* **en bicicleta** to ride a bicycle (11); **montar en bicicleta** to ride a bicycle

bien *adv.* well; **bien frío** very cold (9); **caer** *irreg.* **bien** to make a good impression (7); to agree with (*food*) (7); **llevarse bien** to get along well (5); **para sentirse (ie, i) bien** to feel well (10); **pasarlo bien** to have a good time; **verse** *irreg.* **bien** to look good (16)

bienes *m. pl.* goods, possessions

bienestar *m.* well-being

bife *m. Arg.* steak

bilingüe bilingual

bilingüismo bilingualism

billete *m.* ticket; **billete de ida** one-way ticket (16); **billete de ida y vuelta** round-trip ticket (16)

biográfico/a biographical

biología biology (P)

biológico/a biological

biólogo/a biologist (17)

biosíntesis biosynthesis

bistec *m.* steak (7)

Blancanieves Snow White

blanco/a *adj.* white (7); **pan** *m.* **blanco** white bread (7); **vino blanco** white wine (9)

blando/a soft

bluejeans *m. pl.* jeans (16)

blusa blouse (16)

boca mouth (8)

bocacalle *f.* intersection (15)

boda wedding

boga: en boga in vogue, in style

boletín *m.* news bulletin

boleto ticket; **boleto de ida** one-way ticket (16); **boleto de ida y vuelta** round-trip ticket (16)

boliche *m.:* **jugar (ue) (gu) al boliche** to bowl (10)

bollería assorted breads and rolls (7)

bollo roll (7)

bolsa bag; sack; purse; stock market

bolsillo pocket

bolsita para llevar doggie bag (7)

bombilla *small pipe for drinking mate*

bonito/a pretty (P)

bordado/a embroidered

bordo: a bordo on board

borrador *m.* rough draft

bosque *m.* forest (11)

bosquejo outline

botella bottle

botón *m.* button; **apretar (ie) un botón** to push a button

botones *m. s.* bellhop (16)

boxeo boxing

Brasil: el Brasil Brazil

brazo arm (8)

breve brief

brillante brilliant

bruja witch

brújula compass

bruto: producto nacional bruto Gross National Product

bucear to dive (11)

buen, bueno/a good (P); **buen provecho** enjoy your meal; **(muy) buena idea** a (very) good idea (8); **buenas noches** good evening (P); **buenas tardes** good afternoon (P); **buenos días** good morning (P); **buenos modales** good manners (8); **estar** *irreg.* **de buen humor** to be in a good mood (10); **hace buen tiempo** the weather's good (2); **sacar (qu) una buena nota** to get a good grade (10); **tener** *irreg.* **buena educación** to be well-mannered (8)

buey *m.* ox

bufón, bufona buffoon

búho owl

burdel *m.* brothel

Burdeos Bordeaux

burlarse (de) to make fun (of), laugh (at) (13)

buscar (qu) to look for

C

caballería knighthood; **novelas de caballería** novels about chivalry

caballero gentleman

caballo horse

cabeza head; **(tener** *irreg.***) dolor de cabeza** (to have a) headache (10)

cabina cabin (16)

cable *m.* cable; **televisión** *f.* **por cable** cable television

cabo end; cape; **al fin y al cabo** in the end, when all is said and done; **llevar a cabo** to carry out

cabra goat

cacahuete *m.:* **mantequilla de cacahuete** peanut butter (7)

cada *inv.* each (2); every

cadena chain; channel (*television*)

caer *irreg.* to fall (down); **caer bien/mal** to make a good/bad impression (7); to (dis)agree with (*food*) (7)

café *m.* coffee (7); **café con leche** coffee with milk (7); **café descafeinado** decaffeinated coffee (9);

color *m.* **café** brown; **tomar un café** to drink a cup of coffee (2)

cafeína caffeine (9)

cafetería cafeteria

caimán *m.* alligator

calcetín *m.* sock (16)

calcio calcium (7)

calcular to calculate

cálculo calculus (P); calculation

calendario calendar

calentamiento heating, warming

calentar (ie) to warm up

calidad *f.* quality

caliente hot; **bien caliente** very hot (9); **perrito caliente** hot dog

calificación *f.* rating; assessment; grade; **calificación mínima aprobatoria** minimum passing grade

calificar (qu) to rate; to assess

callar to quiet (down)

callado/a quiet; **permanecer (zc) callado** to keep quiet (10)

calle *f.* street; **cruce la calle** cross the street (15)

calmado/a calm (13)

calmar to soothe

calor *m.* heat; warmth; **hace (mucho) calor** it's (very) hot (*weather*) (2); **tener** *irreg.* **calor** to be (feel) hot (person)

caloría calorie

calórico/a caloric

calvo/a bald (5)

cama bed (16); **hacer** *irreg.* **la cama** to make the bed; **cama matrimonial** double bed (16); **cama sencilla** twin bed (16)

cámara camera; chamber

camarero/a waiter, waitress (8); flight attendant (16)

camarón *m. Lat. Am.* shrimp (7)

cambiar to change; **cambiar de idea/opinión** to change one's mind

cambio change; **en cambio** on the other hand

caminar to walk (10)

camino road, path

camión *m.* truck; *Mex.* bus

camisa shirt (16)

camiseta T-shirt (16)

campeonato championship

cámping: hacer *irreg.* **cámping** to go camping (11)

campo country(side); field (17); **obrero/a del campo** farm worker

campus *m.* campus
Canadá: el Canadá Canada
canadiense *n., adj.* Canadian
canal *m.* channel
canario canary
cancelar to cancel; to strike out
cáncer *m.* cancer
canción *f.* song
canoso/a gray (hair)
cansado/a tired (10); **estar** *irreg.* **cansado/a** to be tired (10)
cansarse *refl.* to get tired (10)
cantante *m., f.* singer
cantar to sing (10)
cantidad *f.* quantity; **de cantidad** *adj.* quantifying (P)
cantina canteen
caña cane; **caña de azúcar** sugar cane
cañaveral *m.* sugar cane field
caótico/a chaotic (13)
capa cape; layer; **capa de ozono** ozone layer
capacidad *f.* ability; capacity; **capacidad para** ability to
capaz (*pl.* **capaces**) capable; **capaz de dirigir a otros** able to direct others (13)
capital *f.* capital (*city*)
capítulo chapter
captar to capture; to understand
cara face (5)
caracol *m.* snail
carácter *m.* (*pl.* **caracteres**) character
característico/a characteristic; **característica de la personalidad** personality trait (5); **característica física** physical characteristic, trait (5)
caracterizar (c) to characterize
carbohidrato carbohydrate
carcajadas: reír(se) (i, i) a carcajadas to laugh loudly (11)
cardíaco/a cardiac; **ataque** *m.* **cardíaco** heart attack
cardo thistle
cargar (gu) to carry
Caribe *m.* Caribbean (Sea)
caribeño/a *adj.* Caribbean
cariñoso/a affectionate
carismático/a charismatic (17); **ser carismático/a** to be charismatic
carne *f.* meat (7); flesh; **carne de res** beef (7); **carne roja** red meat
carnicería meat, butcher shop
carnívoro/a carnivorous
caro/a expensive (16)

carrera major (P); career; race; **¿qué carrera haces?** what's your major? (P)
carretera highway
carro car
carta letter
cartero/a mail carrier
casa house; home; **quedarse en casa** to stay at home (2); **limpiar la casa** to clean the house (2)
casado/a married (4)
casarse *refl.* to get married
cascabel *f.*: **serpiente** *f.* **de cascabel** rattlesnake
casco helmet
casero/a homemade; domestic
casi *adv.* almost
caso case
castaño/a brown (5); **ojos castaños** brown eyes (5)
castigar (gu) to punish (9)
castigo físico corporal punishment
castillo castle
catalán, catalana *n., adj.* Catalan
Cataluña Catalonia
catastrófico/a catastrophic
categoría category; class
categorizar (c) to categorize
catolicismo Catholicism
católico/a Catholic
catorce fourteen (P)
causa cause; **a cause de** because of
causar to cause; **causar risa** to cause laughter, make laugh (11)
caviar *m.* caviar
cazar (c) to hunt
cebolla onion
ceder to yield
ceja eyebrow
celebración *f.* celebration
célebre famous
celos: tener *irreg.* **celos** to be jealous
celoso/a jealous (13)
celular: (teléfono) celular cell phone
cementerio cemetery
cena dinner (7); **preparar la cena** to prepare dinner (3)
cenar to have dinner (1)
censo census
centavo cent
centígrado/a *adj.* centigrade
centro center; **centro comercial** shopping mall
Centroamérica Central America
centroamericano/a *n., adj.* Central American

cerca (de) near, close (15)
cerdo: chuleta de cerdo pork chop (7)
cereal *m.* cereal, grain (7)
cerebro brain
ceremonia ceremony
cero zero (P)
cerrado/a closed
cerrar (ie) to close
certeza certainty
cerveza beer (9)
champán *m.* champagne
champiñón *m.* mushroom
champú *m.* shampoo
chapulín *m. Mex.* grasshopper
chaqueta jacket (16)
charla *n.* conversation, chat
charlar to chat (2)
chat *m.* chat room
chatear to chat, participate in a chat room (2)
chau ciao (P)
Checoslovaquia Czechoslovakia
cheque *m.* check
chicle *m.* gum
chico/a boy, girl (P); *adj.* small
chile *m.* pepper
chileno/a *n., adj.* Chilean
chimenea chimney
chimpancé *m.* chimpanzee
chino/a Chinese; **horóscopo chino** Chinese horoscope
chisme *m.* rumor; gossip
chismoso/a gossipy (13)
chiste *m.* joke; **contar (ue) un chiste** to tell a joke (10); **chiste verde** off-color joke
chistoso/a funny (11)
chocar (qu) con to hit; bump into
chocolate *m.* chocolate
chófer *m.* driver
chorizo sausage
chuleta de cerdo pork chop (7)
churro *type of fried dough* (7)
ciberadicción *f.* addiction to the Internet
cibernauta *m., f. person who spends a lot of time on line surfing the Net*
cien(to) one hundred (6); **por ciento** percent
ciencia science; **ciencia ficción** science fiction; **ciencias** *pl.* **naturales** natural sciences (P); **ciencias** *pl.* **políticas** political science (P); **ciencias** *pl.* **sociales** social sciences (P)
científico/a *n.* scientist (17); *adj.* scientific

cierto/a true; certain (5); **(no) es cierto que** ___ it's (not) certain that ___ (18)

cifra number (6); figure

cinco five (P)

cincuenta fifty (6)

cine *m.* movie theater; **ir** *irreg.* **al cine** to go to the movies (2)

circular to circulate; to move

círculo circle

circunstancia circumstance

cita appointment, date

ciudad *f.* city

ciudadano/a citizen

civil civil; **guerra civil** civil war

civilización *f.* civilization

claramente clearly; **expresarse** *refl.* **claramente** to express oneself clearly (17)

clarificación *f.* clarification

clarificar (qu) to clarify

claro *adv.* clearly; **claro que sí** of course; **está claro** it's clear (5)

claro/a *adj.* clear; light

clase *f.* class (P); type, kind; **clase turística** economy class (16); **compañero/a de clase** classmate (P); **primera clase** first class (16)

clásico/a classic

clasificación *f.* classification

clasificar (qu) to classify

claustrofobia claustrophobia

clave *n. f.; adj. inv.* key

cliente/a customer (8)

clima *m.* climate

climático/a climatic

clínica clinic

club *m.* club

cobarde cowardly (14)

cobija blanket

cocaína cocaine

coche *m.* car

cocido/a cooked

cocina kitchen; cuisine

cocinado/a cooked (7)

cocinar to cook

cocinero/a chef, cook (8)

coco coconut

cóctel *m.* cocktail

codo elbow (8)

cognado cognate

cognitivo/a cognitive

coherente coherent

coincidencia coincidence

coincidir to coincide

cola tail; line; **hacer** *irreg.* **cola** to stand in line (16)

colaborar to collaborate

colapso collapse

colectivo/a collective

colega *m., f.* colleague

colesterol *m.* cholesterol

colgar (ue) (gu) to hang (up)

colmena beehive

colocar (qu) to place, arrange

colombiano/a *n., adj.* Colombian

colonia neighborhood; colony

color *m.* color (5); **color café** brown; **¿de qué color es/son ___?** what color is/are ___? (5)

columna column

comandante commander

combatible combative

combatir to fight

combinación *f.* combination

combinar to combine

comentar to comment on; to discuss

comentario commentary

comenzar (ie) (c) to begin; **comenzar a** + *inf.* to begin to (*do something*)

comer to eat (1); **comerse** *refl.* **las uñas** to bite one's nails (10); **dar** *irreg.* **de comer** to feed; **hábito de comer** eating habit (7)

comercial: anuncio comercial commercial (ad); **centro comercial** shopping mall

comercio commerce

cometer to commit

cómico/a comic(al), funny (P); **tira cómica** comic strip

comida meal (7); food (7); **comida para llevar** food to go (8); **comida rápida** fast food

comienzo beginning

comino: importar un comino not to matter at all

como *prep.* like; **tal como** just as; **tan ___ como** as ___ as (6); **tan pronto como** as soon as (7); **tanto/a ___ como** as much ___ as (6); **tantos/as ___ como** as many ___ as (6)

¿cómo? *adv.* how?; pardon me? (P); **¿cómo te llamas / se llama usted?** what's your name? (P) **¿cómo te sientes** how do you feel? (10); **perdón, ¿cómo se llega a ___?** excuse me, how do you get to ___? (15)

comodidad *f.* convenience, amenity (16)

cómodo/a comfortable

comoquiera *adv.* however

compañero/a companion; **compañero/a de clase** classmate (P); **compañero/a de cuarto** roommate (P)

compañía company; **hacer** *irreg.* **compañía** to keep company

comparación *f.* comparison (6)

comparado/a (con) compared (with)

comparar to compare

compartir to share

compasivo/a compassionate (17)

competitivo/a competitive

compilar to compile

complejo/a complex

completamente completely

completar to complete

completo/a complete; full, no vacancy (16); **pensión** *f.* **completa** room and full board (16)

complexión *f.* complexion

complicado/a complicated

comportamiento behavior

comportarse *refl.* to behave (13)

composición *f.* composition; writing (P)

compra *n.* buying; shopping; purchase; **hacer** *irreg.* **las compras** to go shopping; **ir de compras** to go shopping (1)

comprar to buy

comprender to understand (5); **no comprendo** I don't understand (P)

comprensivo/a understanding

comprobar (ue) to verify, check; to prove

compuesto/a *p.p.* composed

compulsivo/a compulsive (17)

computación *f.* computer science (P)

computadora computer; **usar una computadora** to use a computer (17)

común common

comunicación *f.* communication; **medios de comunicación** means of communication

comunicarse (qu) *refl.* to communicate

comunicativo/a communicative

comunidad *f.* community

comunista *m., f.* communist

con with (1); **con frecuencia** often (1); **con hielo** with ice (9); **¿con qué frecuencia?** how often? (1); **con quien** with whom

concentrar to concentrate; **concentrarse** *refl.* to be focused

concepto concept

concernir (ie) to concern
concierto concert
concluir (y) to conclude
conclusión *f.* conclusion
concordancia concordance, agreement
concordar (ue) to agree
condensación *f.* condensation
condición *f.* condition
condicional *m. gram.* conditional (*tense*)
condimento condiment (7)
cóndor *m.* condor
conducir *irreg.* to drive (1)
conectado/a connected
conejo rabbit
conferencia lecture
confesar (ie) to confess
confianza trust; confidence
confidente trustworthy (13)
confirmar to confirm (16)
conflicto conflict
conformidad *f.* conformity
conformista *m., f.* conformist (14)
confrontar to confront
confundir to mix up; to confuse; to mistake
confusión *f.* confusion
congelado/a frozen
congreso congress
conjugar (gu) to conjugate
conmigo with me
connotación *f.* connotation
conocer (zc) to meet; to know (someone) (1)
conocido/a (well-)known
conocimiento knowledge
conquistador(a) conqueror
consecuencia consequence
conseguir (i, i) (g) to get, obtain
consejo advice
conservador(a) conservative (13)
conservar to maintain
consideración *f.* consideration
considerar to consider
consistir en to consist of (12)
consonante *f.* consonant
constantemente constantly
construcción construction
construir (y) to construct
consultar (con) to consult (17)
consumir to consume
consumo consumption
contabilidad *f.* accounting (P)
contacto contact
contador(a) accountant (17)
contagiado/a contagious; infected
contaminar to contaminate, pollute

contar (ue) to count; to tell; **contar con** to count on; **contar un chiste** to tell a joke (10)
contemporáneo/a contemporary
contenido content
contento/a happy (10); content; **ponerse** *irreg.* **contento/a** to be (get) happy (10)
contestar to answer, reply
contigo with you (*fam.*)
continuación *f.:* **a continuación** following
continuar (continúo) to continue
continuo/a continuous
contra *prep.* against
contrario/a *adj.* contrary; opposite; **al contrario** on the contrary
contrastar to contrast
contraste *m.* contrast; **en contraste** in contrast
contrato contract
contribución *f.* contribution
contribuir (y) to contribute
control *m.* control
controlar to control
controversia controversy
convencer (zc) to convince
conversación *f.* conversation
conversar to converse, chat
convertir (ie, i) to convert; **convertirse** *refl.* to become, turn into; **convertirse en adicto/a** to become addicted (12)
convivir to get together; to live together; to coexist
coordinar to coordinate
copa cup; (wine) glass (8); drink
copia copy
copiar to copy
corazón *m.* heart
corbata tie (16)
cordillera mountain range
corona crown
coronel *m.* colonel
corrección *f.* correction
correcto/a correct
corredor(a) runner, jogger
corregir (i, i,) (j) to correct
correo mail; **correo electrónico** e-mail (1)
correr to run (2); **zapato de correr** running shoe
correspondencia correspondence
corresponder to belong to; to correspond
corrido *Mex.* ballad
corriente *f.* current; *adj. m., f.* current, present; ordinary

corrupción *f.* corruption
corrupto/a corrupt
cortar to cut (8); to cut down; to clip
corte *f.* court; *m.* cut, cutting
cortés *inv.* polite
cortesía courtesy
corto/a short; **pantalones** *m. pl.* **cortos** shorts (16)
cosa thing; **es cosa sabida** it is a known fact (5)
coser to sew
cosmopolita *adj. m., f.* cosmopolitan (P)
costa coast
costar (ue) to cost; to be difficult
costumbre *f.* custom, habit (8)
cotidiano/a daily
creación *f.* creation
crear to create
creatividad *f.* creativity
creativo/a creative (13)
crecer (zc) to grow (up)
crédito credit; **tarjeta de crédito** credit card
creer (y) to believe (5); **(no) creer que ___** I (don't) think that ___ (18); **creo que sí** I think so
crianza nurturing; breeding
criar (crío) to raise
criminal: justicia criminal criminal justice (P)
criollo/a Creole
crisis *f.* crisis
crítica criticism
criticar (qu) to criticize
crítico/a critical
cromosoma chromosome
cronológico/a chronological
croqueta croquette, fritter
cruce *m.* crossing
crucero cruise ship (16)
crudo/a raw (7)
cruz *f.* cross
cruzar (c) to cross; **cruce la calle** cross the street (15)
cuadra block (*of houses*) (15)
cuadro painting; square; table
cual *rel. pron.* which; who; **lo cual** which
¿cuál? which? (4); what? (4); **¿cuál es tu nombre?** what's your (*fam.*) name? (P)
cualidad *f.* quality (17)
cualquier *adj.* any
cuando when; **de vez en cuando** from time to time (1)
¿cuándo? when? (1)

cuanto *adv.* as much as; **en cuanto** as soon as (17); **en cuanto a** as for; as to

cuanto/a: unos/as cuantos/as a few

¿cuánto/a? how much?

¿cuántos/as? how many? (P)

cuarenta forty (6)

cuarto room (1); **compañero/a de cuarto** roommate (P); **encerrarse (ie)** *refl.* **(en su cuarto)** to shut oneself up (in one's room) (10); **menos cuarto** quarter to (1); **servicio de cuarto** room service (16); **y cuarto** quarter past (1)

cuarto/a fourth

cuatro four (P); **hotel** *m.* **de cuatro estrellas** four-star hotel (16)

cuatrocientos four hundred (6)

cubano/a Cuban

cubiertos *pl.* silverware (8)

cubrir (*p.p.* **cubierto/a**) to cover

cucaracha cockroach

cuchara spoon (8)

cuchillo knife (8)

cuello neck

cuenco (earthenware) bowl (8)

cuenta bill, check (8); count; **darse** *irreg.* **cuenta (de)** to realize (*something*); **pagar (gu) la cuenta** to pay the bill (3); **tomar en cuenta** to take into account

cuento story; **cuento de hadas** fairy tale

cuerda: saltar a la cuerda to jump rope (11)

cuerno horn; **¿para qué cuernos?** why the heck?

cuero leather (16)

cuerpo body

cuestión *f.* question

cuestionario questionnaire

cuidado care; **¡cuidado!** watch out!, careful!; **tener** *irreg.* **cuidado** to be careful (12)

cuidar to take care of

cuido care, minding

culona: hormiga culona fat-bottomed ant

cultivar to cultivate

cultivo cultivation

cultura culture

cumpleaños *m. s.* birthday

cumplido compliment

cuñado/a brother-in-law, sister-in-law (4)

curación *f.* treatment; recovery; cure

curar to cure

curiosidad *f.* curiosity

curioso/a curious (14), strange

curso course (*of study*); **cursos electivos** elective courses

cuy *m. Andean* guinea pig

cuyo/a whose

D

dado/a que given that

dama lady; **primera dama** First Lady

danza dance

dañino/a harmful (12)

daño danger; **daño físico** physical injuries (12); **hacer** *irreg.* **daño** to hurt

dar *irreg.* to give (3); **dar asco** to disgust; **dar de comer** to feed; **dar una fiesta** to throw (have) a party (11); **dar hambre/sed** to make hungry/thirsty; **dar igual** to be all the same to (*someone*), not to care; **dar la mano** to shake hands; **dar miedo** to frighten; **dar pena** to sadden; **dar un paseo** to take a walk (2); **dar un paso** to take a step; **dar vuelta** to turn; **darse cuenta (de)** to realize (*something*)

datar de to date from

dato fact; *pl.* data

de *prep.* of, from (P)

debajo (de) *prep.* below; **por debajo** *adv.* underneath

debate *m.* debate

deber to owe; **deber** *v. + inf.* should, must, ought to (*do something*) (1); **deberse a** to be due to; *n. m.* obligation

debido a due to, because of

débil weak

debilitar to weaken

década decade (6)

decapitar to decapitate

decidido/a decisive, decided (13)

decidir to decide

decir *irreg.* (*p.p.* **dicho/a**) to say; to tell (3); **es decir** that is; **¿me podría decir ____?** could you tell me ____? (15)

decisión *f.* decision

declaración *f.* declaration

declarar to declare; **declararse** *refl.* to declare oneself

decorativo/a decorative

dedicación *f.* dedication

dedicar (qu) to dedicate; **dedicarse a** *refl.* to dedicate oneself to (17)

dedo finger

deducir (*like* **conducir**) to deduce

defecto defect

defender (ie) to defend

definición *f.* definition

definido/a defined; **artículo definido** *gram.* definite

definir to define

definitivo/a definitive; **en definitiva** once and for all

dejar to leave; **dejar de** + *inf.* to stop (*doing something*); **dejar propina** to leave a tip (8)

del (*contraction of* **de** + **el**) of, from the

delante de *adv.* in front of

delfín *m.* dolphin

delgado/a thin

delicia delicacy

delicioso/a delicious

demanda demand

demás: los/las demás the others

demasiado/a *adv.* too much

demonio: ¿qué demonios? what the heck?

demora delay (16)

demostrar (ue) to demonstrate, show

demostrativo/a demonstrative

dentista *m., f.* dentist

dentro de *adv.* inside; in; within

denunciar to denounce

depender (de) to depend (on)

dependiente *adj.* dependent

deporte *m.* sport; **practicar (qu) un deporte** to practice, play a sport (2)

depreciarse to depreciate

depresión *f.* depression

deprimido/a depressed (10); **sentirse (ie, i) deprimido/a** to feel depressed

derecha right (8); **a la derecha** to the right

derecho *n.* law (17); right; *adv.* straight; **siga derecho** continue (go) straight (15); *adj.* **derecho/a** right

derramar to spill (8)

derrocar (qu) to defeat

desagradable disagreeable, unpleasant

desamparado/a homeless

desaparecer (zc) to disappear

desarrollar to develop

desarrollo development
desayunar to have breakfast (1)
desayuno breakfast (7)
descafeinado/a decaffeinated; **café descafeinado** decaffeinated coffee (9)
descansar to rest (1)
descanso rest
descender (ie) to go down, descend
descomponer (*like* **poner**) to break down
desconectar to disconnect
desconfiado/a distrusting
desconocido *n.* stranger; **desconocido/a** *adj.* unknown
descremado/a skim, lowfat
describir to describe
descripción *f.* description
descriptivo/a descriptive
descubrimiento discovery
descubrir to discover
desde *prep.* since; from
desear to desire
desempeñar to fulfill, carry out
desempleo unemployment; **tasa de desempleo** unemployment rate
deseo desire
desierto desert (11)
desnacionalizar (c) to denationalize, privatize
desnatado/a skim, lowfat
desnudo/a nude
desocupado/a vacant, unoccupied (16)
despedida leave-taking (P)
despedir(se) (i, i) to say good-bye (5)
despejado/a clear; **está despejado** it's clear (*weather*) (2)
despertador *m.* alarm clock
despertar (ie) (*p.p.* **despierto/a**) to wake; **despertarse** *refl.* to wake up (1)
despierto/a *p.p.* awake; **soñar (ue) despierto/a** to daydream
después *adv.* after, afterward (2)
destacable notable
destacar (qu) to stand out
destino destination
destreza skill, ability
destrucción *f.* destruction
desventaja disadvantage (18)
detalle *m.* detail
detective *m., f.* detective
detergente *m.* detergent
determinado/a definite, specific (14)
determinar to determine
detestar to detest, hate

detrás (de) *adv.* behind (15)
detrimento detriment
deuda debt
devolver (ue) to return (*something*)
día *m.* day; **buenos días** good morning (P); **todo el día** all day; **todos los días** every day (1); **día de fiesta** holiday (11); **día laboral** workday (1); **hoy (en) día** nowadays, today; **menú** *m.* **del día** daily menu (7); **plato del día** daily special (8); **¿qué día es hoy?** what day is today? (1)
diagnóstico diagnosis
diagnóstico/a *adj.* diagnostic
dialectal dialectical
dialecto dialect
diario/a daily
diáspora diaspora (*body of Jews living in regions outside Palestine after the captivity in Babylonia*)
dibujar to draw (11)
dibujo drawing; **dibujo animado** cartoon
diccionario dictionary
diciembre *m.* December (2)
dictador *m.* dictator
diecinueve nineteen
dieciocho eighteen
dieciséis sixteen
diecisiete seventeen
dieta diet
dietético/a *adj.* diet
diez ten
diferencia difference; **a diferencia de** in contrast to
diferente (de) different (from)
difícil difficult
dificultad *f.* difficulty
difundir to diffuse
dinero money; **gastar dinero** to spend money (2)
dinosaurio dinosaur
dios(a) god(dess); **Dios mío** my goodness; **gracias a Dios** thank God
diploma *m.* diploma
dirección *f.* address; direction
directo/a direct; **pensar (ie) de una manera directa** to think in a direct (linear) manner (17)
director(a) director (17)
dirigir (j) to direct; to manage; **capaz de dirigir a otros** able to direct others (13); **dirigirse** *refl.* to address, speak
disciplinado/a disciplined
disco record

discoteca discotheque (2)
discrepancia discrepancy
discreto/a discreet (13)
disculpar to excuse, pardon
discusión *f.* discussion; argument
diseñador(a) designer (17)
diseñar to design
diseño (16)
disfrutar to enjoy
disgusto disagreement
disminución *f.* decrease
disminuir (y) to decrease
disparate *m.* foolish, senseless act
disparo shot
disponer (*like* **poner**) to have available
disponible available
disposición *f.* disposition
distancia distance
distinción *f.* distinction
distinguir (g) to distinguish
distinto/a distinct, different
distraer (*like* **traer**) to distract
distribución *f.* distribution
diversión *f.* diversion, entertainment
divertido/a fun-loving (13); fun
divertir(se) (ie, i) *refl.* to have fun
dividir(se) to divide
divorciado/a divorced
divorciarse to divorce
divorcio divorce
doblar to turn; **doble a la izquierda** turn left (15)
doble double
doce twelve (P)
dócil docile (14)
doctor(a) doctor
doctrina doctrine
documental documentary (*film*)
dólar *m.* dollar
dolor *m.* pain, ache; (**tener** *irreg.*) **dolor de cabeza** (to have a) headache; (**tener** *irreg.*) **dolor de estómago** (to have a) stomachache
doméstico/a domestic; household; **animal** *m.* **doméstico** domestic animal, pet; **quehacer** *m.* **doméstico** household chore; **tarea doméstica** household chore
domicilio home; **servicio a domicilio** home delivery (8)
dominar to dominate
domingo Sunday (1); **domingo pasado** last Sunday
dominicano/a *n., adj.* Dominican; *n.* **República Dominicana** Dominican Republic
dominio dominion

don *m.* title of respect before a man's first name; talent; **tener** *irreg.* **don de gentes** to have a way with people (17); **don de mando** talent for leadership (13)

donativo *m.* donation

donde where

¿dónde? where?; **¿de dónde eres tú / es usted?** where are you from? (P); **¿dónde queda___?** where is ___? (15)

donjuan *m.* libertine man

dorado/a golden

dormir (ue, u) to sleep (1); **dormirse** *refl.* to fall asleep (3)

dormitorio bedroom

dos two (P); **a las dos** at two o'clock (1); **dos mil** two thousand (4); **dos veces** twice; **son las dos** it's two o'clock (1); **los/las dos** *pron.* both

doscientos two hundred (6)

dragón *m.* dragon

drama *m.* drama

dramático/a dramatic

drástico/a drastic

droga drug

ducha shower; **con ducha** with a shower (16)

ducharse *refl.* to shower, take a shower

duda doubt (18); **sin duda** without a doubt

dudar to doubt (18)

dudoso/a doubtful; **es dudoso que...** it's doubtful that (18)

dulce *n. m.* candy (7); *adj.* sweet (7)

duplicar (qu) to duplicate

durante during (1)

durar to last

duro/a hard

DVD *m.* DVD; DVD player

E

e and (*used instead of* **y** *before words beginning with* **i** *or* **hi**)

echar to throw; **echar de menos** to miss (*someone, something*)

ecológico/a ecological

economía *s.* economics (P); economy

económico/a economic; inexpensive

ecoturismo ecotourism

ecuación *f.* equation

ecuatoriano/a Ecuadorean

edad *f.* age (6); **la Edad Media** Middle Ages

edición *f.* edition

edificio building

educación *f.* education; **educación física** physical education (P); **tener** *irreg.* **buena educación** to be well-mannered (8)

educado/a educated; well-mannered, polite (8)

educar (qu) to educate

educativo/a educational

EE.UU. (Estados Unidos) United States

efecto effect; **efecto invernadero** greenhouse effect

efectuar (efectúo) to carry out

eficiencia efficiency

eficiente efficient

egocéntrico/a egocentric

egoísta egotistical, self-centered (13)

ejecutivo/a executive

ejemplo example; **por ejemplo** for example

ejercer (z) to exercise (*one's rights*); to practice (*a profession*)

ejercicio exercise; **hacer** *irreg.* **ejercicio** to exercise (1); **hacer ejercicio aeróbico** to do aerobics (1)

ejército army; **EZLN: Ejército Zapatista de Liberación Nacional** Zapatista National Liberation Army

el *m. s.* the (P)

él *m. sub. pron.* he (P); *obj. of prep.* him

elaboración *f.* production

elaborar to produce

elástico/a flexible

elección *f.* election; choice

electivo: cursos electivos elective courses

electricidad *f.* electricity

electrónico/a electronic; **correo electrónico** e-mail (1)

elegancia elegance

elegante elegant

elegir (i, i) (j) to elect; to choose

elemento element

eliminar to eliminate

ella *f. sub. pron.* she (P); *obj. of prep.* her

ello *neuter pron.* it

ellos/as *sub. pron.* they; *obj. of prep.* them

elogiado/a praised

embargo: sin embargo however, nevertheless

embarque *m.*: **tarjeta de embarque** boarding pass

emborracharse *refl.* to get drunk

embriagado/a intoxicated, drunk

embrión *m.* embryo

emigración *f.* emigration

emigrar to emigrate

emitir to emit

emoción *f.* emotion

emocional emotional

emparejar to match

emperador *m.* swordfish (7)

empezar (ie) (c) to begin (3)

empleado/a *n.* employee; *adj.* employed

emplear to employ, to use

empleo employment, job

emprendedor(a) enterprising, aggressive (17)

empresa company; **administración** *f.* **de empresas** business administration (P)

empujar to push

encantador(a) charming (13)

encantar to delight, to be extremely pleasing (7); **me encanta(n)** I love

encerrarse (ie) to shut or lock in; **encerrarse** *refl.* **(en su cuarto)** to shut oneself up (in one's room) (10)

enciclopedia encyclopedia

encima: por encima on top

encontrar (ue) to find; to meet

encuesta survey; poll

enemigo/a *n., adj.* enemy

energía energy; **energía nuclear** nuclear energy; **energía solar** solar energy

enérgico/a energetic

enero January (2)

enfadado/a angry (10); **ponerse** *irreg.* **enfadado/a** to be (get) angry (10)

enfadar to anger; **enfadarse** *refl.* to get angry

énfasis *m.* emphasis; **poner** *irreg.* **énfasis** to emphasize

enfermedad *f.* illness

enfermería nursing (P)

enfermero/a nurse (17)

enfermo/a ill, sick

enfocarse (qu) to focus

enfoque *m.* focus

enfrentar to confront, face

enfrente (de) in front of (15)

engañar to deceive

engordar to be fattening

enmohecido/a mildewed

enojado/a angry (10); **estar** *irreg.* **enojado/a** to be angry (10)

enojarse *refl.* to get angry (10)

enojo anger
enorme enormous
ensalada salad (7); **ensalada mixta** mixed, tossed salad
ensayar to try
ensayista *m., f.* essayist
ensayo essay
enseñanza teaching
enseñar to teach
ensimismado/a lost in thought
entender (ie) to understand (1); **no entiendo** I don't understand (P)
entero/a entire, whole
entidad *f.* entity
entomología entomology
entonces *adv.* then, next (*in a series*)
entrada entrance
entrar to enter
entre *prep.* between, among
entregar (gu) to give, hand over; **entregarse** *refl.* **(a)** to devote oneself (to)
entrenamiento training
entrenar(se) to train
entrevista interview
entrevistado/a person interviewed
entrevistar to interview
entusiasmarse *refl.* to be enthused
enviar (envío) to send (1)
envidia: tener *irreg.* **envidia** to be envious
época epoch; age; time (*period*) (6)
equilibrado/a balanced (13)
equipaje *m.* luggage (16); **facturar el equipaje** to check the luggage (16)
equipo team; equipment
equivalencia *n.* equivalent
equivocarse (qu) to make a mistake; to be wrong
error *m.* error, mistake
escala scale; **hacer** *irreg.* **escala** to make a stop (*on a flight*) (16)
escalar montañas to mountain climb (11)
escapar to escape
escarabajo beetle
escaso/a scarce
escena scene
esclavo/a slave
escoger (j) to choose
escolar *adj.* school
esconder to hide
escribir (*p.p.*** escrito/a)** to write (1); **escribir a máquina** to type; **escribir la tarea** to write the assignment; **máquina de escribir** typewriter

escrito/a *p.p.* written
escritor(a) writer
escrupuloso/a scrupulous, particular
escuadrón *m.* squadron; **escuadrón de la muerte** death squad
escuchar to listen (to) (1); **escuchar la radio** to listen to the radio
escuela school; **escuela secundaria** secondary school, high school
escultor(a) sculptor (17)
escultura sculpture
ese/a *adj.* that (P)
ese/a *pron.* that one
esfuerzo effort
eso that, that thing, that fact; **por eso** therefore, that's why
esos/as *adj.* those (P)
esos/as *pron.* those ones
espacial spatial
espacio space, blank
espaguetis *m. pl.* spaghetti (7)
espantoso/a scary (P)
España Spain
español *m.* Spanish (*language*); **hablar español** to speak Spanish (P)
español(a) *n.* Spaniard; *adj.* Spanish; **de habla española** Spanish-speaking
especial special; **en especial** especially
especialidad *f.* specialty
especialización *f.* major (P)
especializarse (c) (en) to specialize (in); to major (in)
especie *f.* species
específico/a specific
espectacular spectacular
espejo mirror
espera: sala de espera waiting room (16)
esperanza hope; **esperanza de vida** life expectancy
esperar to expect; to hope; to wait (for)
espinacas *f. pl.* spinach (7)
espíritu *m.* spirit
espiritual spiritual
espléndido/a splendid
esposo/a husband, wife (4); **esposos** *m. pl.* married couple (4)
esquema *m.* chart, outline
esquí *m.* skiing
esquiar (esquío) to ski (11); **esquiar en el agua** to water ski (11); **esquiar en las montañas** to snow ski (11)
estable *adj.* stable

establecer (zc) to establish
establecimiento establishment; settling place
estación *f.* season (2); station (16)
estadio stadium
estadística statistic; statistics
estado state; **estado de ánimo** state of mind (10)
Estados Unidos United States
estadounidense *n. m., f.* American; *adj. of or from the United States*
estanco monopoly
estándar (or **estándard)** standard
estar *irreg.* to be (3); **está claro** it's clear (5); **está despejado** it's clear (*weather*) (2); **está lloviendo** it's raining (2); **está nevando** it's snowing; **está nublado** it's cloudy (2); **estar aburrido/a / asustado/a / cansado/a / enojado/a / nervioso/a / tenso/a** to be bored/afraid/tired/angry/nervous/tense (10); **estar de acuerdo** to agree; **estar de buen/mal humor** to be in a good/bad mood (10); **estar listo/a (para)** to be ready (for); **estar de vacaciones** to be on vacation
estatua statue
estatura height (5); **de estatura mediana** of medium height (5); **¿qué estatura es?** how tall is he/she/you (*form.*)? (5)
estatus status
este *m.* east (15)
este/a *adj.* this (P); **esta noche** tonight
este/a *pron.* this one
estereotípico/a stereotypical
estereotipo stereotype
estilo style
estimado/a esteemed
estimarse *refl.* to have a high opinion of oneself
estimular to stimulate
esto this, this thing, this matter
estofado/a stewed
estómago stomach; **tener** *irreg.* **dolor de estómago** to have a stomachache
estornudar to sneeze
estrella star; **hotel de cuatro estrellas** four-star hotel (16)
estrenarse to debut
estrés *m.* stress
estructura structure
estructurado/a structured

estructural structural

estudiante *m., f.* student (P); **soy estudiante de** _____ I am a(n) _____ student

estudiantil *adj.* student; **residencia estudiantil** student dormitory

estudiar to study (1); **estudio** I am studying _____ (P); **¿qué estudias?** what are you studying (P)

estudio *n.* study

estudioso/a studious

estupefacto/a dumbfounded

etimología etymology

étnico/a ethnic

Europa Europe

europeo/a *n., adj.* European

evaluar (evalúo) to evaluate

evento event

evidencia evidence

evidente evident (5)

evitar to avoid; **tendencia a evitar riesgos** tendency to avoid risks (13)

exacerbar to exacerbate

exacto/a *adj.* exact; *adv.* exactly

exagerado/a exaggerated

examen *n.* test (P); **tener** *irreg.* **un examen** to take a test (3)

examinar to examine

excelente excellent

excéntrico/a eccentric

excepción *f.* exception

excepcional exceptional

excepto *adv.* except

exceso excess

exclamar to exclaim

excluir (y) to exclude

exclusivo/a exclusive

excusa excuse

exhibición *f.* exhibition

exiliado/a *n., adj.* exiled

existencia existence

éxito success; **tener** *irreg.* **éxito** to be successful

expediente transcript

experiencia experience

experimental experimental

experimentar to experience; to experiment

experimento experiment

experto/a *n., adj.* expert

explicación *f.* explanation

explicar (qu) to explain

exploración *f.* exploration

explorar to explore

explosivo/a explosive

exportación *f.* exportation

exportar to export

exposición *f.* exposition

expresar to express; **expresarse** *refl.* **claramente** to express oneself clearly (17)

expresión *f.* expression (P)

expropiado/a expropriated

extendido/a extended; **familia extendida** extended family (4)

extensión *f.* extension

extenuar (extenúo) to tire

externo/a external

extinción *f.* extinction

extinguirse (g) to become extinct

extra *inv.* extra

extracción *f.* extraction

extraer (*like* **traer**) to extract

extranjero abroad (16); **extranjero/a** *n.* foreigner; *adj.* foreign; **idioma** *m.* **extranjero** foreign language (P); **lengua extranjera** foreign language (P)

extraño/a strange

extraordinario/a extraordinary

extravagante extravagant

extroversión *f.* extroversion

extrovertido/a extroverted (5)

EZLN: Ejército Zapatista de Liberación Nacional Zapatista National Liberation Army

F

fábrica factory

fabricación *f.* manufacture

fabricar (qu) to manufacture, make

fabuloso/a fabulous

fachada facade

fácil easy

factor *m.* factor

facturar el equipaje to check the luggage (16)

falda skirt (16)

falso/a false

falta lack

faltar to be missing, lacking (10); to be absent; **faltar a** to miss, not go to

fama fame; **tener** *irreg.* **fama de** to have a reputation for

familia family; **familia extendida** extended family (4); **familia nuclear** nuclear family (4)

familiar *n. m.* relative; *adj.* familiar, pertaining to a family

famoso/a famous (P)

fantástico/a fantastic

farmacéutico/a pharmacist (17)

farmacia pharmacy (17)

fascinante fascinating

fascinar to fascinate

fatal fatal; awful

fauna fauna

favor *m.* favor; **a favor de** in favor of; **por favor** please (P)

favorito/a favorite (P)

faxear to send a fax

febrero February (2)

fecha (*calendar*) date

fechoría villainy, misdeed

fecundación *f.* fertilization

feliz (*pl.* **felices**) happy (5)

femenino/a feminine

fenómeno phenomenon

feo/a ugly (5)

fermentación *f.* fermentation

feroz (*pl.* **feroces**) ferocious

ferroníquel *m.* ferronickel

fertilizante *m.* fertilizer

festival *m.* festival

festividades *pl.* festivities

fibra fiber; **telas de fibras naturales** natural fabrics (16)

ficción *f.* fiction; **ciencia ficción** science fiction

ficticio/a ficticious

fideo noodle

fiesta party (2); **dar** *irreg.* / **hacer** *irreg.* **una fiesta** to throw (have) a party (11); **día** *m.* **de fiesta** holiday (11)

figura figure

figurar to figure, appear

figurativo/a figurative

figurilla figurine

figurina figurine

fijarse to notice

fijo/a fixed

Filipinas Philippines

filosofía philosophy (P)

filosófico/a philosophical

fin *m.* end; **al fin y al cabo** in the end, when all is said and done; **en fin** finally; **fin de semana** weekend (1); **fin de semana pasado** last weekend (3); **por fin** finally

final *m.* end; **al final (de)** at the end (of); *adj.* final

finalista *m., f.* finalist

financiar to finance

financiero/a financial

fino/a fine

firma signature

firmar to sign

firmeza firmness, stability

física physics (P)

físicamente fuerte physically strong (17)

físico/a *n.* physicist (17); *adj.* physical; **característica física** physical characteristic, trait (5); **castigo físico** corporal punishment; **daño físico** physical injuries (12); **educación** *f.* **física** physical education (P); **rasgo físico** physical trait; **terapeuta** *m., f.* **físico/a** physical therapist (17); **terapia física** physical therapy (17)

fisiología physiology

flamenco *a musical and dance form from the region of Andalusia in Spain*

flan *m.* baked custard (7)

flexibilidad *f.* flexibility

flexible flexible

flor *f.* flower

flora flora

fobia phobia

folclor folklore

folklórico/a folkloric

folleto pamphlet

fomentar to encourage

forma form; way; **de todas formas** in any case; **en forma** in shape

formación *f.* formation; training, education

formal formal

formar to form

fórmula formula

formular to formulate

formulario form

foro forum

fósil *m.* fossil

foto(grafía) *f.* photo(graph); **sacar (qu) fotos** to take pictures (16)

fotógrafo/a photographer (17)

fracaso failure

fragmento fragment

francés *m.* French (*language*) (P)

francés, francesa *n.* Frenchman, Frenchwoman; *adj.* French

Francia France

franquicia exemption

frase *f.* phrase; sentence

frecuencia frequency; **con frecuencia** often (1); **¿con qué frecuencia?** how often? (1)

frecuentar to frequent

frecuente frequent

frecuentemente frequently (1)

freír (i, i) to fry

frente *prep.* in front of; **frente a** facing; compared with

fresa strawberry (7)

fresco/a fresh (7); cool; **hace fresco** it's cool (*weather*) (2)

frijol *m.* bean (7)

frío cold (9); **bien frío** very cold (9); **hace (mucho) frío** it's (very) cold (*weather*) (2)

frito/a *p.p.* fried; **huevo frito** fried egg (7); **papas fritas** *Lat. Am.* potato chips (7); French fries; **patatas fritas** *Sp.* potato chips (7); French fries

frívolo/a frivolous (14)

frontera border

frustrar to frustrate

fruta fruit (7)

fuente *f.* source; fountain

fuera (de) *adv.* outside (of)

fuerte strong; **físicamente fuerte** physically strong (17); **licor** *m.* **fuerte** hard alcohol (9)

fuerza strength; force; **fuerzas armadas** armed forces

fulano/a so-and-so

fumar to smoke (9); **sección** *f.* **de (no) fumar** (no) smoking section (16)

función *f.* function

funcionamiento *n.* functioning, operation

funcionar to function, work

fundamento foundation

funeral *m.* funeral

furioso/a furious

fútbol *m.* soccer; **fútbol americano** football; **jugar (ue) (gu) al fútbol** to play soccer (2); **jugar (ue) (gu) al fútbol americano** to play football (2)

futuro *n.* future

futuro/a *adj.* future

G

Galápagos: Islas Galápagos Galapagos Islands

Galicia *region in northwest Spain*

gallego *m.* Galician (*language*)

gallego/a *n., adj.* Galician

galleta cookie (7)

gallina hen

gallo rooster

gamba *Sp.* shrimp

gana desire, wish; **tener** *irreg.* **ganas de** + *inf.* to feel like (*doing something*)

ganar to earn; to win; **ganar peso** to gain weight; **ganarse la vida** to support oneself (*financially*)

garantía guarantee

gasolina gasoline

gastar (dinero) to spend (money) (2)

gasto expense

gastronomía gastronomy

gastronómico/a gastronomical

gato/a cat

gaucho *cowboy of the pampas in Argentina*

gelatina gelatin

gemelo/a *n., adj.* twin (4)

gen *m.* gene

genealógico: árbol *m.* **genealógico** family tree

generación *f.* generation

general general; **en general** in general; **por lo general** generally

generalizar (c) to generalize

generalmente generally (1)

género gender; genre

genética *n.* genetics

genético/a genetic; **herencia genética** genetic inheritance

genio genious; temper; mood

gente *f. s.* people (6); **tener** *irreg.* **don de gentes** to have a way with people (17)

geografía geography (P)

geográfico/a geographical

geométrico/a geometric

gerente *m., f.* manager (17)

gerundio gerund

gesto gesture

gigante *n. m.* giant; *adj.* gigantic, huge

gimnasio gymnasium

gitano/a *n., adj.* Gypsy

glamoroso/a glamorous

globalización *f.* globalization

gnomo gnome

gobernado/a governed

gobernador(a) governor

gobernar to govern

gobierno government (17)

golf *m.* golf; **jugar (ue) (gu) al golf** to golf (11)

golondrina swallow

golpe *m.* blow

gordo/a fat (5)

gorila *m.* gorilla

gótico/a Gothic

gozar (c) to enjoy, have

gracia humor; **hacerle** *irreg.* **gracia a uno** to strike someone as funny (11); **tener** *irreg.* **gracia** to be funny, charming (11)

gracias thank you, thanks (P); **gracias a Dios** thank God

gracioso/a funny, amusing (11)

grado grade, degree

graduado/a: recién graduado recent graduate

graduarse *refl.* **(me gradúo) (de)** to graduate (from)

gráfico *n.* graphic

gráfico/a *adj.* graphic

gramática grammar

gramatical grammatical

gran, grande big (5); impressive, great; **el/la menos grande** the smallest (5); **menos grande (que)** smaller (than) (5)

granjero/a farmer (17)

grasa fat (7)

gratis *inv.* free

grave serious (12)

Grecia Greece

gregario/a gregarious (5)

griego/a Greek (*person*)

grifo faucet

gringo/a *n., adj.* American (*often pejorative*)

gris gray

gritar to shout (10)

grupo group

gua gua *f.* baby (*male or female*)

guano fertilizer

guapo/a handsome, pretty

guaraní Guarani (*an indigenous language*)

guardar to keep; **guardar silencio** to keep quiet

guardia guard

guatemalteco/a *n., adj.* Guatemalan

guerra war; **guerra civil** civil war

guerrero/a warrior

guerrillero/a guerilla

guiado/a guided

guiarse *refl.* **(me guío)** to be guided

guisante *m.* pea (7)

guitarra guitar; **tocar (qu) la guitarra** to play the guitar (1)

gusano worm

gustar to be pleasing; **no me gusta(n) _____** I don't like _____ (P); **sí, me gusta(n) _____** yes, I like _____ (P); **¿te gusta(n) _____?** do you like _____? (P); **no, no me gusta(n) para nada** no, I don't like it (them) at all (P)

gusto taste, preference (7); **al gusto** according to taste; **mucho gusto** pleased to meet you (P)

H

ha (*aux.*) has/have + *p.p.*

haber *irreg.* to have (*aux.*)

hábil para las matemáticas good at math (17)

habilidad *f.* ability (17); **habilidad manual** ability to work with one's hands (17)

habitación *f.* room (16); **habitación con baño privado** room with a private bath (16); **habitación con ducha** room with a shower (16)

habitante *m., f.* inhabitant

habitar to inhabit; to live

hábitat *m.* (*pl.* **hábitats**) habitat

hábito habit; **hábito de comer** eating habit (7)

habitué *n. m., f.* regular; habitual customer

habla *n. f.* (*but* **el habla**) language; **de habla española** Spanish-speaking

hablador(a) talkative (13)

hablante *m., f.* speaker

hablar to speak (1); **hablar español** to speak Spanish (P); **hablar otro idioma** to speak another language (17); **hablar por teléfono** to talk on the telephone (1)

hacendado landed property owner

hacer *irreg.* (*p.p.* **hecho/a**) to do (1); to make (1); **hace +** *time* _____ ago (3); **hace buen/mal tiempo** the weather's good/bad (2); **hace (mucho) calor/frío** it's (very) hot/cold (*weather*) (2); **hace fresco** it's cool (*weather*) (2); **hace sol** it's sunny (2); **hace unos años** a few years ago; **hace varios meses** several months ago; **hace viento** it's windy (2); **hacer autostop** to hitchhike (16); **hacer cámping** to go camping (11); **hacer cola** to stand in line (16); **hacer compañía** to keep company; **hacer daño** to hurt; **hacer el papel** to play the role; **hacer ejercicio** to exercise (1); **hacer ejercicio aeróbico** to do aerobics (1); **hacer escala** to make a stop (*on a flight*) (16); **hacer la cama** to make the bed; **hacer la maleta** to pack one's suitcase (16); **hacer la tarea** to do the homework/assignment; **hacer las compras** to go shopping; **hacer memoria** to try to remember; **hacer preguntas** to ask questions (4); **hacer reír** to make laugh (11); **hacer ruido** to make noise (10); **hacer un viaje** to take a trip (16); **hacer una fiesta** to throw (have) a party; **hacer yoga** to do yoga (11); **hacerle gracia a uno** to strike someone as funny (11); **no hacer nada** to do nothing (2); **¿qué carrera haces?** what's your major? (P); **¿qué tiempo hace?** what's the weather like? (2)

hacia *prep.* toward

hada *f.* (*but* **el hada**) fairy; **cuento de hadas** fairy tale

hamaca hammock

hambre *f.* (*but* **el hambre**) hunger; **dar** *irreg.* **hambre** to make hungry; **tener** *irreg.* **hambre** to be hungry (7)

hamburguesa hamburger (7)

han (*aux.*) have + *p.p.*

hasta *adv.* even; *prep.* until; **hasta mañana** see you tomorrow (P); **hasta pronto** see you soon (P); **hasta que** until (17); **hasta (muy) tarde** until (very) late (2)

hay there is, there are (P); **hay que** it's necessary to (8)

hazaña deed

hecho fact; deed; reason; **de hecho** in fact

hecho/a *p.p.* made, done

helado ice cream (7)

helado/a *p.p.* frozen; iced; **té** *m.* **helado** iced tea (9)

hemisferio hemisphere

hemofilia hemophilia

heredar to inherit

hereditario/a hereditary

herencia inheritance; **herencia genética** genetic inheritance

herida wound, injury (12)

herir (ie, i) to wound (12)

hermanastro/a stepbrother, stepsister (4)

hermano/a brother, sister (4); *pl.* brothers and sisters, siblings (4); **medio/a hermano/a** half brother, half sister (4)

hidalgo nobleman

hielo ice; **con hielo** with ice (9); **sin hielo** without ice (9)

hierba herb; **té** *m.* **de hierbas** herbal tea (9)

hígado liver

hijo/a son, daughter (4); junior; *pl.* children; **hijo/a único/a** only child; **hijo/a adoptivo/a** adopted child

hilaza yarn
himno nacional national anthem
hipotético/a hypothetical
hispánico/a Hispanic
hispano/a Hispanic
Hispanoamérica Latin America
hispanoamericano/a *n., adj.* Latin American
hispanohablante *m., f.* Spanish speaker; *adj.* Spanish-speaking
historia history (P); story
histórico/a historical
hogar *m.* home
hoja sheet (*of paper*); leaf
hola hello (P)
hombre *m.* man; **hombre de negocios** businessman (17)
homicidio homicide
honestidad *f.* honorableness, honesty
honesto/a upright, honorable, honest
honorable honorable, honest
hora hour; time; **¿a qué hora?** at what time? (1); **hora límite** time limit; **¿qué hora es?** what time is it? (1)
horario schedule
hormiga ant; **hormiga culona** fat-bottomed ant
hormona hormone
horno: al horno baked (7)
horóscopo horoscope; **horóscopo chino** Chinese horoscope
hospital *m.* hospital
hotel *m.* hotel; **hotel de cuatro estrellas** four-star hotel (16); **hotel de lujo** luxury hotel (16)
hoy *adv.* today (1); **hoy (en) día** nowadays, today; **hoy es ___** today is ___ (1); **¿qué día es hoy?** what day is today? (1)
huele a it smells like
huella footstep; footprint
hueso bone
huésped(a) guest (16)
huevo egg (7); **huevo frito** fried egg (7); **huevo revuelto** scrambled egg (7)
huir (y) to flee
humanidad *f.* humanity; *pl.* humanities (P)
humano/a human; **raza humana** human race; **ser** *m.* **humano** human being
humedad *f.* humidity
húmedo/a humid

humilde humble (13)
humor *m.* humor; mood; **estar** *irreg.* **de buen/mal humor** to be in a good/bad mood (10)

I

ida: boleto/billete *m.* **de ida** one-way ticket (16); **boleto/billete** *m.* **de ida y vuelta** round-trip ticket (16)
idea idea; **(muy) buena idea** a (very) good idea (8); **cambiar de idea** to change one's mind (8)
ideal *n. m.* ideal; *adj. m., f.* ideal
idealista *n. m., f.* idealist; *adj. m., f.* idealistic
idéntico/a identical
identidad *f.* identity
identificar (qu) to identify
ideología ideology
idioma *m.* language (P); **hablar otro idioma** to speak another language (17); **idioma extranjero** foreign language (P)
iglesia church; **ir** *irreg.* **a la iglesia** to go to church (2)
igual equal, same; **dar** *irreg.* **igual** to be all the same to (*someone*), not to care; **por igual** equally, the same (P)
igualitario/a egalitarian
igualmente likewise (P)
ilógico/a illogical
iluminación *f.* illumination
imagen *f.* image; statue
imaginación *f.* imagination
imaginar to imagine
imaginativo/a imaginative
imitar to imitate
impaciente impatient
impacto impact
imperfecto *gram.* imperfect (*tense*)
imperio empire
impersonal impersonal
impetuoso/a impetuous
implicar (qu) to implicate
imponer (*like* **poner**) to impose (5)
importación *f.* importation
importancia importance
importante important
importar to be important (7); to matter (7); to import; **importar un comino** not to matter at all
imposible impossible
imprescindible essential (8)
impresión *f.* impression

impresionante impressive
impresionar to impress
imprimir to print
impuesto tax
impulsividad *f.* impulsiveness
impulsivo/a impulsive
impulso impulse
inapropiado/a inappropriate
inca *n. m., f.* Inca; *adj.* Incan
incendio fire
incesante incessant
incidencia incidence
incidente *m.* incident
incierto/a uncertain (14)
inclinación *f.* inclination
inclinado/a inclined
incluir (y) to include
inclusive including
incluso *adv.* even
inconformidad *f.* nonconformity
incontrolable incontrollable
incorporar to incorporate; **incorporarse** *refl.* to join
incorrecto/a incorrect
incrementar to increase
indeciso/a indecisive (13)
indefinido/a indefinite
independencia independence
independiente independent
independizarse (c) *refl.* to become independent
India India
indicación *f.* indication
indicar (qu) to indicate
indicativo *gram.* indicative (*mood*)
indiferente indifferent (14)
indígena *n. m., f.* indigenous person; *adj. m., f.* indigenous
indirecto/a indirect
indispensable indispensable, essential
individual *adj.* individual
individualista individualistic (14)
individuo *n.* individual
indudable without a doubt (5)
indumentaria apparel
industria industry
inesperado/a unexpected
inestabilidad *f.* instability
inevitable unavoidable
infancia infancy; childhood
infante/a *any son or daughter of a king of Spain or Portugal, except the eldest*
infierno hell
infinitivo *gram.* infinitive
inflado/a inflated
influencia influence

influido/a influenced
influir (y) to influence
información *f.* information
informar to inform
informática computer science (P)
informe *m.* report
ingeniería engineering (P)
ingeniero/a engineer (17)
ingenioso/a ingenious, clever
ingenuo/a naive (13)
ingerir (ie, i) to ingest, eat
Inglaterra England
inglés *m.* English (*language*) (P)
inglés, inglesa *adj.* English
ingrato/a ungrateful
ingrediente *m.* ingredient
iniciar to initiate
iniciativa initiative
injusticia injustice
inmediato/a immediate
inmenso/a immense
inmigración *f.* immigration
inmigrante *m., f.* immigrant
inmigrar to immigrate
inmortalidad *f.* immortality
inmunología immunology
innato/a innate
innecesario/a unnecessary
inocente innocent
inocuo/a harmless
inquieto/a restless (13)
insatisfacción *f.* dissatisfaction
inscribir (*p. p.* **inscrito/a**) to enroll in
inscripción *f.* enrollment
insecto insect
inseguro/a insecure (13)
insensible insensitive (13)
insincero/a insincere (P)
insistir to insist
insomnio insomnia
inspeccionar to inspect
inspirar to inspire
instalarse to settle
instantánea *n.* snapshot
instante *m.* instant
instintivo/a instinctive
instinto instinct
institución *f.* institution
instituto institute
instrucción *f.* instruction; *pl.* directions
instrumento instrument
insultar to insult
integral: pan *m.* **integral** whole-wheat bread (7)
integrar to integrate
íntegro/a honorable (17)

intelectual intellectual
inteligencia intelligence
inteligente intelligent (P)
intención *f.* intention
intensidad *f.* intensity
intenso/a intense
intentar to try, attempt
intento attempt
interacción *f.* interaction
intercambiar to exchange
intercambio exchange
interés *m.* interest
interesante interesting (P)
interesar to interest, be interesting (7)
internacional international
interno/a internal
interpretación *f.* interpretation
interrumpir to interrupt
íntimo/a close
introducción *f.* introduction
introducir (*like* **conducir**) to introduce, bring in; to put (into)
introvertido/a introverted
inundación *f.* flood
inventar to invent
invento invention
invernadero: efecto invernadero greenhouse effect
invernal *adj.* winter; **síndrome** *m.* **invernal** winter syndrome (*depression*)
inversión *f.* investment
inversionista *m., f.* investor
invertido/a invested
investigación *f.* investigation
investigador(a) investigator
investigar (gu) to investigate
invierno winter
invitado/a *n.* guest
invitar to invite; to treat (pay) (8)
involucrado/a involved
involuntariamente involuntarily
ir *irreg.* to go; **ir a la iglesia** to go to church (2); **ir al cine** to go to the movies; **ir al teatro** to go to the theater (11); **ir de compras** to go shopping (1)
irritado/a irritated
irritarse to be (get) irritated (10)
isla island; **Islas Baleares** Balearic Islands; **Islas Galápagos** Galapagos Islands
Italia Italy
italiano *n.* Italian (*language*) (P)
italiano/a *n., adj.* Italian
itinerario itinerary

izquierda *f.* left; **doble a la izquierda** turn left (15)
izquierdo/a left (8)

J

¡ja! ha!
jabón *m.* soap
jactarse (de) *refl.* to boast, brag (about)
jacuzzi *m.* jacuzzi; **bañarse** *refl.* **en un jacuzzi** to bathe in a jacuzzi (11)
jaguar *m.* jaguar
jamás never (2)
jamón *m.* ham (7); **jamón serrano** *cured Spanish ham*
Jánuca *m.* Hanukkah
Japón *m.* Japan
japonés *m.* Japanese (*language*) (P)
japonés, japonesa *n., adj.* Japanese
jardín *m.* garden; yard; **trabajar en el jardín** to garden (11)
jarra pitcher (8)
jaula cage
jefe/a boss (17)
jerarquía hierarchy
jerez *m.* (*pl.* **jereces**) sherry
jirafa giraffe
joven *n. m., f.* young person; *adj.* young (5)
joyería jewelry store
jubilado/a retired
jubilarse *refl.* to retire
judía bean; **judía verde** green bean (7)
judío/a *n.* Jew; *adj.* Jewish
juego game
jueves Thursday (1)
jugador(a) player (17)
jugar (ue) (gu) to play (*sports*) (1); **jugar a los naipes** to play cards (11); **jugar a los videojuegos** to play video games (3); **jugar al basquetbol** to play basketball (10); **jugar al béisbol** to play baseball (10); **jugar al boliche** to bowl (10); **jugar al fútbol** to play soccer (2); **jugar al fútbol americano** to play football (2); **jugar al golf** to golf (11); **jugar al tenis** to play tennis (10); **jugar al voleibol** to play volleyball (11)
jugo juice (7); **jugo de limón** lemon juice; **jugo de manzana** apple juice (9); **jugo de naranja** orange juice (7); **jugo de tomate** tomato juice (9); **jugo de toronja** grapefruit juice

juicio judgment, sanity: **perder el juicio** to lose one's mind; **recobrar el juicio** to recover one's sanity
julio July (2)
junio June (2)
junto *adv.* near; **junto con** together with
junto/a *adj.* together
justicia justice; **justicia criminal** criminal justice (P)
justo/a just, fair (14)
juzgar (gu) to judge

K

kilo kilogram
kilómetro kilometer

L

la *f. s.* the; *d.o. f. s.* you (*form.*); her; it
labio lip
laboral *adj.* labor; work; **día laboral** workday (1)
laboratorio laboratory (1)
lacio/a straight (*hair*) (5)
lácteo/a: producto lácteo dairy product (7)
lado side; **al lado (de)** next to, alongside (15); **por otro lado** on the other hand; **por un lado** on the one hand
ladrar to bark
lago lake (11)
lágrima tear
lámpara lamp
lana wool (16)
las *f. pl.* the; *d.o. f. pl.* you (*form.*); them
latino/a Hispanic; Latin
Latinoamérica Latin America
latinoamericano/a *n., adj.* Latin American
lavabo bathroom sink
lavar to wash; **lavar la ropa** to wash clothes (2); **lavar los platos** to wash the dishes (8)
lazo tie (*link*)
le *i.o. s.* to/for him, her, it, you (*form.*)
leal loyal (13)
lección *f.* lesson
leche *f.* milk (7); **café** *m.* **con leche** coffee with milk (7); **leche semidescremada** 2% milk
lechuga lettuce (7)
lector(a) reader (*person*)
lectura *n.* reading

leer (y) to read (1)
legalización *f.* legalization
legalizar (c) to legalize
legumbre *f.* vegetable
lejano/a faraway; remote, distant
lejos (de) far away (from) (15)
lengua tongue; language; **lengua extranjera** foreign language (P)
lenguado sole (*fish*)
lenguaje *m.* language
lentamente *adv.* slowly
lenteja lentil (7)
león, leona lion, lioness
les *i.o. pl.* to/for you (*form.*); them
lesión *f.* wound, injury (12)
letargo lethargy
letra letter; handwriting; lyrics; *pl.* letters (*humanities*) (P)
levantamiento de pesas weightlifting
levantar to raise; to lift; **levantar la mesa** to clear the table (8); **levantar pesas** to lift weights (10); **levantarse** *refl.* to get up (1)
léxico/a lexical
ley *f.* law
leyenda legend
liberación *f.* liberation
libertad *f.* liberty
libertino/a libertine (*free of moral and sexual restraint*)
libra pound
libre free; **al aire libre** outdoors; **tiempo libre** free (spare) time (11)
librería bookstore
libro book (P)
licencia license; **licencia de manejar** driver's license
licor *m.* liquor; **licor fuerte** hard alcohol (9)
líder *m.* leader
liga league
ligero/a light
lima lime
limitar(se) to limit (oneself)
límite *m.* limit; boundary; **hora límite** time limit
limón *m.* lemon (7); **jugo de limón** lemon juice
limonada lemonade
limosidad *f.* muddiness, sliminess
limoso/a muddy, slimy
limpiar to clean; **limpiar la casa / el apartamento** to clean the house/apartment (2)
limpieza: mujer *f.* **de limpieza** cleaning lady

limpio/a clean
lindo/a pretty
línea line; **patinar en línea** to in-line skate (11)
lingüístico/a linguistic
líquido liquid
lista list
listo/a clever; smart (17); **estar** *irreg.* **listo/a (para)** to be ready (for)
literario/a literary
literatura literature; **literatura mágico realista** magic realist literature
litro liter
llamada call; **llamada telefónica** telephone call
llamar to call; **¿cómo se llama usted?** what's your (*form.*) name? (P); **¿cómo te llamas?** what's your (*fam.*) name? (P); **llamar la atención** to attract attention; **llamar por teléfono** to call on the phone (3); **llamarse** *refl.* to be called, named; **me llamo** my name is (P); **se llama** his, her name is (P)
llave *f.* key
llegada arrival (16)
llegar (gu) to arrive (3); to reach; **llegar a ser** to become; **perdón, ¿cómo se llega a ____?** excuse me, how do you get to ____? (15)
llenar to fill; to fill out
llevar to take; to carry (5); to keep; to wear (16); **bolsita para llevar** doggie bag (7); **comida para llevar** food to go (8); **llevar a cabo** to carry out; **llevar una vida** to lead a life; **llevarse bien/mal** to get along well/poorly (5)
llorar to cry (10)
llover (ue) to rain; **llueve** it's raining (2); **está lloviendo** it's raining (2)
lluvia rain
lo *d.o. m. s.* you (*form.*); him; it; **lo cual** which; **por lo general** generally; **por lo menos** at least; **por lo tanto** therefore
lobo wolf
loco/a *n.* crazy person; *adj.* crazy
locura crazy, insane action
lodo mud
lógico/a logical
lograr to attain, achieve
lomo back (*of an animal*)
Londres *m.* London

los *m. pl.* the; *d.o. m. pl.* you (*form.*); them

lotería lottery

lucha fight

luchador(a) fighter (14)

luchar to fight, struggle

lucrativo/a lucrative

luego then, therefore (2)

lugar *m.* place (11); **en primer lugar** in the first place; **lugares de asentamiento** settling places

lujo luxury; **hotel** *m.* **de lujo** luxury hotel (16)

luna moon

lunes *m.* Monday (1)

luz *f.* (*pl.* **luces**) light

M

madera wood

madrastra stepmother (4)

madre *f.* mother (4); **madre soltera** single mother (4)

madrugada dawn; early morning

maestro/a teacher (*elementary or secondary school*) (17); master

mágico/a magical

mágico realista: literatura mágico realista magic realist literature

magnífico/a magnificent

magnitud *f.* magnitude

maíz *m.* corn (7); **aceite** *m.* **de maíz** corn oil (7)

mal *n. m.* evil; damage; *adv.* badly

mal, malo/a *adj.* bad (P); **caer** *irreg.* **mal** to make a bad impression (7); to disagree with (*food*) (7); **estar** *irreg.* **de mal humor** to be in a bad mood (10); **hace mal tiempo** the weather's bad (2); **llevarse mal** to get along poorly (5); **pasarlo (muy) mal** to have a (very) bad time (10); **sacar (qu) una mala nota** to get a bad grade (10)

malestar *m.* malaise, indisposition

maleta suitcase; **hacer** *irreg.* **la maleta** to pack one's suitcase (16)

maletero porter; skycap (16)

malévolo/a evil (14)

malicioso/a malicious

mamá mom, mother

manada herd, pack

mandar to send (1); to direct others (17); to lead, command

mandato order; command

mando command, leadership; control, order (13); **don** *m.* **de mando** talent for leadership (13)

manejar to drive (1); to manage; **licencia de manejar** driver's license

manera manner; way; **de tal manera** in such a manner; **pensar (ie) de una manera directa** to think in a direct (linear) manner (17)

manga sleeve

manifestar (ie) to manifest, show

manipular to manipulate

mano *f.* hand (8); **dar** *irreg.* **la mano** to shake hands

manta blanket

mantel *m.* tablecloth (8)

mantener (*like* **tener**) to maintain; to support (*financially*) (5); **mantenerse** *refl.* to support oneself

mantequilla butter (7); **mantequilla de cacahuete** peanut butter (7)

manual *n. m.* manual; *adj. m., f.* manual; **habilidad** *f.* **manual** ability to work with one's hands (17)

manzana apple (7); block (*of houses*) (15); **jugo de manzana** apple juice (9)

mañana morning; tomorrow (1); **ayer por la mañana** yesterday morning; **hasta mañana** see you tomorrow (P); **mañana es ____** tomorrow is ____ (1); **por la mañana** in the morning (1); **todas las mañanas** every morning (1)

mapa *m.* mapa

maquiladora *U.S.-owned factory in Mexico along the border between Mexico and the United States*

máquina machine; **escribir a máquina** to type; **máquina de escribir** typewriter; **máquina vendedora** vending machine (7)

mar *m.* sea (11)

marca brand; mark

marcado/a marked

marcar (qu) to mark

marchar to go, proceed; **marcharse** *refl.* to leave

marearse *refl.* to get dizzy, sick, nauseated

margen *m.* margin

marido husband (4)

marihuana marijuana

mariposa butterfly

marisco shellfish (7)

marrón (dark) brown (7)

Marte *m.* Mars

martes *m.* Tuesday (1)

marzo March (2)

más more (1); **el/la más alto/a (de)** the tallest (5); **más alto/a (que)** taller (than) (5); **más o menos** more or less; **más tarde** later; **más vale prevenir que arrepentir** an ounce of prevention is worth a pound of cure; **es más** what's more, moreover

mascota pet

masculino/a masculine

masticar (qu) to chew

matar to kill

mate *m. an herbal tea typical of Argentina*

matemáticas *pl.* mathematics (P); **hábil para las matemáticas** good at math (17)

materia subject (P); material

material *m.* material (16)

materno/a maternal

matrimonial: cama matrimonial double bed (16)

matrimonio marriage; married couple

máximo *n.* maximum

máximo/a *adj.* maximum

maya *n. m.* Mayan (*language*); *n., adj. m., f.* Mayan

mayo May (2)

mayonesa mayonnaise (7)

mayor older (4); greater; main; **el/la mayor** the older, oldest (4); **la mayor parte** majority

mayoría majority

me *d.o.* me; *i.o.* to/for me; *refl. pron.* myself

media: ____ y media half past (1)

mediano/a *adj.* medium; middle; **de estatura mediana** of medium height (5)

medianoche *f.* midnight

mediante by means of, through

medias *pl.* stockings (16)

medicina medicine (17)

médico/a *n.* doctor (17); *adj.* medical

medida measure, measurement; **a medida que** as

medieval medieval, about the Middle Ages

medio *n.* half; *pl.* means; resources; **medio ambiente** environment, surroundings; **medios de comunicación** means of communication; **por medio de** by means of

medio/a *adj.* half; **la Edad Media** Middle Ages; **media pensión** room and breakfast (*often with*

medio/a (*continued*) one other meal); **medio pollo asado** half a roasted chicken (7)
meditar to meditate
mediterráneo/a Mediterranean
mejilla cheek (5)
mejillón *m.* mussel
mejor better; **el/la mejor** the best
mejorana marjoram
mejorar to improve
melón *m.* melon
memoria memory; **hacer** *irreg.* **memoria** to try to remember
memorizar (c) to memorize
mencionar to mention
menos less (1); least; **al menos** at least; **echar de menos** to miss (*someone, something*); **el/la menos grande** the smallest (5); **más o menos** more or less; **menos cuarto** quarter to (1); **menos grande (que)** smaller (than) (5); **por lo menos** at least
mensaje *m.* (e-mail) message (1)
mente *f.*: **tener** *irreg.* **en mente** to keep in mind
mentir (ie, i) to lie
mentira lie
mentón *m.* chin (5)
menú *m.* menu; **menú del día** daily menu (7)
menudo: a menudo often
mercadeo marketing (P)
mercado market
merendar (ie) to snack (on) (7); **¿qué meriendas?** what do you snack on? (7)
merienda snack (7)
mermelada jam, marmalade (7)
mes *m.* month (2); **hace varios meses** several months ago
mesa table (8); **levantar la mesa** to clear the table (8); **poner** *irreg.* **la mesa** to set the table (8)
mesero/a waiter, waitress (8)
mestizaje the mixing of races
meta goal (17)
metabolismo metabolism
meter to put; **meterse** *refl.* to involve oneself; **meterse en lo suyo** to do one's own thing
metereológico/a meteorological
metido/a involved, wrapped up in
metódico/a methodical
metro subway; meter
mexicano/a *n., adj.* Mexican
México Mexico
mezcla mixture

mí *obj. of prep.* me
mi(s) *poss.* my (P)
miedo fear; **dar** *irreg.* **miedo** to frighten; **tener** *irreg.* **miedo** to be afraid (10)
miel *f.* honey
miembro member
mientras *adv.* while; **mientras tanto** meanwhile
miércoles *m.* Wednesday (1)
mil one thousand (6); **dos mil** two thousand (4)
militar *m.* soldier; *adj.* military; **servicio militar** military service
milla mile
millón *m.* million
mina mine
mineral: agua *f.* (*but* **el agua**) **mineral** mineral water
minería *n.* mining
minero/a *adj.* mining
mínimo *m.* minimum
mínimo/a *adj.* minimum; **calificación** *f.* **mínima aprobatoria** minimum passing grade
ministerio ministry (*government*)
minoría minority
minoritario/a *adj.* minority
minuto *n.* minute
mío/a *poss.* mine, of mine; **Dios mío** my goodness
mirar to look, look at, watch; **mirar la televisión** to look at, watch TV (1); **mirar un vídeo** to watch a video; **mirar una película** to watch a movie; **mirarse** *refl.* to look at oneself
misa mass (*religious*)
misión *f.* mission
mismo/a same; **por sí mismo** per se
misterio mystery
mitad *f.* half
mito myth
mixto/a mixed; **ensalada mixta** mixed, tossed salad
moda fashion (17)
modales *m. pl.* manners (8); **buenos modales** good manners (8)
modelo *m.* model; *m., f.* fashion model
moderación *f.* moderation
moderado/a moderate
modernismo modernism
modernista modernist
modernización *f.* modernization
moderno/a modern
modificación *f.* modification
modificar (qu) to modify

modismo slang
modo manner
molestar to bother, annoy
molino windmill
momento moment
moneda coin; **moneda nacional** national currency
mono monkey
monopatín scooter; skateboard (11); **andar** *irreg.* **en monopatín** to ride a scooter, skateboard (11)
monopolio monopoly
monotonía monotony
monótono/a monotonous
montaña mountain (11); **escalar montañas** to mountain climb (11); **esquiar (esquío) en las montañas** to snow ski (11)
montar to ride; **montar en bicicleta/motocicleta** to ride a bicycle/motorcycle
monumento monument
morado/a purple
moraleja moral (*of a story*)
morder (ue) to bite
moreno/a dark (5); dark-haired (5); dark-skinned (5)
morir (ue, u) (*p.p.* **muerto/a**) to die; **ya murió** he (she) already died (4)
mostaza mustard (7)
mostrar (ue) to show
motel *m.* motel
motivo motive, reason
motocicleta motorcycle; **montar en motocicleta** to ride a motorcycle
moverse to move
movimiento movement
mozo bellhop (16)
mucho *adv.* a lot (P)
mucho/a much (P); **mucho gusto** pleased to meet you (P)
mudarse to move
muerte *f.* death; **escuadrón** *m.* **de la muerte** death squad
muerto/a *p.p.* dead (4); died
muestra indication
mujer *f.* woman; wife (4); **mujer de limpieza** cleaning lady; **mujer de negocios** businesswoman (17); **mujer policía** female police officer; **mujer político** female politician; **mujer soldado** female soldier
multinacional multinational
multiplicarse (qu) to multiply
mundial *adj.* world

mundo *n.* world
muñeca doll; wrist
muñeco stuffed animal
museo museum
música music (P)
músico/a *n.* musician (17)
muy very (P); **muy tarde** very late (1); **muy temprano** very early (1)

N

nacer (zc) to be born
nacido/a *p.p.* born
nacimiento birth
nación *f.* nation
nacional national; **himno nacional** national anthem; **moneda nacional** national currency; **vuelo nacional** domestic flight
nacionalista *m., f.* nationalist
nacionalización *f.* nationalization
nada nothing, not anything (2); **no hacer nada** to do nothing (2); **no, no me gusta(n) para nada** no, I don't like it (them) at all (P)
nadar to swim (2)
nadie no one, not anyone (5)
naipe *m.* playing card; **jugar (ue) (gu) a los naipes** to play cards (11)
naranja *n.* orange (7); **jugo de naranja** orange juice (7)
narcisista *adj. m., f.* narcissistic
narcotraficante *m., f.* drug dealer
nariz *f.* (*pl.* **narices**) nose (5)
narración *f.* narration, story
narrar to tell, recount
narrativa narrative
nata whipped cream
natación *f.* swimming
nativo/a native
natural natural; plain; **ciencias naturales** natural sciences (P); **telas de fibras naturales** natural fabrics (16)
naturaleza nature
naturalidad: actuar (actúo) con naturalidad to act naturally
navegar (gu) to navigate; **navegar en un barco** to sail (11); **navegar la Red** to surf the Web (World Wide Web) / net (Internet) (1)
Navidad *f.* Christmas
navideño/a *adj.* Christmas
necesario/a necessary (8); **es necesario** it's necessary (8)
necesidad *f.* necessity
necesitar to need
negación *f.* negation (2)

negativo/a negative
negocio business (17); **hombre** *m.*, **mujer** *f.* **de negocios** businessman, businesswoman (17)
negro/a black (5)
nene/a baby; small child
nervioso/a nervous (10); **estar** *irreg.* **nervioso/a** to be nervous (10)
nevar (ie) to snow; **está nevando** it's snowing (2); **nieva** it's snowing (2)
ni neither; nor
nicaragüense *n., adj. m., f.* Nicaraguan
nieto/a grandson, granddaughter (4); *m. pl.* grandchildren (4)
ningún, ninguno/a none, not any (2); **ninguna parte** nowhere
niñez *f.* childhood
niño/a boy, girl, child
nivel *m.* level
no no, not (P)
nobleza nobility
noche *f.* night; **ayer por la noche** last night; **buenas noches** good evening (P); **esta noche** tonight; **por la noche** in the evening, at night (1); **todas las noches** every night (1)
nocturno/a nocturnal
nombrar to name
nombre *m.* name; **¿cuál es tu nombre?** what's your (*fam.*) name? (P); **mi nombre es ___** my name is ___ (P); **su nombre es ___** his (her) name is ___ (P)
nórdico/a Nordic
noreste *m.* northeast (1)
norte *m.* north (15); **América del Norte** North America
Norteamérica North America
norteamericano/a *n., adj.* North American
nos *d.o.* us; *i.o.* to/for us; *refl. pron.* ourselves; **nos vemos** we'll be seeing each other (P)
nosotros/as we (P)
nota note; grade; **sacar (qu) una buena (mala) nota** to get a good (bad) grade (10)
notar to notice; to jot down
noticia(s) news
novecientos/as nine hundred (6)
novela *n.* novel; **novelas de caballería** novels about chivalry
noventa ninety (6)
noviembre *m.* November (2)
novio/a boyfriend, girlfriend

nublado/a cloudy; **está nublado** it's cloudy (2)
nuclear: energía nuclear nuclear energy; **familia nuclear** nuclear family (4)
nucléico/a: ácido nucléico nucleic acid
nuestro/a *poss.* our
nueve nine (P)
nuez *f.* (*pl.* **nueces**) nut (7)
numérico/a numerical
número number; **número de teléfono** telephone number
numeroso/a numerous
nunca never (1)
nutricionista *m., f.* nutritionist
nutritivo/a nutritious

Ñ

ñoquis *m. pl.* gnocchi

O

o or (P)
obedecer (zc) to obey
objetivo objective
objeto object; **objeto de arte** work of art (P)
obligación *f.* obligation
obligar (gu) to obligate
obligatorio/a obligatory
obra work; **obra de teatro** play
obrero/a worker; **obrero/a del campo** farm worker
observación *f.* observation
observador(a) *n.* observer; *adj.* observant
observar to observe
obsesión *f.* obsession
obsesionarse *refl.* to be obsessed
obstante: no obstante nevertheless
obtener (*like* **tener**) to obtain
obvio/a obvious
ocasión *f.* occasion
occidental western
océano ocean (11)
ochenta eighty (6)
ochocientos eight hundred (6)
ocio leisure; leisure time (18)
octubre October (2)
ocupación *f.* occupation
ocupar to occupy; **ocuparse de** to take charge of
ocurrencia occurrence
ocurrir(se) to occur
odiar to hate
oeste *m.* west (15)
ofenderse *refl.* to be (get) offended (10)

oficina office; **oficina de turismo** tourism office

oficio job

ofrecer (zc) to offer

oír *irreg.* to hear

ojo eye; **¡ojo!** careful!, watch out!; **ojos azules/castaños/verdes** blue/brown/green eyes (5)

oliva olive; **aceite** *m.* **de oliva** olive oil (7)

olor *m.* smell, odor

oloroso/a odorous

olvidar to forget

once eleven (P)

onza ounce

opción *f.* option

ópera opera

opinar to think, have the opinion (5)

opinión *f.* opinion; **cambiar de opinión** to change one's mind

oponente *m., f.* opponent

oportunidad *f.* opportunity

opresión *f.* oppression

optar to choose

optativo/a optional

optimista *m., f.* optimistic (P)

opuesto/a opposite

oración *f.* sentence

oratoria speech (*school subject*) (P)

orden *m.* order

ordenado/a orderly, tidy

ordenador *m. Sp.* computer (18)

ordenar to order (8); to put in order

orégano oregano

oreja ear (5)

organismo organism

organización *f.* organization

organizado/a organized (17)

organizar (c) to organize

órgano organ

orgulloso/a proud (10); **sentirse (ie, i) orgulloso/a** to feel proud (10)

orientación *f.* orientation, direction

oriental eastern, from the Orient

orientar to orientate; **orientarse** *refl.* to get one's bearings; to stay on course

oriente *m.* east

origen *m.* origin

originarse originate

oro gold

os *d.o. pl. Sp.* you (*fam.*); *i.o. pl. Sp.* to/for you (*fam.*); *refl. pron. pl. Sp.* yourselves (*fam.*)

oscuro/a dark

oso bear

ostra oyster

otoño fall, autumn (2)

otro/a other; another; **capaz** (*pl.* **capaces**) **de dirigir a otros** able to direct others (13); **hablar otro idioma** to speak another language (17); **otra parte** somewhere else; **otra vez, por favor** again, please (P); **por otra parte / otro lado** on the other hand; **el/la uno/a al / a la otro/a** each other

oveja sheep

ozono ozone; **capa de ozono** ozone layer

P

paciencia patience

paciente *n., adj. m., f.* patient (17)

pacífico/a peaceful, pacific

padecer (zc) de to suffer from

padrastro stepfather (4)

padre *m.* father (4); *pl.* parents (4); **padre soltero** single father (4)

paella *Valencian rice dish with meat, fish, or shellfish and vegetables*

pagar (gu) to pay (3); **pagar la cuenta** to pay the bill (3)

página page

país *m.* country (P)

pájaro bird

palabra word (P); **palabras útiles** useful words

palacio palace

paleontología paleontology

palo stick; **de tal palo, tal astilla** a chip off the old block

paloma pigeon, dove

palomitas *pl.* popcorn (7)

pampa grassy plain

pan *m.* bread; **pan blanco** white bread (7); **pan integral** whole-wheat bread (7); **pan tostado** toast (7)

panqueque *m.* pancake (7)

pantalones *m. pl.* pants (16); **pantalones cortos** shorts (16)

papa *Lat. Am.* potato (7); **papas fritas** *Lat. Am.* potato chips (7); French fries (7); **puré** *m.* **de papas** mashed potatoes (7)

papá *m. fam.* Dad

papalote *m. Mex.* kite

papel *m.* paper; role; **hacer** *irreg.* **el papel** to play the role

par *m.* pair; couple

para *prep.* for (1); in order to; **bolsita para llevar** doggie bag (8); **capacidad** *f.* **para** ability to; **comida para llevar** food to go

(8); **de aquí para allá** from here to there (15); **hábil para las matemáticas** good at math (17); **no, no me gusta(n) para nada** no, I don't like it (them) at all (P); **para que** so that; **¿para qué cuernos?** Why the heck?; **¿y para tomar?** and to drink? (7)

paracaídas *m. s.* parachute

paracaidismo *n.* skydiving

parador *m.* inn

paraguas *m. s.* umbrella

paramilitar paramilitary

parar to stop

parcialmente partially

parecer (zc) to seem, appear (5); **parecerse** *refl.* to resemble, look alike

parecido/a similar (5)

pared *f.* wall

pareja couple (4); partner (4)

pariente *m.* relative (4)

parmesano/a Parmesan (cheese)

parque *m.* park (11); **parque zoológico** zoo

párrafo paragraph

parrillada *Arg.* mixed grill

parte *f.* part; **la mayor parte** majority; **ninguna parte** nowhere; **otra parte** somewhere else; **por otra parte** on the other hand; **por todas partes** everywhere

participante *n. m., f.* participant

participar to participate

partícula particle

particular personal; private; particular

partido game; **partido político** political party

pasado/a *adj.* last; past; spoiled, old (7); **fin** *m.* **de semana pasado** last weekend (3); **sábado (domingo) pasado** last Saturday (Sunday) (11); **semana pasada** last week (3); **siglo pasado** last century (6)

pasaje *m.* ticket, passage (16)

pasajero/a passenger (16)

pasar to spend (time) (1); to happen; to pass; **pasar tiempo** to spend time; **pasarlo bien** to have a good time; **pasarlo (muy) mal** to have a (very) bad time (10); **¿qué te pasa?** what's the matter? (10)

pasatiempo pastime, hobby (2)

paseo walk; avenue; **dar** *irreg.* **un paseo** to take a walk (2)

pasillo hallway
pasivo/a passive
paso step; passage (*time*); **dar** *irreg.* **un paso** to take a step
pasta alimenticia pasta (7)
pastel *m.* pastry (7); pie
pastilla pill
pata paw; leg (*of an animal*)
patata *Sp.* potato (7); **patatas fritas** *Sp.* potato chips (7); French fries (7)
paterno/a paternal
patín *m.* skate
patinar to skate; **patinar en línea** to inline skate (11)
patineta skateboard; **andar** *irreg.* **en patineta** to skateboard (11)
paulatinamente slowly
pavo turkey; teetotaler
paz *f.* (*pl.* **paces**) peace
peca freckle (5)
pedalear to pedal (*a bike*)
pedaleo *n.* pedaling
pedazo piece
pedir (i, i) to ask for; request (1); to order (8)
peinar to comb; **peinarse** *refl.* to comb one's hair; to do up one's hair
película film, movie; **mirar una película** to watch a movie
peligro danger (12)
peligroso/a dangerous (12)
pelirrojo/a redheaded (5)
pelo hair (5); **tomarle el pelo a uno** to pull someone's leg
pelota ball
pena: dar *irreg.* **pena** to sadden
pensamiento thought
pensar (ie) (en) to think (about) (1); **pensar de una manera directa** to think in a direct (linear) manner (17)
pensión *f.* boardinghouse, bed and breakfast (16); **media pensión** room and breakfast (*often with one other meal*); **pensión completa** room and full board (16)
peor worse; **lo peor** the worst thing
pequeño/a small (4)
perder (ie) to lose; **perder el juicio** to lose one's mind; **perderse** *refl.* to get lost
perdón *m.* pardon; excuse me; **perdón, ¿cómo se llega a ____?** excuse me, how do you get to ____? (15)
perezoso/a lazy

perfección *f.* perfection
perfeccionista *n., adj. m., f.* perfectionist
perfecto/a perfect
perfil *m.* profile
periódico newspaper (1)
periodismo journalism (P)
periodista *m., f.* journalist (17)
período period
perjudicar (qu) to jeopardize
permanecer (zc) to stay, remain; **permanecer callado/a** to keep quiet (10)
permanente permanent
permisivo/a permissive
permitir to permit, allow (9)
pero *conj.* but (1)
perplejo/a perplexed
perrito caliente hot dog
perro/a dog (4)
persecución *f.* persecution
perseguir (i, i) (g) to pursue; to chase
persistente persistent
persona person
personaje *m.* character
personalidad *f.* personality; **característica de la personalidad** personality trait (5)
pertenecer (zc) to belong
peruano/a *n., adj.* Peruvian
pesa weight; **levantamiento de pesas** weightlifting; **levantar pesas** to lift weights (10)
pesar to weigh; **a pesar de** in spite of
pescado fish (*food*) (7)
pescar (qu) to fish (11)
pesimista *n., adj. m., f.* pessimist (P)
peso weight; burden; **ganar peso** to gain weight
pesquero/a *adj.* fishing
petróleo petroleum, oil
pez *m.* (*pl.* **peces**) fish (*alive*)
picante spicy, hot
picar (qu) to nibble
pie *m.* foot
piedad *f.* pity, compassion
piel *f.* skin
pierna leg
pilotar to pilot
piloto *m., f.* pilot
pimentero pepper shaker (8)
pimienta pepper (7)
pintar to paint (10)
pintor(a) painter (17)
pintura *n.* paint; painting
pionero/a pioneer

piscina swimming pool
piso apartment; floor
pistola pistol
pizarra chalkboard
pizzería pizza parlor
placer *m.* pleasure
plan *m.* plan
plancha: a la plancha grilled
planeta *m.* planet
plano city map
plano/a *adj.* plain
planta plant
plata silver
plátano banana; plantain
platillo saucer (8)
plato plate (8); dish; **lavar los platos** to wash the dishes (8); **plato del día** daily special (8); **plato principal** main dish (8); **primer (segundo, tercer) plato** the first (second, third) course (7)
playa beach
plaza plaza, square
población *f.* population
pobre *n. m.* poor person; *adj.* poor
pobrecito/a poor thing
pobreza poverty
poco/a little (P); **pocas veces** rarely (2)
poder *v. irreg.* to be able, can (1); **¿me podría decir ____?** could you tell me ____? (15); **¿me podría traer ____?** could you bring me ____? (8); **no se puede ____ sin ____** you (one) can't ____ without ____ (8)
poema *m.* poem
poesía poetry
poeta *m., f.* poet
policía *f.* the police
policía *m.*, **mujer** *f.* **policía** female police officer
poliéster *m.* polyester (16)
política *s.* politics (17)
político *m.*, **una mujer** *f.* **político** female politician (17)
político/a political; **ciencias** *pl.* **políticas** political science (P); **partido político** political party
pollo chicken (7); **(medio) pollo asado** (half a) roasted chicken (7)
Polonia Poland
polvo: en polvo powdered
pomelo grapefruit
poner *irreg.* to put, place (7); **poner el televisor** to turn on the TV; **poner énfasis** to emphasize; **poner la mesa** to set the table

poner (*continued*)
(8); **ponerse** *refl.* to put on (*clothing*) (16); **ponerse contento/a / enfadado/a / triste** to be (get) happy/angry/sad (10); **ponerse de acuerdo** to come to an agreement; **ponerse rojo/a** to blush (10)

poniente *m.* west

popular popular

popularidad *f.* popularity

popularizar (c) to popularize

por *prep.* for (1); by; through; during (1); on account of; per; **ayer por la mañana/tarde/noche** yesterday morning/afternoon; last night; **otra vez, por favor** again, please (P); **por ciento** percent; **por ejemplo** for example; **por encima** on top; **por eso** therefore, that's why; **por favor** please (P); **por fin** finally; **por igual** equally, the same (P); **por la mañana/tarde/noche** in the morning / afternoon / evening, night (1); **por lo general** generally; **por lo menos** at least; **por lo tanto** therefore; **por medio de** by means of; **por otra parte / otro lado** on the other hand; **por primera vez** for the first time; **¿por qué?** why?; **por sí mismo** per se; **por supuesto** of course; **por todas partes** everywhere; **por última vez** for the last time; **por último** finally; **por un lado** on the one hand; **repita, por favor** repeat, please (P); **siga (Ud.) por** continue, follow (15); **tengo una pregunta, por favor** I have a question, please (P)

porcentaje *m.* percentage

porción *f.* portion

porque because (1)

portarse to behave (13)

portugués *m.* Portuguese (*language*) (P)

poseer (y) to possess

posesión *f.*: **adjetivo de posesión** possessive adjective (P)

posesivo/a possessive

posibilidad *f.* possibility

posible possible; **(no) es posible que** ___ it's (not) possible that ___ (18)

posición *f.* position

positivo/a positive

postre *m.* dessert (7)

postura posture

pozole *Mexican dish made of hominy and pork*

práctica *n.* practice

practicar (qu) to practice; **practicar un deporte** to practice, play a sport (2)

práctico/a practical (14)

precaución *f.* precaution

preceder to precede

preciado/a esteemed

precio price

precioso/a precious

preciso/a necessary (8); **es preciso** it's necessary (8)

precolombino/a pre-Columbian

predecir *irreg.* to predict

predeterminado/a predetermined

predicción *f.* prediction

predominar to predominate

preferencia preference

preferentemente preferably

preferible preferable

preferido/a favorite

preferir (ie, i) to prefer (1)

pregunta question; **hacer** *irreg.* **preguntas** to ask questions (4); **tengo una pregunta, por favor** I have a question, please (P)

preguntar to ask a question (1); **preguntarse** *refl.* to wonder

prehispánico/a prehispanic (*before the arrival of the Spanish in the New World*)

prehispano/a prehispanic (*before the arrival of the Spanish in the New World*)

prehistórico/a prehistoric

preliminar *adj.* preliminary

premio prize

prenda garment; **prenda de ropa** article of clothing; **prenda de vestir** article of clothing (16)

prender to turn on (*switch, light*)

preocupación *f.* worry; preoccupation

preocupado/a worried

preocuparse *refl.* to worry, get worried (10)

preparación *f.* preparation

preparado/a prepared

preparar to prepare; **preparar la cena** to prepare dinner (3)

preparatoria high school

preposición *f.* preposition

presencia presence

presentación *f.* presentation

presentar to present, to introduce

presente *n. m.; adj. m., f.* present

presidente/a president (17)

presión *f.* pressure; **presión atmosférica** atmospheric pressure

presionar to press, push

prestar to lend; to render; **prestar atención** to pay attention

prestigio prestige

prestigioso/a prestigious

pretérito *gram.* preterite, past (*tense*)

prevenir (*like* **venir**): **más vale prevenir que arrepentir** an ounce of prevention is worth a pound of cure

previo/a previous

primaria primary (*school*)

primavera spring (2)

primer, primero/a first; **en primer lugar** in the first place; **por primera vez** for the first time; **primer plato** first course (7); **primera clase** first class (16); **primera dama** First Lady

primitivo/a primitive

primo/a cousin (4)

principal main, principal; **plato principal** main dish (8)

principalmente mainly

príncipe *m.* prince

principio *n.* beginning; principle

privado/a private; **con baño privado** with a private bath (16); **vida privada** privacy

privilegio privilege

probabilidad *f.* probability

probable probable; **(no) es probable que** ___ it is (not) probable that ___ (18)

probar (ue) to try, taste (8); **probarse** *refl.* to try on (*clothes*)

problema *m.* problem

problemático/a problematic

proceso process

producción *f.* production

producir (*like* **conducir**) to produce

productivo/a productive

producto product; **producto lácteo** dairy product (7)

productor(a) producer (17)

profecía prophecy

profesión *f.* profession (17)

profesional *n., adj. m., f.* professional (17)

profesor(a) professor (P)

proficiencia proficiency

profundo/a profound; deep

programa *m.* program
programador(a) programmer (17)
progresista *adj. m., f.* progressive
progreso progress
prohibición *f.* prohibition
prohibir (prohíbo) to prohibit (9)
promedio average (6); **tamaño promedio** average size
prometer to promise
promiscuo/a promiscuous
pronombre *m.* pronoun (P)
pronóstico prediction; **pronóstico del tiempo** weather forecast
pronto soon; **hasta pronto** see you soon (P); **tan pronto como** as soon as (17)
pronunciar to pronounce
propina tip (8); **dejar propina** to leave a tip (8)
propio/a *adj.* own
proponer (*like* **poner**) to propose
propósito purpose; **a propósito** on purpose; by the way
propuesto/a (*p.p. of* **proponer**) *adj.* proposed
prórroga extension
prosa prose
prospectivista *m., f.* futurist
protagonista *m., f.* protagonist (*lead character in a film*)
protección *f.* protection
proteger (j) to protect
protegido/a protected
proteína protein (7)
protestar to protest
provecho: buen provecho enjoy your meal
provenir (*like* **venir**) to originate
proverbio proverb
provincia province
provocar (qu) to provoke; to cause
próximo/a next
proyecto project
prudente prudent
prueba proof; test, quiz; **prueba de sorpresa** pop quiz
psicoanálisis *m.* psychoanalysis
psicología psychology (P)
psicológico/a psychological
psicólogo/a psychologist (17)
psiquiatra *m., f.* psychiatrist
psiquiatría psychiatry
publicación *f.* publication
publicado/a published
publicar (qu) to publish
publicidad *f.* publicity
público *n.* public

público/a public; **transporte** *m.* **público** public transportation
pueblo town; people
puerco pig
puerta door
puerto port
puertorriqueño/a *n., adj.* Puerto Rican
pues... well . . .
puesta de sol sunset
puesto position, job (17); **puesto que** since, because
pulgada inch
pulpo octopus
punto point; period; **punto de vista** point of view
puré *m.* **de papas** mashed potatoes (7)
puro/a pure
púrpura purple

Q

que *rel. pron.* that, which (P); *conj.* that; **hay que** it's necessary to (8)
¿qué? what? (P); which? **¿a qué hora?** at what time? (1); **¿con qué frecuencia?** how often? (2); **¿de qué color es/son ___?** what color is/are ___? (5) **¿por qué?** why?; **¿qué carrera haces?** what's your major? (P); **¿qué demonios?** what the heck?; **¿qué día es hoy?** what day is today? (1); **¿qué estatura es?** how tall is he/she/you (*form.*)? (5); **¿qué hora es?** what time is it? (1); **¿qué meriendas?** what do you (*fam.*) snack on? (7); **¿qué tal?** what's up? (P); **¿qué te pasa?** what's the matter? (10); **¿qué tiempo hace?** what's the weather like? (2)
quedar to be remaining (10); to be located (15); **¿dónde queda ___?** where is ___? (15); **quedarse** *refl.* to stay (2); **quedarse en casa** to stay at home (2)
quehacer *m.* **doméstico** household chore
quejarse (de) *refl.* to complain (about) (10)
querer *irreg.* to want (1); to like, love
queso cheese (7)
quien *rel. pron.* who, whom; **con quien** with whom; **¿quién(es)?** who?, whom? (P); **¿a quién?** to whom?

química chemistry (P)
químico/a chemist (17); *adj.* chemical
quince fifteen (P)
quinientos/as five hundred (6)
quitar to remove, take away (7); **quitarse** *refl.* to take off (16)
quizás perhaps

R

rábano radish
radio *f.* radio (*broadcasting*); *m.* radio (*set*); **escuchar la radio** to listen to the radio
radio *m.* radius
raíz *f.* (*pl.* **raíces**) root
rana frog; **ancas** *pl.* **de rana** frog's legs
ranchero/a *n.* rancher; *adj.* ranch
rango rank
rápido rapid, fast; **comida rápida** fast food
raqueta racket
raquetbol *m.* racquetball
raro/a strange (P); **raras veces** rarely (1)
rasgo trait (5); **rasgo físico** physical trait
rata rat
rato little while, short time (3)
rayón *m.* rayon (16)
raza breed, race; **raza humana** human race
razón *f.*: **tener** *irreg.* **razón** to be right
razonable reasonable
reacción *f.* reaction (10)
reaccionar to react
real real; royal
realidad *f.* reality; **en realidad** in fact, actually
realismo *m.* realism
realista *n. m., f.* realist; *adj. m., f.* realistic (P)
realización *f.*: **afán** *m.* **de realización** eagerness to get things done (13)
realizar (c) to carry out; to achieve; **realizarse** *refl.* to happen; to take place
realmente really
rebanada slice
rebelarse *refl.* to rebel
rebelde rebellious (13)
rebelión *f.* rebellion
recado note
recepción *f.* front desk (16)
recepcionista *m., f.* receptionist

recesión *f.* recession
receta recipe
rechazar (c) to refuse
recibir to receive (1)
recién *adv.* recently; **recién graduado** recent graduate
reciente recent
recíproco/a reciprocal
recobrar to recover; **recobrar el juicio** to recover one's sanity
recoger (j) to pick up; to retrieve
recomendación *f.* recommendation
recomendar (ie) to recommend
reconocido/a recognized
récord *m.* record (*sports*)
recordar (ue) to remember (3)
recorrido journey
recto: siga recto continue (go) straight (15)
recuerdo souvenir; memory
recuperar to regain; **recuperarse** *refl.* to recover
recurrir to resort to
recurso resource
red *f.* network; net; World Wide Web, Internet; **navegar (gu) la Red** to surf the Web (World Wide Web) / Net (Internet) (1)
redacción *f.* editing, revising
reducir (*like* **conducir**) to reduce
reemplazar (c) to replace
reescribir to rewrite
referencia reference
referéndum *m.* referendum
referirse (ie, i) a *refl.* to refer to
reflejar to reflect
reflexivo/a *gram.* reflexive
reforma reform
refresco soft drink (7)
refrigerador *m.* refrigerator
refugiado/a refugee
refutar to refute
regalo gift
regazo lap
régimen *m.* regime
región *f.* region
regla rule
regresar to return (*to a place*) (1)
regular to regulate
regularmente regularly; usually (1)
rehabilitación *f.* rehabilitation
reina queen
reinterpretación *f.* reinterpretation
reír(se) (i, i) to laugh (10); **hacer** *irreg.* **reír** to make laugh (11); **reír(se) a caracajadas** to laugh loudly (11)
relación *f.* relation; relationship

relacionar to relate; to associate
relajación *f.* relaxation
relajado/a relaxed (10); **sentirse (ie, i) relajado** to feel relaxed (10)
relajarse *refl.* to relax (10)
relativo/a *adj.* relative
relato story
relegado/a relegated
relevante relevant
religión *f.* religion (P)
religioso/a religious
relleno/a stuffed; filled
reloj *m.* clock; watch
remedio cure
remolacha sugar beet
remontar a to date back to
renegado/a renegade
repasar to review
repaso review
repente: de repente suddenly
repetir (i, i) to repeat; **repita, por favor** repeat, please (P)
repetitivo/a repetitive
réplica replica
reponerse (*like* **poner**) to recover
reportado/a reported
reportar to report
reportero/a reporter
reposo rest
representación *f.* representation
representante *m., f.* representative (17)
representar to represent
reptil *m.* reptile
república republic; **República Dominicana** Dominican Republic
republicano/a republican
repugnante disgusting
requerir (ie, i) to require
requisito requirement
res *f.*: **carne** *f.* **de res** beef (7)
reseña review (*restaurant, book, etc.*)
reserva reservation
reservación *f.* reservation
reservado/a reserved (5)
reservar to reserve (16); **reservar con (un mes de) anticipación** to reserve (a month) in advance (16)
resfriado *n.* cold (*illness*)
residencia residency; dormitory; **residencia estudiantil** student dormitory
resignar to resign; **resignarse** *refl.* **a** to resign oneself to
resistir to be able to withstand
resolver (ue) (*p.p.* **resuelto/a**) to resolve

respectivo/a respective
respecto: al respecto about the matter; **(con) respecto a** with respect to, concerning
respetar to respect
respetuoso/a respectful
responder to respond
responsabilidad *f.* responsibility
responsable responsible
respuesta answer
restaurante *m.* restaurant
resto rest, remainder
restricción *f.* restriction
restrictivo/a restrictive
resultado result
resultar to result; to turn out
resumen *m.* summary
resumir to summarize
retirar to remove, withdraw; **retirarse** *refl.* to leave
retórica rhetoric
retraído/a solitary, reclusive (13)
retraimiento reclusiveness
reunir (reúno) to assemble, unite
revelado/a revealed
revelar to reveal
revisar to review
revisión *f.* revision
revista magazine
revolución *f.* revolution
revolucionario/a revolutionary
revuelto: huevo revuelto scrambled egg (7)
rey *m.* king
rezar (c) to pray
rico/a rich; delicious
ricurita *fam.* beautiful girl
ridículo/a ridiculous
riesgo: tendencia a evitar riesgos tendency to avoid risks (13)
rifle *m.* rifle
río river (11)
risa laugh, laughter (11); **causar risa** to cause laughter, make laugh (11)
rítmico/a rhythmical
ritmo rhythm
rizado/a curly (5)
robótica *s.* robotics
roca rock
rocín *m.* nag, old workhorse
rodear to surround
rojo/a red (7); **carne** *f.* **roja** red meat; **ponerse** *irreg.* **rojo/a** to blush (10)
romano/a Roman
romántico/a romantic
ron *m.* rum

ropa clothes; **lavar la ropa** to wash clothes (2); **prenda de ropa** article of clothing
rosado/a pink (7)
rosbif *m.* roast beef
rosquilla donut
roto/a *p.p.* broken
rueda wheel
ruido noise; **hacer** *irreg.* **ruido** to make noise (10)
ruina ruin
rusia Russia
ruta route
rutina routine (11)

S

sábado Saturday (1); **sábado pasado** last Saturday (11)
saber *irreg.* to know (*facts, information*) (3); **no lo sé todavía** I don't know yet (P); **no sé** I don't know (P); **que yo sepa** as far as I know (17); **sabe a ____** it tastes like (7); **saber expresarse** *refl.* **claramente** to know how to express oneself clearly (17); **saber** + *inf.* to know how (*to do something*) (17); **supe que ____** I found out that ____
sabido/a: es cosa sabida it is a known fact (5)
sabio/a wise
sabor *m.* taste, flavor (7)
sabroso/a tasty, delicious
sacar (qu) to take out; to rent (2); **sacar fotos** to take pictures (16); **sacar una buena (mala) nota** to get a good (bad) grade (10); **sacar vídeos** to rent videos
sacerdote *m.* priest
sacrificarse (qu) *refl.* to sacrifice oneself
sagrado/a sacred
sal *f.* salt (7)
sala room; **sala de espera** waiting room (16)
salado/a salty
salamandra salamander
salchicha sausage (7)
saldo balance (*of money*)
salero salt shaker (8)
salida departure (16); exit
salir *irreg.* to go out, leave (1); to come out; **salir de una adicción** to overcome an addiction (12)
salsa sauce; salsa (*music*); **salsa de tomate** ketchup (7)

saltar to jump; to spring; **saltar a la cuerda** to jump rope (11)
salud *f.* health
saludable healthy
saludar to greet (5)
saludo greeting (P)
salvar to save
san *apocopated form of* **Santo**
sándwich *m.* sandwich (7)
sangre *f.* blood
santo/a saint
satélite *m.* satellite
satira satire
satisfacción *f.* satisfaction
satisfecho/a *p.p.* satisfied
se *refl. pron.* yourself (*form.*); himself, herself, yourselves (*form.*); themselves; (*impersonal*) one
sección *f.* section; **sección de (no) fumar** (no) smoking section (16)
secretario/a secretary
secreto *n.* secret
secreto/a *adj.* secret
secuencia: en secuencia in sequence
secuestro kidnapping
secundaria secondary; **escuela secundaria** secondary school, high school
sed *f.* thirst; (**dar** *irreg.* **sed** to make thirsty; **tener** *irreg.* **sed** to be thirsty (9)
seda silk (16)
sedentario/a sedentary
seductor(a) seductive (14)
segmento segment
seguido/a followed; **en seguida** right away
seguir (i, i) (g) to follow; to continue; **siga (Ud.) por ____** continue, follow ____ (15); **siga derecho (recto)** continue (go) straight (15)
según according to
segundo *n.* second
segundo/a *adj.* second; **segundo plato** second course (7)
seguro/a sure, secure (13)
seis six (P)
seiscientos six hundred (6)
selección *f.* selection
seleccionar to select, choose
semáforo traffic light (15)
semana week; **fin** *m.* **de semana** weekend (1); **fin** *m.* **de semana pasado** last weekend (3); **semana pasada** last week (3)
semanal weekly
semejante similar

semejanza similarity
semestre *m.* semester
semidescremado/a: leche *f.* **semidescremada** 2% milk
senador(a) senator (17)
sencillo/a simple; **cama sencilla** twin bed (16)
sensible sensitive (13)
sentarse (ie) *refl.* to sit down
sentido sense
sentimiento feeling
sentir (ie, i) to feel; to feel sorry; **sentirse** *refl.* to feel (10); **¿cómo te sientes?** how do you feel? (10); **para sentirse bien** to feel well (10); **sentirse alegre / avergonzado/a / deprimido/a / orgulloso/a / relajado/a** to feel happy/ashamed, embarrassed/depressed/proud/relaxed (10)
señor *m.* sir, Mr.; man
señora ma'am, Mrs.; woman
separado/a separated
separar to separate
septiembre *m.* September (2)
sequía drought
ser *irreg.* to be (P); **¿de dónde eres tú / es usted?** where are you from? (P); **¿de qué color es/son ____?** what color is/are ____? (5); **es decir** that is; **es la una** it's one o'clock (1); **es más** what's more, moreover; **llegar (gu) a ser** to become; **o sea** that is to say (17); **¿qué estatura es?** how tall is he/she/you (*form.*)? (5); **sea lo que sea** be that as it may (17); **ser adicto/a** to be addicted (12); **ser carismático/a** to be charismatic (17); **si no fuera por** if it weren't for; **son las dos (tres)** it's two (three) o'clock (1); **soy** I am (P); **soy de** I'm from (P); **soy estudiante de ____** I am a(n) ____ student (P)
ser *n. m.* being; **ser humano** human being
serie *f.* series
serio/a serious (P); **en serio** seriously
serpiente *f.* snake; **serpiente de cascabel** rattlesnake
serrano/a *adj.* mountain; **jamón** *m.* **serrano** *cured Spanish ham*
servicio service; **servicio a domicilio** home delivery (8); **servicio de cuarto** room service (16); **servicio militar** military service

servilleta napkin (8)
servir (i, i) to serve
sesenta sixty (6)
setecientos seven hundred (6)
setenta seventy (6)
sexo sex
si if
sí yes (P); **claro que sí** of course; **creo que sí** I think so; **por sí mismo** per se
SIDA *m.* AIDS
siempre always (1)
siete seven (P)
siglo century; **siglo pasado** last century (6)
significado meaning
significar (qu) to mean
signo sign
siguiente following, next
silbar to whistle (10)
silencio silence; **guardar silencio** to keep quiet
silla chair
símbolo symbol
simpatía congeniality, friendliness
simpático/a nice, pleasant (4)
simplemente simply; merely
sin *prep.* without; **no se puede ___ sin ___** you (one) can't ___ without ___ (8); **sin duda** without a doubt; **sin embargo** however, nevertheless; **sin hielo** without ice (9)
sincero/a sincere (P)
sincretismo synthesis
síndrome *m.* syndrome; **síndrome invernal** winter syndrome (*depression*)
sinfonía symphony
sino *conj.* but, instead
sinónimo synonym
síntesis synthesis
sintético/a synthetic
síntoma *m.* symptom
siquiera *adv.* even; **ni siquiera** not even
sirviente/a servant
sistema *m.* system
sitio place
situación *f.* situation
situarse *refl.* to be located
SMS *m.* Short Message Service, text messaging
sobras *pl.* leftovers
sobre *prep.* about; on; **sobre todo** above all
sobreevaluado/a overvalued
sobresaliente outstanding

sobrino/a nephew, niece (4)
social social; **asistencia social** social work (17); **asistente social** social worker; **ciencias** *pl.* **sociales** social sciences (P); **trabajador(a) social** social worker (17)
socialista *m., f.* socialist
socializar (c) to socialize
sociedad *f.* society
sociología sociology (P)
sociológico/a sociological
sol *m.* sun; **hace sol** it's sunny (2); **puesta de sol** sunset; **tomar el sol** to sunbathe
solamente only
solar: energía solar solar energy
soldado / mujer *f.* **soldado** female soldier
soleado/a sunny
soler (ue) + *inf.* to be in the habit of (*doing something*) (1)
solicitante *m., f.* person surveyed (*opinion poll*)
solitario/a solitary
sólo *adv.* only
solo/a alone; single, sole; **a solas** alone
soltero/a *adj.* single (4); **madre** *f.* **soltera** single mother (4); **padre** *m.* **soltero** single father (4)
solución *f.* solution
sombra shade; shadow
sombrero hat (16)
sonar (ue) to sound; to ring
sonido sound
sonreír (i, i) to smile (10)
sonrojarse *refl.* to blush (10)
soñador(a) *n., adj.* dreamer (14)
soñar (ue) to dream; **soñar despierto/a** to daydream
sopa soup
sorber to taste
sorprendente surprising
sorprender to surprise
sorpresa surprise; **prueba de sorpresa** pop quiz
sospechar to suspect
sostener (*like* **tener**) to sustain, hold up
su(s) *poss.* his, her, its, your (*form. pl., s.*), their (P)
suave soft
subir to go up; to lift up; **subir a** to get on/in (*a bus, car, plane, etc.*)
subjuntivo *gram.* subjunctive
sublevar to stir up; to incite to anger or rebellion; **sublevarse** *refl.* to rise up, rebel

subproducto byproduct
subrayar to underline
subsección *f.* subsection
sucio/a dirty
sudadera *s.* sweats (*clothing*) (16)
Sudamérica South America
sudamericano/a *n., adj.* South American
sudar to sweat
suegro/a father-in-law, mother-in-law (4); *m. pl.* in-laws (4)
sueldo salary
suelo ground; floor
sueño dream
suerte *f.* luck; **tener** *irreg.* **suerte** to be lucky
suéter *m.* sweater (16)
suficiente sufficient
sufijo *gram.* suffix
sufrir to suffer (12); to experience (12)
sugerencia suggestion
sugerir (ie, i) to suggest
sujeto subject
superficial superficial (13)
superfluo/a superfluous, unnecessarily excessive
supermercado supermarket
supremo/a supreme
supuesto: por supuesto of course
sur *m.* south (15); **América del Sur** South America
Suráfrica South Africa
Suramérica South America
suramericano/a *n., adj.* South American
surgir (j) to spring up, present itself
suroeste *m.* southwest
suspender to suspend; to fail (*an exam*)
suspenso suspense
sustantivo *gram.* noun
sustituir (y) to substitute
suyo/a your, yours (*form. pl., s.*); his, of his, her, of hers; its; their, of theirs; **meterse en lo suyo** to do one's own thing

T

tabaco tobacco
tabernero/a tavern keeper
tabla table
tacaño/a stingy (13)
tacón *m.* heel; **zapato de tacón alto** high-heeled shoe (16)
tal such; **de tal manera** in such a manner; **de tal palo, tal astilla**

a chip off the old block; **¿qué tal?** what's up (P); **tal como** just as; **tal vez** perhaps

talento talent

tamaño size (6); **tamaño promedio** average size

tampoco neither; not either (2)

tan as, so; **tan ____ como** as ____ as (6); **tan pronto como** as soon as (17)

tanto/a as much, so much; **mientras tanto** meanwhile; **por lo tanto** therefore; **tanto/a ____ como** as much ____ as (6)

tantos/as as many; so many; **tantos/as ____ como** as many ____ as (6)

tapa *Sp.* snack, appetizer

tapiz *m.* (*pl.* **tapices**) tapestries

tardar to take a long time

tarde *n. f.* afternoon; *adv.* late; **ayer por la tarde** yesterday afternoon; **buenas tardes** good afternoon (P); **hasta (muy) tarde** until (very) late (2); **más tarde** later; **(muy) tarde** (very) late (1); **por la tarde** in the afternoon (1); **todas las tardes** every afternoon (1)

tarea homework (1); **escribir la tarea** to write the assignment; **hacer** *irreg.* **la tarea** to do the homework/assignment; **tarea doméstica** household chore

tarjeta card; **tarjeta de embarque** boarding pass; **tarjeta de crédito** credit card

tarta pie (20)

tasa rate; **tasa de desempleo** unemployment rate

taxi *m.* taxi

taxista *m., f.* taxi driver

taza cup (8)

te *d.o.* you (*fam. s.*); *i.o.* for you (*fam. s.*); *refl. pron.* yourself (*fam. s.*)

té *m.* tea (7); **té de hierbas** herbal tea (9); **té helado** iced tea (9)

teatral theatrical

teatro theater (P); **ir** *irreg.* **al teatro** to go to the theater (11); **obra de teatro** play

técnica technique

técnico/a *n.* technician (17); *adj.* technical

tecnología technology

tecnólogo/a technologist

tejano/a *n., adj.* Texan

tejido fabric

tela fabric (16); **telas de fibras naturales** natural fabrics (16)

tele *f.* (*colloquial*) TV

telefónico/a: llamada telefónica telephone call

teléfono telephone; **hablar por teléfono** to talk on the phone (1); **llamar por teléfono** to call on the phone (3); **número de teléfono** telephone number; **teléfono celular** cell phone

telenovela soap opera; **ver** *irreg.* **una telenovela** to watch a soap opera (3)

telescopio telescope

televidente television viewer

televisión *f.* television; **mirar la televisión** to look at, watch TV (1); **televisión por cable** cable TV; **ver** *irreg.* **la televisión** to watch television (2)

televisor *m.* television (*set*); **poner** *irreg.* **el televisor** to turn on the TV

tema *m.* topic, theme

temperamento temperament

temperatura temperature (2)

templo temple

temporada season

temprano/a early (1); **(muy) temprano** (very) early (1)

tenaz (*pl.* **tenaces**) tenacious (14)

tendencia tendency; **tendencia a evitar riesgos** tendency to avoid risks (13)

tenedor *m.* fork (8)

tener *irreg.* to have (1); **tener ____ años** to be ____ years old (4); **tener buena educación** to be well-mannered (8); **tener calor** to be (feel) hot (*person*); **tener celos** to be jealous; **tener cuidado** to be careful (12); **tener dolor de cabeza** to have a headache (10); **tener dolor de estómago** to have a stomachache; **tener don de gentes** to have a way with people (17); **tener en mente** to keep in mind; **tener envidia** to be envious; **tener éxito** to be successful; **tener fama de** to have a reputation for; **tener ganas de** + *inf.* to feel like (*doing something*); **tener gracia** to be funny, charming (11); **tener habilidad manual** to have the ability to work with one's hands (17); **tener hambre** to be hungry (7); **tener miedo** to be afraid (10); **tener que** + *inf.* to have to (*do something*) (1); **tener que ver con** to have to do with; to concern; **tener razón** to be right; **tener sed** to be thirsty (9); **tener suerte** to be lucky; **tener un examen** to take a test (3); **tener vergüenza** to be ashamed, embarrassed (10); **tener vista** to have a view (16); **tengo** I have (P); **tengo una pregunta, por favor** I have a question, please (P); **tienes** you have (P)

tenis *m.* tennis; **jugar (ue) (gu) al tenis** to play tennis (10); **zapato de tenis** tennis shoe

tenista *m., f.* tennis player

tensión *f.* tension

tenso/a tense (10); **estar tenso/a** to be tense (10)

tentación *f.* temptation

tentativo/a tentative

tequila *m.* tequila

terapeuta físico/a *m., f.* physical therapist (17)

terapia therapy; **terapia física** physical therapy (17)

tercer, tercero/a third; **tercer plato** third course (8)

terminar to finish, end

término term; end

ternera veal (7)

terraza terrace

terremoto earthquake

territorio territory

terrorista *m., f.* terrorist

tesis *f.* thesis

tesoro treasure

testarudo/a stubborn (13)

textiles *pl.* textiles

texto text

textura texture

tez *f.* (*pl.* **teces**) complexion

ti *obj. of prep.* you (*fam. s.*)

tiburón *m.* shark

tiempo time; weather; tense; **hace buen/mal tiempo** the weather's good/bad (2); **pasar tiempo** to spend time; **pronóstico del tiempo** weather forecast; **¿qué tiempo hace?** what's the weather like? (2); **tiempo libre** free (spare) time (11)

tienda store

tierra land; earth; *pl.* lands

tigre *m.* tiger

timidez *f.* timidity

tímido/a timid, shy (5)

tinto/a: vino tinto red wine (9)

tío/a uncle, aunt (4); *pl.* aunts and uncles (4)

típico/a typical

tipo type

tira cómica comic strip

titulado/a titled

título title

toalla towel (16)

tobillo ankle

tocar (qu) to touch; to play; to knock; to toll; **tocar la guitarra** to play the guitar (1); **tocarle a uno** to be one's turn

tocino bacon (7)

todavía *adv.* yet, still; **no lo sé todavía** I don't know yet (P)

todo/a all, every; **de todas formas** in any case; **por todas partes** everywhere; **sobre todo** above all; **todo el día** all day; **todos los días** every day (1); **todas las mañanas/tardes/ noches** every morning/afternoon/ night (1)

tolerancia tolerance

tomar to take; to drink (7); **tomar apuntes** to take notes; **tomar asiento** to take a seat; **tomar el sol** to sunbathe; **tomar en cuenta** to take into account; **tomar un café** to drink a cup of coffee (2); **tomar unas vacaciones** to take a vacation; **tomarle el pelo a uno** to pull someone's leg; **¿y para tomar?** and to drink? (7)

tomate *m.* tomato (7); **jugo de tomate** tomato juice (9); **salsa de tomate** ketchup (7)

tonelada ton

tono tone

tonto/a foolish (P)

tormenta storm

torneo tournament

toronja: jugo de toronja grapefruit juice

torpe clumsy

torrencial torrential

torta cake

tortilla *Lat. Am.* tortilla; *Sp.* omelette (7)

tortuga turtle

tostada toast (7)

tostado/a toasted; **pan** *m.* **tostado** toast (7)

total *m.* total

trabajador(a) worker; **trabajador(a) social** social worker (17)

trabajar to work (1); **trabajar en el jardín** to garden (11)

trabajo work; job

tradición *f.* tradition

tradicional traditional

traducir (*like* **conducir**) to translate; to express

traer *irreg.* to bring (8); **¿me podría traer ____?** could you bring me ____? (8); **¿qué trae ____?** what does ____ come with? (8)

tráfico traffic

tragar (gu) to swallow

trágico/a tragic

trago drink

traje *m.* suit (16); costume; **traje de baño** bathing suit (16)

tranquilidad *f.* tranquility

tranquilizante *m.* tranquilizer

tranquilo/a tranquil, calm

transformarse *refl.* to become transformed

transición *f.* transition

transmitir to transmit

transporte *m.* transport, transportation; **transporte público** public transportation

tratamiento treatment

tratar to treat; to discuss; **tratar de** to try; to speak about

trato treatment

través: a través de through

trece thirteen (P)

treinta thirty (6)

tremendo/a tremendous

tren *m.* train (16)

tres three (P)

trescientos/as three hundred (6)

tribu *f.* tribe

trimestre *m.* trimester

triste sad (10); **ponerse** *irreg.* **triste** to be (get) sad (10)

tristeza sadness

triunfar to be successful

triunfo triumph

trompeta trumpet

tropas *pl.* troops

tropezarse (ie) (c) con *refl.* to trip over

trucha trout

truco trick

túnel *m.* tunnel

turismo: agencia de turismo travel agency; **oficina de turismo** tourism office

turista *n. m., f.* tourist

turístico/a: clase *f.* **turística** economy class (16)

tutear *to address with the familiar form* **tú**

tuyo/a *poss.* your, of yours (*fam. s.*)

U

u or (*used instead of* **o** *before words beginning with* **o** *or* **ho**)

Ud. *form. s.* you (P)

Uds. *form. pl.* you (P)

último/a last; highest; **por último** finally; **por última vez** for the last time (3)

un, uno/a one, an (P); **a la una** at one o'clock (1); **es la una** it's one o'clock (1); **el/la uno/a al / a la otro/a** each other

único/a only; unique; **hijo/a único/a** only child

unidad *f.* unit

unido/a united, close-knit; **Estados Unidos** United States

uniforme *m.* uniform

unisexual unisex

universidad *f.* university

universitario/a *n.* university student; *adj.* university

unos/as some (P); **unos/as cuantos/as** a few

uña fingernail; **comerse** *refl.* **las uñas** to bite one's nails (10)

urbano/a urban

usar to use; **usar una computadora** to use a computer (17)

uso use

usuario/a user

útil useful; **palabras útiles** useful words

utilizar (c) to use; **utilizar la aromaterapia** to use aromatherapy (11)

uva grape (7)

V

vacaciones *f. pl.* vacation; **estar** *irreg.* **de vacaciones** to be on vacation; **tomar unas vacaciones** to take a vacation

vacilón, vacilona funny

vacuna vaccine

valer *irreg.* to be worth; **más vale prevenir que arrepentir** an ounce of prevention is worth a pound of cure

valle *m.* valley

valor *m.* value; courage

vanidoso/a vain

vapor *m.*: **al vapor** steamed (7)

variación *f.* variation

variado/a varied

variar (varío) to vary

variedad *f.* variety

varios/as *pl.* various, several; **hace varios meses** several months ago

vasco/a *n., adj. m., f.* Basque; *m.* Basque (*language*); **País Vasco** Basque Provinces

vaso (water) glass (8)

vasto/a vast

vecino/a neighbor

vegetariano/a *n., adj.* vegetarian

veinte twenty (P)

veinticinco twenty-five (P)

veinticuatro twenty-four (P)

veintidós twenty-two (P)

veintinueve twenty-nine (P)

veintiocho twenty-eight (P)

veintiséis twenty-six (P)

veintisiete twenty-seven (P)

veintitrés twenty-three (P)

veintiún, veintiuno/a twenty-one (P)

vendedor(a) salesperson; **máquina vendedora** vending machine (7); **vendedora automática** vending machine

vender to sell

venir *irreg.* to come (1)

venta sale

ventaja advantage (18)

ventana window

ver *irreg.* (*p.p.* **visto/a**) to see; **verse** *refl.* (**bien**) to look (good) (16); **a ver** let's see; **nos vemos** we'll be seeing each other (P); **ver la televisión** to watch television (2); **ver una telenovela** to watch a soap opera (3); **tener** *irreg.* **que ver con** to have to do with; to concern

verano summer (2)

veras: de veras truly, really

verbo verb (P)

verdad *f.* truth

verdadero/a true

verde green; **chiste verde** off-color joke; **judía verde** green bean (7); **ojos verdes** green eyes (5)

verdeo: de verdeo unripened

verdura vegetable (7)

vergonzoso/a shameful

vergüenza: tener *irreg.* **vergüenza** to be ashamed, embarrassed (10)

verificar (qu) to verify; to check

versión *f.* version

vestido dress (16)

vestimenta apparel

vestir (i, i) to wear (16); **prenda de vestir** article of clothing (16); **vestirse** *refl.* to dress, get dressed

veterinario/a veterinarian (17)

vez *f.* (*pl.* **veces**) time; **a veces** sometimes; **a la vez** at the same time; **algunas veces** sometimes; **de vez en cuando** from time to time (P); **en vez de** instead of; **otra vez, por favor** again, please (P); **pocas (raras) veces** rarely; **tal vez** perhaps; **última vez** last time (3); **una vez** once (3)

viajar to travel (16)

viaje *m.* trip (16); **agente** *m., f.* **de viajes** travel agent (16); **hacer** *irreg.* **un viaje** to take a trip (16)

vicepresidente/a vice president

viceversa vice versa

vicio vice, bad habit

víctima *m., f.* victim

vida life; **esperanza de vida** life expectancy; **ganarse la vida** to support oneself (*financially*); **llevar una vida** to lead a life; **vida privada** privacy

vídeo video; **mirar un vídeo** to watch a video; **sacar (qu) vídeos** to rent videos

videoclub *m.* video rental store

videojuego video game; **jugar (ue) (gu) a los videojuegos** to play video games (3)

viejo/a *n.* old person; *adj.* old (6)

viento wind; **hace viento** it's windy (2)

vientre *m.* belly

viernes *m.* Friday (1)

villa municipality

vinagre *m.* vinegar

vinculado/a connected

vino wine (7); **vino blanco** white wine (9); **vino tinto** red wine (9)

violencia violence

violento/a violent

violín *m.* violin

virreinato viceroyalty

viruela smallpox

virus *m. pl., s.* virus(es)

visibilidad *f.* visibility

visita visit

visitar to visit

vista view; **punto de vista** point of view; **tener** *irreg.* **vista** to have a view (16)

vistazo glance

vitamina vitamin (7)

viudo/a widower; widow (4)

vivienda housing; house

vivo/a alive (4); vivid

vocabulario vocabulary

voleibol *m.* volleyball; **jugar (ue) (gu) al voleibol** to play volleyball (11)

volumen *m.* volume; size

voluminoso/a voluminous

voluntario/a *n.* volunteer; *adj.* voluntary

volver (ue) to return (*to a place*) (1); **volver a** + *inf.* to do (*something*) again; **volverse** *refl.* to become; to turn

vomitar to vomit

vos *s. fam.* you (*used instead of* **tú** *in certain countries of Central and South America*)

vosotros/as *pl. fam.* you *Sp.* (P)

votar to vote

voto vote

voz *f.* (*pl.* **voces**) voice; **en voz alta** aloud

vudú *m.* voodoo

vuelo flight (16); **auxiliar** *m., f.* **de vuelo** flight attendant (16); **vuelo nacional** domestic flight

vuelta turn; return; **boleto/billete** *m.* **de ida y vuelta** round-trip ticket (16); **dar** *irreg.* **vuelta** to turn

vulnerabilidad *f.* vulnerability

Y

y and (P); **y cuarto/media** quarter/half past (1); **¿y tú/ usted?** and you? (P)

ya now, already; **ya murió** he (she) already died (4)

yo *sub. pron.* I (P)

yoga *m.* yoga; **hacer** *irreg.* **yoga** to do yoga

yogur *m.* yogurt (7)

Z

zanahoria carrot (7)

Zapatista: EZLN: Ejército Zapatista de Liberación Nacional Zapatista National Liberation Movement

zapato shoe (16); **zapato de correr** running shoe; **zapato de tacón alto** high-heeled shoe (16); **zapato de tenis** tennis shoe

zona zone

zoológico zoo; **parque** *m.* **zoológico** zoo

English-Spanish Vocabulary

A

a **un(a)** (P)
ability to work with one's hands **habilidad** *f.* **manual** (17)
able **capaz** (*pl.* **capaces**); able to direct (others) **capaz de dirigir (a otros)** (13); to be able **poder** *irreg.* (1)
about **sobre** (P)
abroad **extranjero** (16)
abuse *n.* **abuso** (12); *v.* **abusar de** (12); drug abuse **abuso de las drogas** (12)
accountant **contador(a)** (17)
accounting **contabilidad** *f.* (P) (17)
actor **actor** *m.* (17)
actress **actriz** *f.* (17)
adapt **adaptar** (5)
add **agregar** (7)
addicted: to be addicted **ser** *irreg.* **adicto/a** (12); to become addicted **convertirse (ie, i) en adicto/a** (12)
addiction **adicción** (12); to overcome an addiction **salir** *irreg.* **de una adicción** (12)
adjective **adjetivo** (P); demonstrative adjective **adjetivo demostrativo** (P); descriptive adjective **adjetivo descriptivo** (P); possessive adjective **adjetivo de posesión** (P); quantifying adjective **adjetivo de cantidad** (P)
adjust **adaptar** (5)
advance: in advance **con anticipación** (16)
advantage **ventaja** (18)
adventurous **aventurero/a** (5)
aerobic **aeróbico;** to do aerobics **hacer** *irreg.* **ejercicio aeróbico** (1)
afraid: to be afraid **estar** (*irreg.*) **asustado/a** (10); **tener** *irreg.* **miedo** (10)
after *adv.* **después** (2); *conj.* **después (de) que** (17)
afternoon **tarde** *f.* (1); every afternoon **todas las tardes** (1); good afternoon **buenas tardes** (P); in the afternoon **por la tarde** (10)
again **otra vez** (P); again, please **otra vez, por favor** (P)
age **edad** *f.* (16)

agent **agente** *m., f.* (16); travel agent **agente de viajes** (16)
ago: ___ ago **hace** + *time* (3)
agriculture **agricultura** (P), **agronomía** (P)
airplane **avión** *m.* (16)
airport **aeropuerto** (16)
alcohol: hard alcohol **licor** *m.* **fuerte** (9)
alcoholism **alcoholismo** (12)
alive **vivo/a** (4)
alongside **al lado (de)** (15)
also **también** (2)
always **siempre** (1)
ambicious **ambicioso/a** (14)
amenities **comodidades** *f.* (16)
an **un(a)** (P)
and **y** (P); and you? **¿y tú?** (P); and you? **¿y usted?** (P)
angry **enojado/a** (10), **enfadado/a** (10); to be angry **estar** *irreg.* **enojado** (10), **ponerse** *irreg.* **enfadado/a** (10); to get angry **enojarse** (10)
another: to speak another language **hablar otro idioma** *m.* (17)
anthropology **antropología** (P)
any: not any **ninguno/a** (2)
anyone: not anyone **nadie** (2)
anything: not anything **nada** (2)
apartment **apartamento** (2)
apathetic **apático/a** (14)
to be appetizing (*appealing*) **apetecer (zc)** (7)
apple **manzana** (7); apple juice **jugo de manzana** (9)
April **abril** (2)
architecture **arquitectura** (17)
arm **brazo** (8)
aromatherapy **aromaterapia** (11); to use aromatherapy **utilizar (c) la aromaterapia** (11)
arquitect **arquitecto/a** (17)
arrival **llegada** (16)
arrive **llegar (gu)** (3)
art **arte** *m.* (P)
article **artículo** (P); article of clothing **prenda de vestir** (16); definite article **artículo definido** (P); indefinite article **artículo indefinido** (P)
as . . . as **tan... como** (6); as far as I know **que yo sepa** (17); as

many . . . as **tantos/as... como** (6); as much . . . as **tanto/a... como** (6); as soon as **tan pronto como** (17), **en cuanto** (17)
ashamed: to be ashamed **tener** *irreg.* **vergüenza** (10); to feel ashamed **sentirse (ie, i) avergonzado/a** (10)
ask (*a question*) **preguntar** (1); to ask a question **hacer** *irreg.* **una pregunta** (4); to ask for **pedir (i, i)** (1)
asleep: to fall asleep **dormirse (ue, u)** (3)
assistant **ayudante** *m., f.* (17)
astronomer **astrónomo/a** (17)
astronomy **astronomía** (P)
astute **astutuo/a** (14)
at **en** (1); at home **en casa** (1); at night **por la noche** (1); at one o'clock **a la una** (1); at three o'clock **a las tres** (1); at two o'clock **a las dos** (1); at what time? **¿a qué hora?** (1)
athlete **atleta** *m., f.* (17)
attend **asistir (a)** (1)
attendant: flight attendant **aeromozo/a** (16), **auxiliar** *m., f.* **de vuelo** (16), **camarero/a** (16)
attractive **atractivo/a** (P)
August **agosto** (2)
aunt **tía** (4); aunts and uncles **tíos** (4)
autumn **otoño** (2)
average **promedio** (6)
avocado **aguacate** *m.* (7)
away: to take away **quitar** (7)

B

bacon **tocino** (7)
bad **malo/a** (P); to be in a bad mood **estar** *irreg.* **de mal humor** *m.* (10); to get a bad grade **sacar (qu) una mala nota** (10); to have a bad time **pasarlo mal** (10); to make a bad impression **caer** *irreg.* **mal** (7)
baked **al horno** (7); baked custard **flan** *m.* (7)
balanced **equilibrado/a** (13)
bald **calvo/a** (5)
banana **banana** (7)

baseball **béisbol** *m.* (10); to play baseball **jugar (ue) (gu) al béisbol** (10)

basic **básico/a** (7)

basketball **basquetbol** *m.* (10); to play basketball **jugar (ue) (gu) al basquetbol** *m.* (10)

bathe (*someone or something*) **bañar** (5); to bathe oneself **bañarse** (11); to bathe in a jacuzzi **bañarse en el jacuzzi** (11)

bathing suit **traje** *m.* **de baño** (16)

bathroom **baño** (16); room with a private bath **habitación** *f.* **con baño privado** (16)

be **ser** *irreg.* (P); **estar** *irreg.* (3); be that as it may **sea lo que sea** (17); to be able **poder** *irreg.* (1); to be addicted **ser** *irreg.* **adicto/a** (12); to be afraid **estar** *irreg.* **asustado/a** (10), **tener** *irreg.* **miedo** (10); to be angry **estar** *irreg.* **enojado/a** (10), **ponerse** *irreg.* **enfadado/a** (10); to be appetizing/appealing **apetecer (zc)** (7); to be ashamed of **tener** *irreg.* **vergüenza** (10); to be bored **estar** *irreg.* **aburrido** (10); to be careful **tener** *irreg.* **cuidado** (12); to be charming **tener** *irreg.* **gracia** (11); to be embarrassed **tener** *irreg.* **vergüenza** (10); to be happy **ponerse** *irreg.* **contento/a** (10); to be hungry **tener** *irreg.* **hambre** *f.* (7); to be important **importar** (7); to be in a good (bad) mood **estar** *irreg.* **de buen (mal) humor** *m.* (10); to be interesting **interesar** (7); to be in the habit of (*doing something*) **soler (ue)** (*+ inf.*) (1); to be irritated **irritarse** (10); to be located **quedar** (15); to be missing/lacking **faltar** (10); to be nervous **estar** *irreg.* **nervioso/a** (10); to be offended **ofenderse** (10); to be remaining **quedar** (10); to be sad **ponerse** *irreg.* **triste** (10); to be tense **estar** *irreg.* **tenso/a** (10); to be thirsty **tener** *irreg.* **sed** *f.* (9); to be tired **estar** *irreg.* **cansado/a** (10); to be very/extremely pleasing **encantar** (7); to be well-mannered **tener** *irreg.* **buena educación** (8); to be ____ years old **tener** *irreg.* ____ **años** (4)

bean **frijol** *m.* (7); green bean **judía verde** (7)

because **porque** (1)

become addicted **convertirse (ie, i) en adicto/a** (12); to become nauseated **marearse** (16)

bed **cama** (16); bed and breakfast **pensión** *f.* (16); double bed **cama matrimonial** (16); to go to bed **acostarse (ue)** (1); twin bed **cama sencilla** (16)

beef **carne** *f.* **de res** (7)

beer **cerveza** (7)

before *conj.* **antes (de) que** (17)

begin **empezar (ie) (c)** (3)

behave **comportarse** (13), **portarse** (13)

behind **detrás (de)** (15)

believe **creer (y)** (5)

bellhop **botones** *m. s.* (16), **mozo** (16)

beneficial **beneficioso/a** (18)

benefit **beneficio** (18)

beverage **bebida** (9); alcoholic beverage **bebida alcohólica** (9)

bicycle: to ride a bicycle **andar** *irreg.* **en bicicleta** (11)

big **grande** (5)

bill **cuenta** (3); to pay the bill **pagar (ue) la cuenta** (3)

biologist **biólogo/a** (17)

biology **biología** (P)

bite one's fingernails **comerse las uñas** (10)

bitter **amargo/a** (7)

black **negro/a** (5); black hair **pelo negro**

block (*of houses*) **cuadra, manzana** *Sp., Central America* (15)

blond hair **rubio/a** (5)

blouse **blusa** (16)

blue **azul** (5)

blush *v.* **ponerse** *irreg.* **rojo/a** (10), **sonrojarse** (10)

board: room and full board **pensión** *f.* **completa** (16)

boardinghouse **pensión** *f.* (16)

boast (about) **jactarse (de)** (13)

boat **barco** (16)

bold **arriesgado/a** (13)

book **libro** (P)

bored: to be bored **estar** *irreg.* **aburrido/a;** to get bored **aburrirse** (10)

boring **aburrido/a** (P) (14)

boss **jefe/a** (17)

bowl *v.* **jugar (ue) (gu) al boliche** (10); *n.* (earthenware) **cuenco** (8)

boy **chico** (P)

brag (about) **jactarse (de)** (13)

bread: assorted breads and rolls **bollería** (7); white bread **pan** *m.* **blanco** (7); whole-wheat bread **pan** *m.* **integral** (7)

breakfast **desayuno** (7); bed and breakfast **pensión** *f.* (16); room and breakfast (*often with one other meal*) **media pensión** *f.* (16); to have breakfast **desayunar** (1)

bring **traer** *irreg.* (8); could you bring me ____? **¿me podría traer... ?** (8)

brother **hermano** (4); brothers and sisters, siblings **hermanos** (4); half brother **medio hermano** (4)

brother-in-law **cuñado** (4)

brown **castaño/a** (5); brown eyes **ojos castaños** (5); dark brown **marrón** (7)

bus **autobús** *m.* (16)

business **negocios** (17); business administration **administración** *f.* **de empresas** (P)

businessman **hombre** *m.* **de negocios** (17)

businesswoman **mujer** *f.* **de negocios** (18)

but **pero** (1)

butter **mantequilla** (7); peanut butter **mantequilla de cacahuete** (7)

C

cabin **cabina** (16)

caffeine **cafeína** (9)

calcium **calcio** (7)

calculus **cálculo** (P)

call **llamar** (3); to call on the phone **llamar por teléfono** (3)

calm **calmado/a** (13)

camping: to go camping **acampar** (11), **hacer** *irreg.* **cámping** (11)

can *v.*: one/you (*impersonal*) can't ____ without ____ **no se puede ____ sin ____** (8)

candy **dulce** *m.* (7)

carbohydrate **carbohidrato** (7)

card (*playing*) **naipe** *m.* (11); to play cards **jugar (ue) (gu) a los naipes** (11)

careful: to be careful **tener** *irreg.* **cuidado** (12)

carrot **zanahoria** (7)

carry **llevar** (5)

cause laughter **causar risa** (11)

century **siglo**; last century **siglo pasado** (6)

cereal **cereal** *m.* (7)

English-Spanish Vocabulary **V33**

certain **cierto/a** (5); it's (not) certain that **(no) es cierto que** (18)

charismatic **carismático/a** (17)

charming **encantador(a)** (13); to be charming **tener** *irreg.* **gracia** (11)

chat **charlar** (2); to participate in a chat room **chatear** (2)

check *n.* (*restaurant*) **cuenta** (8); *v.* to check luggage **facturar el equipaje** (16)

cheek **mejilla** (5)

cheese **queso** (7)

chef **cocinero/a** (8)

chemist **químico/a** (17)

chemistry **química** (P)

chicken **pollo** (7); (half a) roasted chicken **(medio) pollo asado** (7)

children **hijos** (4)

chin **mentón** *m.* (5)

chips: potato chips **papas fritas** *Lat. Am.* (7), **patatas fritas** *Sp.* (7)

chop: pork chop **chuleta de cerdo** (7)

church **iglesia**; to go to church **ir** *irreg.* **a la iglesia** (2)

ciao **chau** (P)

class **clase** *f.* (P); economy class **clase turística** (16); first class **primera clase** (16); in class **en la clase** (P)

classmate **compañero/a de clase** (P)

clean (the apartment) **limpiar (el apartamento)** (2)

clear *v.*: to clear the table **levantar la mesa** (8); *adj.* it's clear (*obvious*) **está claro** (5); (*weather*) **está despejado** (2)

clever **listo/a** (17)

climb: to mountain climb **escalar montañas** (11)

close **cerca (de)** (15)

closet **armario** (16)

clothes: to wash clothes **lavar la ropa** (2)

clothing: article of clothing **prenda de vestir** (16)

coffee **café** *m.* (2); coffee with milk **café con leche** (7); decaffeinated coffee **café descafeinado** (9)

cognate **cognado** (P)

cold **frío** (9); it's cold (*weather*) **hace frío** (2); very cold **bien frío** (9)

color **color** *m.* (5); what color is/are _____? **¿de qué color es/son _____?** (5)

come **venir** *irreg.* (1); what does _____ come with? **¿qué trae _____?** (8)

comic(al) **cómico/a** (P)

communications **comunicaciones** *f.* (P)

compassionate **compasivo/a** (17)

complain (about) **quejarse (de)** (10)

compulsive **compulsivo/a** (17)

computer **computadora** *Lat. Am.* (18), **ordenador** *m.* (18); computer science **computación** *f.* (P), **informática** (P); to use a computer **usar una computadora** (17)

confirm **confirmar** (16)

conformist **conformista** (14)

consequence **consecuencia** (12)

conservative **conservador(a)** (13)

consist of **consistir en** (12)

consult **consultar (con)** (17)

consultant **asesor(a)** (17)

continue: continue _____ **siga (Ud.) por _____** (15); continue straight **siga derecho/recto** (15)

conveniences **comodidades** *f. pl.* (16)

cook *n.* **cocinero/a** (8)

cooked **cocinado/a** (7)

cookie **galleta** (7)

cool: it's cool (*weather*) **hace fresco** (2)

corn **maíz** *m.* (7); corn oil **aceite** *m.* **de maíz** (7)

corner **esquina** (15)

cosmopolitan **cosmopolita** (P)

cotton **algodón** *m.* (16)

could: could you bring me . . . ? **¿me podría traer... ?** (8); could you tell me _____? **¿me podría decir _____?** (15)

country **país** (P)

couple **pareja** (4); married couple **esposos** (4)

courageous **valiente** (14)

course (*meal*) **plato** (7); first/second/third course **primer/segundo/tercer plato** (7)

cousin **primo/a** (4)

coward, cowardly **cobarde** (14)

cream: ice cream **helado** (7)

creative **creativo/a** (13)

criminal justice **justicia criminal** (P)

cross the street **cruce la calle** (15)

cruise ship **crucero** (16)

cry *v.* **llorar** (10)

cup **taza** (8)

curious **curioso/a** (14)

curly hair **pelo rizado/a** (5)

custard: baked custard **flan** *m.* (7)

custom **costumbre** *f.* (8)

customer **cliente/a** (8)

cut *v.* **cortar** (8)

D

daily: daily menu **menú** *m.* **del día** (7); daily special **plato del día** (8)

dairy product **producto lácteo** (7)

dance **bailar** (2)

danger **peligro** (12)

dangerous **peligroso/a** (12)

dare (to) (*do something*) **atreverse (a)** + *inf.* (13)

daring **arriesgado/a** (13)

dark: dark brown **marrón** (7); dark-haired **moreno/a** (5); dark-skinned **moreno/a** (5)

day **día** *m.* (1); good morning, good day **buenos días** (P); every day **todos los días** (1); what day is it today? **¿qué día es hoy?** (1)

dead **muerto/a** (4)

decade **década** (6)

decaffeinated **descafeinado** (9); decaffeinated coffee **café** *m.* **descafeinado** (9)

December **diciembre** (2)

decided; decisive **decidido/a** (13)

dedicate oneself to **dedicarse (qu) a** (17)

definite article **artículo definido** (P)

delay *n.* **demora** (16)

delight *v.* **encantar** (7)

delivery: home delivery **servicio a domicilio** (8)

depressed **deprimido/a** (10); to feel depressed **sentirse (ie, i) deprimido/a** (10)

describe **describir** (5)

descriptive adjective **adjetivo descriptivo** (P)

desert **desierto** (11)

design **diseño** (16)

designer **diseñador(a)** (17)

desk: front desk **recepción** *f.* (16)

dessert **postre** *m.* (7)

determined **determinado/a** (14)

died: he/she already died **ya murió** (4)

dinner **cena** (3); to have dinner **cenar** (1); to prepare dinner **preparar la cena** (3)

direct: to be able to direct (others) **capaz de dirigir (a otros)** (13)

director **director(a)** (17)

disadvantage **desventaja** (18)

disagree: to disagree with (*food*) **caer** *irreg.* **mal** (7) discotheque **discoteca** (2)

discreet **discreto/a** (13)

dish **plato** (8); main dish **plato principal** (8); to wash the dishes **lavar los platos** (8)

dive (*scuba*) *v.* **bucear** (11)

divorced: he/she is divorced **está divorciado/a** (4)

do **hacer** *irreg.* (1); to do aerobics **hacer ejercicio aeróbico** (1); to do nothing **no hacer nada** (2); do yoga **hacer yoga** (11); do you like ___? **¿te gusta(n) ___?** (P)

docile **dócil** (14)

doctor **médico/a** (17)

dog **perro** (4)

doggie bag **bolsita para llevar** (8)

double bed **cama matrimonial** (16)

doubt *n.* **duda** (18); *v.* **dudar** (18); it is without a doubt **es indudable** (5)

doubtful: it's doubtful that ___ **es dudoso que ___** (18)

dough: *type of fried dough* **churro** (7)

draw **dibujar** (11)

dreamer **soñador(a)** (14)

dress *n.* **vestido** (16); *v.* **vestirse (i, i)** (1); to get dressed **vestirse (i, i)** (1)

drink *n.* soft drink **refresco** (7); *v.* **tomar** (2), **beber** (9); to drink a cup of coffee **tomar un café** (2); and to drink? **¿y para tomar?** (7)

drive **conducir** *irreg. Sp.* (1), **manejar** (1)

during **por** (1)

E

each **cada** (2); we'll be seeing each other **nos vemos** (P)

eagerness to get things done **afán** *m.* **de realización** (13)

ear **oreja** (5)

early **temprano** (1); very early **muy temprano** (1)

earthenware bowl **cuenco** (8)

east **este** *m.* (15)

eat **comer** (1); to eat breakfast **desayunar** (1)

eating habit **hábito de comer** (7)

eccentric **excéntrico/a** (14)

economics **economía** (P)

economy class **clase** *f.* **turística** (16)

education: physical education **educación** *f.* **física** (P)

egg **huevo** (7); fried egg **huevo frito** (7); scrambled egg **huevo revuelto** (7)

egotistical **egoísta** (13)

eight **ocho** (P)

eight hundred **ochocientos** (6)

eighteen **dieciocho** (P)

eighty **ochenta** (6)

either: not either **tampoco** (2)

elbow **codo** (8)

eleven **once** (P)

(e-mail) message **mensaje** *m.* (1)

embarrassed: to be embarrassed **tener** *irreg.* **vergüenza** (10); to feel embarrassed **sentirse (ie, i) avergonzado/a** (10)

embarrassment **vergüenza** (10)

engineer **ingeniero/a** (17)

engineering **ingeniería** (P)

English (*language*) **inglés** (P)

enterprising **emprendedor(a)** (17)

essential: it's essential **es imprescindible** (8)

evening: good evening **buenas noches** (P); in the evening **por la noche** (1)

every: every afternoon **todas las tardes** (1); every morning **todas las mañanas** (1); every night **todas las noches** (1)

everyday life **la vida de todos los días** (1)

everything: is everything OK? **¿está todo bien?** (8)

evident: it is evident **es evidente** (5)

evil **malévolo/a** (14)

excuse: excuse me, how do you get to . . . ? **¿perdón, ¿cómo se llega a... ?** (15)

exercise *v.* **hacer** *irreg.* **ejercicio** (1); to do aerobics **hacer** *irreg.* **ejercicio aeróbico** (1)

exit **salida** (16)

expensive **caro/a** (16)

experience *v.* **sufrir** (12)

express oneself clearly **expresarse claramente** (17)

expression **expresión** *f.* (P)

extroverted **extrovertido/a** (5)

eye **ojo** (5); blue/brown/green eyes **ojos azules/castaños/verdes** (5)

F

fabric **tela** (16)

face **cara** (5)

fact: it's a known fact **es cosa sabida** (5)

fair **justo/a** (14)

fall *n.* (*season*) **otoño** (2); *v.* to fall asleep **dormirse (ue, u)** (3)

family **familia** (4); extended family **familia extendida** (4); nuclear family **familia nuclear** (4)

famous **famoso/a** (P)

far (from) **lejos (de)** (15); as far as I know **que yo sepa** (17)

farmer **granjero/a** (17)

fashion **moda** (17)

fat *adj.* **gordo/a** (5); *n.* **grasa** (7)

father **padre** *m.* (4)

father-in-law **suegro** (4)

favorite **favorito/a** (P)

fear **miedo** (10)

February **febrero** (2)

feel **sentirse (ie, i)** (10); how do you feel? **¿cómo te sientes?** (10); to feel ashamed (depressed, embarrassed, happy, proud, relaxed) **sentirse (ie, i) avergonzado/a (deprimido/a, avergonzado/a, alegre, orgulloso/a, relajado/a)** (10); to feel like (*doing something*) **tener** *irreg.* **ganas de** (+ *inf.*) (10); to feel well **para sentirse (ie, i) bien** (10)

few **pocos/as** (P)

fiber **fibra** (7)

field **campo** (17)

fifteen **quince** (P)

fifty **cincuenta** (6)

fighter **luchador(a)** (14)

film **cine** *m.* (17)

fingernails **uñas** (10); to bite one's nails **comerse las uñas** (10)

first **primero/a (primer)** (7); first class **primera clase** *f.* (16); first course **primer plato** (7)

fish *n.* **pescado** (*food*) (7); *v.* **pescar (qu)** (11)

five **cinco** (P)

five hundred **quinientos** (6)

flavor **sabor** *m.* (7)

flight **vuelo** (16); flight attendant **aeromozo/a** (16), **auxiliar** *m., f.* **de vuelo** (16), **camarero/a** (16)

follow ___ **siga (Ud.) por** ___ (15)

food **alimento** (7); food to go **comida para llevar** (8)

foolish **tonto/a** (P)

football **fútbol** *m.* **americano** (2); to play football **jugar (ue) (gu) al fútbol americano** (2)

for **para** (1); **por** (1)

foreign language **lengua extranjera** (P)

forest **bosque** *m.* (11)

fork **tenedor** *m.* (8)

forty **cuarenta** (6)

four **cuatro** (P); four-star hotel **hotel** *m.* **de cuatro estrellas** (16)

four hundred **cuatrocientos** (6)

fourteen **catorce** (P)

freckle **peca** (5)

French (*language*) **francés** *m.* (P)

French fries **papas fritas** *Lat. Am.* (7); **patatas fritas** *Sp.* (7)

frequently **con frecuencia** (1), **frequentemente** (1)

fresh **fresco/a** (7)

Friday **viernes** *m.* (1)

fried egg **huevo frito** (7)

friend **amigo/a** (P); to go out with friends **salir** *irreg.* **con los amigos** (10)

fries: French fries **papas fritas** *Lat. Am.* (7); **patatas fritas** *Sp.* (7)

frighten **asustar** (10)

frivolous **frívolo/a** (14)

from **de** (P); from here to there **de aquí para allá** (15); I'm from _____ **soy de** _____ (P); where are you from? **¿de dónde eres?** (P), **¿de dónde es usted?** (P)

front: front desk **recepción** *f.* (16); in front (of) **enfrente (de)** (15)

fruit **fruta** (7)

full (*no vacancy*) **completo/a** (16)

fun: to make fun (of) **burlarse (de)** (13); fun-loving **divertido/a** (13)

funny **chistoso/a** (11); **cómico/a** (P); **gracioso/a** (11); to be funny **tener** *irreg.* **gracia** (11); to strike someone as funny **hacerle** *irreg.* **gracia a uno** (11)

future **futuro** (18)

G

garden **trabajar en el jardín** (11)

generally **generalmente** (1)

geography **geografía** (P)

German (*language*) **alemán** *m.* (P)

get: to get a good (bad) grade **sacar (qu) una buena (mala) nota** (10); to get along well (poorly) **llevarse bien (mal)** (5); to get angry **enojarse** (10); to get bored **aburrirse** (10); to get dressed **vestirse (i, i)** (1); to get happy **alegrarse** (10), **ponerse** *irreg.* **contento/a** (10); to get mad **ponerse** *irreg.* **enfadado/a** (10); to get nauseated **marearse** (16); to get off / out of (*a bus, car, plane, etc.*) **bajar de** (16); to get on/in (*a bus, car, plane, etc.*) **subir a** (16);

to get sad **ponerse** *irreg.* **triste** (10); to get sick **marearse** (16); to get tired **cansarse** (10); to get up **levantarse** (1)

girl **chica** (P)

give **dar** *irreg.* (3); to give opinions **para dar opiniones** (5)

glass: water glass **vaso** (8); wine glass **copa** (8)

go **ir** *irreg.* (1); food to go **comida para llevar** (8); go straight **siga derecho/recto** (16); to go camping **acampar** (11), **hacer** *irreg.* **cámping** (11); to go out (with friends) **salir** *irreg.* **(con los amigos)** (1); to go shopping **ir de compras** (1); to go to bed **acostarse (ue)** (1); to go to church **ir a la iglesia** (2); to go to the movies **ir al cine** (2); to go to the theater **ir al teatro** (2)

golf: to play golf **jugar (ue) (gu) al golf** (11)

good **bueno/a (buen)** (P); good afternoon **buenas tardes** (P); good at math **hábil para las matemáticas** (17); good-bye **adiós** (P); good evening **buenas noches** (P); good manners **buenos modales** (8); good morning **buenos días** (P); it's a good idea **es buena idea** (8); to be in a good mood **estar** *irreg.* **de buen humor** (10); to get a good grade **sacar (qu) una buena nota** (10); to make a good impression **caer** *irreg.* **bien** (7); to say good-bye **despedir (i, i) (de)** (5)

good-bye **adiós** (P)

good-looking **guapo/a** (5)

gossipy **chismoso/a** (13)

government **gobierno** (17)

grade **nota** (10); to get a good (bad) grade **sacar (qu) una buena (mala) nota** (10)

grains **cereales** *m.* (7)

grandchildren **nietos** (4)

granddaughter **nieta** (4)

grandfather **abuelo** (4)

grandmother **abuela** (4)

grandparents **abuelos** (4)

grandson **nieto** (4)

grape **uva** (7)

grapefruit **toronja** (7)

gray hair **canoso/a** (5)

green (*color*) **verde** (5); green bean **judía verde** (7); green eyes **ojos verdes** (5)

greet **saludar** (5)

greetings **saludos** (P)

gregarious **gregario/a** (5)

guest **huésped(a)** (16)

guitar: to play the guitar **tocar (qu) la guitarra** (1)

H

habit **costumbre** *f.* (8); eating habit **hábito de comer** (7); to be in the habit of (*doing something*) **soler (ue)** (+ *inf.*) (1)

hair **pelo** (5); straight/curly hair **pelo lacio/rizado** (5); gray/dark/ black/blond hair **pelo canoso/ moreno/ negro/rubio** (5)

half: half a roasted chicken **medio pollo asado** (7); half brother / half sister **medio/a hermano/a** (4); half past **y media** (1)

ham **jamón** *m.* (7)

hamburger **hamburguesa** (7)

hand **mano** *f.* (8); ability to work with one's hands **habilidad** *f.* **manual** (17)

happy **alegre** (10), **contento/a** (10), **feliz** (*pl.* **felices**) (5); to be happy **ponerse** *irreg.* **contento/a** (10); to feel happy **sentirse (ie, i) alegre** (10); to get happy **alegrarse** (10), **ponerse** *irreg.* **contento/a** (10)

hard alcohol **licor** *m.* **fuerte** (9)

hard-working **trabajador(a)** (13)

harmful **dañino/a** (12)

hat **sombrero** (16)

have **tener** *irreg.* (1); I have a question, please **tengo una pregunta, por favor** (P); to have a bad time **pasarlo mal** (10); to have a headache **tener dolor de cabeza** (10); to have a party **dar** *irreg.* **una fiesta** (11); to have a picnic **tener un picnic** (11); to have a view **tener vista** (16); to have a way with people **tener don de gentes** (17); to have breakfast **desayunar** (1); to have dinner **cenar** (1); to have just (*done something*) **acabar de** (+ *inf.*) (10); to have lunch **almorzar (ue) (c)** (1); to have the opinion **opinar** (5); to have to (*do something*) **tener que** (+ *inf.*) (1)

he **él** (P)

headache **dolor** *m.* **de cabeza** (10); to have a headache **tener** *irreg.* **dolor de cabeza** (10) heel **tacón** *m.* (16); high heel **tacón alto** (16)

height **estatura** (5)

her *poss.* **su(s)** (P)

herbal tea **té** *m.* **de hierbas** (9)

here **aquí** (P); from here to there **de aquí para allá** (15)

his *poss.* **su(s)** (P)

history **historia** (P)

hitchhike **hacer** *irreg.* **autostop** (16)

home: at home **en casa** (2); home delivery **servicio a domicilio** (8); to stay at home **quedarse en casa** (2)

homework **tarea** (1)

honest **honesto/a** (17)

honorable **íntegro/a** (17)

hot **caliente** (9); it's (very) hot (*weather*) **hace (mucho) calor** (2); very hot **bien caliente** (9)

hotel **hotel** *m.* (16); four-star hotel **hotel de cuatro estrellas** (16); luxury hotel **hotel de lujo** (16)

house **casa** (2); boardinghouse **pensión** *f.* (16)

how **¿cómo?** (4); how are you? **¿qué tal?** (P); how do you feel? **¿cómo te sientes?** (10); how do you get to ___? **¿cómo se llega a ___?** (15); how do you say ___ in Spanish? **¿cómo se dice ___ en español?** (P); how many? **¿cuántos/as?** (P); how often? **¿con qué frecuencia?** (1); how's it going? **¿qué tal?** (P)

hug *v.* **abrazar (c)** (5)

humanities **humanidades** *f.* (P)

humble **humilde** (13)

hungry: to be hungry **tener** *irreg.* **hambre** *f.* (7)

husband **esposo** (4), **marido** (4)

I

I **yo** (P)

ice **hielo** (9); ice cream **helado** (7); iced tea **té** *m.* **helado** (9); with ice **con hielo** (9); without ice **sin hielo** (9)

iced tea **té** *m.* **helado** (9)

idea: it's a good idea **es buena idea** (8)

important: to be important **importar** (7)

impose **imponer** (*like* **poner**) (5)

impression: to make a good impression **caer** *irreg.* **bien** (7)

in **en** (1); in class **en la clase** *f.* (P); in front (of) **enfrente (de)** (15);

in the morning/afternoon/evening **por la mañana/tarde/noche** (1)

indecisive **indeciso/a** (13)

indefinite article **artículo indefinido** (P)

indifferent **indiferente** (14)

individualistic **individualista** (14)

inexpensive **barato/a** (16)

injury **herida** (12), **lesión** *f.* (12); **daño físico** (12)

in-laws **suegros** (4)

inline skate *v.* **patinar en línea** (11); *n. pl.* **patines en línea** (11)

insecure **inseguro/a** (13)

insensitive **insensible** (13)

insincere **insincero/a** (P)

intelligent **inteligente** (P)

interesting **interesante** (P); to be interesting (*to someone*) **interesarle (a alguien)** (7)

intersection **bocacalle** *f.* (15)

invite (to treat, pay) **invitar** (8)

irritated: to be (get) irritated **irritarse** (10)

Italian (*language*) **italiano** (P)

J

jacket **chaqueta** (16)

jacuzzi **jacuzzi** *m.* (11); to bathe in a jacuzzi **bañarse en el jacuzzi** (11)

jam **mermelada** (7)

January **enero** (2)

Japanese (*language*) **japonés** *m.* (P)

jealous **celoso/a** (13)

jeans **bluejeans** *m. pl.* (16)

job **puesto** (17)

joke **chiste** *m.* (10); to tell a joke **contar (ue) un chiste** (10)

journalism **periodismo** (P)

journalist **periodista** *m., f.* (17)

juice **jugo** (7); apple juice **jugo de manzana** (9); orange juice **jugo de naranja** (7); tomato juice **jugo de tomate** (9)

July **julio** (2)

jump *v.* **saltar** (11); to jump rope **saltar a la cuerda** (11)

June **junio** (2)

just: to have just (*done something*) **acabar de** (+ *inf.*) (10)

K

keep quiet **permanecer (zc) callado/a** (10)

ketchup **salsa de tomate** (7)

kiss *v.* **besar** (5)

knife **cuchillo** (8)

know (*facts, information*) **saber** *irreg.* (3); as far as I know **que yo sepa** (17); it is a known fact **es cosa sabida** (5); to know (*someone*) **conocer (zc)**

L

laboratory **laboratorio** (1)

lacking: to be lacking **faltar** (10)

lake **lago** (11)

language **idioma** *m.* (P); foreign language **lengua extranjera** (P); to speak another language **hablar otro idioma** *m.* (17)

last: last century **siglo pasado** (6); last name **apellido** (4); last night **anoche** (3); last time **última vez** (3); last week **semana pasada** (3); last weekend **fin** *m.* **de semana pasado** (3)

late **tarde** (1); until (very) late **hasta (muy) tarde** (2); very late **muy tarde**

laugh *n.* **risa** (11); *v.* **reírse (i, i)** (10); to laugh (at) **burlarse (de)** (13); to laugh loudly **reírse (i, i) a carcajadas** (11); to make laugh **causar risa** (11), **hacer** *irreg.* **reír** (11)

laughter **risa** (11); to cause laughter **causar risa** (11)

law **derecho** (17)

lawyer **abogado/a** (17)

leadership: talent for leadership **don** *m.* **de mando** (13)

leather **cuero** (16)

leave **salir** *irreg.* (1); to leave a tip **dejar propina** (8); leave-takings **despedidas** (P)

left *adj.* **izquierdo/a** (8); turn left **doble a la izquierda** (15)

leisure time **ocio** (18)

lemon **limón** *m.* (7)

lentils **lentejas** (7)

less **menos** (1)

letters **letras** (P)

lettuce **lechuga** (7)

life: everyday life **la vida de todos los días** (1)

lift weights **levantar pesas** (10)

like: do you like ___? **¿te gusta(n) ___?** (P); I don't like it (them) at all **no me gusta(n) para nada** (P); to look like **parecerse (zc)** (5); to feel like (*doing something*) **tener** *irreg.* **ganas de** (+ *inf.*) (10); what are you like? **¿cómo eres?** (13)

likewise **igualmente** (P)

line: to stand in line **hacer** *irreg.* **cola** (16)

linear: to think in a linear (direct) manner **pensar (ie) de una manera directa** (17)

listen (to) **escuchar** (1)

literature **literatura** (P)

little **poco/a** (P); little while **un rato** (3)

located: to be located **quedar** (15)

lodge *v.* **alojarse** (16)

lodging **alojamiento** (16)

look: to look at **mirar** (1); to look for **buscar (qu)** (3); to look (good) **verse** *irreg.* **(bien)** (16); to look like **parecerse (zc)** (5); what does he/she look like? **¿cómo es?** (5)

lot: a lot **mucho** (P)

loudly: to laugh loudly **reírse (ie, i) a carcajadas** (11)

loyal **leal** (13)

luggage **equipaje** *m.* (16); to check luggage **facturar el equipaje** (16)

lunch *n.* **almuerzo** (7); to have lunch **almorzar (ue) (c)** (1)

luxury hotel **hotel** *m.* **de lujo** (16)

M

machine: vending machine **máquina vendedora** (7)

main dish **plato principal** (8)

major **carrera** (P), **especialización** (P); what is your major? **¿qué carrera haces?** (P)

make **hacer** *irreg.* to make a good (bad) impression **caer** *irreg.* **bien (mal)** (7); to make a stop (*on a flight*) **hacer escala** (16); to make fun (of) **burlarse (de)** (13); to make laugh **causar risa** (11), **hacer reír** (11); to make noise **hacer ruido** (10)

manager **gerente** *m., f.* (17)

manner: good manners **buenos modales** (8); to think in a direct (linear) manner **pensar (ie) de una manera directa** (17)

manual: ability to work with one's hands **habilidad** *f.* **manual** (17)

many **muchos/as** (P); how many? **¿cuántos/as?** (P)

March **marzo** (2)

marketing **mercadeo** (P)

marmalade **mermelada** (7)

married: he/she is married **está casado/a** (4); married couple **esposos** (4)

material **material** *m.* (16)

math(ematics) **matemáticas** (P); good at math **hábil para las matemáticas** (17)

matter *v.* **importar** (7); what's the matter (with you)? **¿qué te pasa?** (10)

May **mayo** (2)

may: be that as it may **sea lo que sea** (17)

mayonnaise **mayonesa** (7)

meal **comida** (7)

meat **carne** *f.* (7)

medicine **medicina** (17)

meditate **meditar** (11)

medium: of medium height **de estatura mediana** (5)

meet: pleased to meet you **encantado/a** (P), **mucho gusto** (P)

melancholy **melancólico/a** (14)

menu **menú** *m.* (7); daily menu **menú del día** (7)

message: (e-mail) message **mensaje** *m.* (1)

messy **caótico/a** (13)

methodical **metódico/a** (13)

milk **leche** *f.* (7)

mind: state of mind **estado de ánimo** (10)

missing: to be missing (*lacking*) **faltar** (10)

Monday **lunes** *m.* (1)

month **mes** *m.* (2)

mood: to be in a good (bad) mood **estar** *irreg.* **de buen (mal) humor** *m.* (10)

more **más** (1)

morning: **mañana** (1); every morning **todas las mañanas** (1); good morning **buenos días** (P); in the morning **por la mañana** (1)

mother **madre** *f.* (4); single mother **madre soltera** (4)

mother-in-law **suegra** (4)

mountain **montaña** (11); to mountain climb **escalar montañas** (11)

mouth **boca** (8)

movie **cine** *m.* (2); to go to the movies **ir** *irreg.* **al cine** (2)

much **mucho/a** (P); very much **mucho** (P)

museum **museo** (11)

music **música** (P)

musician **músico** *m., f.* (17)

mustard **mostaza** (7)

my *poss.* **mi(s)** (P)

N

nails: to bite one's nails **comerse la uñas** (10)

naive **ingenuo/a** (13)

name **nombre** *m.* (P); his/her name is ____ **se llama** ____(P), **su nombre es** ____ (P); last name **apellido** (4); my name is ____ **me llamo** (P), **mi nombre es** ____(P); what's your name? **¿cómo te llamas?** (P), **¿como se llama usted?** (P), **¿cuál es tu/su nombre?** (P)

napkin **servilleta** (8)

natural fabric **tela de fibras naturales** (16)

natural sciences **ciencias naturales** (P)

nauseated: to get nauseated **marearse** (16)

near **cerca (de)** (15)

necessary **necesario/a** (8); it's necessary **es necesario** (8), **es preciso** (8); **hay que** (8)

need *v.* **necesitar** (1)

negation: word of negation **palabra de negación** (2)

neither **tampoco** (2)

nephew **sobrino** (4)

nervous **nervioso/a** (10); to be nervous **estar** *irreg.* **nervioso/a** (10)

net **red** *f.* (1)

never **jamás** (2), **nunca** (2)

new **nuevo/a** (4)

newspaper **periódico** (1)

next **luego** (2); next to **al lado (de)** (15)

niece **sobrina** (4)

night: at night **por la noche** (1); every night **todas las noches** (1); last night **anoche** (3)

nine **nueve** (P)

nine hundred **novecientos** (6)

nineteen **diecinueve** (P)

ninety **noventa** (6)

no **no** (P); no one **nadie** (2)

noise **ruido** (10); to make noise **hacer** *irreg.* **ruido** (10)

none, not any **ninguno/a** (2)

normally **normalmente** (1)

north **norte** *m.* (15)

nose **nariz** *f.* (5)

nothing **nada** (2)

November **noviembre** (2)
number **cifra** (6), **número** (P)
nurse **enfermero/a** (17)
nursing **enfermería** (P)
nut **nuez** *f.* (*pl.* **nueces**) (7)

O

obligation **obligación** *f.* (8); impersonal obligation **obligación impersonal** (8)
obvious: it is obvious **es obvio** (5)
ocean **océano** (11)
o'clock: at one o'clock **a la una** (10); at two (three) o'clock **a las dos (tres)** (1); it's one o'clock **es la una** (1); it's two (three) o'clock **son las dos (tres)** (1)
October **octubre** (2)
of **de** (1); of medium height **de estatura mediana** (5)
off: to get off (*a bus, car, plane, etc.*) **bajar de** (16); to take off (*clothing*) **quitarse** (16)
offended: to be (get) offended **ofenderse** (10)
often **con frecuencia** (1); how often? **¿con qué frecuencia?** (1)
oil **aceite** *m.* (7); corn oil **aceite de maíz** (7); olive oil **aceite de oliva** (7)
OK: is everything OK? **¿está todo bien?** (8)
old **viejo/a** (5); to be ___ years old **tener** *irreg.* ___ **años** (4)
older **mayor** (4)
oldest **el/la mayor** (4)
olive oil **aceite** *m.* **de oliva** (7)
omelette *Sp.* **tortilla** (7)
on: to get on (*a bus, car, plane, etc.*) **subir a** (16); to put on (*clothing*) **ponerse** *irreg.* (16)
once **una vez** (3)
one **uno** (P); at one o'clock **a la una** (1); it's one o'clock **es la una** (1)
one hundred **cien(to)** (6)
one thousand **mil** (6)
one-way ticket *Lat. Am.* **boleto de ida** (16), *Sp.* **billete** *m.* **de ida** (16)
opera: soap opera **telenovela** (3)
opinion **opinión** *f.* (5); to give opinions **para dar opiniones** (5); to have the opinion **opinar** (5)
optimistic **optimista** (P)
or **o** (P)
orange **naranja** (7); orange juice **jugo de naranja** (7)

order (*in a restaurant*) **ordenar** (8), **pedir (i, i)** (8)
organized **organizado/a** (17)
other **otro** (P)
ought to (*do something*) **deber** (+ *inf.*) (1)
overcoat **abrigo** (16)
overcome an addiction **salir** *irreg.* **de una adicción** (12)

P

pack one's suitcase **hacer** *irreg.* **la maleta** (16)
paint *v.* **pintar** (10)
painter **pintor(a)** (17)
pancake **panqueque** *m.* (7)
pants **pantalones** *m.* (16)
pardon me? **¿cómo?** (P)
parents **padres** (4)
park **parque** *m.* (11)
participate: to chat, participate in a chat room **chatear** (2)
partner **pareja** (4)
party **fiesta** (2); to throw/have a party **dar** *irreg.* **una fiesta** (11)
passage (*ticket*) **pasaje** *m.* (16)
passenger **pasajero/a** (16)
passionate **apasionado/a** (14)
past: half past **y media** (1); quarter past **y cuarto** (1)
pasta **pasta alimenticia** (7)
pastry **pastel** *m.* (7)
patient **paciente** (17)
pay **pagar (gu)** (3); to pay the bill **pagar la cuenta** (3)
peanut butter **mantequilla de cacahuete** (7)
peas **guisantes** *m.* (7)
people **gente** *f.* (6); to have a way with people **tener** *irreg.* **don de gentes** (17)
pepper **pimienta** *m.* (7)
pepper shaker **pimentero** (8)
permit **permitir** (9)
personality **personalidad** *f.* (5); personality trait **característica de la personalidad** (5)
pesimistic **pesimista** (P)
pharmacist **farmacéutico/a** (17)
pharmacy **farmacia** (17)
philosophy **filosofía** (P)
phone: to call on the phone **llamar por teléfono** (3)
photographer **fotógrafo/a** (17)
physical **físico/a;** physical characteristic **característica física** (5); physical education **educación** *f.* **física** (P); physical injury **daño**

físico (12); physical therapist **terapeuta** *m., f.* **físico/a** (17); physical therapy **terapia física** (17)
physically strong **físicamente fuerte** (17)
physicist **físico/a** (17)
physics **física** (P)
picnic: to have a picnic **tener** *irreg.* **un picnic** (11)
picture: to take pictures **sacar (qu) fotos** *f.* (16)
pie **tarta** (7)
pink **rosado/a** (7)
pitcher **jarra** (8)
place **lugar** *m.* (11); *v.* **poner** *irreg.* (7)
plate **plato** (8)
play (*sports*) **jugar (ue) (gu)** (1), **practicar (qu);** (*an instrument*) **tocar (qu)** (1); to play basketball/baseball/golf/soccer/volleyball **jugar al basquetbol** (10) / **béisbol** (10) / **golf** (11) / **fútbol** (2) / **voleibol** (11); to play cards **jugar a los naipes** (11); to play football **jugar al fútbol americano** (2); to play the guitar **tocar (qu) la guitarra** (1); to play video games **jugar a los videojuegos** (3)
player: ___ player **jugador(a) de...** (17)
pleasant **simpático/a** (4)
please *v.* **agradar** (7); *adv.* **por favor** (P); again, please **otra vez, por favor** (P); I have a question, please **tengo una pregunta, por favor** (P); repeat, please **repita, por favor** (P)
pleased to meet you **encantado/a** (P), **mucho gusto** (P)
pleasing: to be very/extremely pleasing **encantar** (7)
polite **educado/a** (8)
political science **ciencias políticas** *pl.* (P)
politician **político/a** (17)
politics **política** (17)
polyester **poliéster** *m.* (16)
poorly **mal** (5); to get along poorly **llevarse mal** (5)
popcorn **palomitas** (7)
pork chop **chuleta de cerdo** (7)
porter **maletero/a** (16)
Portuguese (*language*) **portugués** *m.* (P)
position (*job*) **puesto** (17)
possessive adjective **adjetivo de posesión** (P)

possibility **posibilidad** *f.* (18)

possible: it's (not) possible that ____ **(no) es posible que** ____ (18)

potato **papa** *Lat. Am.* (7), **patata** (7) *Sp.;* French fries (*potatoes*) **papas fritas** *Lat. Am.* (7), **patatas fritas** *Sp.* (7); mashed potatoes **puré** *m.* **de papas** (7); potato chips **papas fritas** *Lat. Am.* (7), **patatas fritas** *Sp.* (7)

poultry **aves** *f. pl.* (7)

practical **práctico/a** (14)

practice **practicar (qu)** (2); to practice (*play*) (*a sport*) **practicar (qu) un deporte** (2)

prefer **preferir (ie, i)** (1)

preferences **preferencias** (P)

prepare **preparar;** to prepare dinner **preparar la cena** (3)

president **presidente/a** (17)

pretty **bonito/a** (P)

private: room with a private bath **habitación** *f.* **con baño privado** (16)

probability **probabilidad** *f.* (18)

probable: it's (not) probable that ____ **(no) es probable que** ____ (18)

producer **productor(a)** (17)

professor **profesor(a)** (P)

profession **profesión** *f.* (17)

professional **profesional** *m., f.* (17)

programmer **programador(a)** (17)

prohibit **prohibir (prohíbo)** (9)

pronoun **pronombre** *m.* (P); subject pronoun **pronombre de sujeto** (P)

proteins **proteínas** (7)

proud **orgulloso/a** (10); to feel proud **sentirse (ie, i) orgulloso/a** (10)

psychologist **psicólogo/a** (17)

psychology **psicología** (P)

pullover **jersey** *m.* (16)

punish **castigar (gu)** (9)

put **poner** (7); to put on (*clothing*) **ponerse** *irreg.* (16)

Q

quality **qualidad** *f.* (17)

quantifying adjective **adjetivo de cantidad** (P)

quarter: quarter to **menos cuarto** (1); quarter past **y cuarto** (1)

question: I have a question, please **tengo una pregunta, por favor** (P); to ask a question **hacer** *irreg.* **una pregunta** (4)

quiet: to keep quiet **permanecer (zc) callado/a** (10)

R

rain *v.:* it's raining **llueve** (2), **está lloviendo** (2)

rare **raro/a** (P)

rarely **pocas veces** (1), **raras veces** (1)

raw **crudo/a** (7)

rayon **rayón** *m.* (16)

read **leer (y)** (1)

realistic **realista** (P)

realize (*something*) **darse** *irreg.* **cuenta (de)** (13)

rebellious **rebelde** (13)

receive **recibir** (1)

red **rojo/a** (7); red wine **vino tinto** (9)

redheaded **pelirrojo/a** (5)

regularly **regularmente** (1)

related (to) **relacionado/a (con)** (9)

relative **pariente** (4)

relax **relajarse** (10); to feel relaxed **sentirse (ie, i) relajado/a** (10)

religion **religión** *f.* (P)

remaining: to be remaining **quedar** (10)

remember **recordar (ue)** (3)

remove **quitar** (7)

rent *v.* **alquilar** (16); to rent videos **sacar (qu) vídeos** (2)

repeat, please **repita, por favor** (P)

representative *n.* **representante** *m., f.* (17)

request *v.* **pedir (i, i)** (1)

resemble **parecerse (zc)** (5)

reserve *v.* **reservar** (16); to reserve (*amount of time*) in advance **reservar con** (*time* + **de**) **anticipación** (16)

reserved **reservado/a** (5)

rest *v.* **descansar** (1)

restaurant **restaurante** *m.* (8)

restless **inquieto/a** (13)

retire **jubilarse** (17)

return (*to a place*) **regresar** (1), **volver (ue)** (1)

rice **arroz** *m.* (7)

ride: to ride a bicycle **andar** *irreg.* **en bicicleta** (11); to ride a skateboard **andar** *irreg.* **en patineta** (11); to ride a scooter, skateboard **andar** *irreg.* **en monopatín** (11)

right (*direction*) *adj.* **derecho/a** (8); turn right **doble a la derecha** (15)

risk: tendency to avoid risks **tendencia a evitar riesgos** (13)

river **río** (11)

roast(ed) **asado/a** (7); (half a) roasted chicken **(medio) pollo asado** (7)

roll **bollo** (7); assorted breads and rolls **bollería** (7)

room **cuarto** (1), **habitación** *f.* (16); to chat, participate in a chat room **chatear** (2); room and breakfast (*often with one other meal*) **media pensión** *f.* (16); room and full board **pensión** *f.* **completa** (16); room service **servicio de cuarto** (16); room with a (private) bath **habitación con baño (privado)** (16); room with a shower **habitación con ducha** (16); shut oneself up in one's room **encerrarse (ie) en su cuarto** (10)

roommate **compañero/a de cuarto** (P)

rope: to jump rope **saltar a la cuerda** (11)

round-trip ticket **boleto de ida y vuelta** *Lat. Am.* (16); **billete** *m.* **de ida y vuelta** *Sp.* (16)

routine **rutina** (1)

run **correr** (2)

S

sad **triste** (5); to be (get) sad **ponerse** *irreg.* **triste** (10)

sail *v.* **navegar (gu) en un barco** (11)

salad **ensalada** (7)

salt **sal** *f.* (7)

salt shaker **salero** (8)

sandwich **sándwich** *m.* (7)

Saturday **sábado** (1)

saucer **platillo** (8)

sausage **salchicha** (7)

say **decir** *irreg.* (3); to say good-bye **despedirse (i, i) (de)** (5); how do you say ____ in Spanish? **¿cómo se dice** ____ **en español?** (P); that is to say **o sea** (17); what did you say? **¿cómo dice?** (P)

scary **espantoso/a** (P)

science **ciencia** (P); computer science **computación** *f.* (P), **informática** (P); natural sciences **ciencias naturales** (P); political science **ciencias políticas** *pl.* (P); social sciences **ciencias sociales** (P)

scientist **científico/a** (17)

scooter **monopatín** *m.* (11); to ride a scooter **andar** *irreg.* **en monopatín** (11)

scrambled egg **huevo revuelto** (7)

sculptor **escultor(a)** (17)

sea **mar** *m.* (11)

season (*of the year*) **estación** *f.* (2)

seat **asiento** (16)

second course **segundo plato** (7)

section: (no) smoking section **sección** *f.* **de (no) fumar** (16)

secure **seguro/a** (13)

seductive **seductor(a)** (14)

see **ver** *irreg.* (2); see you soon **hasta pronto** (P); see you tomorrow **hasta mañana** (P); we'll be seeing each other **nos vemos** (P)

seem **parecer (zc)** (5)

self-centered **egoísta** (13)

self-esteem **autoestima** (12)

senator **senador(a)** (17)

send **enviar (envío)** (1), **mandar** (1)

sensitive **sensible** (13)

September **septiembre** (2)

serious (*person*) **serio/a** (P); (*situation*) **grave** (12)

service: room service **servicio de cuarto** (16)

set the table **poner** *irreg.* **la mesa** (8)

seven **siete** (P)

seven hundred **setecientos** (6)

seventeen **diecisiete** (P)

seventy **setenta** (6)

shaker: pepper shaker **pimentero** (8); salt shaker **salero** (8)

shame **vergüenza** (10)

shave (*someone*) **afeitar** (5)

she *pron.* **ella** (P)

shellfish **mariscos** *m. pl.* (7)

ship: cruise ship **crucero** (16)

shirt **camisa** (16)

shoe **zapato** (16); high-heeled shoe **zapato de tacón alto** (16)

shopping: to go shopping **ir** *irreg.* **de compras** (1)

short **bajo/a** (5); short time **un rato** (3)

shorts **pantalones cortos** (16)

should (*do something*) **deber** (+ *inf.*) (1); one/you (*impersonal*) should **se debe** (8)

shout *v.* **gritar** (10)

shower: room with a shower **habitación** *f.* **con ducha** (16)

shrimp **camarones** *m. pl.* (7)

shut oneself up in one's room **encerrarse (ie) en su cuarto** (10)

shy **tímido/a** (13)

sick: to get sick (*nauseated*) **marearse** (16)

silk **seda** (16)

silverware **cubiertos** *pl.* (8)

similar **parecido/a** (5)

sincere **sincero/a** (P)

sing **cantar** (10)

single: he/she is single **es soltero/a** (4); single father **padre** *m.* **soltero** (4); single mother **madre** *f.* **soltera** (4)

sister **hermana** (4); half sister **media hermana** (4); sisters and brothers, siblings **hermanos** (4)

sister-in-law **cuñada** (4)

six **seis** (P)

six hundred **seiscientos** (6)

sixteen **dieciséis** (P)

sixty **sesenta** (6)

size **tamaño** (6)

skate **patín** *m.* (*pl.* **patines**) (11); inline skates **patines en línea**; *v.* **patinar**; to inline skate **patinar en línea** (11)

skateboard *n.* **patineta** (11); *v.* **andar** *irreg.* **en patineta/ monopatín** (11)

ski: to snow ski **esquiar (esquío) en las montañas** (11); to water ski **esquiar en el agua** (11)

skin **pelo**; dark-skinned **moreno/a** (5)

skirt **falda** (16)

skycap **maletero/a** (16)

sleep **dormir (ue, u)** (1)

small **pequeño/a** (4)

smaller (than) **menos grande (que)** (5)

smart **listo/a** (17)

smile **sonreír (i, i)** (10)

smoke **fumar** (9)

smoking: (no) smoking section **sección** *f.* **de (no) fumar** (16)

snack *n.* **merienda** (7); *v.* to snack on **merendar (ie)** (7)

snow: *v.* it's snowing **nieva** (2), **está nevando** (2); to snow ski **esquiar (esquío) en las montañas** (11)

soap opera **telenovela** (3); to watch a soap opera **ver** *irreg.* **una telenovela** (3)

soccer **fútbol** *m.* (2); to play soccer **jugar (ue) (gu) al fútbol** (2)

social **social** (P); social sciences **ciencias sociales** (P); social

work **asistencia social** (17); social worker **trabajador(a) social** (17)

sociology **sociología** (P)

sock (*for foot*) **calcetín** *m.* (*pl.* **calcetines**) (16)

soft drink **refresco** (7)

solitary **retraído/a** (5)

some **algunos/as** (P), **unos/as** (P)

sometimes **a veces** (1)

son **hijo** (4)

soon: as soon as **en cuanto** (17), **tan pronto como** (17); see you soon **hasta pronto** (P)

sour **agrio/a**

south **sur** *m.* (15)

spaghetti **espaguetis** *pl.* (7)

Spanish (*language*) **español** *m.* (P); how do you say ___ in Spanish? **¿cómo se dice ___ en español?** (P)

speak **hablar** (1); to speak another language **hablar otro idioma** *m.* (17)

special: daily special **plato del día** (8)

specialist (*in something*) **especialista** *m., f.* **(en algo)** (17)

speech (*school subject*) **oratoria** (P)

spend (*money*) **gastar** (2); (*time*) **pasar** (1)

spill **derramar** (8)

spinach **espinacas** *pl.* (7)

spoiled **pasado/a** (7)

spoon **cuchara** (8)

sport **deporte** *m.*; to play/practice a sport **jugar (ue) (gu) un deporte** (1), **practicar (qu) un deporte** (2)

spring (*season*) **primavera** (2)

stand in line **hacer** *irreg.* **cola** (16)

star: four-star hotel **hotel** *m.* **de cuatro estrellas** (16)

state of mind **estado de ánimo** (10)

station **estación** *f.* (16)

stay **quedarse** (2); (*in a hotel or boardinghouse*) **alojarse** (16); to stay at home **quedarse en casa** (2)

steak **bistec** *m.* (7)

steamed **al vapor** (7)

stepbrother **hermanastro** (4)

stepfather **padrastro** (4)

stepmother **madrastra** (4)

stepsister **hermanastra** (4)

stingy **tacaño/a** (13)

stockings **medias** (16)

stop: to make a stop (*on a flight*) **hacer** *irreg.* **escala** (16) straight **derecho** (15), **recto** (15); continue/go straight **siga derecho/recto** (15); straight hair **pelo lacio** (5)

strange **raro/a** (P)

strawberry **fresa** (7)

street **calle** *f.* (15); cross the street **cruce la calle** (15)

strike someone as funny **hacerle** *irreg.* **gracia a uno** (11)

strong **fuerte** (17); physically strong **físicamente fuerte** (17)

stubborn **testarudo/a** (13)

student **estudiante** *m., f.* (P); I am a(n) ___ student **soy estudiante de ___** (P)

study **estudiar** (1); I'm studying ___ **estudio ___** (P); what are you studying? **¿qué estudias?** (P)

subject (*class*) **materia** (P); subject pronoun **pronombre** *m.* **de sujeto** (P)

suffer (*experience*) **sufrir** (12)

sugar **azúcar** (7)

suit **traje** *m.* (16); bathing suit **traje de baño** (16)

suitcase **maleta** (16); to pack one's suitcase **hacer** *irreg.* **la maleta** (16)

summer **verano** (2)

Sunday **domingo** (1)

superficial **superficial** (14)

support *v.* (*emotionally*) **apoyar** (5); (*financially*) **mantener** (*like* **tener**) (5)

surf the Web (*Internet*) **navegar (gu) la Red** (1)

sweater **suéter** *m.* (16)

sweats, sweat pants **sudadera** (16)

sweet *adj.* **dulce** (7)

swim **nadar** (2)

swordfish **emperador** *m.* (7)

synthetic fabric **tela de fibras sintéticas** (16)

T

table **mesa** (8); to clear the table **levantar la mesa** (8); to set the table **poner** *irreg.* **la mesa** (8)

tablecloth **mantel** *m.* (8)

take: to take a test **tener** *irreg.* **un examen** (3); to take a trip **hacer** *irreg.* **un viaje** (16); to take a walk **dar** *irreg.* **un paseo** (2); to take away **quitar** (7); to take off (*clothing*) **quitarse** (16); to take pictures **sacar (qu) fotos** *f.* (16)

talent for leadership **don** *m.* **de mando** (13)

talk *v.* **hablar;** to talk on the phone **hablar por teléfono** (1)

talkative **hablador(a)** (13)

tall **alto/a** (5)

taller (than) **más alto/a (que)** (5)

tallest **el/la más alto/a (de)** (5)

taste *n.* (*flavor*) **sabor** *m.* (7); (*preference*) **gusto** (7)

taste *v.* (*sample, try*) **probar (ue)** (8); it tastes like ___ **sabe a ___** (7)

tea **té** *m.* (7); herbal tea **té de hierbas** (9); iced tea **té helado** (9)

teacher (*elementary school*) **maestro/a** (17)

teaching (*profession*) **enseñanza** (17)

technician **técnico** *m., f.* (17)

telephone **teléfono** (3); to talk on the phone **hablar por teléfono** (1)

television **televisión** *f.* (1)

tell **decir** *irreg.* (3); to tell a joke **contar (ue) un chiste** (10); could you tell me ___? **¿me podría decir ___?** (15)

temperature **temperatura** (2)

ten **diez** (P)

tenacious **tenaz** (14)

tendency to avoid risks **tendencia a evitar riesgos** (13)

tennis **tenis** *m.* (10); to play tennis **jugar (ue) (gu) al tenis** (10)

tense **tenso/a** (10); to be tense **estar** *irreg.* **tenso/a** (10)

test **examen** *m.* (*pl.* **exámenes**) (P); to take a test **tener** *irreg.* **un examen** (3)

thank you, thanks **gracias** (P)

that **ese/a** *adj.* (P); **que** *conj.* (P); that is to say **o sea** (17)

the **el** *m. s.* (P); **la** *f. s.* (P); **los** *m. pl.* (P); **las** *f. pl.* (P)

theater (*school subject*) **teatro** (P); to go to the theater **ir** *irreg.* **al teatro** (11)

their *poss.* **su(s)** (P)

then **luego** (2)

therapist: physical therapist **terapeuta** *m., f.* **físico/a** (17)

there: from here to there **de aquí para allá** (15); there is, there are **hay** (P)

these **estos/as** *adj.* (P)

they *pron.* **ellos/as** (P)

thin **delgado/a** (5)

thing **cosa** (5)

think **pensar (ie)** (1); (*have the opinion*) **opinar** (5); to think about **pensar (ie) en** (1); to think in a direct (linear) manner **pensar (ie) de una manera directa** (17); I (don't) think that ___ **(no) creo que ___** (18)

third course **tercer plato** (7)

thirsty: to be thirsty **tener** *irreg.* **sed** *f.* (9)

thirteen **trece** (P)

thirty **treinta** (P)

this **este/a** *adj.* (P)

those **esos/as** *adj.* (P)

thousand: one thousand **mil** (6); two thousand **dos mil** (6)

three **tres** (P); at three o'clock **a las tres** (1); it's three o'clock **son las tres** (1)

three hundred **trescientos** (6)

throw (have) a party **dar** *irreg.* **una fiesta** (11)

Thursday **jueves** *m.* (1)

ticket **billete** *m. Sp.* (16), **boleto** *Lat. Am.* (16); ticket (*passage*) **pasaje** (16); one-way ticket **billete/boleto de ida** (16); round-trip ticket **billete/boleto de ida y vuelta** (16)

tie **corbata** (16)

time: at what time? **¿a qué hora?** (1); from time to time **de vez en cuando** (2); last time **última vez** (3); short time **un rato** (3); time period **época** (6); to have a (very) bad time **pasarlo (muy) mal** (10); what time is it? **¿qué hora es?** (1)

timid **tímido/a** (5)

tip *n.* **propina** (8); to leave a tip **dejar propina** (8)

tired **cansado/a** (10); to be tired **estar** *irreg.* **cansado/a** (10); to get tired **cansarse** (10)

toast **pan** *m.* **tostado** (7), **tostada** (7)

today **hoy** (1); today is ___ **hoy es ___** (1)

tomato **tomate** *m.* (7); tomato juice **jugo de tomate** (9)

tomorrow **mañana** (1); see you tomorrow **hasta mañana** (P); tomorrow is ___ **mañana es ___** (1)

traffic light **semáforo** (15)

train **tren** *m.* (16)

trait **característica** (5), (*usually facial features*) **rasgo** (5); personality trait **característica de la personalidad** (5); physical characteristic **característica física** (5)

travel **viajar** (16)

travel agent **agente** *m., f.* **de viajes** (16)

treat *v.* (*pay for someone*) **invitar** (8)

trip *n.* **viaje** *m.* (16); on a trip **de viaje** (16); to take a trip **hacer** *irreg.* **un viaje** (16)

trustworthy **confidente** (13)

try (*taste*) **probar (ue)** (8)

T-shirt **camiseta** (16)

Tuesday **martes** *m.* (1)

tuna **atún** *m.* (7)

turn right/left **doble a la derecha/izquierda** (15)

twelve **doce** (P)

twenties **los años 20** (6)

twenty **veinte** (P)

twenty-eight **veintiocho** (P)

twenty-five **veinticinco** (P)

twenty-four **veinticuatro** (P)

twenty-nine **veintinueve** (P)

twenty-one *m.* **veintiún** (P), **veintiuno** (P); *f.* **veintiuna** (P)

twenty-seven **veintisiete** (P)

twenty-six **veintiséis** (P)

twenty-three **veintitrés** (P)

twenty-two **veintidós** (P)

twin **gemelo/a** (4); twin bed **cama sencilla** (16)

two **dos** (P); at two o'clock **a las dos** (1); it's two o'clock **son las dos** (1); two hundred **doscientos** (6); two thousand **dos mil** (6)

U

ugly **feo/a** (5)

uncertain **incierto/a** (14)

uncle/aunt **tío/a** (4)

understand **comprender** (5), **entender (ie)** (1); I don't understand **no comprendo** (P), **no entiendo** (P)

unoccupied **desocupado/a** (16)

until *conj.* **hasta que** (17); until (very) late **hasta (muy) tarde** (2)

up: to get up **levantarse** (1) what's up? **¿qué tal?** (P)

use: to use a computer **usar una computadora** (17); to use aromatherapy **utilizar (c) la aromaterapia** (11)

V

vacancy: no vacancy **completo/a** (16)

vacant **desocupado/a** (16)

veal **ternera** (7)

vegetable **verdura** (7)

vending machine **máquina vendedora** (7)

verb **verbo** (P)

very **muy** (P); very cold **bien frío/a** (9); very hot **bien caliente** (9)

veterinarian **veterinario/a** (17)

video **vídeo** (2); to rent videos **sacar (qu) vídeos** (2)

video game **videojuego** (3); to play video games **jugar (ue) (gu) a los videojuegos** (3)

view: to have a view **tener** *irreg.* **vista** (16)

visionary **visionario/a** (14)

vitamin **vitamina** (7)

vocabulary **vocabulario** (P)

volleyball: to play volleyball **jugar (ue) (gu) al voleibol** (11)

W

wait on (*a customer*) **atender (ie)** (8)

waiter **camarero** (8), **mesero** (8)

waiting room **sala de espera** (16)

waitress **camarera** (8), **mesera** (8)

wake up **despertarse (ie)** (1)

walk **andar** *irreg.* (3), **caminar** (10); to take a walk **dar** *irreg.* **un paseo** (2)

want *v.* **querer** *irreg.* (1)

wash *v.*: to wash clothes **lavar la ropa** (2); to wash the dishes **lavar los platos** (8)

watch *v.* **mirar** (1), **ver** *irreg.* (2); to watch a soap opera **ver** *irreg.* **una telenovela** (3); to watch television **mirar la televisión** (1), **ver** *irreg.* **la televisión** (2)

water **agua** *f.* (*but* **el agua**) (7); to water ski **esquiar (esquío) en el agua** (11); water glass **vaso** (8)

way: one-way ticket **billete** *m.*/ **boleto de ida** (16); to have a way with people **tener** *irreg.* **don de gentes** (17)

we *pron.* **nosotros/as** (P); we'll be seeing each other **nos vemos** (P)

wear **llevar** (16), **vestir (i, i)** (16)

weather **tiempo** (2); the weather's bad **hace mal tiempo** (2); the weather's good **hace buen tiempo** (2); what's the weather like? **¿qué tiempo hace?** (2)

Wednesday **miércoles** (1)

week **semana** (3); last week **semana pasada** (3)

weekend **fin** *m.* **de semana** (1); last weekend **fin de semana pasado** (3); weekend activities **actividades** *f.* **para el fin de semana** (2)

weights: to lift weights **levantar pesas** (10)

well **bien** (5); to feel well **para sentirse (ie, i) bien** (10); to get along well **llevarse bien** (5)

well-mannered **educado** (8); to be well-mannered **tener** *irreg.* **buena educación** (8)

west **oeste** *m.* (15)

what? **¿qué?** (P); **¿cuál(es)?** (4); what are you like? **¿cómo eres?** (13); what are you studying? **¿qué estudias?** (P); what color is/are ____? **¿de qué color es/son ____?** (5); what did you say? **¿cómo dice?** (P); what does ___ come with? **¿qué trae ____?** (8); what does he/she look like? **¿cómo es?** (5); what height is he/she? **¿de qué estatura es?** (5); what is your major? **¿qué carrera haces?** (P); what time is it? **¿qué hora es?** (1); what's on the table? **¿qué hay en la mesa?** (8); what's the matter with you? **¿qué te pasa?** (10); what's up? **¿qué tal?** (P); what's your name? **¿cómo te llamas?** (P), **¿cómo se llama usted?** (P), **¿cuál es tu/su nombre?** (P); what time is it? **¿qué hora es?** (1)

wheat: whole-wheat bread **pan** *m.* **integral** (7)

when? **¿cuándo?** (1); **¿a qué hora?** (1)

where? **¿dónde?** (1); where are you from? **¿de dónde eres?** (P), **¿de dónde es usted?** (P); where is ____? **¿dónde está ____?** (15), **¿dónde queda ____?** (15)

which? **¿cuál(es)?** (4); **¿qué?** (4)

while: little while **un rato** (3)

whistle *v.* **silbar** (10)

white **blanco/a** (7); white bread **pan** *m.* **blanco** (7); white wine **vino blanco** (9)

who/whom **¿quién(es)?** (P)

whole-wheat bread **pan** *m.* **integral** (7)

widow: she is a widow **es viuda** (4)

widower: he is a widower **es viudo** (4)

wife **esposa** (4), **mujer** *f.* (4)

windy: it's windy **hace viento** (2)

wine **vino** (7); red/white wine **vino tinto/blanco** (9); wine glass **copa** (8)

winter **invierno** (2)
wise **sabio/a** (13)
with **con** (1); with ice **con hielo** (9)
without **sin** (9); without a doubt **indudable** (5); one/you (*impersonal*) can't ___ without ___ **no se puede ___ sin ___** (8); without ice **sin hielo** (9)
wool **lana** (16)
word **palabra** (P)
work *v.* **trabajar** (1); ability to work with one's hands **habilidad** *f.* **manual** (17); *n.* social work **asistencia social** (17)

workday **día** *m.* **de trabajo** (1), **día laboral** (1)
worry *v.* **preocuparse (por)** (10)
wound *n.* **herida** (12), **lesión** (12); *v.* **herir (ie, i)** (12)
write **escribir** (1)
writing *n.* **composición** *f.* (P)

Y

year **año** (2); to be ___ years old **tener** *irreg.* ___ **años** (4)
yellow **amarillo/a** (7)
yes **sí** (P)
yesterday **ayer** (3)
yoga **yoga** (11); to do/practice yoga **hacer** *irreg.* **yoga** (11)

yogurt **yogur** *m.* (7)
you *pron.* **tú** *fam. s.* (P), **usted (Ud.)** *form. s.* (P), **ustedes (Uds.)** *form. pl.*, **vosotros/as** *fam. pl. Sp.;* and you? **¿y tú?** (P), **¿y usted?** (P)
young **joven** *m., f.* (*pl.* **jóvenes**) (6)
younger **menor** (4)
youngest **el/la menor** (4)
your (*form. s., pl.*) his, her, their **su(s)** (P)
your **tu(s)** *fam. poss.* (P), **su(s)** *form. s., pl. poss.* (P)

Z

zero **cero** (P)

INDEX

This index is divided into two parts: Part I (Grammar) covers topics in grammar, structure, and usage. Part II (Topics) lists cultural topics, everyday language (functional topics), maps, reading strategies, and vocabulary topics treated in the text. Topics in Part II appear as groups; they are not cross-referenced.

Part I: Grammar

a, personal, 124, 125, 184, 247, 373, 403
  with **conocer**, 147
  with **gustar**, 11, 60, 374–375
  importance of, 131
acabar de + infinitive, 347
accent marks. *See* written accent marks
acostarse (ue), 34, 39–40, 64
adjectives
  after **ser** and **estar**, 5, 122
  corresponding nouns, 344
  demonstrative, 18, 26
  describing people, 363
  describing personalities, 340, 343
  descriptive, 14–15, 107, 122
  gender and number of, 14–15, 107, 142, 264
  personal qualities, 381
  possessive, 15, 26, 107, 116
  preceding nouns, 18
  quantifying, 26
  superlative forms, 133
  used as nouns after **lo**, 402
  veintiún and **veintiuna**, 18
  word order with, 18
adverbs
  of frequency, 35, 48
  of time, 32
age, 161, 183
  with **tener**, 112
andar (*irreg.*), 108, 297, 300, 336. *See also* Appendix
apocopation
  mal, 66
  ningún, 59
  un/un(a), 162
  veintiún, 18
articles
  definite, 9, 27
  indefinite, 9, 27
-ar verbs. *See specific tenses and* Appendix

caer (*irreg.*), 256
  idioms with, 375
  See also Appendix

commands
  affirmative, 324, 337, 418–419, 472
  defined, 325
  negative, 326, 337, 419, 472
  softened, 325
  spelling changes in, 327, 337
  tú form, 324, 325, 326, 337
  Ud. form, 418–419, 472
  Uds. form, 324, 326, 418–419, 472
  vosotros form, 324, 326
  word order with pronouns, 324, 326, 337, 419
  See also Appendix (imperative)
¿cómo?, 115, 198
¿Cómo es... ?, 113
comparisons
  of equality, 176, 183, 185
  of more or less with adjectives, 139, 141, 159
comprender, preterite meaning of, 240
conditional, 367–368, 402, 420–421, 472.
  See also Appendix
conducir (zc), 40, 107
conjugation, formation, 33–34
conjunctions
  of time, 443
  use of subjunctive after, 443–444
conocer (zc), 40, 107, 114, 147, 240, 300
  versus **saber,** 147, 185
  See also Appendix
construir (y). *See* Appendix
¿cuál(es)?, 115, 197
¿cuándo?, 115
¿cuántos/as?, 18, 115

dar (*irreg.*)
  commands with, 326, 419
  with direct object pronoun, 196
  idioms with, 57
  present subjunctive of, 436, 474
  present tense of, 107
  preterite of, 300, 336
  See also Appendix
days of the week, 38, 53
de, used with prepositions of location, 383

decir (*irreg.*)
  in commands, 324, 326, 337
  conditional of, 367, 402, 421
  future tense of, 455, 474
  with indirect object, 196
  past subjunctive of, 370
  present perfect of, 40
  preterite of, 100, 336
  See also Appendix
definite article, 9, 27
  used to express generalizations, 190
describing, 14–15, 107, 122, 139, 144, 260
  using subordinate clauses, 435
  verbs used in, 145–146
  See also adjectives, descriptive
descriptive adjectives, 14–15, 107, 122
direct object pronouns, 123–125, 128, 184
  with commands, 324
  word order of, 207
do, 34, 109, 126
¿dónde?, 115
dormir (ue, u)
  present perfect of, 345
  present subjunctive of, 445, 474
  present tense of, 34, 39–40, 107
  preterite of, 89, 240, 257, 336
  See also Appendix

ellos/ellas, 66
encantar, 191, 256, 271
entender (ie), 34
-er verbs. *See specific tenses and* Appendix
escribir, 170, 173, 345, 401
estar (*irreg.*)
  with adjectives, 122, 184–185, 257, 260–261, 262, 335
  + adjectives, 207
  future tense of, 474
  with **-ndo** forms, 71, 165, 185
  past subjunctive of, 370
  with prepositions of location, 383, 402
  present subjunctive of, 436, 474
  present tense of, 107
  preterite of, 108, 297, 336
  quedar versus, 383, 402

ser versus, 5, 145–146, 207, 262
uses of, 67, 71, 106, 145–146, 207,
   335, 402
See also Appendix
estudiar, 39–40

faltar, 270–271, 334
future meaning
   deadline expressed with **para,** 58
   intent expressed by present tense of
      pensar/esperar/ir a + infinitive, 454
   ir + **a** form of, 73
   present indicative used to express, 165
      subjunctive used to express, 443–444
future tense, 454–455
   summarized, 474
   See also Appendix

gender, 9, 14
   of adjectives, 14–15, 264
   of nouns ending with **-a** or **-o,** 219
   of nouns with two meanings, 219
   of numbers, 162, 164
   of occupations, 430–431
   of words ending in **-ista,** 431
generalizations (impersonal expressions)
   followed by subjunctive, 457–458
   with **se,** 246, 256–257
gustar, 10–11, 26, 60, 106, 125, 191–192,
   195, 270–271, 374–375, 403
   uses of, 375

haber (*irreg.*)
   as auxiliary, 345, 347
   conditional of, 368, 402, 421
   future tense of, 455, 474
   present subjunctive of, 436, 474
   See also Appendix
hacer (*irreg.*)
   in commands, 326, 337
   commands with, 324
   conditional of, 367, 402, 421
   idioms with, 66–67, 79, 100, 311,
      411–412
   past subjunctive of, 370
   present perfect of, 345, 401
   present tense of, 40, 62, 64, 66–67, 107
   preterite of, 83, 89, 90, 96, 100, 108,
      239, 300, 336
   + **que** + present tense, 346
   time expressions with, 346
   with weather expressions, 66–67, 79
   See also Appendix
hay
   + **que,** 222
   uses of, 19, 108

idioms
   with **dar,** 57
   with **hacer,** 66–67, 79, 311
   with **tener,** 311
if clauses, 368
imperative. *See* commands; Appendix

imperfect indicative
   English equivalents of, 170–171
   of irregular verbs, 278, 316
   preterite versus, 302–303, 335–336
   of regular verbs, 170–171, 173, 185
   thinking about how to use, 302
   uses of, 170–171, 177, 185, 278, 297,
      335–336
   See also Appendix
imperfect subjunctive. *See* past
   subjunctive
impersonal expressions
   (generalizations), followed by
   subjunctive, 457–458
impersonal **se.** *See* **se,** impersonal
importar, 191, 194, 256
indefinite antecedents, followed by
   subjunctive, 435–436
indefinite articles, 9, 27
   with occupations, 432
indicative, subjunctive versus, 458, 473
indirect object pronouns, 11, 60, 125,
   191–192, 194–195, 196, 204, 207,
   256, 270–271
   with commands, 324
   word order of, 207
infinitive
   after **ir a,** 73
   how it is indicated, 33
   types in Spanish, 33
   when to use, 73, 295, 335
information questions, 115, 140, 159,
   184, 197
interrogative words, 115, 140, 159, 184,
   197, 198
invitar, uses of, 227
ir (*irreg.*)
   + **a** + infinitive, 73, 109, 454
   in commands, 324, 326, 337, 419
   imperfect, 171, 173, 185, 316
   present perfect of, 345
   present subjunctive of, 436, 444, 474
   present tense of, 36, 40, 62, 64, 107
   preterite of, 83, 89, 90, 96, 98, 100,
      108, 300
   See also Appendix
-ir verbs. *See specific tenses and* Appendix
-ista, words ending in, 142, 431
it, 68, 109, 130

jamás, 58
jugar (ue) (gu), 34, 62, 89, 336

le, 87
llegar, preterite of, 299
llegar a ser, concept of, 455
llevar(se), 153, 174
lo, 128, 130, 389, 402

mal(o), 66
más..., 135, 139, 141, 159
menos..., 133, 139, 141, 159
morir (ue, u), 345, 401, 445

nada, 58–59
nadie, 58–59
-ndo form of verbs. *See* present
   participle; Appendix
necesitar + infinitive, 108
negation
   in expressions of doubt when using
      subjunctive, 458
   of sentences, 34
   of **tú** commands, 326
   words expressing, 58–59, 107
ningún(o), 58, 59
no, use of in negations, 58
nominalization, **lo** + adjective, 389, 402
nonexistent antecedents followed by
   subjunctive, 441
nouns
   comparison of, 176, 183, 185
   gender of, 9, 219, 430–431
number
   of adjectives, 14–15
   of nouns, 9
   ser +, 5
   See also gender
numbers, cardinal, 18, 26, 161, 162, 163,
   164, 183. *See also* years, how to read
nunca, 58
object pronouns, position of, 195, 196,
   204, 207, 324, 373, 419. *See also*
   direct object pronouns; indirect
   object pronouns; reflexive pronouns

oír (*irreg.*). *See* Appendix
order. *See* word order
orthographic changes. *See* spelling
   changes

para, 413, 458
   mí and **ti** with, 230
   por versus, 59, 229–230, 257, 388, 402
   uses of, 229–230, 257, 388, 402, 413,
      458
para que, 230
parecerse (zc), 142
pasar, with **-ndo** forms, 72
passive **se.** *See* **se,** passive
past participle, 345–346, 401. *See also*
   Appendix
past perfect indicative. *See* Appendix
past perfect subjunctive. *See* Appendix
past subjunctive
   formation of, 369–370, 402
   of **tener,** 402
   used in conditional sentences, 368,
      369–370, 402
   See also present subjunctive; Appendix
   (imperfect subjunctive)
past tense. *See* imperfect subjunctive;
   preterite
pedir (i, i), 34. *See also* Appendix
pensar (ie), 34. *See also* Appendix
perfect tenses, present perfect indicative,
   345–346, 401. *See also* Appendix

personal pronouns. *See* pronouns
pluperfect subjunctive. *See* Appendix
    (past perfect subjunctive)
plural. *See* number
poder (*irreg.*)
    conditional of, 367, 402, 421
    future tense of, 455, 474
    meaning in the preterite, 108, 240
    past subjunctive of, 370
    present tense of, 34
    preterite of, 90, 108, 300, 336
    uses of, 108, 240, 440
    See also Appendix
poner(se) (*irreg.*)
    in commands, 324, 337
    to express change in mood or
      emotion, 260–261, 264, 334
    with indirect object pronouns, 204, 256
    present perfect of, 345, 401
    preterite of, 336
    reflexive, 408
    to talk about getting dressed, 408
    See also Appendix
por
    para versus, 59, 229–230, 257, 388, 402
    uses of, 40, 59, 229, 257, 261, 384,
      385, 388, 389, 402
position. *See* word order
possession
    adjectives of, 15, 26, 107, 116
    with **ser,** 5
preferir (ie, i), 34
prepositions
    after certain verbs, 409
    of location, 383, 400
    used for destination, 413
present indicative
    to express future intent, 454
    first personal plural, 64
    first person singular of, 39–40
    irregular verbs summarized, 107
    present perfect versus, 401
    of regular verbs, 33–34, 39–40, 45–46,
      61–62, 64, 106–107
    second person plural of, 106
    second person singular of, 45–46
    of stem-changing verbs, 33–34,
      39–40, 107
    summarized, 106–107
    third person plural, 61–62
    third person singular, 33–34
    uses of, 34, 165, 345
    See also specific verbs and Appendix
present participle, 71, 72, 295, 335.
    See also Appendix
present perfect indicative, 345, 401.
    See also Appendix
    English and Spanish uses
      compared, 346
    present perfect of **-ar** verbs, 345
    present perfect of **-er** verbs, 345
present perfect subjunctive. *See* Appendix
present progressive, 165

present subjunctive
    after conjunctions of time that express
      future intent, 443–444, 473
    after expressions of doubt and
      uncertainty, 457–458, 473
    after indefinite antecedents, 435–436,
      472–473
    after negative and nonexistent
      antecedents, 441, 473
    formation of, 436, 438, 444, 473–474
    in formulaic expressions, 444
    of **tener,** 474
    used to express future, 443–444
    uses summarized, 472–474
    See also past subjunctive; Appendix
preterite
    changes in meaning of, 89
    first person plural of, 99, 108
    first person singular of, 89–90, 108
    imperfect versus, 302–303, 335–336
    of irregular verbs, 85, 89–90, 98, 100,
      108, 240, 299–300, 336
    meanings of, 84, 240, 336
    of regular verbs, 81–82, 84, 89, 96, 98,
      99, 108, 238–239, 257, 336
    second person plural of, 108
    second person singular of, 96, 108
    spelling changes in, 98, 100, 300, 336
    of stem-changing verbs, 84, 85, 89–90,
      98, 100, 240, 300, 336
    summarized, 108
    third person plural of, 98, 108
    third person singular of, 85, 108
    uses of, 84, 96, 98, 99, 108, 239, 335–336
    See also Appendix
producir (zc), 40. *See also* Appendix
pronouns. *See* direct object pronouns;
    indirect object pronouns; reciprocal
    pronouns; reflexive pronouns;
    subject pronouns
pronunciation, 19, 21, 25

¿qué?
    ¿cómo? versus, 198
    ¿cuál(es)? versus, 115, 197
quedar(se), 62, 63, 96, 270–271, 334
    estar versus, 383, 402
querer (*irreg.*), 34, 108, 336
    uses of, 375
    See also Appendix
questions
    conversational, 154
    information, 115, 159, 226
    question words, 115, 159, 184, 197, 200,
      226, 271
¿quién(es)?, 115
quitar, with indirect object pronouns, 204

reciprocal pronouns, 184
reciprocal verbs, 152, 153, 184
reflexive verbs
    to express reciprocal actions, 152,
      153, 184

present tense of, 33, 39–40, 46, 64
reflexive versus nonreflexive uses of
    se, 149, 268, 351–352
true reflexive constructions, 148–149,
    289, 401, 408
use of pronouns with, 33, 40, 62,
    148–149, 184, 263–264, 268, 324,
    326, 334, 349
verbs, 142, 221, 409, 472
verbs that require reflexive pronouns,
    334, 351–352, 401
verbs used without reflexive
    pronouns, 334
reír (i, i). *See* Appendix
responses, shortened, 126

saber (*irreg.*)
    + **a,** 200
    conocer versus, 147, 185
    + infinitive, 440
    meaning in the preterite, 108, 240
    past subjunctive of, 370
    poder + infinitive versus, 440
    present subjunctive of, 436, 474
    present tense of, 107
    preterite of, 108, 300, 336
    uses of, 114, 147, 200, 240, 439–440
    See also Appendix
salir (*irreg.*)
    in commands, 324, 337
    conditional of, 368, 402, 421
    future tense of, 455, 474
    present tense of, 33, 40, 64, 108
    preterite of, 89, 96, 97, 336
    See also Appendix
se
    impersonal (*one*), 220, 222, 224, 226,
      245–246, 247, 256–257
    passive, 223–224, 245–246, 247, 256–257
    as reflexive pronoun, 33, 40, 62,
      148–149, 150, 351–352
    reflexive versus nonreflexive use of,
      268, 351–352
    to replace **le** or **les** as the indirect
      object pronoun, 207
seguir (i, i) (g). *See* Appendix
sentir(se) (ie, i)
    to express state of being, 260–261, 263
    present subjunctive of, 474
    preterite of, 336
    See also Appendix
ser (*irreg.*)
    commands with, 326, 337, 419
    conditional of, 367
    estar versus, 5, 145–146, 207, 262
    to express origins, 2, 5
    future tense of, 474
    imperfect, 316
    imperfect of, 171, 173, 185
    present subjunctive of, 436, 444, 474
    present tense of, 4–5, 64, 108
    preterite of, 89, 100, 108
    uses of, 5, 145–146, 207, 262

shortened forms. *See* apocopation
si clauses, 370
singular. *See* number
soler (ue)
  forms, 48, 64
  + infinitive, 48
spelling changes
  in commands, 327
  in preterite, 89, 98, 100, 336
  in subjunctive, 436, 473–474
  See also stem-changing verbs;
    Appendix
stem-changing verbs
  past participles, 401
  present indicative, 33–34, 40, 64, 107
  present progressive, 165
  preterite, 89–90, 98, 100, 336
  subjunctive, 445, 474
  See also Appendix
stress. *See* written accent marks
subject pronouns, 5, 26, 33, 39, 124
subjunctive, concept of, 435, 472–474
  with expressions of uncertainty,
    457–458
  See also past subjunctive; present
    subjunctive
superlatives, 133, 159, 390
su(s), agreement of, 15, 116
tag questions, 200, 271

tampoco, 58–59
tan... como, 176
tanto/a, tantos/as... como, 176
tener (*irreg.*)
  in commands, 324, 337
  conditional of, 368, 402, 421
  future tense of, 455, 474
  idioms with, 172, 202, 237, 265, 267,
    311, 335
  + noun, 265
  + nouns, 335
  past subjunctive of, 370, 402
  present subjunctive of, 436, 474
  present tense of, 34, 40, 107

preterite of, 100, 108, 300, 336
  + **que** + infinitive, 47, 108
  stating age with, 112
  See also Appendix

tiempo, 66–67
time expressions, 82
  in the past, 298
time of day (telling time), 32, 42–43, 51,
  53, 54, 67, 304, 336
todo/a, todos/as, 35
traducir (zc), 40
traer (*irreg.*)
  with indirect object, 196
  preterite of, 336
  See also Appendix
tú, 5
  use of, 45–46
  usted versus, 45–46
  vos versus, 23
tú form commands, 324, 325, 326, 337

un, un(a), 162
unos/unas, 9
used to, equivalent of imperfect, 171,
  278
usted
  tú versus, 45–46
  uses of, 2, 45–46, 96, 106
usted form commands, 418–419, 472
ustedes
  ellos/ellas versus, 62
  uses of, 62, 98, 106
  vosotros versus, 23, 62, 324, 326

venir (*irreg.*)
  in commands, 324, 326, 337
  present tense of, 34, 107
  preterite of, 100, 108, 300, 336
  See also Appendix
verbs
  followed by an infinitive, 47, 108, 109
  requiring indirect objects, 191–192.
    See also **gustar**

used reflexively and nonreflexively,
  149, 351–352
ver (*irreg.*)
  in commands, 324
  imperfect, 316
  present perfect of, 345, 401
  See also Appendix
vestir(se) (i, i), 34, 97, 107, 408, 409
volver(se) (ue), 34, 99. *See also*
  Appendix
vosotros, 4, 23, 62
vosotros form commands, 324, 326
vos versus **tú,** 23

weather expressions, 66–67, 79
will, in future tense, 454
word order
  with adjectives, 15
  in commands, 324, 327, 337,
    419, 472
  with **gustar,** 374–375, 403
  with object pronouns, 125, 196, 204,
    207, 324, 373, 419, 472
would
  in conditional tense, 367–368
  meaning *used to* as equivalent of
    imperfect, 171, 278
  as soft command, 325
written accent marks, 21
  with commands, 337
  to denote meaning, 21
  in past participles, 345
  in preterite tense, 257
  when pronouns are attached to
    present participles, 125
  in regular preterite tense, 238
  used in imperfect tense, 173
  when unnecessary, 90

years, how to read, 163

Part II: Topics

Culture
addictions, 325, 327, 333
afternoon snacks, 201, 216
animals
  sense of direction in, 386
  as symbols, 354
Argentina, 72, 244, 379. *See also*
  Hispanic world; **Latinoamérica**
art, 186, 258, 338, 404
artists, 253
Aztec. *See also* pre-Hispanic America

beverages, 41, 243–244, 248
Caribe (Caribbean), 294. *See also*
  Hispanic world; **Latinoamérica**
cellular telephones, 321
Celsius and Fahrenheit
  temperatures, 67
Chile, 244. *See also* Hispanic world;
  Latinoamérica
coffee drinking, 41
Colombia, 213. *See also* Hispanic world;
  Latinoamérica

Cuba, 243. *See also* Hispanic world;
  Latinoamérica
daily routines, 51. *See Vocabulary index*
dance, 76–77
eating and mealtimes, 193, 196, 203,
  208, 212–213, 218, 225, 227,
  284–285
ecotourism, 358–359
education, 14, 20
El Niño, 358
embracing, 153

endangered species, 359
environment, importance of, 358–359
España (Spain)
  breakfast time in, 196
  daily schedules in, 44, 50–51
  jerez in, 243
  lodging in, 417
  meals in, 199
  television viewing in, 317
  traditional cooking in, 212
  use of **vosotros** and **Uds.** in, 62
  See also specific topics; Hispanic world
Estados Unidos (United States)
  bilingual education in, 468
  Census 2000 on families, 168
  daily schedules compared to those in
    Spain and Mexico, 50–51
  family size in, 168
  influence of Spanish language, 232
  Latina superstars in, 94
  life expectancy in, 162
  Spanish language in, 22, 468–469
  See also Hispanic world; **Latinoamérica**
family life and relationships, 129, 168
fashion, 409, 424–425
folk art, 103
folklore, 102–103
futurism, 457, 461, 463, 468–469
globalization, 284–285
good manners, 218
greetings and leave-takings, 2–3, 153
Guatemala, 252. *See also* Hispanic
  world; **Latinoamérica**
health, interest in, 225
heredity and genetics, 392–393
higher education, 14
Hispanic world
  24-hour clock and daily schedules, 51
  art and literature, 252–253
  bilingualism, 134–135
  cooking, 212–213
  daily life in, 50–51
  economy in, 398–399
  environmentalism, 358–359
  fashion, 424–425
  folklore and folk art, 102–103
  globalization, 284–285
  immigration/emigration, 180–181
  indigenous populations, 330–331
  influence of, 232–233
  life expectancy, 162
  literary and artistic talent, 252–253
  music and dance, 76–77
  population of countries, 22
  pre-Hispanic civilizations, 308–309
  racial mixing, 156–157
  religion, 103
  revolution and civil war in 20th
    century, 448–449
  science, 378–379
  Spanish language, 22–23, 468–469
  See also specific countries;
    Latinoamérica

history. *See specific countries*; Hispanic
  world; **Latinoamérica;** pre-Hispanic
  America
hotels, 417
Inca. *See* pre-Hispanic America
indigenous cultures in Latin America,
  330–331
languages, indigenous, 330–331
Latinoamérica, 398–399
  bilingualism, 135
  clothing traditions, 425
  daily schedules, 51
  ecotourism, 358–359
  effects of **El Niño,** 358
  folk art, 103
  indigenous cultures, 330–331
  life expectancy, 162
  music and dance, 76–77
  popular academic majors, 14
  population of countries, 22
  racial mixing, 156–157
  religion in, 103
  revolution and war in 20th century,
    448–449
  use of **Uds.,** 62
  See also specific countries, topics;
    Hispanic world
life expectancy, 162
literature, 91, 233, 252, 331, 366
la Llorona, 102
Mafalda (cartoon), 5, 132, 430, 433, 443
maps. *See Maps index*
Maya. *See* pre-Hispanic America
Mediterranean diet, 225
mestizos, 156–157
México, 50–51, 212–213, 248. *See also*
  Hispanic world; **Latinoamérica**
music, 76–77, 94
nightlife, 51
Nobel prizewinners, 252, 378
Perú, 213, 244. *See also* Hispanic world;
  Latinoamérica
physical appearance, 141
physical contact, 153
politics, 331
population of Spanish-speaking
  countries, 22
Popul Vuh, 102
pre-Hispanic America, 308–309
professional life and gender, 434, 457
Puerto Rico, 243. *See also* Hispanic
  world; **Latinoamérica**
racial mixing, 156–157
religion, 103
rum, 243
Sábato, Ernesto, 91
santería, 103
schedules, 51
science, 378–379
seasons in Argentina, 72
shopping, 51, 285
siesta, 51
snack foods, 203

Spanish language, 22–23, 468–469
  influence in the world, 232–233
sports, 275, 294
surnames, 117
tapas, 203
technology, 463
television viewing, 317
tequila, 248
time, 50
tú, versus **usted,** 45–46
twins, 392–393
Uruguay, 244. *See also* Hispanic world;
  Latinoamérica
usted versus **tú,** 45–46
winter depression, 272
women in the workplace, 434, 457
work
  employment trends, 434, 457
  workday, 51

Everyday language

addressing others, 45–46, 106
clarification and verification, asking for,
  6, 9, 200, 202, 394
classroom expressions, 4, 9
commands, softening, 325
details, asking for, 155
directions, giving and receiving,
  384–385, 388
doubt, expressing, 459
emotions and feelings, expressing,
  260–262, 262, 263–264, 266–267
family resemblances, talking about,
  142, 144
family size, talking about, 169
final point, expressing a, 178
frequency, expressing, 35, 48
getting dressed, talking about, 408, 409
information, asking for, 115
introductions, 2–3, 13
keeping a conversation going, 154
likes and dislikes, expressing, 10–11, 60,
  191–192, 193–194, 374–375
noncommittal attitude, expressing, 444
obligation, expressing, 222, 235
occupation, talking about someone's, 432
opinions, requesting or giving, 154
permission to enter, asking, 222
referent, emphasizing or clarifying a, 5
slang expressions, 266
stalling, 444
states of mind and being, expressing,
  262, 265, 266–267, 271, 287, 340
studies, talking about one's, 7–8, 10–11, 13
taste, describing a, 200
time, talking about, 42–43, 48, 51, 67,
  100, 304, 458
transition words and expressions,
  250, 444
unknown words, asking for, 226
unknown words, looking up, 229
using visualization to memorize, 34
what you do, saying, 126

Maps

Argentina, 69
Caribbean region, 77
South America, 135
Spain, 22, 134
world, 22

Reading strategies (*Vamos a ver* and *Consejo práctico*)

associating a word's meaning with context, 83
consolidating information you've just read, 241
guessing meaning from context, 395
making an outline, 167
predicting content from titles, subtitles, visuals, and introductory sentences and paragraphs, 93, 167, 241, 394
reading and then thinking about one section at a time, 241
recognizing cognates, 95, 242
reviewing your notes, 395
scanning for information, 93, 394
semantic mapping for predicting content and reviewing what you've read, 319–320, 322
skimming, 93
skipping over unknown words, 93, 242, 395
summarizing by outlining, 395
summarizing in your own words, 242, 395
summarizing using key phrases, names, and numbers, 167

Vocabulary

academic subjects, 7–8, 13, 25–26, 430–431, 451
activities. *See* daily activities; leisure activities; weekend activities
adjectives, 14–15, 18, 26, 122, 137, 139, 144, 159, 189, 215, 260–262, 287, 343, 344, 355, 361, 363, 381, 440, 451
beverages, 197, 216, 237, 243–244, 255
body, parts of, 139, 159
classroom expressions, 4, 6, 9, 25, 26
clothing, 406–407, 427
cognates, 6, 95, 188, 189, 218. *See also* false cognates
colors, 189, 216
  of eyes and hair, 140
daily activities, 30–31, 53, 81–82, 105
days of the week, 38, 53
descriptions
  food, 189, 215
  general qualities, 14–15, 26
  personality, 144, 159, 343, 355, 361, 363, 381
  personal qualities, 363, 381, 439–440, 451
  personal situations, 122, 137
  physical appearance, 139, 159
  state of mind, 260–262, 287
dialect differences, 23
directions, 384–385, 388, 400
doubt, expressions of, 457–458, 459
education, 7–8, 13
emotions, personality, and behavior, 144, 145–146, 260–262, 263–264, 266–267, 287, 349, 361, 440, 451
false cognates, 6, 218
family, 112–113, 118–119, 121, 137
food and drink
  beverages, 237, 255
  foods, 188–189, 198, 215
  meals, 196–197, 199, 201, 215–216
  table setting, 218, 235
frequency expressions, 35, 48, 53
fruit, 189, 215
future, 463, 471
geographical landforms and locations, 291–292, 311
greetings and leave-takings, 2–3, 25
hotels, 414–415
injuries, 313, 333
introductions, 2–3, 13
leisure activities, 79, 274–275, 287, 289–290, 291–292, 297, 311
manners, 218
meals, 196–197, 199, 201, 215–216, 218
meat, poultry, and seafood, 188, 215
months, 71, 79
negation, words of, 79
numbers, 18, 26, 161, 162, 163, 183
obligation, expressions of, 222, 235
occupations and work, 430–431, 439–440, 451–452
personality descriptions, 144, 145–146, 159, 361
physical description, 139, 159
prepositions, 383, 413
question words, 137
restaurants, 227, 235
seasons, 71, 79
skills, 439–440, 451
sports and pastimes, 274–275, 287, 289–290, 291–292, 311
subjects (academic), 7–8, 13, 25–26, 430–431, 454
table setting, 218, 235
time
  clocks, 42–43, 51, 54
  of day, 32, 54
  expressions, 35, 105
  periods, 163
  por versus **para**, 40, 59, 458
time expressions, 48, 67, 100, 163
  in the past, 298
transition words, 250, 444
travel and transportation, 411–412, 414–415, 427–428
vegetables, 189, 215
weather, 66–67, 68, 79
weekend activities, 56–57, 79, 297, 311
work
  professional fields, 430–431, 454
  qualities and skills, 439–440, 454
  years, 163

CREDITS

Photos

Page 1 © Rhoda Sidney/Stock Boston; **21** © PhotoDisc/Getty Images; **28T** Kahlo, Frida (1907–1954) © Banco de México Trust. The Bus (El Camión), 1929. Oil on canvas, 26 × 55 cm. Fundación Dolores Olmedo, Mexico City, D.F., Mexico.; **28B** © Bettmann/Corbis; **29** © Frerck/Odyssey/Chicago; **41** © PhotoDisc/Getty Images; **50** © Bob Daemmrich/Stock Boston; **51** © Marco Cristofori/Corbis; **55** © Frerck/Odyssey/Chicago; **76** © Frerck/Odyssey/Chicago; **77** © Nik Wheeler/Corbis; **80** © Frerck/Odyssey/Chicago; **94** © Photo by CBS Photo Archive/Courtesy of Getty Images; **102** © Diana Bryer; **103T** © Dave G. Houser/Corbis; **103B** © Courtesy of the artist, Felipe Potosme and A Different Approach; **110T** © Courtesy of the Marlborough Gallery; **110B** © Eric Robert/VIP Production/Corbis; **111** © Ulrike Welsch; **116** © Ulrike Welsch; **138** © Ariel Skelley/Corbis; **141TL** © Jeremy Horner/Corbis; **141BL** © LWA-Sharie Kennedy/Corbis; **141TR** © David Simson/Stock Boston; **141BR** © Jan Butchofsky-Houser/Corbis; **143L** © Nick Stockbridge/Camera Press/Retna; **143R** © Sainlouis/Retna; **151** © Scala/Art Resource; **151** © Scala/Art Resource; **153** © Beryl Goldberg; **157BL** © Bob Krist/Corbis; **157BR** © Ulrike Welsch/Stock Boston; **157TL** © Frerck/Odyssey/Chicago; **157TR** © Dave Houser/Corbis; **160** © David Wells/The Image Works; **161** © Stuart Cohen; **162** © Jay Dickman/Corbis; **180** © Inga Spence/DDB Stock Photo; **181** © Glen Allison/Getty Images; **186T** © Diana Bryer; **186B** © Lynn Lown; **187** © Nik Wheeler/Corbis; **202** © Reg Charity/Corbis; **203** © Dennis Gottlieb/FoodPix/Jupiter Images; **210** © Jack Kurtz/The Image Works; **212TR** © John Burwell/FoodPix/Jupiter Images; **212BR** © Ben Fink/FoodPix/Jupiter Images; **212BL** © Wolfgang Kaehler/Corbis; **213T** © AFP/Getty Images; **213B** © Jan Butchofsky-Houser/Corbis; **217** © Frerck/Odyssey/Chicago; **225** © Kevin Sanchez/Cole Group/Getty Images; **227** © Stuart Cohen; **232** © H.Huntly Hersch/DDB Stock Photo; **233** © Carol Roseff/AP Images; **236** © Schulle/BASF/DDB Stock Photo; **243** © Jimmy Dorantes/LatinFocus.com; **244T** © Frerck/Odyssey/Chicago; **244B** © Jimmy Dorantes/LatinFocus.com; **246** © Beryl Goldberg; **248** © Douglas Peebles/Corbis; **252** © Timothy Ross/The Image Works; **253T** © Courtesy of the Marlborough Gallery; **253M** © Diana Bryer; **253B** © Courtesy of Ramón Lombarte; **258T** © Courtesy of Ramón Lombarte; **258B** © Courtesy of Ramón Lombarte. Photo by José Luis Pelegrín.; **259** © Frerck/Odyssey/Chicago; **270** © Stuart Cohen; **285B** © Frerck/Odyssey/Chicago; **285TL** © Bob Krist/Corbis; **285TR** © Keith Dannemiller/Corbis; **288** © David Stoecklein/Corbis; **294** © Reuters NewMedia/Corbis; **295** © Peter Menzel; **306** © Frerck/Odyssey/Chicago; **307** © PhotoDisc/Getty Images; **309T** © Frerck/Odyssey/Chicago; **309B** © Corbis; **309B** © Hans Georg Roth/Corbis; **312** © José Luis Peláez Inc./Corbis; **317** © Peter Menzel/Stock Boston; **321** © Rick Gómez/Corbis; **323** © Javier Pierini/Corbis; **330L** © Robert van der Hilst/Corbis; **330R** © Robert van der Hilst/Corbis; **331B** © Alfredo Aldai/Corbis; **331T** © Gregory Bull/AP Images; **338T** © Cecilia Concepción Álvarez.; **338B** © Courtesy of Cecilia Concepción Álvarez. Photo: Albert Smalls; **339** © José Luis Peláez Inc./Corbis; **353** © José Luis Peláez Inc./Corbis; **354** © Filmteam/DDB Stock Photo; **358** © Bates Littlehales/Corbis; **359T** © Wolfgang Kaehler/Corbis; **359B** © Kevin Schafer/Corbis; **362** © Collection Kipa/Corbis; **366** © Swim Ink/Corbis; **378** © William Coupon/Corbis; **379B** © Nik Wheeler/Corbis; **379T** © Anthony John West/Corbis; **382** © Courtesy of Pedro Alfonso Ochoa Ledesma; **387** © PhotoDisc/Getty Images; **392** © Dennis Degnan/Corbis; **398** © Richard Bickel/Corbis; **399** © Bernard Bisson/Corbis; **404T** © James Prigoff; **404B** © Courtesy of the artists and James Prigoff; **405** © Fernando Alda/Corbis; **406TL** © Corbis; **406TM** © Scala /Art Resource, NY; **406TR** © Erich Lessing/Art Resource; **406BL** © Rob Lewine/Corbis; **406BM** © Will and Deni McIntyre/Photo Researchers Inc.; **406BR** © Sergio Carmona/Corbis; **415L** © Buddy Mays/Corbis; **415R** © Michael Busselle/Corbis; **417** © Marc Anderson/Photographers Direct; **424T** © Patrick Roncen/Kipa/Corbis; **424B** © Kathy Willens/AP Images; **425T** © Dave G. Houser/Post-Houserstock/Corbis; **425B** © Hubert Stadler/Corbis; **425M** © John Moore/AP Images; **429** © Andrew Brookes/Corbis; **434** © Owen Franken/Stock Boston; **448** © Reuters NewMedia Inc./Corbis; **449T** © Corbis; **449B** © Scott Sady/AP Images; **449M** © Alejandro Ernesto/Corbis; **453** © Pablo Corral Vega/Corbis; **463** © Bob Daemmrich/Stock Boston; **468** © Jeff Hutchens/Getty Images News; **469R** © Bob Daemmrich/Stock Boston; **469L** © Rachel Epstein/PhotoEdit Inc.

Realia

Page 5 © Quino/Quipos; **8** *Hombre Internacional;* **37** Televisió de Catalunya; **132** © Quino/Quipos; **143** *Miami Mensual* magazine; **198** Courtesy of The Quaker Oats Company; **220** Editorial Televisa, S.A.; **272** Courtesy of *Muy Interesante;* **316** © Quino/Quipos; **318** © Quino/Quipos; **430** © Quino/Quipos; **433** © Quino/Quipos; **443** © Quino/Quipos.

Readings

Page 193 Text and photos: © *Noticias,* Editorial Perfil, Argentina; **325** Editorial Televisa, S.A.; **327** "El trabajo como adicción" by Christina Peri Rossi. Reprinted with permission of International Editors; **461** "Apocalipsis" in *Falsificaciones, Obras Completas,* by Marco Denevi, Buenos Aires, Corregidor 2005. Used by permission; **464T** *Conocer;* **464B** *Conocer.*

ABOUT THE AUTHORS

BILL VANPATTEN was, until recently, Professor of Spanish and Linguistics at the University of Illinois at Chicago. His areas of research are input and input processing in second language acquisition, sentence professing in a second language, and the effects of formal instruction on acquisition processes. He has published widely in the fields of second language acquisition and second language teaching and is a frequent conference speaker and presenter. His publications include *Making Communicative Language Teaching Happen,* Second Edition (with James F. Lee, 2003, McGraw-Hill), *From Input to Output: A Teacher's Guide to Second Language Acquisition* (2003, McGraw-Hill), *Processing Instruction: Theory, Research, and Practice* (2004, Lawrence Erlbaum Associates), and most recently, *Theories in Second Language Acquisition: An Introduction* (with Jessica Williams, 2007, Lawrence Erlbaum Associates). In addition to *¿Sabías que... ?,* he is also the lead author and designer of both *Destinos* and *Sol y viento.*

JAMES F. LEE is Head of the Department of Spanish and Latin American Studies at the University of New South Wales, Sydney, Australia. His research interests are in the areas of second language reading comprehension, input processing, and exploring the relationship between the two. His research has appeared in a number of scholarly journals and publications. His previous publications include the book *Tasks and Communicating in Language Classrooms* (2000, McGraw-Hill) and the co-authored book *Making Communicative Language Teaching Happen,* Second Edition (2003, McGraw-Hill). He has also co-authored several textbooks, including this Fifth Edition of *¿Sabias que... ?* and *Ideas: Lecturas, estrategias actividades y composiciones* (1994, McGraw-Hill). He and Bill VanPatten are series editors for the McGraw-Hill Second Language Professional Series.

TERRY L. BALLMAN is Professor of Spanish and founding faculty member and coordinator of Spanish/Languages at California State University, Channel Islands. Her teaching experience includes Spanish language and linguistics courses as well as methods courses for foreign language, ESL, and bilingual teachers. She has also coordinated lower-division language programs and supervised student teachers. A recipient of several teaching awards, Dr. Ballman is a frequent presenter of workshops and papers. She has published articles in research volumes and journals. She is a co-author of this Fifth Edition of *¿Sabías que... ?* as well as project leader and co-author of *The Communicative Classroom,* a volume of the American Association of Teachers of Spanish and Portuguese Professional Development Series for K–16 Teachers.

ANDREW P. FARLEY is Associate Professor of Applied Linguistics and Concurrent Associate Professor of Curriculum and Instruction at Texas Tech University. He received his Ph.D. in Second Language Acquisition and Teacher Education (SLATE) from the University of Illinois at Urbana-Champaign. His areas of research are input processing in second language acquisition, the effects of instruction on second language acquisition, lexical access in early bilinguals, and the acquisition of second language morphology. He has taught a variety of courses ranging from beginning Spanish language courses to graduate seminars on applied linguistics and second language acquisition. He has authored and co-authored numerous articles and book chapters and is the author of *Structured Input: Grammar Instruction for the Acquisition Oriented Classroom* (2005, McGraw-Hill), a book in the McGraw-Hill Second Language Professional Series.